POSTMODERNISM, ECONOMICS AND KNOWLEDGE

It is only in the past ten years that the debates surrounding modernism and postmodernism have emerged within the discipline of economics. This new way of thinking moves beyond the prior emphasis of the philosophy of science – challenging the belief in the progressivity and modernity of economics and rejecting claims that science and mathematics provide the only models for the structure of economic knowledge.

This highly important volume is the first to bring together the essays of top theorists to debate issues in the following areas:

- Modernism and postmodernism: Sheila Dow, Arjo Klamer, Deirdre McCloskey and Jack Amariglio
- Reading symbols, changing subjects and discerning bodies in economic discourse: Jack Amariglio, David F. Ruccio, Jean-Joseph Goux, Regenia Gagnier and John Dupré
- Gendered subjectivities in neoclassical economics: S. Charusheela, Gillian Hewitson and Brian Cooper
- Feminist/postmodern economics: Ulla Grapard, Julie Nelson, Jane Rossetti and Suzanne Bergeron
- Postmodernism, economic rationality and the problem of 'representation': Stephen Cullenberg, Indraneel Dasgupta, Shaun Hargreaves-Heap, Judith Mehta and Henry Krips
- Is there a (postmodern) alternative in economics? From markets to gifts: William Milberg, Philip Mirowski, Stephen Gudeman and John Davis

Postmodernism, Economics and Knowledge does not require the reader to have an economics background; it is an accessible text providing diverse views of each topic, followed by critical commentary to end each section. From the editors' introductory essay through the individual contributions, this book will serve as an invaluable reference tool for all studying economic methodology, postmodernism and the history of economic thought.

Stephen Cullenberg is Chair of the Department of Economics at the University of California, Riverside. **Jack Amariglio** is Professor of Economics at Merrimack College. **David F. Ruccio** is Associate Professor of Economics at the University of Notre Dame.

ECONOMICS AS SOCIAL THEORY
Tony Lawson
University of Cambridge

Social Theory is experiencing something of a revival within economics. Critical analyses of the particular nature of the subject matter of social studies and of the types of method, categories and modes of explanation that can legitimately be endorsed for the scientific study of social objects, are reemerging. Economists are again addressing such issues as the relationship between agency and structure, between economy and the rest of society, and between the enquirer and the object of enquiry. There is a renewed interest in elaborating basic categories such as causation, competition, culture, discrimination, evolution, money, need, order, organization, power, probability, process, rationality, technology, time, truth, uncertainty, value, etc.

The objective for this series is to facilitate this revival further. In contemporary economics, the label 'theory' has been appropriated by a group that confines itself to largely asocial, ahistorical, mathematical 'modeling'. *Economics as Social Theory* thus reclaims the 'Theory' label, offering a platform for alternative rigorous, but broader and more critical conceptions of theorizing.

Other titles in this series include:

ECONOMICS AND LANGUAGE
Edited by Willie Henderson

RATIONALITY, INSTITUTIONS
AND ECONOMIC METHODOLOGY
Edited by Uskali Mäki, Bo Gustafsson, and Christian Knudsen

NEW DIRECTIONS IN ECONOMIC
METHODOLOGY
Edited by Roger Backhouse

WHO PAYS FOR THE KIDS?
Nancy Folbre

RULES AND CHOICE IN
ECONOMICS
Viktor Vanberg

BEYOND RHETORIC AND REALISM
IN ECONOMICS
Thomas A. Boylan and Paschal F. O'Gorman

FEMINISM, OBJECTIVITY AND
ECONOMICS
Julie A. Nelson

ECONOMIC EVOLUTION
Jack J. Vromen

ECONOMICS AND REALITY
Tony Lawson

THE MARKET
John O' Neill

ECONOMICS AND UTOPIA
Geoff Hodgson

CRITICAL REALISM IN
ECONOMICS
Edited by Steve Fleetwood

THE NEW ECONOMIC CRITICISM
Edited by Martha Woodmansee and Mark Osteen

WHAT DO ECONOMISTS KNOW?
Edited by Robert F. Garnett, Jr

POSTMODERNISM, ECONOMICS
AND KNOWLEDGE
Edited by Stephen Cullenberg, Jack Amariglio and David F. Ruccio

THE VALUES OF ECONOMICS
An Aristotelian perspective
Irene van Staveren

POSTMODERNISM, ECONOMICS AND KNOWLEDGE

*Stephen Cullenberg,
Jack Amariglio and
David F. Ruccio*

London and New York

First published 2001
by Routledge
11 New Fetter Lane, London EC4P 4EE

Simultaneously published in the USA and Canada
by Routledge
29 West 35th Street, New York, NY 10001

Routledge is an imprint of the Taylor & Francis Group

© 2001 Selection and editorial matter, Stephen Cullenberg, Jack Amariglio and David F. Ruccio; individual chapters, the respective contributors.

Typeset in Palatino by Taylor & Francis
Printed and bound in Great Britain by
Biddles Ltd, Guildford and King's Lynn

All rights reserved. No part of this book may be reprinted or reproduced or utilised in any form or by any electronic, mechanical, or other means, now known or hereafter invented, including photocopying and recording, or in any information storage or retrieval system, without permission in writing from the publishers.

British Library Cataloguing in Publication Data
A catalogue record for this book is available from the British Library

Library of Congress Cataloging in Publication Data
Postmodern, economics and knowledge/ edited by Stephen Cullenberg,
Jack Amariglio and David F. Ruccio
p. cm – (Economics as social theory)
Simultaneously published in the USA and Canada.
Includes bibliographical references and index.
1. Economics–Philoosophy. 2. Postmodernism–social aspects. I. Cullenberg, Stephen. II. Amariglio, Jack. III. Ruccio, David F. IV. Series.

HB72 .P64 2001

330.1–dc21   00-045954

ISBN 0–415–11025–4 (hbk)
ISBN 0–415–11026–2 (pbk)

CONTENTS

List of illustrations   ix
Notes on Contributors   x
Acknowledgements   xv

PART I
Introduction

1 **Introduction**   3
   STEPHEN CULLENBERG, JACK AMARIGLIO AND DAVID F. RUCCIO

PART II
Modernism and postmodernism

2 **Modernism and postmodernism: A dialectical analysis**   61
   SHEILA DOW

3 **Late modernism and the loss of character in economics**   77
   ARJO KLAMER

4 **The genealogy of postmodernism: An economist's guide**   102
   DEIRDRE McCLOSKEY

5 **Writing in thirds**   129
   JACK AMARIGLIO

CONTENTS

PART III
Reading symbols, changing subjects and discerning bodies in economic discourse

6 From unity to dispersion: The body in modern economic discourse   143
JACK AMARIGLIO AND DAVID F. RUCCIO

7 Ideality, symbolicity, and reality in postmodern capitalism   166
JEAN-JOSEPH GOUX

8 Chacun son Goux? Or, some skeptical reflections on flat bodies and heavy metal   182
REGENIA GAGNIER AND JOHN DUPRÉ

PART IV
Gendered subjectivities in neoclassical economics

9 Women's choices and the ethnocentrism/relativism dilemma   197
S. CHARUSHEELA

10 The disavowal of the sexed body in neoclassical economics   221
GILLIAN HEWITSON

11 Comment on Charusheela and Hewitson   246
BRIAN COOPER

PART V
Feminist/postmodern economics

12 The trouble with women and economics: A postmodern perspective on Charlotte Perkins Gilman   261
ULLA GRAPARD

13 Feminist economics: Objective, activist, *and* postmodern?   286
JULIE A. NELSON

CONTENTS

14 Postmodernism and feminist economics   305
JANE ROSSETTI

15 No more nice girls? Feminism, economics, and postmodern encounters   327
SUZANNE BERGERON

PART VI
Postmodernism, economic rationality and the problem of 'representation'

16 From myth to metaphor: A semiological analysis of the Cambridge capital controversy   337
STEPHEN CULLENBERG AND INDRANEEL DASGUPTA

17 Postmodernity, rationality and justice   354
SHAUN HARGREAVES HEAP

18 A disorderly household – voicing the noise   374
JUDITH MEHTA

19 Postmodern encounters   399
HENRY KRIPS

PART VII
Is there a (postmodern) alternative in economics? From markets to gifts

20 Decentering the market metaphor in international economics   407
WILLIAM MILBERG

21 Refusing the gift   431
PHILIP MIROWSKI

22 Postmodern gifts   459
STEPHEN GUDEMAN

CONTENTS

23 Gifts and trade: Mirowskian, Gudemanian, and Milbergian themes 475
JOHN DAVIS

Name index 483
Subject index 487

ILLUSTRATIONS

Tables

2.1	Pluralism in economics	63
13.1	The contemporary definition of economics	289
13.2	Extremist binary oppositions in the modernism/ postmodernism debate	300
18.1	Summary of results	383
20.1	Intra-firm trade, USA, Japan and Sweden	418
20.2	Cumulative current account balance, selected countries	423

Figures

9.1	Analyzing decisions in a choice-theoretic framework: decision tree showing the analyst's choices and decisions in deciphering agent actions	201
13.1	The hierarchical dualism	291
13.2	The gender/value compass	292
13.3	Separation and connection	294
13.4	Detachment and engagement	298
13.5	Unity and multiplicity	301
16.1	Reswitching and capital reversal	342
16.2	The semiology of myth	345
17.1	Conflict over a resource	359
17.2	Conflict between a Utilitarian and a Rawlsian	361
17.3	Equal relative concession	370
20.1	Organization and location of a transnational corporation: hypothetical case	417
20.2	Varieties of international intra-firm integration of production	420
20.3	Alliances among airline computer reservation systems	422
21.1	Sahlins causal structure	443

CONTRIBUTORS

Jack Amariglio is Professor of Economics at Merrimack College. He was one of the founders of the interdisciplinary journal, *Rethinking Marxism*, and served as its initial Editor from 1988 to 1997. He has published widely on the philosophy and history of economic thought, as well as on the intersection of economics and culture. His book with David Ruccio, entitled *Postmodern Moments of Modern Economics*, is forthcoming from Princeton University Press.

Suzanne Bergeron is an Assistant Professor of Women's Studies and Social Sciences at the University of Michigan, Dearborn. She received her Ph.D. in Economics at the University of Notre Dame. She has written on postmodernism and economics, gender and development, and globalization.

S. Charusheela is Assistant Professor of Women's Studies at the University of Hawaii at Manoa. She received her doctorate in economics from the University of Massachusetts, Amherst. She served on the editorial board of the journal *Rethinking Marxism*, and is an active member of the Association for Economic and Social Analysis (AESA) and the International Association for Feminist Economics (IAFFE).

Brian Cooper is Assistant Professor of Economics at State University of New York at Oswego. He has research interests in and has published articles on the economics of the family, the history of economics, the economics of race, gender, and class, and the intersections between literary theory and economic theory. He is currently finishing a book, *Family Fictions and Family Facts: Harriet Martineau, Adolphe Quetelet, and the Population Question in England, 1798–1859*, to be published by Routledge.

CONTRIBUTORS

Stephen Cullenberg is Chair of the Department of Economics at the University of California, Riverside. He is the author of *The Falling Rate of Profit* (Pluto, 1994) and co-author of *Economics and the Historian* (University of California Press, 1995) and co-editor of Marxism in the *Postmodern Age* (Guilford, 1994) and *Whither Marxism?* (Routledge, 1994).

Indraneel Dasgupta is Lecturer, School of Economics, University of Nottingham, UK. His research interests lie primarily in the fields of microeconomic theory and development economics. Publications include papers in the *Journal of Economic Theory*, *European Economic Review* and *Oxford Economic Papers*.

John Davis, Professor of Economics and International Business, Ph.D. in Philosophy (University of Illinois-Urbana, 1983) and Ph.D. in Economics (Michigan State University, 1985), teaches International Trade and International Economics at Marquette University. He is the author of *Keynes's Philosophical Development* (Cambridge, 1994), editor of *New Economics and Its History* (Duke, 1998), and co-editor of *The Handbook of Economic Methodology* (Elgar, 1998). He is President-Elect of the History of Economics Society, and has been the editor of the *Review of Social Economy* since 1987. Currently he is working on a book to be published by Routledge on theories of the individual in economics.

Sheila Dow holds a Personal Chair in Economics at the University of Stirling, having previously worked as a government economist. She has published widely in the areas of history of thought, methodology of economics, monetary theory, and regional finance. She is author of several books, the latest being *The Methodology of Macroeconomic Thought* (Elgar, 1996).

John Dupré is a Professor of Philosophy at the University of Exeter. He works in the philosophy of science, specializing in the philosophy of biology and the philosophy of economics. As well as numerous articles in philosophical journals and anthologies, he is the author of *The Disorder of Things: Metaphysical Foundations of the Disunity of Science* (Harvard, 1993), and the editor of *The Latest on the Best: Essays on Evolution and Optimality* (MIT, 1987).

Regenia Gagnier is Professor of English at the University of Exeter and has written extensively on culture and economics. Her books include *Idylls of the Marketplace: Oscar Wilde and the Victorian Public* (Stanford, 1986); *Subjectivities: A History of Self-Representation in Britain 1832–1920* (Oxford, 1991); and *The Insatiability of Human Wants: Economics and Aesthetics in Market Society* (Chicago, 2000).

CONTRIBUTORS

Jean-Joseph Goux is the Lawrence Favrot Chair at Rice University where he currently teaches French philosophy in the Department of French Studies. He has also taught at the University of California (San Diego, Berkeley), the University of Montreal, Brown University and Duke University. His major books translated into English are: *Symbolic Economies* (Cornell University Press, 1990), *Oedipus, Philosopher* (Stanford University Press, 1993), *The Coiners of Language*, (Oklahoma University Press, 1994). He is co-editor of *Terror and Consensus: The Vicissitudes of French Thought* (Stanford University, 1998) and *Frivolité de la valeur: essai sur l'imaginaire du capitalisme*, (Paris: Blusson, 2000).

Ulla Grapard is Associate Professor of Economics at Colgate University. Her teaching specialties include gender in the economy and the political economy of the Scandinavian welfare state. Her publications and research are focused on theoretical issues of gender in the history of economic thought and feminist economic methodology.

Stephen Gudeman is a Professor and Chair of the Department of Anthropology at the University of Minnesota. He has carried out fieldwork in several Latin American nations focusing on Spanish-speaking peoples in the countryside and, more recently, in urban areas. He examines social and symbolic organization but has a special interest in economic anthropology and local models of economic life.

Shaun Hargreaves Heap teaches at the University of East Anglia. His research is in macroeconomics and philosophy and economics. He is particularly interested in the role of rationality assumptions in economics and his most recent research is in the economics of the media.

Gillian Hewitson is a lecturer in the School of Business at La Trobe University, and teaches macroeconomics and money and banking subjects. Her Ph.D. was a metatheoretical discussion of neoclassical and feminist economics from the perspective of feminist poststructuralism (published by Edward Elgar, 1999). She has also published in the area of endogenous monetary theory.

Arjo Klamer is currently Professor in the Economics of Art and Culture at the Erasmus University. Recently he edited the volume *The Value of Culture: On the Relationship Between Economics and the Arts* (Amsterdam/Michigan University Press, 1996). Before returning to the Netherlands, he taught at The George Washington University, University of Iowa and Wellesley College. During his American period he pushed hard for the rhetorical perspective on economics. His best-known book is *Conversations with Economists* (1984).

CONTRIBUTORS

Henry Krips is Professor of Communication and of History and Philosophy of Science at the University of Pittsburgh. He has published extensively in the areas of cultural studies and philosophy of science. His major publications are *The Metaphysics of Quantum Theory* (Oxford University Press, 1989), and *Fetish: An Erotics of Culture* (Cornell University Press, 1999).

Deirdre McCloskey is Professor of the Human Sciences at the University of Illinois-Chicago and Tinbergen Professor at Erasmus University of Rotterdam. She has written many books, some with postmodern themes, such as *The Rhetoric of Economics* (2nd ed. 1998), *If You're So Smart: The Narrative of Economics Expertise* (1990), and *Knowledge and Persuasion in Economics* (1994). Her latest book, about her change of gender, is *Crossing: A Memoir*.

Judith Mehta is a Lecturer in Economics at the Open University. Her teaching and research focus on decision-making and economic organization, overlaid with a concern to locate new kinds of conversations in response to challenges posed by recent French philosophy.

William Milberg is Associate Professor and Chair of Economics at the Graduate Faculty of Political and Social Science at New School University in New York. He has worked on the staff of the Federal Reserve Bank of New York, the Council of Economic Advisors and UNCTAD. His research focuses on international trade, technological change, trade policy and economic methodology.

Philip Mirowski is Carl Koch Professor of Economics and the History and Philosophy of Science at the University of Notre Dame. He is the author of *Against Mechanism* and *More Heat than Light*, and the editor of *Natural Images in Economics*, *Edgeworth on Chance* and *The Collected Economic Works of William Thomas Thornton*. His book *Machine Dreams: Economics Becomes a Cyborg Science* is forthcoming from Cambridge University Press, and a reader on the economics of science, prepared jointly with Esther-Mirjam Sent, entitled *Science Bought and Sold*, will be appearing from the University of Chicago Press. While not himself a post-boasty, he is convinced that economics has been more influenced by cultural movements like poststructuralism than it likes to make out.

Julie A. Nelson does research on the relation of feminist theory to economics and the analysis of household behavior. She is the author of *Feminism, Objectivity, and Economics* (Routledge, 1996), coeditor (with Marianne A. Ferber) of *Beyond Economic Man: Feminist Theory and Economics* (University of Chicago Press, 1993), and author of articles in journals including the *Journal of Economic Perspectives* and the *Journal of*

Labor Economics. She currently has a fellowship at the Center for the Study of Values in Public Life, Harvard Divinity School, Cambridge, Massachusetts.

Jane Rossetti has taught Economics at Williams College, Occidental College, and Franklin & Marshall College. She is currently an unaffiliated scholar.

David F. Ruccio is Associate Professor of Economics at the University of Notre Dame and editor of the journal *Rethinking Marxism*. He is the author of numerous articles and essays on economic development and postmodernism and economics and the coeditor of *Postmodern Materialism and the Future of Marxist Theory* (Wesleyan, 1996). He is currently working (with Jack Amariglio) on a book manuscript for Princeton University Press entitled *Postmodern Moments in Modern Economics*.

ACKNOWLEDGEMENTS

The authors and publishers would like to thank the following for granting permission to reproduce material in this work:

Cambridge University Press for permission to reproduce extracts from Deirdre McCloskey (1994) *Knowledge and Persuasion in Economics*.

Critical Review for permission to reproduce extracts from Deirdre McCloskey (1991) 'The Essential Rhetoric of Law, Literature and Liberty', 5 (Spring) 202–23.

Every effort has been made to contact copyright holders for their permission to reprint material in this book. The publishers would be grateful to hear from any copyright holder who is not here acknowledged and will undertake to rectify any errors or omissions in future editions.

PART I

INTRODUCTION

1
INTRODUCTION

Stephen Cullenberg, Jack Amariglio, and David F. Ruccio

> Funeral by funeral, economics does make progress
> (Paul Samuelson 1997: 159)

Modernism as dirge; economic knowledge as its fossil remains. Borrowing from Max Planck with just the minor addition of his own bailiwick (substituting 'economics' for 'science'), the doyen of modernist economics, Paul Samuelson, motivates even Keynes's gloomy dictum about economics one step further in this cautionary epigraph, or epitaph, as the case may be.[1] Economics is not only the 'dismal science'. Its ascension to the level of the 'queen of the social sciences' is by virtue of one shovelful after another, as the 'Darwinian impact of reality melts away even the prettiest of fanciful theories and the hottest of ideological frenzies' (1997: 159).

Samuelson, of course, is only the latest to conclude with morbid optimism that, in the end, the evolutionary nature of scientific practice amongst economists does lead to the growth of economic knowledge, even if, revisiting the spirits of Smith, Ferguson, and the Enlightenment Scots, it grows as an unintended consequence of its practitioners' practice. There is a kind of utopia in this dystopic rendition; a kind of faith nonetheless in the idea that as long as economists remain committed to the norms of (some) scientific practice, the knowledge they produce, almost at times in spite of themselves, will prove to illuminate historical reality and enlighten future generations.[2] This grizzled confidence – no matter how tempered it may be as the new century and millennium is upon us – is a hallmark of modernism itself, those discourses and practices that have been associated with such ideas as 'progress' and 'knowledge' arguably throughout much of the post-Enlightenment period in the West.[3]

Yet, no matter how optimistic time and again throughout the past 100 and more years economists and the philosophers among them have remained, many of them come back somewhat nervously to survey the standing of economic knowledge in the landscape of modernist culture and science. Thus, we may say with the distinguished historian of economic thought, T. W. Hutchison, that 'claimed to be the most "effective" or "mature" of the social or human sciences, or described as the 'hardest' of the "soft" sciences, economics seems destined for a somewhat ambiguous and problematic place in the spectrum of knowledge' (1979: 1).

There is no need to sing lamentations about this ambiguity. Instead, we can see that it speaks to the effervescent life (and not Samuelson's recursive life through incessant death) of economics as a set of discourses. And this life may be most attributable to the 'undecidables' and 'aporia' that can be said to characterize modern economics' 'ambiguity', the fact that pure scientificity always seems out of reach as the ostensible achievement of the discipline.[4] Now, of course, in some versions of this perceived ambiguity, the point is to clean up economics by removing the vestiges of past 'errors' ('prettiest of fanciful theories') and opinion ('hottest of ideological frenzies') that are seen to still remain in the debates among and between various schools.[5] This, we take it, is mostly Samuelson's vision. Still other versions have it that as long as economics remains a 'human' science, then it will forever be impossible to accurately model economic behavior since humans, it is said, confound models in their resort to just plain inexplicable or indefensible actions, at times.[6] And there are others who, in fact, speak to what they consider the pure blasphemy in economists' trying to model human behavior at all, seeing such desire for mechanistic control in economic models as a violation of the basic freedom of human beings and of the fundamental dignity and meaning of human life.

We are not partial to any of these ways of thinking through the problematic of 'ambiguity' that Hutchison announces. Instead, in this book we take up the challenge that unearthing and engaging the 'undecidables' and 'aporia' of economic discourse is part of a broader realization of a new phase of self-conscious thought, a new phase even perhaps of society and history: that which has been labeled the 'postmodern'.[7]

Categorizing the postmodern

The postmodern and its cognates (postmodernism, postmodernity, etc.) are notorious by now for the plethora of meanings that have been attached to them. One major difficulty then in engaging the theoretical and practical horizons sketched by the term postmodern is that ambiguity and undecidability reside even in the realm of their fundamental definition. Yet, in our view, there are ways to categorize the various literatures that have sprawled in the past 20 or more years in relation to this concept. We attempt such a tentative categorization below, trying as best we can to provide unfamiliar readers with some guidelines to key debates as well as to illuminate the partial context within which the essays that comprise this collection have been written.

INTRODUCTION

For, as we see it, postmodernism is a relatively new development within economics, but one that has great promise in calling economists' attention not only to the epistemological conditions of existence for their theorizing, but also to the general cultural milieu within which modern economics has both expanded and contracted. Modern economics has certainly had a right to claim, as Samuelson says, the 'growth of knowledge'. But it also can be said that modern economics has run up against certain anomalies and fragmentations that have proliferated diverse knowledges in addition to putting on the agenda concepts and approaches that lead away from rather than toward a universalist science. While some may regard the current state of economic discourse as closer to 'convergence', we see and argue something rather different. That over a century after the marginalist revolution, economic discourse is more heterogeneous than one might expect from a supposedly 'unified' science.[8] Again, this heterogeneity is nothing to bemoan, in our view. It might speak instead to the limits of modernism in economics, and just as much to the emergence of what we call the 'postmodern moments' within the official discipline.

The categories around which we discuss postmodernism are historical phase, existential state or 'condition', style, and critique. That is, we think it is possible to render intelligible most of the debates surrounding the term 'postmodern' and its implications according to these four categories.[9] Postmodernism has been seen, by some critics, as a particular stage in the life history of modern capitalist economies. Postmodernism has also been seen, by these and others, as a 'condition', or a state of existence, describing the cultural/social dominant within which we experience the contemporaneous. There are also some writers who view postmodernism as a kind of literary/rhetorical or practical style (especially in the arts and architecture), one that affects even the philosophical stances that are seen to characterize much current discussion regarding the possibility and nature of knowledge and scientific method. Finally, we think that in relation to these previous notions and sometimes distinct from them, postmodernism has been intended and utilized as a critique, that is, as a critical stance attempting to create thought and action 'outside' of the perceived constraints of modernism (and here, modernism ranges from modernization and economic development strategies in a post-colonial world to the 'high modernism' of formalist literature and mathematics). In what follows, we elucidate each of these categories. This helps us to set the stage for a brief synopsis of the postmodern moments that we think have arisen within economic discourse as well as to provide a context for the papers included in this volume.

Postmodernity: the latest phase of capitalism?

In this vein, it needs to be said straightaway that the category of analysis that is represented least in the papers in this volume is the one that treats postmodernism more or less as a particular world-historical phase. Or rather, there is just a little here that will address what has become an entire literary industry within other disciplines, which is characterizing as 'postmodern' the latest stage in 'late capitalist' economies and especially the process of 'globalization'. Some of the papers included here touch on these topics (certainly the papers by Milberg and Charusheela), but for the most part, the notion that we live in a new phase of human history brought about by the latest mutation of capitalism is primarily backdrop, and may even be refused as a preconception by many of the authors here. In any event, as we say, there is a vast literature by now that treats postmodernism as a name for the economic and cultural forms that have supposedly marked the onset of global capitalism.

Arguably, the best known advocate of this approach is the American cultural theorist Fredric Jameson. Jameson (1991) captures well the flavor of treating postmodernism as the cultural form of the latest phase of capitalist development in his frequent reference to three identifying aspects of 'late capitalism': mass commodification, a shift in the location and conditions of global production, and the rise of new industries (mostly in information technologies) that allow for the unbroken worldwide expansion of capitalist markets and, hence, profitability.[10] Jameson, it should be noted, is a devotee of the late Belgian Marxist economist Ernest Mandel (1978), whose book on 'late capitalism' serves as the veritable bible for those (mostly cultural critics) who are looking to describe and define, from the Left, capitalism's most recent trajectory.[11] Following in the footsteps of both the Marxian-inspired Frankfurt School of sociocultural analysis (whose members included Theodor Adorno, Max Horkheimer, and Herbert Marcuse, among others) and the writings of the great Hungarian cultural theorist Georg Lukács, Jameson seeks to analyze, from a critical perspective, the forms of cultural expression that have aided, partly by becoming commodities themselves, this phase of capitalist development.[12] Hence, everything from the arts to philosophical thinking in this age, in some way or other, is seen to have a relationship to unyielding commodification and the post-industrialization of the previously industrialized nations, the latter of which is matched by the shift in economic production and ecological impact brought about by the globalization of capital.[13]

But perhaps it is the idea of commodification that has been most clearly identified as that which marks a new cultural phase, postmodernism, that corresponds to the new economic phase, late capitalism.[14] And here, what is meant is not only that capitalism has inexorably expanded markets, both in terms of geographical location and in terms of what objects become marketed. But, this has also meant that culture has lost its relative autonomy (if this ever existed) and has now become almost entirely oriented toward the sale of commodities. This can be seen, according to some critics, in the growth of markets for cultural artifacts (and the fact that so little now is produced outside of an exchange economy), but more importantly in the fact that the arts and thought itself have become more shallow and slick, as they either uncritically mimic (as with Andy Warhol's 'pop art') or help to further the spread of commercial images. Indeed, the rise of 'image' or 'surface' as opposed to 'content' or 'depth', is said to mark most recent art forms that express this postmodern shift.[15]

It is interesting in this light to note that Jameson identifies, not surprisingly, Gary Becker (1991) as the quintessential postmodern economist, a view, paradoxically, that is almost the exact opposite of that which is expressed by most of the contributors to this volume. The reason for Jameson's attribution is fairly straightforward. Becker represents, in Jameson's view, the recognition among economists that most if not all areas of contemporary life are now prone to the logic of capital, and mostly to the vagaries of market forces. In fact, in a way according to Jameson, Becker captures the spirit of the age, as everything from marriage to drug addiction to death becomes a matter for market-inspired calculations. It is not so much that Becker is the latest disciplinary 'imperialist', seeking to speculatively displace most other non-economic approaches to culture by advocating economically rational principles, especially individual choice, as the foundation of all social life.[16] It is, instead, that Becker gives voice in his theoretical oeuvre to that which has transpired 'in reality': the unfettered spread in the last century of capitalist markets and the commodification of just about everything. Becker's postmodernism, in Jameson's eyes, consists mainly in marking the extent to which market logics have in fact taken over for any and all non-capitalist, non-market social domains.

As we have said, this take on Becker's work is in contrast to much that is contained in this collection. Becker is treated, to the extent his work is considered, more in the vein of 'high modernism', a representative (along with the New Classical Economists) of the dominant neoclassical paradigm committed to formal modeling and the reduction of most human motives to a single purpose: individual gain (and this includes 'psychic income' from such motivations as 'altruism').[17] Be that as it may, we note again that for many literary and cultural theorists like Jameson, the realm of the postmodern denotes rampant commodification, unchecked by oppositional forces – avant-gardes, say – that find themselves subverted or even co-opted by the very power and allure of the market. And, again, this world structured according to the object-life of the commodity has been thought to have received an enormous recent boost by the emergence of new information technologies, especially the internet. According to this view, computers have made commodity time and space ultimately traversable in ways unthinkable for past generations of producers and consumers. In addition to the use of computer technology in such 'post-Fordist' production methods as 'flexible specialization', it is claimed that one need not leave one's chair (in front of one's screen, of course) to be bombarded by commodity images and the cornucopia of goods that exist and are transacted in cyberspace. This obliteration of previous constraints of time and geographical location in buying and selling (lowering considerably transactions costs and reducing to rubble other past barriers to the international flow of financial capital and goods) reconstructs all notions and experiences pertaining to community and nation, hence the idea of the 'global economy' that is said to be the hallmark of the postmodern.

We note that opponents of this global spread of capitalist commodity production are often among those whose form of resistance, to the extent this is conceivable, includes seeking spaces for economic life, if not for economic theorizing, in pre- or non-capitalist social processes.[18] Among other things, the sense that capitalism threatens to seep into every existing pore of the worldwide social skin leads some cultural critics to hail the gift, and any realm of economic activity not reducible to market exchange, as offering one possible way out. This set of concerns arises in this volume in papers by Mirowski, Gudeman, Davis, and in a way Goux, as they all touch upon the degree to which the commodity and/or discourse about the commodity is omnipresent, even in the attempts to construct the 'anti-economics' of gift theory. If the postmodern age is one in which culture is merely an accompaniment to capitalist economic expansion, then it is a legitimate question if it is possible under the circumstances to think such issues as value and exchange in any register 'outside' the regime of the commodity as, in Marx's phrase, 'the general equivalent'.

Postmodernism as the 'condition' of the contemporary

The idea of the postmodern as a 'condition' or the state of life today is sometimes connected to the previous notion of postmodernism as a historical stage. Yet, in the work of the best known theorist of this 'condition', Jean-François Lyotard (1984), most of the baggage of 'late capitalist' discourse is discarded for a different emphasis, one that connects living in a postmodern world with changes in discourse itself, including (and perhaps especially) those that concern knowledge and science. Lyotard's focus on science and knowledge is matched by still others who describe the current state of social existence (mostly in developed

Western capitalist nations) as characterized by the decentering of individual selves and society, a shift from 'global' to 'local' politics and ethics, the 'saturation' of psyches and imaginations by an amazing array of discontinuous images and events, and much else. In Lyotard's important book *The Postmodern Condition*, however, the central themes have to do with a shift in the ways in which knowledge and science are both conceptualized and practiced. A shift, we note, that opens up a chasm between modernity and postmodernity.[19]

Lyotard's 'report on knowledge', as he calls it, is concerned largely with two interrelated issues. One is rejection and (hoped-for) disappearance of what he terms the 'grand metanarratives' that have structured much thought and practice since the Enlightenment. Hence, to the degree that 'modernity' may be said to be contemporaneous with the rise and spread of Enlightenment thinking, Lyotard is offering a diagnosis of life after modernism. These metanarratives have ranged in their overarching scope from the promise of political independence and human liberation through representative democracy and/or the victory of the masses to the claims for the efficacy of scientific knowledge as the harbinger of social progress through victory over a now mostly tamed nature and through social engineering. Lyotard calls particular attention to those metanarratives, like liberalism and Marxism, that have held out the hope for total change in society and culture (and economy) through advocacy of particular principles and perspectives. In both liberalism and Marxism, for example, there has been the tendency to measure human progress partly in terms of the ability of humankind to harness technology and science to human designs, most especially the end of political oppression and/or economic exploitation. Lyotard is hostile to such stories insofar as they themselves contribute to a 'totalizing' vision of the world, one in which progress is in the nature of history, and in which social practices are linked in a kind of reinforcing signifying chain in the name (or cause) of freedom, happiness, and autonomy. That is, Lyotard sees that much damage has been done in the advent of such grand causes, and he identifies them with the narratives, broadly held and interpreted, that give them their extra-discursive power. But, additionally, Lyotard sees as well the attempt to reduce the relative autonomy of science and culture in the service of these master narratives as either illusory or dangerous, or both.

Thus Lyotard eschews the story, so prevalent, for example, in the history and philosophy of economics, that knowledge has both simply progressed and that it has been the dynamic force behind social progress, as truth inevitably drives out error and knowledge comes to increasingly replace ideology.[20] Indeed, a distinguishing aspect of modernist thought is the widely and fiercely held belief in the narratives about the clear benefits and merits of scientific knowledge. (A chemist who is a colleague of one of us declared recently in a public audience that the only thing in the entire past century he could identify as clearly contributing to a 'better' world was science; his evaluation of every other sphere of human endeavor, from the arts to social and political movements for enfranchisement to sexual revolutions to the spread of the marketplace, have resulted in mixed results, at best, and most probably social devolution!) Lyotard seems more intent to talk about what he perceives as the fact that current scientific preoccupations and practices are no longer (in his view) wedded to narratives about the ultimate knowability of the world and the beneficial dimension of such knowledge. The world of science that he consequently describes is more taken with images, concepts, and activities of discontinuity. It is a world of nearly infinite and diverse information flows (of course, made possible by the computer revolution) and it is rife with scientific 'games'[21] in which meaning and consequence (of these games) are always in play or at stake. This is a world, he feels, that is developing more along the lines of considerations of chaos and uncertainty, of indeterminacies and fracta, rather than in accordance with a view of the unified structure of nature and of the predictably sanguine (and utilitarian) results of scientific knowledge.[22] This is a world, too, in which the fundamental discursivity of science is not only celebrated, but becomes almost a new master narrative enlivening current scientific endeavors, as everything from biotechnology and human genome research to contemporary astrophysics may increasingly be seen as a 'reading' or a Wittgensteinian game of particular fields as inscribed within a kind of ultralinguistic system. Lyotard identifies these considerations and games as constituting, to a large degree, the postmodern condition, at least where knowledge production and dissemination are concerned.

The postmodern condition Lyotard describes has its corollaries in a variety of fields of human activity. Regardless of the originating causes of this condition (whether it reflects capitalism's most recent developments, or the information revolution, or the decline of community and the evaporation of universal moral norms, or the effects of affluence for some and continued agony for others, and so forth), many others in addition to Lyotard have joined in to note the changed conditions of life in more developed societies during the past 40 or more years.[23] Lyotard's 'report' highlights in many ways the central terms of this altered life experience (that is, compared to the modernism that is said to either precede or coexist with it).[24] These terms include a sense that individual lives and social entities have been 'decentered'; that we live in a variety of psychological and social states/positions, each of which 'overdetermine' our identities and subjectivities; that modern science and technology contribute possibly as much to 'barbarism' and destruction (the atom bomb, pollution, germ warfare, etc.) as they do to the betterment of human life and the natural environment; that the metanarratives of progress and liberation have either failed or have contributed to sociopolitical outcomes that are repulsive; that knowledge and ethics are context-specific and time-specific; that there are radical discontinuities in the way we experience most everything we encounter; that there is little that can be considered 'original' or 'authentic' in culture (nor ought there to be); that power is dispersed rather than concentrated; that the search for unique meaning and transcendent truth are no longer meaningful or constructive quests; and that social inequalities and race, class, gender, and ethnic oppression continue in direct contrast to modernism's promises of freedom, justice, and equality for all.

This brief list speaks to modernism's putative exhaustion and anomie, but it also speaks to altered circumstances, some of which are happily embraced by theorists of postmodernism. These changed circumstances, expressed perhaps most fully in recent art and literature, speak to the extent to which many of the touchstones of modernist culture and society have been or are now being decomposed, discarded, or 'deconstructed'. Therefore, while the 'postmodern condition' can and often does span a wide spectrum of social, cultural, and even economic currents, let us spend a few more moments talking about three areas in particular that are of primary concern for many of the papers in this volume: the nature of the contemporary 'subject', the state of scientific knowledge, and the sense that we live in a world pervaded by uncertainty.

As we mention above, so much talk about postmodernism has been about the human subject and the dissolution of psychosocial unity in the face of an increasingly fragmented existence.[25] In some postmodern strands of writing, the subject is said to be overloaded, or 'saturated', by images and identities that are made possible today – indeed are forced on the poor subject – by the excess of images, cultural events, and social relationships that are the result of everything from the increased volume and pace of market transactions to MTV. Again, the idea here is that changes in how we experience time and space have both paradoxically expanded the social world and, in a way, themselves been compressed as a result of this same world getting smaller (because becoming increasingly 'global'). The cultural psychologist Kenneth Gergen (1991) gives numerous examples that depict this saturation of the prototypical postmodern subject through the 'lengthening' of social experience and the shortening of time and space. Here are just a few:

> a call to a Philadelphia lawyer is answered by a message recorded in three languages.
>
> (2)

I gave a short speech at a birthday party in Heidelberg last year. When I returned to the United States three days later, a friend on the opposite coast called to tell me about the guests' reactions to the talk. He had gotten the gossip two days earlier via electronic mail.

(2)

Fred is a neurologist who spends many of his spare hours working to aid families from El Salvador. Although he is married to Tina, on Tuesday and Thursday nights he lives with an Asian friend with whom he has a child. On weekends he drives his BMW to Atlantic City for gambling.

(171)

Leaving aside any consideration for the moment of the class, race, gender, nationality or any other 'privilege' that these examples may exemplify, Gergen claims to be describing a growing phenomenon. In his view, the compression of time and space accomplished by technological achievements like jet travel and the internet, along with the accompanying possibilities of crossing, or even living in, a variety of 'cultures' has now pervaded the everyday lives of a vast world-wide populace. The assault on singular personality and focused rationality, and the dispersion of the putative 'unity' of the ego and the intentional subject, are the consequence of the fragmenting of social life that is considered the hallmark of postmodernity.[26]

Now, this fragmentation is either celebrated or lamented, determining to a large degree whether or not one sees the postmodern condition as a beneficial or negative development. Yet, for those who believe that the condition of existence for most of the world's population has indeed changed in the direction of increased fragmentation but also increased 'possibility', the passing of the unified subject and its replacement by the 'decentered subject' is a defining moment of a world-historical change. As we have said, the emergence of the decentered subject has been hailed or reviled. And these alternative evaluations have often depended on whether or not one sees the resulting dispersion of self and society as an evil, brought about by the insidious commodification that those like Jameson describe, or a good, announcing the abandonment of the great modernist, humanist metanarratives that Lyotard has attempted to elucidate. Be it as it may, the perception that the subject may not be as unified and rational as modernist science and literature had once supposed marks one of the key ways to trace the impact (perhaps potential) on such fields of social theory as economics.

For there is no question that for generations of mainstream economists, the rational subject who is capable of identifying or at least representing a consistent (at a moment in time) set of preferences is the starting point of much consequent economic theorizing.[27] Yet, it is possible that the postmodern condition is one that has been dimly grasped in some corners of the profession (even in some unlikely places, like game theory). More importantly, the postmodern condition may be said to open up a very different research agenda for economic scientists should they choose to disown what many regard as the necessary 'fiction' (defended by many, in the end, for containing more than just a grain of truth about human subjects) of the unified self and move, instead, to a different fiction (but one supposedly more in tune with contemporary reality), the decentered self. We return to these issues below. For now, suffice it to say that the idea that psychic fragmentation – and here we are not describing a supposed 'irrational pathology', as is said to be the case with schizophrenics – and the decentering of selves might alter economic analysis considerably is one that is represented to a degree in some of the essays in this collection (see footnote 25), and is, after all, one of the strongest challenges that the postmodern condition, if one accepts its 'reality', poses to the discipline.[28]

The recognition that subjects may in fact be 'decentered' in the contemporary world has considerable spillover effects on notions of the status and nature of knowledge in the postmodern condition. There is a sort of paradox operating here. On the one hand, subjects are seen to occupy so many different positions and to hold a bewildering variety of perspectives that the possibility of stable and commensurable knowledge among and between people is seen as highly questionable. In this view, knowledge is seen to be local (not universal) and subject to persistent uncertainty. The fragmentation of subjects (within themselves as well as among themselves) leads each and every one to hold mostly incommensurable concepts and notions, as universal truths retreat into the background or remain a thing of a supposed past, one in which homogenizing forces were presumed to be more determinative in constituting a horizon of transcendental intelligibility.

On the other hand, subjects may also be seen to reflect the particular locations in which they find themselves, thus leading to the idea that the unique experiences either of individuals or the groups to which they belong are today productive of 'situated' knowledges that, while not entirely translatable or transmittable, are at least stable enough to contribute to well-developed, 'standpoint'-based understandings. This view is based on the idea that fragmentation or decenteredness is not a matter of pure solipsism. Instead, the view is that knowledge may be 'relative' to the diversity of cultures and set of experiences – which may be widely shared, but not universally so – that are thought to determine human consciousnesses. The plurality of such identity-based knowledges – often reflecting the particular experiences people may have because of race or gender or class or national distinctions – makes it impossible for knowledge to pass itself off as 'unsituated' and 'uninterested'. In this view, the 'god's eye perspective' or the Platonic desire for a view from nowhere that were thought, alternatively, to be the underlying premises of modernist notions of the possibility of knowledge and science are rejected in favor of the notion that knowledge is always/already influenced by, if not an outright expression of, the 'standpoints' that various and discrete subjects may hold.

The standpoint approach to knowledge and science is one that, perhaps, brings certain postmodern theorists close to the perspectives brought to bear by feminists, multiculturalists, and those who stress the importance of post-coloniality for the 'social construction' of knowledge and science. Thus, while one may argue that the postmodern condition is characterized by rampant globalization, caused primarily by multinational capital flows and the increased mobility of worldwide labor, an irony may be that different voices – or at least their 'breakthrough' into the discourse and consciousness of Western societies and cultures – have remained intransigent in rejecting and blocking easy assimilation and formation into a globally agreed upon knowledge. The globalization that Jameson and others have described may be occurring apace, but this has only meant increased differentiation in the field of discourse and culture, as identities and standpoints turn out to be more resistant to integration than is often thought.

Hence, the postmodern condition may be one that not only calls attention to the race, gender, class, and national privilege that allowed for the 'scientific revolution' brought about by the Enlightenment to occur. It may also be one that keeps in play irreducible differences as the bases for all contemporary knowledge, even in fields that are self-described as 'hard science'. As subjects and societies are decentered by the proliferation of experiences and cultural identities, so too is knowledge and science in this postmodern world. And, note that the effects of such a decentering accompanied by a profusion of voices, in which one's standpoint matters, includes the possible indeterminacy and/or multiplicity of knowledge(s) not only for the subjects described within any field of thought, but of course (and perhaps even more importantly) for the scientist/observers themselves.

Economic agents, living in a postmodern world, are thus considered to be both situated and saturated. Giving voice to the confusion, but also the clarity, that results from an overload of possibilities, situated nonetheless in the multiple positions and identities that globalization has enhanced rather than eliminated. Agents are not irrational. They possess different, simultaneously experienced rationalities, expressing the likely cultural locations and histories whence they arise. Choice in this scenario often appears like a crap shoot, or something even more random than this (some Marxian theorists would call such a situation an 'overdetermined conjuncture'). Scientists, too, are confronted with a welter of choices. Theories contend and overlap, but they also are just plain different and non-reducible or transcendable by a transdiscursive Method. Theory choice may be more a matter of aesthetic taste, as the playing field for all such knowledge games is constituted as a collage of relatively autonomous strategies, tactics, and their outcomes. Thus, the postmodern condition for knowledge production is often represented as a kind of relativism, a situation in which there can be no ultimate appeal to a predetermined or attainable Truth, but in which taste and power and interest are shown to be part and parcel of why one theory flourishes while another may dwell in the shadows (see Foucault [1980] on the relationship between power and knowledge).

As we say above, the postmodern condition, as it is often described, is one that evinces indeterminacy and uncertainty rather than limpidity and predictability. Agents and observers of their behavior are constantly thinking and acting in the face of 'just not knowing'. So, then, as might be expected, the issues of how to behave or how to theorize under conditions of uncertainty have risen to the top of the agenda for natural and social scientists, that is if postmodern theorists like Lyotard are to be believed. Indeed, it is arguable that for the past 75 or more years the theme of uncertainty has been central to so many new developments in the arts and sciences, and this includes economics of course.[29] From the sheer randomness of Dada poetry to the indeterminacy of quantum physics to the role of uncertain expectations in organizing agent behavior in a market economy, this theme emerged during the twentieth century as opening up a new range of creative possibilities for thought and action.[30] Thus, some argue, postmodernism is simply the recognition of this reality, as theory brings up the rear in self-reflection on already changed world historical circumstances.

The style of the postmodern: self-reflecting and deconstructing

The preceding comments bring us to our third category for postmodernism. That is, postmodernism as a 'style' of writing, thinking, acting, and creating. In this vein, postmodernism has been associated once again not surprisingly with a vast number of different stances, genres, and movements, encompassing many things from self-reflexivity and bricolage to deconstruction and pastiche.[31]

Postmodern styles in music, art, architecture, literature, philosophy, and culture have brought to the fore the undecidability of meaning, the discursivity of the non-discursive, the inconceivability of pure 'presence', the irrelevance of intention, the insuperability of authenticity, the impossibility of representation, along with the celebration of play, difference, plurality, chance, inconsequence, and marginality. Postmodernism, as an agglomeration of styles, contributes to the sense that there is indeed a postmodern condition to which all these styles are directly or obliquely referring. And, of course, some of these styles are intended as well as oppositional to – as critiques of – the prevailing sensibilities and formations that are thought to make up the various modernisms in these fields and disciplines. But, whether or not these all speak to a set of changed historical and empirical circumstances, and indeed whether or not the emergence of these styles speaks too to some central historical cause, like the spread of global capitalist commodity culture, it remains the case that within the past 40 or more years, one can successfully document the rise of the 'postmodern' in aesthetics and ethics. That is, postmodernism as style affects the fundamental determinations of 'value' and 'meaning' as they are encountered throughout the social and cultural landscape.[32]

It is, of course, impossible for us to render intelligible such diverse stylistic movements in the questions of value and meaning in a brief introduction like this. Yet, since in fact some of the essays here draw upon certain strands of postmodern styles of thought and presentation, we will dwell upon just a few. One, of course, is the style that goes under the name of deconstruction.[33] This style, sometimes converted into a method, was pioneered and made famous by the French philosopher Jacques Derrida (1976, 1978). Now, like everything else discussed under the rubric of postmodernism (and its close relation, poststructuralism), deconstruction as literary/philosophical style has meant many different things to many different people. We encounter it most often, though, as a textual reading in which the play of words and signs within a text, presumed to produce stable and intelligible meanings, is shown to the contrary to precisely undo such stability and significance. For many who practice deconstruction, the goal is to demonstrate the impossibility of pure presence, that is, the inability of any sentence or text to stand for singular meanings and, hence, to eliminate contradiction, ambiguity, multiplicity, and so forth. In this view, texts can be 'deconstructed' by means of a close and careful analysis to reveal the 'aporia' and the 'undecidables' that are everpresent. Hence, a text is always gesturing – mostly in spite of itself – to other texts and to other referents, as it is shown to be the site of 'differance' (a mixed word that attempts to connote both 'difference' and 'deference' – the act of deferring).[34]

Deconstruction as a style of textual analysis calls attention to the radical indeterminacy of meaning, the inability to reduce the incessant play between signifiers (such as words and symbols) that never settles down into univocality. Deconstruction as a style of writing is a deliberate attempt to bring forth all those things that can be said to undermine – deconstruct – the supposed central and fixed meanings of textual compositions. So, for example, Derrida and others have often composed texts that are seemingly dialogic in nature, with simultaneous columns that in some way refer (or defer) to one another (if for no reason other than they occupy a privileged space on the same page). Likewise, these columns and other devices (marginal notes, cross-outs, and so forth) are utilized as means to show that there is something both arbitrary and even concealing about textual composition. Arbitrary, since the juxtaposition of words and images produces certain random possibilities simply by occupying the same space; concealing, since the eradication of erasures and the placing in margins of notes and other references often hides the conditions of production of texts and the importance of this marginalia in determining the range of possible meanings. That is, deconstruction as literary/philosophical style is often employed to show that what at first seems secondary or even superfluous to the main meanings turns out, in many ways, to either unsettle those meanings or, more seriously, displace those meanings in a reversal of signification.

Two texts by the economist Judith Mehta (one published here) show some of these elements at work in the composition of a piece of economics writing. In 'Look at Me Look at You' (1999), Mehta makes use of by now familiar deconstructionist textual strategies of composition. She combines images with texts, and has fragments of text overlapping on the page. At times, there are multiple columns. She writes with a variety of typefaces and font sizes. She intersperses quotations that, at first, may seem to be tangential to some other parts of the text. The 'voice' of the text toggles back and forth from more 'personal' to more 'objective' modes of presentation. There is little if any deference to disciplinary bounds, as economic ideas freely mingle with discourse concerned mainly with photography, art history, and much else. And so forth. Indeed, looking over her text, it is hard to 'center' it either on the page or even in terms of what constitutes a primary argument (thus, deconstruction as a style of literary or artistic creation deliberately conjures up the notion of 'decentering' we discuss above).

Yet, of course, it is possible to see this text as being concerned with several points. One is the idea that all texts achieve whatever meaning possible by reference and deference to other texts (hence the deliberate use of quotation). Another is that knowledge production is a messy affair, one that has as a condition of existence a multiplicity of sources and strategies. There is no single or sure road to meaning. Another is that readers are active (rather than passive) in constructing meanings in and out of texts. This is achieved largely by making the text unfamiliar in ways that challenge readers to be more engaged and conscious of their roles in 'discovering' what a text is trying to say.

In her essay for this volume, Mehta stages for readers the 'noise' that she finds expressed in most experiments involving economic bargaining games. Rather than the neat formulaic representations that game theorists are used to in modeling such strategic situations, Mehta chooses to run dual columns in certain parts of her text, one of which contains the 'actual words' of participants in a bargaining game experiment she and other colleagues ran, the other containing a typical neoclassical game theorist's abstract rendering of such a game. The point is, as Mehta maintains, to 'voice the noise', and to show that these two columns of text cannot be reducible to one another and that, in some important way, they signify quite different things that are unrecoverable in acts of 'translation' and synthesis. In opposition to the idea that there are few authorized and acceptable ways to 'represent' such experiments and their results, Mehta invokes a cacophony of voices in order to model in a different way deconstructing a game theorist's modernist text.

Indeed, more generally, deconstructive styles of writing give vent to discursive and semiotic play. But a kind of play in which discursive layers are tossed down on top of other layers with no particularly clear 'reason' for doing so. Thus, while some deconstructionist texts are quite deliberately created to embody indeterminacy, other texts are seemingly more slapdash and randomly constructed and take the form of a bricolage, a mishmash of presumably unrelated elements and images. The 'jokey', 'ersatz', and even 'nihilistic' quality of such writing and construction (as with postmodern architecture, which is often linked to an excess of 'quotation', ornament, and playfulness in contrast to a primary concern with function) unleashes a host of possible reevaluations, or, if one is critical of these strategies, the very demise of value itself. As opposed to the minimalism and parsimony thought to be characteristic of many 'high modernist' moments in culture and theory, postmodernist, deconstructionist style is overflowing with meanings, causes, and effects galore. The saturation we describe above is an effect of some postmodern creations, and this excess of everything is seen, alternatively, to signal a new age of possibility, a proliferation of meanings, a voicing of previously repressed desires, the cultural emergence of marginalized 'others', or the destruction of intelligibility, knowledge, and community.

While deconstruction may be a preferred stylistic strategy within what could be considered postmodernism, there is also no question that a similarly adopted stance is what has been called 'self-reflexivity'. One rendition of this idea is the practice that any agent or author 'locate' themselves in the process of producing artifacts, actions, and their effects. Agents and authors, then, seek to show not only that they are themselves 'implicated' in their works and deeds, but also that these productions cannot be entirely separated from such constituting aspects as one's histories, identities, interests, values, and so forth. Warren Samuels states that in matters of knowledge, postmodernism 'points out the fundamental assumptions of all claims to knowledge, including, in a self-reflexive manner, its own' (1996: 66).

Self-reflexivity may be something other than subjective self-awareness. It is more concerned with the argument that all things, from politics to philosophy, are intimately bound up with the situatedness of those engaged in these activities. And that identifying the locations from which people speak, write, and act matters for the kinds of meanings and values that can be produced. In our own field, E. Roy Weintraub argues, for example, that 'all knowledge, a fortiori economic knowledge, is local and contingent and connected to a community in which that knowledge was produced or interpreted or otherwise made significant', and he goes on to state that it is 'not useful to speak about economic knowledge without also speaking about economists and the communities in which economic knowledge was produced and communicated' (1992: 53–4).

A number of essays in this volume speak or employ, either directly or in passing, a self-reflexive style. It is believed, for example, that it simply will not do to 'hide' the desires and wills of economic scientists that can be seen to determine their own 'preferences' in theory choice, methodology, and so much else besides.[35] So, not only do several authors here make clear the positions from which they believe they are writing, and what privilege or authority they seek, express, or are trying to subvert,[36] but, they also want to 'out' all other economists, especially those who maintain that one's politics or morals or cultural identities have had or should have no bearing on the kinds of economic analysis that they have been disseminating.

In a different way, a self-reflexive style can be said to be at the heart of the 'discursive turn' that many commentators of postmodernism and poststructuralism have noted for the past 20 years. In this view, postmodern forms of theorizing and fictionalizing have in common an inward focus, a focus on the conditions of writing and discoursing as opposed to the connection of the word with the world or to just 'revealing' the world in all its fullness and glory. Thus, postmodernism has been very closely associated with the self-conscious, incessant play with words and images that comprise an assault for some and a celebration for others of modes of discursive creation and representation. The 'self-consciousness' of many postmodern writers and thinkers that takes the form of showing the discursive conditions of a text's existence, and a showing that one is showing, and so on sometimes into potentially infinite recursiveness has been seen either as a retreat of philosophy, art, and social theory away from the pressing issues of the day (presumed to exist 'outside' of these realms) or, more benignly, as a new appreciation for the way rhetoric, metaphor, speech acts, and other figures of writing and speech shape fundamentally the ideas and events of both the discursive and the non-discursive world.

Whatever the case may be, there is strong evidence that one important way that postmodernist style has entered a field like economics has been through exhortations and explications of the ways language and sign systems in general (like mathematics) are or should be most under scrutiny in the formation of economic analysis. Monographs and collections in economics with titles such as *Adam Smith's Discourse* (Brown 1994), *Economics as Discourse* (Samuels, ed. 1990), *Economics and Language* (Henderson, Dudley-Evans, and Backhouse, eds. 1993), *Economics and Hermeneutics* (Lavoie 1991), *The New Economic Criticism* (whose subtitle is *Studies at the Intersection of Literature and Economics*) (Woodmansee and Osteen 1999), and of course *The Rhetoric of Economics* (McCloskey 1985), *The Consequences of Economic Rhetoric* (Klamer, McCloskey, and Solow, eds. 1988), *Knowledge and Persuasion in Economics* (McCloskey 1994), and *Conversations with Economists* (Klamer 1983) have appeared in the past 20 years and mark this kind of self-reflexive moment in economic thought.[37] And, of course, many if not all of the essays in this volume are marked as well by this type of self-reflexivity, by a consideration of the ways economists write and think according to well-known literary and semiotic devices, all of which supposedly give the lie to the claim, then, that words are simple transparencies allowing privileged economic scientists to apprehend truths that are just simply 'out there'.

Perhaps self-reflexivity is witnessed as well in the extent to which the problem of knowledge within postmodern circles is posed largely in non- or anti-epistemological terms. Or rather, the problem of knowledge, for many postmodernists, is not an issue at all since there is a wholesale refusal of the polar opposites that structure most epistemological dissertations at least since the Enlightenment (and likely going back much further in historical time). The problem of knowledge for so many 'modernist' philosophers of knowledge had been to specify how a knowing subject could apprehend a mostly dumb and intractable world of objects. But, postmodernists have often written on the question of knowledge from the point of view that this problem is really a red herring. That is, postmodernists often claim that the problem of knowledge in classical epistemology is built upon a misspecification of the nature of the subject and ignores the impossibility of ever pulling apart the knower from the known.

In this light, postmodernists have argued that knowledge production is not a matter of a subject/scientist finding the right 'tools' to 'penetrate' the world of objects, finding the nuggets of truth contained within the outer sheaths of extraneous dross. To the contrary, subjects are active in the construction of truths, and their very observations and perceptions structure those truths irresistibly.[38] Subjects therefore can see themselves or their practices and their effects in the truths they produce (a classic reference is to Heisenberg's uncertainty principle), and this gives rise, then, to another moment of self-reflexivity.[39] Unable to claim any disengagement and disentanglement from the world under analysis, postmodernist practitioners give full voice to their own 'presence' in their constructions. Again, this style of writing and analysis is in evidence in several of the essays presented here.

Postmodernism as critique: from antimodernism to 'postmodern moments'

Self-reflexive and deconstructive styles of writing are most often used in the service of critique. Modernism is the object of the critical stances and styles that comprise postmodernism. Now, of course, there are diverse and divergent understandings about what modernism means in all of its manifestations. For our purposes, we refer readers to several texts that attempt to summarize those aspects and understandings of modernism that are of most concern for a large number of postmodern theorists and practitioners.[40] We will specify, though, some of those aspects insofar as they show up as the likely foil for many of the essays contained here. First, however, we need to clarify exactly what it means to regard postmodernism as a critique of modernism and modernity.

For some postmodernists, the forms of social and cultural life that have been ushered in as part of the 'modern age' are sufficiently debilitating and faulty as to warrant simple opposition. That is, postmodernism is sometimes encountered as an anti-modernism. In this case, postmodernism often joins forces with neo-traditionalists (neo-Aristotelians, for example – see the discussion of this tendency in Klamer's essay in this collection) who see modernism in many of its forms as having brought about the demise in older values – some even promised as a feature of modernism – that stressed (local) community, moral goodness, tolerance, social justice, and individual freedom. Since modernism is seen to have failed, either partially or catastrophically, in cultivating and upholding such values, postmodernism then provides a perspective from which to critically evaluate and ultimately transcend modernity. The tendencies to be sensitive to difference and alterity, to question expertise and authority, especially in the name of the state or science, to value conversation and discourse, to desire ecological conservation rather than economic transformation, to refuse the prerogatives usually according to supposedly inexorable technological progress, to criticize the fiction of the self as an independent, unified entity, and to see the murderous flaws in grandiose, global schemes for human liberation, are all thought to be dimensions of postmodernism in its critical moments. As we say, often these moments amount to a hope of recovering elements of a pre-modern world of values and characters and community and sociality. At the very least, modernism is seen here as presenting the opportunity for a future, not in its 'completion', but rather in suggesting exactly the points at which it can be opposed.[41] Postmodernism as anti-modernism takes modernity as the negative blueprint for much of what it hopes to erect.

Yet, for other postmodernists, being simply 'against' modernism is both impossible and besides the point (see, e.g., Dow in this book). In this view, postmodernism's critical bearing leads towards a 'non-modernism', that is, an attempt to escape in some way the oppositions – seen to be caught within modernism – that are seen to structure so much of modernist thought (subject/object, essence/appearance, and so forth). The pressure to be 'either/or' is seen to be precisely what modernisms present as the only real options. Hence, postmodernism, to be truly 'other', cannot be reduced to the play of modernism's oppositions, just the other side of the modernist coin. And, for many writing and creating in this postmodern critical mode, the point *is* to be 'truly other'. To be radically different is to suggest a sea-change rather than a search and recovery mission (finding the remnants of a discarded pre-modernism at the bottom of the vast modernist ocean). The critical edge then in this type of postmodern work consists of elisions, of somehow escaping the snares that are presented by modernist ways of thinking and behaving, of being just out of reach of either/or couplets. This type of non-modernism is often infuriating to modernist and other critics since postmodernists seem to avoid the kinds of battle that their critics desire. Hence, postmodernism as a non-modernism often appears as avoidance behavior, a retreat into non-confrontational stances distinguished by an emphasis on play, the relativity of perspectives, self-absorption, and the inconsequence of theory, interest, value, and meaning.

Elements of both these attitudes – postmodernism as an anti- and non-modernism – appear in our own work and in the papers in this book. There is, however, another possibility which we think worth exploring. This is to view modernism and postmodernism to always be 'incomplete', unable to achieve the pure presence that we discuss above. That is, we take seriously the deconstructionist idea that it is impossible for various modernisms to ever totalize any field of discourse, art, or work to the extent that their meanings and effects are unequivocal and determinate. To the contrary, we prefer to think of modernism and postmodernism as constituting horizons or, better said, moments that are, themselves, transient and porous, lacking the ability to suture time and space – to create discernible boundary lines for historical ages and within the vast terrain of the social – in discursive and non-discursive realms. One critical component of such a view lies in the idea that one can show the tenuous, even if tenacious, hold on imaginations and institutions that attend the appearance of modernism (or postmodernism for that matter) in any field of inquiry or action. Another critical element consists of demonstrating that, despite its best efforts, modernism is unable to close the circle, to completely hegemonize political, economic, and cultural spaces, and that crucial postmodern moments arise and are effective in beckoning us toward alternative ways of thinking 'beyond' modernism. Showing then the postmodern moments that have emerged within fields dominated (but only partially) by modernism can give rise to adumbrating the paths of its supercession. Thus, to the extent that modernism is seen to produce less than salutary effects, highlighting the postmodern moments within a field can be tantamount to a kind of immanent critique.[42]

Two additional remarks. One is that our interest in exhibiting the postmodern moments within economics is not much directed to the obvious point that modernism and postmodernism coexist in the present. Nor, really, it is directed to the point that postmodernism might be profitably viewed as the latest stage of modernism, a continuation in some sense of many of the themes developed over the course of the past century in art, literature, philosophy and so forth. Indeed, some cultural critics have belittled the overarching notion of modernism and postmodernism found in other non-literary fields (in economics, for instance) since, in their view, including such elements as indeterminacy, the critique of representation, and the decentered (if not the alienated) subject within the confines of postmodernism misses badly the emergence of these and other themes within what they regard as the 'high modernism' of their own fields of work and study. In this view, postmodernism may be said to be a strengthening rather than a weakening of certain crucial components of modernism, that is, a moment in the continuous development of modernism. Or, the term postmodern might be reserved to describe still other irruptions.

This brings us to the second remark. Our use of the term postmodern moments is also directed at the idea that there are what we perceive as 'uneven developments' within and between fields of thought and practice. So, perhaps it makes more sense to label as postmodern the attack on the unified subject and notions of more or less certain knowledge within a field like economics, where modernism may appear as a strict and dogged adherence by a majority of practitioners to such notions. Yet, in other fields, literary studies say, postmodernism may be more concerned with issues having to do with deconstructive techniques, reader response, canonical texts, and still other concerns. Hence, to bring forth the postmodern moments in any field or endeavor is to acknowledge that modernism(s) may have many faces that appear here and there, with no necessity for a single visage ever to emerge 'full-blown' (whatever this fullness may be thought to consist of). And, by extension, postmodernism(s) are likewise dispersed and multiple and follow no logic that mandates they appear everywhere in the same form at the same time. Since much of our interest in this volume is discipline-specific, we steer the remainder of our remarks toward the postmodern moments within economics, paying attention to the extent to which postmodernism as critique is directed at the forms of modernism we can identify within economic discourses.

The objects of postmodern critique: modernity's 'isms'

Whether anti- or non-modernist or dedicated to showing postmodern moments, what does it mean to treat postmodernism chiefly as a critique of modernism? What elements of modernism within economics are found by critics to warrant opposition and/or transcendence? What moments of postmodernism can be discerned as disturbing the modernist waters of economics as a discipline?

First, we enumerate what we regard as among the primary objects of postmodern critique within this field. These include essentialism, foundationalism, scientism, determinism, formalism, and humanism in addition to the notion of the unified, intentional, rational agent.[43] In some ways, postmodernism shares with other viewpoints and whole schools of thought (and here we include feminism, Marxism, institutionalism, and other 'heterodox' approaches within economics) an attack on one or another of these objects. Yet, there is also a connection between some of the critiques that are considered specifically postmodern, and so we attempt to show how, for example, the postmodern critique of the unified agent may weigh heavily as well on postmodern considerations of the content and process of producing knowledge.

Representation and essentialism

Modernism is thought to be imbued with representational logics and forms of display. Here, what we mean is the idea that there are at least two levels of thought and/or practice for each and every object. A shorthand way of looking at the relationship between these levels is to call them 'appearance' and 'essence'. Now, it is possible to show that so much of modernist notions of science and culture speaks to this crucial distinction. In much modernist philosophy of science, for example, the world of appearances is said to be incapable of yielding up the 'meaning' and/or 'true nature' of objects and their relationships among themselves. The role of the trained scientist is then to be able to perceive the patterns or meanings that reside either within objects themselves or in the interactions between them. 'Discovery' is a practice which is all about finding the essential order that lies beneath a presumed chaotic and even ornamental surface. Indeed, the scientific critique of common sense, ersatz, and/or other supposedly non-scientific thought consists of showing that, in these discourses, appearances are mistaken for essences (or rather that there is no discernible difference observed between them).

Representation structures as well the self-consciousness of scientific practice. The scientist's words are thought to correspond, in some important way, to the world they are intended to describe. That is, language is seen to be mostly representational, at least in the hands of scientists who are trained not to let 'mere words' obfuscate the truths that have been thus discovered.[44]

Whether that language is professional prose, or mathematics, or formal logic, and so forth, the view that many regard as exemplary of a modernist conceit or prejudice is that language is a second-order condition. Language and signs are only useful or necessary to communicate truths that have been discovered and that require representation through language. The idea here is that language can be utilized in a way where it does not 'distort' the essential truths that scientific practice and thought have unearthed.[45] Hence, language is reduced to appearance (not essence), but a necessary one if the gems of truth excavated in the world are going to be put on display and allowed to shine.

One form of this cult of representation, then, is what has been called essentialism – the idea that there are essences to discover, that there are tried-and-true methods of uncovering these essences, and that appearances are to be suspected but also probed for the hidden truths or meanings lying beneath their surface. There is no question that so much postmodern critique has been in the form of a refusal of representational schemas and logics, and of course a rejection and/or subversion of essentialism. In place of these schemas and logics has been an aesthetic or ethic of 'depthlessness'. Postmodernism can be distinguished in many different arenas as repudiating the search for and representation of essences, proclaiming in contrast notions of juxtaposition, simultaneity, and so forth. That is, for many postmodernists, there are no meanings hidden in texts or in the world, and therefore there are no hierarchies of elements, some living as appearances and others as essences, or alternatively, some occupying the space of cause while others simply effects. While there may be nothing, therefore, waiting for just the right technique or act of genius (or accident) to be discovered in this non-representational logic, there is instead an appreciation of the play of elements that comprise pure surface. It is attention to the constructedness as well as the arbitrariness of any given meaning or value that marks many postmodern approaches. It may not be that the world is meaningless or valueless. It may just be that meaning and value are not 'essential' or at least implicit in objects and their relations. The shift to looking at how knowledge is produced from how a subject/scientist comes to extract truth from a world of simultaneously glittery but also inarticulate appearances distinguishes, once again, the postmodern turn.[46]

Note that so much else is implied in this postmodern critique of representation and essentialism. For example, formalism as a preferred mode of presentation is based on the presumption that there are languages better suited than others for representing discovered truths.[47] The idea that there is, in fact, an important distinction between form and content belies the notion that form can be adequate to content if and when the appropriate linguistic or semiotic devices are employed. The defense of formal modeling and the heavy reliance on mathematics in economics, for example, depends crucially on the view that such forms of presentation are better able to allow truths to shine through (or at least hypotheses to be tested for their potential veracity or acceptability) than non-formal devices.[48] If there are no truths waiting to be apprehended and displayed by the right formal language, then the power and privilege accorded to mathematics in fields like economics are likely denied. Formal presentation and modeling become just 'other' discursive means of economic knowledge production, with no better access to underlying essential truths than any other such means. Which is simply to say that formalism may be important in producing economic knowledge, but it is production once again (and not representation) that is in evidence.[49]

The postmodern critique of essentialism resounds as well in thwarting attempts to escape some forms of representation, as can be seen in some versions of economic philosophy in which words and numbers are said not so much to represent or describe a real world outside of discourse as to present testable propositions for their ability to predict outcomes. The shift from the 'realism' of assumptions to the 'as if' hypotheses of Milton Friedman and his followers is often defended as an implicit critique of essentialism. This is because Friedman and others may claim not to have any particular notion of the correlation between words, numbers and underlying truths but, instead, seek accuracy (or at least less falsehood) in prediction that follows from a causal hypothesis. Yet, this response fails to eliminate the recourse to some notion that it is possible to discern transdiscursive truth via a method of ascertaining regularities through scientific observation. Such observation 'reads' essences (now discussed in the form of abstractions) in the myriad perceptions that are picked over for what is necessary or useful in testing the proposition and what is not. Appearances still are suspect, and need to be arranged and interpreted properly in order for the scientist to verify or falsify the proposition in question.

Foundations for knowledge

Postmodern critique in areas dominated by ideas concerning scientific knowledge has concentrated largely on an assault on foundationalism, the notion that there is a transdiscursive basis upon which such knowledge can be erected.[50] The foundations in question usually range from certain modernist epistemological positions (which include empiricism and rationalism and their offshoots, like positivism) to 'proper' experimental methods. What postmodern criticism amounts to, in light of the refusal of essentialism, includes an alternative view that there are multiple bases for the production of knowledge; that there can be no ultimate conceptual arbiter of different truth claims (though there may indeed be the perception that these claims have different effects, some of which can be preferred to others); that discourses concerned with knowledge production are often irreducible, largely non-translatable, and therefore mostly incommensurate; and that settling the priority or hierarchy of different truth claims must always be connected to persuasiveness and power. Though relativist nihilism is certainly one possible outcome of this anti-foundationalism, it is not the only one.[51] Postmodern critique calls attention not only to the play of power and persuasion in the current or past status quo within scientific practice.[52] It also calls attention to the fact that such forces are considered, in a sense, legitimate in the adjudication amongst and between discourses.[53]

Rather than shying away from, or simply decrying, the way rhetoric, privilege, authority, and networks of power are all entwined in knowledge production and especially in claims for any one discourse's superiority in constituting truth, an alternative position, one embraced by the French philosopher Michel Foucault (1972, 1980), is to acknowledge precisely that this is the way the world of knowing and convincing (and enforcing) works. The imbrication of power and knowledge, in fact, was the focus of much of Foucault's work, and postmodern critics have taken from him the view that there is nothing much to be ashamed of in the recognition that there are 'wills' and 'desires' to knowledge that have as much to do with power as they do with anything else.[54] Power can be contended over; it can be the object of struggle over who gets to speak and produce authoritative knowledge and who does not. This, of course, is exactly what is at stake in the attempts to storm the citadels of knowledge production occupied and controlled by those (usually Western and white men) who disseminate their 'normal sciences' in the form of canonical knowledge. That is, power to produce, speak, and disseminate, as well as to subvert and displace traditional notions of knowledge and particular conceptual content are often the objectives of oppositional forces – in economics comprised of heterodox thinkers and doers, including Marxists, feminists, postcolonialists, and many others.[55] It is true that some of this opposition holds precisely the same modernist view that scientific knowledge ought to be disinterested, unsusceptible to power, unmoved by rhetorical flourishes, unattached to other networks of power in society, and so forth. But, in effect, the postmodern position à la Foucault is that power and persuasion are *not* science's dirty little secret, and postmodern critique has attempted to bring them into the light (sort of like a previously perceived deviant behavior, which has now been shown to be undeserving of ostracism), not in the form of sensational revelation or staged revulsion, but as an assertion of the norms necessarily operating in the everyday life of scientific disciplines.

Science or scientism?

What this postmodern critique makes possible though is a sweeping rejection of scientism, the view that scientific concepts, methods, protocols, and the like are exclusively entitled to the power and privilege they have achieved with modernization. If the growth of scientific knowledge is the key accomplishment of the past three centuries in the West, it has been accompanied by an elaborate philosophical defense of a variety of exclusionary practices by which those deemed to be untrained or unreceptive to such science are shunted aside and oftentimes even denied opportunities to speak (since they are the voice of unreason). We need not belabor this point here since so much of the controversy surrounding postmodernism – indeed, many of the visceral reactions it has provoked – has been in the challenges it has thrown up in contending over the exalted status of science within modernism. However, again, it should be noted that the attack on scientific privilege does not necessarily imply a disinterest in or refusal of scientific practice.[56]

Indeed, the postmodern critique has often been more on the self-congratulatory aspects of the philosophy of science and the attempts to insulate scientific practice from scrutiny of its own rules of discursive formation, its implicit epistemological norms, its own situatedness in contemporary culture and social life, and much else. In many of the essays included here, inspired to greater or lesser degrees by postmodernism, so-called scientific practice in economics is investigated through a critical lens for its rhetorical structure, for its values and norms, for its connections to other centers of power and authority, as well as for the construction and interplay of the 'internal' elements that give any particular theory or approach discursive force. Postmodernism as critique of scientism then connects up with other, perhaps non-postmodern, critics of science and the philosophy of science, such as Thomas Kuhn (1970), Paul Feyerabend (1978), Bruno Latour (1993), Sandra Harding (1986), and Barry Barnes (1985), who can each be read in different ways to have promoted the idea that 'agreement' (voluntary, forced, and every combination inbetween) in science is what needs to be understood and investigated, and that those theories that often succeed at any given moment in time in shaping a field of thought are either bound to more general social institutions and patterns of status, wealth, and power, or are able to hegemonize the field by 'normalizing' the conditions under which that theory arises, and maybe both. The postmodern critique of scientism is close as well to the view of Feyerabend that there are no singularly exceptional methods that are productive of science, and even that actual scientific 'progress' is the result of scientists' refusal to codify and obediently follow any philosophically prescribed road toward truth.[57] As we have said, when one empties the world of the distinction between appearance and essence, and any method that claims to uniquely bridge the gap, one gives vent to a plurality of approaches that are potentially productive of knowledge, scientific or otherwise.

The critique of essentialism and foundations opens up the question then of the privileged status of scientific discourse. If science has no prior purchase on uncovering embedded and veiled truths, then it is not possible to sustain the hierarchy of discourses in which only science is productive of knowledge and all else – opinion, faith, ideology, art, etc. – is productive of, well, all else. If postmodernist critique is effective in the attack on essentialism, then one possible repercussion may be the leveling of the field of knowledge. Thus, as argued elsewhere (Amariglio and Ruccio, 1999), postmodern critique makes one start from the premise that what are today regarded as 'ersatz' or 'commonsense' or 'everyday' – read: confused, aberrant, and irrational – understandings of economics can be shown to be likewise productive of knowledge worthy of analysis and consideration, if not acceptance.[58] In other words, the trappings of science do not amount to a protective shield, and much of importance would be achieved, we think, if all would-be knowers treated seriously the possibility that truth and useful knowledge can perhaps come from these 'other' discursive formations and locations.

We note that this leveling of the field of knowledge makes it also impossible to sustain a meaningful distinction between metadiscourse and discourse. To take just one example, there exists a hierarchy well established and respected within academic economics such that talk about economic discourse (which includes such specializations as the history of economic thought and the philosophy and methodology of economics) is seen once again as 'second-order', and 'doing' economics (which involves mostly building and testing economic models) is seen as primary, the stuff the discipline is essentially made of.

Now, one presumption here is that economic model building and even 'high theory' (which often has no particular testable model as its consequence) have a priority in defining professional economic discourse since they are not commentary on texts but, in contrast, have direct access in some way, shape, or form to economics' 'content' (either the 'real world' or mathematically derived abstract truths). Here we see that if we conjoin the critique of essentialism with other poststructuralist tenets regarding the textuality of any world 'read' by a scientist/observer, then we can appreciate the impossibility of maintaining the 'meta' distinction that accords, once again, so much power and privilege to those thought capable of 'doing' economics as opposed to merely 'talking' about it. If doing economics is just one other means of 'reading' the world, and consists no more nor less of 'commentary' on it, then one can at least challenge the first-order, epistemological privilege that is accorded to high economic theory and/or econometric analysis. Admittedly, the objects of such discourse may be different from that which is the object of the history of economic thought, but perhaps that is all that can be said. Neither tells the truth better or worse, and neither is closer (or further) from the supposedly primordial 'real' with its hidden meanings.

Determinism

Modernism is accused by postmodern critics for its persistent recourse to deterministic arguments where questions of cause and effect are concerned. In some versions of this critique, modernist explanation consists mostly of establishing the necessary or, less strongly, contingent patterns that link particular events as causes with other events as effects. Indeed, theory is the realm in which such explanations reign, and the absence of causal explanations is often viewed as the absence of theoretical activity. Now, while it is by no means necessary for causal explanation to be consistent, unilinear, and determinate, postmodern critics see the reduction of causation to these elements in most of what they observe in modernist discourses and disciplines. Determinism is a way of summing up these elements, as deterministic arguments are characterized by the search for principal causes that are said to have the largest weight (sometimes the only weight) in consistently bringing about a particular cause. In the idealized world of the 'marketplace of ideas', some causal explanations are preferred if they either identify an essential, underlying, and necessary cause (hence, determinism can be another form of essentialism) or capture a statistically predictable correlation between two distinct events, where one event is seen to nearly almost always 'follow' in time and perhaps in space from the other. Postmodernist thinkers, though, have proposed alternative ways of conceiving of causation that avoid, in their view, the destructive consequences of determinism (and these range from the intolerant fanaticism of those who feel that they have found the one and only explanation for events to the passivity produced in human agency and social action when deterministic understandings posit the impossibility of alternative courses of behavior).

Determinism comes in many shapes and sizes. Within modernist social and natural sciences, everything from biology to culture to the economy to subjectivity has been pronounced, often simultaneously, to be the first, last, and perhaps efficient cause of many different events and human actions. In economics, of course, determinism has a variety of familiar forms, the most common being economic determinism, in which the economy or some sub-particle of it is seen to structure an array of predictable effects. Hence, 'it's the economy, stupid' is not just taken by many economists as an adage of what should count in the political opinions of social agents. It's taken even more to describe a grand chain of social causation, in which 'the economy' (here including alternative entry points as labor, utility, rational choice, and so forth) is seen as the motivating agency behind all consequent social outcomes. Indeed, as we discussed above, the extension by Becker, Richard Posner (1992), and others of economic reasoning into cultural spheres is based on a type of privilege economists think redounds to economic explanation, since, by this logic, most human activity can be reduced in explanation to a matter of economizing, maximizing choices.[59]

The attack on determinisms of all sorts has been among the main contributions of postmodern critique. Alternative, specifically postmodern interrogations have emphasized the randomness of causation and the effectivity of chance, the indeterminacy of events, the multiplicity of possible causes, the fluidity of the relationship between seeming causes and their effects, and the reversibility of positions between putative causes and effects. Such interrogations have proceeded through the use of such notions as 'overdetermination', juxtaposition, synchronic simultaneity, fundamental uncertainty, and so forth. But, rather than surrender to the claim that theory is all but impossible if causation is not rendered in some form of determinism, postmodern non-determinists have answered by stressing the role of theory in positing rich conjunctural analyses, limited, of course, to more 'local' and specific occurrences. Some, for example the Marxist economists Stephen Resnick and Richard Wolff (1987), have argued further that the rejection of determinism does not require even a different 'entry point' into analysis. What it does require, though, is the idea that this entry point – which is a discursive 'choice', often connected to a multitude of other values and desires – not be presented as favored 'cause' in the world one is describing. Borrowing the term 'overdetermination' from the French Marxist philosopher Louis Althusser, Resnick and Wolff show how entering a discourse with any privileged concept such as class does not mandate causal explanations in which class then is said to determine (either directly or even in a mediated but distinguishable form) other social processes and events.

In economics, of course, economic determinism is less a function of the reduction of the social world to effects of class but much more a similar reduction to the effects of individual economic agency. Postmodern critique adds one more voice to an already noisy chorus of objections to the idea of homo economicus.[60] The notion of subjectivity that founds much economic (particularly neoclassical) theorizing has been railed against and dissected for its faultiness by dissenting voices for most of the past century. Postmodern critique, though, identifies the rational, maximizing agent as only one element within the context of a broader theoretical humanism, another distinguishing aspect (according to postmodernists) of the rise and dominance of modernist modes of thinking and being.

Theoretical humanism

Much of the postmodern critique of theoretical humanism has been closely connected to the writings of Foucault, Althusser, Lyotard, Derrida, and other 'poststructuralist' analysts. Perhaps Foucault, though, is best known for his thoroughgoing offensive against humanism, or rather, his claim that recent writing and philosophizing (in the postmodern vein) has shown glimmers, blessedly, of the 'death of Man'.[61] Foucault (1973) outlines what he terms certain 'epistemes' that he believes have structured much of Western thought since the Middle Ages, and when he gets to the Enlightenment and thereafter, he sees many roads in thought and practice leading to representational modes in which what is represented and/or signified is most often humanity as the originating subject of all knowledge and consequent history. Placing humanity, rather than god, say, at the center of a discursive universe is, in Foucault's writings, one noticeable characteristic of post-Enlightenment thinking (that is, perhaps until the middle of the twentieth century). Foucault argues that so much social thinking and cultural activity is directed to knowledge of and control over human subjectivity (and here, subjectivity becomes again the motivating agency in tracing all historical movement). Foucault (1979) goes further and identifies the human body as the site of so much surveillance and discipline, and he sees this desire to 'know Man' and his/her body as behind projects of knowledge and social ordering – the exercise of power – varying in subject matter from utilitarianism to existentialism.[62]

The idea that the human subject is the sine qua non – the bottom line – for all thought and practice in the modern era is taken up as well by Althusser (1970; Althusser and Balibar 1970), who concentrates some of his own critique on the idea that history is most frequently understood within modern thought as a process with a subject (usually, but not exclusively, a human subjectivity, like individuals seeking progressive freedom from natural or social constraint, or classes seeking the overthrow of exploitation and oppression). Placing humans at the center of schemas of progress and history and meaning is what distinguishes theoretical humanism, as the human subject is thus the beginning and ending point of all movement from the growth of knowledge (which is now understood as undertaken by, for, and through human subjectivity) to the transformation of the natural world (through science and technology orientated to human desires and ends, such as happiness).

Poststructuralist feminism contributes another major voice to this critique of humanism. While of course not all feminisms have been interested in challenging the presumptions of the essential commonality of humans and/or the notion that progress must be human-centered, quite a few strands of contemporary feminist thought move beyond expanded enfranchisement and 'equal rights' (battles still mandatory to fight) to interrogations of the humanist (read masculinist) assumptions and practices that followed in the wake of the Enlightenment. One group most committed to rethinking issues of subjectivity and identity through a focus on the ambiguous meanings of sex and gender has been poststructuralist feminists. Here we have in mind such writers as Judith Butler (1990 and 1993), Jane Flax (1990 and 1993), and Elizabeth Grosz (1994), among others.[63] While differing in important ways, each of these thinkers takes on the assumption that progress for women is a matter of establishing a stable subjective identity of their own – looking a lot like the model of the human subject that was formulated with modernity, or based on the modernist assumption of irreducible biological difference. Butler and the others trouble the notion that subject positions and identities could be (or ever were) stable, and thereby challenge the essentialism (either in the form of cultural determinism or biological destiny) that sometimes accompanies the claim that gender produces clearly distinguishable subjects. Not only, then, do poststructuralist feminists call attention to the implied or often explicit and enforced masculinism (or 'phallocentrism') that one can 'read' in the notion of the human subject and the cult of Reason as they have evolved over the past 300 years in the West.[64] But, poststructuralist feminists go on to question the possibility of finding an alternative construct of the human, and certainly one that fixes sexual and gender identity in a bipolar fashion, that can be utilized strategically or not for current and future struggles against sexism, discrimination, and the oppression of women. As Gillian Hewitson (1999) has described it, stressing 'performed' as opposed to inherited or natural gender difference (and actually placing heightened emphasis on the body than on 'consciousness in the determination of performed identity'), poststructuralist feminists have refused the 'add women and stir' conception of expanding the modernist notion of humanity as a way to remedy how and where sex and gender identity become marks of affliction. Thus, such feminists 'view the ideal of equality, which involves reducing difference to sameness, and the ideal of difference, when reduced to biological difference, as problematic, since both replicate phallocentrism' (Hewitson, 1999: 128).

If nothing else, postmodern critique has identified the ubiquity of theoretical humanism in characterizing the modern age, but it goes on to propose a much-needed decentering in which the human subject is not only displaced from its structuring role as entry and exit point (and 'represented' at every stage along the way), but also in which human subjectivity is shown in all its varieties to be capable of deconstruction and fragmentation. Not only, then, are 'forces', 'processes', and 'wills' (along the lines specified by Nietzsche) disembodied in some postmodern thought – going even beyond 'structuralism' – and shown to construct subjects rather than being 'emissions' or manifestations of subjectivity, but, subjectivity itself is seen to be indeterminate and unstable, as much in flux as in an incessant process of de- and recomposition. The decentered subject, found in Foucault, Althusser, Butler, and others, and the decentered social totality (with the subject no longer that which seeks its own representation in and through art, philosophy, technology, etc.) are unsuitable because troubling essences for much existing modernist social thought, and this is why for some critics of postmodernism, the assault on theoretical humanism is viewed as making theorizing itself simply impossible.

Yet, of course, postmodern critique shows precisely how one can incorporate the ideas that human subjectivity is complex, uncertain, and irreducible and that this same subjectivity is as much effect as it is cause in scenarios of historical movement. We note, by the way, that the attack on humanism is one that implicates many critics of the notion of homo economicus along with its mostly neoclassical purveyors. So, for example, complaints that neoclassicals and others haven't captured the 'real' human subject in championing homo economicus starts from similar premises that there is some such previously unrepresented, unified, and distinguishable human subjectivity that can and should, if properly specified, begin or at least make an appearance within all economic thought. Postmodern critique, then, should be distinguished from those forms of humanism (found in all sorts of heterodox schools of economic thought, including Marxism, feminism, institutionalism, and so forth) that seek to reinstall rather than end the primacy of a 'lost' or missing human subjectivity in economic discourse. One can see in the essays in this volume, for example, the tensions felt by those unhappy with neoclassical (and often masculinist and Western) notions of economic agency, but hesitant to go the way of an anti-humanism. We expect these tensions to persist into the foreseeable future.

Postmodernism and economics: a stylized genealogy

Most surveys of postmodernism in the contemporary scholarly landscape have little or nothing to say about the discipline of economics, though as we have stated, there are lots of attempts mostly in cultural fields to talk about a postmodern economy. In her 1991 article, Sheila Dow in fact asked the question of whether there were signs of postmodernism with economics. A decade later, we can answer this vigorously in the affirmative. For, not only have there been important essays, like McCloskey's 1983 article on the 'rhetoric of economics' that have set off a wave of subsequent debates and discussions about modernism within economics, but as this volume attests, there are by now a significant number of different scholars within the field of economics who are either writing about postmodernism or who, consciously or otherwise, employ postmodern approaches within their works. For some of these economists, and this is true of many of those represented here, postmodernism enters in its critical guise, as the modernism of mainstream economics is roundly censured in their writings.

While not all those who are attracted to postmodern critique are outside of the mainstream of the profession, it has been the case that postmodernism has been useful for those who seek more visibility for their approaches or who wish to displace entirely the long tradition of neoclassical economic theory as dominant within the field.[65] Much is at stake, some of the critics feel, in the struggle to obviate the centrality of homo economicus, to decenter notions of economic totalities, to revive interest in morality and values and power as determinants in economic discourse, to scale down the pretensions of economics as a 'science', to open up spaces for plural perspectives, and to resist the 'imperialism' of economics as a master discourse capable of shaping cultural fields (see especially the essays by Klamer, Milberg, and Hewitson in this volume).[66] These are often, and rightly we feel, linked to other struggles, such as those dedicated to breaking down barriers to entry of women and minorities into the economics profession, or those that attempt to redress the excessive exercise of expertise and authority, with their pervasive exclusionary effects, that can be found within pecking orders of universities, journals, and so forth.[67] It is no accident, then, that many of the papers in this volume have multiple purposes. They not only weigh the import (and come up with different judgments, we should add) of postmodernism within economics, but they often take up additional or related causes – decanonization, as one instance, or the elimination of gender bias, as another – that are either highlighted or obscured by postmodern critiques.

Parts of what we describe here as postmodern critique can be traced to different movements within economics over the past 25 years. Certainly, if one is looking for progenitors, then one must mention at the very least Keith Tribe's often overlooked 1978 treatise on Smithian and pre-Smithian economic discourse. In this book, Tribe employed specifically poststructuralist critiques of humanism and other forms of essentialism in modernist histories of economic thought (shaped by the idea, which we saw in Samuelson, of the inexorable growth of knowledge, funeral by funeral) to rethink the claim that Smith was the initiator of a new, modernist economics. And, one can look at the entire body of work of Resnick and Wolff over the past 25 years as well, as they have advocated, with others, everything from the critique of classical epistemology to economic determinism in their attempt to refound a postmodern Marxian theory as something distinct from neoclassical and other mainstream economic thought, as well as distinct from Marxism's own inscription within its past modernist projects. And, of course, for many McCloskey's 1983 article on the rhetoric of economics pointedly criticized at least the official methodologists and epistemologists among economic philosophers for their modernism, even if it didn't make the concepts and constructs of neoclassical economics its primary object of scorn.

There may be other progenitors as well, and in fact the onset of postmodernism has led some historians of economics to find similar critiques of the tenets of modernism in a wide variety of writers and thinkers, often, however, out of the mainstream (this, for example, is much of what Ulla Grapard does in her paper for this volume by locating Charlotte Perkins Gilman's 'social constructivism' as an early expression of this more or less postmodern element). And, of course, there is fertile ground in economics to find such critiques since, in fact, the braggadocio that has accompanied 'advances' made possible by formalism and other supposedly 'scientific' methods of analysis and proof has often been met with annoyance and resistance by those left out of the resulting conversations. Perhaps then the next few decades of work in the history and philosophy of economics will be dedicated at least in part to 'unearthing' the mostly anti- or non-modernist sympathies of past and present economists and others made to live in the margins of the official discipline.[68]

While postmodernism has been mainly available to economists as anti- or non-modernist critique of the modernist mainstream, the 'postmodern moments' approach has a somewhat different emphasis. Here, the point has been to show those elements of postmodernism that have arisen in the midst of economics as a modernist enterprise. That is, in addition to evaluating and criticizing neoclassical and other schools for their pervasive adherence to modernism, 'finding' the postmodern moments with these schools of thought has been tantamount to deconstructing economic discourse to demonstrate, in the end, troublesome anomalies that pertain to uncertainty, the instability of subjectivity, the possibility of various rationalities, simultaneous multicausality, persistent and irreducible disequilibrium and still more. In some cases, calling attention to these postmodern moments has been with the intent to show that, despite proclamations to the contrary, economic discourse in much of the past half century has not been able to build a stable consensus around a 'core' of supposedly superior ideas and approaches.

Or, differently, discussing postmodern moments is likewise aimed at depicting even mainstream economic discourse as, perhaps unwittingly, increasingly preoccupied with postmodern themes and ideas despite the claims that fundamental uncertainty, decentered subjects, and so forth are either negligible or manageable within existing theoretical approaches. There are now numerous articles, for example (three that immediately come to mind are by Varoufakis (1993), Mehta (1993), and Hargreaves Heap (1993)) that attempt to show the lacunae pertaining to problems of assuming stable, directed, contained, and unfragmented rationalities that become evident in economic game theoretical approaches. Varoufakis, in particular, argues that anxiety about modernist rationality assumptions are increasingly pervading the field, and that in their wake postmodernist approaches to subjectivity have been considered, even if still underrepresented.

In our own past work, we have tried to show the postmodern moments of uncertainty, of the economy as a decentered totality, of the human body as a site of fragmentation, and much else that is not only evident in heterodox schools of economic thought, but perhaps is just as much evident within neoclassical orthodoxy.[69] Again, the point here has been to call attention to these elements both as recognition of just how much modernist economics has been unable to exclude, let alone address, its own aporia and undecidables, and as a prolegomena to a research program, in which these postmodern moments are finally embraced as worthy of direct consideration. We realize of course the 'threat' that such an embrace represents. The historian of economic thought, Mark Blaug, puts it succinctly: 'in one way or another, postmodern arguments always amount to "anything goes"' (1998: 29). But, from our perspective the dissolving effects of uncertainty, decentering, epistemological relativism, and the like on well-formulated economic models are already in process, for better or worse, and are just as much the unintended consequences of modernist formalism, essentialism, scientism, and so forth as they are 'importations' from postmodern critics. Though we are not interested in prognostication (our postmodern training, perhaps) we do propose at least one improbable hypothesis: modernist economic discourse, so intent on maintaining its scientific identity, may be seen through the perspective of postmodern moments to be in the process of becoming 'other'.

Perhaps then postmodernism in economics allows for a restatement of Samuelson's paraphrased maxim: funeral by funeral, economics does become other. While modernism still has a death grip on the imaginations of many in the profession, postmodernism beckons those with breath left in them to another site, another graveyard, possibly. Be that as it may, the economists, philosophers, anthropologists, and cultural theorists who are published in this volume have been willing, at least for now, to pick up their shovels and temporarily consider relocating – some as diggers, others as mourners – to this other site. Postmodernism cannot, and will not, promise 'progress' in economic knowledge as a result of all that repositioned digging. All it can do is show that even if the quest for progress is dead and buried, still the excavation goes on, and transformations of this different terrain present new opportunities and new discourses for economic knowledge, funeral by funeral.

This volume had its inception in a conference entitled 'Postmodernism, Economics, and Knowledge' at the University of California, Riverside in March, 1995. The conference was generously supported by the University of California Humanities Research Institute and the Center for Ideas and Society at the University of California, Riverside. The conference stimulated the idea for a book that would take off from the papers presented at this conference. In addition to soliciting papers from the conference, we sought out wherever necessary additional contributions and commentary in order to include more and different perspectives. The conference had as one of its premises a beginning of a cross-disciplinary discussion of the postmodern turn in economics, and both the original list of presenters and discussants and the present line-up include scholars who do not earn their living by the sweat of an economics brow. In the time leading up to the publication of this book, the papers originally presented at the conference were revised and edited and can be read then, along with the additional contributions, as an up-to-date précis of where the discussion of postmodernism within much of the economics profession stands. We would like to thank all the authors here for their cooperation and patience, and we want to thank as well Carlos Vélez-Ibáñez, Barbara Herrnstein Smith, Stanley Fish, Bernd Magnus, Susan Feiner, Joseph Childers, Marc Herold, Warren Samuels, and Diana Strassmann, all of whom participated in the 1995 conference. We would also like to thank Ayesha Khanna for invaluable bibliographic and research support.

Notes

1   While Samuelson's reformulation – with a difference – of Planck's credo occurs in this 1997 essay paying tribute to his *Economics* textbook, it occurs as well in his (1998) fiftieth anniversary paean to his 'lucky' book (*Foundations of Economic Analysis*). This time, though, he not only credits Planck for the loan, but also proceeds in paraphrasing a different adage, as when he tells us that in economics, 'often the dance must proceed Two Steps Forward and One Step Back' (1998: 1379). Whether digging or dancing, though, Samuelson

labors just the same in his confident assertion that 'soft and hard sciences are cumulative disciplines' in which 'we each bring our contributions of 'value added' to the pot of progress' (1998: 1378).

2 It seems that there must be thousands (perhaps tens of thousands) of easily accessible statements by economists in which this optimism is a necessary component. One does wonder why it is necessary to keep incanting such confidence. One of these thousands is the following. Talking about his own theory of 'bounded rationality' and its relative neglect to date by practicing economists, Herbert Simon (1991) reflects that 'science, viewed as competition among theories, has an unmatched advantage over all other forms of intellectual competition. In the long run (no more than centuries), the winner succeeds, not by superior rhetoric, not by the ability to convince or dazzle a lay audience, not by political influence, but by the support of data, facts as they are gradually and cumulatively revealed. As long as its factual veridicality is unchallenged, one can remain calm about the future of a theory' (364–5).

3 In the course of his discussion of the citing of precursors for one's own authoritative stance, E. Roy Weintraub summarizes 'Whig' histories of the history of economic thought like this: 'Science as the exemplar of the march of reason, and economics, as science, leads the Whiggish historian of economics and the typical economic scientist to think in terms of successes and failures, precursors and blind alleys, heroes sung and unsung, and all manner of retrospective gold medals and booby prizes' (1997: 186).

4 Compare the view that ambiguity means absence of scientific precision (and thereby progress) with the comment by Paul Feyerabend where he emphasizes 'the essential ambiguity of all concepts, images, and notions that presuppose change. Without ambiguity, no change, ever. The quantum theory, as interpreted by Niels Bohr, is a perfect example of that' (1999: viii).

5 Consider, for example, this blast at 'neowalrasian theory' leveled by Robert Clower (1994). After declaring this theory 'scientifically vacuous' and concluding that there 'is no way to make progress in economic science except by first discarding neowalrasian analysis' (810), Clower really gets down to business: 'in my opinion, what we presently possess by way of so-called pure economic theory is objectively indistinguishable from what the physicist Richard Feynman, in an unflattering sketch of nonsense "science" called "cargo cult science"' (809). Clower, by the way, goes on to make a pitch for a reversion to 'induction', as though this would indeed provide a straight shot to science.

6 This confounding of science due to human behavior includes, of course, the all-too-humanness of the economic scientists themselves. Or, at least this is the gentle conclusion of Tjalling Koopmans (1957), who sees in the supposed discrepancy between the logic of correct scientific procedures and the persistent departures from this norm by economists a kind of understandable human failing in wanting to cut to the chase, a failing that could be called uncharitably the 'will to distort'. In Koopmans's own (understated) words: 'often we are more preoccupied with arriving at what we deem to be true statements or best predictions, in the light of such knowledge as we have of the phenomena in question, than in exhibiting the postulational basis, and thereby the ultimate observational evidence, on which our statements rest' (143).

7 We have found the following surveys of postmodernism useful in our teaching and research: Bertens (1995), Rosenau (1992), Best and Kellner (1991), Docherty (1993), Connor (1989), Rose (1991), and Nicholson (1990).

Our depiction here of postmodernism thus draws on all of these, but also differs in some important respects, as readers can check.

8 Though, of course, there are studies (e.g., Alston, Kearl, and Vaughan 1992) showing a great degree of 'consensus' among a sample of economists on numerous theoretical issues. As Fuchs, Krueger, and Poterba (1998) argue, though, their own studies dealing with questions of policy based on parameter estimation techniques demonstrate considerable amounts of disagreement among economists within particular fields. This result is interesting since it suggests that the empirical and practical implications one draws from common theoretical outlooks (that is, even if one concedes this point) can vary widely among aspiring scientists because of differences in estimates, but even more so because of the economists' 'values'.

9 Stephen Brown (1995) speaks of the seven 'key features' of postmodernism. He lists them as 'fragmentation, de-differentiation, hyperreality, chronology, pastiche, anti-foundationalism, and pluralism' (106). As readers can ascertain, these features are dispersed throughout our treatment of the 'four categories' that follow. For another list of distinguishing characteristics of postmodernism (or at least of poststructuralism), see Amariglio (1998).

10 Manuel Castells's monumental recent three volume analysis (1996–98) of globalization, information, and identity foretells a new global information age that might be understood as the phase of postmodernity par excellence.

11 For a first-rate depiction of the way Jameson utilizes Mandel, see Norton (1995). Norton also argues that Jameson 'contains postmodernism within a modernist narrative' (66) by invoking the unifying vision of a stage-theory of capitalism.

12 Culture here should be understood to include the forms of subjectivity that global capitalism is said to produce. Needless to say, in the Jamesonian vision, post-colonials seem increasingly to hold identical subject (or should we say, subjected) positions , including of course that of class. Kayatekin and Ruccio (1998) challenge the idea that processes of globalization create a single subjectivity and argue, instead, that it is both possible and desirable to locate/produce multiple social (including class) identities in the post-colonial world.

13 A similar frame of analysis marks David Harvey's 1989 book, *The Condition of Postmodernity*. If not on a par with the influence of Jameson, then Harvey must be seen as not far behind in affecting investigations of postmodernism in terms of the latest phase of capitalism. For an alternative take on capitalism and globalization, one that challenges from a feminist, poststructuralist viewpoint the totalizing vision implicit in Jameson and Harvey, see Gibson-Graham (1996).

14 Bruce Pietrykowski (1994) provides a different reading from Jameson and others who have argued for a one-to-one correspondence between consumer culture and postmodernism. Pietrykowski presents evidence that many of the elements of 'fast capitalism' and 'ephemerality, fragmentation, juxtaposition, surface, and depthlessness' that are currently attributed to post-Fordism and postmodernism can be seen clearly in the rise of consumer services and the particular aesthetics or designs of many commercial sites, from gas stations to department stores, during the heyday of Fordism in the early twentieth century in the USA. Pietrykowski's main point is that there is no clear-cut division, when it comes to commodity culture, between modernity and postmodernity.

INTRODUCTION

15 For an excellent overview of the many art forms that have characterized the postmodern from diverse postminimal styles to deconstruction and commodity art during the last thirty years, see Sandler (1996).
16 For an excellent evaluation of Becker's notion of culture as it enters economic analysis, see Koritz and Koritz (1999). Amartya Sen names Becker as one example of economists whose understanding of establishing 'close relations' with different disciplines takes an 'imperialist' form. As Sen states more generally, 'Sometimes the proposed relation has been given a rather "imperialist" form, with economic theorists adhering strictly to their astonishingly narrow methodology and then applying, with remarkable confidence, that slim methodology to other disciplines as well' (1991: 76).
17 Charusheela and Hargreaves Heap in this volume challenge the formal modeling of the neoclassical paradigm and its reduction of human motives to rationality. McCloskey, while critical of the strategies of formal modeling, or 'blackboard economics' as she has called it elsewhere (1996), supports the neoclassical metaphor of the rational individual, at least in major part.
18 Or, consider, for example, this understanding of postmodernity as resistance to 'economics', a resistance that is informed by the experience of post-colonial subjectivity: 'Post-modernity already exists where people refuse to be seduced and controlled by economic laws. It exists for peoples rediscovering and reinventing their traditional commons by re-embedding the economy (to use Polanyi's expression) into society and culture; subordinating it again to politics and ethics; marginalizing it – putting it at their margins: which is precisely what it means to be "marginal" in modern times' (Esteva and Prakash, 1998).
19 Dow and Klamer in this volume both interrogate the tenuous links between modernity and postmodernity as it affects discourse. For Dow, the postmodern is the dialectical emergence of the antimodern, while for Klamer neoclassical economics' turn to 'high modernism' augurs its imma(i)nent implosion. Amariglio's commentary treats the ultimate success or not of Dow, Klamer, and also McCloskey to steer a path between or away from modernism and postmodernism.
20 Cullenberg and Dasgupta's paper for this volume shows that the 'high modernist' debate over capital theory between the two Cambridges was as much about a contestation of mythologies as it was about the logical correctness of various theoretical propositions put forth. McCloskey, among others, also challenges in her paper here the view of the progressive and inevitable triumph of 'better' theory.
21 If there is an icon of postmodernism, it is likely the computer. According to Wise (1995), computer science ironically holds much the same position in regard to high theoretical science as did mathematics before the last part of the nineteenth century. Wise states: 'Not until the end of the nineteenth century did mathematical expression by itself attain high status among natural philosophers, ultimately as the very foundation of "modern" physics. (Its formerly suspect boundary position has now been taken over by computer science, halfway between proper science and practical engineering, which in turn is rapidly becoming the foundation of "postmodern" science' (357).
22 Paul Cilliers in his recent book *Complexity and the Postmodern* (1998) brings together developments in neurosciences logic, linguistics, computer science, the philosophy of science and deconstruction and poststructuralism to provide an interdisciplinary approach to questions of representation and organization in postmodernity. Building explicitly upon Lyotard, Cilliers

argues that postmodern societies meet all of what he specifies as the main criteria for 'complex systems'.

23 In his 1986 book, *The Control Revolution*, which treats the rise of 'the information society' during the past 40 or so years, James Beniger produces a daunting list (on pages 4 and 5) of names given by a wide range of social theorists to the 'major social transformations identified since 1950'. This list, which stops at 1984, includes such labels as 'postindustrial society', 'postliberal age', the 'age of discontinuity', the 'new service economy', and much more, posited by such writers as Peter Drucker, Alvin Toffler, Daniel Bell, Michael Piore and Charles Sabel, just to name a few. Of course, the past 15 years have seen even more terms and many other authors that could easily be added to his list.

24 In an earlier text, *Libidinal Economy*, Lyotard (1993, original French edition in 1974) ventures into discussions about the nature of economic crises during the past century (though, of course, this venture follows a different agenda of subjecting modernist economic discourses to poststructuralist interrogation). Brian Cooper and Margueritte Murphy (1999) conduct an insightful close reading of Lyotard's libidinal economics.

25 The idea of the decentered or fragmented subject has certainly received much attention in feminist literature. In this volume, Hewitson, Charusheela, Nelson, Bergeron, and Rossetti all consider the role of the feminist subject – fragmented or not – in its relationship to neoclassical economics. In a related way, Amariglio and Ruccio develop in their chapter Judith Butler's work on the body to show how a decentered body can be seen both in opposition to and in terms of the leading traditions in the history of economic thought. In contrast, Dupré and Gagnier take issue with Amariglio and Ruccio's claim that the body can be read in terms of a decentered subjectivity in the high modernism of the Arrow-Debreu model of general equilibrium.

26 Simon (1991), no theorist of postmodernism, yet describes the situation of a less-than-unified, dispersed self (our words, not his) this way: each of us is 'a committee of urges, wants, and needs, housed in body and mind' (362); 'each of us "time-shares", alternating our many selves' (363).

27 We have chosen to keep our comments about the rationality assumption to a minimum and instead focus attention on the presumption of a unified form of subjectivity for the economic agent. One reason for our choice is that there is a vast literature by now defending and contending against the notion of rationality as the starting point for economic analysis. This theme has been overworked to a degree that we feel confident that postmodernist approaches add little to what has already been said on one side or another of this debate. However, here is a smattering of references presenting different points of view for those who are looking for a place to start mulling over this issue: Arrow (1987), Sen (1977 and 1987), Bausor (1985), Simon (1978), Sugden (1991), Sent (1997), Gerrard (1993), England (1993), and Hollis and Nell (1975). For some who explicitly consider postmodernism and rationality as it is used in economics, see Hargreaves Heap (1993), Varoufakis (1993), and Sofianou (1995).

28 Louis Sass (1992) is a clinical psychologist who has years of experience working with schizophrenics in institutional settings. His book constitutes the most serious treatment of the loose claim that schizophrenia is an apt trope for describing the general state of 'postmodern' subjectivity and its manifestation in the arts. An example of the more casual (but not necessarily incorrect) use of this idea is the following discussion of channel surfing – a prototype for postmodern subjective activity – from the composition theorist,

Lester Faigley (1992): 'The experience of flipping across television programming approximates the consciousness of the schizophrenic living in the intense, eternal present. The viewer watches a series of spectacles from around the world – "smart" bombs exploding buildings, sports heroes in the elation of victory, royal marriages, plane crashes, assassinations, rock concerts, ranting dictators, shuttle launches, hurricanes, scandals, earthquakes, revolutions, eclipses, and international terrorism – all issued in an economy of images competing for attention' (13).

29 Sizing up the state of economic analysis in the mid-1950s, Koopmans concluded that 'our economic knowledge has not yet been carried to the point where it sheds much light on the core problem of the economic organization of society: the problem of how to face and deal with uncertainty' (1957: 147). Writing 30 years later, Amartya Sen indicates the degree to which the issue of uncertainty had become the primary context for much economic analysis such that the all-important notion of agent rationality had to be framed in terms of the general case of decision-making in the face of uncertainty. As Sen puts it: 'behaviour under certainty can be formally seen as an extreme case of behaviour under uncertainty…in this sense, rational behaviour under certainty must be subsumed by any theory that deals with rational behaviour in the presence of uncertainty' (1987, 1999)

30 Some reading on the question of how uncertainty, 'indeterminism', and disorder became central themes across the cultural and disciplinary landscape during the past two centuries includes Hacking (1990), Stigler (1986), Plotnitsky (1994), Dupré (1993), Sass (1992), Kern (1983), Hayles (1991), Krüger, Daston and Heidelberger (1987), Krüger, Gigerenzer, and Morgan (1987), and Krips (1987).

31 Nigel Wheale (1995) attempts a summary of postmodern style in the arts like so: 'A definable group of strategies and forms recur in the description of postmodern arts and this lexicon orders them into a hierarchy. An all purpose postmodern item might be constructed like this: it uses eclecticism to generate parody and irony; its style may owe something to schlock, kitsch or camp taste. It may be partly allegorical, certainly self-reflexive and contain some kind of list. It will not be realistic. Now construct your own program to meet these demands' (42–3).

32 For a recent collection of essays that interrogates the relationship among value, culture, meaning, and art, see Klamer (1996).

33 Essays in this volume where deconstruction is a major motif include those by Hargreaves Heap, Mehta, and Rossetti. Krips offers a critical reading of the essays by Cullenberg and Dasgupta, Mehta, and Hargreaves Heap for not pushing poststructuralism and deconstruction far enough. Krips's critique speaks perhaps in part to the more fully developed use of deconstruction and poststructuralism in fields like communications studies and cultural theory.

34 Useful overviews of Derrida's work include Caputo (1997), Norris (1988, 1991), Norris and Benjamin (1989), Gasché (1986), and Culler (1983). For an introduction by an economist to the concept of deconstruction and the discussion of this notion of 'differance', see Ruccio (1998). Jane Rossetti must be named as among the first to declare a deliberately deconstructive reading of economics texts, as she does in her important 1990 essay on Robert Lucas. See also Rossetti (1992).

35 One common criticism, which is not at all limited to those who pledge allegiance to postmodernism, is that the desires and wills of economists, like others, is largely a function of prestige, power, and even relative wealth. Donald Katzner (1991a), in his thoughtful defense of formalization within

economics, admits the point that at least some of the obsession with formal modes of presentation in economics is because 'that is where the rewards of publication, recognition, support money, promotion, and tenure are...even the selection of the problem to work on is subject to the same reward pressures. And the structure of these rewards tends to be set by the established standards of what constitutes relevant and significant questions, and what makes up the appropriate assumption-content of analyses which purport to provide answers. Clearly the existence of established standards provides a powerful rationalization for the continued use of formalization' (22).

36 See especially the essays in this volume by Klamer, Amariglio and Ruccio, Goux, Milberg, and Mehta.
37 Though the title may not be as suggestive as the others we cite, we should add Salanti and Screpanti's edited volume, *Pluralism in Economics*, in which some of the essays call for or employ self-reflexivity within economics. In addition to McCloskey (1983), an important early article reflecting on language in economics that is cognizant of postmodernism and poststructuralist thought is Milberg (1988).
38 Cullenberg (1994) discusses this issue in more general terms as the 'co-determination' of theoretical discourse and material reality. He concludes that this co- or over-determination implies the impossibility of an independent standard of truth since 'a standard of truth requires an independent or absolute point of reference. But in this case the independence has been corrupted by the mutual interaction between theoretical discourse and material reality' (13).
39 Indeed, the very meaning of a 'fact' has been shown in a number of instances to be socially constructed, thus imbricating the subject/scientist in what modernist discourse considers the objective character of natural or social reality. See Latour and Woolgar (1986), Poovey (1998), and Porter (1995) for detailed studies of the construction of social and natural facts.
40 A sampling of these texts are Toulmin (1990), Kern (1983), Gablik (1984), Sass (1992), Xenos (1989), Ross (1994), and Berman (1982).
41 The sociologist Anthony Giddens is one who has argued that the modernist project (e.g., justifying a commitment to reason in the name of reason) fails to complete itself: 'modernity turns out to be enigmatic at its core' (1990: 49).
42 Hargreaves Heap's critique of justice and rationality in his essay, along with the essays by Mirowski, Gudeman, and Davis's commentary in this volume, provides such an immanent critique, we would argue.
43 In what follows, we discuss formalism (or, rather, mathematical formalism) in passing. We note though that, for many commentators and critics, the rise of modernity has grown up hand-in-hand with a mathematized culture. And modernism in certain disciplines certainly has meant the move from prose to probability distributions. There are some excellent and diverse discussions, such as Ruccio (1988), Mirowski (1989), Morgan (1990), Porter (1995), and Stigler (1986), of this and related theoretical moves and what they have meant within the discipline of economics and elsewhere. In addition, we provide the following sentences from Katzner, a respected mathematical economist, who nicely links modernity and math: 'we moderns, it seems, attempt to measure everything...measurement is relatively easy and convenient. It has become natural for us. It makes us feel good because it imparts the (frequently illusory) impression that we know something. And it is often not difficult, and even tempting, to ignore what cannot be measured. We seem to be caught up in a culture of measurement which we are unable to let go' (1991b: 18).

44 Compare this view with that of the Physiocrat disciple and French state bureaucrat Turgot, who saw language as the essential ingredient, bar none, for the emergence of genius. Manuel and Manuel summarize Turgot's theory which postulated that the progress of language would make it 'destined to become an even better instrument; it would be stripped of its rhetoric, cleansed of its ambiguities, so that the only means of communication for true knowledge would be the mathematical symbol, verifiable, unchanging, eternal' (1979: 471). Manuel and Manuel proceed with this wonderful account of Turgot's view of what happened to scientific genius with the fall of the Roman Empire: 'In the past one of the unfortunate consequences of the conquest of a decadent higher civilization by vigorous barbarisms had been the linguistic confusion which followed the disaster. A long period of time elapsed before the victors and the vanquished merged their different forms of speech and, during the interval, language, the only receptacle for the storing of scientific progress then available, was lacking. Geniuses continued to perceive new phenomena, but since they were deprived of a stable body of rational linguistic symbols their observations were stillborn...The babel of languages resulted in a protracted period of intellectual sterility during which it was impossible for a creative genius to express himself because there was no settled linguistic medium for scientific thought' (471–2).

45 Robert Solo, in fact, criticizes the use of mathematics in economics and advocates the use of a 'natural language' precisely because the latter 'alone conveys an image in the mind that can be checked against the observed and experienced' (1991: 103).

46 One good example is Andrew Pickering's 'posthumanist' account of Rowan Hamilton's construction of the mathematical system of quarternions in which 'the center of gravity...is positioned between Hamilton as a classical human agent, a locus of free moves, and the disciplines that carried him along' (1997: 63). There are, of course, many more examples, as during the past 20 years, there has been much written about the 'social construction' of knowledge, though not all of which embraces postmodernism. For just two accounts with different foci, see Longino (1990) and the essays in Lynch and Woolgar (1990).

47 Formalism also connotes, for many, 'rigor'. And this attribute is often seen to comprise the acid test for deciding if a statement is possibly scientific or otherwise. It is interesting to note that in the same issue of *Methodus*, we get two different accounts of the place of the value of rigor for modern economic science. The first, by Sen (1991), amounts to the claim that furors about formalization sometimes are blown out of proportion since, by now, most economists have some formal training. And, 'furthermore, the aura of glory that was associated once with being "rigorous" "exact", and "modern" – available only to the chosen mathematical few – has rather dimmed in recent years' (73). The second, by Solow (1991), is directed to the confusion sometimes between 'abstraction' and 'rigor'. Losing patience (Solow's comments come as a response to a 'debate' of sorts between McCloskey and Katzner over formalization in economics), Solow blares, 'there is no excuse for lack of rigor. You can never have too much rigor. To make non-rigorous statements is to make false statements' (31). And finally, 'there is not a category of non-rigorous truths, not in theory' (31). It seems Professor Sen hadn't yet spoken to Professor Solow. One more view on rigor will suffice. This is from Mark Blaug's recent salvo fired at formalism in economics: 'If there is such a thing as "original sin" in economic methodology, it is the worship of the idol of mathematical rigor, more or less invented by Arrow and Debreu in 1954 and then canonized by Debreu in his *Theory of Value* five years later, probably the

most arid and pointless book in the entire literature of economics' (1998: 17). Professors Sen and Solow, meet Professor Blaug.

48 We have gotten used to the very familiar soliloquy in which famous economists, many of whom pioneered the use of these models and near-pyrotechnical mathematics, late in their careers wonder how in the world such 'tools' ever got so out of hand in the training and consequent work of economists as to displace all other forms of argumentation, a concern for 'reality', and discursive borrowings. One such example is the recent confession by the new economic historian Richard Easterlin (1997), in which he bemoans that 'model building is the name of the game. Empirical reality enters, if at all, chiefly in the form of "stylized fact". Econometrics, though a formal course requirement everywhere, plays a surprisingly small part in economic research – showing up in perhaps one dissertation in five. There is no such thing as descriptive dissertations or theses devoted to the measurement of economic magnitudes. Although topics in disciplines other than economics are not uncommon, there is little or no use of the work done in the other disciplines' (15).

49 On this point, postmodern approaches in economics have much in common with critical realists, such as Tony Lawson who emphasizes that 'knowledge is a social product, actively produced by means of antecedent social products' (1997: 25). Indeed, while there are obvious disagreements one can find between postmodernists and critical realists, we are moved here more by important similarities regarding the social production and distribution of economic knowledge, a commitment to (at least some forms of) non-reductionism, a dislike of scientism, and much else. For more on critical realism, see also Fleetwood (1999).

50 There is no question that a defense of foundations for knowledge consists largely of the view that establishing bases expands the realm of what can be considered worthy of scientific study. Yet, postmodernists often follow the line of reasoning found in Rorty (1979), in which foundationalism is seen to be about constraint and exclusion. In Rorty's words, 'the desire for a theory of knowledge is a desire for constraint – a desire to find "foundations" to which one might cling, frameworks beyond which one must not stray, objects which impose themselves, representations which cannot be gainsaid' (315). We can not overemphasize, by the way, the impact of Rorty's work on postmodern philosophies.

51 Indeed, Bruna Ingrao charges E. Roy Weintraub with plunging into an 'extreme relativism' because of his insistence that the 'sequence of 'facts' in the history of the discipline is fluid and mutable, according to the contingent problems with which each community of scholars is concerned' (1997: 227). In our view, Weintraub's work does not lead to 'extreme', 'radical', or 'nihilistic' relativism precisely because it involves the production of concrete stories about specific episodes in the history of economic thought.

52 The mathematical microeconomist David Kreps admits that 'the rise of mathematics' in economics can be explained, at least in part, by the fact that 'the use of a powerful and somewhat obscure tool confers power on the user. As economists became convinced of the value of mathematical rigor, the reward system (based on peer review) reinforced this tendency' (1997: 64).

53 Weintraub (1992) asserts, 'power does matter' (55). Yet, of course, some like Roger Backhouse (1992) aren't persuaded. Though Backhouse admits that the dependence of knowledge on power may be a 'fact of life', he concludes there is still 'no place' (by which he means no legitimate place) for power in economic methodology (73).

54 As Chris Weedon explains, 'the theory that all discursive practices and all forms of subjectivity constitute and are constituted by relations of power is…only disabling if power is seen as always necessarily repressive' (1997: 175).

55 Postcolonial theory has become an important literature over the last twenty years and shares in many ways the concerns of some postmodernists, feminists, and Marxists, though, of course, there are important differences as well (for one comparative treatment, see Appiah 1992). Postcolonial theorists are concerned with the literary and cultural constructions of those in the former colonized nations as well as those diasporic locations outside these countries. Postcolonial theory often builds upon the idea of 'sub-alternity', 'otherness', and 'resistance'. The idea of the subaltern and otherness refuses the binary of the postcolonial subject and experience in simple opposition or contrast to the West. Rather, otherness is often conceived in a nonessentialist and nontotalizing recognition of the myriad differences between and among postcolonial people and groups and their colonial pasts and postcolonial presents. Resistance is often thought of as subversion or mimicry, often with the recognition that the act of resistance not be fully separated from that being resisted. The idea of hybridity is an important conceptual marker signaling a recognition of the integration of cultures and practices and the impossibility of a fully self-referential or 'authentic' postcolonial life. Postcolonial writers are also concerned with many of the other concepts that have occupied postmodern theory, such as identity and difference, subjectivity, fragmentation, and representation. For an excellent collection of essays dealing with many aspects of postcolonial theory, see McClintock, Mufti, and Shohat (1997). Gayatri Chakravorty Spivak (1999) provides a brilliant critique of postcolonial studies, and she pushes the field to consider seriously the conditions of transnational culture and globality.

56 David Hollinger (1994) is right in his claim that 'scientism is sometimes taken to cover a range of ideas broader than either naturalism or positivism, but the common denominator of its many definitions is a highly censorious tone…scientism is normally an opprobrious epithet directed at what the speaker regards as an arrogant or naive effort to extend the methods or authority of science into a field of experience where it does not belong' (34). Hollinger, in his defense of some variant of modernism in the human sciences, is also correct in stating that not all 'aspirations toward a scientific culture' have been scientistic. But, again, we argue that the negative connotation in the term scientism is precisely oriented toward defenses of science that, when faced with people who do not buy into this form of thinking or its presumed results, lead either to a sneer or the advice (often followed by an enforcement) to 'shut up'.

57 Of course, one does not have to buy into postmodernist critique to hold a methodological pluralist position. For a spirited defense of methodological pluralism in economics, see Caldwell (1982).

58 In his interesting and valuable collection of Austrian, neo-Austrian, and libertarian essays about the possible and actual contributions of economists to public discourse, Daniel Klein (1999) describes the practitioner of economics as 'Everyman'. Now, this label is a tip-off for what is to follow: 'the practitioner of political economy is typically highly ignorant of basic economic ideas' (2). This diagnosis leads surely to a prescription. Klein quotes Adam Wildavsky: 'It is up to the wise to undo the damage done by the merely good' (7). We hope that readers will forgive us for wincing when we read Klein's follow-up: 'The economist's good works rarely bare fruit in any direct way. The economist's advice seems to fall on deaf ears. When good advice is

rejected, the rejection is brusque and ignorant. Even in the rare case when the advice takes root, the sage's influence is long lost and he receives no credit. For the most part, participation in public discourse is like tutoring an ornery and spoiled child. The economist must plead to get attention; once he has attention, his appeals consist of elementary ideas, rehearsed earnestly and painstakingly, and illustrated by imaginative stories and examples. Just when he thinks the public and policymakers are taking his precepts to heart, they suddenly abandon his instruction and for no good reason. His only recourse is to keep on hoping and pleading' (8). For a different story about the possible ways economists might interact with 'everymen' (and women), see the essays in Garnett (1999a).

59 The latest variant of this extension, of course, is the claim that all human behavior worth studying can be crammed into game theory. As the Nobel Prize winner John Harsanyi (1995) states, for himself and for many economists 'in principle, *every* social situation involves strategic interaction among the participants' (293). In fact, Harsanyi argues that, paradoxically, the assumption of perfect competition in markets was one of the chief obstacles to the ascendance of game theory since it implied the inability of any particular agent to effect much in the way of change in market price.

60 Among more recent critics, feminist economists have been prominent. Some readings include Feiner (1999), Grapard (1995), Strassmann (1993), Nelson (1996), and Hewitson (1999). Hewitson's book, especially, is written from a self-consciously poststructuralist point of view, as is her essay for this volume. The journal *Feminist Economics* is a good place to find such critical takes on homo economicus.

61 There is an enormous literature that treats Foucault's work. We recommend the following as an introduction to this commentary: Rabinow (1984), Dreyfus and Rabinow (1983), Smart (1993), and Shumway (1992).

62 For one discussion within economics that evaluates the Foucaultian themes of power/knowledge and their effects on the human body, see Amariglio (1988).

63 Readers can also evaluate arguments for and against poststructuralist feminism and postmodernism more broadly in Nicholson (1990). Carole Biewener (1999) offers a valuable assessment of the hoped-for effects of poststructuralist feminism on a decentered Marxism (and vice versa).

64 The essays in this volume by Grapard and Cooper consider the manner that early feminists like Charlotte Perkins Gilman and Harriet Martineau confronted the enforced masculinism of their day. The essays by Charusheela, Hewitson, Nelson, and Rossetti explore many of the issues of poststructuralist feminists in the field of economics, albeit in different ways.

65 This is true of most of the essays that composed the special symposium entitled 'Postmodernism, Economics, and Canon Creation' that appeared in the *Journal of Post Keynesian Economics* in 1991 (see Beed et al. 1991). Post Keynesianism has turned out to be a welcome ground (relatively speaking) to raise issues of postmodernism, as the influence of Keynes (especially his 1937 article) and Shackle (1961, 1966, 1990) in particular on questions of uncertainty and the indeterminacy of agent choice , not to mention ideas stemming from Keynes on persistent tendencies toward disequilibria, have been felt within some branches of this school.

66 Once more on disciplinary imperialism. Consider this one from Jack Hirshliefer: 'There is only one social science…What gives economics its imperialist invasive power is that our analytical categories – scarcity, cost, preferences, opportunities, etc. – are truly universal in applicability…Thus

economics really does constitute the universal grammar of social science' (1985: 53).

67 Easterlin (1997) captures again nicely some of the arrogance and exclusions, supposedly in the name of science, practiced by economists in this summary of what he terms his own 'indoctrination' to the economics profession in graduate school: 'And then there was my education in the values of the economics profession. I learned that economics is the queen of the social sciences. I learned that theory is the capstone of the status hierarchy in economics. I learned the brand names whose research I was to revere and respect. I learned that tastes are unobservable and never change. I learned that subjective testimony and survey research responses are not admissible evidence in economic research. I learned that what was then called "institutional economics" (Commons, Veblen, etc.) was beyond the pale, as were other social sciences more generally. I learned that there is a mere handful of economics journals really worth publishing in, and that articles in inter- or extra-disciplinary journals count for naught. I learned that economic measurement as then practiced by the National Bureau of Economic Research was to be denigrated as "measurement without theory" (13).

68 In addition to work we have already cited, and the essays in this book, such work includes Hands's (1997) rediscovery of Frank Knight's contextualist pluralism and Burczak's (1994) focus on the postmodern moments in Friedrich von Hayek's work. In a similar way, Cullenberg (1999) points to the postmodern moments and similarities in certain traditions within Marxism and institutionalism by emphasizing their decentered affinities, and Garnett (1999b) takes this Marxist-Institutionalist dialogue about postmodernity a step further in his consideration of heterogeneous approaches to non-neoclassical value theory.

69 On uncertainty, see for example Amariglio (1990), Ruccio (1991), and Amariglio and Ruccio (1995); on the decentered totality, see Cullenberg (1994 and 1996); on the fragmented body, in addition to the paper in this volume, see Amariglio and Ruccio (forthcoming).

References

Alston, Richard M.; Kearl, J. R.; and Vaughan, Michael B. (1992) 'Is There a Consensus Among Economists in the 1990s?' *American Economic Review*, 82 (2): 203–9.

Althusser, Louis (1970) *For Marx*, trans. Ben Brewster, New York: Vintage.

Althusser, Louis and Balibar, Etienne (1970) *Reading Capital*, trans. Ben Brewster, London: New Left Books.

Amariglio, Jack (1988) 'The Body, Economic Discourse, and Power: An Economist's Introduction to Foucault' *History of Political Economy*, 20 (4): 583–613.

—— (1990) 'Economics as a Postmodern Discourse', in Warren J. Samuels (ed.) *Economics as Discourse: An Analysis of the Language of Economists*, Boston: Kluwer Academic Publishers, 15–46.

—— (1998) 'Poststructuralism', in John B. Davis, D. Wade Hands, and Uskali Maki (eds) *The Handbook of Economic Methodology*, Northampton, MA: Edward Elgar, 382–88.

Amariglio, Jack and Ruccio, David F. (1995) 'Keynes, Postmodernism, Uncertainty', in Sheila Dow and John Hillard (eds) *Keynes, Knowledge, and Uncertainty*, Aldershot: Edward Elgar, 334–356.
—— (1999) 'The Transgressive Knowledge of "Ersatz" Economics', in Robert F. Garnett, Jr. (ed.) *What Do Economists Know? New Economics of Knowledge*, New York: Routledge.
—— (forthcoming) 'Modern Economics: The Case of the Disappearing Body?' *Cambridge Journal of Economics*.
Appiah, Kwame Anthony (1992) *In My Father's House: Africa in the Philosophy of Culture*, Oxford: Oxford University Press.
Arrow, Kenneth J. (1987) 'Economic Theory and the Hypothesis of Rationality', in John Eatwell, Murray Milgate, and Peter Newman (eds) *The New Palgrave: Utility and Probability*, New York: W. W. Norton, 25–37.
Backhouse, Roger (1992) 'The Constructivist Critique of Economic Methodology' *Methodus* 4 (1): 65–82.
Barnes, Barry (1985) *About Science*, Oxford: Basil Blackwell.
Bausor, Randall (1985) 'The Limits of Rationality' *Social Concept* 2 (2): 66–83.
Becker, Gary (1991) *A Treatise on the Family*, enlarged edn, Cambridge: Harvard University Press.
Beed, Clive *et al.* (1991) 'Symposium: Postmodernism, Economics, and Canon Creation' *Journal of Post Keynesian Economics* 13 (4).
Beniger, James R. (1986) *The Control Revolution: Technological and Economic Origins of the Information Society*, Cambridge: Harvard University Press.
Berman, Marshall (1982) *All That Is Solid Melts Into Air: The Experience of Modernity*, New York: Simon and Schuster.
Bertens, Hans (1995) *The Idea of the Postmodern: A History*, New York: Routledge.
Best, Steven, and Kellner, Douglas (1991) *Postmodern Theory: Critical Interrogations*, New York: Guilford Press.
Biewener, Carole (1999) 'A Postmodern Encounter: Poststructuralist Feminism and the Decentering of Marxism' *Socialist Review* 27 (1 and 2): 71–97 .
Blaug, Mark (1998) 'Disturbing Currents in Modern Economics' *Challenge*, 41 (3) (May/June), 11–34.
Brown, Stephen (1995) *Postmodern Marketing*, New York: Routledge.
Brown, Vivienne (1994) *Adam Smith's Discourse: Canonicity, Commerce and Conscience*, New York: Routledge.
Burczak, Theodore (1994) 'The Postmodern Moments of F. A. Hayek's Economics' *Economics and Philosophy* 10: 31–58.
Butler, Judith (1990) *Gender Trouble: Feminism and the Subversion of Identity*, New York: Routledge.
—— (1993) *Bodies that Matter: On the Discursive Limits of Sex*, New York: Routledge.
Caldwell, Bruce (1982) *Beyond Positivism: Economic Methodology in the Twentieth Century*, London: Allen and Unwin.
Caputo, John D. (ed.) (1997) *Deconstruction in a Nutshell: A Conversation with Jacques Derrida*, New York: Fordham University Press.
Castells, Manuel (1996–8) *The Information Age: Economy, Society and Culture* Volumes 1–3, Malden, MA: Blackwell Publishers.
Cilliers, Paul (1998) *Complexity and Postmodernism: Understanding Complex Systems*, London: Routledge.

Clower, Robert W. (1994) 'Economics as an Inductive Science' *Southern Economic Journal*, 60 (4) (April): 805–14.
Connor, Steven (1989) *Postmodernist Culture: An Introduction to Theories of the Contemporary*, Oxford: Basil Blackwell.
Cooper, Brian P., and Murphy, Margueritte S. (1999) '"Libidinal Economics": Lyotard and Accounting for the Unaccountable', in *The New Economic Criticism: Studies at the Intersection of Literature and Economics*, (eds) Martha Woodmansee and Mark Osteen, New York: Routledge, 229–41.
Cullenberg, Stephen (1994) *The Falling Rate of Profit: Recasting the Marxian Debate*, London: Pluto Press.
—— (1996) 'Althusser and the Decentering of the Marxist Totality', in *Postmodern Materialism and the Future of Marxist Theory: Essays in the Althusserian Tradition*, (eds) Antonio Callari and David F. Ruccio, Hanover, NH: Wesleyan University Press, 120–49.
—— (1999) 'Overdetermination, Totality and Institutions: A Genealogy of a Marxist Institutionalist Economics' *Journal of Economic Issues* 33 (4): 801–15.
Culler, Jonathan (1983) *On Deconstruction: Theory and Criticism after Structuralism*, Ithaca: Cornell University Press.
Derrida, Jacques (1976) *Of Grammatology*, trans. Gayatri Chakravorty Spivak, Baltimore: Johns Hopkins University Press.
—— (1978) *Writing and Difference*, trans. Alan Bass, Chicago: University of Chicago Press.
Docherty, Thomas (ed.) (1993) *Postmodernism: A Reader*, New York: Columbia University Press.
Dow, Sheila, C. (1991) 'Are There Any Signs of Postmodernism with Economics?' *Methodus*, 3 (1) (June): 81–5.
Dreyfus, Hubert and Rabinow, Paul (1983) *Michel Foucault: Beyond Structuralism and Hermeneutics*, Chicago: University of Chicago Press.
Dupré, John (1993) *The Disorder of Things: Metaphysical Foundations of the Disunity of Science*, Cambridge: Harvard University Press.
Easterlin, Richard A. (1997) 'The Story of a Reluctant Economist' *The American Economist*, 41 (2) Fall: 11–21.
England, Paula (1993) 'The Separative Self: Androcentric Bias in Neoclassical Assumptions', in Marianne A. Ferber and Julie A. Nelson (eds) *Beyond Economic Man: Feminist Theory and Economics*, Chicago: University of Chicago Press, 37–53.
Esteva, Gustavo, and Prakash, Madhu Suri (1998) *Grassroots Post-Modernism: Remaking the Soil of Cultures*, London: Zed Books.
Faigley, Lester (1992) *Fragments of Rationality: Postmodernity and the Subject of Composition*, Pittsburgh: University of Pittsburgh Press.
Feiner, Susan F. (1999) 'A Portrait of Homo Economicus as a Young Man', in Martha Woodmansee and Mark Osteen (eds) *The New Economic Criticism: Studies at the Intersection of Literature and Economics*, New York: Routledge, 193–209.
Feyerabend, Paul (1978) *Against Method*, London: Verso.
—— (1999) *Conquest of Abundance: A Tale of Abstraction versus the Richness of Being*, Chicago: University of Chicago Press.

Flax, Jane (1990) *Thinking Fragments: Psychoanalysis, Feminism and Postmodernism in the Contemporary West*, Berkeley: University of California Press.

—— (1993) *Disputed Subjects: Essays on Psychoanalysis, Politics and Philosophy*, New York: Routledge.

Fleetwood, Steve (ed.) (1999) *Critical Realism in Economics: Development and Debate*, London: Routledge.

Foucault, Michel (1972) *The Archaeology of Knowledge and The Discourse on Language*, trans. A. M. Sheridan Smith, New York: Harper and Row.

—— (1973) *The Order of Things: An Archaeology of the Human Sciences*, New York: Vintage.

—— (1979) *Discipline and Punish: The Birth of the Prison*, trans. Alan Sheridan, New York: Vintage.

—— (1980) *Power/Knowledge: Selected Interviews and Other Writings, 1972–1977*, trans. Colin Gordon, Leo Marshall, John Mepham, and Kate Soper, New York: Pantheon.

Fuchs, Victor R.; Krueger, Alan B.; and Poterba, James M. (1998) "'Economists' Views about Parameters, Values, and Policies: Survey Results in Labor and Public Economics' *Journal of Economic Literature* 36 (3): 1387–425.

Gablik, Suzi (1984) *Has Modernism Failed?* New York: Thames and Hudson.

Garnett, Jr., Robert F. (1999a) *What Do Economists Know? New Economics of Knowledge*, New York: Routledge.

—— (1999b) 'Postmodernism and Theories of Value: New Grounds for Institutionalist/Marxist Dialogue?' *Journal of Economic Issues* 33 (4): 817–34.

Gasché, Rodolphe (1986) *The Tain of the Mirror: Derrida and the Philosophy of Reflection*, Cambridge: Harvard University Press.

Gergen, Kenneth J. (1991) *The Saturated Self: Dilemmas of Identity in Contemporary Life*, Basic Books.

Gerrard, Bill (ed.) (1993) *The Economics of Rationality*, London: Routledge.

Gibson-Graham, J. K. (1996) *The End of Capitalism (as we knew it): A Feminist Critique of Political Economy*, Oxford: Blackwell.

Giddens, Anthony (1990) *The Consequences of Modernity*, Stanford: Stanford University Press.

Grapard, Ulla (1995) 'Robinson Crusoe: The Quintessential Economic Man?' *Feminist Economics*, 1 (1): 32–53.

Grosz, Elizabeth (1994) *Volatile Bodies: Toward a Corporeal Feminism*, Bloomington: University of Indiana Press.

Hacking, Ian (1990) *The Taming of Chance*, Cambridge: Cambridge University Press.

Hands, D. Wade (1997) 'Frank Knight's Pluralism', in Andrea Salanti and Ernesto Screpanti (eds) *Pluralism and Economics: New Perspectives in History and Methodology*, Cheltenham: Edward Elgar, 194–206.

Harding, Sandra (1986) *The Science Question in Feminism*, Ithaca: Cornell University Press.

Hargreaves Heap, Shaun (1993) 'Post-Modernity and New Conceptions of Rationality in Economics', in Bill Gerrard (ed.) *The Economics of Rationality*, London: Routledge, 68–90.

Harsanyi, John C. (1995) 'Games with Incomplete Information' *The American Economic Review*, 85 (3) 291–303.

Harvey, David (1989) *The Condition of Postmodernity*, Oxford: Basil Blackwell.
Hayles, N. Katherine (ed.) (1991) *Chaos and Order: Complex Dynamics in Literature and Science*, Chicago: University of Chicago Press.
Henderson, Willie; Dudley-Evans, Tony; and Backhouse, Roger (eds) (1993) *Economics and Language*, London: Routledge.
Hewitson, Gillian J. (1999) *Feminist Economics: Interrogating the Masculinity of Rational Economic Man*, Cheltenham: Edward Elgar.
Hirshliefer, Jack (1985) 'The Expanding Domain of Economics' *American Economic Review* 75 (6): 53–68.
Hollinger, David A. (1994) 'The Knower and the Artificer, with Postscript 1993', in Dorothy Ross (ed.) *Modernist Impulses in the Human Sciences, 1870–1930*, Baltimore: Johns Hopkins University Press, 26–53.
Hollis, Martin, and Nell, Edward (1975) *Rational Economic Man: A Philosophical Critique of Neo-Classical Economics*, Cambridge: Cambridge University Press.
Hutchison, T. W. (1979) *Knowledge and Ignorance in Economics*, Chicago: University of Chicago Press.
Ingrao, Bruna (1997) 'Comment' in 'Frank Knight's Pluralism', in *Pluralism and Economics: New Perspectives in History and Methodology*, Cheltenham: Edward Elgar, 227–31.
Jameson, Fredric (1991) *Postmodernism, or The Cultural Logic of Late Capitalism*, Durham: Duke University Press.
Katzner, Donald W. (1991a) 'In Defense of Formalization in Economics' *Methodus*, 3 (1): 17–24.
—— (1991b) 'Our Mad Rush to Measure: How Did we Get into This Mess?' *Methodus*, 3 (2) December: 18–26.
Kayatekin, Serap, and Ruccio, David F. (1998) 'Global Fragments: Subjectivity and Class Politics in Discourses of Globalization' *Economy and Society* 27 (February).
Kern, Stephen (1983) *The Culture of Time and Space, 1880–1918*, Cambridge: Harvard University Press.
Keynes, John Maynard (1937) 'The General Theory of Employment' *Quarterly Journal of Economics* 51 (2): 209–23.
Klamer, Arjo (1983) *Conversations with Economists: New Classical Economists and Opponents Speak Out on the Current Controversy in Macroeconomics*, Totowa, NJ: Rowman and Allanheld.
—— (ed.) (1996) *The Value of Culture: On the Relationship between Economics and the Arts*, Amsterdam: Amsterdam University Press.
Klamer, Arjo, McCloskey, D. N.; and Solow, Robert M., (eds) (1988) *The Consequences of Economic Rhetoric*, Cambridge: Cambridge University Press.
Klein, Daniel B. (ed) (1999) 'Introduction: What Do Economists Contribute?' in *What Do Economists Contribute?*, New York: New York University Press, 1–26.
Koopmans, Tjalling C. (1957) *Three Essays on the State of Economic Science*, New York: McGraw Hill.
Koritz, Amy, and Koritz, Douglas (1999) 'Symbolic Economics: Adventures in the Metaphorical Marketplace', in Martha Woodmansee and Mark Osteen (eds) *The New Economic Criticism: Studies at the Intersection of Literature and Economics*, New York: Routledge.

Kreps, David M. (1997) 'Economics – The Current Position' *Daedalus* 126 (1): 59–85.
Krips, Henry (1987) *The Metaphysics of Quantum Theory*, New York: Oxford University Press.
Krüger, Lorenz; Daston, Lorraine J.; and Heidelberger, Michael (1987) *The Probabilistic Revolution, 1: Ideas in History*, Cambridge: MIT Press.
Krüger, Lorenz, Gigerenzer, Gerd; and Morgan, Mary S. (1987) *The Probabilistic Revolution, 2: Ideas in the Sciences*, Cambridge: MIT Press.
Kuhn, Thomas S. (1970) *The Structure of Scientific Revolutions*, 2nd edn, Chicago: University of Chicago Press.
Latour, Bruno (1993) *We Have Never Been Modern*, trans. Catherine Porter. Cambridge: Harvard University Press.
Latour, Bruno and Woolgar, Steve (1986) *Laboratory Life: The Social Construction of Facts*, Princeton: Princeton University Press.
Lavoie, Don, (ed.) (1991) *Economics and Hermeneutics*, London: Routledge.
Lawson, Tony (1997) *Economics and Reality*, London: Routledge.
Longino, Helen (1990) *Science as Social Knowledge: Values and Objectivity in Scientific Inquiry*, Princeton: Princeton University Press.
Lynch, Michael, and Woolgar, Steve (eds) (1990) *Representation in Scientific Practice*, Cambridge: MIT Press.
Lyotard, Jean-François (1984) *The Postmodern Condition: A Report on Knowledge*, trans. Geoff Bennington and Brian Massumi, Foreword by Fredric Jameson, Minneapolis: University of Minnesota Press.
—— (1993) *Libidinal Economy*, trans. Ian Hamilton Grant, Bloomington: Indiana University Press.
Mandel, Ernest (1978) *Late Capitalism*, London: Verso.
Manuel, Frank E., and Manuel, Fritzie P. (1979) *Utopian Thought in the Western World*, Cambridge: Harvard University Press.
McClintock, Anne; Mufti, Aamir; and Shohat, Ella (eds) (1997) *Dangerous Liaisons: Gender, Nation, and Postcolonial Perspectives*, Minneapolis: University of Minnesota Press.
McCloskey, D. N. (1983) 'The Rhetoric of Economics' *Journal of Economic Literature* 31(June): 434–61.
—— (1985) *The Rhetoric of Economics*, Madison: University of Wisconsin Press.
—— (1994) *Knowledge and Persuasion in Economics*, Cambridge: Cambridge University Press.
—— (1996) *The Vices of Economists, The Virtues of the Bourgeoisie*, Amsterdam: Amsterdam University Press.
Mehta, Judith (1993) 'Meaning in the Context of Bargaining Games – Narratives in Opposition', in *Economics and Language*, (eds) by Willie Henderson, Tony Dudley-Evans, and Roger Backhouse. London: Routledge.
—— (1999) 'Look at me look at you', in *What Do Economists Know?: New Economics of Knowledge*, (ed.) by Robert F. Garnett, 37–59. New York: Routledge.
Milberg, William (1988) 'The Language of Economics: Deconstructing the Neoclassical Text' *Social Concept* 4 (June): 33–57.
Mirowski, Philip (1989) *More Heat than Light: Economics as Social Physics, Physics as Nature's Economics*, Cambridge: Cambridge University Press.

Morgan, Mary S. (1990) *The History of Econometric Ideas*, Cambridge: Cambridge University Press.
Nelson, Julie A. (1996) *Feminism, Objectivity and Economics*, New York: Routledge.
Nicholson, Linda, (ed.) (1990) *Feminism/Postmodernism*, New York: Routledge.
Norris, Christopher (1988) *Derrida*, Cambridge: Harvard University Press.
—— (1991) *Deconstruction: Theory and Practice*, London: Routledge.
—— and Benjamin, Andrew (1989) *What is Deconstruction?* New York: John Wiley and Son.
Norton, Bruce (1995) 'Late Capitalism and Postmodernism: Jameson/Mandel', In *Marxism in the Postmodern Age: Confronting the New World Order*, Antonio Callari, Stephen Cullenberg, and Carole Biewener (eds), 59–70. New York: Guilford Press.
Pickering, Andrew (1997) 'Concepts and the Mangle of Practice: Constructing Quaternions', in *Mathematics, Science, and Postclassical Theory*, (eds) Barbara Herrnstein Smith and Arkady Plotnitsky, Durham: Duke University Press.
Pietrykowski, Bruce (1994) 'Consuming Culture: Postmodernism, Post-Fordism, and Economics' *Rethinking Marxism* 7 (1): 62–80.
Plotnitsky, Arkady (1994) *Complementarity: Anti-Epistemology after Bohr and Derrida*, Durham: Duke University Press.
Poovey, Mary (1998) *A History of the Modern Fact: Problems of Knowledge in the Sciences of Wealth and Society*, Chicago: University of Chicago Press.
Porter, Theodore M. (1995) *Trust in Numbers: The Pursuit of Objectivity in Science and Public Life*, Princeton: Princeton University Press.
Posner, Richard A. (1992) *Sex and Reason*, Cambridge: Harvard University Press.
Rabinow, Paul, ed. (1984) *The Foucault Reader*, New York: Random House.
Resnick, Stephen A. and Wolff, Richard D. (1987) *Knowledge and Class: A Marxian Critique of Political Economy*, Chicago; University of Chicago Press.
Rorty, Richard (1979) *Philosophy and the Mirror of Nature*, Princeton: Princeton University Press.
Rose, Margaret A. (1991) *The Post-Modern and the Post-Industrial: A Critical Analysis*, Cambridge: Cambridge University Press.
Rosenau, Pauline Marie (1992) *Post-Modernism and the Social Sciences: Insights, Inroads, and Intrusions*, Princeton: Princeton University Press.
Ross, Dorothy, (ed.) (1994) *Modernist Impulses in the Human Sciences, 1870–1930*, Baltimore: Johns Hopkins University Press.
Rossetti, Jane (1990) 'Deconstructing Robert Lucas', in *Economics as Discourse: An Analysis of the Language of Economists*, Warren Samuel (ed.), 225–43. Boston: Kluwer Academic Publishers.
—— (1992) 'Deconstruction, Rhetoric, and Economics', in *Post-Popperian Methodology of Economics: Recovering Practice*, Neil de Marchi (ed.), 211–34. Boston: Kluwer Academic Publishers.
Ruccio, David F. (1988) 'The Merchant of Venice, or Marxism in the Mathematical Mode' *Rethinking Marxism*, 1 (4): 37–68.
—— (1991) 'Postmodernism and Economics' *Journal of Post Keynesian Economics*, 13(4): 495–510.
—— (1998) 'Deconstruction', in *The Handbook of Economic Methodology*, John B. Davis, D. Wade Hands, and Uskali Maki (eds), 89–93, Northampton, MA: Edward Elgar.

Salanti, Andrea, and Screpanti, Ernesto, (eds) (1997) *Pluralism and Economics: New Perspectives in History and Methodology*, Cheltenham: Edward Elgar.
Samuels,Warren J., (ed.) (1990) *Economics as Discourse: An Analysis of the Language of Economists*, Boston: Kluwer Academic Publishers.
—— (1996) 'Postmodernism and Economics: A Middlebrow View' *Journal of Economic Methodology* 3 (1): 113–20.
Samuelson, Paul A. (1997) 'Credo of a Lucky Textbook Author' *The Journal of Economic Perspectives*, 11 (Spring), 153–60.
—— (1998) 'How *Foundations* Came To Be' *Journal of Economic Literature*, 36 (September), 1375–1386.
Sandler, Irving (1996) *Art of the Postmodern Era: From the Late 1960s to the Early 1990s*, New York: Harper and Row.
Sass, Louis A. (1992) *Madness and Modernism: Insanity in the Light of Modern Art, Literature, and Thought*, Cambridge: Harvard University Press.
Sen, Amartya (1977) 'Rational Fools: A Critique of the Behavioural Foundations of Economic Theory' *Philosophy and Public Affairs* 6 (4): 317–44.
—— (1987) 'Rational Behaviour', in *The New Palgrave: Utility and Probability* John Eatwell, Murray Milgate, and Peter Newman (eds), 198–216. New York: W. W. Norton.
—— (1991) 'Economic Methodology: Heterogeneity and Relevance' *Methodus* 3 (1): 67–80.
Sent, Esther-Mirjam (1997) 'Sargent versus Simon: Bounded Rationality Unbound' *Cambridge Journal of Economics* 21: 323–38.
Shackle, G. L. S. (1961) *Decision, Order, and Time in Human Affairs*, Cambridge: Cambridge University Press.
—— (1966) *The Nature of Economic Thought: Selected Papers 1955–64*, Cambridge: Cambridge University Press.
—— (1990) *Time, Expectations, and Uncertainty in Economics: Selected Essays* by J. L. Ford (ed.). Aldershot: Edward Elgar.
Shumway, David (1993) *Michel Foucault*, Charlottesville: University Press of Virginia.
Simon, Herbert A. (1978) 'Rationality as Process and Product of Thought' *American Economic Review* 68 (May), 1–16.
—— (1991) *Models of My Life*, New York: Basic Books.
Smart, Barry (1993) *Michel Foucault*, London: Routledge.
Sofianou, Evanthia (1995) 'Postmodernism and the Notion of Rationality in Economics' *Cambridge Journal of Economics* 19: 373–89.
Solo, Robert A. (1991) *The Philosophy of Science and Economics*, Armonk, NY: M. E. Sharpe.
Solow, Robert M. (1991) 'Discussion Notes on "Formalization" *Methodus*, 3(1), 30–1.
Spivak, Gayatri Chakravorty (1999) *A Critique of Postcolonial Reason: A Critique of the Vanishing Present*, Cambridge: Harvard University Press.
Stigler, Stephen M. (1986) *The History of Statistics: The Measurement of Uncertainty before 1900*, Cambridge: Harvard University Press.
Strassmann, Diana (1993) 'Not a Free Market: The Rhetoric of Disciplinary Authority in Economics', in *Beyond Economic Man: Feminist Theory and*

Economics, Marianne A. Ferber and Julie A. Nelson, (eds) Chicago: University of Chicago Press 54–68.
Sugden, Robert (1991) 'Rational Choice: A Survey' *Economic Journal* 101:751–83.
Toulmin, Stephen (1990) *Cosmopolis: The Hidden Agenda of Modernity*, Chicago: University of Chicago Press.
Tribe, Keith (1978) *Land, Labour and Economic Discourse*, London: Routledge & Kegan Paul.
Varoufakis, Yanis (1993) 'Modern and Postmodern Challenges to Game Theory' *Erkenntnis* 38, 371–404.
Weedon, Chris (1997) *Feminist Practice and Poststructuralist Theory*, 2nd edn Cambridge: Blackwell.
Weintraub, E. Roy (1992) 'Roger Backhouse's Straw Herring' *Methodus* 4(2): 53–7.
—— (1997) 'Is '"Is a Precursor of" a Transitive Relation?' In *Mathematics, Science, and Postclassical Thought* Barbara Herrnstein Smith and Arkady Plotnitsky. (eds), Durham: Duke University Press.
Wheale, Nigel (ed.) (1995) *The Postmodern Arts: An Introductory Reader*, London: Routledge.
Wise, M. Norton (1995) *The Values of Precision*, Princeton: Princeton University Press.
Xenos, Nicholas (1989) *Scarcity and Modernity*, New York: Routledge.

PART II

MODERNISM AND POSTMODERNISM

2
MODERNISM AND POSTMODERNISM
A dialectical analysis

Sheila Dow

Postmodernism addresses the fragmented nature of meaning arising from discursive processes. This chapter takes a process approach to postmodernism itself, seeing it, not as an end-state, but as being itself part of a discursive process. The 'post' in postmodernism is thus taken seriously as referring to the temporal framework of discourse. The premise is that modes of thought in economics, or any discipline, arise from the wider cultural/political/technological context, so that the focus is on broad trends; this approach is not incompatible with 'moments' of reaction, which may be part of the engine for change in thought.

It will be argued here that postmodernism evolved out of modernism as the antithesis to modernism's thesis. Postmodernism is also antimodernism; it will be argued that postmodernism has carried forward modernism's dualism and it is the consequences of this dualism which are driving thought beyond postmodernism. In other words, just as implosion is immanent in modernism, so implosion is immanent in postmodernism. Already apparent in postmodernism is evidence of a transition to the next, synthetic, stage which goes beyond the dualism of modernism/postmodernism.

The argument will be introduced first in terms of monism and pluralism, where monism is understood as the ideal of unity and pluralism the ideal of plurality (see Salanti and Screpanti, eds, 1997, for a discourse on pluralism). Modernism's monism will be depicted as giving way to postmodernism's pure form of pluralism, which in turn is giving way to a modified form of pluralism which transcends both sides of the previous dual. In the following section, the argument is made more generally for a dialectical interpretation of this process. Finally, the process is put in historical context by suggesting comparison with earlier periods in which ideas may be seen as evolving according to a similar process: the period of the Scottish Enlightenment, with its influence on

Smith, and the period immediately following the First World War, with its influence on Keynes.

I am conscious, in the process of presenting this argument, of employing categories which may be regarded as incompatible with postmodernism. The notion of broad sweeps of thought may smack of modernism. Also I shall refer to modernist, postmodernist and synthetic thought as entities, in spite of their obvious diversity, in order to emphasise the key elements in common which allow us to construct these categories. Indeed attitude to singularity and plurality will be a key distinguishing feature. I shall employ the categories of ontology, epistemology and methodology in the discussion of pluralism, categories which many postmodernists may regard as inadmissible. But there is no escape from using some set of categories. The best we can do is to be aware of the particularities of the categories we are using and be clear in explaining to which approach they belong. My approach in this chapter is the synthetic approach which it is partly the purpose of this chapter to explain.

Pluralism

Identifying different strands of discourse in thought has become confused by different usage of common terms. We focus here on the term 'pluralism', which is associated with postmodernism, but which has been employed increasingly outside postmodernism. Not only does it have different meanings depending on the mode of thought employed, but it also has different meanings depending on the level of analysis: ontological, epistemological, methodological or method. In what follows we attempt to distinguish between these levels for each of three modes of thought: modernist, postmodernist and what I shall call for want of a better term 'synthetic'. (This approach could also usefully be termed 'political economy', but a concern with political economy as such is not the issue here; see Dow, 1990a.) The different positions with respect to pluralism are set out in Table 2.1.

Vision of reality

At the ontological level, the *modernist* vision of reality is monist in the sense that reality has an objective existence, and its nature is that there are unifying forces which it is the business of science to discover, and encapsulate in laws. For universal laws to be justified, reality must be understood to be a closed system, precluding the emergence over time of new forces, other than as exogenous shocks. Modernism involves a pervasive application of dualism; in the case of vision of reality, monism is understood dualistically and justified by the presumption that, if there were not unifying principles, then there would be chaos.

Table 2.1 Pluralism in economics

	Modernism	Postmodernism	Synthesis
Vision of reality	*Monist*; unifying forces in nature; scope for discovering laws from objective facts	*Pure pluralist*; fragmentation of nature. Or deny ontology altogether	Each school *monist*; but open system; regularities rather than laws
Theory of knowledge	*Monist* Words have fixed meanings; test re. facts; only one best way of gathering knowledge	*Pure pluralist* No means of comparing understandings. No regularities so no schools of thought	*Modified pluralist* Open system of knowledge means scope for schools of thought
Methodology	*Monist*, prescriptive Identifies best way of gathering knowledge. Pluralist, descriptive if cannot identify best way	No role. Or *pure pluralist*	*Modified pluralist.* Can have reasoned debate on different methodologies, by criteria of any one school of thought.
Method	*Monist* Pluralist if cannot identify best way of gathering knowledge	Nothing to say since no methodology. Or *pure pluralist*	*Modified pluralist* Range of methods limited by vision of reality and theory of knowledge

The *postmodern* reaction to modernism is completely different in terms of the vision of reality. As Rosetti (see Chapter 14) explains, the view is taken that there is no essence; meaning is taken from context and conveyed by language. From this comes the view that it is illegitimate to distinguish the ontological level from the epistemological level (see Amariglio, 1990). Thus statements may still be made in the postmodern literature as to the nature of reality, as embodied in discourse. These statements suggest the dual of the modernist vision of reality, most notably that reality is fragmented. Our understanding of reality arising from discourse is thus fragmented (which we shall come on to again at the next, epistemological, level). It is therefore in the nature of reality itself to be fragmented, since reality takes its meaning from discourse. Thus for example Amariglio (1988) discusses the fragmentation of the self. Reality further is understood, through discourse, as an open system, whereby fragmentation and lack of determinism hold the potential to disturb any regularities. While there is a refusal within postmodernism explicitly to distinguish a postmodern position on ontology, as distinct from epistemology, we can nevertheless think of postmodernism as being founded on a particular ontological position, which is bound up with the distinctive position taken in turn on epistemology, methodology and method. Postmodernism thus generates a pure pluralist understanding of reality.

The *synthetic* approach transcends the opposition of monism and pluralism by incorporating aspects of each to create a third vision of reality. The synthetic approach sees reality as being an open system, subject to new and unexplained influences, and evolving in undeterministic ways. But there is scope for a wide range of visions of this economic process; indeed difference of vision is inevitable if the economic system is seen as open, and complex; then there is scope for seeing the essence of the process in very different ways. Marxians, for example, see the economic process in totally different ways from neo-Austrians, while both may see the economy in open system terms. From openness it follows that no school of thought can be said to presume unifying forces which can yield universal laws. Rather, there can at best be a presumption that reality involves some regularities. Nevertheless, the existence of regularities may be regarded as the *sine qua non* of science. The synthetic approach is thus pluralist in its vision of reality in that scope is seen for a plurality of regularities from which schools of thought may select what they see as the essence of the economic process. Nevertheless, each school of thought is monist in the sense that each has its own, singular, vision of reality. Indeed I define schools of thought according to the particular vision of reality held (see Dow, 1990a), the implication being that different visions of reality cannot be sustained within a school of thought. (From this perspective, the fragmentation of vision in postmodern discourse limits the scope for theoretical development.)

Theory of knowledge

The theory of knowledge associated with *modernism* is, like the vision of reality, monist in the sense that knowledge is built up with reference to 'the facts', where these facts are objective representations of reality. The words used to convey these facts have fixed, singular, meanings (see Hacking, 1981). The facts are used to identify the universal laws which would reflect the unifying forces of nature. Indeed, testability against the facts is defined as the identifying feature of science. The goal of science is to develop true knowledge; science progresses (unidirectionally) as its stock of true knowledge grows. Further, because the economic system is seen as being closed, a closed system of knowledge is applied to it, modelled on the world of classical mechanics (see Mirowski, 1989).

Again, we can tease out from the composite ontology/epistemology of *postmodernism* a distinctive approach to epistemology. The postmodern approach reacts against the monism of modernism with a pure pluralist theory of knowledge. Since there are no real essences to discover, there is no subject-matter for knowledge other than discourse itself. Within this discourse there is a plurality of understandings and no independent means for comparing them because language is so context-specific. There is no scope whatsoever for classifying any piece of knowledge as true, because of the incommensurability of knowledge among different economists, and by the same economist with respect to different circumstances (see Amariglio, 1990). There is thus no common ground of shared knowledge on which to build schools of thought. Indeed, McCloskey (1994) argues that the use of schools of thought labels impedes conversation. The postmodern approach thus advocates tolerance on the grounds that no one economist can lay claim to the truth.

The *synthetic* approach again employs a modified pluralist position. Starting from the view that the economic system is (to human eyes, at least) an open system, the synthetic approach applies to this system an open system of knowledge. This implies that not all relevant variables are known, or knowable, requiring that any system of knowledge itself be partial. This opens up the scope for different schools of thought to choose to develop different partial systems of knowledge; these systems correspond to the vision of the economic process of each school. The theory of knowledge is thus pluralist in that pluralism of knowledge is entailed in an open system. Further, the synthetic approach has absorbed from postmodernism the argument that language is not neutral and the reporting of facts not a purely objective process. As a consequence it has inherited from postmodernism a tolerance of alternative systems of economic knowledge on the grounds that none has a prior claim on the truth. On the other hand, the synthetic approach takes from modernism a concern with criteria for good practice in generating knowledge. Thus, *from the perspective of a school of thought*, it is regarded as legitimate to argue for the system of knowledge chosen by that school. But, unlike modernism, there is no presumption that any one school has identified the route to true knowledge.

Methodology

Methodology refers to the system of techniques employed in order to generate knowledge. There has been some confusion generated by using the term 'methodological pluralism' when what is meant is 'pluralism of method'; the latter refers to the methodological choice in favour of a plurality of techniques; this will be discussed below. I shall use 'methodological pluralism' to refer to what methodologists do. As far as the *modernist* approach to methodology is concerned, again the approach is the dual of pluralist: it is monist. Traditionally, methodology was seen as being prescriptive, i.e. as setting out rules for good scientific practice.

Implicit was the notion that it was possible to identify one set of rules as being the best – hence the long-running battles between inductivists and deductivists, for example. But this approach to methodology has lost force, not least because it took its lead from the philosophy of science, which has long since moved beyond methodological monism. Now Blaug (1980 and 1991) is one of the few remaining standard-bearers of traditional methodology in economics.

It is in methodology that postmodernism has had its greatest (or at least its most direct) impact, deflating the confidence previously held in the capacity to identify best practice. Traditional methodology has thus gone through a sea-change by emphasising description over prescription (see, for example, Weintraub, 1989). But the field gives the impression of being in limbo, with the modernist predilection for rules for best practice periodically being voiced as something which might still come out of all the descriptive work (see de Marchi, 1991). The orthodox methodology approach is thus now predominantly pluralist, with methodologists providing accounts of theorising; but monism, as the wish to return to a single, preferred set of rules, is still evident.

For all the influence of *postmodernism* on modernist methodology, postmodernism does not in fact espouse a pluralist methodology; it denies the role of methodology altogether. This point was made most forcefully by McCloskey (1983). She argued that, once the contextual role of language was appreciated, it would become apparent that there was no role for methodology (by which she meant prescriptive methodology). But of course, as became apparent from the *furore* that she caused in methodological circles, McCloskey could not avoid methodology, even in denying methodology. The sense in which postmodernism also denies even descriptive methodology is that the concept of methodology requires some regularity in techniques for acquiring knowledge. Knowledge acquisition is too fragmented in the postmodern approach to identify methodologies. But even the act of identifying modernism requires the perception of modernist methodology as a regularity; criticising it goes even further down the methodological path. Indeed, Amariglio (1990) explains the difference between McCloskey and most postmodernists in that the latter explain the implications of modernist rhetoric for its methodology. But it is difficult at times to identify what postmodernists wish to put in its place (see Wendt, 1990). This follows from the postmodern conclusion that an overarching methodology is rendered impossible by the fragmented nature of discourse-based knowledge.

The *synthetic* approach adopts a pluralist approach to methodology, in that methodologists accept that there are no external criteria for arriving at the best methodology. The methodology of each school of thought, therefore, should be analysed critically in its own terms. However, pluralist methodology derives from a pluralist ontology and epistemology. Just as there is no ultimate objective account of reality in general, there are no grounds for expecting that a methodologist can somehow escape this in describing a plurality of methodologies. For the methodologist, the language used to analyse methodologies is specific to the context and the methodologist's perspective. Pure description is thus not feasible. Any methodologist brings to the analysis some criteria which correspond to a particular methodology. On these grounds the methodologist is equipped for critical analysis, on the basis of these criteria; as these are the methodologist's preferred criteria then the methodologist can engage in argument about the relative merits of different methodologies. It is not a question of whether or not this is desirable; it is a question of it being inevitable. But it is less harmful the more explicit the methodologist is about her starting point. In contrast to the modernist search for universal criteria, the synthetic approach entails a plurality of criteria, combined with the basis for argument as to the relative merits of different sets of criteria.

Method

Modernist economics is generally identified with general equilibrium economics; the unifying method is thus the equilibrium method (see Weintraub, 1985 and Hausman, 1992). Yet mainstream economics has been characterised lately by some degree of fragmentation (see Dow, 1996). This is due in part to the reassurance from McCloskey (1983) that methodology was no longer an issue; although it has to be said that economic practice had not generally conformed at all closely to professed methodology (as Blaug, 1980, demonstrated). Some leading mainstream economists such as Solow (1988) and methodologists such as Boland (1982) have indeed advocated pluralism of method, because of the difficulties involved in theorising about the complexities of the economic system. However, if the ontological and epistemological positions have not changed, then the hope must still be there, as with methodology, that the single best set of techniques will again be identified. Otherwise, pluralism of method lacks foundation and is thus antithetical to the foundationalist approach of modernism.

Because *postmodernism* denies the prescriptive role of methodology, it is consistent that nothing may be said about method. Nevertheless, it can be argued that, implicit in the postmodern critique of the monist modernist general equilibrium method as a means of establishing general laws in economics is an advocacy of pluralism of method. Certainly there is no explicit advocacy of an alternative range of methods, leaving pure pluralism of method as the only remaining possibility. But on what grounds may pure pluralism of method be justified? If reality is indeed fragmented, then there is no scope for identifying any regularities on which to theorise; if the fragmentation is only partial, then the nature of the fragmentation requires explicit discussion. If knowledge is pluralist also in the pure sense, there is no common ground for discussion among theorists; if it is not purely pluralist, then again the scope for regularities requires explicit discussion. If a pure pluralist position is taken on methodology, again there is no basis for discussion, but further, there are no grounds for preferring something other than the monism of method of modernism. If on the other hand there are grounds, on the basis of agreed views on reality, on knowledge or on methodology (i.e., departures from pure pluralism), for advocating either pure pluralism of method, or a modified pluralism, then these require discussion.

The *synthetic* approach is consistent with its positions at the other levels by adopting a modified pluralist approach to method as to everything else. Modified pluralism of method is indeed entailed by the modified pluralist methodology. Where an open system form of theorising is advocated, a range of methods is entailed to capture different aspects of the system in a partial manner, which is all that any theorist can aspire to. These methods may well be incommensurate because of the incommensurability of different parts of an open system. The range of methods adopted by any school of thought will be determined by the vision of reality and theory of knowledge peculiar to that school. Thus for example, neo-Austrians might rule out formalism and employ other methods more suited to focusing on behaviour within firms, households and governments. Orthodox Marxians may rule out market analysis as being of minor relevance to their vision, while allowing a limited degree of formalism to represent causal processes in historical time. An open system epistemology allows for, and indeed encourages, debate within and between schools of thought as to the appropriate range of methods. But the starting point is a chosen methodology which is part of what defines a school of thought.

A dialectial interpretation

Having characterised modernism, postmodernism and the synthetic approach in terms of pluralism, the next stage of the argument is to make the case that the three can be understood as stages in a dialectical process. The argument to be made is that, just as modernism proved to be unsustainable, so the postmodernism that grew out of it will ultimately also prove to be unsustainable; there is a third, synthetic, approach which can be seen as growing out of modernism and postmodernism and which is sustainable.

Klamer (1988) has referred to postmodernism as representing a 'moment' in the development of economics (see also pp. 83). Similarly,

Amariglio (1990) and Amariglio and Ruccio (1995) identify points at which uncertainty has been addressed as postmodern moments within modernism. Further, it is noted that attention to pure uncertainty and its implications have been gaining increasing attention of late. Postmodernism entails impermanence, and more generally the rejection of the notion of universal truths. So it comes naturally to think of postmodernism itself in transient terms, rather than itself involving some final truth. It is this feature of postmodernism, however, and the difficulties postmodern economists face in adhering to it, which means that its implosion is immanent, just as it was for modernism.

The first question to address is how applicable is the chronology of modernism-as-thesis and postmodernism-as-antithesis. McCloskey (Chapter 4) quite correctly points out the ancient origins of both; something like modernism and postmodernism have jostled for position over the centuries. Further, the synthetic position also has firm roots in the history of economics (notably in the work of the founder of modern economics, Adam Smith, and the major figure of twentieth-century economics, Keynes; we shall focus on the context of their thought in the next section). Nevertheless, McCloskey argues that the twentieth century can be understood in terms of a particular flowering of modernism and its reaction in postmodernism. It is possible to identify this development in broad cultural terms, within which economics is only a part. (How far it was influenced by external developments, and how much it influenced them, is a different, and large, question.) The implication of this historical perspective is that the dialectic can be expected to play itself out again and again. But we concern ourselves here only with the current dialectic. Certainly the bulk of the postmodern literature seems to identify modernism with the early years of the twentieth century, and postmodernism with developments in the second half of the century (the exact decade varying with the field of enquiry).

To what extent can postmodernism be considered as the antithesis of modernism's thesis? Such a construction requires that postmodernism can be shown to have evolved out of modernism, so that postmodernism contains some elements of modernism and cannot be understood other than as a reaction against modernism, i.e., postmodernism entails opposition to modernism in terms of particular principles. Klamer (Chapter 3) and McCloskey (Chapter 4) both refer to the evolutionary aspects of postmodernism. Klamer cites Jencks as noting the technological improvements of modernist architecture being carried forward into postmodern architecture. He then proceeds to list the features of modernism which postmodernists reject. I would argue that it is in this rejection that a key element of modernism is continued in postmodernism: dualism. As Chick (1995) argues, there is a range of reactions open to those who choose not to adopt the dualistic, modernist approach, of which rejection is only one (the others being containment, paradox and synthesis). But of course, rejection is a dualistic reaction. And it is dualism, I would argue, which was unsustainable in modernism, and which will prove unsustainable in postmodernism.

Dualism in modernism and postmodernism can be discussed with reference to the different positions of the two approaches with respect to pluralism. Modernists have a dualist vision of reality: either it conforms to order or it conforms to chaos. The dualist position on knowledge is that there is one best way of observing reality and theorising about it in terms of a closed system; closed systems in turn entail dualism in the concepts of endogeneity and exogeneity, known and unknown, etc. Modernist methodology is dualist: either there are absolute rules for good science, or there are none (in which case methodology can only be purely descriptive). Even the view on method is dualist: either there is one best method, or set of methods, or else any method may be employed.

The discussion in the previous section suggested some ambiguity in the postmodern position on pluralism, which arises in large part from the postmodern view that these categories are themselves modernist. In the case of each level (vision of reality, theory of knowledge, methodology, and method) the position is either the dual of modernist monism in the form of pure pluralism, or it is that nothing may be said. Certainly 'nothing may be said' is something other than the dual of monism. (It is however the dual of the more general position that 'things may be said'.) But if indeed this second possibility does represent postmodernism more accurately than pure pluralism, then nothing may be said. Full stop.

Herein lies the unsustainability of postmodernism. If the position is one of pure pluralism at any of the levels, then it requires justification in terms of the other levels of analysis. That such justification is required finds support in Klamer's criticism of modernism for lacking a philosophical foundation (see Chapter 3). On the other hand, if 'nothing may be said', then postmodernism is a purely negative position with respect to any knowledge, and any grounds for action, in general as well as in science. Postmodernism is, as Amariglio (1990) points out, nihilist.

That such a position is unsustainable is evident in the fact that much (and much that is useful) is said by postmodernists. It is for this reason that many postmodernists might not recognise themselves in the above account. In a way this is the point. Discourse is unsustainable if either nothing, or absolutely anything, may be said. Thus, Nelson (Chapter 13) offers an account of the way forward for feminist thought, starting from postmodernism but moving beyond it, which is compatible with the synthetic approach being presented here. Further, Milberg (Chapter 20) offers a very constructive analysis within international trade theory which advocates a preferred approach which corresponds with what I would identify with the postmodern vision of reality as fragmented and evolving; but Milberg suggests regularities to that fragmentation and evolution which provide the basis for theorising. Indeed this identification of regularities and advocacy of theoretical approach inevitably appear whenever postmodern economists address a particular field of enquiry in economics.

Many postmodernists' work corresponds more closely to the synthetic approach outlined here simply because the professed postmodern approach is unsustainable when it comes to discussions of methodology, theory or method. Just as it has proved very unhelpful for modernist economists not to address the foundations for their theorising, the same applies to postmodernists. To assert, as many postmodernists do, that foundations are irrelevant is to ignore the position on vision of reality, theory of knowledge and methodology implicit in any economic analysis. Since the 'nothing may be said' position removes any justification for analysis, and is in any case itself a foundationalist position, it does require discussion; further, in order for 'things to be said' there needs to be discussion of the basis for such things to be said.

But a return to the monism of modernism is not required in a discussion of foundations; the synthetic position outlined above is well articulated within heterodox economics. By definition, as a synthetic position, it has absorbed much of what is good in postmodernism: the tolerance of different approaches, the awareness of the need to develop theory within context, the need to encompass human creativity and unknowability into economic theory, and so on. It is also a sustainable position because it avoids the dualisms of modernism and postmodernism (see Dow, 1990b, and 1996). The synthetic position is explicit in non-orthodox schools of thought and is, I would argue, implicit in postmodernist applied economics. It is also possible to argue that it is implicit in much of modern neo-classical economics. As McCloskey (1983) points out, modernists find it impossible in practice to live up to their modernist principles. What is alarming however is the refusal by most neo-classical economists to recognise the disjunction and its implications (see Dow, 1997a).

Further, there is evidence in other fields of such a move beyond dualism. In chemistry, for example, Prigogine and Stengers' (1984) theory of self-organising systems avoids the order/chaos dual by considering chemical systems as open systems. Then, rather than order and chaos being mutually exclusive as in orthodox science, chaos is the precondition for order; under certain conditions, chaos generates processes which reinstate order in a new form. Mathematics too has been addressing issues raised by open systems. Fuzzy mathematics (see for example Dubois and Prade, 1980) avoids the dualism entailed in known boundaries of sets. Indeed Chick (1995), in exploring developments in fields other than economics, has argued that there is evidence of a physiological evolution among humans which is shifting the balance between dualistic (left brain) thought processes and non-dualistic (right brain) thought processes in favour of the latter. The rise of postmodernism can be seen as early evidence of this change; but, in that it itself entails dualism in its rejection of dualism, it will ultimately be inconsistent with non-dualistic modes of thought.

Earlier dialectics

It may be helpful in considering the current process of development in modes of thought if we consider briefly two earlier periods when similar processes were at work. The first period we consider here is the period of the Scottish Enlightenment, building up to Smith's contributions to the development both of philosophy and economics. The second is the period building up to the philosophic and economic contributions of Keynes. Both cases are admittedly controversial given the debate over the relationship between the Enlightenment and modernism, and over whether or not Keynes should be regarded as a modernist.

Both periods were characterised by the rejection of authority: in the case of the Enlightenment, Church dogma, and in the case of the early twentieth century, Victorian values. In the first case, the rejection of authority arose from the social, political and technological upheavals of the emerging Industrial Revolution while in the latter case it was the result of a disillusionment about the inevitability of progress brought on by the experience of the First World War and the shifting disposition of economic and political power. The Newtonian era saw the emergence of rationalism and an increasing faith in the power of science to uncover truth. Similarly, economics at the turn of the twentieth century was in the throes of mimicking classical mechanics in an attempt to portray economics as a science rather than a moral science (see Drakopoulos, 1991). The philosophical reaction among the sceptics in the Enlightenment period (such as Locke and Berkeley) was to point out the severe limits to the scope for rationally grounded knowledge. Bertrand Russell in many ways can be understood in similar terms at the turn of this century. Both periods were ones of intellectual ferment, not only over particular questions about scientific knowledge, but also about how to ask and answer questions, i.e., about the foundations of knowledge.

The Scottish Enlightenment was distinctive in a way which is captured in the denomination of the key figures as 'sceptical whigs' (see also Chapter 4). While Hume and Smith were keenly aware of the limits to certain knowledge, they were driven by practical concerns to theorise in any case, backed up by detailed observation of real historical processes. The aim was to establish some connecting principles as a basis for theory, but it was recognised that these could not be regarded as 'true' and that they required careful adaptation in the light of the detail of particular contexts. Fundamental was a theory of the commonality of human nature; but because that nature was social, it manifested itself differently in different contexts. Further, while behaviour was governed to a considerable extent by social convention, it was at times intentional, but even then was often deluded. The theory of knowledge as being limited and social was thus incorporated directly into theory. Smith's (and Hume's) work can thus be understood as conforming to the synthetic position outlined above, reacting against the scepticism of the rationalists. (See Dow, 1997b, for a fuller expression of this general argument.)

The characterisation of the early twentieth century is more difficult, in that it is often seen as signalling the beginnings of modernism proper (see for example Klamer, 1995). In fact, it would be possible to identify elements of postmodernism in philosophy, physics and in literature. But Keynes can be seen as combining elements of what we now know as postmodernism with elements of modernism in a synthesis which belies his characterisation as either modernist (Phelps, 1990) or postmodernist (see Amariglio and Ruccio, 1995, and Klamer, 1995). Keynes came to economics from philosophy, and a concern to establish the basis for action in belief under uncertainty. Like Smith, Keynes appreciated the importance of rhetoric as a vehicle for persuasion in the absence of demonstrable propositions. His discussion of uncertainty, further, countered the deterministic analysis of the orthodox economics of the time. Nevertheless, he proceeded to theorise about decision making under uncertainty, albeit in a social context, and to draw some generalisations at the macro level. Keynes thus employed postmodern ideas about the nature of knowledge but used them creatively in his analysis of economic behaviour in order to arrive at some explanations for observed regularities. Keynes thus also conformed, I would argue, to the synthetic approach outlined above.

But of course ideas in economics moved on. In philosophy, eighteenth-century scepticism turned into a focus on rational knowledge, whatever its scope, as exemplified by the French Enlightenment (see McCloskey, pp. 108). In the case of classical economics, Smith's approach was overtaken by the formalism of Ricardo which had much in common with modernism. The competing interpretations of Smith to that offered above are interpretations from a modernist perspective (see for example Arrow and Hahn, 1971; see Winch, 1997, for a detailed critique). Similarly, Russell's scepticism turned into an undue focus on certain, rationally grounded knowledge, whatever its scope, an approach from which Keynes (1972) explicitly distanced himself in terms of an alternative view of human nature as entailing passion as well as reason. Keynes's ideas were more clearly overtaken by modernism in a manner which is well documented (see Coddington, 1976, for example). In the case of both periods, the crucial elements of uncertain knowledge and the social nature of behaviour were squeezed out, allowing a deterministic theory of atomistic behaviour which purported to demonstrate truth with certainty. It is only in the last twenty years or so that there has been a postmodern reaction to this modernism, and now an attempt at synthesis.

Does this historical experience suggest an inevitable cycle, with modernism or something akin to it repeatedly gaining control? One possible way of addressing this question is to consider that the synthetic approach has been the victim of its own success. When economies and societies are stable (or growing in a stable fashion) then the uncertainty of knowledge, and changes in the social nature of knowledge, assume less importance. Only in times of turmoil, as in eighteenth-century Europe, or the turn of the twentieth century, do established grounds for belief come under suspicion, and the foundational questions again come to the surface. This is much more than a postmodern moment – it is something which can persist for decades, and requires some resolution. What has been suggested here is that the resolution of the postmodern reaction to the failures of modernism has taken the form of a synthesis which provides for theorising, but incorporates fundamentally postmodern ideas about knowledge and discourse. The argument here is that we are reaching this stage again now and, if the transition to the synthetic stage is to be successful in the sense of not reverting to modernism, it would be helpful for postmodernists to move even further in the direction of constructing new theories, even if this requires abandonment of what were originally the hallmarks of postmodernism, defined by its rejection of modernism.

Conclusion

This contribution is offered in the spirit of postmodernism, applying the process-of-knowledge approach to postmodernism itself. Postmodernism represents an advance on modernism with its critique of the idea that regularities in nature could be identified by means of unitary facts, analysed within methodologies conforming to rules of best practice; that the resulting theories had universal application in time and space; and that science necessarily progresses. The result has been a much greater awareness of the inevitability of differing perspectives generating different theories, none of which could lay claim to truth; the need for theory to be context-specific; and the view of science as sometimes taking wrong turnings.

But the contribution has in many ways been a negative one, in the sense that it is expressed as the justification for rejecting modernism. As far as alternative approaches to economics are concerned, postmodernism can be interpreted as saying either that anything is acceptable, or that nothing may be said on the subject. In practice, either has been an impossible position for postmodern economists to take. Postmodernists do make statements, and they do, explicitly or implicitly, express judgements about alternative approaches (to methodology, or theory). In practice, therefore, postmodern economists tend to adopt the modified pluralist position of the synthetic approach which does have an articulated position on vision of reality, theory of knowledge, methodology and method. To build constructively on this synthetic development would be welcome as a way of moving economics forward in a way which might forestall a reversion to modernism.

References

Amariglio, J. L. (1988) 'The Body, Economic Discourse and Power: An Economist's Introduction to Foucault', *History of Political Economy*, 29(4).
—— (1990) 'Economics as a Postmodern Discourse' in W. J. Samuels (ed.) *Economics as Discourse: An Analysis of the Language of Economics*, Boston: Kluwer.
Amariglio, J. L. and Ruccio, D. F. (1995) 'Keynes, Postmodernism and Uncertainty' in S. C. Dow and J. Hillard (eds) *Keynes, Knowledge and Uncertainty*, Aldershot: Elgar.
Arrow, K. J. and Hahn, F. H. (1971) *General Competitive Analysis*, Edinburgh: Oliver and Boyd.
Blaug, M. (1980) *The Methodology of Economics; Or How Economists Explain*, Cambridge: Cambridge University Press; 2nd edn 1992.
—— (1991) 'Afterward' in N. de Marchi and M. Blaug (eds) *Appraising Economic Theories*, Aldershot: Elgar.
Boland, L. A. (1982) *Beyond Positivism*, London: Allen and Unwin.
Chick, V. (1995) ' "Order out of Chaos" in Economics?' in S. C. Dow and J. Hillard (eds) *Keynes, Knowledge and Uncertainty*, Aldershot: Elgar.
Coddington, A. (1976) 'Keynesian Economics: The Search for First Principles', *Journal of Economic Literature*, 14(4).
de Marchi, N. (1991) 'Introduction' in N. de Marchi and M. Blaug (eds) *Appraising Economic Theories*, Aldershot: Elgar.
Dow, S. C. (1990a) 'Post Keynesianism as Political Economy: A Methodoogical Discussion', *Review of Political Economy*, 2(3).
—— (1990b) 'Beyond Dualism', *Cambridge Journal of Economics*, 14(2).
—— (1996) *The Methodology of Macroeconomics: A Conceptual Analysis of Schools of Thought in Economics*, Aldershot,: Elgar.
—— (1997a) 'Mainstream Economic Methdology', *Cambridge Journal of Economics*, 21(1).
—— (1997b) 'Hume, Smith and Critical Realism', University of Stirling *mimeo*.
Drakopoulos, S. (1991) *Values in Ecoomic Theory*, Aldershot: Gower.
Dubois, D. and Prade, H. (1980) *Fuzzy Sets and Systems: Theory and Applications*, London: Academic Press.

Hacking, I. (1981) 'Introduction' to *Scientific Revolutions*, Oxford: Oxford University Press.

Hausman, D. (1992) *The Inexact and Separate Science of Economics*, Cambridge: Cambridge University Press.

Keynes, J. M. (1972) 'My Early Beliefs' in *Essays in Biography: Collected Writings X*, London: Macmillan, for the Royal Economic Society.

Klamer, A. (1988) 'Economics as Discourse' in N. de Marchi (ed.) *The Popperian Legacy in Economics*, Cambridge: Cambridge University Press.

—— (1995) 'The Conceptions of Modernism in Economics: Samuelson, Keynes and Harrod' in S. C. Dow and J. Hillard (eds) *Keynes, Knowledge and Uncertainty*, Aldershot: Elgar.

McCloskey, D. N. (1983) 'The Rhetoric of Economics', *Journal of Economic Literature*, 21 (June).

—— (1994) *Knowledge and Persuasion in Economics*, Cambridge: Cambridge University Press.

Mirowski, P. (1989) *More Heat than Light*, Cambridge: Cambridge University Press.

Phelps, E. S. (1990) *Seven Schools of Thought in Macroeconomics*, Oxford: Oxford University Press.

Prigogine, I. and Stengers, I. (1984) *Order Out of Chaos: Man's Dialogue with Nature*, London: Heinemann.

Salanti, A. and Screpanti, E. (eds) (1997) *Pluralism in Economics*, Aldershot: Elgar.

Solow, R. M. (1988) 'Comments from Inside Economics' in A. Klamer, D. McCloskey and R. M. Solow (eds) *The Consequences of Economic Rhetoric*, Cambridge: Cambridge University Press.

Weintraub, E. R. (1985) *General Equilibrium Analysis*, Cambridge: Cambridge University Press.

—— (1989) 'Methodology Doesn't Matter. But History of Economic Thought Might', *Scandinavian Journal of Economics*, 91.

Wendt, P. (1990) 'Comment' on Amariglio (1990), in W. J. Samuels (ed.) *Economics as Discourse: An Analysis of the Language of Economics*, Boston: Kluwer.

Winch, D. (1997) 'Adam Smith's Problems and Ours', *Scottish Journal of Political Economy*, 44(4).

3

LATE MODERNISM AND THE LOSS OF CHARACTER IN ECONOMICS

Arjo Klamer

Modernism continues to characterize dominant economic discourse. Yet, its implosion must be imminent. The epistemological foundations in shambles, modernist economics is without a coherent philosophical justification. Consistent implementation of its strategies and heuristics has led to a gradual deconstruction of fundamental concepts. Undermining it further is the incredibility of the metanarrative that motivated the modernist project in economics. Original motivations have unravelled and turned into ironic commentary. Without credible hope of affecting the worlds around them, including the everyday lifeworld, modernists are left to their own devices and doomed to find gratification only within their own community.

Even so, modernism continues to characterize dominant economic discourse.

> There we go again: Bold conjectures, if not gross generalities, followed by a long monological exposition in support. Take the postmodernist sensitivity only half seriously, and such a presentation becomes suspect for pretending what it is not: a straight argument carefully articulated and composed. In the pomo vein we are led to think of this as a performance that we put on to impress, entertain and intimidate other academics, the only possible implied audience. Let's face it, staking out one more claim in this field of chaos and adding another noise to the cacophony of academic babble is futile and presumptuous. Yet the show must go on.

In the following I intend to diagnose the tensions and contradictions within modern neoclassical economics that augur its imminent implosion. But before getting to that, I am compelled to deal with the problem of characterization.

> William Ashmore (1989) and others of the Edinburgh school of sociology of knowledge ironized academic practices by interrupting their own monologues with dissenting voices. The interruptions underscore the inevitable ambiguity of making assertions about the world while withholding epistemological and ontological judgements at the same time.

The problem of characterization

The buzz about modernism and postmodernism seems to indicate that there are real presences of 'modernisms' and 'postmodernisms' out there. Use the terms a lot and they become real. In the meantime they are characterizations that are meant to capture elusive and complex 'realities'. In line with the postmodernist stance, we come to think of them as social constructions that serve as tools to sustain endless conversations in support of mainly academic communities.

Ironically, both in postmodernist and modernist moments characterizations are suspect, including the characterization of 'postmodernist' and 'modernist'. Yet the reasons for the resistance appear to differ. In the postmodernist spirit the complexity of a phenomenon such as 'postmodernist discourse' overwhelms so much so that no single category, no term, refers unequivocally. The pluriformity and the fragmented nature of things resists any single label. Apply the label 'postmodernism' to characterize a practice in economics, and the knee-jerk reaction will be to turn the characterization inside out, confront it with its own inconsistencies (as I am doing here), and expose its incompleteness. No characterization will withstand a well executed deconstructive move, certainly not a simple one like 'postmodernist economics'. So what are we talking about? The least we can do in the postmodernist spirit is to erase the concept as soon as we use it.

Within alleged modernist circles the application of 'modernism' does not make sense because it is in the character of modernist discourse to resist any characterization for its superficiality. National characters and moral characters are of no use in modernist treatises and novels. In search for deep structures that reveal universal characteristics (like *the* structure of a dynamic general equilibrium system) there is no need for differentiation in the form of characterizations of surface phenomena. Any character dissolves in the process.

The same happens in modernist economics. The representation of *the* market structure is successful only if it transcends contingent properties and identifies the invariant underneath unstable appearances. The only persuasive characterization would be in terms of the deep structure exposed, as in *syntactics* and *semantics*. Accordingly, the modernist project aims beyond characterizations of temporal and particular phenomena to cast its nets in the deep waters where the truth must lurk.

Modernist critic: What other way is there?
Postmodernist critic: You're falling into the modernist trap with your desire to characterize. Give it up!

    Maybe. Maybe not. I am in the business of characterizing a very complex reality even while I sense the ubiquitous presence of traps and suspect disapproval and dissent all around. How can we avoid characterizations anyway? We do it all the time. We do it for example when conveying our impressions about a person to someone who does not know that person. Surely, we could benefit from an analysis of the DNA structure of that person ('Please, do you mind if I take a hair from you?') or submit that person to a psychological test. Even so, the information will not suffice and may not be in the form that our audience will comprehend. So we interpret, inducing and abducting features from the confrontations between what we observe and what we know and then assimilating our findings into a characterization, that is, the verbal representation. As is common knowledge in the hermeneutic tradition, we make the same moves when coping with phenomena in general. Critical is the conveying of our findings as the need to communicate forces us to wring our vague, fuzzy, and multidimensional understanding into the straitjacket of language. Forced to communicate our undoubtedly complex and nuanced comprehension of the phenomena under discussion, we will do the same in this paper. Characterization is what this paper is, to a great extent, all about.

    It should be possible to characterize without the modernist claim to capture the invariant, or the essential, features. At the same time we can resist the postmodernist hypersensitivity to the overdetermined and complex character of everything existing by taking the *pragmatic* stance. For it is in communicative action that characterizations operate, receive resistance and get reformulated. In action we necessarily and inevitably fall back on characterizations, their imperfection being a condition for action. Let Erasmus be the example with his *Praise of Folly*; all action, after all, requires a suspension of disbelief as well as a momentary erasure of systemic knowledge to make room for the Fool in us. Contrary to what is commonly believed, the Fool does not condemn us to the merely irrational (whatever that may mean), but encourages us to act in accordance with principles, ideas and values which, if put to the modernist and postmodernist tests, would crumble and dissolve. The Fool can be reasonable and pragmatic.

Intermezzos

The interest in characterization is similar to the recent interest in character. On the latter MacIntyre notes in *After Virtue*:

> To understand [characters] is to be provided with a means of interpreting the behavior of actors who play them, just because a similar understanding informs intentions of actors themselves; and other actors may define their parts with special reference to these central characters.
>
> (MacIntyre, 1981: 26)

Exceptions support the characterization of modernists as resisting the characterization of modernist. One exception is Edmund Phelps, who in his introductory textbook (1985) identifies modernism in the 'new vocabulary' with concepts such as incomplete information, transaction costs, customer markets, 'asymmetric' information, rational expectations, and credibility. The question is why he sees these concepts as modernist. The reference to architecture on the front cover indicates that the modernism as it is identified in that practice is on his mind. The reader is left to wonder how the organic forms of Wright's Guggenheim museum and the rectangular buildings of Van Der Rohe compare to the forms of rational expectations and transaction costs.

Another exception is McCloskey, who put the concept of modernism on the agenda in her seminal work on rhetoric in economics (1985). But then she is not quite the conventional economist given her Old Chicago stance and attention to our classical heritage, literature, and rhetoric. Her attacks on modernism in economics, which she mainly recognizes in positivist beliefs, and her attention to rhetoric have earned her the reputation of being a relativist. When the only terms available to us are 'modernist' and 'postmodernist', her critique of modernism should make her a postmodernist. Yet she is not. The relativist label does not stick very well either.

Neo-traditionalism McCloskey's case calls for alternative labels. Calling her an Old Chicago economist, as she herself prefers, may do fine in the context of economics, but fails to capture the more global sentiment that her work reflects. The label that I prefer is that of the neo-traditionalist. Currently, it represents respect for tradition, place, authority, values and roots coupled with the (postmodern) recognition that all these entities are socially constructed and subject to change. The neo-traditionalist urge is to revisit the pasts of family, of nation, of discipline and take along what seems of value for the

> present life – to activate memory, as Christopher Lasch puts it in his last work (1995). It makes one suspicious of radical programs, yet at the same time makes one susceptible to change. It makes one oppose any form of fundamentalism including the fundamentalist adherence to what once was. Neo-traditionalism cuts through modernist dualisms, twentieth-century ideological oppositions; it encapsulates modernist elements together with postmodernist sensibilities and then some more, such as interest in, and concern for, the traditions that frame our lives.

Modernism and economics

In earlier exercises (Klamer, 1987 and 1993), I have attempted a characterization of modernism in economics with the visual arts and architecture as bases for comparison. After a great deal of testing against texts and skeptical audiences, I settled on the following eight characteristics:

Eight characteristics of modernism

1 *Problematization of representation*. Appearances deceive: reality is not as it presents itself. When appearances deceive, the representation of reality becomes a problem. (cf. physics, Marx, Freud.)
2 *Exploration of the invariant structure of reality while recognizing its ephemeral appearance*. In order to highlight the problem of representation some modernists wanted to express the 'transient, the fleeting, the contingent'. Others were intent in exploring and determining the fundamental, invariant structure that underlies the appearances.
3 *Predilection for formal, reductionistic and axiomatic representations*. For those looking for the invariant, logic, geometry and mathematics were the preferred languages; the dominant heuristic prescribes the development of formal systems from a minimal set of axioms, of which at least some concern the characteristics of the most basic units of the system (particles, individual decision makers).
4 *The machine as a dominant root metaphor*. The machine suggests the possibility of perfection and control. As such, it answers the ideal of a better life.
5 *A break with history*. Commitment to the new called for a liberation from tradition. The future, and not the past, should determine the present (cf. the avant-garde, the shock of the new, the bulldozer).
6 *The turn inwards*. The medium becomes the issue. The significant audience comprises the initiated, the insiders, that is, colleagues and knowledgeable critics. Much of modernist work is self-referential

and reflexive. One implication is the distinction between high-brow and low-brow, that is, academic art (or economics) from popular art (or economics). Another implication is the professionalization of the arts and sciences, and the departmentalization of their instruction in universities.

7 *The square versus the circle.* Modernism operates both in the square and the circle. The square is the domain of the scientific, the circle of the therapeutic. The sharp distinction of the square and the circle in modernist consciousness accounts for a basic tension within modernism. It is responsible for the gulf that separates the humanities and the sciences in modern academia, as well as professional and personal life in general.

8 *Endorsement of the Enlightenment metanarrative.* Modernists seek to overcome historical and cultural barriers in the search for universal truth, peace, a better world, or all three.

According to this characterization, the problem of representation is the central theme in modernism. Exemplary in economics is the work of Paul Samuelson. Highly abstract, reductionistic and formalistic, it seeks to expose the deep structures of economies in forms that transcend historical and cultural, and hence all contingent conditions to claim universal validity. Whether it is the theory of revealed preferences, international trade or business cycles, Samuelson's theory is devoid of references to historical situations or human subjects. His theory is reflexive in the sense that the main subject is the medium, that is, the theoretical strategy itself. Modernist economics, as in Samuelson's work, is foremost about itself. The only real character that inhabits its world is its author, that is, the economist him-, or herself (as I have tried to show in Klamer, 1995).

The bulldozer (see point 5 above) symbolizes the levelling strategies within modernism. Like Corbusier in architecture, Samuelson and his modernist colleagues appear to erase old frameworks to level their playing field so that they can build new models from first principles. They speak of liberating the discipline from the verbiose and empiricist practices that dominated into the 1940s.

The purpose of this scientific revolution in economics was world improvement, in accordance with the Enlightenment narrative. Before I can claim confidently that modernist economists actually subscribed to this metanarrative, more research is needed. General impressions derived from textbook presentations, perusal of academic articles, research proposals, and endless conversations with academic economists indicate that economic policy has been the legitimating and motivating factor in academic economic research. Abstract arguments found their justification in possible policy consequences. In a survey among graduate students, world improvement continues to be a rationale for studying economics. This rationale speaks to the continuing strength of the Enlightenment narrative in economics. Yet that strength appears to be waning: and with it the persuasiveness of the complex of values, strategies, attitudes, and sentiments that define modernism in economics.

Moments

There are plenty of problems with my characterization of modernism. One of these is the narrative that accompanies the eight-point list. A narrative needs to begin somewhere, but it is unclear how to begin *this* narrative. It has been customary to begin with Descartes, who is credited with the introduction of various dualisms into the collective modern consciousness. In the table above these dualisms are captured in the square–circle opposition, which sets apart factors such as the rational, the objective, and the public from the emotional, the moral, the subjective, and the personal. Toulmin (1990) problematized this beginning – how could anyone not do so? – and proposed to begin the narrative of the genesis of modernism with Montaigne. The great advantage of Toulmin's narrative is that it generates a better transition to postmodernism, since Montaigne seems to anticipate postmodern sentiments.

Another, related problem is that of periodization. Claim modernism in economics and the question is 'When did it start?' followed by 'If it has ended, when was that?' Should we mark the beginning with Von Thunen, or is Walras the modernist pioneer in economics? No to both, I would argue, because their formal and reductionistic approach was incidental and did not inform the *dominant practice* of their respective times, which continued to be historical, empirical and conceptual. If formalism and reductionism are the criteria, we should go back to at least Pythagoras! So dominance – or, to use Gramsci's term, hegemony – is what counts. Whereas art changed apparently around 1910, with painting turning to abstract or surreal techniques and concerns, modernism began to affect the representation in economics only in the 1930s. For it is then that formal annotations started to crowd out empirical tables and historical descriptions from the journal pages.

Throw in the numerous instances of economic work during the twentieth century that take exception to my listed characteristics, and the characterization appears to blow up in our faces. What shall we do with Keynes, Schumpeter, and Hayek, to name just a few paragons of twentieth-century economics? Their work is insufficiently formal, reductionistic, mechanistic, and self-referential to be called modernist. Amariglio and Ruccio (1995) would even go as far as to label Keynes and Knight as postmodernists. Milton Friedman's work resists the characterization too, as does the entire oeuvre of the Old Chicago school. When one of its avowed members, Deirdre McCloskey, fulminates against modernist economics, something is amiss. So what are they if not modernists? Are they 'pomos'?

Amariglio provides a sensible way out of this conundrum in his important paper 'Economics as a Postmodern Discourse' (1990) with the notion of 'moments'. In an allegedly postmodernist move he suggests that 'while economic discourse is characterized by a self-consciousness of modernism, within this modernism we can discern various postmodern "moments"' (1990: 15). As one of such postmodern moments, he identifies the concern with uncertainty in the work of Keynes and Knight because that concern would undermine, he purports, the epistemological foundations on which modernist economics is built. By highlighting the postmodern moments in modernist economics, Amariglio's characterization avoids the wholesale character of modernism outlined in the list above. It furthermore brings out the tensions and contradictions within modernism that may lead to its implosion.

The notion of moments has the additional advantage that it alerts us to the possibility that modernism, postmodernism and something like traditionalism are indeed just that: moments that can operate simultaneously. Accordingly, when modernist moments are perceived to dominate, postmodern and traditionalist moments may very well continue to operate, or vice versa. The avowed modernist may know moments of radical doubt – the postmodern moment. They may subsequently return to a reductionistic analysis of an economists' problem (like the equilibrium solution in a non-cooperative game) – the modernist moment. And on the side they may be indignant about sneering in the profession – conceivably a traditionalist moment. It may be even in the nature of discursive activities that all three, and possibly more, moments concur. Further speculation on this count I leave for another occasion.

Late modernism

Apart from allowing for postmodern and traditional moments, my characterization of modernism behoves further differentiation to distinguish Samuelsonian modernism from more recent forms, as in game theory, new classical and new Keynesian economics, new growth theory, chaos theory and so on. To characterize these more recent forms as postmodern would not be appropriate. For none of them exhibit the radical doubt, the fragmentation, the duplicities, the stylistic mixtures that are typical for postmodernist practices (or moments). It would be more appropriate to call these forms 'late modernist' in imitation of the nomenclature applied by readers of the scenes in the arts and architecture. A brief detour through the world of the arts may clarify this move.

Conventional wisdom in art history presents Andy Warhol as the artist who broke with modernism in the arts. His reproduction of familiar images is interpreted as an argument against the internal, self-referential, and abstract language of modernism (as in abstract expressionism and neo-plasticism). Not a modernist, he has to be a postmodernist. What else could he be? In architecture we witness a trend away from the taut, formal buildings of Mies Van der Rohe and the Bauhaus towards buildings with relief, intricate forms, and display of technological devices, such as the Centre Pompidou in Paris. Are such buildings to be named postmodern? Is Warhol a postmodernist? The answer on both counts is no.

Jean-François Lyotard (1984), in his characterization of the 'postmodern condition', emphasizes the loss of *metanarratives* that accompanied modernism. According to one such metanarrative, as interpreted by Lyotard, 'the rule of consensus between the sender and addressee of a statement with truth-value is deemed acceptable if it is cast in terms of a possible unanimity between rational minds: this is the Enlightenment narrative, in which the hero of knowledge works toward a good ethics-political end – universal peace' (1984: xxiii–iv). The inhabitants of a postmodern world, he claims, do not believe in such a possibility anymore. They do not believe in the possibility of universal truth and beauty and in the value of monolithic methodologies; they also have given up the modernist conviction that intellectuals and artists can reform the world and shape a better future. Postmoderns instead practise plural methods. In their world a thousand flowers bloom.

The critic Suzi Gablik (1984) considers a significant segment of Lyotard's postmodernism still as part of modernism. The search for the new, she claims, reflects a modernist spirit. The same could be said about the attachment to abstract representations and the use of exclusive jargon. In his little book *What is Post-Modernism?* Charles Jencks sorts out some of the confusion. He proposes that we label pop-art, minimalism and buildings such as the Centre Pompidou 'Late Modern'. His characterization is as follows: 'in architecture it is pragmatic and technocratic in its social ideology and from 1960 takes many of the stylistic ideas and values of Modernism to an extreme in order to resuscitate a dull (or clichéd) language' (1986: 35). Late moderns, according to Jencks, may have lost the original faith of moderns, but still practise much of what the moderns preached. Although many late moderns abandon the formalism of modern methodology, they still celebrate the future (through their appreciation of the 'new') and the abstract. Some may have tried to popularize their discourse, but many late moderns, especially the minimalist and conceptual artists, continue to operate for a select, well-informed audience. These artists construct 'strange objects', fill a gallery with sand, throw a heap of cloth in the corner of a museum, that is, they do things that an amateur will find hard to understand. 'The morality of Late Modernism consists in [...] integrity of invention and usage; like Clement Greenberg's defense of Modernist morality the work has to be judged as a hermetic, internally related world where the meanings are self-referential' (Jencks, 1986: 39). Jencks's Late Modernism is the Post-Modernism that Ihab Hassan describes as 'essentially subversive in form and anarchic in its cultural spirit...[Post-Modernism] dramatizes its lack of faith in art even as it produces new works of art intended to hasten both cultural and artistic dissolution' (cited by Jencks, 1986: 33).

Accordingly, in Jencks's characterization, late modernism, although often a reaction against modernism, still adheres to its critical values. Postmodernism is the label we best reserve for those expressions which intend to reclaim the territory that modernism erased. Jencks terms postmodernism 'that paradoxical dualism, or double coding, which its hybrid name entails; the continuation of Modernism and its transcendence;...an architecture [Jencks's main subject] that was professionally based *and* popular as well as one that was based on new techniques *and* old patterns' (1986: 7, 15). He refers to classical patterns in otherwise stylistic buildings, to the reintroduction of symbolism and allegories in painting. Among painters, the Italians Enzo Cucchi and Sandro Chia, and the Americans David Salle and Eric Fischl provide good examples of the postmodern interest in culture, history and symbolism. They have brought back figures into their painting: Cucchi paints the sacredness of the land in which he grew up; Fischl takes his viewer behind the façade of American middle-class life (cf. also the movie *Blue Velvet*); Salle divides his canvas into a modernist and a postmodernist part, thereby asking the viewer to make the connection.

Recent developments in the world of the arts attest to the strength of modernist sentiments, as late modernist work maintains a strong presence. The work of conceptual artists, such as Donald Judd and Joseph Beuys, is still going strong. The neo-expressionists (Cucchi and Chia) and neo-traditionalists (Fischl?, April) have retreated into relative obscurity. Nobody seems to know what the art scene is about right now. Confusion, maybe. Loss of direction, perhaps.

Late modernism in economics: the case of new classical economics

I have provided a story for the arts, or at least an impression of it. Now we can return to the world of economics. The argumentative strategy that Hicks, Samuelson *et al.* introduced into macroeconomic discourse requires the writing down of models and, in a later version, the derivation of macrorelations from the neoclassical assumption of individual maximizing behavior. The intent is the construction of a universal model that, after adjustment for the values of parameters, can apply to any situation in any period of history in any culture. The favored expression is formal, i.e. a series of equations that facilitate mathematical solution procedures.

New classical economists take over this strategy from the Keynesians, but 'take it to an extreme'. Their argument is that neo-Keynesians have not been consistent and strict in their adherence to this strategy. Robert Lucas, for example, argues that the dynamic properties of neo-Keynesian models were ad hoc. 'While Keynes and the other founders of what we now call macroeconomics were obliged to rely on Marshallian ingenuity to tease some useful dynamics out of purely static theory, the modern theorist is much better equipped to state exactly the problem he wants to study and then to study it' (Lucas, 1987: 2). He means that the new classical strategy has produced models that are dynamic *and* make rational choice explicit, which is what the Keynesian dynamic models (cf. the models of the Phillips curve) failed to do.

In conversation, new classical economists make clear that they want to talk in terms of models. 'I want to write down a model', thus goes a standard expression of intention, 'that makes explicit the structural properties (is grounded) and accounts for...'. New classicals want to be explicit, precise, and exact. Being in the mathematical mode, they expect logical consistency, that is, consistency which can be checked through mathematical operations.

I distrust discursive analyses.
Why is that?
They are vague and speculative. Later, after more careful analysis, we often discover that they contain inconsistencies. I think that we ought to write down models that are explicit and so can be shown to be consistent.
Aren't you afraid that if you adhere strictly to this strategy, you end up not being able to say anything.
No.

Thus new classicals have picked up and run amok with the mathematical values that Samuelson *et al.* instilled, leaving Keynesians to say: 'Yes, but we didn't mean it that way'. In addition new classicals carried through the axiomatic approach in the traditions of Hicks-Samuelson and Arrow-Debreu. While physicists are still looking for the most elementary particle and the unified force, economists appear to have found their fundamental axiom in the notion of the maximizing individual unit. New classicals resemble the minimalists in the arts in the sense that they strive to construct complex models with a minimal number of assumptions. They are conceptual artists in the sense that their work communicates abstract ideas which only those within the inner circles can grasp.

Deconstruction

Much of the work that critics place under the label 'late modernism' turns to preceding work – usually modernist work – to do a number on it. The intent is critical; the idea is to show the contradictions within that work by turning the work against itself. This is the art of deconstruction, an art that was theorized and perfected by Derrida. When pursued with persistence, deconstruction leaves the critic and the reader lost in the rubbles and illusions of modernist constructions.

Deconstruction is an important element in new classical economics, too. New classical economists do not subvert the Keynesian strategy – they do not seek distinction by returning to, say, institutionalism or historicism. No, they use the Keynesian strategy to turn it against the Keynesian edifice. Taking the Keynesian search for microfoundations to an extreme, new classicals dismantle macroeconomics, the preeminent Keynesian construction. Lucas writes:

> The most interesting recent developments in macroeconomic theory seem to be describable as the reincorporation of aggregative problems such as inflation and the business cycle within the general framework of 'microeconomic' theory. If these developments succeed, the term 'macroeconomic' will simply disappear from use and the modifier 'micro' will become superfluous. We will simply speak, as did Smith, Ricardo, Marshall and Walras, of economic theory.
>
> (Lucas, 1987: 108)

Furthermore, by giving a radical interpretation of the Keynesian strategy to connect macro with neoclassical economics and by grounding the theory of expectations in this way, new classicals took away the footing upon which Keynesian policy conclusions rested. But that is an old story by now.

Naturally, economists operate under conditions that are to a great extent very different from those that operate in the world of artists and literary critics. The differences are important; one does not step without consequences, social and personal, from one world into the other. Nevertheless, when we eavesdrop on 'conversations' in both worlds – as I have been doing – common strategies, values and intentions become too obvious to be ignored. They are even more remarkable because the worlds are so different.

Turning inwards

One characteristic of modernism, revealed in the disciplines of the arts as well as economics, is the conscious separation of the discipline from others. Painters historically separated themselves from sculptors; they also separated themselves from the 'public' and continue to consider other painters their main audience. Thus they have produced a highbrow culture, only to be fully understood by the initiated.

A similar trend is discernible in economics. Along with professionalization, the language of economics has become more complex and difficult. When the mathematical strategy took over from institutional, empirical and discursive approaches (in the US this happened sometime in the 1950s), academic economics got out of reach for non-Ph.D.s or those Ph.D.s who work outside academia or the major research institutes. Thus, communication turned inward.

In the art world this product of modernism was challenged in, for example, pop-art. The attempt was to de-academicize art and bridge the gap with the public. It is not unreasonable to assume that in this cultural climate, challenges to the abstract and 'obscure' nature of economics could also surface during the 1960s and have some impact on the profession. But just as in the art world, attempts to connect high with low brow enjoyed only brief popular support. Artists returned to their explorations of form and to intricate internal discussions (cf. minimalism and conceptual art); art became difficult again. ('What does that heap of old cloth in the corner of a museum room mean?'). The most devastating criticism of a work was, and still is, the charge of it being entertaining or decorative.

Entertainment was certainly not on the mind of new classical economists either. They may not have set out to make economics difficult, but that is what it became (unless one enjoys and is good at topology, differential calculus and all that). To become a 'serious economist' (a common way of putting it) one needs to undergo a rigorous mathematical training. New classical economics is for 'serious economists', and thus not for anyone who is 'simply' interested in economics. Politicians, for example, can expect little support from economic practitioners.

Reflexivity

Deconstruction, which is, as we saw, an integral element of late modernist practice, tends to stimulate self-consciousness, a mode in which one reflects on one's own constructions. Often mentioned in this context is Saussure's linguistics. Saussure conceives of language as a system of signs in which the signs derive meaning not from connections to external or non-linguistic 'objects', but through differences with other signs. Language would thus be a *self-referential* system in which meanings are interdependent. (Saussure was inspired by the sign 'money', which signified not because it stood for something, but because of the way in which it operated within a system of signs, i.e. an economic system.)

Modernist economists, too, adopted the notion of an interdependent system. Signs such as 'market', 'price', 'demand', 'supply', 'money', 'equilibrium' derive their meanings from the context within economic discourse in which they are used. Their precise meanings vary with variations in the system. (Economists usually call these self-referential signs theoretical terms.) When meanings are attributed through references to the 'real' world, the modernist economist is likely to be uncomfortable, if not dismissive.

New classicals took the self-referential character of the modernist model one step further. In Keynesian (and monetarist) models, expectations referred to 'objects' outside the theoretical model. The rational expectations hypothesis incorporated expectations into the model; in a new classical model expectations are consistent with the predictions of the model itself and thus come to refer to the model. Game theory and the applications of the rationality assumption in the analysis of government behavior are the next steps in the development towards a self-referential system.

Current Keynesians are made nervous by this development, even though their older generation made significant contributions in its early stages. Samuelson *et al.* showed the power of abstraction, of the movement away from direct representation. Samuelson's multiplier-accelerator model is a good example of a self-referential system that generates a business cycle with minimal reference to extra-theoretical factors. His notion of 'revealed preference' is another; it served as a ploy to eliminate the need for references to subjective and thus extra-theoretical preferences. In his work one hears the echo of Mondrian's statement that 'life is becoming more and more abstract'.

The Keynesian commitment to the creation of abstract, self-referential systems, however, was not complete. This became clear when Keynesians had to deal with Milton Friedman's challenge regarding the probable (and desirable) unreality of initial theoretical assumptions. Samuelson and others came out to assert the importance of the realism of their assumptions. Friedman went too far for them. But he did not go too far for the new classical economists; they continue to use his epistemological argument to justify their highly abstract and self-referential models. Lucas refers to his models as analogies, which is the rhetorical term for 'as if' devices. The step towards a rhetorical interpretation seems small from here.

Most new classical models still allow for an interpretation that links the theoretical terms with 'real' phenomena. Such an interpretation is made impossible in time-series analysis; in this strategy, which is closely connected with the new classical program, virtually all reference to economic 'reality' is erased.

The rejection of the modernist metanarrative

> I will use the term modern to designate any science that legitimates itself with reference to a metadiscourse [which makes] an explicit appeal to some grand narrative, such as the dialectics of Spirit, the hermeneutics of reasoning, the emancipation of the rational or working subject, or the creation of wealth...I define postmodern as incredulity toward metanarrative.
> (Lyotard, 1984: xxiii–iv)

> On the final truth of economics I am completely agnostic. Until such truth is unequivocally revealed I hold all coherent theorising as worth of attention and respect.
> (Hahn, 1984:19, 20)

As stated above the introduction of modernism into economics was accompanied by a metanarrative that glorified:

the character of the enlightened and reasonable person;
the possibility that reasonable people would be able to comprehend economic processes through scientific methods;
and thus the possibility that armed with scientific knowledge reasonable people could withstand ideological fanaticism and plain stupidities to stabilize the economy and make the world a better place to live.

To recognize this metanarrative at work we only need to remind ourselves of the large econometric models, the notion of 'fine tuning', and the involvement of economists in the Keynesian Camelot days during the early 1960s.

The belief in the scientific possibilities of economics, however, gradually eroded beginning with the realization that the validity of theories could not be proven empirically. Many economists probably still adhere to the Popperian falsification criterion but the avant-garde appears to have come to recognize the impossibility of the falsification of general theories. Econometric practice has become suspect, as robust results and empirical constants fail to materialize. Consequently, one may hear agnostic comments such as the one by Hahn cited above.

New classicals might still believe in economics as a science (they say they do), but they seem to deny the possibility or, better still, the desirability of realistic representations of the economy. Thus they dismantle the major part of one side of the Keynesian metanarrative. The dismantling of the other side appears even more far-reaching. The dominant tone in new classical discourse is against government intervention and, hence, against the belief that we can stabilize the economy and thus improve the world. Typical is Lucas's comment to the question of what he would do if he were on the Council of Economic Advisors: 'I would resign'. New classicals take the line that our knowledge of the economy is imperfect and that we therefore cannot know how to tinker with the economy. The Keynesian presence in Washington seems to annoy them; they perceive pretensions which are unjustified given the state of economic knowledge.

Consequently, new classicals do not volunteer advice to politicians. They stay away from the political realm and prefer communication among themselves.

The great disappearing acts

The new classical project shows some similarities with Wittgenstein's project in philosophy. While Wittgenstein applied the tools of logic and 'precise' statements, he realized that little, if anything, constructive could be said with certainty. He stripped the positivistic project from its positivities and left an emptiness that frightens some and excites others. New classicals, too, appear to work towards such an emptiness where nothing positive or constructive can stand. Pursuing consistency and exactness, they show us more and more what we cannot say. Carrying their arguments to their logical extreme, we could end up with the deconstruction of economics as a discipline.

We have noticed already several disappearing acts. Macroeconomics as an autonomous subject would disappear if economists would only consistently 'ground' general relations in microeconomics. Furthermore, in line with the modernist intent, new classicals have erased the human subject from their discourse. Although they may be aware of the subjective and the psychological factors in their own lives, as Lucas is, they consider them out of bounds in their discussion of 'individual' behavior. The individual in their analysis is nothing more than an isolated unit that operates according to a rational strategy; possible associations with human beings are of no relevance.

The disappearance of the human subject demands more attention. Here it is.

The loss of character in economics

> And all at once, in the midst of these reflections, Ulrich had to confess to himself, smiling, that for all this he was, after all, a 'character', even without having one.
>
> (Musil, [1930] 1979: 175)

> 'To understand' means to grasp the total intention …the unique way of existing, that finds expression in the properties of the public, the glass, or the piece of wax, in all the deeds of a revolution, in all the thoughts of a philosopher …Everything has a meaning; we find, beneath all its relationships, the same structure of being.
>
> (Merleau-Ponty, 1969: xiii–iv)

The main character in the new classical story is Max U (although it could be argued that the story is really about 'us', the scientific community). Max U is a silent character who is certainly not preoccupied with his ends. These are given to him, and he is supposed to know. Insofar as he talks, it is to consider the constraints under which he operates and to assess the benefits of the best alternatives. Subsequently, he is deleted with a few key strokes to re-emerge in the form of a constrained maximization problem. 'The cultivated man of today is gradually turning away from natural things, and life is becoming more and more abstract', declared the Dutch painter Piet Mondriaan in 1919. Starting in the 1930s, economists followed suit and, just like Mondriaan in his paintings, conceived the abstract as a system of stylized forms. Max U became their main character.[1]

No matter how effective the character of Max U has proven to be – it certainly has stimulated plenty of writing – he remains an odd character. For Max is a character that has none. Like Musil's Ulrich, Max is a man without the qualities that would make a subject human; Max U has no history, is devoid of moral sentiments, does not know tradition, and is oblivious to the uncertainties and insecurities that plague anyone who has to make choices.

Max U is caught up in lifeless problem-solving exercises. He is not a particular individual being, conceived to represent a deeper structure. In his Hamiltonian form, Max U reminds one of a scientific representation of physical phenomena: energy fields, if we believe Philip Mirowski.[2] The furious response by neoclassical economists to Mirowski's thesis, however, suggests that the metaphor of energy fields is rejected by those who are interested in weaving plots with Max U's character. Has Max become a mere form, the absent subject in a formal structure that has meanings because of its own formal properties? If the answer is yes, and Max U makes one think 'as if' the formal problems posed by the constrained maximization set-up are all that really matter, then the human subject in economics is dead. A formal Max U is lifeless. Just like a cartographic map cannot tell us human mortals how to find a path through life, this Max U cannot tell us how to live. He also cannot tell me why I am writing this paper.

Max U is characteristic of the late modernist phase in economics, although the advanced stage of deconstruction in new classical economics and other contemporary research programs may announce the arrival of postmodernist moments in the discourse. I venture that if Max U is taken to his perfect expression, Max U will deal the death blow to economics as a living subject in the world at large.

Thinking human action

The character of Max U shows a life reduced to a string of choices. As if moments of choice are what life is about. Could we conceive of life in any other way? Is it possible within economics to figure a character that is endowed with moral qualities, has a history, is connected with traditions, and deliberates, just like the characters we live with in the world outside neoclassical economics?

Within the constraints of neoclassical discourse alternative characters prove to be difficult to imagine. In spite of the badgering of the figure of Max U, the numerous expositions of its unrealistic and silly nature, it remains a very obstinate character. And justly so. Take it away and much of the work done by economists over the last sixty years will add up to a big heap of insignificant mumblings, on a level of the work of the cameralists. For Max U is the metaphor around which the neoclassical narrative revolves.

The resilience of Max U owes a great deal to the conviction of the community of its creators. Apparently, academic economists find meaning in the numerous exercises that the analysis of Max U produces. Max U, I would argue, is the subject that allows them to sustain the metanarrative that Lyotard (1984) identified as characteristic of the Enlightenment project. It is the metanarrative of the scientist who, through the applications of stylized reconstructions of reality, knows how to intervene in and improve on that reality. Max U gives its manipulators a sense of control.

Methodologically, Max U enables the application of analytical skills. It prods the analytical mind to set up problems, work out an algorithm, and find the solution. Max U makes for what Schumacher called 'convergent thinking' (Schumacher, 1977).

But is there another character that makes for a mode of thinking that more closely mimics the thinking of those involved in markets and writing papers? I do think so. Oddly enough, my assertion is bold only in the world populated by Max U. In virtually any other world this assertion is a commonplace. In reconstructing the alternative character – for that is what is called for under the current circumstances – we need to begin, so I propose, with thinking of human *action*. The question is: what makes us act?

The proposal, which I have worked out elsewhere (Klamer, 1991), is to imagine action as a way of coping with a problem. Something is amiss, something is problematic, and we act to solve or remedy the problem. The action can be a gesture, a movement, a fleeting thought, a verbal expression or whatever people do. Through the action we ignore the problem, subsume it into what is in place in the form of concepts, interpretative frameworks, traditions, and models; or we work with the problem, allowing it to transform the existing arrangements and thus give cause for further actions.

In this framework Max U is the agent that by its definition subsumes each problem by solving it with a predetermined algorithm. Analysis defines this action. Incidentally, no real choice is involved, the neoclassical characterization notwithstanding. At best, Max U may choose not to do what his character tells him to, namely the act upon the solution of the constrained-maximization problem. The action is mechanic; the subject that acts solely in this manner is lifeless.

Similar to Max U is the subject submerged in structuralist thinking. Philosophers and novelists respond by exclaiming that the subject is dead. Left without real choices, without meaningful subjectivity, Max U may be declared a dead subject as well.

It is only if we allow uncertainty, including the probable that cannot be translated in stochastic arithmetics, that human action will come back to life. This is the action through which individuals call attention to the problems they are facing, the problems of experiencing, knowing, seeing, and believing. This is the action that produces narratives, metaphors, 'artistic' images; this is the action that can cause the 'shock of the new' as it is said in the art world. This also produces 'the moral character'.

If Max U motivates its manipulator to be preoccupied with the constraints for action and to assume Max's objectives – to be given in the form of the utility function– the moral character makes these objectives the problem. Thinking about moral actions starts from the recognition that individuals do not know the consequences of their actions. Values enter as a way of coping with this uncertainty. We value honesty and say we do so for its own sake because, the observer will note, we cannot foresee what follows when we lie. If the value were to be clear cut and clearly identifiable, the character of Max U might be saved by simply subsuming it to its utility function. Yet, following Aristotle, the value as such is problematic; as stated it is vague and requires further interpretation in every situation where it is applied. ('One does not tell the truth to one's enemy, so do we tell the truth to one's teacher?') Characteristic of the moral character is the engagement in interpretative acts (this point is elaborated upon in both Nussbaum, 1986 and MacIntyre, 1981).

This is the character featured by Aristotle in *Politics* and *Nichomachean Ethics*. Behavior in his books is moral behavior; the acting subject is supposed to ask what is called for *given* his character and to act in accordance with the virtues associated with that character. The liberal man will not be mean, nor will he be prodigal, but by means of giving he will want to be somewhere in between – since giving determines his virtue as a liberal man. Somehow he has to interpret what that golden mean – or perhaps third dimension – is. No book, no algorithm, will tell him that. In contemporary terms, it is only through knowledge of the discursive context, including its history and traditions, that he or she will be able to do so.

This character is still alive in Adam Smith, although in an enlightened form. Adam Smith, too, thinks of human action with that third dimension. In *The Theory of Moral Sentiments*, Smith instructs his 15 and 16-year-old students that it is in their nature to feel 'sympathy' towards their fellow being, and that 'to feel much for others and little for ourselves, that to restrain our selfish, and to indulge our benevolent affections, constitutes the perfection of human nature; and can alone produce among mankind that harmony of sentiments and passions in which consists their whole grace and propriety' (Smith, 1969). Like Aristotle, Smith stresses our need for praise; like Aristotle his characters have no resolute solutions to their problems; and he even seems to think, like Aristotle, that individuals enact roles in their lives. That is how the following paragraph reads, a paragraph, incidentally, that was added after completion of *The Wealth of Nations*:

> We desire to be respectable and to be respected. We dread both to be contemptible and to be contemned. But upon coming into the world, we soon find that wisdom and virtue are by no means the sole objects of respect; nor vice and folly, of contempt. We frequently see the respectful attentions of the world more strongly directed towards the rich and the great, than towards the wise and the virtuous. We see frequently the vices and follies of the powerful much less despised than the poverty and weakness of the innocent. To deserve, to acquire, and to enjoy the respect and admiration of mankind, are the great objects of ambition and emulation. Two different roads are presented to us, equally leading to the attainment of this so much desired object; the one, by the study of wisdom and the practice of virtue; the other, by the acquisition of wealth and greatness. Two different characters are presented to our emulation; the one, of proud ambition and ostentatious avidity; the other of humble modesty

and equitable justice. Two different models, two different pictures, are held out to us, according to which we may fashion our own character and behaviour; the one more gaudy and glittering in its colouring; the other more correct and more exquisitely beautiful in its outline; the one forcing itself upon the notice of every wandering eye; the other, attracting the attention of scarce any body but the most studious and careful observer.
([1853] 1976: pt I, section III, ch. III)

Yet, in this eloquent presentation of two characters, Smith suggests to his audience a choice. It should be clear which choice is deserving of his praise, but, he continues to tell them later, even if they pursue selfish ends, the invisible hand will turn their action to the good of society. In other words, although people's actions may be lacking in virtue – woe the follies of men – God's design is such that those actions turn out to serve good ends anyway, unintentionally.

This does not free his audience to do as they wish and pursue their vain desires as they wish. Smith's hero is the prudent man:

The prudent man is always sincere, and feels horror at the very thought of exposing himself to the disgrace which attends upon the detection of falsehood. But although always sincere, he is not always frank and open... The prudent man, though not always distinguished by the most exquisite sensibility, is always capable of friendship. But this friendship is not that ardent and passionate, but too often transitory affection, which appears so delicious to the generosity of youth and inexperience.
([1853] 1976: pt VI, section I)

He continues that the prudent man is guided by 'the sober esteem of modesty, discretion, and good conduct'. It is the self-interested man, but not the selfish man for which Smith is so often held accountable. The prudent man pursues his interest because he knows he cannot know the consequences of his actions. But the prudent man also is endowed with the moral sentiments that will make him act, when appropriate, with benevolence towards his fellow beings.

In this characterization, Adam Smith does not derive virtuous behavior, as did Aristotle, from the role one has in the theatre of life. Smith shows himself to be part of the Scottish Enlightenment project in which human reason and passions overtake the will of the gods. The Deity oversees the world as he deems necessary, but the individual fills it. Yet, in Smith's discussion of moral character, Max U is hard to detect. With the seeming implosion of late modernist economics, are we moving into a stage of economic discourse in which the moral subject will rise again?

Conclusion

Late modernism in economics has ushered in the disappearances both of the Keynesian metanarrative of public welfare and the long-standing concern in economic discourse – at least since Smith – about the character of the economic subject. In its ultimate expression, with the erasure of the Keynesian metanarrative, new classical economics makes the economic enterprise seem absurd for anyone who still wants to believe in the public activist's way of perceiving, defining, and influencing the world. Radical interpretation of the rationality assumption by the new classicals, for example, eliminates the possibility of any contribution to the improvement of economic behavior. If individual units act optimally, there is no reason for any input of economic knowledge – there is no way of improving actions that are already optimal. In a recent vintage of new classical models, the same reasoning is applied to the behavior of policy-makers. Accordingly, if economic policy-makers act optimally, further economic knowledge becomes irrelevant. Voilà, the end of any social responsibility of economic science! All that is left to economists is the intellectual enjoyment of 'neat' and aesthetic systems. Late modernism in economics means the most extreme formalism, which implies in turn the most extreme passivity in the public sphere on the part of economists. The moral character of the economist is reduced to that of the voyeur.

The disappearance – or loss – of moral character in late modernist economics has at least one further implication. This can be seen in the recent fascination of new classicals with computer language as a metalinguistics to guide economic analysis. Even though new classical discourse seeks to establish a self-referential system in which meanings are generated 'internally', this ideal of complete self-referentiality is ultimately unattainable. (It has become cliché to mention Gödel's theorem in support of a statement such as this.) Thus, new classicals signify through connections – mostly intentional – to other late modernist discourses and practices, such as artificial intelligence and the 'information revolution'. In particular, new classical economic discourse signifies in relation to a continuing fascination with machines – not the productivist machines that stood as the central metaphor for many of the Keynesian models, but instead the new information-processing machines, specifically computers. New classical models are largely about information processes and the 'noises' that regularly occur within these processes.

On the one hand, this fascination has rendered the new classical economist into a new kind of technocrat, one who is intrigued by the intricacies of fully articulated systems, just like a computer analyst who is intrigued by the 'possibilities' of a computer program. The desire of the new classicals to speak in a purely technical language which requires only precision and allows primarily for mathematical operations to take place. In this way, new classicals increasingly take on the attributes of their favorite character, the problem-solving, soulless Max U. On the other hand, again, new classicals are increasingly likely as well to divorce information from the subject him/herself. This explains, for example, how and why Shannon has become important for new classicals. New classicals are inclined to follow Shannon's lead in perceiving information as entirely self-referential, without any need to figure out how such things as values and morality might in fact permeate 'information' in and through the human subject. So, new classicals remain active in emptying the subject of economics of any and every form or moral character. Max U becomes morally thinner and thinner over (late modernist) time.

Perhaps we are between ages. Perhaps again the late modernist project will simply implode due to its own irrelevance or absurdity. Perhaps finally late modernism in economics will embrace one moment in the postmodern age, that of neo-traditionalism. One thing is clear, however, late modernism – for all its technical skill and virtuosity – has impoverished economics by its erasure of the Keynesian metanarrative, and even more by the loss of moral character it has championed. We can only hope for a next stage, whatever it may be called.

Notes

1 The credit for the name 'Max U' goes to Deirdre McCloskey. The analogy between painting and economics is explored further in my unpublished 1987 paper, 'The Advent of Modernism'.
2 Mirowski eloquently expounds upon this thesis in his 1990 book, *More Heat than Light*.

References

Amariglio, Jack (1988) 'The Body, Economic Discourse, and Power: An Economist's Introduction to Foucault', *History of Political Economy*, 20(4): 583–613.
—— (1990) 'Economics as a Postmodern Discourse' in Warren J. Samuels (ed.) *Economics as Discourse*, Boston: Kluwer Academic Publishers.
Amariglio, Jack and Ruccio, David (1995) 'Keynes, Postmodernism, Uncertainty', in Sheila Dow and John Hillard (eds) *Keynes, Knowledge and Uncertainty*, Aldershot: Edward Elgar.
Ashmore, William (1989) *The Reflexive Thesis: Writing Sociology of Knowledge*, Chicago: University of Chicago Press.
Connolly, William E. (1983) *The Terms of Political Discourse*, Princeton: Princeton University Press.
Connor, Steven (1989) *Postmodernist Culture*, Cambridge: Basil Blackwell.
Foster, Hal (ed.) (1983) *The Anti-Aesthetic: Essays on Postmodern Culture*, Port Townsend, Washington: Bay Press.
Franscina, Francis and Harrison, Charles (eds) (1982) *Modern Art and Modernism*, New York: Harper and Row.
Gablik, Suzi (1984) *Has Modernism Failed?* New York: Thames and Hudson.

Hahn, Frank (1984) *Equilibrium and Macroconomics*, Cambridge: MIT Press.
Harvey, David (1989) *The Condition of Postmodernity*, Cambridge: Basil Blackwell.
Jencks, Charles (1973) *Modern Movements in Architecture*, New York: Anchor Books.
—— (1986) *What is Post-Modernism?* New York: St Martin Press.
Kern, Stephen (1983) *The Culture of Time and Space*, Cambridge: Cambridge University Press.
Klamer, Arjo (1984) *Conversations with Economists*, Totowa: Rowman and Allanheld.
—— (1987) 'The Advent of Modernism in Economics', unpublished manuscript.
—— (1991) 'Towards the Native Point of View, or How to Change the Conversation' in Don Lavoie (ed.) *Economics and Hermeneutics*, London: Routledge.
—— (1993) 'Modernism in Economics: An Interpretation Beyond Physics' in Neil de Marchi (ed.) *Non-Natural Social Science: Reflecting on the Enterprise of More Heat than Light*, Durham: Duke University Press.
—— (1995) 'The Conception of Modernism in Economics: Samuelson versus Keynes' in Sheila Dow and John Hillard (eds) *Keynes, Knowledge and Uncertainty*, Aldershot: Edward Elgar.
Klamer, Arjo, and Leonard, Thomas (1993) 'So What's an Economic Metaphor?' in Philip Mirowski (ed.) *Natural Images in Economics*, New York: Cambridge University Press.
Lasch, Christopher (1995) *The Revolt of the Elites and the Betrayal of Democracy*, New York: Norton.
Lucas, Robert E. Jr. (1987) *Studies in Business-Cycle Theory*, Cambridge: MIT Press.
Lyotard, J. F. (1984) *The Postmodern Condition: A Report on Knowledge*, Minneapolis: University of Minnesota Press.
McCloskey, D. N. (1985) *The Rhetoric of Economics*, Madison: University of Wisconsin Press.
—— (1990) *If You're So Smart: The Narrative of Economic Expertise*, Chicago: University of Chicago Press.
MacIntyre, Alisdair (1981) *After Virtue*, Notre Dame: University Of Notre Dame Press.
Merleau-Ponty (1969) *Phenomenology de la Perception*, Paris:
Mirowski, Philip (1989) *More Heat than Light*, New York: Cambridge University Press.
—— (1991) 'Postmodernism and the Social Theory of Value', *Journal of Post Keynesian Economics* (Summer): 511–24.
Musil, Robert (1930) trans. as *The Man Without Qualities*, vol. 1, London: Pan Books, 1979.
Nussbaum, Martha (1986) *The Fragility of Goodness*, Cambridge: Cambridge University Press.
Phelps, Edmund (1985) *Political Economy*, New York: Norton.
Rabinbach, Anson (1990) *The Human Motor*, New York: Basic Books.
Ruccio, David (1991) 'Postmodernism and Economics', *Journal of Post Keynesian Economics* (Summer): 511–24.
Samuels, Warren J. (ed.) (1990) *Economics as Discourse*, Boston: Kluwer Academic Publishers.

—— (1991) '"Truth" and "Discourse" in the Social Construction of Economic Reality: An Essay on the Relation of Knowledge to Socioeconomic Policy', *Journal of Post Keynesian Economics* (Summer): 511–24.

Samuelson, Paul (1939) 'Interactions Between the Multiplier Analysis and the Principle of Acceleration', *The Review of Economic Statistics*, XXI: 75–8

Schorske, Carl E. (1981) *Fin-de-Siècle Vienna*, New York: Vintage Press.

Schumacher, E. F. (1977) *A Guide for the Perplexed*, London: Gate.

Skidelski, Robert (1983) *John Maynard Keynes*, vol. 1, New York: Viking Penguin.

Smith, Adam (1853) *The Theory of Moral Sentiments*, Indianapolis: Liberty Classics, 1976.

Szostak, Rick (1992) 'The History of Art and the Art in Economics', *History of Economics Review* (Summer): 70–107.

Toulmin, Stephen (1990) *Cosmopolis :The Hidden Agenda of Modernity*, New York: The Free Press.

Wallis, Brian (ed.) (1984) *Art After Modernism: Rethinking Representation*, New York: The New Museum of Contemporary Art.

Zola, Emile (1867) 'Edouard Manet', reprinted in Franscina and Harrison (eds) *Modern Art and Modernism*, New York: Harper and Row, 1982.

4

THE GENEALOGY OF POSTMODERNISM

An economist's guide

Deirdre McCloskey[1]

> I suppose that what I am asking, without being entirely sure that it is possible, is for a leap over modernist battlefields to the postmodern rediscovery that the primal symbolic act is saying yes to processes like the wrenching one in which you are engaging.
>
> (Booth, 1974: 204)

As directly as it can be put, 'postmodernism' names a tendency since 1970 or so to doubt the tenets of 'modernism'. In economics it would be against the high modernism, for example, of Paul Samuelson's program. Though postmodernism more generally has been appropriated by writers innocent of economics or maths or statistics, there is nothing inevitable in this. I am saying that in adopting a pomo attitude an economist need not fear contamination from literary critics, psychoanalysts, and the politically correct. Postmodernism can be given an economic and classical liberal – I did not say 'conservative' or 'reactionary' – reading.

1910 Modernism

The definition of 'postmodernism' depends on what one means by 'modernism'. 'On or about December 1910', declared Virginia Woolf in 1924, 'human character changed' (Woolf, 1924: 320). As the word 'modernism' is usually employed, then, it refers to scientific and artistic movements beginning in the decades around the First World War, among them cubism, futurism, philosophical neopositivism, stream-of-consciousness fiction, functionalism, surrealism, behaviorism. Modernism was for half a century the faith of élite culture in Europe and its offshoots, replaced only in the 1960s, and then not completely. It filled the gap left in the élite culture by the decline of religion.

Two kinds of 1910 modernism need to be distinguished at the outset, one artistic in origin and the other scientific. They need to be distinguished because in the modernist theory they come from opposite cultural worlds. One kind, usually called 'literary modernism' and instanced by Woolf, Joyce, Picasso, and Stravinsky, attacked Science with a big-S. It attacked, that is, the elevation of Science to a religion. It was anti-rational, or more exactly it appealed to the deeper rationality of the myth or the unconscious. Literary modernism entailed 'dislocation of conventional syntax, radical breaches of decorum, disturbance of chronology and spatial order, ambiguity, polysemy, obscurity, mythopoeic allusion, primitivism' (Lodge, 1981: 71).

The other modernism might be called 'architectural'. Instanced by Le Corbusier, Mondrian, Bertrand Russell, and Paul A. Samuelson, it worshipped Science with a big-S. It was pro-rational, appealing to the surface rationality of proof, logic, axiom, explicitness. Look at the downtown of a modern city, the glass towers circa 1970, and you see modernism built, called in this version the 'international style' (flourished 1945–75; cf. Jencks, 1973; Brolin, 1976; Kolb, 1990). It simplified conventional syntax, stressed Scientific decorum, elevated chronology and spatial order to mechanical rules, and fled from ambiguity, polysemy, obscurity, mythopoeic allusion, and primitivism.

Economics has been influenced by the architectural kind of modernism. Economists call it by various names, not all of them accurate: positive economics, scientific economics, rigor, serious work. In a word it is 'Samuelsonian'. What Paul Samuelson conceived in the late 1930s and published in 1948 – such as 'the problem of stability of equilibrium cannot be discussed except with reference to dynamical considerations' (Samuelson, 1947: 262) – was carried out by, for example, Robert Lucas in the 1960s. A standard paper in economics looks now like a building in downtown Dallas. It defines itself as the opposite of *The Waste Land* or *Sacre du Printemps*.

The two modernisms, however, come from the same intellectual culture. One of the pair sometimes drops out of discussions of 1910 modernism, but it is a commonplace to link them. The literary critic Wayne Booth, for example, uses the word to describe both Bertrand Russell and James Joyce (Booth, 1974: 43 and throughout; Booth 1988: 246–51). The literary and architectural modernism share an optimism about form, a distaste for the ungeneralizable, an obsession with provability, a fascination with novelty, a celebration of the future, an affection for timeless axioms, a glorification of the individual, an aversion to ethical reasoning, a high value on separating fact from value, a belief in the theory that facts are independent of theory, and above all a strong feeling that reason and feeling are opposed realms.

Arjo Klamer has an illuminating way of talking about the two kinds of modernism (Klamer, 1991). He draws side-by-side a square and a circle, representing the two ways of talking according to the modern theory. Either you are square, rigid, and logical or you are circular, loose, and illogical. (Feminists will note the gender valence.) Modernists adopt a sensibility that dissociates the two. Science or art, numbers or words, fact or value, work or play. Klamer's point, and Booth's also, is that the two are necessary for each other, defining each by its opposite. In more ways than one they are like stereotypical men and women.

The two kinds of modernism were formed out of a Marriage of Modernism, which in its popular version left a mechanical notion of Science with one half of the culture and a romantic notion of Art with the other half. (The feminine associations of Art in 1910 modernism troubled artists like Ernest Hemingway or Jackson Pollock, who compensated by drinking too much; the feminine associations of artistic story telling troubled social scientists, who compensated by measuring too much [cf. Laslett, 1990: 429].) An example of the dichotomizing of modernism is the micro-culture of the Institute for Advanced Study in Princeton, the Einstein institute. On the one hand the Institute provides space (suitably modernist) for serious work, either mathematical physics or traditional history (wedged between the two is the School of Social Science, in whose postmodern appointments the physicists and historians routinely interfere). On the other hand, after 5:00 there are concerts, treated as sacred rites, to which the ladies are invited. Robert Oppenheimer, later Director of the Institute, builds a bomb and then quotes Sanskrit religious texts at the site. The mathematician proves theorems and then plays the violin sublimely, or at least competently.

Literary and architectural modernism of 1910 are two sides of the same dichotomizing impulse. In economic terms they are dual and primal. When I told Robert Fogel some years ago that since about 1980 I had been reading in the humanities he asked me amiably whether I had 'become a mystic'. Fogel, whose brother was a professor of English and who is a cultivated man, was using the mental categories of 1955, at the high tide of 1910 modernism. In 1955 you were either a scientist or a touchie-feelie. You could be rational, scientific, empirical; or alternatively you could be into Zen and emotion. Einstein or Ezra Pound. Man of science or mystic. That was it.

The mental categories of 1955 are symbolized in a fact of geography. The world capital of rationality since about 1955 has been the Rand Corporation, which is located in the world capital of irrationality since about 1955, Santa Monica. The Rand people have got along fine with the City, called in the old days 'The People's Republic of Santa Monica'. The getting along fine fits the categories of 1955 (they were nothing like all bad in their effects). In 1955 you would choose sides, scientism or humanism, physics or tao, but then you were not supposed to bother the other people, or make them read your stuff. The ideal was an amiable lack of contact or understanding, which Fogel was reflecting. Humanities? You mean 'mysticism'. Hey, man, whatever turns you on.

Jack Amariglio notes that both kinds of 1910 modernism were determined to shake off history, to transcend time and space (Amariglio, 1990: 18). In science or in art, or both, modernism is the elevation of being modern to the acme of creative work. It is the triumph of the avant garde and the defeat of tradition. The virtue of hope takes all. Wayne Booth notes the modernist 'belief in the future as somehow more real than the past or present' (1974: 22n). 'The avant-garde destroys, defaces the past', writes Umberto Eco, 'then...destroys the figure, cancels it, arrives at the abstract.... In architecture and the visual arts, it will be the curtain wall, the building as stele, pure parallelepiped, minimal art; in literature, the destruction of the flow of discourse, the Burroughs-like collage, silence, the white page; in music, the passage from atonality to noise to absolute silence' (Eco, 1985: 66; cf. Klamer, 1991).

Modernism of both kinds believes that form and content can be divorced, leaving formality to do the work, letting 'the business be done', as Francis Bacon put it at one of the numerous dawns of modernism, 'as if by machinery' (Bacon [1620] 1965: 327). Ornament, history, culture are in modernism mere error terms. Its characteristic projects are Hilbertian mathematics, imagist poetry, twelve-tone music, and abstract general equilibrium.

An instance is the stick-figure international language, elaborated at successive Olympic Games (quick: what's the stick figure for the women's luge?). It is most commonly seen on the door to the gents'. The figures could just as well be realistic representations, even photographs – of a woman zooming down a hill on a sled or of a man striding into a men's room; or for that matter the words in English 'Women's Luge' and 'Men's Room', which are widely understood. Someone had to invent the notion that it would be better, more up-to-date, more modern, to simplify, axiomatize, standardize, deculturalize, universalize along modernist lines. Consider: it is the future we are serving. As one might have expected, the inventor of the stick figures was a leading positivist thinker, Otto Neurath (1882–1945), in the metropolis of modernism, Vienna during the 1920s. In answering the question, Why not *words* on the men's room door?

> He saw verbal language...as a disfiguring medium for knowledge, because be believed its structure and vocabulary fail to be a consistent, logical model of objects and relations in the physical world.... Sociology on a materialist basis...knows only of such behavior of men that one can observe and 'photograph' scientifically. ...The silhouette [*on the men's room*] emulates the

shadow...a rationalized theatre of shadows, in which signs are necessary geometric formulae cast by material things – Plato's cave renovated into an empiricist laboratory. Flatness suggests a factual honesty, as opposed to the illusionism of perspective drawing.

(Lupton, 1989: 145, 150, 152)

The stick figures are like the mathematics in economics or the formulas in social engineering. In modernism of either type, words fail.

Postmodernism

The postmodernism in the late twentieth century, then, is the doubt that 1910 modernism in such matters had it entirely right. In deciding whether it has been a good idea or not to have such a doubt, one needs to exercise humility. The radicals and the conservatives in the Culture Wars have not always done so. 'We are *within* the culture of postmodernism', observes the critic Fredric Jameson, 'to the point where its facile repudiation is as impossible as any equally facile celebration of it as complacent and corrupt' (1984: 381). In light of this wisdom it is surprising that the critics of postmodernism, of pragmatism, of rhetoric, and the like are so confident they have grasped the writings they disdain. Consider for instance the writings of Richard Rorty – the same applies to Paul Feyerabend, Jacques Derrida, the Modern Language Association, and other bogeymen in the conservative night. The conservatives (and some of the Marxist materialist radicals and a lot of newspaper people who do not like to give credit for common sense to a professor anyway) think Rorty is trivially easy to contradict. But does it seem plausible that Rorty cannot handle the points that simpletons writing for the *Wall Street Journal* or the *New York Times* are able to devise after a few minutes of thinking lite? The hypothesis does not seem plausible on its face: Rorty, eminent philosopher, well-known as an analyst, full professor at Princeton, university professor at Virginia and now at Stanford, first of the MacArthur Fellows, scourge of his profession, president of the Eastern Division of the philosophers, etc., etc., is trivially easily shown to be guilty of circularity, confusion, contradiction, naïveté, and falsehood.

The critic Charles Altieri noted recently that the *modernists* used 'ironic strategies to undo the expectations elicited by representational art' in aid of realizing experience directly, 'rebuilding a formal site where the spirit learns to dwell reflexively within its own deepest powers' (Altieri, 1993: 793). Notice that this is *not* postmodernism, but is on the contrary as old as Van Gogh or Henry James. Some have never recovered from the insult of Picasso's painting the eyes of a woman on the same side of her face.

Their indignation against what they take to be postmodernism ('It doesn't *say* or *show* anything') is better directed at modernism itself.

On the other hand, the radicals need to admit that architectural modernism in, say, economics was a worthwhile and even noble teaching, from which much has been learned. Literary modernists such as early Eliot or late Yeats or early and late Wallace Stevens will endure. Getting beyond modernism does not mean tossing out the modernists, ignoring their rat experiments or burning their paint-splattered canvases or forgetting how to solve a dynamic programming problem. It does not mean being against *modernity*, taking the fruits and running. It is merely against the elevation of modernity to a religion, *modernism*. As the architectural historian Brent Brolin writes, 'Although these truths were represented as logical deductions from the spirit of the times [viz., modernity], they were actually articles of faith, rhetorical statements whose moral overtones made them as unquestionable as Divine Law' (Brolin, 1976: 45). Postmodernism means questioning whether a stick figure on the men's room is the only possible way to solve a practical problem.

Note that Altieri's words – non-representational art providing 'a formal site…to dwell reflexively' – would serve as a description of music or of pure mathematics. Modernist art and science aspired to the condition of music and pure mathematics. The two were correlated in modernist culture. The joke of the Oppenheimer generation was, 'At the Institute, what's the definition of a string quartet? Three physicists and a mathematician'.

The postmodernist has doubts that poetry or economics is best reduced entirely to music or pure mathematics. Postmodernism aspires to the condition of…what? Nothing in general, because it does not believe in timeless generalities. At most it aspires to a civilized conversation among equals, what the German sociologist Jürgen Habermas calls 'the ideal speech situation' and what the British political philosopher Michael Oakeshott called 'the conversation of mankind'. The chief problem with modernism, say the postmodernists, is its loony aspiration to speechlessness. Shut up: I have a proof. Shut up: this is avant-garde painting. Shut up.

The aspiration to this or that transcendent and ineffable Truth made for much of modernism's guff. Modernism was a reaction to Romance, but it clutched to the Romantic striving for the infinite, *das Streben nach dem Unendlichen*, which has done so much mischief in the twentieth century. When otherwise hardnosed astrophysicists become dewy eyed about the High Frontier one is hearing an echo of Romance (and of a cash register). No eighteenth-century astrophysicist would have thought of making such an airy appeal. He justified his projects as providing better time-keeping for ocean navigation. The point was the same in the art business at the time. Samuel Johnson had no more patience than did Andy Warhol with the assumption that art and commerce conflicted. In 1776 (about a month, it happens, after the appearance of *The Wealth of Nations*) Johnson remarked that 'no man but a blockhead ever wrote, except for money'. The Artist separated from bourgeois culture is a recent and romantic invention, *c.* 1780 in Germany, universalized in England *c.* 1800. Martha Woodmansee has recently shown its close connections to the economics of copyright and publishing (Woodmansee, 1994), and I have written on the longer history of the divorce of art from money (McCloskey, 1994b).

Postmodernism might therefore be called irony or self-awareness or merely sophistication about the way we talk – anything but the earnest romanticism and modernism, romance tied to chemistry, that led to the Somme and Auschwitz and the Gulag. Umberto Eco has given a characteristically postmodern definition. Postmodernism, he writes, is the attitude of:

> a man who loves a very cultivated woman and knows he cannot say to her, 'I love you madly', because he knows that she knows (and that she knows that he knows) that these words have already been written by Barbara Cartland. Still, there is a solution. He can say, 'As Barbara Cartland would put it, I love you madly'.... He will have said...that he loves her, but he loves her in an age of lost innocence.
>
> (Eco, 1985: 65)

The earlier modernisms: the Enlightenment, the Scientific Revolution, and Plato

Any age of lost innocence will do. There were modernisms before 1910. In consequence there were also earlier *post*modernisms. I want to make a lot of this simple point.

To speak of *the* postmodern without some argument is to commit a characteristically modernist mistake of believing that we moderns are of course unique. Postmodernism by contrast doubts that on or about December 1910, or any other date, human character changed and became once-and-for-all modern. In the form of this mistaken conviction that *Now* We Have It, modernisms keep being reinvented. The theory that theory can do it, that we are about to have a unified science, has been invented and reinvented dozens of times, first by Plato, then by Aquinas, then by Bacon, then by Rousseau and Condorcet, then by Comte, then by Pearson, then by Russell, then by Neurath, then by Samuelson, then by some other bossy genius.

John Ruskin, the nineteenth-century art critic (I do not on the whole recommend his views on economics, though recently I am beginning to see that they have something to say even to economists), noted that the search for a crystalline ideal has been an incubus on classical and Renaissance – and now one may say modernist – architecture. He attacked the tyranny of the lonely genius, seeking by contemplation in a warm room a system to impose upon us all. Of the Renaissance he wrote:

> its main mistake…was the unwholesome demand for perfection at any cost.… Men like Verrocchio and Ghiberti [*consider Marx or Samuelson*] were not to be had every day.… Their strength was great enough to enable them to join science with invention, method with emotion, finish with fire.… Europe saw in them only the method and the finish. This was new to the minds of men, and they pursued it to the neglect of everything else. 'This', they cried, 'we must have in our work henceforward': and they were obeyed. The lower workman secured method and finish, and lost, in exchange for them, his soul.
>
> (Ruskin [1853] 1960: 228–9)

Ruskin's argument also fits modernism (in economics and elsewhere) which seeks an all-embracing, testable Theory apart from the practical skills of the statesman or of the economic scientist. An 'interpretive economics', as Arjo Klamer, Metin Cosgel, and Don Lavoie began to call it at the end of the 1980s, would turn the other way, as economists do in practical work (see Lavoie, 1990a, 1990b; Cosgel and Klamer, 1990). It is in Ruskin's term 'Gothic economics', an end to searching for a grail of a unified field theory, an awakening from Descartes's Dream. In such terms, interpretive economics is another postmodernism. The Gothic spirit is seen in the best works of applied economics, from the economic historian Robert Fogel, say, or the agricultural economist Theodore Schultz, from the financial economist Robert Shiller or the statistical economist Edward Leamer. It is not seen in the routine science of the field nowadays, servile to the undoubted genius of Paul Samuelson, Kenneth Arrow, and Lawrence Klein.

The point of postmodernism is that the program of the genius to subordinate everyone to his conveniently brief plan never quite works out. Expressing such a doubt is not the same thing as saying that it was stupid to try, merely that it is wrong to use a claim of transcendence as a stick to batter the opposition. The same Otto Neurath became Editor-in-Chief of a transcendent project on the Foundations of the Unity of Science: Toward an International Encyclopedia of Unified Science. The project died, though nineteen of its volumes were published by the University of Chicago Press from 1938 to 1971 (among them Gerhard

Tintner's *Methodology of Mathematical Economics and Econometrics*, 1968). The most important book in the series, ironically, was Thomas Kuhn's *The Structure of Scientific Revolutions* (1962), which showed why such attempts to end the scientific conversation once and for all are impossible. Reinstating history and politics in science studies, Kuhn showed why we do *not* now Have the Transcendent It.

So there have been as many modernisms as there have been spectacularly successful geniuses claiming transcendence. And therefore one can find corresponding postmodernisms in Greek rhetoric or Elizabethan urbanity or early eighteenth-century equipoise or American philosophical pragmatism c. 1900. But there's something to be said for taking the present-day reaction to modernism as special, as the end of some history. (I see the danger in this move that I will end up committing the modernist fallacy of thinking that Now We Have It; I will take care). It is a matter, to be pomo about it, of choosing the story that makes most sense to us.

For example, an alternative date to December 1910 for the onset of modernism is the French Enlightenment about 1751 to 1775. Such a story gives modernism longer standing, dating from the French *philosophes* rather than from the Italian futurists. Amariglio has argued that modernist economics, like modernist everything else, contained a contradiction, what Paul Wendt calls in a comment on Amariglio 'the immanence thesis', that 'postmodernism is immanent in [1910] modernist economics' (Wendt, 1990: 47). But in essentials the contradiction is of two centuries standing, though heightened in the latest, 1910 modernism. The contradiction is known as 'the aporia [indecision] of the Enlightenment project', a phrase that every young person anxious to do well on the cocktail-party circuit should commit to memory. The philosopher Stanley Rosen describes it as 'a conflict between mathematics and Newtonian science on the one hand and the desire for individual and political freedom on the other.... The understanding is in essence the formulation of and obedience to rules. Since there are no rules for the following of rules...the understanding must be a spontaneous "project"...of freedom...Kant's unstable attempt to ground reason in spontaneity' (Rosen, 1987: 3, 4, 8). In a sentence: being unreasonably rational will eventually enslave us to rules (compare Ruskin on the Renaissance, or Lucas on the Federal Reserve). As Amariglio puts it, 'the desire to know Man, to control him for purposes of efficiency and utility through this increased knowledge, produces the notorious exercises of power in the modern age' (Amariglio, 1990: 21).

Amariglio's story is a good one, fitting economics well. In line with the immanence thesis, modern economics has turned back on itself in a postmodern way, especially (as Amariglio points out) in the treatment of uncertainty. Uncertainty evokes prediction. Economics is a particularly thoroughgoing example of Enlightenment rationality, turning back on itself for example in the conflict between an Austrian and the earlier neoclassical views of prediction. Thus Robert Lucas and the other developers of rational expectations pointed out in an Austrian style that a predictable economy is not one in which government policy can work. If economics is a good imitation of (some high-status branches of) physics, a capital-S Science in the definition offered by philosophers around 1955, or as understood by eighteenth-century admirers of Newton, then it should predict. But then we are thrown into paradox, aporia, indecision: if economics is Scientific, we can predict; but a predictable future is a freedomless nightmare; and is anyway impossible when the predictor can invest in her predictions (McCloskey, 1990).

Friedrich Hayek said once that 'I believe I can now...explain why...[the] masterly critique by Mises of socialism has not really been effective. Because Mises remained in the end himself a rationalist-utilitarian, and with a rationalist-utilitarianism, the rejection of socialism is irreconcilable.... If we remain strictly rationalists, utilitarians, that implies we can arrange everything according to our pleasure.... In one place he says we can't do it, in another place he argues, being rational people, we must try to do it' (Hayek 1994). It is what is wrong with some of modern economics, this utilitarian rationalism – in Stigler's political economy as against Friedman's, or in Richard Posner's law and economics as against Ronald Coase's. Utilitarianism is the French element in British thought, so contrary to British empiricism. Jeremy Bentham was the problem, tempting economics away from its Scottish common sense about the world. Hayek was in this respect two centuries behind the times, a product of the quite different Scottish rather than the French Enlightenment, a spiritual resident of Edinburgh rather than Paris, an exponent of bourgeois virtue rather than aristocratic expertise. By the end of the twentieth century he became old-fashioned enough to be postmodern. You read it here (and in Burczak, 1994 and Don Lavoie in many places): Hayek has more in common with Jacques Derrida and Richard Rorty than with Bentham and Comte and Russell.

A still earlier dating pushes the onset of modernism back to Descartes, and makes our present postmodernism the culmination of a three-and-half-century genesis. The men (I choose the word carefully) of the seventeenth century were in this history the patriarchs of modernism (cf. Bordo, 1987). A case can certainly be made that modernist ideas have ruled since Descartes. What is emphasized by choosing a seventeenth-century birthdate for modernism is the fall of rhetoric, which had been for 2,000 years the education of the West. The inventors of rationalism in the seventeenth century – Descartes, Bacon, Hobbes, Spinoza – had a paradoxically low opinion of the power of reasoning in human affairs. Ancient and medieval writers had more faith in the power of speech to move people towards the light. The men of the seventeenth century had seen words induce people to kill over the doctrine of transubstantiation, and they sought therefore a way to disarm the words. Their refuge was 'crushing' proof and 'compelling' demonstration, that which cannot possibly be doubted, 'putting Nature to the rack', as Bacon delicately put it. They assigned everything else, as for example Hobbes did in his book of 1681 on rhetoric, to mere ornament, suited only to arousing a feminine passion. We fellow moderns have inherited their low opinion of reasoning.

Actually, all the modernisms are suspicious of reasonable persuasion. In 1910 modernism, for example, the studies in the 1930s of propaganda and public opinion and the hardening in 1950s of an American intellectual contempt for commercial free speech called for conviction rather than persuasion. 'Conviction' comes from a Latin legalism, itself from *vincere, victus*, 'to defeat, defeated'. 'Persuade' by contrast comes from *per* [thoroughly] + *suadere*, the latter meaning 'to seek to persuade that', and is from the same Indo-European root as English 'sweet'. Persuasion, like free exchange, is sweet and mutually beneficial. The anti-bourgeois character of modernism in all its forms testifies to a lordly tendency among intellectuals to spurn persuasion. Intellectuals make up modernisms, and want them to be exclusive and regulated. Modernism is proudly, even obnoxiously, élitist.

The Amariglio/Wendt 'immanence thesis' says that postmodernism grew out of 1910 modernism. I have a second immanence thesis. The modernisms were attacks on bourgeois culture. 'The noblest acts of mind [in modernist theory] would be those resisting the triumphant bourgeois order' (Altieri, 1993: 792). But – here is the immanence – out of each attack from the earliest modernism to the present grew a defense, successively stronger, and now strongest.

The antibourgeois character of modernism has taken many forms: scientific elitism, standard Marxism, the anti-capitalist line that élite literature in Europe and its offshoots began to follow around 1848. In 1910 modernism the exclusivity was directed more at the lower middle class than at captains of industry. The anti-modernist English poet Philip Larkin in the 1960s complained about the 'irresponsible exploitations of technique in contradiction to human life as we know it. This is my essential criticism of modernism, whether perpetrated by Parker, Pound or Picasso'. (Or the fourth P, Paul [Samuelson].) Larkin explained the [Charlie 'Bird'] Parker reference in one of his columns on jazz:

> [Said another jazz critic] 'After Parker, you had to be something of a musician to follow the best jazz of the day'. Of course! After Picasso! After Pound! There could hardly have been a conciser summary of what I don't believe in art.... The artist has become over-concerned with his material (hence an age of technical

experiment), and, in isolation, has busied himself with the two principal themes of modernism, mystification and outrage. Piqued at being neglected, he has painted portraits with both eyes on the same side of the nose,...or a novel in gibberish.... And parallel to this activity...there has grown up a kind of critical journalism designed to put it over.... Basically the message is: don't trust your eyes, or ears, or understanding.... You've got to work at this.... I mean, this is pretty complex stuff.... [After Parker, jazz] was split into two, intelligence without beat and beat without intelligence.

Larkin, 1985: 22–5

Modernism does that, dissociating the sensibilities. Francis Bacon warned against persuasion:

For it is a false assertion [of Protagoras, the Greek sophist] that the sense of man is the measure of all things. On the contrary, all perceptions as well as of the sense as of the mind are according to the measure of the individual and not according to the measure of the universe. And the human understanding is like a false mirror, which, receiving rays irregularly, distorts and discolours the nature of things by mingling its own nature with it.

(Bacon, [1620] 1965: XVI)

Modernism's main mode of operation in both its literary and architectural kind was and is to exploit the charm of what's difficult. I mean, this is pretty complex stuff. When T. S. Eliot versified in *The Waste Land* about the lower middle-class suburbanites coming to work – 'Unreal City,/ Under the brown fog of a winter dawn,/ A crowd flowed over London Bridge, so many,/ I had not thought death had undone so many' – he required two footnote references, one to Baudelaire and the other to the *Inferno*, III, 55–7.

The avant-garde was in this way fleeing its bourgeois origins and keeping clear of the masses. It was making itself, at any rate in its imaginings, into a new aristocracy. John Carey writes in a book chronicling the élitism of literary modernism, 'The intellectuals could not, of course, actually prevent the masses from attaining literacy. But they could prevent them from reading literature by making it too difficult for them to understand' (Carey, 1993: 16). The obscurity of modernism kept literature (and music and painting) in the hands of cultured chaps. It kept it out of the hands of suburbanites, clerks, Eastern European immigrants, and the other nasty creatures growing in such numbers.

'All those damn little clerks', says a character in an H. G. Wells novel of 1901 quoted by Carey. They have 'no proud dreams and no proud lusts'. The 'swarms of black, brown, and dirty-white, and yellow people...have to go'. George Bernard Shaw wrote the same way in 1910: 'Extermination must be put on a scientific basis'. And D. H. Lawrence, who in *Aaron's Rod* (1922, quoted again in Carey), advocated 'a proper and healthy and energetic slavery', in 1908 had written presciently, 'If I had my way, I would build a lethal chamber as big as the Crystal Palace, with a military band playing softly.... Then I'd go into the back streets and bring them all in, all the sick, the halt, and the maimed'.

Carey piles up the evidence for the proposition that fascism and modernism were more than merely chronologically linked. George Moore, a leading figure in the Irish renaissance, wrote in 1888, 'Injustice we worship.... What care I that some millions of wretched Israelites died under Pharaoh's lash or Egypt's sun? It was well that they died that I might have the pyramids to look upon.... I would give many lives to save one sonnet by Baudelaire'. Lordly indeed. Clive Bell, an art critic and friend to Woolf and to Maynard Keynes, had this to say in 1928 about political theory: 'To discredit a civilization it is not enough to show that it is based on slavery and injustice; you must show that liberty and justice would produce something better'.

It was not just modernist literary men who talked this way, of course. They were seconded by modernist scientists – and not, as is sometimes claimed by old-fashioned philosophers of science, by mere 'pseudo-scientists', either. In 1900 the great Karl Pearson, who invented modern statistics, wrote in his neopositivist bible *The Grammar of Science*: 'What we need is a check to the fecundity of inferior stocks.... It is a false view of human solidarity, which regrets that a capable and stalwart race of white men should advocate replacing a dark-skinned tribe' (1900: 369). In 1925 he advocated in a scientific paper stopping Jewish immigration to Britain.

Postmodernism by contrast is plebeian and 'middle class', at least in the sense that 91 per cent of Americans call themselves 'middle class'. Carey's antimodernist hero, the novelist Arnold Bennett (1867–1931), wrote in 1901 that 'everyone is an artist, more or less', in their lives and perceptions. This would be an impossible sentiment in Virginia Woolf. Unlike Woolf's modernism, postmodernism is proudly, even obnoxiously, democratic, deriving more from Atlantic City than from Princeton. When a French critic described the Disney World outside Paris as 'une catastrophe culturale', the postmodernists merely giggled.

The anti-élitism is what drives cultural conservatives into a rage about the latest postmodernism, a critical literature discussing reruns of the Brady Bunch. It is horrible to say that movies or (shudder!) TV or (gak!) style in clothing and automobiles can be studied seriously and then compared seriously, or for that matter unseriously, with the sacred cultural products of high modernism. Charles Newman's book attempting to bring a (non-economic) theory of inflation to a criticism of postmodernism has this difficulty, that it has no cultural interests beyond the modernist high canon. Postmodernists by contrast delight in such absurdities as the movie *I.Q.*, with Walter Matthau as a postmodern Einstein fascinated by 1950s-style convertible cars and rock music. The movie was shot on the very grounds of the Institute for Advanced Study. The Director (of the Institute, not the movie, which was amusing and pointed) must be losing his grip.

One can of course find exceptions to these propositions. Not all modernists are élitists (that is, aspiring aristocrats) or anti-bourgeois, either in their theories of themselves or in their actual effects. But the institutions of high modernism were, I think, hostile to capitalism even as they used it, angry at the middle class even as they relied on it, ignorant of the economy even as they lived in it.

The first modernist

All this leads back to the earliest possible dating of the onset of 'modernism', at old aristocratic Plato himself four centuries before Christ, and therefore of an ancient 'postmodernism' in opposition to Plato. Such a choice of origin makes modernism nearly two and half millennia old, and makes it identical to the philosophical as against (always 'against') the parallel rhetorical tradition. The modernisms of 1910 or of the Enlightenment or of the seventeenth century were recycled Plato, attempts to get underneath merely human persuasion to the bedrock of certitude. Therefore postmodernism in this biggest of stories is the denial of certitude.

Plato the system builder detested the sophists – the lawyers and law professors of his time – and detested the democracy their talk supported. Through his influence, 'rhetoric' (he may have invented the very word) and 'sophistry' were identified with clever fallacy. Plato separates belief (*pistis*; or *doxa*, mere things heard, common opinion) from knowledge (*episteme*; or *eidenai*, the thing seen, certitude):

Socrates: Then would you have us assume two forms of persuasion—one providing belief without knowledge [without the thing seen], and the other sure knowledge [*episteme*]?
Gorgias: Certainly.
Socrates: Now which kind of persuasion [*peithô*] is it that rhetoric creates in law courts or any public meeting on matters of right or wrong?
Gorgias: Obviously, I presume, Socrates, that from which we get belief [*pisteuein*].

Socrates: Thus rhetoric, it seems, is a producer of persuasion for belief [*peithoûs...pisteutikês*], not for instruction in the matter of right and wrong.

Gorgias 454E-455A

The attempt to lay down the law once and for all is aristocratic, and in modern times has taken the form of a lofty expertise. The historian of ideas Isaiah Berlin quoted once a revealing remark by Comte, who like Plato and the rest in the anti-rhetorical tradition was quite certain he had his hands on the transcendent (cf. *Phaedrus*, 247E): 'If we do not allow free thinking in chemistry or biology', asked Comte, 'why should we allow it in morals or politics?' (Berlin, 1958: 151). Why indeed? The editor of *Science* could not express the dogmatism of science as religion more flatly.

This is what is wrong with the notion that we can ascertain a Truth which all must obey for ever and ever. It is right to try to persuade each other and right to ask for an audience – this against the modernist suspicion of attempts to persuade an audience of, say, cold fusion. It is not right to contemplate, with Comte, 'allowing' free thought, as some sort of luxury. As Berlin pointed out, Comte's question exposes the rot in political rationalism – that is, in Platonism: 'first, that all men have one true purpose...; second, that the ends of all rational beings must of necessity fit into a single universal, harmonious pattern, which some men are able to discern more clearly than others; third, that all conflict...is due solely to the clash of reason with the irrational' (1958: 154). Where in economics have you heard such premises?

Berlin explains that the 'rule of experts' comes from the argument, prominent in Plato, and then in worshippers of experts such as Bentham and Comte, that my 'real' self must be rational and 'would' want me to obey the guardians or confess in a show trial. The expert therefore, in my own real interest, issues the order for my execution. In the Spanish Inquisition, that exemplar of paternal expertise, if a Jew under torture renounced his religion he was baptized and immediately executed, as ready now to enter Paradise.

Free persuasion, unlike the coercions of modernism, shares many qualities with free exchange. Speech is a deal between the speaker and his audience. Persuasion and exchange share the unique feature as devices of altering other people's behavior that the people so altered are glad the alteration was made. It's not surprising to find aristocratic Plato equally outraged at the 'flattery' of *hoi polloi* by democratic orators and at the taking of fees by the professors of rhetoric. In the *Republic* he showed, consistently, that he was opposed to free exchange in the market place as well.

The postmodernism of the sophists was, against Plato's authoritarianism, the chief support of Athenian (and Greek Sicilian) democracy and commerce (Jaeger, [1933] 1965; Guthrie, 1971; Kerferd, 1981). A new free politics and capitalist economics, as in Eastern Europe now, required a new art of persuasion in law courts and legislative assemblies. The Greeks, being reflective sorts (they had adapted the Phoenician alphabet a couple of centuries before, and were mad to use it), made the give and take of persuasion into a theory of language. It was a theory of language as an autonomous influence on free people, rhetoric, 'the first humanism which the world had seen', which 'made Greece conscious of her own culture' (Jaeger, [1933] 1965: 302–3).

Anti-rhetorical thinking, in ancient times the dogma that truth is transcendent and in modern times the dogma that truth is ideological, claims that the persuasion [*peithos*] of free men is merely another coercion. The modernist theory of persuasion is that there's no such thing as persuasion, only interests. The modernist philosopher P. H. Partridge stipulates that 'uncoerced' entails 'unmanipulated', where 'manipulation' includes 'the persuasive machinery of totalitarian governments'. One imagines a right of a free man to unmanipulated opinions, a world free from beer commercials and sound bites, free from dishonest appeals to read my lips and free from governmental programs for bringing children up as environmental radicals. Such a world is impossible to legislate. Trying to achieve it by dropping the distinction between physical and verbal coercion is a mistake. If Goebbels merely talks persuasively to the German people, even lies to them, or even runs a splendid film about Nazi successes in the Berlin Olympics in their presence, he is not in a useful sense engaged in 'coercion'. Michael Taylor has argued that 'coercion' must be confined to physical action or to 'the successful making of credible, substantial threats' backed by physical coercion (1979: 11–21, 147). Otherwise blackjacks and prisons are 'merely' rhetoric. We had better stick with a distinction between rhetoric and coercion. Keeping the distinction does not deny that rhetoric works within structures of power – in academic economics itself, for example. But a gun is different from a denial of promotion.

The claim to do for others through the state what they cannot do themselves – since after all coercion is merely another persuasion if people would only look on it rightly – justifies modernist social engineering. It was Bentham's obsession. No advocate of *laissez faire* was he, who saw levers in the state for law reform and the construction of rational prisons. In Berlin's terms, social engineering of the Benthamite sort seeks 'positive' freedom, such as the freedom to eat well, as against the 'negative' freedom of the Smithian sort, such as the freedom from oppression by Benthamite social engineers. In 1929 Frank Knight noted the rhetorical contradiction in the idea that we can be helped by social engineers: 'natural science in the "prediction-and-control" sense of the laboratory disciplines is relevant to action only for a dictator standing in a one-sided relation of control to a society, which is the negation of liberalism – and of all that liberalism has called morality' (1929: 38). It is again the aporia of the Enlightenment project.

The postmodern liberalist in the late twentieth century has plenty of reason to doubt that we have the knowledge for prediction and control (as Comte put it: 'savoir pour prévoir, prévoir pour pouvoir'). To doubt in this postmodern way that the Federal Reserve can fine tune the economy (thus Milton Friedman the postmodernist) is not 'mere relativism' or 'irrationalism' or an advocacy of 'anything goes'. A recent student of the sophists noted that 'The time is surely long past when the rejection of any transcendent reality can be taken as evidence that the search for truth has been abandoned' (Kerferd, 1981: 175). A claim that one has found the way to determine a transcendent Truth diverts effort from the search for terrestrial truths. It is the intellectual's substitute for theism. Only in God's eyes is the Truth settled now and forever.

Deconstruction

The mention of 'relativism' will bring swimming into the mind of most American readers of the *New York Times* the D word, 'Deconstruction'. It may be surprising that I haven't mentioned it yet, considering how the op-ed pages view literary criticism. In truth 'deconstruction' is now elderly in literary criticism, long since pushed from the center of the stage by feminism and the new historicism. And there is a minority view inside literary criticism, with which I agree, that in any case deconstruction was a reinvention of ancient rhetoric, acquired by the French inventors of deconstruction during Greek class at their *lyceés*. The rhetorician Richard Lanham complains that 'the "theory" world is forever taking bits of classical rhetoric and tarting them up in new French frocks' (Lanham, 1993: 263). He notes too that the American Kenneth Burke invented deconstruction forty years before Jacques Derrida. Only willful ignorance keeps the Parisians and their epigones from recognizing it.

Only willful ignorance of another sort, however, keeps the editorialists snarling at deconstruction. People have a way of seeing a novelty through the strangest version with which they imagine they are familiar. Thus outsiders to economics think they can reject a modest version of supply side economics by attacking what they imagine to be the opinions of Arthur Laffer. Richard Posner in his egregious book *Law and Literature: A Misunderstood Relation* (1988) used this rhetorical trick in dismissing literary criticism as applied to law. When explaining to his conservative readers among lawyers Everything You Need to Know About Literary Studies But Were Terrified to Ask you can imagine the terrifying subfield he started with: Chapter Five, Section 1, 'Deconstruction and Other Schools of Literary Criticism'. One hopes that his decisions as a federal judge are not so transparently rigged.

The reason people play such mind games is that they are conservative, intellectually speaking, and would rather avoid investing in a new set of thinking tools if they can get away with it. Thinking gives one the headache. It has to be admitted, though, in extenuation of the conservatives' nonthinking, that the deconstructionists do not make it easy. Many academics these days adhere to the modernist conviction that obscurity is the same thing as profundity, and therefore write with trowels. You've got to work at this. I mean, this is pretty complex stuff.

Still, deconstruction in substance is not all that hard. Jane Rossetti has given some examples (Rossetti, 1990 and 1992). Here I can illustrate one of its main points, using a couple of sentence she quotes but does not deconstruct from the great and dangerous American economist Wesley Clair Mitchell (1874–1948): 'it must never be forgotten that the development of the social sciences (including economics) is still a social process. Recognition of that view...leads one to study these sciences...[as] the product not merely of sober thinking but also subconscious wishing'. The sentences contain at least these half-spoken hierarchies ready for liberating deconstruction (reading back to front, the terms in square brackets being those implied but not mentioned): sober-subconscious; thought-wishing; product-[mere ephemera]; sciences-[mere humanities]; study-[beach reading]; one-[you personally]; leads-[compels]; view-[grounded conviction]; sciences-[mere] processes; development-[mere chaotic change]; must-[can]. The first term of each is the privileged one – except that in the pairs leads-[compels] and view-[grounded conviction] they are in fact polite self-deprecation, with ironic force: Mitchell is on the contrary claiming the commanding heights of compelling and grounded conviction, in modernist style, not the soft valleys of mere gently leading 'views'.

That's quite a haul for two sentences, and suggests that deconstruction (or for that matter the Greek rhetoric from which it derives) might be onto something of use to the economic reader. It's worth doing with Mitchell – and always easier to do with figures from olden times than from the present (for an English professor's interesting attempt to deconstruct Thatcherian economic rhetoric, see Selden, 1991). To put it in the vernacular, Mitchell is playing all kinds of mind games on his readers and we had better watch out. Mitchell, of course, is not special in this. He espoused, for example, an erotic fascism that was nothing special among modernists in the 1920s but needs deconstruction: 'In economics as in other sciences we desire knowledge mainly as an instrument of control. Control means the alluring possibility of shaping the evolution of economic life to fit the developing purposes of the race' (quoted in Adelstein, 1991: 13). Savoir pour pouvoir.

You will notice that nothing in deconstruction says that the world does not exist or that you cannot say anything about anything or that we do not look both ways when crossing the street. What it does say is the message of postmodernists from the Greek sophists to the present. As Wayne Booth puts it, 'Man is essentially...a self-making-and-remaking, symbol manipulating creature, an exchanger of information, a communicator, a persuader and manipulator, an inquirer. The terms will differ depending on one's philosophical vocabulary, but what will not vary is the central notion that man's value-embedded symbolic processes are as real as anything we know' (Booth, 1974: 136).

The proposals of postmodernism: toggling in the market place of ideas

To put it another way, postmodernism is and always has been thoroughly rhetorical. Richard Lanham use the notion of a 'toggle', that is, in computerese the keystroke that allows one to move from, say, looking at a stripped-down version of a text on a screen to looking at a fully formatted version with all ornaments in place (Lanham, 1993). The age of oratory before Gutenberg and the age of keyboarding after the silicon chip, Lanham argues, both elevated toggling to the master art. They reacted to a modernism, which wants the toggle always *off*. Modernism is flatfooted. Postmodernism is ironic.

Lanham quotes the American pragmatist George Herbert Mead on the multiple roles played by graceful living in the world: 'It is the social process itself that is responsible for the appearance of the self; it is not there as a self apart from this type of experience. A multiple personality is in a certain sense normal' (Mead, 1934, quoted in Lanham, 1976: 153). In being a self and a citizen, argues Lanham, 'the same technique is required – holding opposite worlds in the mind at once' (1976: 154), an attitude that 'oscillates from realism to idealism and back again' (Lanham, 1974: 39). You must know that the President's inaugural address is *merely* a speech, and note its figures at the same time that you grasp its values, for what they are worth. To be unable to toggle between the two knowings is to be either a cynic or a fool.

Lanham contrasts the rhetorical looking *at* the words with the philosophical looking *through*. Modernism of whatever era is the theory that the two should be separated, one for Art and the other for Science. But a rhetorical education offers the ability to toggle between the two. In a comment on my writings on rhetoric, Lanham explains how a strong defense of the rhetorical tradition can be constructed out of this idea:

> [McCloskey's] stated defense [of rhetoric] is the weak one: 'Rhetoric is merely a tool, no bad thing in itself'. [...] But what she succeeds in doing, with her...close readings of the rhetoric of economics in action, is to suggest the Strong Defense we began

to see emerging with [the Chicago Aristotelian Richard] McKeon. To read economics as McCloskey suggests is always to be toggling between looking at the prose and through it, reading it 'rhetorically' and reading it 'philosophically', and this toggling attitude toward utterance is what the rhetorical paideia was after all along. Train someone in it and, according to [the Roman rhetorician] Quintilian's way of thinking, you have trained that person to be virtuous.

(Lanham, 1993: 169–70.)

Lanham argues persuasively that someone educated in modernist style without the toggle, so to speak, is not only not automatically a good person (though perhaps skilled at a certain specialized way of speaking) but is likely to be bad. Being educated in rhetoric, acquiring skill in speaking across the culture, is usually to acquire the toggle.

The argument can be made more precise, economically speaking. Having two views allows one to toggle. Toggling allows one to see that one's view is a view. Monists are likely at this point to scream 'mere relativism' and call for the guards. But being able to toggle from view to view does not imply indifference between the views. Economically speaking it is the index number problem. You can evaluate the standard of living in America and India using either the point of view of American prices (cheap cars, expensive servants) or of Indian prices (expensive cars, cheap servants). Knowing that there are two sets of prices at which one might evaluate the difference does not paralyze thought or lead to nihilism. On the contrary, it is necessary for wisdom. Pick one view, know what you're doing, and from time to time, for the hell of it, toggle.

A liberalist and economic postmodernism

I have been suggesting that postmodernism need not be expressed only in post-Marxist ways (thus Baudrillard or Lyotard) or late Freudian ways (thus Lacan and Irigaray). It can be expressed in post-Marshallian or post-Keynesian or late Mengerian ways, too. I have given some examples in a conversation with Gayatri Chakravorty Spivak (McCloskey, 2001). French thinkers and their followers in the USA have tended to assume that a postmodernism must deal with exactly and only the questions that French intellectuals are most worried about: How can we bear life without Cartesianism? How can we escape from the rigidities of the French bourgeoisie? How will the Revolution come? How can we be 'critics' if we are not 'critics' in the adolescent's sense of sneering at everything we see? How can we avoid becoming American?

One reason that economists should come to terms with postmodernism is that many prominent theorists of postmodernism (theorists, not necessarily advocates), such as the American Fredric Jameson or the Frenchman Jean Baudrillard, have definite ideas about the economy, ideas they believe important. Yet the ideas are detached from modern economics, even when of Marxist origin (that is, even the Marxist economists have no impact on what the literary Marxists say). This is odd on its face. One would think the professors of literature would want to learn more about what they are talking about. They are confident they understand the modern economy, yet know little of its history and nothing about the main conversation in which the economy is discussed, our very own economics (take it how you will: neoclassical or Marxist or Austrian or institutionalist). True, literary critics and their artist subjects see things about the economy that economists miss. The point is that there is an occasion here for serious, beneficial trade. Economists if they would set their minds to it, and see that postmodernism is an adult's way to be a scientist, could reunify the cultures of science and literature.

The missing ingredient in liberalist thought, I am arguing, is rhetoric, to be supplied by the professors of literature in exchange for lessons in economics. As John of Salisbury wrote eight centuries ago in its defense: 'Rhetoric is the beautiful and the fruitful union between reason and expression. Through harmony, it holds human communities together' (quoted in Vickers, 1970: 30). Charles Altieri, like many critics still under the spell of Marxism, has difficulties with the unfoundedness of a rhetoric. He has a nostalgia for certitude and a hatred of capitalism. Charles, my good man: surrender, to Lanham's toggling and to capitalism. Rhetoric, the first postmodernism, was born with capitalism in the marketplaces of Greece.

Refutation

But what of the weighty objections to the postmodern, such as those supplied by those ingenious writers I mentioned in *The New York Times*? A little dispute about postmodernism and classical liberalism I had recently with Jeffrey Friedman, the editor of the admirable journal *Critical Inquiry*, can serve. Friedman asks (Friedman, 1991), 'without the discipline imposed by a putatively objective, non-metaphorical reality, is not each interpretive community licensed to convert its instincts into sacred cows on the ground that there is no higher standard of truth than whatever is arbitrarily self-imposed?'

Briefly, No: to admit that our only standard is our interpretive community is not to surrender to *arbitrary* standards, but to standards. There are no timeless standards outside those of an interpretive community. As Aristotle put the point, 'Since the persuasive is persuasive *to someone*...rhetoric theorize[s]...about what seems true to people of a certain sort, as is also true with dialectic' (*Rhetoric*, I, ii, 11; 1356b). The literary critic and law professor and now dean Stanley Fish attacks Critical Legal Studies. Fish is well known for his relativism and postmodernism and trendy leftism. Why then does he not thrill to the late-1960s leftwing tactics of Critical Legal Studies? Because the Crits do not reach the standards of the interpretive community. Fish, the notorious constructivist, complains that for the Crits, 'all of a sudden "constructed" means "fabricated" or "made up"' (Fish, 1989: 227). Fish is consistent and Fish is correct. 'Rational debate', he says, 'is always possible; not, however, because it is anchored in a reality outside it, but because it occurs in a history' (Fish, 1989: 196). Yes. Fish believes that modernism, whether rationalist or irrationalist, has some deliberative screws loose. We postmodernists propose to tighten them up. The conservatives want to carry screwily on.

But what about, in Friedman's words, 'the discipline imposed by a putatively objective, non-metaphorical reality'? I would argue that the 'discipline' of 'non-metaphoric reality' is phony. For one thing, since Mary Hesse's *Models and Analogies in Science* (1963), or for that matter since Immanuel Kant, it has been hard to claim that scientists get along without metaphor. In the early 1960s the philosopher Max Black wrote of metaphor 'since philosophers...have so neglected the subject, I must get what help I can from the literary critics. They, at least, do not accept the commandment, "Thou shalt not commit metaphor," or assume that metaphor is incompatible with serious thought' (1962: 25).

For another, the metaphor of 'discipline' doesn't bite in practice. Modernists talk a lot about 'discipline' and 'rigor' and 'compelling proof', in a vocabulary approaching the sadomasochistic, but when it gets down to the whips and chains they don't carry through. In this they follow their master: Plato's arguments, when examined closely, hinge on myths. Any practitioner of a subject like economics under the sway of modernism knows in her heart that this is so, and can offer examples in practice. We can have a real discipline based on a serious rhetoric, a discipline admitting that we cannot achieve Truths but affirming that we can come to agree on some truths. We cannot have a transcendent discipline, since we cannot ground it as the transcendentalists demand. The groundings proffered in the successive modernisms since Plato have proven to be fakes. So the 'discipline' is fake, too. Unlike the real discipline of rhetoric, which demands we persuade each other, the fake discipline escapes in the end all demands. 'Anything goes' was a conservative technique long before it was, putatively, a postmodern theory.

Friedman asserts that interpretive communities must in practice act as though their standards were 'transcendent'. There's the word, and there's the 'discipline'. Only children and platonists need transcendence. The children in *The Lord of the Flies* must worship absolutely the pig's, and Piggy's, head. Communities of adults by contrast have in practice no difficulty recognizing that their standards are not God's own, not transcendent and not ahistorical, while affirming that the standards are still worth discussing and implementing. It's not the case empirically, as philosophical and political conservatives have always feared, that adults will descend into a war of all against all if they lose their faith in God or the divine right of kings or the synthetic a priori or some other principle of transcendence. The engineering standard for the height of road crowns is nowhere inscribed by the finger of God, and yet a contractor who fails to abide by it will accept that he needs to rebuild the road. The standard of replicability in biological experiment is not absolute, and cannot in principle be so. Yet the community of biologists can recognize conjecturally, well enough for scientific purposes, when an experiment on oxidative phosphorylation has gone wrong (Mulkay, 1985). Friedman thinks that without a belief in transcendence we 'would have no criteria of what counts as persuasive'. Huh? Come again? Why so? He does not say, nor do the other worried critics of postmodernism. I say, Relax: the end of civilization is not near, and if there is a threat it comes from the barbarians already inside the gates, the modernists of Princeton or Pasadena.

The philosopher of postmodernism Gary Madison is quoted by Friedman saying that modernism subscribes to a 'Promethean illusion that by means of theory we can manipulate and control human affairs however we desire'. Friedman calls this a 'dubious reading of modern history', but again does not pause to say why. Yet Madison's description would satisfy empirically most members of a speech community who have lived through communism and anti-communism, Vietnam and the expansion of the modern state. Someone accurately described the illusion of architectural modernism or the modernism of the Enlightenment as the notion that we can in fact accomplish everything we rationally propose to do. (Compare Hayek: 'If we remain strictly rationalist, utilitarian, we can arrange everything according to our pleasure'.)

With such a rationalism who needs *ir*rationalism? And what else would you call such lunacy but a 'Promethean illusion'? 'All their doings were indeed without intelligent calculation until I showed them the rising of the stars, and the settings, hard to observe. And further I discovered to them numbering, pre-eminent among subtle devices.... It was I who arranged all the ways of seercraft, and I first adjudged what things come verily true from dreams' (Aeschylus, *Prometheus Bound*, ll. 452–61, 478). Prometheus might as well have been justifying a forecast from the social engineers of next year's interest rate. It is the Promethean, and modernist, illusion. It denies scarcity and it denies the rationality that the easy predictions have already been exploited.

Such modernism is bad economics. Fixing it is another reason for economists to get on with the postmodern project. Somehow we've got to bring along with us in the back of the pickup the terrified conservatives, mumbling their rosaries of 'standards', 'transcendence', and 'discipline', none of which they have seen or practiced in their scientific lives.

Notes

1 Parts of the following have appeared in (1994a) *Knowledge and Persuasion in Economics*, Cambridge: Cambridge University Press, and in (1991) 'The Essential Rhetoric of Law, Literature, and Liberty' (Review of Posner's *Law as Literature*, Fish's *Doing What Comes Naturally* and White's *Justice as Translation*)' *Critical Review* 5 (Spring): 203–23. I thank David Ruccio for comments on a draft.

References

Adelstein, Richard P. (1991) '"The Nation as an Economic Unit": Keynes, Roosevelt and the Managerial Ideal', *Journal of American History* 78 (June): 160–87.
Aeschylus (1942) *Prometheus Bound*, trans. David Greene, in David Greene and Richard Lattimore (eds) *Greek Tragedies*, vol. 1, Chicago and London: University of Chicago Press, 1960.
Altieri, Charles (1993) 'Modernism and Postmodernism', in Alex Preminger and T. V. F. Brogan (eds) *The New Princeton Encyclopedia of Poetry and Poetics*, Princeton: Princeton University Press, pp. 792–96.
Amariglio, Jack (1990) 'Economics as a Postmodern Discourse', in Warren J. Samuels (ed.) *Economics as Discourse: An Analysis of the Language of Economists*, Boston: Kluwer Academic Publishers, 15–46.
Aristotle (1991) *Rhetoric*, trans. George A. Kennedy, New York: Oxford University Press.
Bacon, Francis (1620) 'The New Organon and The Great Instauration [Instauratio Magna]', in S. Warhaft (ed.) *Francis Bacon: A Selection of His Works*, Indianapolis: Bobbs-Merrill, 1965.
Berlin, Isaiah. [1958] (1970) 'Two Concepts of Liberty', inaugural lecture, pp. 118–72 in Berlin, *Four Essays on Liberty*, New York: Oxford University Press 1969.
Black, Max (1962) *Models and Metaphors*, Ithaca: Cornell University Press.
Booth, Wayne C. (1974) *Modern Dogma and the Rhetoric of Assent*, Chicago: University of Chicago Press.
—— (1988) *The Company We Keep: An Ethics of Fiction*, Berkeley and Los Angeles: University of California Press.
Bordo, Susan (1987) *The Flight to Objectivity: Essays on Cartesianism and Culture*, Albany: State University of New York Press.
Brolin, Brent C. (1976) *The Failure of Modern Architecture*, New York: Van Nostrand Reinhold.
Burczack, Ted (1994) 'The Postmodern Moments of F. A. Hayek's Economics', *Economics and Philosophy* 10: 31–58.
Carey, John (1993) *The Intellectuals: Pride and Prejudice Among the Literary Intelligentsia, 1880–1939*, New York: St Martin's Press.
Cosgel, Metin, and Klamer, Arjo (1990) 'Entrepreneurship as Discourse', unpublished manuscript, Departments of Economics, University of Connecticut/-George Washington University.

Eagleton, Terry (1985) 'Capitalism, Modernism and Postmodernism', *New Left Review*; reprinted as pp. 385–98 in Lodge, ed.

Eco, Umberto (1985) *Reflections on the Name of the Rose*, trans. W. Weaver, London: Secker and Warburg.

Fish, Stanley (1989) *Doing What Comes Naturally : Change, Rhetoric, and the Practice of Theory in Literary and Legal Studies*, Durham, NC : Duke University Press.

Friedman, Jeffrey (1991) 'Postmodernism vs. Postlibertarianism', *Critical Review* 5, no. 2 (Spring): 145–58.

Guthrie, W. K. C. (1971) *The Sophists*, London: Cambridge University Press.

Hayek, Friedrich (1994) *Hayek on Hayek*, in Stephen Kresge and Leif Wener (eds), Chicago and London: University of Chicago Press.

Hesse, Mary (1963) *Models and Analogies in Science*, Notre Dame: University of Notre Dame Press.

Jaeger, Werner (1933) *Paideia: The Ideals of Greek Culture*, vol. 1, *Archaic Greece: The Mind of Athens*, trans. G. Highet, New York: Oxford University Press, 1965.

Jameson, Fredric (1984) 'The Politics of Theory: Ideological Positions in the Postmodernism Debate', repr. in David Lodge, (ed.) *Modern Criticism and Theory: A Reader*, London and New York: Longman, 1988: pp. 373–83.

Jencks, Charles (1973) *Modern Movements in Architecture*, London and New York: Penguin; 2nd edn 1985.

Kerferd, G. B. (1981) *The Sophistic Movement*, Cambridge: Cambridge University Press.

Klamer, Arjo (1991) 'The Advent of Modernism in Economics', unpublished manuscript. Department of Economics, George Washington University, Washington, D.C.

Knight, Frank ([1929] 1947) 'Freedom as Fact and Criterion' in *Freedom and Reform: Essays in Economics and Social Philosophy*, New York: Harper and Row, pp. 1–18; reissued by Port Washington, NY: Kennikat Press, 1969.

Kolb, David (1990) *Postmodern Sophistications: Philosophy, Architecture, and Tradition*, Chicago and London: University of Chicago Press.

Kuhn, Thomas (1962) *The Structure of Scientific Revolutions*, 2nd edn, Chicago: University of Chicago Press, 1970.

Lanham, Richard A. (1974) *Style: An Anti-Textbook*, New Haven: Yale University Press.

—— (1976) *The Motives of Eloquence: Literary Rhetoric in the Renaissance*, New Haven: Yale University Press.

—— (1992) 'The Extraordinary Convergence: Democracy, Technology, Theory, and the University Curriculum' in Darryl J. Gless and Barbara Herrnstein Smith (eds) *The Politics of Liberal Education*, Durham: Duke University Press, pp. 33–56.

—— (1993) *The Electronic Word: Democracy, Technology, and the Arts*, Chicago: University of Chicago Press.

Larkin, Philip (1970) *All What Jazz: A Record Diary*, London: Faber and Faber, 1985.

Laslett, Barbara (1990) 'Unfeeling Knowledge: Emotion and Objectivity in the History of Sociology', *Sociological Forum* 5 (3): 413–33.

Lavoie, Don C. (1990a) 'The Discovery and Interpretation of Profit Opportunities: Culture and the Kirznerian Entrepreneur', unpublished manuscript, Department of Economics, George Mason University, Fairfax, Virginia.

—— (1990b) 'Hermeneutics, Subjectivity, and the Lester/Machlup Debate: Toward a More Anthropological Approach to Empirical Economics' in Samuels (ed.) *Economics as Discourse*, Boston: Kluwer Academis Press, pp. 167–184.

Lodge, David (1981) *Working with Structuralism: Essays and Reviews on Nineteenth and Twentieth-Century Literature*, London: Routledge, 1991.

Lupton, Ellen (1989) 'Reading Isotype' in Victor Margolin (ed.) *Design Discourse: History, Theory, Criticism*, Chicago: University of Chicago Press, pp. 145–156.

McCloskey, Deirdre (1990) *If You're So Smart: The Narrative of Economic Expertise*, Chicago and London: University of Chicago Press.

—— (1991) 'The Essential Rhetoric of Law, Literature, and Liberty' (Review of Posner's Law as Literature, Fish's Doing What Comes Naturally and White's Justice as Translation)', *Critical Review* 5 (Spring): 203–23.

—— (1994a) *Knowledge and Persuasion in Economics*, Cambridge: Cambridge University Press.

—— (1994b) 'Bourgeois Virtue', *The American Scholar* 63 (2): 177–91.

—— (1999) 'Postmodern Market Feminism: Half of a Conversation with Gayatri Chakravorty Spivak', forthcoming *Rethinking Marxism*, spring 2001.

Mulkay, Michael (1985) *The Word and the World: Explorations in the Form of Sociological Analysis*, Winchester, Mass.: Allen and Unwin.

Newman, Charles (1985) *The Post-Modern Aura: The Act of Fiction in an Age of Inflation*, Evanston: Northwestern University Press.

Partridge, P. H. (1967) 'Liberty' in *The Encyclopedia of Philosophy*, vol. 3, New York: Free Press, pp. 222–3.

Pearson, Karl (1892) *The Grammar of Science*, 2nd edn, London: Black, 1900.

Plato (1925) *Gorgias*, trans. W. R. M. Lamb, Cambridge: Harvard University Press.

—— (1914) *Phaedrus*, trans. H. N. Fowler, Cambridge: Harvard University Press.

Posner, Richard (1988) *Law and Literature: A Misunderstood Relation*, Cambridge: Harvard University Press.

Rosen, Stanley (1987) *Hermeneutics as Politics*, New York: Oxford University Press.

Rossetti, Jane (1990) 'Deconstructing Robert Lucas' in Samuels, (ed) *Economics as Discourse*, Boston: Kluwer Academis Press, pp. 225–43.

—— (1992) 'Deconstruction, Rhetoric, and Economics', in de Marchi, (ed.) *Post-Popperian Methodology*, Boston : Kluwer Academic Publishers, pp. 211–34 .

Ruskin, John (1851–3) *The Stones of Venice*, 3 vols, New York: Peter Fenelon Collier, 1890.

Samuelson, Paul A. (1947) *The Foundations of Economics Analysis*, Cambridge: Harvard University Press.

Selden, Raman (1991) 'The Rhetoric of Enterprise' in R. Keat and N. Abercrombie, (eds) *Enterprise Culture*, London: Routledge, pp. 58–71.

Taylor, Charles (1979) 'What's Wrong with Negative Liberty' in Alan Ryan (ed.) *The Idea of Freedom: Essays in Honour of Isaiah Berlin*, Oxford: Oxford University Press, pp. 175–93.

Tintner, Gerhard (1968) *Methodology of Mathematical Economics and Econometrics*, Chicago and London: University of Chicago Press.

Wendt, Paul (1990) 'Comment on Amariglio's "Economics as a Postmodern Discourse"' in Samuels, (ed.) *Economics as Discourse*, pp. 47–64.

Woodmansee, Martha (1994) *The Author, Art, and the Market: Rereading the History Aesthetics*, New York: Columbia University Press.

Woolf, Virginia (1924) *Collected Essays*, vol. 1. New York: Harcourt, Brace, World, 1967.

5

WRITING IN THIRDS

Jack Amariglio

Sheila Dow, Arjo Klamer, and Deirdre McCloskey are a venerable threesome. The three are among the few economists who started talking about modernism and postmodernism back in the 1980s. Early on, each contributed several noteworthy papers that specified one (among many) problems within contemporary economics to be about modernism and its excesses. These papers, taken together, constitute some of the first and finest work from economists about the impending 'implosion' of modernist economics – its impossibility to go on blithely and securely – and the equally impending emergence of 'something else', postmodernism perhaps, or perhaps not. The papers Dow, Klamer, and McCloskey have written for this volume have the tone of a wisened and collective re-evaluation, a taking stock and look back at where their own concerns about modernism and the economics profession's trajectory in the past two decades have left this something else.

Their papers, as both retrospection and prospection, share something deep and abiding. It is what I will call the desire for 'the third'. Without spending too much time on establishing attribution or periodization, I will hazard a thesis: that the desire for a third, a way out of either/or oppositions – what Dow identifies as 'dualism' – has been part of many economists' self-consciousness during the reign of modernism within economics. That such a desire may also be part and parcel of postmodernism I readily acknowledge. Or rather, I think it is correct to say that many postmodernists (myself and my own past work included) internalize such a desire. This being the case, a question arises if such a desire is central to postmodern movements within economics or other fields, or simply belies the strong effects of modernism and its characteristic modes of posing problems within any of these fields. I will leave this question mostly unanswered for the present.

I am convinced, though, that third ways speak most clearly to the historical legacies of transcendental philosophies, and that the desire for this 'other', where the other is posed as a third, has an honorable genealogy in the dialectics that are the bequeathment of ancient Greece and, more recently, Hegel and Marx and beyond. Of course, not all schemes for third ways are inscribed within or bear as much weighty baggage as the creaky thesis/antithesis/synthesis dialectic of history and knowledge, or the similarly constituted dialectic of nature, for that matter. Third ways are operative in all sorts of transcendence scripts that don't seek to employ thesis, antithesis, and synthesis as the dynamic forces behind ruptures and continuities (but mostly ruptures). Modernist escapism (and here I do not mean this pejoratively) hasn't needed the Hegelian or any other dialectic to suggest that each time an opposition is posited, the path to the truth lies in some conjoined or orthogonal movement away from the either/or couplet.

Yet, there is something so familiar within the field of economics (and I would dare say, within so much academic, and perhaps non-academic, discourse) about performatives to establish at least one's own position as a third, and different, way. I have been struck, for example, at the recurring and widespread resistance of many economists to 'own' and publicly perform the labels of any particular school of thought, or any particular theoretical approach. As Klamer suggests in his paper here (Chapter 3), the characterization of a school of thought, and claiming that one is a devotee, nay, a disciple of such a school, runs up against the modernist countertendency of refusing general (if they are not universal and transhistorical) attributions. Among other reasons, this refusal is bolstered by the perceived need to disclaim that one thinks 'narrowly' within and from a particular (hence non-universal) perspective. Who among contemporary economists has worn consistently throughout his/her career, for example, the label of neoclassical? Who bears, with regularity, the appellation of 'modernist'? Would Samuelson, for example, who appears as the bane of modernism and even formalist neoclassicism in Klamer's and McCloskey's papers, proudly self-ascribe under these labels? Would Arrow? Solow?

Now, as Dow, Klamer, and McCloskey make evident in their papers, there are of course names that one can wear, for a time, with pride and even aggression. But, what is also true is that the closer one gets to being seen as a central figure in some aging school of thought, and certainly those that are showing rips and tears and appear time-worn if not just plain shop-worn, so repudiations begin to proliferate stating that one is not what one once was comfortable with as a self-description (so many radicals just love to repeat Marx's comment at one later stage that he was not a Marxist). There appears to be something unseemly, and upsetting to personal integrity as well as the growth of science, to be at the 'core' of a discipline or even a school of thought, to be viewed as a paragon of the 'mainstream' and a representative of hoary authority. Montaigne summed up this unsettled self-consciousness quite well in the following:

> Incessantly to follow one's own track, to be so close a prisoner to one's own inclinations that one cannot stray from them, or give them a twist, is to be no friend to oneself, still less to be one's master; it is to be one's own slave.
>
> (1958: 251)

We are right to read this as an appeal to difference, if not tolerance. But, we would also be right to read it as a desire to transcend one's own 'initial' place of intellectual standing, if only to avoid the appearance, even to ourselves, that we have indeed fallen slave to our own pet thoughts, which, by the way, occur often as habit and ritual (thus establishing the important anti-modernist postulate that all theory is invested with such discursive and non-discursive culturally formed regularities). Our fear of being both drones *and* heavies, or at least as being seen this way, occasions as its opposite a notion of personal freedom, individual moral dignity, and social *development* that has had enormous power during periods pervaded by modernist sensibilities. As Marshall Berman (1982) has indicated, indeed, here in this notion of development as transcendence is the character of modern men and women. This is a character, one might add, that can still be gleaned even in the late modernism of new classical economics, if not in the formal theorems and axioms, then at least in the conversations that Klamer has previously recorded with new classical practitioners.

The modernist conceit to move developmentally forward, even if this consists of a move backward (by claiming that progress requires we dig up and revive our discredited ancestors), powers the impulse away from anything that can be called a center. In this view, though, it is not just the center that does not hold. The poles – the either/ors – lose their magnetism as well.

The amusing idiosyncrasies and courageous individualities (self-perceived) of those whom others believe are at the center of a discourse or discipline like economics are precisely what one reads interminably in their own self-stories. They were and remained rebels, they claim. They were and remained true to the pursuit of truth. They could never be labeled and tied to any one school of thought or research project. Their students and followers are mostly acolytes, and often got the 'received word' wrong. They transcend even their own reputation and authority. The crucial point is that they transcend. They just transcend.

This, I think, is a mostly modernist story, though there are 'moments' of the same in the postmodernisms that seek to escape precisely the either/or-ism of modernity (as Dow rightly notes). And by this I take fully McCloskey's point in her paper (Chapter 4) that modernisms (and postmodernisms) have appeared in so many different ages in the West. One could easily read the story of transcendence here as deflecting blame and eliding responsibility by an act of outrageous dissemblance, but I shall leave that for now to others if they wish to make the case. Instead, I want to focus on the aspect of transcendence that sees the way out of either/or-ism as the introduction of a third element, even when this third is still marked with the sign of the original couplet.

It is interesting then that Sheila Dow offers as resistance to both modernist and postmodernist dualism such a third way, what she calls the 'synthetic approach'. Dow arrives at this particular form of transcendence through an adaptation of traditional dialectics (or at least one familiar version of it). In their papers, Dow, Klamer, and McCloskey all make visible their mental struggles with the problem of such synthesis or transcendence in trying to figure out if it makes any sense at all to treat modernism and postmodernism as exhaustive of the field of possibilities in economics or, for that matter, in any field of thought and practice. For Dow, though, this struggle leads to ways out of modernist and postmodernist dead-ends (such as she finds in the dualisms with which they each operate) through something which is both and neither of the original poles of the opposition. It seems important for Dow to establish the grounds for synthesis partly in the impossibility of something entirely 'new' – and here, I take it that Dow is skeptical and perhaps even critical of the modernist and postmodernist boasts to encapsulate fully what could ever be 'new' in the world of thought – emerging without identifiable birth parents. But, just as importantly, Dow's desire for synthesis appears to be accounted for by her view that there is much of value and also non-value, perhaps even to equal degrees (though this is left ambiguous), in modernism and postmodernism as they have been introduced into economics.

Dow's point of departure in much of her paper concerns the status of diverse schools of economic thought. In fact, her advocacy of a 'synthetic approach' rests more on her commitment to a particular notion of a 'school of thought' as coherent and mostly unified than on a complete exposition of the problems inherent within what she perceives to be modernism and postmodernism as they appear and are defended within economics. What I mean here is that Dow makes plain her concern, for example, that the possibility of rampant diversity or pluralism within a school of thought would be a contradiction in terms. Hence, for example, Dow argues that despite postmodernist claims to the contrary, there is always a limit to pluralism of 'vision of reality', epistemology, and certainly of method within any school of thought worthy of the name. Pluralism may be unbounded in the entire field of economic theory, but it has little or no place within any of the schools of thought that make up this field. If pluralism is the key term in postmodernism, and monism the key term in modernism, then the synthetic approach retains elements of both. Thus, in what is in fact a familiar and shared move in all three papers, Dow asserts that the third way she is championing is something that already exists and, in some ways, couldn't be otherwise since both modernists and postmodernists could never live up to the strong monist and/or pluralist positions on ontology, knowledge, and methodology that they pledge allegiance to (and then proceed to violate naively, guiltily, or with impassible intentionality).

Dow's rendition of the synthetic approach is a powerful one, and she is right in claiming that many modernists and certainly postmodernists will see themselves in her description of diversity, plurality, openness, and tolerance in their actual work, if not in their desires, but within largely modernist limits proscribed by belonging to one school of thought or another. Dow too stakes out a way ahead (though she is well-attuned to the problem with claims of progress) through her assertion that postmodernism, following modernism, is imploding – or at least this implosion is imminent and immanent. Indeed, with all of the necessity of the analogous Hegelian-inspired Marxist dialectic of history, Dow's synthetic approach is not just preferred (though it is), it is proven in the pudding, like it or not (and this reader claims to like it – at least more than modernist suet). But, along the way, as I have suggested, Dow treats certain modernist precepts as unexceptional, at least if one is to still have theoretical sciences, and postmodernist positions as extreme or nonsensical, if taken to so-called 'logical' conclusions. This is seen most acutely in her discussions of the necessity for schools of thought to be monist, even though the field of theory in a discipline can be pluralist without any necessary end.

Here, Dow is in direct contradiction to those who claim no particular unity at all inherent in loosely defined schools of thought. To the contrary, in these counterclaims, made by both modernists and postmodernists, unity is often viewed as the aggressive action of one approach to hegemonize the school (since the unity often reflects exactly that approach's internal protocols and procedures) through a supposed neutral 'description' of the present state of affairs. As a Marxist, I feel I could give lessons on such intra-disciplinary moves of inclusion and exclusion, since so much internecine struggle is precisely over what should be 'allowed' to be thought of as 'in' or 'out' of Marxism itself. I would have thought this to be true for Post-Keynesians as well, or indeed any other such school. To my way of thinking, there is no more artificiality or authenticity to any and every disciplinary boundary marker, school of thought included. Dow's view, for example, contrasts significantly with that of Stephen Resnick and Richard Wolff (1987), who understand well the fact that while boundary discussions may occupy so much of our time (and perhaps even rightly so), there is no need to claim that scientific, theoretical work depends crucially on uniformity in any aspect of a theory's composition (from vision of reality to method).

It is one thing to say that schools – loosely – may be perceived or self-identified as having a shared vision of reality, or at least what Resnick and Wolff have called an entry point into the real-in-thought. But, what this says is merely (and strongly) a comment on the perceived state of perception, the view (by some) that some agreements seem possible and appear to hold at a moment in time. What is provocative about Dow's view, though, is the implication that without such agreement, theory becomes impossible, as though, in her words, the proliferation of views within a school of thought (but not outside?) amounts to 'nothing can be said'. One can easily believe that there are conjunctures in which agreements exist and hold within and between perceived schools of thought. This is a matter of historical narrative, which I assume will be different, at least often, depending on who is doing the story-telling. Or sociological 'fact' (with all of the usual social constructionist caveats about such facts). But, this has little, if anything, to do with the true nature (read non-discursive – accessed by whom and how?) of reality within any school. And it certainly has little, if anything, to do with the necessity of unity as a requirement of scientific practice from within any so-called school.

However, in another way Dow is gesturing at a serious problem in versions of postmodernism that assert, as Dow nicely puts it, 'pure pluralism' (though how any postmodernist could be caught dead defending 'pure' anything is surely a question). It is true that some of us have, at times, drawn the incommensurability argument too tight, thus making it possible to be read as believing in the boundary limits that Dow is partly defending, at least in terms of the existence of heterodox economics. For, I think Dow is onto something in the view that the situation may be 'synthetic' or rather neither and both – in this case, schools of economic thought might be seen as porous, always leaking out and 'infecting' each other (and in this sense, always within each other), while they can be seen, for some purposes and from some perspectives, as distinctly different. It is the constant 'toggling', as both McCloskey and Klamer have liked to call it, between these views that seems to be in play in postmodernism, if not in the synthetic approach (which does seem to want to resolve the back and forth – the ambiguity).

Arjo Klamer attempts to move away from the modernism/postmodernism dualism also by seeking a third way. Yet, Klamer is less interested in periodizing this moving away since he accepts the idea that it may be best to think of modernism and postmodernism as 'moments' that can (but need not) occupy the same time and space within the field of economic thought. Likewise, Klamer's interest in what he calls 'neo-traditionalism', which avoids the 'modernist claim to capture the invariant' and also the 'postmodernist hypersensitivity to the overdetermined and complex character of everything existing', is located in the present, past, and future, living in a simultaneity with modern and postmodern moments. Klamer's transcendence scheme, then, is less orientated toward a historical dialectic (one certainly doesn't feel the force of the necessity for neo-traditionalism to succeed modernism and postmodernism) than it is toward a simple escape, though of course one can see in Klamer's construction of the neo-traditionalist alternative a kind of synthesis similar to Dow's of the 'best' of modern and postmodern moments.

More to the point, transcendence is not fanciful for Klamer since, like Dow and McCloskey, the alternative moment of neo-traditionalism always/already exists (or at least has been around in earlier forms of economic thinking since at least Adam Smith). If neo-traditionalism makes possible the recovery of the human subject, a loss or disappearance Klamer is certain has occurred with the rise to glory of Max U – the stick figure of mathematically-derived utility calculation now formalized to the extreme in new classical economics – then this move amounts really to a re-appreciation of the legacies of Smith and others who were concerned primarily with the moral character of economic agents. As is befitting the name, neo-traditionalism is established by reference back to traditions of thought about the moral character of economic agents, although Klamer accedes that the imperative to now do so is largely because of the introduction of fundamental uncertainty – a postmodern moment par excellence – into modernist economic models. In a Keynes/Shackle-like move, Klamer is clear that uncertainty may provide the necessary impetus to overcome both Samuelsonian modernist and new classical 'late modernist' mechanism and formalism, each of which reduce human action to robot-gestures requiring no thought at all to the moral constitution or outcomes of human subjectivity. The freedom once again to be a moral character may reside largely in the fact that fundamental uncertainty cannot be modeled mechanically or even formally, so that finally (and again) economic theory can treat the subject as having real choice.

Klamer's attempt to establish his third way is constructed as a rebirth of sorts of an older tradition in economic thinking, though with the postmodern twist of true uncertainty. There is much to recommend in Klamer's path toward revitalizing economics through explicitly moral and political discourse. And there is nothing particularly 'wrong' with this third way, that is, unless you are unconvinced that human subjectivity has taken the hit Klamer describes as one of the great disappearing acts attendant upon the rise since the 1970s of new classical theory (a view that is challenged in Amariglio and Ruccio, forthcoming). And unless you are less enamored of the 'return' to a 'respect for tradition, place, authority, values and roots' than is Klamer. And finally, unless you do not believe that a primary problem for economic theory is in being the decisive motivating force for agent action.

In fact, it is this last problem that motivates in large part the writing of all three papers, since there seems to be a common agreement (I think of this as a modernist bias that so many of us share) that action follows from thought, and that action without theory is either impossible or dangerous (or at least unpredictable – precisely!). On this last point, by now we can see that one familiar tenet for some postmodernists is the denial of the necessary primary effectivity of theory on human action. While Klamer is not comfortable with the 'overdetermined and complex character of everything existing', it is true that a commitment to thinking about the potentially infinite determinations of just about anything makes it impossible to privilege theory – economic or otherwise – as the key to morally preferable human action. To be fair, Klamer presents his concern in an ambiguous and, hence to me, interesting way. Klamer states: 'The question is what makes us act? The proposal…is to imagine action as a way of coping with a problem. Something is amiss, something is problematic, and we act to solve or remedy the problem'. And in this statement, we are uncertain ourselves if action is motivated by prior theorizing, by a conscious, rational choice to solve a problem, or if action happens and, among its effects, so-called 'problems' are addressed as a way of coping.

But, whether Klamer represents a good example or not, it still is the case that modernism hangs heavy in the discipline at large and even in the criticisms of economic modernism in the prejudice that theory (as McCloskey well notes, the specialized province in modernity claimed by intellectuals and other experts) always must precede action for it to accomplish any particular goal. The point of the postmodern caution is not that theory 'doesn't matter', a view that is similar to Dow's worry that 'nothing can be said'. It is, instead, to warn us against the modernist self-flattery that theory – and those who have it as opposed to those who don't – is both a scarce commodity and a primary, necessary means of production for a just (because rational) society. Theory matters, but it does so as part of a combinatory of causes and effects, and one of the postmodern moments possible for economics is to see any and every third way that is constituted as a theoretically-inspired master discourse or plan as less than what its avant-garde or traditionalist purveyors suggest is mandatory. Klamer is right to be unhappy with the unmediated attack on public activism and social intervention that he sees in the new classical economists' revolt against Keynesianism. But, to rethink the efficacy and advisability of any form of action argued for on theoretical grounds does not require the view – held by the Samuelsonian modernists, as Klamer and McCloskey astutely point out – that only professionals and experts trained in theoretical work can be relied upon to stimulate beneficial actions. And, more to the point, it does not require the view that theory is first and foremost the predecessor to human action, whether morally acceptable or not. While a third way may be transcendent then of the either/or-isms it finds in the modern/postmodern alternatives, to the extent that the third way requires a belief in the privilege of economic theory to motivate action, we haven't yet left one pole to even begin to explore the other.

Deirdre McCloskey's paper is situated in the hinge or joint of the problem of theory and action. McCloskey's third way – her way of transcending unacceptable either/ors – turns out to be rhetoric, though here rhetoric both is and is not given the label of postmodernism. And rhetoric makes visible to a heightened extent the problem of talk, action, and morality, the same issues found at the heart of Klamer's neo-traditionalism (McCloskey, of course, is counted among Klamer's adherents to this view). Yet, different from Klamer, rhetoric, which for some can be the hallmark of rationalism (at least in the sense that discourse matters and matters and matters), is rendered by McCloskey as something imperative (all we can do is talk to try to persuade and/or listen and be persuaded if we wish to avoid the authoritarianism of those who have 'the word') but also resistant – or at least it should be – to social engineering.

In McCloskey's view, social engineering – putting expert theory into practice by shaping society consciously (and mostly through the state) according to certain 'laws' or moral precepts – is a modernist outrage, even though it is not clear why she thinks that the rhetoricians among postmodernists would be less inclined to want to move people to social action and establish institutional structures through sweet persuasion. Be that as it may, rhetoric may not have the same status as 'theory' in modernist versions of these terms, but one certainly feels the force of McCloskey's pleas on behalf of argument and counterargument as a stimulus (a necessary one?) to individual and social action. Rhetoric does not escape the modernist bias of thinking that discourse – whether theoretically informed or not – is a prerequisite for moral behavior as well as decision and choice. But, as McCloskey shows colorfully, an appreciation of rhetoric does move us past other modernist biases that monumentalize some kinds of thought and talk in preference to others as the only acceptable bases for such behavior and action.

McCloskey's third way transcends by being identical to an eternal recurrence, the reiteration into the present of a battle between modernism and postmodernism. In this way, it is different from a more 'progressivist' version of synthesis, as can be seen in Dow. In fact, it is doubtful that McCloskey's third way attempts synthesis in the main, though she does in fact applaud, among other things, some modernist advances in economic theory. In this recurring struggle between modernism and postmodernism, which McCloskey traces through at least four iterations of modernism (moving backwards from 1910 to the

French Enlightenment to Descartes and finally, or originally, to Plato), rhetoric appears as unifying some if not all of the postmodernisms that were 'immanent' in their modernisms. Hence, as McCloskey describes it, the current postmodernism – with all its fancy Frenchisms, such as deconstruction – revisits the older scene of rhetorical reaction against Plato and all other philosopher-kings who have sought to halt discourse in the name of the best and last word on the topic. Yet, McCloskey's third way of rhetoric, while called 'postmodern', is also at a distance from some aspects of current postmodern theory, especially those that do not share McCloskey's view that free talk is morally equivalent and perhaps inextricably intertwined with free exchange.

McCloskey's postmodernism, then, surprisingly (for some) is announced in the name of the bourgeoisie, since it is clear that what McCloskey decries in the authoritarianism of past and present intellectual fascists is the 'aristocratic' bearing that they take on in marking the distance between themselves and those of lesser intellectual and moral stature. McCloskey's third way through rhetoric relives what she perceives perhaps to be the great socioeconomic struggle in the West since the ancient Greeks, that between nascent or full-blown capitalism, and those forms of feudalism that reduce to authoritarianism either with or without a centralized state (in this way, McCloskey is very close to Hayek in seeing communism as something that existed as a form of state-enforced serfdom). We leave for another time the problem, of course, of the questionable identification of markets and exchange with capitalism (this is certainly something that many Marxists would have serious misgivings about). We leave as well the fact that subsuming the struggles between modernisms and postmodernisms within a metanarrative of a world historical battle between the bourgeoisie and the aristocracy (at least as these are defined as 'social' or 'cultural' positions, if not economic ones) can be subject to postmodern criticism on numerous grounds, not the least of which is the lingering issue of the exact status of the working classes in all of this debate. McCloskey's third way is really a revival of classical liberalism, as she acknowledges, and it is distanced from current modernity only to the degree that one accepts the idea that freedom and choice and morality are blocked by the aristocrats who, in McCloskey's view, preside over Princeton and the Pentagon.

Rhetoric's homology with free market exchange calls up, as McCloskey wisely notes, reactions to what exactly is free (the opposite one supposes to 'coerced') about either talk or trade. Here, McCloskey may be seen to depart most fully from those postmodernists who have always been suspicious of concepts of freedom if what is meant by this is freedom from power and coercion. Unlike Foucault, for example, McCloskey's discussions of rhetoric continue to stress the 'sweetness' of it all, including the community of free thinkers and believers, who potentially converse in ways that recognize the right of the 'other' to exist as a talker and listener too. Again, McCloskey sees in free exchange such a similar rhetorical move, as trade establishes civility and even compassion (via a Smithian sympathy). McCloskey is used to, by now, challenges to her defense of persuasion and markets as too innocent and unconcerned with issues of power and exploitation. She demonstrates this in her rebuff to those (she claims they are modernists) who see coercion in rhetoric, no different from modernist science, and confound, in her view, that 'a gun is different from a denial of promotion'. Leaving aside the caricature upon which this dismissal is based (the deck is certainly stacked), one can certainly wonder if there is an obvious set of values to which we all ascribe that would always answer the question of which is the lesser of two evils. Of course, once we insert denial of a job or housing or education or whatever for 'promotion' in this sentence, we see that the choice with which we are faced can be less obvious for some. That is, if it is true that rhetoric assures nothing in particular (nor does free exchange) that these denials of job, etc. may be outcomes of rhetorical and trading practices (a view I hold), then it is less frivolous than we might first think to wonder about and interrogate the forms of exclusion and coercion that can exist with and constitute persuasion and exchange.

In this sense, McCloskey is right when she says that her advocacy of the rhetorical approach can be different from other current postmodernisms that see in most capitalisms, no less than most communisms, forms of modernism that would better be left for dead. But, economic theory aside (and here, Dow may be right when she notes that people who agree on the need for a plurality of views can disagree on matters of theory stemming from their adherence to one school or another of economic thought), McCloskey's third way has as much right to claim ownership of the label postmodernism – and also to transcend this label through a critical distance. McCloskey's postmodernism consists largely of a thoroughgoing rebuttal of so much of modernist huffing and puffing, as McCloskey notes, about such things as "discipline" and "rigor" and "compelling proof", in a vocabulary approaching the sadomasochistic'. McCloskey's punchline – similar to Dow's – is that 'when it gets down to the whips and chains', modernists are not able to carry through is based again on the perception that modernism is strictly impossible, and that in the end what most modernist economists do engage in is rhetorical practice anyway.

It is interesting that Dow, Klamer, and McCloskey all pursue third ways that turn out to be there all along. Transcendence through the familiar. Perhaps in some way this is the fate of all transcendence schemes, even those that announce themselves as 'the new'. To show that one need not ever leave Kansas in order to, well, leave Kansas. Dow, Klamer, and McCloskey produce here three compelling stories about the ways modernism and even postmodernism may leave those looking for relief from either/or-ism lukewarm, if not cold. The warmth of some home is surely inviting. But then, we can wonder if the desire to be elsewhere and home at the same time is fulfilled by the alternatives they sketch. Perhaps at least a visit is in order. In each case, in my view, it would do economic modernists, and some postmodernists as well, a world of good to take the trip.

References

Amariglio, Jack, and Ruccio, David F. (forthcoming) 'Modern Economics: The Case of the Disappearing Body?', *Cambridge Journal of Economics*.

Berman, Marshall (1982) *All That Is Solid Melts Into Air: The Experience of Modernity*, New York: Simon and Schuster.

Montaigne, Michel de (1958) *Essays*, trans. J. M. Cohen, Harmondsworth, Middlesex: Penguin.

Resnick, Stephen A., and Wolff, Richard D. (1987) *Knowledge and Class: A Marxian Critique of Political Economy*, Chicago: University of Chicago Press.

PART III

READING SYMBOLS, CHANGING SUBJECTS AND DISCERNING BODIES IN ECONOMIC DISCOURSE

6
FROM UNITY TO DISPERSION
The body in modern economic discourse

Jack Amariglio and David F. Ruccio

The body (in economics) vanishes?

Here is one story about the body and its relation to the history of economic discourse. From the early beginnings of modern economics in the late eighteenth century to the early decades of the twentieth century, economic theory was grounded in different but explicit theories of the body, its disposition, and its effects. The classical political economists, from Adam Smith to John Stuart Mill, were inclined to formulate the categories and concepts of economic analysis as expressions of personal sensations and sensibilities, regardless of whether the individuals thus constituted by the senses were perceived as entities whose bodies' unity could be organized and represented by their desires or, alternatively, by their capacity to labor. The birth of modern economics, therefore, saw the corporeal, sensate body elevated to the privileged status of a first principle. The virtue of classical political economy, in this story, is that it was a coherent, centered discourse in which the 'whole human', with all his/her natural sentiments, emotions, affections, and sensations – nowhere better presented than in Smith's *Theory of Moral Sentiments* (1759) – became the organizing principle to understand, traverse the landscape of, and manipulate individual bodies within the social body.

In contrast to the period of the birth of modern economics, as this story continues, the formalization of economic thought during the twentieth century, in conjunction with the rise to predominance of the neoclassical school of thought, has subsequently pushed the question of the body to (and perhaps beyond) the margins. While presumably originating from the idea of the desiring body – the body that seeks to maximize utility in all domains of economic activity – whose very fluidity is controlled and channeled by the rational mind, neoclassical economics has increasingly obscured the nature and effects of bodily desire as it has moved in the direction of axiomatizing the rules of human behavior. As our storytellers would have it, the human subject –

the thinking, feeling, working organic individual, the 'sympathetic' and 'prudent' individual whose body comprises chapter after chapter of Smith's *Moral Sentiments* – has simply disappeared in the contemporary neoclassical clamor for parsimony, simplicity, and elegance in high theoretical (read: mathematical) expression. In an interesting development, the aesthetics of high modernism – in economics, associated largely with the norms imposed by the application of calculus, topology, set theory, and, more recently, game theory – came to dominate the very constitution of scientific economic discourse itself, determining largely not only the form but also the content of economic concepts and forms of analysis.

The formalization of economic discourse in this century has thus come at a cost: human bodies are no longer recognizable as the site at which the various economic 'capacities' and 'functions' do their work. The full discussion of sensation and sentiment, passions and interests which informed so much of the theoretical legacy handed down to today's economists is not so much reduced in importance with the onset of axiomatization as it is completely ignored or even renounced as extraneous to the methods and procedures of contemporary economics. The 'scientizing' of economics in the twentieth century jettisoned the human body and its complicated excesses from the domain of legitimate economic discussion and debate.

In seeking the origins of this displacement and even obliteration of the human body and, with it, a 'full' human subject in contemporary economics, our storytellers point especially to the period after the Second World War during which economics reached its high modern, formalist stage (which, we should add, has yet to pass). One of the key players in this movement to finally discard the human body as the appropriate foundation for economic discourse was Paul Samuelson. In his *Foundations of Economic Analysis* (1948), published shortly after the war, Samuelson tried to carry through to completion, and thus bring to a close, earlier attempts to displace 'value theory' (the theory or theories of the origin and primary causes of economic value or price) from its prior importance in economic thought. The move to 'hide' the body can be seen to result to some degree from the embarrassment Samuelson and other neoclassical economists (such as John Hicks and R. G. D. Allen [1934]) felt in being inscribed within an economic discourse that had at the center of its analysis the desiring body or psyche as the initiating, first cause of economic value. Samuelson's famous 'revealed preference' theoretical approach to demand theory (originally presented in 1938 and further elaborated in 1948 and 1950), and therefore his demonstration that the theoretical determination of price did not logically require 'unobservable' utility as the premise from which all other concepts need derive, removed for many economists the last remaining link to the more corporeal and psychological theories of the eighteenth- and nineteenth-century utilitarian predecessors, for whom, as this story goes, the body was a central preoccupation. Increasingly, and partly upon Samuelson's example, neoclassical economists since the 1940s have treated the question of the body's place in determining or even registering the effects of economic activities as 'exogenous' to the main tasks of economic theory. Among other things, the claim that a theory of the body and its order did not need to be part and parcel of a properly 'economic' analysis may explain the disdain some US economists expressed in encountering Keynes's investment theory of the 1930s and 1940s, which reduced the portfolio decisions of entrepeneurs, in the end, to 'animal spirits' (and, therefore, to that which is most base because it suggests the power of the body to supersede rationality in cases where reason simply fails). Bluntly stated, it appears that for many modern economists since Samuelson the study of the body and its many effects within economic discourse has vanished or has been driven underground or has simply been ignored.

In this critical narrative, the transitional moment in the 'fall from grace' was the emergence in Europe in the 1860s and 1870s of the neoclassical paradigm. The neoclassical revolution, which instated a marginalist approach to all economic categories capable of being quantified, took over from the classicals the utilitarian premise regarding the centrality of the desiring body for economic theory. Yet, it is also true that the different renditions of marginal utility or *rareté* that were put forward by Carl Menger, W. Stanley Jevons, Léon Walras, and others were accompanied by at least two significant departures from the classicals. First, utility was clearly raised to an exclusive initiating cause so that the inscription within economic theory of labor as a primary source of value (found to varying degrees in Smith, David Ricardo, Mill, and others) was mostly eschewed. It is interesting to note that Jevons is known to have toyed with the idea of labor as a source of value (White, 1994: 220) but, in his landmark *Theory of Political Economy* (1871), he moved instead to the view that labor and the decisions concerning its use, efficacy, and expenditure (its cost) could be reduced mostly to a question of bodily desire – in this case, to the disutility (the pain) that a subject would endure in the time s/he allotted to work. In any event, the marginalist revolution was the occasion for a rupture with previous 'objective' theories of value in which the laboring body was seen as the privileged origin (or, at least, one of several prime causes) for the determination of value, price, profit, and much else. Desire and the mental calculation of utility and disutility (in Jevons's text, of pleasure and pain) replaced energetic and labor expenditure as the body's determinant cause, at least in the context of the choices that were available to subjects regarding how to utilize their bodies in ways that could bring ultimate satisfaction in consumption, production, and so forth.

Second, as Philip Mirowski (1991) has so carefully shown – and for many critics this is the crux of the matter – the neoclassicals sought to model their new marginalist theoretical apparatus on nineteenth-century mechanics and energetics. In this regard, Jevons and Walras certainly stand out in proselytizing for a thorough-going mathematization of the field of economics in line with contemporaneous changes wrought in the studies of motion and energy. The notion of calculating most economic quantities at the margin, amenable to and best expressed in modern calculus, was joined to the concepts of equilibrium and much else that was borrowed, in some cases wholesale, from nineteenth-century physics. The mathematics and physics envy emboldened neoclassical economists to think of re-establishing their discipline (or, at least, large parts of it) on a modern scientific basis. Such a move required the shift in deriving and expressing economic concepts in more 'imprecise' notions of social and economic value – grounded in a discourse in which the body in its many aspects and appearances was present – to representing the changes in language and conceptual framework in more recent recognizably scientific trappings. This strong belief that science required quantifiable entities and formal analysis for its primary legitimacy was responsible, therefore, for a fetishism of mathematics that has since run amok in modern economics.

Yet, despite the insistence on utilizing mathematical formulations that worked primarily for and with objectively quantifiable entities, the founders of neoclassicism curiously insisted on the principle of utility which they were soon forced to admit was anything but representable in 'objective' terms. The subjective value theory which was enshrined then with the neoclassical revolution was and continued to be a sore spot for those economists in subsequent years who were determined to rid economics of all nonscientifically established (read: empirically observable or verifiable) concepts and terms. Nineteenth-century neoclassical economics, then, only marked a partial transition from the classicals in as much as it allowed economic theory to be thought of as having a point of origin in a theory of value and as it sought to ground this theory of value in some metaphysical discussion of the desiring body. Thus, for early neoclassicals, the body was foreshortened in its dimensions and effects (at least in so far as value determination is concerned: labor and all other actions and sensibilities relevant to economic theory largely became subcategories of utility, just as utility became less and less dependent on a full-blown psychological theory for its expression). Desire became a primary cause, but it was tendentiously linked with the equally strong interest of neoclassical economists to organize the field of economic discourse into a modern scientific discipline. As the developments in the twentieth century have demonstrated, the desiring body became more oblique and extraneous to the scientific concepts and protocols of economic theory. And so, while the early neoclassicals may have intended otherwise, the revolution they set off has led to the current state in which the body has, for the most part, disappeared in economic analysis.

The differential 'orders' of the body

The preceding is a story that we have heard quite frequently (albeit in a variety of forms and registers) in talking with other critics of mainstream, particularly neoclassical, economic theory. Our view is that this story is deficient in some important respects. One goal of our work, then, is to recompose this story into something different. Anticipating somewhat our conclusion, we believe that no such disappearing act has occurred in the two hundred years of passage through modern economics. To the contrary, our reading of the traditions discussed above indicates to us simply that mainstream and neoclassical economic discourses have proffered distinct 'orders' of the body in each of the three phases of modernism in economics. Or, to put this differently, we discern different conceptions of the body, and perhaps different places within discourse that the body has appeared, in the constitution of these phases. To help illuminate our view, we call attention first to several aspects of the above story that stand in contrast to our own reading.

First, the historical narrative offered above is constructed as a teleology. As we have represented it, the story's structure is familiar in that it proceeds like all historical narratives that seek or trace a progressive regression or, as we put it, a deepening fall from grace. Historians of economic thought, regardless of their training within and allegiance to whatever school of economics, are often prone to tell their stories of changes in economic thinking or to trace movements in the discipline as either culmination or descent. The normative elements of the story of the downfall of economics in regard to the disappearance of the body – and, with it, of human subjectivity – are apparent in the narrative of regression. The differences among 'leading' economists, or between the parts of their work within each of the historical phases, are swept away by forcefitting the 'key developments' in economic discourse into the constraints of the narrative of expulsion and exile from Eden. Modernity, in economics, emerges as a progressive nightmare, one in which the 'whole subject' and his/her 'real' self – a living, breathing, needing and thinking subject – is replaced by theoretical and formal abstraction. Indeed, the teleology of this story gives rise to the view that the victory of 'humanity' represented by the Enlightenment has been dismantled and deconstructed to such a degree, at least in economics, that simultaneously precise but shapeless functions and forms are now hailed in preference to the messy but distinct corporeality and subjectivity that were the innovations of the birth of the modern age in the seventeenth and eighteenth centuries.

In our reading of the history of economic thought, such a teleology has no place. As we describe below, there is neither a simple (or even complex) progression or regression on questions of the body in economics over the past two centuries. Measured according to a different scale, the passage of mainstream neoclassical economics through various discursive forms has not meant the displacement of the body or of subjectivity. Nor, for that matter, has it meant the increasing unreality of representations of the body (as we discuss below, the fragmentation of the body and the emergence within contemporary neoclassical thinking of a body without center or origin can be thought of, ironically, as more in tune with recent 'postmodern' cultural representations of the body and subjectivity). Our reading suggests that relatively discrete views of the body and its order and distribution have existed within mainstream economics and each can be seen, from different vantage points, as either a development or retrogression in theories of the body.

Let us put this last point differently. Since we do not have in mind a particular notion of the body and its order (or orders) as 'correct' or as corresponding to any specific historically determined objective reality, we have no interest in preserving the idea that contemporary neoclassicals have systematically misrepresented or displaced 'the body'. Based upon our reading of several representative texts and our adherence to a Foucauldean notion of the constitution of bodies within particular discursive formations, we find no basis for the claim that one representation of the body in the history of economics is empirically grounded, closer to or better able to capture 'actual' human behavior, than others. The view that allows critics of neoclassicism to detect the disappearance of the human body from economic discourse is one that often presumes that an observer would know the body in its appearances in economic theory if s/he did in fact see it. As Louis Althusser (Althusser and Balibar, 1977: 158–93) argued in relation to Marx's privileged 'sight' regarding the errors of Smith and Ricardo, the ability to see or not to see a body in discourse depends primarily on the discursive 'problematic' that is employed. It is not a matter of discovering, and therefore of producing an economic discourse which adequately captures, the always-already existing body by performing a magical act of conjuration. It is rather a matter of seeing that there is no fixity to the body and its forms of appearance as we move from one discourse to another. Thus, the view that the human body must be presented as a whole rather than dispersed, as sensual instead of ethereal, congealed and not fluid, bounded and not excessive, prevents the possibility of 'seeing' the body's appearance in economic discourses, such as contemporary neoclassicism, in which previous conceptions of sense, sensibility, psychology, and much else are pushed to the background.

This brings us to our second observation, and our second objection to the story of the disappearance of the body from modern economics. It must be remarked that this story is, of course, one that shapes many criticisms of and the framing of alternatives to neoclassical economic discourse. That is, it is a narrative that arises in Austrian, institutionalist, radical, Marxian, feminist, post-Keynesian, and other 'heterodox' discursive traditions within economics. Despite differences of emphasis and detail, the common thread in all such criticisms of mainstream theory is that economics has moved increasingly over the past century, and especially in the postwar period, away from the observable and that which can be intuited about actual human beings and their behavior. What we find usually in most of these critical traditions is the charge that neoclassicals – with their preference for formalization, abstraction, and 'elegant' results, and their desire to celebrate free markets – have lost the 'real' human being as the agent of economic activity and behavior. Small wonder, then, that the story of the neoclassical fall from grace is dependent on a nostalgia for a time, located roughly in the early days of classical political economy (or in Marx or in the early institutionalists such as Thorstein Veblen), in which human beings and their fully corporeal bodies were the point of departure and ground for economic analysis. From this standpoint, the debates over objective versus subjective theories of value in exchange or over the laboring body versus the desiring body (in other words, over labor versus utility) as the origin of economic activities and institutions (and, therefore, of economic categories) are of greater pertinence and reality than today's axiomatizing would allow for. The classical economists, and certainly the Smith of the *Moral Sentiments*, are hailed in terms of their respect for and understanding of the complex ways in which human bodies are constituted as economic agents.

This nostalgia for the true humanist beginnings of modern economics is one we do not share. In addition to our belief that the concept of the human body has no particular form of representation that correctly captures the state of human existence (whether actual or desirable), we think that the humanism which informs the critics of neoclassicism is problematic in numerous ways. We have registered our objections to humanism both within and outside of economics in several places (Amariglio 1987, 1988, 1990; Ruccio 1988, 1991). Here we note that the notion of the centered subject in which sense experience or rational control of the body or desire or affection or any other presumed attribute of human bodies is seen as the essential and often natural determinant of the unity of the body has a long and varied history. While some of that history has been one of 'liberation', as Michel Foucault, Althusser,

Etienne Balibar, and others have rightly shown, it is also one in which the notion of the 'true' human body is notorious for its complicity in some of the more heinous exercises of power and violence of the modern age. These include not only the forms of discipline and punishment that are recorded in Foucault's writings, but also the definitions and practices to seek out and control deviance that have structured Western knowledge from the birth of modern psychology to theories of colonial administration. That the early modern notions of the 'normal' and/or 'natural' human body and its essentialized effects have played critical roles in the elaboration of gender, race, class, and sexual differences and their perversions is by now well established in the humanities and social sciences.

In any event, we do not find the views of the body proffered by classical political economists (or, for that matter, by Marxists or institutionalists) to be 'fuller' or more descriptive of reality in any sense, and we certainly hold no hope for criticisms of the neoclassical school that chastises it for its possible abandonment of the idea of the 'truly human'. Indeed, there is a certain refreshing quality to recent neoclassical thinking in that it mostly displaces the question of the body as origin and proliferates, instead, a differentiated, fragmented body according to various functions which do not necessarily impinge upon or govern each other. To say this differently, we are interested and regard with some degree of approval the appearance of a body in high-level neoclassical theory (as, for example, in Gerard Debreu's *Theory of Value* 1959, or in Kenneth Arrow and Frank Hahn's *General Competitive Analysis* 1971), of bodily functions and capabilities (of consumption, production, and distribution, not to mention, in subsequent works by them and other neoclassicals, the formation of institutions, strategic interaction, and so forth), that only obliquely relate to a central, unifying dimension. In these theoretical formulations, consumption, production, and so on emerge as composites of various elements and, as separable realms, do not inform one another either in their respective determinations (the consuming body, or its functions, can be rendered independent of the producing body, or its functions) or in their respective effects (outcomes of these discrete functions imply nothing about the unity that may be presumed to hold them together). The dispersed map of the body that some contemporary neoclassical economists have produced is one that can lead to a distinctly nonessentialist view of the body and its inscription within both discourse and society. While it may still be true that there is often an obligatory nod to the 'rational/desiring/maximizing subject' as the appropriate agent in contemporary neoclassical theory, it is also true, in our view, that the consequence of axiomatizing economic behavior has been to render as discrete and distributed the forms of behavior – and thus to attribute agency to these forms themselves – that are henceforth being described.

This, we think, is precisely the importance of general equilibrium theory for neoclassical economists: it serves to coordinate (at least in principle) the various dimensions or behaviors of the body, and thus the different agencies attached to such bodily orders, at a level separate from any individual body. The insistent expressions of admiration for the 'refinement' and 'power' of the Arrow-Debreu model betray a certain nervousness that, once value is unhinged from the 'deep' structure of the classical and early neoclassical laboring and/or desiring bodies, a set of prices and agent plans that would reconcile the economic agencies dispersed throughout the economic space might not (logically) exist. In this sense, contemporary neoclassicals' own narratives of theoretical continuity (not to mention improvement) from Smith's 'invisible hand' through Walras's 'equation counting' to the axiomatic logic of postwar general equilibrium theory are not only teleological but disingenuous: while all three systems can be said to demonstrate the existence of coherence and harmony within a market/capitalist economy (in contrast, for example, to the tension and conflict portrayed in Marxian and other approaches), the conception of the body for which each serves as the expression and 'solution' is fundamentally different. In the case of contemporary neoclassicals, the attempt to break both from the complex, prereconciled individual agent of the classicals and from the hierarchically arranged 'psychologistic' or 'rational' subject portrayed by the early marginalists in order to create what they considered to be a mathematically sophisticated, more scientific conception of value, one that did not simply represent the 'unobservable' internal order of the body, required a new approach. It is the search for this new approach, and then its refinement and further elaboration, which has dominated neoclassical theory in the postwar period.

One of the important conditions, as we have noted above, for this 'problem' to emerge was the discomfiture occasioned by the seeming identification of value with an inner (physiological and/or psychological) pleasure-seeking drive on the part of market participants. The great merit of Samuelson's contribution, whether or not it can be judged ultimately successful on strictly behavioralist grounds,[1] was to focus attention on the conditions associated with or required by consumer choice rather than the extent to which the actions of economic agents could be said to be governed by, and thus to adequately represent, some set of underlying processes. In Samuelson's own words:

> there has been a shift in emphasis away from the physiological and psychological hedonistic, introspective aspects of utility. Originally great importance was attached to the ability of goods to fill basic biological needs; but in almost every case this view has undergone extreme modification. At the same time, there has

been a similar movement away from the concept of utility as a sensation, as an introspective magnitude.

(1948: 91)

Initial pretensions to the contrary,[2] Samuelson's approach does not completely foretell of the disappearance of utility – that magnificently dense concept which, in the history of economics, has been rendered differently according to whether the 'body' or the 'mind' (either separately or in combination) was in favor as the privileged origin of all consequent economic behavior:

> It is not merely that the modern economist replaces experienced sensation or satisfaction with anticipated sensation, desire, according to the now familiar distinction between *ex post* and *ex ante* analysis. But much more than this, many writers have ceased to believe in the existence of any introspective magnitude or quantity of a cardinal, numerical kind. With this skepticism has come the recognition that a cardinal measure of utility is in any case unnecessary; that only an ordinal preference, involving 'more' or 'less' but not 'how much', is required for the analysis of consumer's behavior.
>
> (1948: 91)

Still, as Samuelson himself perhaps saw coming, the substitution of 'ordinal' for 'cardinal' utility was only one important step in the move to the eventual denunciation of any recourse to the desiring body in producing economic analysis as a theory of choice.

In our view, revealed preference theory (along with the proof of its weak or strong equivalence to ordinal utility scales or indifference curves) created the conditions for invoking a 'flat' body, one without depth. Subsequently, in many quarters of neoclassicism, there would be nothing but the surface, the (internally consistent) choices made in each particular context based on the feasible alternatives available and the relevant constraints. Or as Amartya Sen has formulated it, the binary relations that are the 'stuff' of rational choice would come to be seen as *reflections* of choice rather than *determinants* of it (1990: 202).

One way of understanding the effects of the neoclassical axiomatization of economic behavior, then, is to see it as having turned the body inside out. Instead of attempting to discover the hidden, because internal, driving force or self-regulating principles of the body, it has derived the body from its externality. The focus of neoclassical value theory has, in this sense, moved to the outside, to the ways in which choices are displayed on, rather than emanating from deep within, the observable planes and superficies of the body. Departing both from the classicals, for whom what was interesting and important about the body was its ability to organize and order its various rational, emotional, and physical needs and impulses, and from the early neoclassicals, for whom the body was moved and directed by the intensity of its potential energy, later neoclassical economists focused on the diverse and separable behaviors and functions of the body as they are revealed in their interactions with external objects.

If this 'second marginalist revolution' of Samuelson and company began the process of dissociating consumer demand (and economic decision-making more generally) from the 'amount' of utility felt or envisioned by economic agents, it also created the problem of seemingly unhinging the determination of value itself from its original human(ist) origins. Value could no longer be said to be caused by or to represent the internal order or force of the body, whether labor (embodied or commanded) or desire; instead, it was conceived to be a consequence of the consistency among otherwise uncoordinated actions and plans of different agents. The project taken up by Arrow, Debreu, and other neoclassical economists from the 1950s onward was how to fragment and distribute the body across the economic space, invoking one or another of the various bodily orders or functions where appropriate, and, at the same time, to determine the conditions under which a 'competitive equilibrium' for such an economy could be said to exist.

The proposed (general equilibrium) solution has become the standard for all subsequent developments in neoclassical theory. In its simplest formulations, the economy is divided into two groups of agents: producers (or firms) and consumers (or households). Avoiding unnecessary detail (and purposely shunning the mathematical formalisms prevalent in this literature), we can see that the role of producers is to choose a production plan (quantities of inputs and outputs) from the feasible set of production plans (determined by the available technology) in order to maximize profits. Consumers, on the other hand, are characterized by a set of preference relations (defined over the entire set of available commodities); their goal is to choose a consumption plan to which none is preferred, subject to the constraint that their total expenditures not exceed their total wealth. Once the total resources are introduced, and under various sets of restrictions on technology and the choice criterion, it is possible to show that a set of prices exists according to which all agents can carry out their respective plans.

This relatively simple 'economy' can be, and has been, refined and extended (becoming, we should add, a veritable neoclassical industry) to include a wide variety of additional dimensions: uncertainty, savings, capital, international trade, exchange, and so on. Our point is not to review the history or what are considered to be the respective successes and failures of general equilibrium theory.[3] Rather, we hope to explain the sense in which, if only in a preliminary fashion, the body has not only *not* disappeared from the Arrow-Debreu model but that the multiple ways in which bodies are implicitly assumed and explicitly summoned presage what we mean by a postmodern conception of the body. We should note that whatever body is presumed by and/or produced through this axiomatic treatment of value is likely not the unified, 'natural' body which was invoked as the ground for economic discourse in earlier periods (and, as we show below, by other schools of thought today). To presume such a body is to misrecognize other discursive existences of the body, to rule out from the start the presence of other bodies.

What we are interested in, then, is what happens to readers when they confront the theorems, equations, and verbal explanations in and through which the Arrow-Debreu model is presented. What do we see, what kind of narrative do we construct? In particular, what images of the body emerge from our engagement with the text? In many cases, as we have discussed above, readers do not see a body at all – or at least a body which conforms to their expectations. Therefore, in searching for a particular set of familiar images, they conclude that the body is missing. Our own reading is, as we have indicated, quite different: because we refuse to make assumptions about a 'naturalized' or 'full' body, and thus a body which must serve as a ground for representation in economic discourse, we come away with a rich and diverse set of corporeal images. Therefore, in our view, neoclassical value theory does represent an extended allegory about the mechanisms and capabilities of the body.

We can see this in the treatment of both the 'producer' and the 'consumer'. As we follow the presentation of the nature and role of each in the texts of neoclassical theory, we are struck by the extent to which they are treated as distinct, 'relatively autonomous' sites in which various and differentiated bodily orders reside and function. Producers, for example, are often defined as operating within a commodity space in which inputs are transformed into outputs according to technological possibilites and the rule of profit-maximization. Clearly – and this we grant to the critical stories concerning neoclassical theory we referred to above – this kind of 'activity' analysis (and the 'netput' vector conception of the location of the results of production in commodity space) rules out some of the most famous bodies that have populated the history of treatments of production. We do not find, for example, the value-creating laboring bodies of classical theory or the pain-avoiding bodies of the early neoclassicals – or, for that matter, the heroic entrepeneurs of the Austrian economists. Indeed, the familiar outlines of laboring, pleasure-seeking, and entrepeneurial bodies, along with the (legal, sectoral) boundaries of the enterprise itself, tend to fade into the background or disappear altogether. What does emerge, however, is a different set of bodily functions, for example, those associated with the meticulous bookkeeping necesssary (if only implicitly) to choose, from among all the possible production sets, those that meet the criterion of profit maximization. Without this practice of accounting, of keeping track of inputs and outputs (and their respective 'given' prices), no choice of profit-maximizing production plans would be possible. Perhaps even more important (certainly in terms of explicit discussion), we see the bodily orders and capabilities associated with the assembly, transformation, repackaging, and so on of one set of objects (inputs) in order to end up with a different set of objects (outputs, including new potential inputs for the next round of production). Neoclassical production is thus rendered as a collection or assemblage of heterogeneous elements and materials, a set of operational linkages and external relations between things, machine connections (if not a 'whole' machine), in which a discontinuous series of bodily organs, processes, and flows (for example, 'the labor of a coal miner, of a truck driver, of a member of some category of teachers, of engineers, of draftsmen, of executives, etc.' [Debreu, 1959: 30–1]) come together with other things (the divisible 'raw materials, semifinished products; land and equipment or their uses...at various dates and locations' [1959: 38]) according to the available codes, the technologies of production.

It is the characteristics of these codes which tend to receive the most attention in neoclassical theories of production. Here we find the ubiquitous discussions of the assumptions, conventions, and restrictions required to define a 'closed, convex cone' of production possibilities. Technology, in this scheme, plays the dual role of being an extension of the body, the ability to coordinate the alignment of services and other inputs at particular points in space and time in order to produce ouputs, and a way of writing on the body, to the extent that neoclassical economists have taken on the project of specifying the rules that these technologies must adhere to so that firms' output supply functions assume the appropriate forms. In the first case, then, the technical codes invoke a body or corporeal agency which determines the possible linkages among and between factor services and (produced and nonproduced) inputs. In the second case, the body operates as a surface on which the requirements proposed by the theorists can be inscribed. Both are central to the neoclassical theory of production.

What is apparent (at least to us) in this treatment is that production itself is deprived of any depth (with respect to other, classical or early neoclassical theories, that is). It serves merely to determine a particular vector of outputs from the set of all possible outputs. Production is not conceived to be governed, for example, by the bodily imperative of reproduction (as it was for the classicals and still is for the Sraffians) or of the body's experience of pain or disutility (which could be compensated by a corresponding increase in utility in consumption for Jevons and the other early neoclassicals). Instead, the realm of production in contemporary neoclassical theory consists of a diverse set of bodily functions and activities – the calculations of profit-maximizing conditions, the flows and intensities of factor services, the ability to assemble or bring together disparate body movements and objects, and so on – which have no 'underlying' purpose or 'compensating' relief other than to move from one point to another through commodity space. In our view, then, neoclassical economists' theory of production, in eschewing both the unity of a single 'productive' or 'entrepeneurial' body and any hierarchy of functions and requirements, creates an open-ended terrain in which distinct and separate bodily orders literally meet and engage in activities that result in the supply of new commodity outputs.

What, then, on the consumer side? Here we encounter, once again, a diverse set of bodily surfaces that are written on and of bodily functions and orders that are invoked as economic agencies in their own right. We recall that the role of consumers in neoclassical theory is to choose, from the array of available commodities, a plan of consumption whose monetary value is less than or equal to their total wealth. That wealth derives from the sale of factor services and any other goods to, plus the receipt of profits (if and when they are shareholders) from, producers. Consumers' bodies therefore enact a variety of different agencies. For example, they are conceived to be endowed with, and thus are capable of performing, factor services. According to Arrow and Hahn (1971: 75), 'among the endowments of the household, the most important in practice are the capacities to perform different types of labor'. The kind and amount of labor that any consumer decides to demand and supply are seen to be constrained by such factors as the kinds of skills they possess, the amount of time of which they dispose, and their ability to withstand the 'arduousness' of the tasks involved. Consumers are not only characterized by the ability to furnish and execute labor services; they also enjoy nonlaboring time in the form of leisure. Thus, for example, if a consumer is capable of teaching for 12 hours, s/he can decide to teach for 8 hours and enjoy 'teaching leisure' for 4 hours (ibid.). In addition, since consumption is assumed to take time, consumers are, in effect, conceived to pass through or enact different bodily orders during any given period of time (day, year, or lifetime): they can perform some or all of different kinds of labor, spend their time not working, and/or consume commodities. Each of these activities is based on qualitatively different and changing capabilities and orders of the body, various processes, intensities, and organs, as an individual passes through and experiences each of these ways of spending time. Presumably, the only thing that the different orders and combinations of laboring/not working/consuming bodies have in common is that they have to endure, enjoy, and so on these activities within the constraints of the available time.

FROM UNITY TO DISPERSION

Not surprisingly – given the importance they attribute to consumer choice and, at the same time, their aversion to invoking the inner, 'psychologistic' assumptions of early neoclassical theory – neoclassicals devote the major part of their time in this area to discussing the conditions under which consumers decide how much and what kinds of (net) labor services to offer and commodities to purchase. The focus here is on the nature of the preference (pre)orderings that are seen to guide and thus to be expressed in the choices that consumers make. Thus, 'the preference ordering of the ith consumer completely expresses his tastes with regard to food, clothing, housing...labor and also to consumption at some date or some location rather than another' (Debreu, 1959: 54). As in the case of technology, consuming bodies are invoked in two different senses: on one hand, they consist of the specific and differentiated tastes or preferences, the particular consumption codes, whereby individuals express their interest in performing factor services and in consuming outputs over all possibilities; on the other hand, they represent the material on which neoclassical economists can write the appropriate codes (expressed, e.g., as insatiability, continuity, and convexity) such that the resulting demands and supplies are 'well behaved'. The importance of these codes is that it becomes unnecessary to peer inside, to invoke any kind of deep structure of 'utility' which can be said to govern, the bodies of consumers. Instead, the utility functions that consumers are seen to 'maximize' are merely the numerical representations of their stated (or revealed) preferences. In this sense, everything that consumers do (or are restricted to do) resides on the surface.

Of course, the focus on the choices that consumers make in the different domains of offering factor services and demanding commodities, constrained solely by wealth or budgetary considerations (along with restrictions on preference orderings), leaves open the possibility that the separable decision units, and hence the bodily functions to which they refer, may not cohere in any simple or smooth fashion. A similar issue arises in the case of production: even in the presence of technological codes which serve to align the bodies and inputs so that a profit-maximizing netput vector can be said to exist, the different bodily orders may operate with greater or lesser degrees of autonomy than a unified, fully machine-like, body would allow. In both cases, we may observe what Jon Elster (1986) has referred to as the 'multiple self'. Elster, who is far from being a critic of neoclassicism and its conception of methodological individualism and rational choice, and the other contributors to his important edited volume recognize that when the unified, singular body (as traditionally understood) is fragmented into different orders or functions and scattered within any individual sphere and throughout the economic space as a whole (as we have seen in general equilibrium theory), a wide variety of possible new agencies emerge.

And when economists (and other rational choice theorists) attempt to account for the interaction among and between these body parts, they begin to challenge the usual presumption of combination and coordination, leading to a proliferation of forms of disunity – from the 'loosely integrated self' to an infinitely fragmented, 'no self' conception of the body. In our view, it is precisely the attempt on the part of Samuelson, Arrow, Debreu, and others to displace the deep, hierarchical ordering of the body in favor of theories of consumption, production, and distribution based on the horizontal linkages among a wide variety of bodily functions that leads to a view of the differentiated and dispersed (what we prefer to call a postmodern) body.[4]

Marxian, post-Keynesian, and feminist resurrections of the classical body

We compare this fragmentation and diffusion with the view put forward by the classical political economists who, we believe, were also able to produce a rich theory of the differentiated body. In fact, Smith leads us to believe that economics has suffered a relative impoverishment, at least in the language of description of the body if not in the ultimate conceptions of human bodies. While for Smith and several of the others (especially Malthus and his discussions of laboring, consuming, and reproducing bodies)[5] the complexly differentiated human body, with its imperatives, instincts, artifices, and constraints is a site of mutual effectivity, the body and subject find at the point of ultimate determination an organic totality in which all elements seem to cohere. One way of seeing this in Smith's approach, for example, is by seeing how his vision of society and the body come to mirror and determine one another. Just as the social body is or can be the harmonious outcome of the principle of the division of labor (and here, we note that the division of labor is the key to the material abundance for the satisfaction of individual bodies promised by the expansion of markets and industrial rule), so the body itself is divided into various components that are or can be harmoniously conjoined in the person of discretion and moral sensibility. The body as organic unity is one that has depth (in contrast to the horizontal arrangement of bodily functions in the neoclassical version) because of the principles of utility (or labor, if one prefers a more Marxian reading of the classicals, including Smith), sympathy, and affection. That is, the classical body can be viewed as an expressive totality in that it can always signify the essential determinants of its constitution and disposition. Hence, as we saw above, despite its beautiful complexity, especially in the hands of Smith, the body in classical political economy is one in which difference is always sublated or resolved by subsumption into a higher unity. It is clearly not a discontinuous body. Again, the mischief caused by such a notion of the organically unified, though internally differentiated, body – a body with an ultimate center and usually, therefore, signifying a particular 'normal' gender, race, sexuality, nationality, and so forth – has been extensive. We leave the enumeration of the crimes committed in the name of such a conception to others.

It is striking, then, to see the extent to which the humanist bias gives rise to the view that mainstream economics has all but made the human body disappear, and the extent to which a return to the body, as per the classicals, is advocated. We conclude this essay with a brief discussion of how the alternative outline we propose conflicts with the humanist purposes of several of the schools of thought – here we concentrate on some parts of the Marxian, post-Keynesian, and feminist enterprises in economics – that purportedly seek to reinscribe the 'whole' human body within economic discourse.

As we have noted, one crucial element of classical political economy that was eventually displaced in the neoclassical revolution of the nineteenth century was the idea that labor was a primary or even exclusive determinant of value. Now, readings of Marx that posit him either as the last of the great classicals or as the leading left-wing critic of classical political economy often share the claim that Marx extracted from the classicals the view that labor is the sole source of value. Thus, as we get even in such a sophisticated reader of Marx and the classicals as Maurice Dobb (1973), Marx is applauded for his consistent formulation of a labor theory of value and, thus, for his adherence to the view that social relations of production (which are observable) determine the distribution of social labor and the value and exchange-value of commodities. That is, for Dobb as for many other Marxists, the fact that individuals may be desiring beings and motivated in their economic behaviors by instinct, affection, emotion, and so forth is relegated to the status of secondary phenomena insofar as the determination of value, the social allocation of labor, and the distribution of income and wealth are involved. For many Marxists, the essential causes of economic activity are labor and production. Thus, the laboring body, rendered in some versions of this story as a truly transhistorical corporeal entity, is given pride of place in establishing the conditions for that which is uniquely human and thereby economic. As Jean Baudrillard (1975, 1981) and others such as Georges Bataille (1991, 1993) and Gilles Deleuze and Felix Guattari (1983) have pointed out, this 'productionist' bias of Marxists has constituted the grounds by which Marxism has discursively ignored or excluded libido, excess, and true expenditure in the economic theory to which it has given rise.

Contemporary Marxian critics in the field of economics, then, often prefer to resurrect the nineteenth-century debates over the correct attribution of value to either 'subjective' desire or 'objective' labor. Their critique of neoclassical theory devolves on the claim that the bourgeois individualism, naturalism, and arcane abstraction consequent upon the use of axiomatic formulations in neoclassicism obscure the true (because substantial and transhistorical) conditions under which economic activities and institutions arise. Whereas production is viewed as ubiquitous across epochs and geographical boundaries, desire and utility maximization are seen as limited in historical importance to capitalist societies and, even there, they are more a consequence of a hegemonic false consciousness imposed by the self-promotion of the bourgeoisie (for example, to hide the 'fact' of exploitation or to explain away the waste and inefficiency of unplanned markets) than the objective conditions of life under capitalism. The modernism of much Marxism consists, at least partly, in its insistence in finding an ontological referent for the essential cause – labor – that emerges in Marxian economics as the source of value. The laboring body and the conditions of work, then, take precedence in everything from determining the nature of subjectivity (the individual who produces him/herself in the course of participating in social labor) and estimating the 'good life' (the elimination of alienation in work) to the primacy of certain struggles (especially those associated with factories and 'productive' laborers) in the movements to transform and move beyond capitalism.

We leave for another paper the full explication of our view that, rather than codifying the classicals' laboring body as a first principle, Marx can be said to have disrupted the order of the body established in classical political economy and in much Marxism. For us, Marx is not the inventor of a new anthropology (his work, we believe along with Althusser, represents a sharp rupture from the humanist anthropology that preceded – and, in the pretensions of the early neoclassicals, followed – him). Briefly stated, we view Marx's contributions to be more along the lines of presenting the human body as a register of class and other economic and social processes, a place where the effects of capitalism are largely inscribed, rather than the site of the privileged origin (through labor) of subjectivity, agency, or socioeconomic relations. In other words, the body that Marx presents in his writings is overdetermined and has no center or essential unity other than that which is the effect of the historical conditions of production, consumption, circulation, distribution, and so forth. In this sense, the body in Marx's work is closer to some current neoclassical renditions, at least insofar as it is differentiated, dispersed, and brought to temporary unity by specific productions rather than by the presumption of its essentiality.

The problem, then, for some of the Marxian critics of neoclassical theory is that the story they prefer revives a view of the body and subjectivity that are fully part of the modernist project to promote an overarching and exhaustive notion of 'man'. In this regard, the postmodern moments of Marxism are suppressed and the affinity that

Marxists may have with other developments within which the humanism of the classicals is finally displaced is largely ignored. To put this otherwise, the retention of the laboring body as prime cause of social and economic relations does little to undermine the humanist essentialism that, purportedly, many Marxists have been at pains to attack over the course of the last century. While recent neoclassicals and Marxists may make absurd bedmates, there is a sense in which Marxists can augment rather than blunt their attacks on bourgeois social order by acknowledging the fragmentation of the human body and the dismemberment of theoretical humanism that may have been accomplished by some neoclassicals.

A similar issue confronts post-Keynesian critics of neoclassical economics. Instead of using their trenchant questioning of the notions of certainty (and of probabilistic certainty), rationality, and much else that still abounds within neoclassical theory, together with their own exploration of the significance and effects of uncertainty, as the initial steps in decentering the body, post-Keynesian economists have largely resisted such a move. As we see it, the 'radical uncertainty' originally focused on by Keynes (and also by G. L. S. Shackle) and now embraced by post-Keynesian economists has the potential of disrupting the modernist unity of the body, for example, by severing the necessary connection between, the presumed sequence of, some set of initial anticipations and the actions of economic agents as well as by 'relativizing' even the recognition of the degrees and forms of certain and uncertain knowledge on the part of those agents, making uncertainty into a variable and heterogeneous constitutent and effect of bodily capabilities and orders.[6]

Post-Keynesians, however, tend to emphasize the extradiscursive 'brute nature' of uncertainty, reducing it to the limits on knowledge imposed by an unforeseeable future. Their view is that neoclassical economists (and, with them, others such as new Keynesian economists), by emphasizing certain (or, again, probabilistically certain) knowledge, have simply exaggerated the role and possibilities of rational calculation and diminished the 'animal spirits', 'spontaneous optimism', and other nonrational, corporeal determinants of economic behavior. In this sense, post-Keynesian economists seek to reinscribe a more 'balanced' human body – one which, if not exactly derivative of the classicals, both recognizes the limitations of the body (for example, in terms of the ability to gather and process information) and recovers the kind of profusion of sentiments and emotions, conventions and habits, that were seen to be central to the activities and practices of economic agents prior to the marginalist revolution. It is this body which, for post-Keynesians, serves both to replace the 'sterility' of disembodied neoclassical decision-makers and to avoid the 'nihilism' occasioned by the postmodern decentering of the body.

Turning to the recent emergence of feminism in economics, we are struck by how some of the leading thinkers in this field neither wish to replace the hierarchical model of subjectivity and the body represented by the nineteenth-century neoclassicals nor wish to challenge the idea that economic theory can indeed capture and express a view of the 'total' and real human body. The brilliance of the feminist critique, of course, has been to show that the concepts of the body that have characterized all of the schools of modern economic thought – from the mainstream to the most radical – have been gendered and, therefore, 'partial' in their implications. Both the early neoclassicals' desiring body (along with its rational monitor) and the traditional Marxists' laboring body, to consider but two examples, have been aptly shown to express degrees of maleness (and whiteness and Europeanness) that have henceforth been downplayed or completely ignored in economic discourse. How strange it is, then, that one motivating force behind a good deal of feminism in economics has been an additive model of the human body so as to now 'include' female functions and affections, bodily attributes that are thought to be mostly feminine, in the existing models of economic behavior. While feminists may be loath to regard the classicals as the 'fathers' of the discipline, there is still a tendency to find favor in the discussions of altruism, sympathy, emotion, and much else that had their discursive appearance with the classicals and have faded from view since then.

To be clear, it is not that the inclusion of the female body into economic discourse is any way objectionable to us. To the contrary, it marks for us one of the most potentially powerful contributions to economic theory of which we are aware. It is the case, however, that we regard as problematic the insistence that such an inclusion of one or another of the previously excluded bodily orders or attributes will give us a 'better' (in the sense of more accurate) picture of the effects of the body in economic activities and the view that a revamped, consciously gendered but centered body can now take its place, as the nineteenth-century neoclassicals clearly wanted, as the point of origin of economic theory. It is still unclear how many feminists in economics will go the route of other critics of modernism in simply insisting upon a more inclusive and complete view of the human body, as though the discursive construction of different types and orders of the body could somehow resolve into a singular formulation, and how many others will push forward the project of dispersing and multiplying the bodily orders – both actual and possible – thus radically recasting the body and, with it, the contours of existing economic theory.

Conclusion: the postmodern body in economics

In conclusion, we believe that the challenge to economic theory that the introduction of the decentered, discontinuous body has suggested has yet to be picked up. So as not to avoid misunderstanding, while we think that it is plausible to entertain the idea that the body has not disappeared but has been recomposed in recent neoclassical thinking along the lines of fragmentation and differentiation, we also think that the neoclassical rendition of the postmodern body is stunted and meager at best. The richness of the classicals has not been replicated by today's neoclassicals because of the latters' reluctance to treat directly the dispersion of the body and its effects as an object of economic theory. That is, we contend that the neoclassicals have been unaware in the main of the changes in the concept of the body that their formal analyses have implied, and they remain largely uninterested in considering, for example, how the processes of gendering and so forth may alter the kinds of theoretical work that they are willing to recognize as 'economics' proper. And, of course, we acknowledge as well that when pushed to defend the integrity and unity of their work, many neoclassicals still resort to homo economicus as the starting presupposition despite the fact that, as we see it, even this belabored idea has been reduced in scope and given new meaning in the conglomeration of behavioral assumptions and theorems that now comprises the profile of economic agency for today's model builders.

The challenge of introducing postmodern bodies for different economic schools of thought remains, not only for neoclassicals but also for their critics, a largely unrealized project. While it may be the case that each school of thought has had its postmodern 'moments' in the disruption of the eighteenth- and nineteenth-century forms of modernism and humanism,[7] the reliance on modernism and humanism to reconstitute the human body and/or the mourning of the body's purported disappearance from view reproduces a critical narrative that avoids rather than faces the innovations that are underway outside economics in recomposing the body in terms of postmodernism.[8] Coming to terms with these innovations within economics is, in any event, the project we hope to have begun in this chapter.

Notes

1 Stanley Wong (1978) declares Samuelson's approach to have been unsuccessful because it was not ultimately able to eliminate all non-observational concepts from consumer theory.
2 Wong (1978) discusses the changes over time in Samuelson's claims for revealed preference theory.
3 Comprehensive histories are provided by Ingrao and Israel (1990) and Weintraub (1979, 1985, 1991).

4 This is not to say, because we view with a great deal of interest the emergence of a postmodern treatment of the body in at least some of the 'classic' texts by neoclassical economists, that we simply applaud their efforts or the results of their work. Quite the contrary. We regard the relative lack of interest on the part of neoclassicals in exploring the ways in which bodies are produced and inscribed not only in the discipline of economics (including by their own work) but also in 'real' economies as indicative of the degree to which we will have to borrow and invent metaphors and languages beyond those of neoclassical economics in order to develop appropriate conceptions of the body.
5 See, for example, the discussion by Gallagher (1986).
6 For an exploration of these and related dimensions of uncertainty, see Amariglio and Ruccio (1995).
7 See, for example, our analysis of the postmodern moments in Marxian and Keynesian theories (Amariglio and Ruccio 1994, 1995).
8 We are thinking of the discussions of the body by, among others, Brooks (1993), Butler (1993), Grosz (1994), and the various authors in the edited collection by MacCannell and Zakarin (1994). We have devoted considerably more attention to the conceptions of the body in feminism and in literary and cultural theory in Amariglio and Ruccio (forthcoming).

References

Althusser, L. and Balibar, E. (1977) *Reading Capital*, trans. B. Brewster, London: New Left Books, 2nd edn.

Amariglio, J. (1987) 'Marxism Against Economic Science: Althusser's Legacy', *Research in Political Economy* 10:159–94.

—— (1988) 'The Body, Econonomic Discourse, and Power: An Economist's Introduction to Foucault', *History of Political Economy* 20 (4): 583–613.

—— (1990) 'Economics as a Postmodern Discourse', in W. Samuels (ed.) *Economics as Discourse*, Boston: Kluwer Academic Press, 15–46.

Amariglio, J. and Ruccio, D. F. (1994) 'Postmodernism, Marxism, and the Critique of Modern Economic Thought', *Rethinking Marxism* 7 (Fall): 7–35.

—— (1995) 'Keynes, Postmodernism, Uncertainty', in S. Dow and J. Hillard (eds) *Keynes, Knowledge, and Uncertainty*, Aldershot: Edward Elgar, 334–56.

—— (Forthcoming) 'Modern Economics: The Case of the Disappearing Body?' *Cambridge Journal of Economics*.

Arrow, K. and Hahn, F. (1971) *General Competitive Analysis*, San Francisco: Holden Day.

Bataille, G. (1991) *The Accursed Share: An Essay on General Economy*, vol. 1, trans. R. Hurley, New York: Zone Books.

—— (1993) *The Accursed Share: An Essay on General Economy*, vols 2 and 3, trans. R. Hurley, New York: Zone Books.

Baudrillard, J. (1975) *The Mirror of Production*, trans. M. Poster, St Louis: Telos Press.

—— (1981) *For a Critique of the Political Economy of the Sign*, trans. C. Levin, St Louis: Telos Press.

Brooks, P. (1993) *Body Works: Objects of Desire in Modern Narrative*, Cambridge: Harvard University Press.

Butler, J. (1993) *Bodies that Matter: On the Discursive Limits of 'Sex'*, New York: Routledge.
Debreu, G. (1959) *Theory of Value*, New York: Wiley.
Deleuze, G. and Guattari, F. (1983) *Anti-Oedipus: Capitalism and Schizophrenia*, trans. R. Hurley *et al.* Minneapolis: University of Minnesota Press.
Dobb, M. (1973) *Theories of Value and Distribution Since Adam Smith*, Cambridge: Cambridge University Press.
Elster, J. (ed.) (1986) *The Multiple Self*, New York: Cambridge University Press.
Gallagher, C. (1986) 'The Body Versus the Social Body in the Works of Thomas Malthus and Henry Mayhew', *Representations* (Spring): 83–106.
Grosz, E. (1994) *Volatile Bodies: Toward a Corporeal Feminism*, Bloomington: Indiana University Press.
Hicks, J. R. and Allen, R. G. D. (1934) 'A Reconsideration of the Theory of Value', *Economica* 1: 52–76, 196–219.
Ingrao, B. and Israel, G. (1990) *The Invisible Hand*, trans. I. McGilvray, Cambridge, MA: MIT Press.
Jevons, W. S. (1871) *The Theory of Political Economy*, New York: Kelley and Millman; 5th edn 1957.
MacCannell, J. F. and Zakarin, L., (eds) (1994) *Thinking Bodies*, Stanford: Stanford University Press.
Mirowski, P. (1991) *More Heat than Light: Economics as Social Physics, Physics as Nature's Economics*, Cambridge: Cambridge University Press.
Ruccio, D. F. (1988) 'The Merchant of Venice, or Marxism in the Mathematical Mode', *Rethinking Marxism* 1 (Winter): 36–68.
—— (1991) 'Postmodernism and Economics', *Journal of Post Keynesian Economics* 13 (Summer): 495–510.
Samuelson, P. A. (1938a) 'A Note on the Pure Theory of Consumer's Behavior', *Economica* 5: 61–71.
—— (1938b) 'A Note on the Pure Theory of Consumer's Behavior: An Addendum', *Economica* 5: 353–4.
—— (1948) *Foundations of Economic Analysis*, Cambridge: Harvard University Press.
—— (1950) 'The Problem of Integrability in Utility Theory', *Economica* 17: 355–85.
Sen, A. (1990) 'Rational Behavior', in J. Eatwell *et al.* (eds) *Utility and Probability*, New York: W. W. Norton and Company, 198–216.
Smith, A. (1759) *The Theory of Moral Sentiments*, Indianapolis: Liberty Classics, 1976.
Weintraub, E. R. (1979) *Microfoundations*, New York: Cambridge University Press.
—— (1985) *General Equilibrium Analysis*, New York: Cambridge University Press.
—— (1991) *Stabilizing Dynamics*, New York: Cambridge University Press.
White, M. V. (1994) 'The Moment of Richard Jennings: The Production of Jevons's Marginalist Economic Agent', in P. Mirowski (ed.) *Natural Images in Economic Thought: 'Markets Read in Tooth and Claw'*, Cambridge: Cambridge University Press, 197–230.
Wong, S. (1978) *The Foundations of Paul Samuelson's Revealed Preference Theory*, Boston: Routledge and Kegan Paul.

7

IDEALITY, SYMBOLICITY, AND REALITY IN POSTMODERN CAPITALISM

Jean-Joseph Goux

From the utilizing of gold coins in the nineteenth century to the present enormous volume of electronic transactions that are almost instantaneously carried out on a global basis, maintaining a permanent uneasiness in the volatility of assets, an unprecedented revolution has occurred in the status of money and, more generally, in every procedure of finance – becoming cyberfinance in a world defined by globalization. It is significant that one economist has counterposed a 'symbol economy' organized by combined movements of intangible transactions, which only has information for support, to a 'real economy' of goods and services that today only represents a small share of economic activity (Drucker, 1981: 8). According to the most recent estimates, the financial or 'symbol economy' is between thirty and fifty times larger than the 'real economy'. For every dollar spent on something 'real' (a car, a bottle of wine, a haircut, and so on), $30 to $50 is spent on a bond, stock, futures, contract, or insurance policy (Kurtzman, 1993: 40).

So, the financial economy, with its global electronic network, has taken nearly complete charge of the 'real economy'. Isn't it in this threatening fracture between the real and the symbolic, between the material and the virtual, between things and signs, that we must find one of the most prominent features – or maybe the determinant feature – of a postmodern conjuncture? What happened in the history of exchanges, in the status of money, that resulted in this hegemony of the 'symbol economy'? And is money still 'money'? What is the meaning of 'reality' and 'symbolicity' in the economic realm?

Precious metal (most often gold, but also silver) becoming money fulfils three very different functions: (1) common measure of values, (2) instrument of exchange, and (3) means of hoarding. The possible confusion of these three functions in the same monetary body sometimes made it difficult to discern this traditional distinction. And it is this distinction (perfectly systematized by Marx at the beginning of *Capital*) which appears to me of a decisive importance in order to grasp the general logic of exchange in all its implications and in order to establish parallels with noneconomic forms of symbolization: language, religion, law, aesthetic representation, and so on. In fact, what will emerge is that these three functions of the general equivalent (which we will soon designate as *archetype, token, treasure*) are placed in very different *ontological* registers. The taking into account of these three registers and their reciprocal (interweaving) relationships can lead to a precise analysis of the regime of communication, including the mode of signifying, in a particular social formation.

As long as gold is a measure of value, its presence or availability is not necessary. For instance, it is possible to estimate the value of a certain amount of commodities in gold units without the real intervention of a gold which serves as a measure. It is sufficient that the quantity of gold which serves as a unit be constant, like a standard to which anyone can refer. As Marx affirms in *Capital*, 'since the expression of the value of commodities in gold is a purely ideal act, we may use purely imaginary or ideal gold to perform this operation' (Marx, 1990: 189–90). The terms 'imaginary gold' or 'ideal money' characterize well this specific register. The difficulty starts when a precise name has to be given to the ontological register of the measure of values. Should we designate it as ideal or as imaginary? The term 'imaginary' suggests a lesser existence, or something secondary, which is not relevant to this function of measure. Even though ideal, this function is not imaginary in the dream-like or fictitious sense. It may be convenient to underline that the function ensured by the monetary standard is in close relationship with the realm of archetypes. It is remarkable that the polysemy of the word 'archetype' attests to this link. Archetype: 'model from which a piece of work, a work of art, etc. is made; the original which is reproduced. Standard for money, weights, and measures' (Larousse 1928–33). Archetype-money is a certain quantity of a precious metal. Its 'intrinsic' value is used as a unit of measure to comparatively estimate any goods or services. Historically, the general equivalent appeared first in the form of archetype-money and not as circulating money. The standard as an ideal unit of measure long precedes coins as a means of exchange. Thus, in ancient Egypt there exists an ideal unit of measure that allows the evaluation of goods that are exchanged, in spite of the appearance of barter (the direct exchange between goods for other goods). The fixed standard that transcends all real exchanges constitutes the archetype unit that can uniformly measure goods and services without being present itself as a commodity. Archetype-money, this unique and fixed standard (generally placed in the *sanctuary*), logically and historically precedes circulating money in the sphere of economic values. Similarly, archetype (in the Platonic sense) precedes the *concept*, which is a product of exchange in the sphere of significations. This precedence does not imply, however, that the function of the archetype of the general equivalent can be suppressed and overcome.

The second function of the general equivalent is that of means of exchange. Money begins to circulate. The general equivalent (for example, in the form of a gold coin) takes part directly in the market. Money is not only a function of evaluation; it is the *medium* that allows real exchanges. Nevertheless, and this is a remarkable characteristic of money considered as simple medium of exchange, the actual *matter* of this money little by little becomes indifferent. It can be *replaced* by any sign or token. Thus, if the general equivalent is *archetype* in its function of measure, it tends to become *token* in its function of medium of exchange. As an intermediary of exchanges, money has only a symbolic existence. Thus, conventional symbols can replace money as such simple tokens without intrinsic value. This is a specific register, one of the symbolic, in the sense of the purely symbolic.

Third, and finally, there are certain functions in which gold has to be present in its metallic body as a *real* equivalent of the commodity or as commodity-money. It is in its function of *means of payment* or *reserve*. Indeed, gold is required *in presencia*, and no longer in its ideal or purely symbolic form, whenever a payment is needed (not on the daily market, but in a transaction in which conventional tokens are no longer accepted). Even more so, gold is required when a 'treasure' is accumulated. Its value will be considered real and not dependent upon a temporary agreement. This is a new register that can be named the real. In this case, token-money is no longer convenient, but only money which is itself a commodity, a fragment of bullion. Thus, this is treasure-money.

Consequently, at the end of the analysis of the triple function of the general equivalent, we have identified three registers of the possible existence of money. They have the particularity and the ability to define three very different ontological regimes, the generality of which can be perceived in order to analyze the conditions of communication: ideality, symbolicity, and reality. It is even remarkable that those economists who are least preoccupied with a general theory of the sign or of communication are led inevitably to foresee these three registers when they analyze the function of money. It is probable that these three registers constitute fundamental categories of the logic of exchange.

Let me say in a direct manner, then: this intertwining reminds us of the Lacanian triplicate of the imaginary, the symbolic, and the real, but does not coincide exactly with it, for the following reasons. The divergence concerns the imaginary. Certainly, account money has often been designated as 'imaginary money', and this can be found in the Lacanian register. But this imaginary has a measuring role which has nothing dream-like or fantastic about it; it is rather of the order of the law, of regulating standard. It would not be impossible for this discrepancy to reveal, in Lacan's work, an excessive devalorization of the register of the ideal, reduced to the imaginary in the weak sense, whereas the register of the pure signifier is promoted to an exorbitant role regarding the law. It is possible that the Lacanian division must be corrected to be more coherent with this logic of exchange. It therefore appears that the three monetary functions are not necessarily united in money. As Pierre Vilar emphasizes, three different things are named 'money': (*a*) 'object-commodity-money', of which, taking into account its matter, its weight has a realizable value on any market. In this register, gold is money 'par excellence'; (*b*) 'sign-money' or fiduciary money, which has, under defined conditions, a certain buying power, even though it is not convertible into gold; and (*c*) 'name-money', which is not circulating coin but allows the expression of the value of other goods (1976: 20–1). It is 'nominal money' or 'account money'. Now, if we consider that 'then as now, monetary problems were produced by the interaction of three kinds of money' (Vilar, 1976: 21), it becomes clear that this interaction combines, associates, dissociates, and interweaves three registers which we have defined as those of the real, the ideal and the symbolic, corresponding respectively to *treasure-money, archetype-money,* and *token-money.*

I cannot underestimate the importance of these distinctions for a sociosymbolic analysis of historical phenomena. Marx did not seize the opportunity to elaborate in a more precise theory the links between exchange and social consciousness, even though he recognized the 'theological subtleties' related to the analysis of the monetary form. If we take as a starting point the distinction among the three registers, it becomes possible to conceive ideology not only as the *content* of ideas, of notions, of concepts, but as the disposition in which ideality, symbolicity, and reality specifically intertwine in a given social formation. It is the constitution or construction mode of the 'real' which can be grasped from the reciprocal relationship among these three functions as they are articulated in social exchange, in the mode of 'communication'.

Thus, it is important to determine the manner in which archetype, token, and treasure exercise their functions at all levels, in the logic of social metabolism for each historical mode of economic and 'sign' exchange. It will appear that there are several possible economies of the general equivalent. These differences are not only economic, but concern exchange in general, the status of value and meaning. They allow us to analyze the main aspects of the 'mode of symbolizing' of a social formation and, especially, the status of religious representations.

In a society such as that of ancient Egypt, the general equivalent already exists but in the noncirculating form of ideal standard, whereas products, evaluated according to this unique measure, are nevertheless exchanged on the market as though it were barter. As far as its mode of symbolizing is concerned, ancient Egypt is very different from ancient Greece. In this latter case, we come across a moment of development of exchanges when, for the first time, the three functions of the general equivalent are accumulated, embodied in the same monetary object, although at the same time they can be differentiated. The piece of gold (or, alternatively, of silver) ensures at the same time: (*a*) the function of archetype (it is identical to the archetype); (*b*) the function of token (it circulates, it has to be accepted in transactions, it has a nominal value guaranteed by the state); and (*c*) the function of treasure or bullion since it retains, as matter, an 'intrinsic' value. This value exactly coincides by law with its nominal value, but it is in fact autonomous with respect to this nominal value because, out of circulation, the coin retains its intrinsic value.

The status of money in the Greco-Roman world is very close to the status of money in the modern world, from the Renaissance to the beginning of the twentieth century. In both cases, we have 'true' money, a fragment of bullion on which an effigy is minted and which is guaranteed by the collectivity or the sovereign, which allows the coin to circulate for a given value without the need to weigh it or estimate its denomination. From the appearance of this type of money at the end of the seventeenth century in Greek cities until the end of the Roman Empire, we always find the conjunction of the three functions of measure, exchange, and reserve in the same monetary body. The monetary unit is embodied in real and circulating coin such that we can refer to it as a regime of *complete* or full general equivalent.

With respect to the Roman monetary system (which, according to Vilar, 'was similar to the best of the nineteenth century' [1976: 30]) the Middle Ages introduce a profound transformation which leads to the disappearance of 'true' money. During this period of limited transactions, coins are almost not minted at all in Europe. Exchanges are thus based on evaluation by account money. The same non-circulating and purely ideal monetary unit serves as measure for the value of goods exchanged and even for the value of metallic coins of very different origin and quality. Thus, as Vilar writes, 'for centuries France and other places too priced all goods by the pound (*livre*), though with rare exceptions no actual unit of currencey had the same value. In each transaction both the goods being sold and the possibly quite different currencies in which payment was made, were calculated in pounds and subdivisions of the pound' (1976: 21). Thus, during this medieval period, whether under the appearance of barter or of monetary exchanges with various coins (copper, gold, silver coins, of all origins and minted with various effigies), a unique but purely ideal measure (the pound) governs the evaluation of what is exchanged and of what is hoarded. There is a cleavage between the functions of the general equivalent in this economic regime of exchange. As Marc Bloch clearly wrote, 'What is the regime of account money if not a system in which the two essential functions of money as measure of value and as means of payment are separated?' (1954: 49). Money as measure (which I have named archetype-money) cannot merge with the different types of commodity-money that circulate. There is no longer any coincidence between the ideal function of measure and the real function of hoarding or direct payment. We are certainly within an economy governed by the principle of the general equivalent, but this one exists only in the mode of archaic ideality and not in the mode of reality and even less in the mode of simple substitute (token).

With a few exceptions (Florence, Genoa, Venice, the commercial cities) it will be necessary to await until the fourteenth century for new gold-money to be again systematically minted as legal tender, in conformity with the circulation principle, which was the one of the Roman Empire. It is then that a monetary regime with a complete or full general equivalent could be instituted. It will be maintained in principle through all the modifications and all the crises, until the end of the nineteenth century.

This brief historical review calls for numerous comments and a detailed analysis, which I cannot undertake here. Nevertheless, let me stress that this is remarkably enlightening for anyone who wishes to establish homologies between the structure of exchanges and the signifying forms which characterize an epoch. The resemblance between the modes of representation of the Greco-Roman world and the modern world since the Renaissance have often been noted. This resemblance is astonishingly corroborated regarding the structure of exchanges. If we consider the disposition of the three registers of the general equivalent, the status of the monetary thing, there is a close resemblance between the Greco-Roman world and the modern world (complete general equivalent with intricacy of the three functions – measure, exchange, reserve). Otherwise, we know that the principle of representative mimesis in arts and in literature characterizes these two great historical periods (in opposition to both ancient Egypt and the Middle Ages). To mention only two arts, ancient painting and sculpture are essentially founded on 'optical realism' as are the paintings and the sculptures of the Renaissance period and of the modern era until the end of the nineteenth century, in spite of the differences. Thus, a close structural link exists between the intricacy of the three functions of the general equivalent within the same body and realistic representation. When the same monetary body is simultaneously measuring, circulating, and has an 'intrinsic value', in other words, when the registers of ideality, symbolicity, and reality are intricate, we are then in a mode of signifying which is based upon 'objective' representation or 'optical realism'. Ideality is embodied in reality.

In turn, when the general equivalent exists only in its measuring form as ideal standard of values, realistic representation is not constituted. This concerns ancient Egypt and also the Middle Ages, in very different conditions. Here, the measuring general equivalent ceases to enter the market; it is only an ideal instance, a transcendent unit to exchange. Everything unfolds as though the ideality register (or the archetype) is separated from the register of real exchanges.

Medieval exchanges are governed by an ideal measure which transcends real exchanges, and which constitutes a unitary principle of evaluation from which not only commodities but different coins (partial general equivalents) express their price. This is a device whose profound homology with the ensemble of manifestations of this social formation cannot be ignored.

Particularly, I notice what an astonishing congruence brings together 'nominal money', which dominates the medieval epoch, and the nominalist theories of language. This account money can be considered a transcendent standard, which governs exchanges (and thus accommodates a Platonic concept of essences, which exist in God). It also can be considered a mere name, a *flatus vocis* without real existence, because it does not enter into the exchange *in presencia*, with no need to be present in order to function as unit of measure. Thus, the theories of language torn between nominalism and conceptualism, providing that we either insist on the value of essence and measure of concepts or on their reduction to mere terms, which have only an 'imaginary' meaning, would correspond to the era of nominal money.

As surprising and indirect as this may seem, it is also the symbolic and not the realistic status of the pictorial and literary figuration during the Middle Ages which is profoundly congruent with this system of exchanges:

1   As much as the general equivalent does not participate in real exchanges – thus, as much as no element has the function to embody measure in these exchanges – the exchanging subjects involved in daily transactions never coincide with the measuring code itself. It remains transcendent as though the place of the measure would not be unable to identify itself with the present exchanging subjectivities. The dissociation between the measuring function and real exchange leads to a radical separation between the immanence of actual transactions (which involves a horizontal relationship between subjects) from the transcendence of measure, as place of the Other. It appears that this difference between the exchanging pole and the measuring pole is not so radical when, as it is the case for minted gold, circulating money is also measuring money. In this case, the measuring place of the Other is directly embodied in each of the exchanging acts and it almost coincides with the subjects of exchange. There is nothing astonishing if in this latter case it is 'man', 'the subject', who is considered as the center of

perspective, the source which confers measure upon things. Whereas in the medieval mode of evaluation it is only from the transcendent site of the Other, which is very different from the subject, that all measure could emerge. In this sense, the philosophy of Descartes, in which the subject becomes the place of measure (unit, point of perspective) could be structurally linked to the circulation of complete or full money, which unites the three functions. The place of measure is no longer transcendent to the exchanging subject, but coincides with him or her, as though the principle of evaluation of treasure and the treasure itself were identical.

2   On the other hand, in the medieval economy real exchange has all the appearance of barter, since a circulating general equivalent is absent. So, no purely and simply exchangeable element (reduced to the functionality of exchange) can be isolated in this commerce. No element representing 'exchangeability' itself, that is to say, belonging to the register of the pure symbolic (token), can appear in its truthfulness.

Similarly, the absence of a radical distinction between commodity and circulating money (and of a real substitution between the two) makes it impossible to institute a system of representation. Indeed, representation is based upon the translation in the 'language' of the circulating general equivalent of that which does not have the status of a general equivalent (but only of a relative form). Representation (by language and also by 'tableau') exists only in the act of evaluating, translating, transposing, 'exchanging' that which is given first as exterior to this form into the form of circulating general equivalent. This is why realistic representation would have a homological relationship with the real exchange of commodities with the general equivalent, as though language, for instance, could directly represent the thing itself, in its objectivity. On the contrary, in the case of medieval barter, the absence of circulating mediation makes the clear-cut opposition between the represented thing (the commodity) and the representing thing (circulating money) impossible to discern. Then, what dominates is the opposition between the evaluated thing and the evaluating site, which remains transcendent. Now, this device in which things (commodity, signs) are evaluated by an outside-of-exchange or transcendent measure no longer corresponds to representation but to the symbolic dimension. Meaning and value (of commodities, of signs) are not adequately translated by their real 'exchange' here and now, with an element which is equally measuring (as though equivalence could be realized in an actual representation), but their meaning and value remain open, suspended at the measuring, transcendent site. Instead of being represented by general equivalents, visible things (signs, commodities) make sense, make value, for the site which gives them measure. In social relations (as in the system of figuration), the vertical dimension of the transcendent evaluation, which constantly refers signs and commodities to the archetype, which measures their meaning and value, prevails over the horizontal dimension in which signs and commodities realize their value through exchange with the circulating general equivalent. In the first case, this direction defines the symbolic dimension (signs remain open to the site of the Other which gives them meaning without ever definitely realizing this meaning in an operation of concrete equivalence) and, in the second case, this direction defines the representational dimension (different signs could be translated by other well-defined and circulating signs which are their general equivalents).

In symbolic figuration, the place of the code (or of the evaluating measure) cannot coincide with any particular subject, but refers to a necessarily enigmatic and transcendent Other. On the contrary, in the regime of representation, the place of the code or measure may seem to coincide with the exchanging subject himself, since the circulating element is at the same time a measuring element. Signifiers, as commodities, can concretely translate, here and now, their meaning and value into the embodied, general equivalent which participates *in presencia* in actual transactions. Their relation to the measuring source is not a relation to an ideality, which transcends concrete exchanges, but this relation realizes itself in the exchange which puts 'relative forms' in a relation of equivalence with a 'general equivalent' form, which represents them. In this respect the medieval concept for which the meaning of any symbol refers finally to God Himself, transcendental signified of all symbols (see, for instance, Chydenius 1975), reveals a remarkable and striking homology with the medieval economic device of exchange in which the general equivalent is measuring (ideality) without being circulating (pure symbolicity or reality).

Otherwise, if the Greco-Roman system of monetary exchange is closer to that of the modern world (from the Renaissance until the beginning of the twentieth century) than to that of the Middle Ages, it becomes understandable that the Stoic theory of the sign, and not the medieval theories, is closer to our triadic concept of the sign. The distinction between signifier, signified, and referent, in the Stoic manner, can only exist in a triadic monetary system, in which circulating money, its value, and the commodity for which it stands are rigorously distinguished. Such a semiotics cannot be formulated in the absence of a circulating general equivalent and of a triadic economy which it institutes.

Thus, there would exist a correlation between realism (in literary and pictorial esthetics) and the circulation of gold-money. What makes this correlation much more convincing is that the nineteenth century, Balzac's and Zola's epoch, is a remarkable period for monetary history and for the history of monetary doctrines as well: 'the economists of the nineteenth century, an era of monetary stability, thought of money as "neutral"' (Vilar, 1976: 17). It is the stage of the triumph of industrial capitalism in

Europe. It is significant that during this same period novelists also believe in the convertibility of language into referential reality. They postulate that language could be exchanged for things, in full and complete equivalence, which constitutes its power of representation. As such, as the economists believe that money is neutral, novelists no longer question the linguistic medium they use, but consider it transparent, because reality presents itself through it in an operation of equivalence, of exchange, in which the word stands for the thing. Balzac's and Zola's language would therefore have the same status as bourgeois money: stable, with an undisputed gold-standard, an ensured convertibility, an immediate exchange which makes it a neutral medium.

This gold-language is not only the one which fully speaks the truth. It is also the one which expresses the speaking subject's truth. Not only can the exterior world be objectively represented, but a soul or a person can be adequately revealed. Victor Hugo makes this comparison: 'Poets are like sovereigns. They have to mint money. Their effigy must remain on ideas they issue into circulation' (1972: 398). Paul Valery develops the same homology between language and money: 'The powerful mind, like powerful politics, mints its own money and allows in its secret empire only coins that bear its sign. The possession of gold is not enough for it, it has to bear its mark. Its wealth rests in its own image. Its capital of fundamental ideas is marked with its effigy; it made or reminted them and gave them so clear a form, created them in so hard a gold that they will travel throughout the world without debasement of their characters and its imprint' (1943: 85). We cannot make a clearer homology between the production of an exchangeable language and the issuing of gold-money. Here, Valery creates a metaphor for a precise historical moment of the linguistic confidence. Gold-language bearing the author's effigy corresponds to definite sociosymbolic circumstances. The sovereign-ego (the great sovereign, the powerful mind) makes itself into a universal measure of values and, at the same time, into the issuer of treasure (its treasure) which, thus coined, becomes negotiable. It is clear that here the functions of measure, reserve, and exchange (the three functions of the general equivalent) are combined, interwoven in the same money, instituting the particular individual at the pole of this economy. Imperialist cogito or romantic genius, this is the moment when the author's powers are revered as source and creative principle of meaning. Hugo and Balzac become the princes of gold-language, in which the triumphant nineteenth century could experience its absolute confidence in sure and well coined gold of linguistic money.

It is the unraveling of the three functions, which we shall see intervene in the beginning of the twentieth century. In the visual arts and literature, as well as in monetary circulation, the problem of reference will arise. We can speak in the world of economy of 'the abandonment of reference to concrete commodity-money' (Vilar, 1976) and, at the same time, of an acute problem of measure of values (standard) and of the relation to bullion (hypothetical convertibility of the token). Similarly, in the visual arts and in literature, the illusion of a possible and direct representation of the real will be replaced by 'abstraction' and by a more acute reflection on the medium itself. Everything unfolds as though a certain privileged moment of the interweaving among archetype, token, and treasure which allowed the 'effect of reality' has vanished before a new play among these three registers is instituted. It is as though an increasing autonomization of the pure symbolic emerges, the drift of a token having cut all links with stable value, which it was supposed to signify, a token which refers only to other tokens, in a general floating of the system of signs.

Thus, the history of the general equivalent, if we consider it from the perspective of the three registers of 'ideality', 'symbolicity', and 'reality' in their intricacy, engendered a periodization in which the European Middle Ages remind us of ancient Egypt, and in which the modern epoch since the Renaissance reminds us of the Greco-Roman world. There would be congruence within the field of aesthetic representation between realism and circulating gold-money, between symbolism and archetype-money, and, finally, between abstraction and token-money. Such a congruence does not imply that money as thing is determinant, but that money as social relation is highly significant of the types of relations which are instituted in a social formation and of the way in which archetype, token, and treasure intertwine.

The beginning of the twentieth century is marked by a decisive crisis that represents a break in relation to the system of the Renaissance. With the disappearance of the full general equivalent, the domination of token-money, which is neither measuring nor 'real' and which loses its convertibility, we witness a new system, the homology of which with the structuralist theories of the pure symbolic or non-figurative arts could be brought into prominence. The indefinite drift of signifiers without any transcendental signified, which could anchor the play of signs in a treasure or standard with absolute meaning, accords well with the circulation of a token without backing, an almost exclusive domination of the pure symbolic over the other two registers. Postmodernity takes place in this new regime of the general equivalent and of exchange. It leads to the so-called symbol economy.

Up to the end of the nineteenth century, the sensible presence of the monetary substance (gold, silver) which guaranteed more or less directly the value of the circulating sign, could lead us to forget that money was also a sign. The gold-standard system implied the circulation of gold by itself (until the Frist World War) or the free convertibility of bank-notes into gold. And this, according to a creed which was almost unanimously shared by all economists and statesmen of the nineteenth century, regardless of their nationality, their religious beliefs, or philosophical opinions: 'banknotes have value only because they represent gold'. Marx himself denied the possibility or the legitimacy of a money which would be a mere sign (against the theory of Berkeley and Steuart). For him, the backing by commodity-money (produced by a certain amount of labor) is necessary. Nowadays, the direct representational possibility of monetary signs is suspended not only for circumstantial reasons, but completely suppressed, as we know, for reasons that became structural. Thus, we passed from a monetary regime where gold circulated *in presencia* to a regime where money was a sign representing gold; and finally to money which is a pure sign, without any reference to a gold-value, a regime of complete nonconvertibility. The logical relationship between the nonconvertibility of money and the dismissal of the labor theory of value by neoclassical economists (Walras, Jevons, *et al.*) and mainstream economics has been stressed. As Fabra (1979) shows, the theory of the 'numéraire' (legal-tender value) developed by Walras allows us not to consider it necessarily as commodity-money, since its value rests only upon our desire, our need. So, this legal-tender can become a sign. There is a deep semiotic, economical, political revolution whose radical bearings we still have not measured.

Money becomes a mere sign, a writing, but this writing is no longer the substitute of something else which guarantees its value. The question of the substitute and of the substitute of the substitute which lies at the heart of the mechanism of symbolicity arises in a new manner. In a very precise way, we are able to date the last moment of this process with reference marks that abruptly become evident in broad daylight, the reverse of relationships between the thing and the sign. It is Richard Nixon's decision of 1971 that suspended the dollar's convertibility into gold. The dollar, that exceptional central money, that had assumed indirectly the gold convertibility of all other currencies, itself became inconvertible. The argument that leads to the decision of the dollar's inconvertibility is remarkable and amazing. The true and only international currency appointed by the financial choices of the public, being already the dollar (and no longer gold) – consequently, the dollar is better than gold and gold is only a substitute for the dollar and not the contrary. We perceive with precision the true semiotic reversal that surely refers to a political and economic conjuncture (and structure) in its entirety, which presides over this historical decision: the sign-dollar becomes a store-value, whereas the function of the reserve of values (treasure, hoarding) could only have been previously conceived as constituted by a 'reality' with an 'intrinsic' value, able to become a commodity-money. It is really an important step in the 'fiduciarization' of money. No one has yet measured all the far-reaching effects of this reversal, the unparalleled regime of exchanges to which it corresponds, the new relationship among reality, symbolicity and ideality which it implies.

The inconvertibility of money is only the most striking and disturbing manifestation of the 'symbol economy'. The entire economy, in its movement of globalization, is based upon gigantic pyramids of debt, each one building on the others, in an incredible equilibrium of promises to pay. By means of credit, we can purchase without paying immediately and we can sell without really being in possession. The notion of 'presence' and of 'property' are called into question. This accumulation of 'promises to pay' implies a referral toward the future, a deferring and an intangible status of the value.

This virtual economy postulates a regime of the sign, or of the symbolic, that can be compared exactly to the one articulated by the philosophy of Jacques Derrida: the structure of the deferred, of the referral, of the non-presence. Never the 'thing' itself, in its present and in its presence, in its full possession and perception, by the drift of signs, a writing of writings (Goux, 1989). In credit, in the indefinite referral of debt, in the inconvertibility, in the floating exchange rate, in the stock-market speculation, and so on – in every financial transaction on which the economy feeds today we encounter the same lack of 'treasure' (if we wish, 'reality') that would give a guaranteed pledge to the referral of signs, one to the other. It is not without reason in the lexicon that we often contrast a 'real economy' to a 'virtual' or financial economy that operates only on signs, writing, and, as of today, exceeds to a great degree the former by the quantity of its intangible transactions. What is new is not the existence of these kinds of abstract procedures but their extent, scope, mode of transmission, and generalization. We might have spoken of a 'symbol economy' opposed to a 'real economy' and this terminology is significant.

The founding economists of the marginalist school (Jevons, Walras) had already taken an interest, more so than their predecessors, concerning the different roles or functions of money, making the distinction, again, between money as medium of exchange, as unit of measure, and as store of value. And they clearly became aware that these roles could logically and historically come apart. But, it is only in the domination of industrial capital by financial capital (theorized by Hilferding in *Finance Capital*, in 1910) that the idea of a financial and monetary system became decisive. Money is not a thing of value, a good, but a sign in a system; it only takes value in that system – parallel to and contemporaneously with the theory of language elaborated by Saussure. It is the predominance of the system, of the structure , that allows the disappearance of gold coins and, later, of the gold-system itself. A word, according to Saussure, does not directly represent a concept and a thing; its value, or meaning, depends on language as a system. Just as the linguistic sign, the monetary sign is 'arbitrary and differential'. The monetary sign does not directly represent a value and a richness of wealth. Money is no more than a mere trace in the indefinite circulation of a debt. Inconvertibility becomes the normal regime of the sign, whether linguistic or monetary.

It is noteworthy that aesthetic modernism (cubism, abstract painting, dadaist poetry, and so on) is in itself strictly contemporary with this breaking-point in the representational conception of money and of language. This historical moment was marked by unprecedented hyperinflation which, we are able to say according to Polanyi, led to the totalitarian disasters (particularly nazism) as a reaction to the floating of 'values' and in its quest for an origin and a foundation that could confront the fluctuations of the time. It is a general crisis of 'values' (aesthetic, ethical) beyond any economic definition.

'Cash, check or charge?' This question, asked every day by cashiers in department stores, enables us to see how the instrument of payment is seized by this movement of representational dismissal. In this question, three modes of payment, belonging to three recent successive stages, correspond to very different regimes of symbolization.

The banknote presents itself as a political symbol marked by the founding and regulating role of the state. The banknote is a civic monument. The state, which has the monopoly of issuing banknotes, guarantees its value. The state illustrates them by the most solemn insignia to assert and reinforce the credibility of this guarantee. The banknote is a mediator between a seller and a buyer who remain anonymous, as if the responsibility of the 'backing' was entirely supported by the state. Using a banknote is still situating oneself in the political space of representation. On the contrary, with a check, then a credit card, and so on, one drifts to another kind of transaction. State mediation disappears. Each party to the transaction is identified by a proper name: the banker, the bearer, the recipient. Instead of a monetary exchange, it is an operation or transaction on values. A check is not money but a 'transfer order'. With this deposit or bank-money and all these account movements 'in writing', a semiotic and praxeological space opens up where the marks are no longer signs of value (in a representational mode) but sign-operations to be carried out. These signs cannot be directly appropriated, but they determine an always-open play of deferral, remittal, reference, postponement, adjournment, with no full and definitive clearing process being conceivable. Strictly speaking, there is no exchange but, instead, information, order, operation so interlinked that the time parameter (the deferring, the delaying) is decisive.

Can 'charge' payments and the 'smartcard' still be considered as the use of 'money'? We are shifting from a representational notion of value to an operative one, which opens up a new problematic regime of symbolization. This corresponds to the power held by banks, and not just by the state, to create 'money' ex nihilo (Allais, 1990). Crashes, inflation, devaluation, boom-and-bust cycles, daily volatility, and other distortions remind us that the relationships between social reality and monetary and financial symbolicity can be a cause of concern, in spite of those who acclaim the novelty and promise of the phenomena (Rachline, 1991;Wriston, 1996). The difference between the 'real economy' and the virtual or symbol economy implies new modes of profits (sometimes questionable) and exploitation (nationally or, overall, internationally, in the global financial system).

The economy becoming an electronic, global cyberfinance is based on this monetary nominalism. This nominalism is not the one that prevailed in the Middle Ages, because it is based on operation, on transaction, and not on an ideal measure. From this angle, the contemporary economy is made up of a nonrepresentational semiotics, a financial 'grammatology', which leads to disarray through the crisis of all the previous conceptions of value and of all the former economic models. Economy has objectively entered into a deconstructive regime of the sign, of value, of the real and time – and, maybe, in the long term, the deconstruction of economy itself.

Speculation on the stock exchange, capitalism at its peak, with its perplexed and paradoxical logic, seems to undo the oppositions between the virtual and the real, the rational and the irrational, the predictable and the aleatory, the real and the simulated, the material and the intangible, and so on (Goux, 1997). We can say that this regime of speculation is an objective deconstructor of traditional oppositions issued from Greek metaphysics and from the age of the Enlightenment. It is a capitalism that has became postmodern. The impact of this sociohistorical conjuncture on the Althusserian approach to Marxism would be interesting and important to consider but it is outside the scope of this paper. (This approach has recently been richly explored by Stephen Cullenberg, David F. Ruccio, Jack Amariglio, Stephen Resnick, and Richard Wolff.)

As far as share values are concerned, even the illusion of a 'real' value becomes impossible. Its credit status, its immateriality, and, most of all, the impossibility of fixing any value whatsoever outside of its instantaneous price make any notion of value-in-itself futile. Here again one cannot help but notice a parallel between the emergence of a stock market paradigm of values (in neoclassical economics) and the anti-Platonist explosion that shook postmodern philosophy. Walras and Nietzsche, let us not forget, were contemporaries.

From this angle, Jacques Derrida's deconstruction is a remarkable philosophical expression, perhaps the most radical and the most coherent, of a sociosymbolic moment dominated by the perplexing paradigm of the stock exchange, the speculative search for 'differential profit' in informational transactions, the inconvertibility of the monetary sign, all the logic of credit and of the 'differing' linked to the operations of financial capitalism in a regime of 'symbolic economy'. But Derrida's philosophical premises do not enable him to recognize this sociohistorical determination.

And yet the distress of economic thought and the risk of chaos can only lead us to restore, beyond the autonomization of the purely symbolic, the historical and social background that these operations are ignoring. The glorification of mathematical models, cut-off from the real (denounced by Maurice Allais, 1990) corresponds to the same moment. The banking, financial, speculative economy relies on a relative autonomization of the symbolic. A new critique of political economy, in a postmodern context, should reintegrate, in a new manner, the articulation of sociopolitical reality with the historical imaginary from which the 'symbol economy', for its own profit, believes itself to have become independent.

References

Allais, M. (1990) 'La science économique et les faits', *Revue des deux mondes* (June).
—— (1993) 'L'Occident au bord du désastre', *Libération* (2 August).
Bloch, M. (1954) *Esquisse d'une histoire monétaire de L'Europe*, Paris: Collin.
Chydenius, J. (1975) 'La théorie du symbolisme medieval', *Poétique*, no. 23.
Drucker, P. (1981) 'Toward the Next Economics', in D. Bell and I. Kristol (eds) *Crisis in Economic Theory*, New York: Basic Books, 4–18.
Fabra, P. (1979) *L'anticapitalisme: essai de rehabilitation de l'économie politique*, Paris: Flammarion.
Goux, J.-J. (1990) *Symbolic Economies*, Ithaca: Cornell University Press.
—— (1989) 'Cash,Check or Charge?' *Communication*, 50: 7–22.
—— (1994) *The Coiners of Language*, Norman: University of Oklahoma Press.
—— (1997) 'Values and Speculations: The Stock Exchange Paradigm', *Cultural Values*, (October).
Hugo, V. (1972) *Choses vues, 1849–1869*, Paris: Gallimard.
Kurtzman, J. (1993) *The Death of Money*, New-York: Little Brown and Company.
Larousse. (1928–33) *Larousse du XXe siècle*, vol. 1, Paris: Librairie Larousse.
Marx, K. (1990) *Capital*, vol. 1, trans. B. Fowkes, London: Penguin.
Rachline, F. (1991) *De Zero à Epsilon: L'économie de la capture*, Paris: Archipel First.
Valery, P. (1943) *Tel quel*, II, Paris: Gallimard.
Vilar, P. (1976) *A History of Gold and Money, 1450 to 1920*, trans. J. White, New York: Verso.
Wriston, W. (1996) 'The Future of Money', *Wired* (October).

8

CHACUN SON GOUX? OR, SOME SKEPTICAL REFLECTIONS ON FLAT BODIES AND HEAVY METAL

Regenia Gagnier and John Dupré

For over a decade now, perhaps since the wide reception of Foucault's *History of Sexuality* (1976), literary and cultural studies have given a prominent place in their discourse to the figure of the body. Originally, as in Foucault's *Discipline and Punish* (1975), the body figured as the site on which ideological and repressive state apparatuses – the Church, the School, the Family, the Clinic, the Prison, and so forth – played out their institutional forms of power and control. More recently, the body has figured as the site of aesthesis – of sense, feeling, emotion, sensibility, taste, etc. – that rejected undue emphasis on rationality, certainty, mind, etc. That is, critical aesthetic discourse used the body, its senses, emotions, feelings, pains, affects, neuroses, and so on, to critique scientific notions of rationality. But this was a critical strategy, not meant to reify a mind/body problem that critical theory had long ago rejected in its Cartesian formulations. We do not see that Amariglio and Ruccio's deployment of the term 'body' connects significantly with either of these usages, and wonder whether their main points might not more clearly be expressed in terms of the concept of a person.

If we substitute the term person in their paper for body, then we might see that since the nineteenth century there has been a decreasing emphasis on 'persons' or 'people' in economic theory culminating in, for example, Arrow and Debreu's formulation of general equilibrium. According to Amariglio and Ruccio, Arrow, Debreu, and other 'high-level neoclassical theorists' have unyoked neoclassical theory from oppressive humanistic notions of normalized persons by redistributing value to different bodily functions and capabilities: to production, consumption, distribution, roles in institutions, strategic interaction and so forth. If such functions and capabilities are indeed the approved body in Amariglio and Ruccio, then there is no reason in the terms discussed above to call them bodies as distinct from minds, for both mind and body operate within these functions and capabilities. (One might think here of P.F.Strawson's (1959) 'double-aspect' theory of the person, as one thing amenable to distinct classes of mental and physical attributions.)

At any rate, the functions and capabilities that Amariglio, Ruccio, Arrow, and Debreu are talking about clearly do not amount to bodies in the sense that literary and cultural critics have talked about the body, for the latter have until very recently (see Halberstam and Livingston, 1995) talked about the *human* body, as in the body in labour or the body in pain, or the body in need, or the tortured body, or the desiring or sexed body; whereas the four economists are not talking about human bodies at all, we think, but about processes that transcend individuals. Rather, they are talking about 'bodies' as components of systems such as the corporate body, the firm, or the economy in equilibrium.

The question is, is the move they approve from normative human bodies to more diverse human bodies, or is it a move toward processes, equations, and systems that make economics a self-contained system that has little or nothing to do with what Adam Smith called the needs and desires of the people? Amariglio and Ruccio think that humanistic individualism is bad, and we certainly agree that both bourgeois and methodological individualism have functioned oppressively; but is Amariglio and Ruccio's postmodern/neoclassical system of functions and capabilities a more liberating conception?

'The rich and diverse set of corporeal images' that Amariglio and Ruccio find in Arrow and Debreu amount to two that are familiar to us: the mind(-body?) of the book-keeper or the accountant, who alone can provide us with information on choice or preference in the form of statistical price lists; and a cyborg body 'associated with assembly, transformation, repackaging, and so on of one set of objects (inputs) in order to end up with a different set of objects (outputs)': 'Neoclassical production is thus rendered as a collection or assemblage of heterogeneous elements and materials, a set of operational linkages and external relations between things, machine connections, in which a discontinuous series of bodily organs, processes, and flows come together with other things' (pp. 155). To a cultural critic, this sounds like Donna Haraway's cyborg, a creature of integrated circuits, fractured identities, the informatics of domination, 'able to be disassembled, reassembled, exploited as a reserve labour force; seen less as workers than as servers; subjected to time arrangements on and off the paid job that make a mockery of a limited work day; leading an existence that always borders on being obscene, out of place, and reducible' (1985: 166). It's down to Amariglio and Ruccio to tell us the difference.

A cultural historian might approach this world of different functions and capabilities differently. Cultural history is not niggardly of different models of humankind, as creative producer or labourer; as consumer, hedonist, or creature of taste; or of different models of value as absolute or relative, as heavy metal (silver, gold) or as a concept like distance, always defined with reference to something else.

The economist Arjo Klamer recently edited a collection called *The Value of Culture: On the Relationship between Economics and Arts* (1996) in which he (though not the other contributors) opposes a romantic idea of cultural value to economic value. Klamer uses aesthetic value to critique the reduction of all value to price. Yet the history of aesthetics offers no unitary conception of aesthetic value, but shows varied models of production, consumption, and value contemporary with economic models. There are models of production, reproduction, and creativity that posit aesthetic man as producer or creator and scrutinize the conditions of creativity and production from the perspective of producers; models of consumption that posit aesthetic man as hedonic or the man of taste and that concern themselves with the calculation of pleasure, the pursuit of happiness, and distinctions of taste. These basic anthropological models roughly correspond to a shift from a labour theory of value to marginal utility or consumer demand. Consider the following quotations from the history of aesthetics:

> Now I maintain that the Beautiful is the symbol of the morally Good; and only because we refer the Beautiful to the morally Good does our liking for it include a claim to everyone else's assent.
> (Immanuel Kant, *Critique of Judgment* [1790] 1987: 228)

Probably the most famous statement in Western aesthetic philosophy, Kant's referral of the beautiful to the moral good is a statement of absolute value; it is universal; it refers to a freedom from desire or self-interest that harmonizes the self and the self in relation to society. The Kantian aesthetic arose with industrialism and concerned itself with self-regulating subjects and autonomous works: it was self-regulating, mechanistic, and bourgeois, like Smith's market that also harmonized self-interest with the social good. The Kantian aesthetic is not about the object (product) or its producer but about a process that occurs between subject and object; it is not about pleasure ('mere liking') but a system of interrelation between the good, the true, and the beautiful.

> Go forth again to gaze upon the old cathedral front, where you have smiled so often at the fantastic ignorance of the old sculptors: examine once more those ugly goblins, and formless monsters, and stern statues, anatomiless and rigid; but do not

mock at them, for they are signs of the life and liberty of every
workman who struck the stone.
>(John Ruskin 'The Nature of Gothic' in
>*Stones of Venice* [1851] 1985: 85)

A classic labour theory of value. The object has value because of the labour mixed in it. A purely economic labour theory of value, as in Locke or Smith, traces value merely to labour as the scarce transformer of natural resources into goods. Ruskin, like Marx, has a deeper account of the value in human labour, so that ultimately the value of goods is determined by the quality of life of the producer.

> Women cannot distinguish between soul and body, whereas the dandy creates a more and more perceptible divorce between the spirit and the brute... The more a man cultivates the arts, the less often he gets an erection... Only the brute gets really good erections. Fucking is the lyricism of the people. (Charles Baudelaire, *My Heart Laid Bare* [1863 pub. 1867] 1986: 175, 210, 213)

In his autobiographical notebooks, *Mon Coeur Mis à Nu*, Baudelaire presented his critique of productionism and reproduction in the form of an attack on the socialist-feminist George Sand. He preferred the more voyeuristic pleasures of the connoisseur *flaneur* to the active life of production and reproduction.

> I shall write no more. Already I feel myself to be a trifle outmoded. I belong to the Beardsley period. Younger men, with months of activity before them, have pressed forward since then. *Cedo junioribus.*
>>(Max Beerbohm's Preface to his *Complete Works* 1896 published when he was 24 years old)

A comic version of the same critique of productionism that illustrates the fin-de-siècle basic stances toward the economy: boredom with production but love of comfort, insatiable desire for new sensation, and the fear of falling behind the competition.

> A cigarette is the perfect type of a perfect pleasure, because it leaves one unsatisfied.
>>(Oscar Wilde, *The Picture of Dorian Gray* [1891] 1978: 228)

This is Wilde's famous definition of a cigarette that also functions as that of a perfect commodity under capitalism, because it creates the desire for more. It continues the emphasis on pleasure, consumption, and insatiability and illustrates a general, but not exclusive, shift from need to desire, what the turn-of-the-century economist Vilfredo Pareto would call 'ophelimities'.

In the following quotation, women are no longer producers or Malthusian reproducers, as above in Baudelaire, but cigarettes or commodities, to 'fulfil' the insatiable desires of men:

> More than ever did he seek women, urged by a nervous erithism which he could not explain or control. Married women and young girls came to him from drawing-rooms, actresses from theatres, shopgirls from the streets, and though seemingly all were as unimportant and accidental as the cigarettes he smoked, each was a drop in the ocean of the immense ennui accumulating in his soul.
> (George Moore, *Mike Fletcher* [1889] 1977: 261)

In the next quotation, the productivist feminist replies. Here the woman as wage earner despises the idle consuming pleasure-seeking man; the parasitic female *produces* the consuming male; consumption appears as decadence, a fall from production:

> Only an able and labouring womanhood can permanently produce an able manhood; only an effete and inactive male can ultimately be produced by an effete and inactive womanhood. The curled darling, scented and languid, with his drawl, his delicate apparel, his devotion to the rarity and variety of his viands, whose severest labour is the search after pleasure;... this male whether found in the late Roman empire, the Turkish harem of today, or in our northern civilisations, is possible only because generations of parasitic women have preceded him. More repulsive than the parasitic female herself, because a yet further product of decay, it is yet only the scent of his mother's boudoir that we smell in his hair.
> (Olive Schreiner, 'The Woman Question' 1899, cited in Ledger, 1997: 76)

Schreiner's emphasis on creative production can be compared with that of other New Women, like the novelist Sarah Grand, whose productivism made her pathologize all French literature as 'vain, hollow, cynical, *barren*' (cited in Richardson, 1999–2000: 244).

The final quotation may be contrasted with Ruskin's valueing of labourers above: here the people going to and from work are only valued for the consumption or 'taste' they provide the aesthete. Unaesthetic in themselves, they supply the pleasures of condescension to the discerning aesthete:

> As I walk to and fro in Edgware Road, I cannot help sometimes wondering why these people exist. Watch their faces, and you will see in them a listlessness, a hard unconcern, a failure to be interested.... In all these faces you will see no beauty, and you will see no beauty in the clothes they wear, or in their attitudes in rest or movement, or in their voices when they speak. They are human beings to whom nature has given no grace or charm, whom life has made vulgar.
>
> (Arthur Symons, *London: A Book of Aspects*, privately printed 1909, cited in Beckson, 1987: 242)

We draw two points from these quotations. First, that while there seems to have been a general shift from production to consumption models in art, as there was in economics, toward the end of the nineteenth century, the dominant models were never uncontested – feminist producers challenged male consumers, socialists challenged capitalists, and so forth. Second, that despite their different models of producers, consumers, and value, the quotations above from cultural history all refer to identifiably human producers, consumers, and values: i.e., stonemasons, women, collectors or connoisseurs, undergraduates, womanizers, *bourgeoises*, gay men. We wonder whether a plurality of different kinds of people in diverse relations of cooperation and opposition may not provide a potentially more liberating image than the fracturing of individuals into a diversity of disembodied and dehumanized functions. Although we share Amariglio and Ruccio's reluctance to essentialize people, and do not intend to reduce people to one-dimensional consumers, producers, reproducers, gays, etc., the transfer of agency from people to their diverse functions (p.147) seems to us to be going too far. People do exhibit agency in the roles of consumers, or of workers, or of gays, but they do so as whole people, not as one among their various 'functions'. Of course – and this is part of the point of de-essentialization – one person may act in several of such roles at different times, and perhaps at other times simply as individuals. We are less enthusiastic than Amariglio and Ruccio about the 'flat' body (p.152) lacking internality. Such a flat body has another notorious instantiation in twentieth-century thought, as Skinnerian behaviorism. Both behaviorism and neoclassical economics derive in large part from classical logical positivism, and its attempts to eliminate all reference to a reality beyond immediate appearances. This intimate association with a failed program in experimental psychology and a discredited philosophical system contributes to our more pessimistic assessment than Amariglio and Ruccio's of the benefits of neoclassical economics.

These quotations also tell us quite a lot about social relations from the eighteenth to the early twentieth century, and they tell us quite a lot about 'the needs and desires of the people', provision for which was Smith's idea of the goal of economics as a profession (Smith, [1776] 1937: 397). How much do Arrow and Debreu tell us about these friends? One wonders whether the move from the human body, or person, to bodies as diverse systems of functional interrelation and conduits for the flow of information, as in Arrow and Debreu, is the same move from money as a system of social relations to money as information. Perhaps postmodernism means the move from persons and people to information systems. That is, Amariglio and Ruccio act as if we are, as sociologists have said, moving from value to difference; but does this amount to moving from people to systems of knowledge? And if this is what postmodernism mandates, should we welcome it?

As it became clear that the possession of money would take the place of other, traditional forms of status, money was criticized because it negated not just the metal referent but all human capacities and therefore all social relations. The referent of the critique was not gold but human capacities and social relations. 'Cash payment', wrote Thomas Carlyle in 'Chartism', 'is the sole nexus between man and man' ([1839] 1971: 199). Contrary to the problem being the absence of the real weight of gold, Carlyle contrasts the ponderous heaviness of wealth with the lightness of being – 'flaccid, imponderous' – without it:

> And now what is thy property? That parchment title-deed, that purse thou buttonest in thy breeches-pocket? Is that thy valuable property? Unhappy brother, most poor insolvent brother, I without parchment at all, with purse oftenest in the flaccid state imponderous, which will not fling against the wind, have quite other property than that! I have the miraculous breath of Life in me, breathed into my nostrils by Almighty God. I have affections, thoughts, a *god-given capability to be and do*; rights, therefore – the right for instance to thy love if I love thee, to thy guidance if I obey thee: the strangest rights, whereof in church pulpits one hears something though almost unintelligible now; rights stretching high into Immensity, far into Eternity!
>
> ([1839] 1971: 194)

At precisely the same time Carlyle was writing, Marx turned to Goethe and Shakespeare to depict 'the real nature of money', drawing on *Faust* and *Timon of Athens* to show how money's properties *become* the properties of its possessor, obliterating other properties altogether. 'Six stallions', Marx cites *Faust*, 'I can afford/ Is not their strength my property?/ I tear along, a sporting lord,/ As if their legs belonged to me'. And Marx cites *Timon*'s hymn to gold (IVii):

> This yellow slave

Will knit and break religions, bless the accursed;
Make the hoar leprosy adored, place thieves
And give them title, knee and approbation
With senators on the bench: This is it
That makes the wappen'd widow wed again;
She, whom the spital-house and ulcerous sores
Would cast the gorge at, this embalms and spices
To the April day again.... Damned earth,
Thou common whore of mankind, that putt'st odds
Among the rout of nations.
                    (*Timon of Athens* IViii)

Marx glosses the passage with an analysis of metaphor. Money makes the ugly attractive, the lame mobile, the bad honoured, the dishonest honest, the stupid talented, the desirous fulfilled. It turns incapacities into their contrary; it obliterates natural qualities and replaces them with social aspects:

> That which is for me through the medium of money — that for which I can pay (i.e., which money can buy) — that am I, the possessor of the money. The extent of the power of money is the extent of my power. Money's properties are my properties and essential powers — the properties and powers of its possessor. Thus what I am and am capable of is by no means determined by my individuality. I am ugly, but I can buy for myself the most beautiful of women. Therefore I am not ugly, for the effect of ugliness — its deterrent power — is nullified by money. I, in my character as an individual, am lame, but money furnishes me with twenty-four feet, therefore I am not lame. I am bad, dishonest, unscrupulous, stupid, but money is honoured, and therefore so is its possessor. Money is the supreme good, therefore its possessor is good. Money, besides, saves me the trouble of being dishonest: I am therefore presumed honest. I am stupid, but money is the real mind of all things and how then should its possessor be stupid? Besides, he can buy talented people for himself, and is he who has power over the talented not more talented than the talented? Do not I, who thanks to money am capable of all that the human heart longs for, possess all human capacities? Does not my money therefore transform all my incapacities into their contrary?
>
> The overturning and confounding of all human and natural qualities, the fraternization of impossibilities — the divine power of money — lies in its character as men's estranged, alienating

and self-disposessing species-nature. Money is the alienated ability of mankind.
(Marx, *Economic and Philosophic Manuscripts* [1844] 1978: 102–5)

The problem for Marx was not whether the money was in the form of cash, check, or charge, but in the replacement of substantive properties with the properties money can buy. And the problem is not that money is necessarily evil, for although Marx probably thinks it an evil that the dishonest should appear honest and that the dishonourable should be honoured, it is probably a good that the ugly should be made attractive, and that the lame should be mobile.

The problem for the Enlightenment critics of money, which as we shall see below was a virtue for the Romantic communitarians, was that the cash nexus should be the sole nexus between man and man, that without money one did not *appear* at all except as ugly, lame, bad, dishonest, or stupid. The problem with money was the havoc it played with social relations, not with the gold standard. People were either commodities, to have their value added by money, or they were creatures with capabilities to be and do, to love and be loved, to guide and be guided. Without that, the particular fetish in which the money, or the commodification of social relations, was embodied, was beside the point. 'Capital', as Marx said, 'was not a thing, but a social relation between persons... Property in money, means of subsistence, machinery, and other means of production, do not yet stamp a man as a capitalist if there be wanting the correlative – the wage-worker' ([1867] 1967: 766).

In fact there was a school of Romantic theorists who did not, like Goethe's *Faust*, associate paper money with the work of the devil, of a diabolical alchemy that produced value out of nothing. These theorists had no interest in metallism, but rather saw money as social glue precisely because it signified not gold but a social, communicative pact. According to the Germanicist Richard T. Gray, Adam Müller argued against the commonly held notion that paper money was a mere second-order representation of metallic money and defended paper currencies and credit money against metallism (Gray, 2000: 298). Indeed, he reverses this relationship, giving priority to the word, 'to the stamp that makes metal into minted coin': 'what by means of a kind of credit, first elevates metal to the status of money, and which in the further development of civil society is represented in bank notes – is the principal thing' (298). Gray concludes, 'Legal tender, in other words, is constituted not by any concrete value, by the worth of the precious metals from which it is made, but by the "credit", the faith, belief, and confidence placed in it and in the state that secures its value.... Money, for Müller, is nothing other than the representative, the symbol, of this natural sociability, this solicitous co-dependence among human beings'. This acccount makes perfect sense of the story Goux tells of the abandonment of the gold standard. Surely the dollar *had* become a more plausible repository of confidence than any mere lump of metal. Against Adam Smith's belief that paper currencies threatened to undermine 'the commercial and moral fabric of European civilization' (cited in Gray, 2000: 299), for these Romantics money could be liberating: Gray cites the German economist Johann Georg Busch's *Treatise on the Circulation of Money* (1780), 'Wherever money is employed, no one is tied any longer to particular individuals in order to satisfy his needs from those individuals' (301).

Gray argues that Müller's theory of money derived from a Romantic theory of interpretive community developed by Novalis and others.

> The Romantics expended a great deal of energy theorizing about just such interpretive or, if you will, semiotic communities. One need only think of their notions of 'symphilosophizing' or 'sympoeticizing', of collective intellectual effort and production, or of their demand for the development of a new mythology... Adam Müller's theory of money is but one more manifestation of this drive for interpretive community. For Müller, money is the symbol of an economic mythology, that is, an economic discourse that provides community and coherence for all the members of a state.
>
> (309)

For Müller, value is relative, like distance; value is a term used in relation to agents; Müller said money was a function of acts of exchange. Property cannot be private, hoarded, but should be a 'hypermarket', a nexus of furious and incessant exchange, holding a community together. Müller objected to classical political economy's overemphasis on economic 'facts' to the detriment of relations, dynamic interdependencies, and reciprocal interactions. Both Müller's relativism, hyperactivity, and semiotics and the 'flat' processes and flows that Amariglio and Ruccio admire in Arrow and Debreu share properties that have been called 'postmodern'; but Müller's 'romantic semiotics' refers at its deepest levels to social relations.

Now, with respect to Goux's paper, the question is whether the forms of hypercredit currently represented in modern finance have much to do with exchange or communities, or whether they operate at a level of abstraction that obliterates agency, exchange, and community for most of us altogether. Do the forms of hypercredit that make up LBOs, Futures, Savings and Loan scandals, hedge funds and the rest since the 1980s have anything to do with the exchange of belief among persons and communities or only with electronic bleeps on a computer screen? Does money's liberation from heavy metal permit forms of wealth transfer that would make Müller and Novalis, not to mention Marx and Smith, turn over in their graves? The least we can say is that monetary transactions have become disembodied and dehumanized. The arbitrageur or investment banker at the computer terminal is far removed indeed from Adam Smith's transactions with the village butcher, the baker, and the brewer, or Marx's ugly rich man's transactions with prostitutes. Only through a neoclassical fantasy is such a person contributing to social cohesion or to 'solicitious codependence among human beings'. The crucial point, however, is that despite this dehumanization of the economic transaction, it seems to us that the fundamental nature of money as a mediator of social relations remains unchanged.

Although as Müller's romanticism suggests, there is no necessary connection between money and harm, a useful parallel in the cases just discussed is with the change from classical warfare through hand-to-hand combat to the remote dispatch of smart bombs in modern warfare. There are no personal interactions in the latter case, but the essence of the relation remains, or indeed is amplified: someone gets killed. Similarly the arbitrageur or investment banker in Boston or New York never comes face-to-face with the Indonesian peasant or small business woman in Hong Kong who loses her livelihood. But the causal relation is nonetheless real. This is our deepest concern with the formalisms, abstractions and disembodiments that Amariglio and Ruccio applaud in contemporary economics and with the abstract distinctions Goux asserts between historical forms of money: they occlude the common thread that runs through this postmodern diversity, that in the end someone is harmed.

References

Baudelaire, Charles (1863) *My Heart Laid Bare and Other Prose Writings*, trans. Norman Cameron, London: Soho, 1986.
Beckson, Karl (1987) *Arthur Symons: A Life*, Oxford: Clarendon.
Beerbohm, Max (1896) *Complete Works*, London: John Lane.
Carlyle, Thomas (1839) *Selected Writings*, London: Penguin, 1971.
Foucault, Michel (1976) *The History of Sexuality*, New York: Random House, 1980.
—— (1975) *Discipline and Punish: The Birth of the Prison*, New York: Random House, 1979.
Gray, Richard (2000) 'Hypersign, Hypermoney, Hypermarket: Adam Müller's Theory of Money and Romantic Semiotics'in 'Economics and Culture', special issue of *New Literary History* 31:2 (Spring): 295–314.
Halberstam, Judith and Livingston, Ira (eds) (1995) *Posthuman Bodies*, Bloomington: Indiana University Press.
Haraway, Donna J. (1985) 'A Cyborg Manifesto', reprinted in *Simians, Cyborgs, and Women: The Reinvention of Nature*, New York: Routledge, 149–182.
Kant, Immanuel (1790) *Critique of Judgment*, trans. Werner S. Pluhar, Indianapolis: Hackett, 1987.

Klamer, Arjo (1996) *The Value of Culture: On the Relationship Between Economics and Art*, Netherlands: Amsterdam University Press.

Ledger, Sally (1997) *The New Woman: Fiction and Feminism at the Fin de Siècle*, Manchester: Manchester University Press.

Marx, Karl (1867) *Capital*, vol. 1, Frederick Engels (ed.), New York: International.

—— (1844) 'Economic and Philosophic Manuscripts' in Robert Tucker (ed.) *The Marx-Engels Reader*, New York: Norton, 1978.

Moore, George (1977) *Mike Fletcher*, New York: Garland.

Richardson, Angelique (1999–2000) 'The Eugenization of Love: Sarah Grand and the Morality of Genealogy', *Victorian Studies* 42 : 227–55

Ruskin, John (1851) *Unto this Last and Other Writings*, London: Penguin, 1985.

Smith, Adam (1776) *The Wealth of Nations*, The Cannan Edition, New York: Modern Library, 1937.

Strawson, P.F. (1959) *Individuals: An Essay in Descriptive Metaphysics*, London: Methuen.

Wilde, Oscar (1891) *The Portable Oscar Wilde*, (ed.) R. Aldington, Middlesex: Penguin, 1978.

PART IV

GENDERED SUBJECTIVITIES IN NEOCLASSICAL ECONOMICS

9
WOMEN'S CHOICES AND THE ETHNOCENTRISM/RELATIVISM DILEMMA

S. Charusheela

Feminism, relativism, ethnocentrism[1]

For the past two decades or more, feminist theorists have been grappling with the criticism that their analyses of women's oppression are ethnocentrically universalist.[2] But while there is broad agreement in principle that ethnocentric universalism is to be avoided, there is disagreement about how to do this without falling into its opposite, a cultural relativism that reinforces patriarchy. The problem is particularly acute for feminist development economists.

This paper addresses one aspect of this difficult path between ethnocentrism and relativism by focusing on theoretical concepts of *choice* used in assessing women's activities and decisions in differing cultural contexts.[3] This assessment highlights fundamental presuppositions of the Enlightenment notions of human nature on which the concept of choice is built, and argues that both ethnocentrism and relativism are historical products of the same underlying conception of human agency.[4] It will be demonstrated that this dilemma results from a fundamental gap, or flaw, in the neoclassical conception of choice. The paper builds on this insight to offer an alternative conception of human subjects which can help feminist economists better negotiate the ethnocentrism/relativism divide.

The location of choice in feminist vision

Feminism as it arose within the context of the Enlightenment and liberalism in the West has always had trouble reconciling the goals of equality and autonomy in assessing women's decisions.[5] *Equality*, specifically the notion that women do not have a socially defined relationship of equality to men, remains a central organizing principle of feminist analysis and politics. The evidence most often offered for the absence of equality is disparity in *aggregate outcomes*. If we assume a universal human nature which informs choices, then systematic disparity in outcomes must be the result of disparity in options. In other words, gender-skewed outcomes are attributed not to a different female nature, but to male oppression and female exclusion.[6] If for some reason women do not, given a chance, make the same choices and attain the same outcomes as men, this is attributed to a socialization that has *created* male–female differences in individual preferences and aspirations to the detriment of women.[7] Once this socialization is removed, the underlying substratum of universal being will take over and the systematic differences in outcomes between men and women should disappear.[8]

Feminism, drawing on the Enlightenment, also values women's *autonomy* to make choices, including their autonomy of being – the right to *differ* from the norm, including the right to differ from men and make choices which reflect the type of female agency envisioned for feminist politics and practice.[9] Once autonomy enters the picture as a highly valued norm, however, we can no longer use disparities in aggregate outcomes as automatic indicators of oppression. Why do women often make decisions that leave them unequal to men? If we put forward socialization or internalized oppression as the answer, we are left with the problem of sorting women into those who suffer from internalized oppression and those who have genuine autonomy, and of doing this sorting based on observing outcomes and judging which choices are right. But once we do this, there is little freedom left in autonomy – women are not autonomous to make choices deemed inappropriate by the analyst/adjudicator. Can we conceive of worlds in which women act differently from men, attain different outcomes based on criteria we do not ourselves agree with, and yet do so as autonomous choosing beings expressing a desired identity for themselves?

This is not to argue that equality and autonomy are necessarily incompatible. But they are fundamentally different ideas, posing a dilemma for the feminist economist who confronts opposing assessments of women's choices and actions which depend on the criteria used in making the assessment. When we look at debates within Western feminism about Western societies, it is clear that this dilemma can be productive and in fact encourages deeper analysis.[10] Western feminists have started with a cultural base that permits sympathy with problematic expressions of autonomy by other Westerners, and generally find that autonomy and equality are either reconcilable, or else capable of generating a productive tension which allows us to have a sympathetic and complex understanding of – without any necessary agreement with – the women whose feminist agency may lead them to a conclusion or decision different from our own.

But the commitment to autonomy and the capacity for a sympathetic and complex understanding of feminist agency that may lead to divergent conclusions and decisions has been harder to maintain as cultural and historical difference widen. What do we do when women in a foreign culture assert as a choice actions or behaviors that do not lead to equality? What do we do when women, in asserting their right to autonomy of cultural identity and national self-determination, do not attack a social construction of gender we deem patriarchal, nor seek to replace it with notions of human autonomy or choice that we consider marks of female emancipation? Here, the explicit assertion of autonomy clashes with the goal of equality, and we are tempted to use the concept of socialization to attribute the choice to the influence of patriarchal ideology.

As above, we can argue that women have become unable, due to internalized oppression, to comprehend what their true interests are and hence lack the appropriate self-consciousness needed for them to undertake proper choice. Unfortunately for feminists working on these issues, such an assertion of inadequate or inappropriate consciousness for women 'elsewhere' is subject to sharp challenge, given the legacy of ethnocentric racial ideology and colonial history in shaping Western views of the non-West. This difficulty is not new. Feminism has been plagued by this question from the moment of its formal self-conception as a simultaneous theoretical and political project. This legacy takes its sharpest form in the ethnocentrism–relativism divide. This paper argues that the divide can be overcome because it is a product of a very particular conception of choice. The next section begins an analysis of this idea in its most common, neoclassical, form.

The concept of choice in neoclassical economics

A feminist analyst assessing women's decisions in the Third World must determine which decisions reflect *lack of choice* or gender-oppression, and which ones reflect *expressive choice* or expression of both opportunity and socio-psychological autonomy by women.[11] This is necessary for any analysis that claims to:

a) assess how and why and in what contexts women in the Third World may be seen as oppressed and lacking choice;
b) assess what *constitutes* freedom from such oppression or a moment of *expressive* choice; and
c) recommend policy actions to move women from 'a' above to 'b' above.

The theorist must decide when specific actions in a given cultural context reflect *constraints* on choice, and when they reflect *desire*. When the theorist decides that the action in question reflects desire, a further adjudication has to be made about whether the desire reflects internalized oppression and inadequate consciousness or *expressive* choice.

In the neoclassical framework, this forces the analyst to create a neat dichotomy between those aspects of an agent's decision which enter *Utility* (the realm of desire) and those that enter *Constraint*. Choice in neoclassical economics assumes constraint. An autonomous individual finds that the external world, whether physical or social, constrains her from getting everything she wants. In this situation she must decide between alternative outcomes – for example, between alternative uses of a scarce resource. Identifying constraints gives us a choice set.

The autonomous individual, or neoclassical agent, chooses that element of the choice set which is most satisfactory based on some internal, subjective, adjudication of desire. The subjective desire is *independent* of the specification of constraints.[12] This moment of choice is understood by neoclassical economists as utility maximization, utility being a ranking of choices from worst to best.[13] Thus, the moment when individual autonomy and external environment come together in neoclassical analysis is when we bring together utility and constraint to describe human choice.

Suppose we observe the outcome that women in some places are less educated than men. Figure 9.1 provides a synopsis of the neoclassical analytical framework which we can use to interpret such an action. The framework gives us two simple explanations: either there are gender constraints that limit women's access to education, or women have freely chosen less education (analytical decision 1 in Figure 9.1). In the second case, the assumption of universality of human nature – if we are to explain such outcome inequality from a feminist lens as discussed earlier – requires us to posit a layer of false consciousness (incorrect ranking of choices) that impairs women's agency (analytical decision 2 in Figure 9.1). The first scenario calls for a policy expanding women's options, the second calls for policies promoting cultural change to bring women to the point where they can rid themselves of a socialization that makes them choose lower educational levels. Where we decide that the action in question reflects *expressive* choice,[14] no policy to push for change need be undertaken.

As seen above, economics has radically *separated* constraint from desire in analyzing choices (analytical decision 1 in Figure 9.1 reflects this separation). This separation rests on the assumption of a universal underlying human nature that is intrinsically autonomous and free, using reason to generate appropriate assessments of both the constraints faced and consequences of choices made, and using reasoned judgment and appropriate criteria to set up the rank orderings of preferences. In other words, this approach rests on a conception of the nature of human agency coming from the Enlightenment theories about the *Reasoning*

WOMEN'S CHOICES

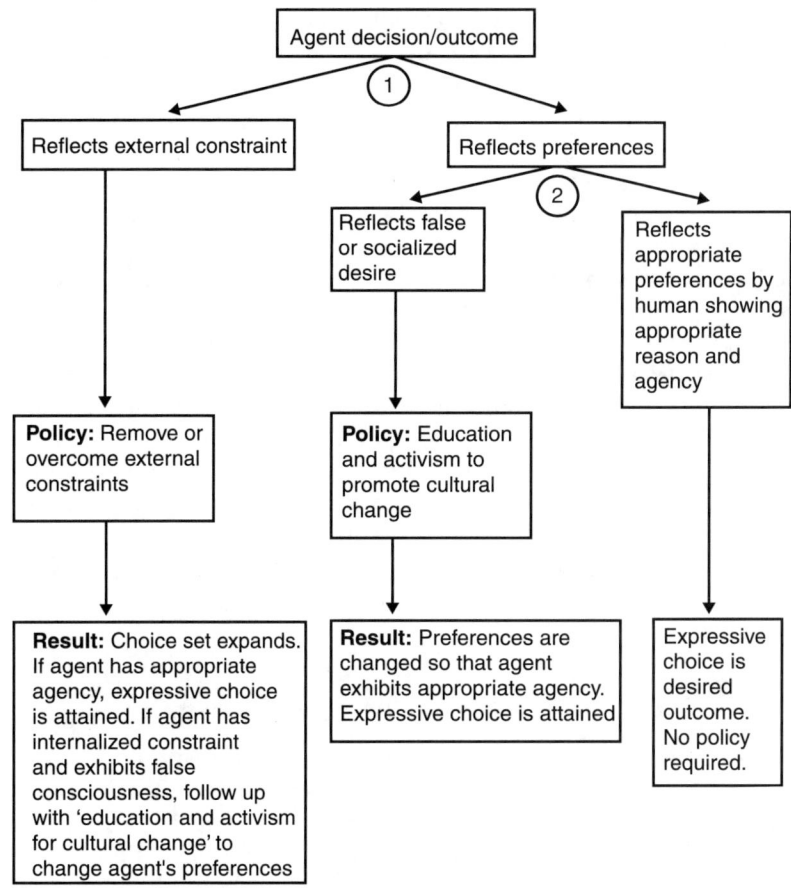

Figure 9.1 Analyzing decisions in a choice-theoretic framework: decision tree showing the analyst's choices and decisions in deciphering agent actions

human being. This conception allows us to locate free choice and autonomy in the individual, and constraint on choice in the external world of nature, market, state/civil society, or cultural norms. But faced with a specific action, there is no *intrinsic* mechanism by which we can decide what component of the agent's action reflects desire, and what component reflects constraint.[15]

Further, feminist theory has *also* argued that gender roles are *socialized*, and that women are trained to *want* certain social locations (analytical decision 2 in Figure 9.1). Socialization, since it rests on the assumption that the individual human being is not really intrinsically autonomous and free, becomes a difficult area for the theory to handle. Fully endogenous preferences cause the theory to break down. Recognizing socialization without positing that *all* preferences are, by their nature, socially and endogenously generated, requires us to look for some substratum of expressive choices.[16] This is usually done by reference to some 'common sense' which tells us that such and such choice should not and cannot be anything but a reflection of false desire, internalized oppression, socialization. This common sense rests on a shared conception of what types of desires a human being free of such socialized oppression would have, based on an assumed universal human nature. Cultural knowledge inevitably informs this conception.

Thus, we face the very difficult question of that ill-theorized realm in neoclassical economics, *appropriate desire* discerned via reasonable or correct preferences. But figuring out a non-ethnocentric utility function that truly reflects autonomous being and appropriate desires is not easy (and is in fact, I will argue, a theoretical impossibility). As far as possible, neoclassical economists have tried to leave the preferences side of the discussion vague, and tried to focus on constraint.[17] This is not a bad strategy, and works well for some very important questions – basic food security, for example, is, I think, safely understood as constraint on choice.[18]

Choice, expressive desire, and constraint

There are, however, situations where the economist cannot so safely stay in the realm of constraint when analyzing women's decisions – one example being female veiling. How would the neoclassical economist proceed to understand the decision to veil? Facing the act of veiling, the neoclassical theorist has to make a decision about whether the veil should enter the set of constraints which limit the agent's choice set, or the utility function as a choice coming from preferences.

Let us start by placing the veil in the set of constraints on choice. Here, we simply start by assuming that the veil is a constraint which limits women's options alongside other constraints. But what is the basis on which we pick out *this* specific clothing norm as a constraint? Unless one decides that *all* social markers of gender-difference are *always* and *everywhere* constraints, there is no *intrinsic* aspect of the veil that can make us decide to locate it *alone* as constraint, while we leave out stockings and skirts and all other markers of female–male difference in apparel norms in other societies.[19] This implies that to avoid ethnocentrism, we may have to designate all gender-based apparel distinctions in all societies as constraint – otherwise, we have to specify some set of criteria (criteria we can reasonably and convincingly argue are non-ethnocentric) by which we make such adjudications across cultures. Lacking such criteria, either we ethnocentrically choose some gender-markers in clothing as oppressive, and some as trivial, or we take a position that all such norms are oppressive (which might be regarded as somewhat arbitrary in itself).

When one examines veiling practices, one finds some women (usually better educated and living in urban areas) who choose not to veil – here enforced veiling is clearly experienced as a constraint on choice. Or, women may veil because the constraint is enforced by punitive sanctions such as state-sponsored edicts mandating veiling – here we can still usefully place veiling in the area of externally imposed constraint. But in many places where women opt for veiling, we do not clearly discern externally imposed constraints. Most commonly, we find women who veil simply as part of their social identity, without much thought about whether they do this because they are forced (constraint) or because they desire to do this (utility). They veil as they go about their daily work (which includes shopping, going to work, or visiting friends in the evening, with gradations around the type of veil and level of veiling), with as much cogitation as found in a Western woman hurriedly pulling on her stockings and checking her lipstick before she rushes to drop off her daughter at day care and reach her workplace on time, or adjusting her appearance according to social context. But further, there are women who actively choose to veil despite the sanctions *for* veiling. For example, some Muslim women in India choose to veil rather than conform to the norms of Hindus around them. Similarly, we come across Muslim women in France, who risk eviction from schools in order to maintain their right to veil. These decisions are taken *despite* sanctions faced for so explicitly marking oneself off as Muslim. One is hard pressed to argue that these women veil *only* because they are forced to veil by social constraint. They seem, instead, to be explicitly upholding the veil as an act of defiance, a *choice* made *despite* the pressures placed on them to abandon the veil and conform to the mores of the dominant culture.

Suppose we put the veil in the arena of preference in all cases where women choose to veil? Here, we have two options – it is a reflection of false consciousness and internalized oppression, or it is expressive choice. If we take the first option, we are arguing that the women have the wrong type of preferences – an argument we might make for those cases where the women veil without much deliberation, but one which is harder to sustain when the women deliberately choose to veil to uphold their identity despite sanctions. But even in the case of non-deliberative veiling, who decides what the correct preferences are? Why is non-deliberative veiling a false preference, when other non-deliberative decisions to abide by gender-divided clothing norms are not false?

Unable to locate a non-ethnocentric mode of picking out veiling as false desire, we are left with putting the veil into the area of expressive choice whenever overt constraints are not discernable. Thus, women choose to veil not because of any constraint or wrong socialization, but simply because they *wish* to. If so, then why is veiling a problem? Come to that, why is any particular cultural practice promoting gender differences and generating outcome-inequality a problem? Neoclassical theory ostentatiously abjures efforts to adjudicate between different utility functions, and we believe that choice exists when the agent is free to act on her preferences or desires. Desire, the expression of underlying and innate universal being, cannot be touched or questioned, since to do so destabilizes the implicit conceptions of individual autonomy underlying this theory. The trouble with this is that we collapse into relativism – any and every cultural practice or social norm which is desired or accepted by a culture's participants is beyond criticism now, since we have no non-ethnocentric basis for judging the goodness or badness of such willing participation or personal desire.

So how do we set up criteria to distinguish between constraint and preference in decoding the actions of women? Further, how do we decide when the preference in question is a reflection of internalized oppression, and when it shows expressive choice by autonomous humans? Usually, we use some unstated notion of underlying, universal, rationalist human *being* as the location of expressive choice, and assume a universal standpoint which can reveal to us what this true choice is. This, of course, is nothing more than the universalist extension of a very specific notion of the nature of the human self coming from the Enlightenment. The assumption that we can simply *know* true choice is what we usually leave unstated within the realm of our political commitment to a specific notion of female agency and autonomy in feminism.

Unfortunately for us, without such an ethnocentric conception within the choice-theoretic framework, we end up unable to adjudicate between various cultural practices and fall into relativism.[20] The problem with the theory is that there is no internal mechanism here which tells us how to divide the terrain of agent action into constraint on choice, socialized false choices, and true freedom and choice. Neoclassical economics may give us analytical tools to deploy *once* we have made some adjudication of these issues, but the assessment of when to put a specific action in one category or the other remains extra-theoretical. And, it is precisely the *ability* to undertake this act of adjudication in an appropriate manner that forms the heart of non-ethnocentric non-relativist feminist analysis.

Ethnocentrism and relativism: two poles of a 'dialectically interlocking sentence'

Gayatri Spivak notes in her 'Can the Subaltern Speak? Speculations on Widow Sacrifice':

Faced with the dialectically interlocking sentences that are constructible: 'White men are saving brown women from brown men' and 'The women wanted to die', the post-colonial woman intellectual asks the question of simple semiosis – 'What does this mean?' – and begins to plot a history.

(Spivak, 1985: 122)

This section follows her lead, examining ethnocentrism and relativism as the two parts of a dialectically interlocking map created by the Enlightenment discourses of equality, autonomy, and choice.

So far, much feminist discussion of the ethnocentrism–relativism divide has proceeded as if the two are clearly demarcated 'opposites' which occupy the entire space of analytical and ethical possibility. One is perforce, as a feminist, forced to choose sides. However, the previous sections' excavation of the neoclassical notion of choice shows us that the *same* conception of an ahistorical universal human nature, in which each individual uses a specific type of asocially defined, universal, human *reason* for making judgements, undertaking decisions, and organizing social and cultural interaction, lies behind both extremes. One is then caught between ethnocentrism and relativism when one tries to judge whether the human being analyzed demonstrates this specific type of agency in making her decisions. So given this shared conception of agency, ethnocentrism and relativism emerge as 'opposites' because they are *historically* created opposites: they form two types of responses from *within* the Western discourse to the process of colonizing non-Western cultures, and to the legacy of colonialism.

Ethnocentrism draws on an Enlightenment notion that humans demonstrate appropriate agency free of constraints of culture and history, only under specific self-conceptions. The parameters of appropriate agency are posited at a high level of abstraction, and one has to give further content to such agency. Discursively and historically, the Enlightenment self gives meaning and content to such agency by creating a margin peopled with backward denizens who lack such agency. The 'other' culture is implicitly assumed to be frozen and incapable of change from internal ethical sources. It is also presumed that the non-Western woman is *unable* to generate a challenge to extant roles *from the internal norms of her culture*. With these assumptions, one finds that an ethnocentric gaze coming from the only culture which *can* articulate a feminist vision is essential for feminist politics. The ethnocentric feminist analyst uses this Enlightenment conception of agency for her analytical and ethical assessment of non-Western women's actions.

At this point, we should note a consequence, however unintended, of ethnocentric feminism: by assuming that a Western ethical basis is necessary for feminist challenge, it strengthens the hand of local patriarchal structures. It *agrees* with them that the non-Western culture is *not* one in which women's roles can change; that this is not a culture *within* which contestation, confrontation, and change can arise; that this is a culture immune to feminist vision, so that any change assessed as feminist *must* reflect the ethical and cultural perspective of the West and cannot be part of the 'authentic' non-Western culture. This refuses the possibility of a serious analytical position called non-Western Third World feminism (as opposed to some women who happen to be of non-Western origin, but uphold some Western cultural import called feminism), since from such a framework, non-Western feminism is an oxymoron: one can either argue against ethnocentrism, or one can be a feminist and judge a culture's practices while espousing a Western Enlightenment conception of agency for ethical judgement, but one cannot be *both* a feminist and a critic of Western ethnocentrism and orientalism.

However, the mere critique of ethnocentrism is insufficient. Because the Enlightenment conception of agency is 'filled' by creating a margin for ethnocentric judgement, a successful attack on this center-margin structure leaves the analyst working from an Enlightenment conception unable to 'fill' the center, and thus unable to render ethical judgements about what constitutes appropriate agency. She collapses into relativism. In our example of veiling, we undertook to show the gaps in the logic by which the margin was assumed to lack agency. As the gaps widened, the neoclassical analyst was left without a margin against which she could 'discern' what the true Enlightenment self looked like, and found herself *unable* to form a critical judgement and so fell into relativism.

Within current debates, relativism does not see itself as partaking in an Enlightenment conception of the self, and usually expresses itself as a 'critical' position, pointing to the racial, gender, class, and ethnic biases which form the constructed margins by which Enlightenment agency is 'filled'. As the gaps are exposed, the center becomes 'decentered' or 'unfilled', and we lose the anchor of a margin against which we decode agency and ethics.[21] Thus, relativism vis-à-vis non-Western cultures is usually concerned with the ways in which cross-cultural judgements about the actions of people in 'other cultures' are undertaken *within* Western discourse. It is in fact the logical conclusion of an Enlightenment self-conception, after exposure of the constructed margin leaves the 'center' empty of content from which judgement can be made.

Relativism draws its *moral* force within the Western discourse by arguing for cultural autonomy and the *rights* to self-determination. Autonomy and the right to self-determination by a populace are morally compelling calls from *within* the Enlightenment conception of agency, and the critiques of orientalism and ethnocentrism carry weight *because* the ethical conceptions of universal agency are morally antithetical to the way in which marginal subjectivities are construed and used in such a framework. Given the legacy of colonialism, and the way in which orientalist conceptions of inadequate reason and inappropriate agency were used to deny people their rights and justify colonialism, what greater argument from *within* the Western ethical precepts can the relativist make than autonomy?

But we must now ask what it means when a relativist *refuses* to make the gesture of cross-cultural judgement. Apart from being *different*, what does the non-Western subject on whose behalf relativism undertakes its internal critique of Western discourse *look* like? Does she – as a human – share with all other humans a (minimally conceived) capacity for (not Enlightenment based) *agency* from within her own culture? Or is she *so* different, that *no* such agency can be ascribed to her without falling into an ethnocentrist trap?[22] Relativism eschews any effort to answer this question, and does not posit any universal ontological notion of human *agency* of even a minimal sort for fear of turning ethnocentric. If such agency is presumed or discerned, it must be because one has mangled the subject and fabricated her into one's own image, or because the person described is not 'authentically' non-Western, not different *enough*.

What is at stake is whether we can seriously argue for the notion of the Third World Woman as an *agent*, not in the Enlightenment sense of the word, but in the minimal sense we need if we are to make any claim for at least the *possibility* of a non-Western feminism which is not simply an 'offshoot' of the Western world view. Without any such minimal conception of agency and an internal cultural capacity for change, the non-Western woman can end up as the frozen, unchanging, helpless subject posited by ethnocentric orientalism, who is fully determined by and reflects a culture which we can no longer *judge*, but who shows no capacity *herself* for purposively reflecting on her world and desiring to change it from *within* her culture.

Relativism, by eschewing any such minimal conception of agency, as somehow purely 'Western', *joins* ethnocentrism in presuming that the 'other' may be *different*, but is not capable of *agency*. The non-Western woman may have *culture*, but she seems to lack the ability for *agency*. Presumably then, feminist judgement is something Westerners do *to* non-Westerners, and non-Western cultures themselves do not undertake ethical judgements of the self-reflective feminist variety. Thus, though the non-West may change, it does not do so in political purposive fashion with members of the community using internal norms to ask for change from within – at most, the non-Westerner can reflect her structural inheritances, or she can hang in limbo as the material world of her culture disintegrates around her under the onslaught of modernity. If she responds to such change from within her culture, she does so in a conservative or reactive fashion, seeking to *conserve* her changing world. If she responds by looking for an active reshaping as an agent, she must do so as an 'inauthentic' member of her community reflecting Western views and mores. Thus, like ethnocentrism, relativism feeds the assumption put forward by patriarchal elites in the non-West, that all who ask for change as non-Western feminists do so as 'outsiders', imposing an 'external' cultural judgement from the West.[23] In deciding to forgo *any* notion of agency shared in common with other humans for those outside the West altogether, it makes the notion of a non-Western feminist who can challenge her own culture's actions from *within* its norms an oxymoron.

Thus, ethnocentrism and relativism emerge as the dialectical conversation *about* the non-West unfolding in the West. Beneath this debate lies the shared Enlightenment metanarrative of a very *particular* notion of universal human being as the *only* basis from which one can have agency or come to *feminist* ethical judgements about one's societal and cultural norms – a substratum never explicitly laid out but implicitly invoked by both sides of the debate. As with Joan Scott's famous deconstruction of 'equality versus difference', (Scott, 1988) we start to see that relativism and ethnocentrism are not mere 'opposing positions', but 'dialectically interlocking' structures which leave no possible space for *non-Western* feminism.

Situated subjects: an alternative conception of subjectivity

One way out of the ethnocentrism–relativism impasse is the notion of 'situated subjects'.[24] Instead of positing abstractly defined autonomous agents, and then examining real human beings to see if they 'match' that highly abstract norm of autonomy, a number of scholars have argued that agency and autonomy are never found in an asocial, ahistorical, trans-cultural, pre-given state of human nature. Instead, these analysts understand agency as something people work toward *within social interaction*. As socially situated, humans are neither fully free nor fully unfree, rather they are always engaged in a struggle to comprehend and achieve autonomy within social engagement, based on the contexts they face, the histories they inherit, and the complex cultural world of ethical and moral norms they inhabit. One of the contexts and histories we inherit in today's world is colonial legacy – a legacy which implies that neither the Western nor the non-Western social subjects can be seen as enacting agency without reference to one another, and which forces us to find ways to excavate the *agency* of the non-Western subject, based on her particular situation and coming from her complex, contradictory, and changing world view, in all our analyses of her actions and decisions.

Situated subjects do not 'lack' agency, but make history under conditions not of their choosing. They enter the world with a history, a social location, a cultural inheritance. Thus, *situated subjectivity* requires that the analyst work toward two things:

a) comprehending the inherited social, cultural and material situation in which the agent lives (her situational location – the easy part), and,
b) seeing her as possessed of agency and capable of reflective and purposive deliberation and action from *within* her world view.

We then decipher her responses to her inherited history and situation (her capacity for agency *within* her own location, the subjectivity part). This is the hard part, but it is necessary if we are to take seriously the possibility of a *non-Western* self-reflective feminist capacity. It requires our readiness to consider that the non-Western discourse is capable of reflective change (she possesses agency), and *also* that the Western discourse is capable of being stretched (we can make a serious effort to make the agency which is currently invisible within Western conceptions – the 'excess' which has escaped speech – if not fully visible, at least partially present in our *own* conceptual maps). This requires an act of imagination on our part, as we force ourselves to create new concepts of human purposive action, new terminology, and rethink our imaginations of agency.

While it is difficult to give further content to such a conception at this level of abstraction, it is possible to provide examples where the analyst-interpreter of non-Western subjects has managed to do this. S. P. Mohanty (1989) gives an example from the anthropological literature, describing how an effort to comprehend religious practices around agriculture could be moved out of the 'is this rational' (ethnocentrism) and 'we cannot understand, but we cannot judge since it would be wrong to assume that rational agency is preferable' (relativism) binarism. Instead, the author not only places the religious practice in the sphere of meaning it inhabits within the culture, but stretches our boundaries for *comprehending* such actions in a sympathetic effort to describe the *agency* here – the meanings and world views by which a human can partake of such a practice in reflecting on and coming to terms with the world around her, without confusing it for a technical practice which enhances production.[25]

To return to the example of veiling, we would first have to 'place' the agent in the situation or context she inhabits. But we must now go further – we need to look at the overall cultural meanings within which veiling takes place, and see if we can consider the agency of the woman making decisions here. I will give just one example of such perspectives. Abu-Lughod (1986) describes the complex conceptions of sentiment, romance, courage, and connection within which veiling takes place among the Bedouin she studies.[26] Here, she conveys not merely that the women veiled and the society was gendered, nor merely that they are 'different'. She stretches our conceptions of emotional expression so we can see how the women look at the world, come to terms with it, and act to change it from within – we see how the women are indeed oppressed within a patriarchal system, but we also comprehend that women here may respond and act to change their world by reflecting on issues of honor, emotional sympathy, and re-negotiate familial obligations and their roles vis-à-vis family and others from *within* such reflections.[27]

There is a rich literature describing the history and diversity of veiling practices among different classes of women in differing regional and social contexts. Within Muslim and Arab feminism, there is a strong debate over veiling which dates back to at least the turn of the twentieth century. It would be a serious mistake to assume that the veil's advocates come from an 'authentic' Muslim view of situated subjectivity, and those critiquing it are 'Westernized, inauthentic', or come from an 'external, ethnocentric' view. Instead, we need to see this as a debate within postcolonial societies, in which both parties to the debate come from that context and that cultural world-view, and adopt or reject the practice as agents reflecting on the world they live in, and coming to some judgement both about their actions and about the organization of their world, from within.[28]

I would like to provide one more example of the way that the ethnocentrism–relativism binarism can make a non-Western feminist voice difficult to hear. M. Nussbaum has made the case for a nuanced, but essentialist conception of agency and Aristotelean values.[29] Nussbaum (1995: 64–6) motivates her attack on relativism by describing encounters with proponents of that position, such as Frederique Apfel-Marglin and Stephen Marglin. I would like to continue those conversations, particularly the conversation about female menstrual seclusion between the Marglins and Sen and Nussbaum (described in Nussbaum, 1995: 64).

The experience of being caught between these two perspectives described here is personal. I have attended lectures given by Stephen Marglin (at the University of Massachusetts, Amherst, in 1987) and Martha Nussbaum (at Franklin and Marshall College in 1997), and in both cases the lecturer invoked the other in his/her answer to my question from the floor – Marglin responded by criticizing Nussbaum's position, and vice versa. Neither could imagine a critique of their position originating from any other perspective.[30]

Conclusion: situated subjects in feminist economics analysis

Though feminist economists have made much progress in moving toward a non-relativist non-ethnocentric vision of agency, we need to press further. Feminist economists have critiqued the neoclassical vision of agency and have examined the way in which neoclassical narratives of subjectivity form margins, spaces within which the actions and decisions and agency of women (and non-Western men, and non-Western women, and racial minorities in the West) reside. Feminist economists have argued that we should pay attention to the context and situation in which women undertake their activities. And feminist economists have examined women's agency, and argued that we need a conception that can take women's own agency from their particular location and experience seriously. So, in many ways, we can argue that feminist economists have indeed pushed for a non-relativist, non-masculinist economics.

But there is one limit that we need to breach – that of a conception of situated subjectivity for women in non-Western contexts. The situated/context part we have taken seriously (though we need to do more, so that the contradictory interaction between economic, social and cultural contexts becomes part of the situation we inherit) for both Western and non-Western contexts. But for the *subject* part, we have not managed to provide an adequate discussion of agency of those from non-Western world views. Most of the assumptions about female agency, such as norms of beauty, motherhood, texture of male–female relations, and the way in which the agent thinks of such issues from her ethical and normative world, derive from a Western conception of role, norm, and moral/social order. Hence, we need to go further than we have in formulating analyses of the contradictory and changing agency of women in non-Western contexts.[31]

Development economics lacks an adequate *theoretical* response to the postcolonial critique – a critique which is now a good twenty years old. For feminist economics in particular, we have not managed to ensure that 'development' (the area where non-Western women's issues reside) is not some special subset of feminist economics theory in general, and have not had a *theory* which can adequately respond to C. Mohanty's and A. Escobar's critique of the orientalism of our field (Mohanty, C. 1988; Escobar 1995) – we do have examples of people who manage to take these critiques seriously in their own work, but we do not have a *theoretical* perspective on (men and) women's roles, oppression, and agency in feminist economics which makes such a response central to its analytical framework. Feminist economics will have to meet the challenge of a theoretical approach which manages to attain a non-relativist, non-ethnocentric, analysis of the situated subjectivity of women – and men – 'elsewhere'. When our analyses move these texts from the realm of relevant classic to the terrain of anachronism, we will know we have succeeded.

Notes

1 The author thanks the participants on the e-lists *Femecon-l* and *Sawnet* for the discussions leading up to this paper. Also, thanks to Diana Strassmann, Steve Gudeman, Lisa Saunders, Colin Danby, Eiman Zein-Elabdin, Brenda Wyss, Jennifer Olmsted, Steve Cullenberg, Drue Barker and Edith Kuiper for discussion and comments on previous drafts of the paper. All errors and omissions, of course, remain the author's responsibility.
2 Here, I refer to the specific theoretical and literary production of a Third World, Womanist, Immigrant, or Black feminism (as opposed to just Feminism without any modifiers) in the past few decades. The particular concerns raised in this paper are related to the feminist scholarship within the broadly defined field of postcolonial studies. Moore-Gilbert (1997) provides a good overview of this field, while Ashcroft, Griffiths and Tiffin (1995), Mongia (1996), and Williams and Chrisman (1994) provide good introductions to the key texts in this tradition.
3 For purposes of analytical clarity, the paper focuses on neoclassical notions of choice (since they are the most commonly deployed notions of choice in economics). The critique raised here extends to some aspects of choice-concepts deployed by other theories of agent decisions as well (for example, this critique would apply to the distinctions made between perceived and objective interests by A. K. Sen [Sen 1990]). This however, does not dispute the usefulness of the critiques of the neoclassical paradigm, or the value of the contributions toward an alternative approach, made by these authors (e.g., this critique would not dispute the usefulness of the concept of commitment in creating a non-ethnocentric, non-relativist analysis of decision-making [Sen 1973, 1974, 1976 and 1985]).
4 The Enlightenment can be seen as the culmination of an intellectual project begun with the Renaissance and carried forward in early Liberalism, with its emphasis on a particular conception of *Reason*. By 'Enlightenment notions of universal human nature or being', I refer to the idea of an atomistic asocial substratum of universal human nature, defining what it means to be a full human being possessing human faculties of reason, a human who is capable of acting appropriately and who is deserving of rights. This conception of human nature emerged in social and historical contexts which resulted in it marking out the European/white/male/west or center, from the margins of non-European/colored-black/female/non-west. This legacy from the Enlightenment project poses specific problems for analysts who wish to use these conceptions of human agency in creating a non-ethnocentric non-relativist assessment of women's choices in non-Western contexts. But while I am critical of the ways in which Enlightenment conceptions of human nature constrain us, this should not be taken as a dismissal of the ethical promise of the Enlightenment. Instead, I view a project of non-ethnocentric non-relativist analysis as crucial for our efforts to *realize* these promises.
5 See Scott (1988) for a discussion of the links between these concepts and the difficulties they raise for feminists assessing women's decisions.
6 For example, average wage levels or average education differ between men and women. This inequity is noted as an indication of male oppression and female exclusion from the spheres of access to high-wage work and education, and not as the result of some aspect of female nature which makes women either incapable or undesirous of attaining the same outcomes as men.

7   For example, we note that though women and men now have similar opportunities for schooling in the USA, women tend to stay away from mathematics, engineering, and other technical subjects which can provide them with access to higher-wage jobs. This can be seen as the result of socialization which creates gender differences in preferred school subjects and envisioned careers for girls and boys. This causes girls to internalize their oppression and prefer to opt for the 'alternative' educational and career tracks, leading to their self-exclusion from those educational avenues which would open up access to higher-wage jobs.

8   Note that the idea that women become socialized to internalize their oppression and accept inequity need not lead to a completely social-constructivist view of human nature which displaces the Enlightenment conceptions of agency – one can argue that girls are socialized to avoid mathematics, and still hold on to the Enlightenment notion of a universal substratum of human agency which lies beneath the socialization (as in the vision of women reaching their true underlying human potential once the socialization is removed). Such an Enlightenment-based notion of socialization is found both in older liberal feminist texts, as in Mary Wollstonecraft's vigorous refutation of Rousseau's descriptions of Sophie in his *Emile* (Wollstonecraft, [1792] 1992, especially chs. 2–5), and in more recent discussions of the need for some type of essentialist conception as an answer to the dangers of relativism (Nussbaum, 1995; Nussbaum and Sen, 1993; Nussbaum and Glover, 1995).

9   In much of radical feminist thought, one finds feminist theorists envisioning and trying to create worlds where they have autonomy to make decisions which would be quite different from norms of outcomes-equity. In the language of the once-popular bumper sticker, 'A Woman Who Wishes to be Equal to Men Lacks Ambition'.

10 Within the US feminist movement, one famous example of such a dilemma was seen in the 'porn wars' of the 1980s. In discussing their approach to pornography, feminists found themselves divided between the goals of eliminating socialization leading to violence against women on the one hand, and the equally legitimate right of women as autonomous beings to diverge from received sexual wisdom and experience a host of sexual acts, including 'taboo' acts. The debate became even more tangled as it was difficult to discern the cluster of feminist goals that informed each perspective. But the dilemma itself proved extremely productive, as feminists began to try to comprehend the differing contexts within which a woman may value one norm over the other, to envision the complexity of feminist agency among women taking opposing positions on this issue, and to develop richer analyses of the processes of gender socialization and sexuality.

11 Choices can be made under conditions which denote a lack of freedom either due to inadequate opportunities or due to socialization leading to internalized oppression on the part of women. Hence, I use the term *expressive choice* to indicate that the expressed decision or outcome can be deemed a *valid* choice. For us to agree that we see expressive choice, we must agree that: a) the agent has equal opportunity/resource access in making her decisions, and b) she has also demonstrated appropriate agency in making her decisions.

12 Economics has always been anxious about endogenous preferences, since its models of choice depend on our ability to define preferences independent of final outcomes and constraints. The models begin to crumble once preferences are endogenous and socially fabricated, shifting according to history, situation, and past outcomes.

13 Since utility is simply a preference ordering, or ranking of choices from worst to best (the assumptions needed to generate a coherent and consistent ranking being no doubt onerous), it would be here that false consciousness and socialization would find their expression. They would show up as an 'incorrect' or inappropriate ranking given to outcomes (as compared to appropriate rankings made by individuals not so socialized against their own interests).
14 Either because the external constraints are inherently unchangeable (say because of women's innate natural capacities), or because the decision was reached after a conscious consideration of alternatives which we reasonably agree were based on appropriate criteria for ranking outcomes.
15 In neoclassical theory, the process of discerning underlying preferences from an agent's actions is done via 'revealed preference'. Sen (1971, 1973, 1974, and 1976) provides a lucid discussion of the problems with the revealed preference approach.
16 The project of Sen and Nussbaum (Sen, 1992; Nussbaum and Sen, 1993; Nussbaum and Glover, 1995) to enunciate alternatives to the neoclassical and relativist frameworks, can be reasonably interpreted as an effort to find some subset or partial area of human life, where we can make a nuanced and muted claim for such a substratum. Here, it is recognized that socialization shapes preferences, that there are social and cultural conflicts in interpreting agent actions, and that ethnocentrism and cultural barriers do impose themselves between analyst and agent when we attempt to decode actions. However, the effort is to reveal a partial ordering we can use for analysis and policy, based on a universal sub-stratum around hunger, death, deprivation and freedom, that we can agree on as forming the basis of such assessments. While I agree with them that the rejection of *any* human commonality proves inadequate for non-ethnocentric non-relativist analyses (see below), I take issue with the particular notions of agency they put forward.
17 Out of the two decisions made by an analyst, decision 1 may be less controversial than decision 2 in some circumstances – in fact, constraint may be put forward even if we disagree with the overall framework of individual choice as described above. The effort to draw out a common human sub-stratum around hunger, deprivation, death, and freedom described in the above footnote, can be seen as an effort to demarcate those areas of human life where we can come to a cross-cultural agreement about which actions and decisions can be reasonably viewed from the lens of constraint. The contexts in which we can agree on the constraints leading to decision 1 cross-culturally, and cross-paradigmatically, however, are not 'obvious' – thus, though death may be agreed to be binaristically opposed to life, the larger map of context and meaning may make death through suicide an act of defiance, related to a constraint or commitment coming from some other area of life than deprivation via lack of access to food.

Decision 2 becomes very difficult to make from a non-ethnocentric, non-relativist perspective since it requires that we accede to a very particular notion of universal underlying human agency which is trans-historical and trans-cultural – and decision 2 becomes necessary if we accept the preference-choice based framework. There has been some recent effort to generate adequate bases for undertaking decision 2 from without the neoclassical framework, so as to have a universal mode of assessing the ethics of actions and outcomes (see Nussbaum and Sen, 1993; and Nussbaum, 1995). Despite their best efforts, however, I argue that Sen and Nussbaum's approach needs to be modified before it can meet its stated goal of creating a non-ethnocentric non-relativist approach (Charusheela, 2000).

18 This assessment is based on a rather casual empiricism. I know of no society that has *preferred* starvation over basic ability to meet food/nutrition needs, and where basic needs are denied to an individual, it is usually understood as either a punishment, or the result of a constraint. As an example, it would be a mistake to confuse the notion of a *fast* in various Eastern religions, which is an expressed choice for abstinence in the *face* of the *availability* of food, and *hunger* or *starvation*, which emerges when this specific choice is absent because food is not accessible. In Hindi, just as in English, the language clearly demarcates the difference between these two, the former being *vrath* and the latter being *bhookh*. In Tamil (my own mother-tongue), the words used are *vratham* and *pasi*. In referring to starvation, the discourse often uses words to denote the number of days one has gone without food (*das din se khana nahin khaya* in Hindi, or *pathu naala sapadu illai* in Tamil, denoting I have not eaten for ten days, or I have had no food for ten days, both easily discernible as meaning something quite distinct from the notion of religious abstinence or fasting). Thus, when women fail to eat and secure basic nutrition, one can usually distinguish between such a lack of food due to abstinence and such a lack due to non-availability of food. However, in places where one finds female starvation (rather than fasting), one still has to assess the *causes* of such a lack of food (source of the constraint) to put forth policies for changing the situation – and assessing the causes of a lack of food availability can be difficult and controversial, and proposed policies for changing the situation can clash dramatically even where one agrees that what we see here is clearly constraint.

19 One could pick out the veil as a clothing norm which should be seen as constraint on the basis of arguments that the veil, by being enforced as a practice through punitive sanctions, acts to prevent women from entering public spaces (and hence constrains choices). That since stockings and other such clothing norms do not so prevent women from entering public spaces and are not enforced via punitive sanctions, they do not act to constrain women the way that veils do. This procedure, however, does not work to pick out the veil alone as a constraint. First, historical examination shows that the veil is adopted to different degrees and in different circumstances in differing locations. In many places, the veil is adopted to *allow* women's entry into the work place. Second, many women adopt the veil despite sanctions for veiling and though there are rewards offered to those women who choose not to veil (as in the case of Muslim women in France who risk educational access in order to veil). Further, while a correlation can be made between practices of veiling and female exclusion, it is not always clear what solutions manage to overcome such exclusion. An example would be the special polling booths for *pardah-nasheen* women as in India, which allows women practicing such veiling to exercise their vote – here, a solution is found which allows women entry into the public domain without requiring us to eliminate veiling. And finally, while stockings and other such norms of apparel in the West do not restrict women's entry into the public arena, we find that *lack* of such clothing restricts women's ability – especially poor, working class women's ability – to find good jobs. That this is not a trivial issue is seen both by the clothing advice and borrowing to finance a set of interview clothes that precedes interviews at the Allied Social Science Associations meetings for those seeking jobs, and by the fact that we find a non-profit organization in New York devoted to helping poor women seeking jobs find appropriate

interview clothing (Dress for Success New York [DSNY], with 20 sister organizations across the USA).

20 There is reason to think that even non-neoclassical notions of choice based on the Enlightenment self find themselves bereft of moorings if they give up ethnocentrism. One example of this is found in the project of Nussbaum and Sen described above. Despite the complex and nuanced conception of self and agency put forward, the care to delimit areas of life which are put forward for universalism, and the role given to social and cultural constructions of meaning in the analytical framework, the issue of ethics proves to be most troubling for the authors. Without some such mooring, they fear that we loose our ability to argue against practices which debilitate women's capacities and capabilities – the notion of Aristotelean values provides one example of such an ethnocentric closure. Charusheela (2000) provides a discussion of the pitfalls that this universalism creates for cross-cultural feminist politics within the Sen-Nussbaum approach.

21 Note that '*de*-centering', or a loss of center/self, is primarily something that emerges for the Enlightenment subject who becomes 'decontent-ified' as she accepts the gaps and starts to give up the margins which fill her self-conception as a reasoning autonomous person possessed of appropriate agency in a superior culture. Thus, it is eminently a description of what happens to the Western self-conception as the gaps and fissures by which it creates its margins are exposed. It is not an accurate description of the transformations taking place in the non-Western subject's world-view or self-conception – since she was not 'centered' or 'selved' in quite this way, she is hardly in a position to lose that which she never possessed.

22 See S. P. Mohanty (1989) for a detailed discussion of the philosophical precepts of relativism, and the need for a minimal, non-Enlightenment conception of universal human capacity for agency if we are to move beyond 'sentimental charity' in Western engagements with non-Western subjectivity.

23 Even among those analysts asking for us to 'recognize' agency in a particular location, we note slippage into the view of non-Westerners in need of external 'help' to become agents for change. The importance of this presumption was noted by Lourdes Beneria, in a discussion of postmodern and postcolonial feminism at the June 1998 'Out of the Margins' conference in Amsterdam. She noted that the postmodernist paper on Latin American women we were discussing presumed that feminists in the West had to 'create discursive spaces which will allow the voices of Latin American and other Third World women to be heard'. This presumes that so far, they have not exactly been agents, and they depend on outsiders to make 'room' for them – apparently lacking the capacity to push on the door themselves. This example provides a sharp reminder of S. P. Mohanty's comment that postmodern relativism, by eschewing any minimal universal conception of agency altogether, reduces Western efforts to comprehend and engage with non-Western subjects, to merely an act of 'sentimental charity'. (S. P. Mohanty, 1989: 23.)

24 This term was originally coined by Steve Cullenberg (personal communication). It refers to the type of subjects described in the analysis of scholars like S. P. Mohanty (1989), C. Mohanty (1988), Escobar (1995), Narayan (1997), and others who work in the loosely defined arena of poststructural, postcolonial, Third World feminist scholarship. The term itself borrows from Haraway's concept of situated knowledges, and the resonances with the broad area of feminist scholarship on epistemic conceptions, ontic locations and agency invoked here are deliberate – though the usage of situated *subjectivities*, rather

than situated *knowledges* (or *epistemologies*) points to some areas of possible difference between the two approaches (Haraway, 1988).

25 In the context of India, I immediately thought of the practice of writing slogans to ward off the evil eye on trucks (*buri nazar vaale tera muh kaala* – oh evil eyed one, may your face turn black). This does not mean that irrational truck drivers confuse the technical mechanisms which make trucks run and think that trucks do not need maintenance. Rather, the realm in which the driver undertakes this practice marks a *different* sphere of relationship to objects, and the agent does not mistake one for the other. If this is difficult to comprehend, an example in the West would be the practice of saying a prayer before exams. This does not mean people who pray *confuse* this with the need to crack the books, and we would be seriously mistaken if we assumed that among Christians, there is a belief, which we cannot explain, that you don't need to study to do well in school. The prayer involves an effort to come to terms with the exam in a different way than studying does.

26 In subsequent work, Abu-Lughod has revisited her discussion in *Veiled Sentiments*, to argue that she did not, in fact, manage to describe the situated subjectivity of the Bedouin women she studied. Indeed, Abu-Lughod argues against any possible space for such types of discursive 'breaching' of limits at all (Abu-Lughod, 1990). I am sympathetic to portions of her argument, and agree with her that we need to beware of imagined and romanticized fabrications of agency and give up dreams of complete cross-cultural universal understanding. However, I do not agree with her implicit assumption that no type of stretching of our own cultural maps in straining toward a conception of situated subjecthood, even of a partial and contingent variety, is possible. A detailed discussion of the epistemological bases on which one may look for a 'space' from which to strive for such a partial, locatable, and contingent knowledge claim is beyond the scope of this paper. See Haraway (1988) for a discussion of ways in which one may approach the problem of epistemology from a non-universalist non-relativist perspective on truth and knowledge claims. Tsing (1993) provides a good example of how one may fruitfully pursue such a project in concrete analysis.

27 This also allows us to see that within the complex codes of gendered clothing in the West, women may respond from 'within' their world view to change things – by helping others gain such clothing, playing with and shifting norms of what may be appropriate work clothing, and so on. They may find it possible to think about and comprehend gender oppression in their world from within the norms they occupy, struggling around work rules, family friendly policies, and so on, without necessarily believing that they can only be feminist if they stop wearing skirts and stockings to work.

28 See Narayan (1997) for a discussion of the limits of a notion of cultural 'authenticity'. The notion of cultural authenticity itself depends on conceptions of cultures 'elsewhere' as not merely different, but frozen, uncontradictory, unreflective, isolated, and incapable of change.

29 And, I hasten to add, her work here has been fruitful in furthering the project of a non-relativist feminism while taking serious and honest note of the critiques of ethnocentrism and essentialism made by various authors. However, her conception of agency is different from the minimal conception put forward by S. P. Mohanty (1989), which I argue for here.

30 In particular, the issue both focused on and responded to was that of the *ethics* of cross-cultural judgement (these ethics drawing on an internal discourse within the West about the non-West, as noted above). Neither seemed to comprehend that the issue at stake in my question was not the

ethics of judging *per se*, but the assumptions about the nature of South Asian women's agency on which the debate rested. While I lack the space to provide an account of the situated subjects found here, I would like to note that the debate as it unfolded made it impossible for me to present an argument that there is nothing 'inauthentic' or 'Western' about the women who dispute the practice, and also that the women who follow or uphold the practice do not do so simply as an expression of some pre-given, unchanging, uncontested, simplistic and frozen concept of 'respect' or 'communal connectedness' within the culture they inhabit. Effectively, the way in which both perspectives 'filled' the agenda disallowed the option of an internal, non-Western capacity for cultural self-reflection and internal change. For myself, at age twelve, I found it perfectly possible to dispute and contest the practice from within the cultural norms of my family. The arguments on which I based my case would sound strange and not particularly 'appropriate' to a Western feminist without some work on my part to explain the context and moral-cultural order from which they came – my unlettered, regional-language speaking, religious grandmother, however, found the arguments quite comprehendible (if not necessarily likable). That she comprehended them and accepted them was an indication of *her* agency just as much as my rebellion was an indication of mine, something the framework deployed so far fails to note.

31 There have been some stellar efforts in this direction – Zein-Elabdin (1996); *Review of Radical Political Economics* (1991, especially the introduction but also many of the articles); Olmsted (1996, 1997) provide some recent examples of such scholarship within feminist economics. Unfortunately, their approaches are seen as particularist/descriptive, relating to a *particular* 'case study', and these works are not treated as serious theoretical interventions in the creation of a feminist economics theory. What we need here is a recognition that there is theoretical context, an overall question of our analytical approach, at stake here. Unless we comprehend the question as one of approach and theory, with a well-conceptualized philosophical position, and not as merely one of 'special examples', 'case studies', 'institutional and historical description', and so on, we will remain trapped in the binarism within which (to borrow from Wahneema Lubiano's plenary at the *Rethinking Marxism* conference on the *Politics and Languages of Marxism*) some women do/have 'theory', and the rest of us have 'special experiences, situations requiring a modification of the theory, particular circumstances'.

References

Abu-Lughod, L. (1986) *Veiled Sentiments: Honor and Poetry in a Bedouin Society*, Berkeley, CA: University of California Press.
—— (1990) 'The Romance of Resistance: Tracing Transformations of Power Through Bedouin Women', *American Ethnologist* 17 (1), pp. 41–55.
Ashcroft, B., Griffiths, G., and Tiffin, H. (eds) (1995) *The Post-Colonial Studies Reader*, New York: Routledge.
Charusheela, S. (2000) *Analyzing Non-Western Women's Choices: Toward a Post-Colonial Feminist Economics*, unpublished paper available from author.
Escobar, A. (1995) *Encountering Development: The Making and Unmaking of the Third World*, Princeton, NJ: Princeton University Press.

Haraway, D. (1988) 'Situated Knowledges: The Science Question in Feminism and the Privilege of Partial Perspective', *Feminist Studies* Fall, 14:3.

Mohanty, C. (1988) 'Under Western Eyes: Feminist Scholarship and Colonial Discourses', *Feminist Review*, no 30, (Autumn).

Mohanty, S. P. (1989) 'Us and Them: On the Philosophical Bases of Political Criticism', *Yale Journal of Criticism* 2 (2), pp. 1–31.

Mongia, P. (ed.) (1996) *Contemporary Postcolonial Theory: A Reader*, New York: Arnold.

Moore-Gilbert, B. (1997) *Postcolonial Theory: Contexts, Practices, Politics*, New York: Verso.

Narayan, U. (1997) *Dislocating Cultures: Identities, Traditions, and Third World Feminism*, New York: Routledge.

Nussbaum, M. (1995) 'Human Capabilities, Female Human Beings', in M. Nussbaum and J. Glover (eds) *Women, Culture and Development*, Oxford: Clarendon Press.

Nussbaum, M. and Glover, J. (eds) (1995) *Women, Culture and Development*, Oxford: Clarendon Press.

Nussbaum, M. and Sen, A. K. (eds) (1993) *The Quality of Life*, Oxford: Clarendon Press.

Olmsted, J. C. (1996) 'Women "Manufacture" Economic Spaces in Bethlehem', *World Development* 24 (December), pp. 141–51.

—— (1997) 'Telling Palestinian Women's Economic Stories', *Feminist Economics* 3 (Summer), pp. 1829–40.

Review of Radical Political Economics (1991) special issue on *Women in the International Economy*, 23 (Fall/Winter).

Scott, J. W. (1988) 'Deconstructing Equality-versus-Difference; or, The Uses of Poststructuralist Theory for Feminism', *Feminist Studies* 14 (Spring), pp. 33–50.

Sen, A. K. (1971) 'Choice Functions and Revealed Preference', *Review of Economic Studies* 38 (July), pp. 307–17: reprinted in Sen 1982.

—— (1973) 'Behaviour and the Concept of Preference', *Econometrica* 40 (August), pp. 241–59: reprinted in Sen 1982.

—— (1974) 'Choice, Orderings and Morality', in S. Körner (ed.) *Practical Reason*, Oxford: Blackwell: reprinted in Sen 1982.

—— (1976) 'Rational Fools: A Critique of the Behavioural Foundations of Economic Theory', *Philosophy and Public Affairs* 6 (Summer), pp. 317–44: reprinted in Sen 1982.

—— (1982) *Choice, Welfare and Measurement*, Cambridge, MA: MIT Press.

—— (1985) 'Goals, Commitment and Identity', *Journal of Law, Economics and Organization*,1 (Fall), pp. 341–55.

—— (1990) 'Gender and Cooperative Conflict', in I. Tinker (ed.) *Persistent Inequalities: Women and World Development*, New York: Oxford University Press.

—— (1992) *Inequality Reexamined*, Cambridge, MA: Harvard University Press.

Spivak, G. C. (1985) 'Can the Subaltern Speak? Speculations on Widow Sacrifice', *Wedge* 7/8 (Winter/Spring), pp. 120–30.

Tsing, A. L. (1993) *In the Realm of the Diamond Queen: Marginality in an Out-of-the-Way Place*, Princeton, NJ: Prtinceton University Press.

Williams, P. and Chrisman, L. (eds) (1994) *Colonial Discourse and Post-Colonial Theory: A Reader*, New York: Columbia University Press.

Wollstonecraft, M. ([1792]1992) *A Vindication of the Rights of Woman*, New York: Penguin.

Zein-Elabdin, E. (1996) 'Development, Gender, and the Environment: Theoretical or Contextual Link? Toward as Institutionalist Analysis of Gender', *Journal of Economic Issues* 30 (December), pp. 929–47.

10

THE DISAVOWAL OF THE SEXED BODY IN NEOCLASSICAL ECONOMICS

Gillian Hewitson[1]

The subject of this chapter is neoclassical economics as a sexually specific discourse or knowledge that constructs sexually specific subject positions. Using the example of the neoclassical conception of the surrogate motherhood exchange, I argue that the female body is constituted as the excluded 'other' of the contracting agent or rational economic man, and hence, more generally, that woman is the constitutive outside of neoclassical economics. I read the neoclassical construction of the surrogate motherhood exchange through the metaphor of the womb-as-capital in order to reveal the way in which the binary opposition of man/not-man supports the claims of economists that neoclassical economics is a universally applicable and sexually-indifferent knowledge. I argue that the womb-as-capital metaphor is essential for the neoclassical conception of the surrogate motherhood exchange, and I situate it within a range of discourses which support the notion of the universal individual and hence a 'one-sex model', or a construction of sexual difference as man and his derivative 'other'. When considering these issues, it is important to note that to argue that a particular discourse constructs sexual difference or femininity in particular ways is not to essentialize sexual difference or femininity, since, as Cornell argues, 'Woman "is" only in language, which means that her "reality" can never be separated from the metaphors and fictions in which she is presented' (1991: 18). I argue, then, that the neoclassical account of the surrogate motherhood exchange produces the female body as meaningful in particular ways, but I do not simultaneously assert another true meaning which I would then compel neoclassical economists to add to their analyses. Meaning is created between texts rather than between texts and the real world, and hence neoclassical economics must be understood as intertextual. It does not produce sexed bodies as meaningful in particular ways within a vacuum, but relies for its intelligibility upon a series of discourses to which it also contributes (on intertextuality, see Culler 1983: 32, 103–4; see also Amariglio and Ruccio, Chapter 6). For this reason, the discussion of the neoclassical construction of the contracting agent within the surrogate motherhood exchange draws upon textual support from a wide range of sources, including the work of feminist legal theorists. The purpose of this chapter, then, is not to accuse neoclassical economics of ignoring some reality of woman which exists independently of its theoretical constructions, and hence neither to advocate nor to oppose surrogate motherhood contracts. Rather, this is a specific case study of the problematic status of 'woman' within the neoclassical account of exchange in general. It is therefore a feminist poststructuralist reading of the neoclassical modelling of the exchange for its production of meaning, but not, I again stress, for the purpose of producing a specific position in relation to surrogate motherhood contracts per se. It is also important to keep in mind that, although I draw upon the extant economic texts on surrogate motherhood (Posner 1989, 1992; Hewitson 1997), the analysis to follow requires neither consistency with the conscious intentions of authors, nor verification from the experience of women and men who have been involved in surrogacy. On this latter point, I endorse Pateman's argument that the existence of smoothly-completed surrogacy contracts (as well as, in the context of the 'sexual contract', happy marriages or satisfied prostitutes) is irrelevant to the productive work of the discourse of the contract or exchange itself (1988: 215).

Feminist poststructuralism is one of several feminist approaches which may be used to analyse the masculinity of neoclassical economics.[2] It differs from the more frequently adopted approaches, such as liberal feminism, 'object relations' feminism, and other 'constructionist' feminisms, in its understanding of the relationship between neoclassical economics and women or the feminine. These alternative feminist approaches, which may be labelled 'gender' feminisms, or feminisms which rely upon a distinction between sex (males and females) and gender (masculine and feminine), view the problem of neoclassical economics as one of partiality.[3] Neoclassical economics is a partial knowledge because it excludes in some way women or feminine characteristics. For example, some feminist economists have argued that neoclassical economics is biased because the occupation of economist is dominated by men.[4] Some also argue that questions of interest to women have been of little interest to male economists (see, for example, Waring 1988; Folbre and Abel 1989). Others propose that women have been excluded from economic analysis through the willful or simply forgetful failure to incorporate constraints which are specific to women (see, for example, Bergmann 1981, 1989; Cohen 1982; Pujol 1992). Still others have suggested that the masculine personality structure has caused men to focus on 'rational economic man' while ignoring those aspects of humanity which reflect the personality structure of the feminine gender (see, for example, England 1993). The solution to these exclusions is one of incorporation. Neoclassical economics will be improved by the incorporation of questions of interest to women, the modelling of economic issues in a way which reflects the specific economic positionings of women, and/or the inclusion of characteristics which have been deemed feminine rather than masculine within the present gender schema (see, for example, England 1993; Nelson 1996). Thus these feminisms argue that neoclassical economics does not properly or fully reflect the real world which it is supposed to describe. A feminist poststructuralist, however, takes a quite different view of the relationship between neoclassical economics and women or the feminine. For a feminist poststructuralist, neoclassical economics is a discourse which actively produces its objects as well as its subjects of knowledge, rather than being a knowledge in relation to which the 'real world' of men and women, or masculinity and femininity, has a separate existence. Further, for feminist poststructuralists, the question of sexual difference is one of embodied difference, the meaning of which is constituted within discourses (see, for example, Irigaray 1985; Grosz 1989; Dallery 1994; Hewitson 1999). The allegedly universal construct of rational economic man, a supposedly disembodied or unsexed figure capable of representing the essence of the economic subject, is not merely a partial representation of humanity: he is already embodied as a man, problematizing both the reliance of feminist economists upon the sex/gender distinction and the 'femininization' of rational economic man for which such a theoretical framework calls (see Hewitson 1994, 1999). For a feminist poststructuralist, it is vital that neoclassical economics be examined for its production, rather than its reflection, of sexual difference or sexed embodiment.

My contention is that the phallocentric nature of neoclassical economics can be seen within the surrogate motherhood exchange in two ways. First, as discussed on pages 224, the pregnant woman's body is rewritten through the womb-as-capital metaphor to enable her to take up the masculine subject position of contracting agent. Hence, 'woman' is constructed as the 'same' as 'man' within a one-sex model. Second, as discussed on pages 232, the 'natural' place of 'woman' as the material foundation of 'rational economic man' is re-established in the face of the breakdown of the boundary between the natural and the social (signified by the 'mercenary' mother) through the elimination of the surrogate mother's status as 'mother'. Thus I contend that the metaphor of the womb-as-capital is the key means by which neoclassical economics maintains the range of binary oppositions which support the one-sex model and hence the 'universal' individual in the face of the embodied difference brought into the realm of exchange through surrogate motherhood.

The metaphor of the womb-as-capital and the one-sex model

The work of the womb-as-capital metaphor

The one-sex model upon which the allegedly universally-applicable 'rational economic man' relies is the product of the binary opposition of man/not-man. The womb-as-capital metaphor plays a key role in the transformation of a pregnant woman, a 'not-man', into 'rational economic man', the calculating, choosing, capital-owning agent. The womb as capital stands in an external relationship to the woman, and she uses it instrumentally to produce services which can be sold on the market and hence to maximize her utility. In this sense, surrogate motherhood is the same as the case of a man renting out his factory. Indeed, the surrogate motherhood exchange is no different to other exchanges which involve bodies, such as labor market exchanges. In each case, the sexed body is disavowed by the transformation of the marketable aspects of the body into capital which is possessed by the mind. Despite this disavowal, necessary for the fantasy of a 'universal' individual, the man/not-man opposition remains, and it is only the female body which disappears. In this section, then, I examine the way in which the metaphor of the womb-as-capital underpins the one-sex model.

The new, but rapidly growing, phenomenon of the surrogate motherhood exchange has been formally modelled by Hewitson (1997; the exchange has also been discussed by Posner 1989, 1992). The essence of this model, as in neoclassical models in general, is the rational calculating agent. The market was constructed on the basis of the utility-maximizing choices of the surrogate mother and the commissioning party. As in any exchange in which the services of the body are the object of the exchange, such as exchanges of labor, sexual services and blood, the exchanger is assumed to own the objects of exchange, which are therefore metaphorically separate or detached from the personhood of the agent. The transformation of the body into capital, and the depiction of exchanges involving the body as the sale of the services derived from this capital, is the central means by which this externalization is achieved. The womb-as-capital metaphor is therefore no more than a specific example of the general underlying metaphor of own-body ownership which is required for any exchange to take place at all within a neoclassical model. Without own-body ownership, the services of the body cannot be sold. The social contract itself, which produces the conditions in which voluntary exchange replaces the rule of the strongest, requires that, in John Locke's words, 'Over himself, his own body and mind, the individual is sovereign' (quoted in Diprose 1996b: 261n; see also Pateman 1988). Thus, in order to be part of a surrogate motherhood exchange, a woman must be in a relationship of possession with her body, and, more specifically, with her womb.

The metaphor of the womb-as-capital therefore constructs the body of the surrogate mother as a possession, the services of which can be sold or given away according to the utility-maximizing calculus. Indeed, if it were not the case that a surrogate mother were renting her womb, she would be selling a baby, an illegal transaction since babies are also own-body owners (Pateman 1988: 212). Posner concurs with this point, arguing that women rent their reproductive services: 'Fertility is just another asset, like a professional degree or other job-market human capital' (1992: 425, see also 1989: 27). The surrogate motherhood exchange must therefore be understood to be the exchange of a service, specifically, the service of gestation, for which the biological father may or may not pay. In this formulation, surrogacy is 'a process which transforms the commissioning parents' goods, that is their gametes, through the service of incubation provided by the surrogate' (Secomb 1995: 20; see also Shanley 1993: 623ff). Hence it is no different from the employment contract, in which the worker's labor transforms the employer's material inputs into products over which the worker has no claim (Pateman 1988: 213). The idea of the body and its parts as capital, then, not only allows exchanges to take place, but also eliminates the possibility of trades in self-possessing persons and therefore overcomes the threat to civil society which such trades, i.e. 'baby-selling' and its attendant denial of the self-possession of certain individuals, would invoke.

The metaphor of the womb-as-capital also divides the surrogate mother into two individuals. This is because the womb as capital takes the form of a rentable space which can be made available for hire – no different from a warehouse or factory floor, or a room in the woman's house. The biological father combines the semen with a rented womb to produce his child. The fetus therefore stands in relation to the surrogate mother in the same way that commodities produced by hired machinery under the direction of an entrepreneur stand in relation to the owners of this machinery. It is evident that the owners of the machinery have no rights to the commodities being produced through the rented services of their capital, assuming the contractual obligations are fulfilled, and that they are certainly not somehow inseparable from the commodities for the period of the production process. Thus, just as the metaphor of the womb-as-capital transforms the womb into something separate and inessential to personhood, it also transforms the fetus housed within that womb into a separate entity. This means that the sexed body is disavowed within the neoclassical framework. An exchange which appears to involve sexed bodies is rewritten through the metaphor of the womb-as-capital as one involving self-possessing capital owners. Neither the womb nor the fetus is essential to the personhood of the surrogate mother, who has been recast as a rational economic agent fortunate enough to own capital of a particular kind. Women as embodied, and hence sexed, subjects are eliminated, and all that is left is the 'universal' individual sometimes known as Robinson Crusoe.

Intertextual support of the womb-as-capital metaphor

There are an immense number of representations which support this neoclassical depiction of the surrogacy exchange and its division of the pregnant body into two persons. These representations shed further light on the problematic status of the female body in economic relations, and point to the intertextuality of neoclassical economics, or the ways in which economics 'makes sense' only within an historically-specific set of discourses. The conceptual separation of the mother from the fetus is especially prominent in the biomedical discourse surrounding technological developments in fetal surgery, ultrasound and fetal photography. Such developments have made the fetus both accessible and visible, providing an image of the fetus as separate from the mother (Secomb, 1995: 20). In her discussion of such imagery and its links to the film *2001: A Space Odyssey* and satellite photography, Petchesky has argued that 'the autonomous, free-floating fetus merely extends to gestation the Hobbesian view of born human beings as disconnected, solitary individuals' (1994: 406). The resulting simultaneous construction of the image of the fetus as 'space-hero' and the pregnant woman as 'empty space' points to the 'disappearance' of the pregnant woman herself within these new technologies (ibid: 414, 416). Secomb has argued that the view of surrogacy as a service also makes the pregnant woman disappear, since 'she becomes an incubator or "the nurse who tends the growth of the young seed planted by the true parent, the male..." rather than a woman or a mother' (1995: 20).

The term 'manthropomorphizing' has been used by Mykitiuk to refer to the process in which 'the importance of the contribution of pregnancy, gestation and birth have vanished with regard to the creation of a child' (1994: 93). Common understanding supports this minimal role of the gestating woman: 'The dominant culture projects pregnancy as a time of quiet waiting. We refer to the woman as "expecting", as though this new life were flying in from another planet and she sat in her rocking chair by the window, occasionally moving the curtain aside to see whether the ship is coming' (Young, 1990: 167). Indeed, in modern 'fetology' the fetus is even ascribed the role of active partner within the pregnancy process, with a will of its own and an ability to dictate the terms of its environment. It is defined, in short, as 'an individual agent, who is separate from the mother and has its own distinct interests of which it is both aware and capable of acting on' (Franklin, 1991: 193). This is the fetus as an egoist, whose aim 'is to see that its own needs are served' (fetologist, quoted in Franklin 1991: 194). This portrait of fetal independence implies a pregnant woman at the biological 'beck and call' of her fetus. It is therefore apparent that certain medical discourses support the neoclassical interpretation of the surrogate mother's womb as capital producing an independent fetus.

The neoclassical interpretation of the surrogate mother also has many similarities with the depiction of the pregnant woman within the various legal and political discourses which have emerged from the US abortion debate. The 'fetal rights' discourse, for example, constructs the fetus as a legal person, and the pregnant body as two self-possessing individuals, who, due to the location of the fetus, are within an antagonistic relationship. The US anti-abortionists construct the fetus as a person 'housed' by another whenever they equate the beginning of life (the moment the fertilized egg comes into existence) with personhood, or whenever a person is equated with their genetic inputs. To argue that 'the individual *is whoever he is going to become from the moment of impregnation*' (Ramsey, quoted in Petchesky 1990: 340; italics in original) is to argue that a fetus *is* a person. The potentially victimized but mute fetus is given voice in the classic anti-abortionist film, *Silent Scream*. Here technologies which 'reveal' the life of the fetus are shown also to be used as instruments of its death, before which it responds with a physically-enacted 'silent scream'. As Karpin remarks, the 'fetus unable to be heard from inside the womb, gains a right to speech when it is technologically given a text' (1994: 57; see also Petchesky 1994). Anti-abortionists, then, tend to depict the fetus as simultaneously an independent legal person and a biological dependent, constructing the pregnant woman as the potentially hostile 'fetal environment'. A bumper sticker used in the US depicts precisely this view, stating that 'The Most Dangerous Place in America to Live is in a Mother's Womb' (Karpin 1994: 36).

Yet another discourse in which the separate personhoods of the pregnant woman and the fetus is constructed is the corpus of legal cases in which pregnant women play a role. For example, those cases in which women have been brought to account regarding their behavior and actions during pregnancy, at least those which 'fail to respect the rights of the fetus', contribute to the construction of the fetus as (legal) person (even if the cases fail). One of the first of these cases was the charging of a woman with criminal neglect for failing to follow medical advice during pregnancy (see Bordo 1993: 81–8; Karpin 1994). In those cases in which the fetal environment is viewed as having actually imposed harm, a child born alive has been given leave to sue. In one case, a child was given leave to sue doctors who had performed surgery on its mother (which subsequently had been held responsible for causing brain damage to the fetus) before it was even conceived (Poovey 1992: 248). In addition, cases in which women are legally required to undergo such treatments as Caesarian section pit the rights, or even the life, of the pregnant woman against those of the fetus (see Young 1993; Bordo 1993: 71–97). These cases rely, as has the US legal debate over abortion, upon the notion of fetal viability. This notion, as Young argues, 'asserts the 'livingness' of the fetus and its independence from the woman. As such, the woman's necessity is diminished: if the fetus is viable it can leave the uterus and live happily ever after outside it' (1993: 292). In each of these cases, the courts or the terms of a contract control and punish the potentially or actually hostile fetal environment in the name of the fetus, thus construed as an individual with rights (for the developing legal status of the fetus in the US, see the discussion in Poovey 1992). This construction of the pregnant woman and the fetus as separate, conflicting entities is also evident in the typical surrogacy contract. Whether or not the specific provisions of such a contract are enforceable, numerous obligations are imposed upon the 'fetal environment' (Keane and Breo 1981: ch.13; Ince 1984). The self-interest of the surrogate mother is thereby mitigated by contractual provisions and monitoring which force her to maintain her capital so that the health of the fetus is ensured.

Perhaps the most important support of the womb-as-capital metaphor and its associated division of the pregnant body into two discrete persons is the liberal paradigm of the self as a self-present rational consciousness with individualized rights and freedoms, basic to which is his ownership of his own body (see Pateman 1988; Diprose 1992, 1994, 1996a; Poovey 1992; Mykitiuk 1994). Indeed, Franklin has described 'patriarchal individualism' as the 'meta-discourse' which 'holds together the construction of fetal personhood in a number of respects, including how it is constructed through power/knowledge or discourse, how it is described through language and metaphor, how it is represented visually, how it is narrated and how it is positioned as a masculine subject' (1991: 201). As pointed out above, this positioning of the body as property owned by the liberal individual is central to the surrogate motherhood exchange. The liberal individual, the essence of which is unsexed consciousness, possesses the body, ruling over it and using it instrumentally to meet its ends. Dodds and Jones point out that accepting that each person has a property right in their own person means accepting a model of an entity which stands in an external relationship with that which it owns, including its own mental capacities, leaving only 'a purely deliberative capacity: a thing which weights and ranks options and preferences....The agent, thus conceived, has no identity' (1992: 13). This is precisely a description of rational economic man, as neoclassical economists would like to view him: he is disembodied, he has no (sexed) identity, he is universally applicable, in short, he is instrumental reason in control of body. In the tradition of Western philosophy as well as neoclassical economics there is therefore a denial that embodiment is critical to personhood, and simultaneously a denial that the specificity of this body is integral to subjectivity.

These discourses show that the neoclassical interpretation of the surrogate mother is not independent of the ways in which Western cultures are structured. Specifically, pregnant women are represented within non-economic discourses as separate persons from the fetuses they house. The surrogate mother is similarly represented within the neoclassical model as separate from the product of the capital she rents out. The womb-as-capital metaphor is instrumental in constructing this representation, which amounts to producing the surrogate mother as a possessive, or liberal, individual. This sheds considerable light on the way in which 'woman' can be incorporated into models of exchange. Representing the womb-as-capital eliminates the specificity of the female body from the economic analysis, it converts the surrogate mother into a rational economic agent, and it produces a one-sex model. This one-sex model is the basis of the neoclassical claim that its object of analysis, rational economic man, is a universal figure. What actually occurs, however, is that the male body is established as the embodiment of the rational economic agent. The female body acts as the foundation for the construction of the masculinity of the economic agent through its exclusion. Woman is incorporated into the subject position of exchanging agent as the same as man: her specificity (in this case, her pregnant embodiment) is eliminated, in the name of the universal contracting agent, but actually in the service of the man/not-man binary opposition. It should be kept in mind that these conclusions rely not only upon a view of neoclassical economics as a productive discourse (a non-empiricist view of language), but also upon a specific focus upon sexed embodiment, and it is these joint considerations which have been largely missing from other feminist economic accounts of the masculinity of economics.

Feminist poststructuralists have already examined the way in which the exclusion of the female body acts as a foundation for various non-economic discourses, and my analysis in this chapter should be considered as an extension of this scholarship. The exclusion of the female body in the construction of the political agent which is central to liberal discourse has particularly close parallels with the exclusion of the female body in the construction of the neoclassical agent. Feminists have argued that the liberal individual is never simply abstract, disembodied or absent, but 'a particular body – one who is white, male, heterosexual, able bodied, young, adult, and it is this body which has been generalized as the normative body of liberal discourse' (Mykitiuk 1994: 80). Other bodies are constructed in reference to this white male body. This power to construct other bodies is elided by the liberal logic of individuals as prior to society, in which 'society has no power to constitute or inscribe itself on embodied subjects' (ibid). Thus the seemingly absent body at the centre of liberal discourse serves to disguise the reality of the particular body which actually operates as the normative body in modern Western societies, positioning other types of bodies only in relation to its own form (ibid: 80–1; see also Eisenstein 1988; Pateman 1988; Gatens 1988, 1991a, 1991b).

This phallocentric construction of sexual difference is central to the myth of the origin of modern liberal states, and although the rights and freedoms of the civil sphere have now largely been extended to women in Western nations, women have not taken up these rights unproblematically, since this seemingly universal subject position was premised upon, and continues to be symbolically linked to, (white) masculinity alone. As in the case of neoclassical economics, the incorporation of sexed (and raced) bodies into the universality of the subject position of the liberal individual has problematized that alleged universality. To maintain the fantasy of universality, such bodies must be incorporated as 'the same' as those of white men. Although the surrogate mother is a contracting agent, then, her taking up of this subject position involves a particular writing of the meaning of her body, a writing which must exclude pregnant embodiment. This is because women, and pregnant women in particular, do not fit the liberal paradigm of the individual. As Franklin points out, the 'very term "individual", meaning *one who cannot be divided*, can only represent the male, as it is precisely the process of one individual becoming two which occurs through a woman's pregnancy' (1991: 203).

In her discussion of the role of the law in maintaining the boundaries of 'the proper' (as analyzed by Derrida), Secomb has similarly pointed out that pregnancy 'is problematic, in part, because the laws of propriety and property relations become ungainly and inadequate in adjudicating on the question of foetal and infant ownership and control. The law must treat that product of pregnancy either as a thing available for exchange on the market like other things or as a human subject which as human is not available for exchange. The neither/nor status of the pregnant woman and foetus confounds the humanistic dichotomy of subject/object, self-conscious/incognizant, human/non-human, and free/predetermined' (1995: 34; see also Dodds and Jones 1992; Poovey 1992; Diprose 1994: ch. 1). In her discussion of the abortion debate in the USA, Mary Poovey (1992) also argues that the concept of the liberal individual can be taken to its *reductio ad absurdum* when applied to pregnant women, rather than independent men. She contends that the Roe vs Wade decision, which set the scene for the discourse of fetal rights, problematized the notion of legal personhood. It 'implicitly granted the fetus some of the properties of a gendered subject even though this subject does not have an autonomous, sexed body' (ibid: 248–9). Poovey points out that this logic would mean that personhood could be granted to an egg or a sperm. On the other hand, if the fetus is not given the status of legal personhood, a neonate would similarly have to be deprived of this status, since it is no more physically independent than a fetus (ibid: 249). Thus pregnant embodiment is inconsistent with the realm of the contracting individual.

In this section it was argued that the metaphor of the womb-as-capital is essential for the establishment of the pregnant body as a self-possessive individual, and hence one capable of sustaining contractual relations with other 'sames'. This manoeuvre relies upon the mind/body and the man/not-man dichotomies. By converting the surrogate mother into two persons, the fetus and the capital-owning contracting agent, the metaphor of the womb-as-capital eliminates the specificity of female embodiment and constructs a one-sex model within the neoclassical paradigm. The surrogate mother becomes the contracting liberal individual, 'rational economic man'. Both the fetus and the surrogate mother are awarded masculine subject positions as self-possessive individuals. The surrogate mother, conceptually separate from the fetus, becomes a 'universal', seemingly disembodied, rational agent with the property rights of a citizen of the civil sphere, who is therefore able to undertake voluntary exchanges in that sphere: she exchanges the rights to her rentable space for a utility gain. Pregnant women, however, remain problematic, especially when they enter contracts to exchange 'sexed body property' (the term is due to Diprose 1996b: 254). In the next section, I discuss the ways in which the impropriety of the pregnant body's presence within the civil realm of contract is reined in.

Maintaining the propriety of motherhood

The opposition between motherhood and contract in Western discourses

The deployment of the womb-as-capital metaphor and the associated construction of the surrogate mother as the allegedly unsexed contracting agent allows the pregnant body, stripped of its sexed specificity, to be incorporated within neoclassical economics. However, this incorporation simultaneously endangers neoclassical economics and other phallocentric knowledges by disrupting the divisions between the natural and the contractual. The impropriety of the presence of the pregnant body within the realm of contract – specifically, the mother as rational economic man – is due to the fundamental conflict between motherhood and contract which is established by the reliance of the liberal and neoclassical paradigms upon a division between the natural and the social/contractual. In order to preserve the phallocentric oppositions upon which neoclassical economics relies, the realm of the natural must be re-established. In other words, the propriety or the proper place of the pregnant body must be maintained, and this occurs through the production of a 'real mother' who is distinct from the surrogate mother and who is therefore not a contracting agent. In this section, then, I argue that neoclassical economics relies upon a division between the realms of the natural and exchange, and discuss the ways in which the transgression of this boundary by the surrogate motherhood exchange is contained in order to maintain a phallocentric construction of sexed identity in which man can function as the universal. To this end I begin with a brief overview of the way in which the opposition between the natural and the social, and the associated opposition between motherhood and contract, are central to Western discourses.

Feminists have argued that the supposedly unsexed contracting agent within the social or civil sphere, together with the associated rights and freedoms which that agent derives from the social contract which brings that sphere into existence, are meaningful only because of the existence of a realm of nature in which such rights and freedoms do not exist (see Tapper 1986; Pateman 1988; Gatens 1991a). That is, the mythical origin of a civil domain and the agents who inhabit that domain (the 'social contract') is not simply a displacement of the 'state of nature'. Rather, the state of nature continues to reside within a binary structure as that which is excluded from the civil realm in order to give the civil realm its meaning. To frame it in a way more familiar to economists, the rights and freedoms of contracting or exchanging agents in the market arena are premised upon another arena, where the so-called natural work of reproduction and care takes place. Under the social contract, these 'natural' functions were allocated to women, who were legally as well as symbolically denied the rights and freedoms of men. In addition to the mind/body binary opposition, then, the identity of the liberal individual relies upon the exclusion of 'nature' from the realm of contract, and hence an opposition between the mother and the contracting agent, where motherhood connotes nature, body and not-man. This means that social practices which shift motherhood into the realm of contract threaten the coherence of this pyramid of oppositions and hence the phallocentric construction of sexual difference which allows the fantasy of the universal individual. The contracting and self-interested mother becomes such a threat if she is introduced into the liberal and neoclassical discourses without first being divested not only of her sexually-specific embodiment, but also of her connections to 'real motherhood'. To preserve the binary opposition between motherhood and contract, then, the incorporation of markets for reproductive services or motherhood into the realm of contract must proceed in a way which excludes 'real motherhood', represented by women who are virtuous, natural and good mothers.

Feminists have drawn upon a range of discourses to reveal the importance of the boundary between contract and motherhood, and the ways in which representations of 'real motherhood' or the virtuous, natural mother, and self-interested motherhood, or the selfish, unnatural mother, uphold this boundary. In other words, feminists have shown that it has been essential to the coherence of such discourses to represent mothers who enter the civil sphere as contracting agents as bad mothers, and hence not mothers at all. The identification of woman with virtuous, natural motherhood has long been central to Western discourses.[5] The constitution of maternity as the essence of the female subject was elaborated and institutionalized in the late seventeenth and eighteenth centuries, and has since been central to an 'entire battery' of social practices (Poovey 1992: 243; see Foucault 1981; Laqueur 1990). Such practices include all those premised upon the nuclear family in which the man is the breadwinner while the woman is the wife and mother, such as 'full-time' work; the idea that married women displace other, more legitimate workers; dependent spouse allowances and other tax and welfare policies; 'fetocentric' employment regulations; in short, the whole apparatus of the division between the public realm of work and exchange and the private realm of family. These practices support the notion that the essence of woman is motherhood: women are either already mothers or they will become mothers. This equation of woman and mother is particularly prominent in representations of pregnant women as already mothers. The discourses of fetal rights, fetal viability and the fetus as a potential or actual person construct the fetus as an unborn *child*, and operate to exclude all possible outcomes of the pregnancy except that the fetus will be brought to term. Thus the pregnant woman is denoted as a mother before she has given birth (see Poovey 1992: 245–6).

The essence of woman, however, is not simply assumed to be maternity. As already indicated, it is the representation of woman as the self-sacrificing mother which operates to preserve the boundary between contract and motherhood. This is particularly evident in medical and legal discourses which focus on the pregnant body. For example, in a judgment dealing with the case of a Caesarian section having been imposed upon an unwilling and dying woman who was 26 weeks pregnant, and who died shortly after the procedure, it was asserted that

> the welfare of the fetus is of the utmost importance to the majority of women; thus only rarely will a conflict arise....The vast majority of women will accept significant risk, pain and inconvenience to give their babies the best chance possible. One obstetrician states that most of the women he sees would 'cut off their heads' to save their babies
> (quoted in Young 1993: 293)

Similarly, King Solomon found the 'real mother' to be the woman prepared to make the greatest sacrifice for the baby. Moreover, woman as the self-sacrificing, indeed, self-*less*, mother is supported by those representations of women as 'mere bodies' (Bordo 1993: 72). For example, when courts refuse to violate the bodily integrity of individuals on the one hand, and fail to uphold this vision of bodily integrity when the subject at issue is a pregnant woman, they construct women as a non-citizen and hence a body without a mind.

Bordo (1993) has discussed these cases at length, comparing those in which bodily integrity is upheld by courts and those in which it is not. Courts have refused to order individuals to make donations such as bone marrow even when those donations could save the lives of others. Similarly, a court likened the forced regurgitation of two capsules swallowed by a suspected drug dealer to medieval torture. On the other hand, courts have failed to uphold the bodily integrity of women when ordering them to undergo major surgery, such as sterilization and Caesarian sections, against their wills (ibid: 73–88). Bordo points to the logical inconsistencies apparent in these bodies of case law. That pregnant women are 'a special class of persons' due to the 'total dependence' of the fetus fails to explain these contradictions, since 'total dependence' for life occurs in other cases where the bodily integrity of, for example, bone marrow donors, has been upheld (ibid: 312n). Bordo argues that such decisions 'are mediated by normative conceptions of the pregnant woman's role and function' (ibid: 78). When women fail to be 'good mothers', when they fail completely to subordinate their own subjectivity to that of the fetus, they are construed by courts as 'excessive [and] wicked': 'The cultural archetype of the cold, selfish mother – the evil goddesses, queens, and stepmothers of myth and fairy tale – clearly lurks in the imaginations of many judges issuing court orders for obstetrical intervention' (ibid: 79). Thus the pregnant woman has been constructed as the opposite 'of the abstract subject whose bodily integrity the law is so determined to protect....The essence of the pregnant woman...is her biological, purely mechanical role in preserving the life of another'. When her subjectivity conflicts with her 'life-support function', her life-support function is privileged (ibid). In short, the pregnant woman is the subject of metonymic as well as metaphoric transformation. Part of her – her body or womb – replaces the whole of her. Thus the pregnant woman as such is excluded from the social contract; she is simply body, with a will that courts have often failed to recognize when this means supporting the woman's subjectivity or right to bodily integrity at the expense of the fetus.

The identification of woman with the self-sacrificing mother is also extended to an identification of this mother with family and nature. This identity is supported by those Western political theories which require a natural counterpoint to the cultural and political endeavours of man. Examples of feminist investigations of such constructions of the nature/culture opposition are numerous, leading Pateman and Shanley to remark that 'Notwithstanding all the differences between theorists from Plato to Habermas, the tradition of Western political thought rests on a conception of the 'political' that is constructed through the exclusion of women and all that is represented by femininity and women's bodies' (1990: 3; see also Lloyd 1984; Pateman 1988; Gatens 1991b; Lake 1992). Poovey has emphasised the danger of undermining this concept of 'mother-nature' in her discussion of the abortion debate. She states that: 'if the normative woman is a mother, then the mother-nature of woman is one of the linchpins of sexed identity and therefore, by the oppositional logic of gender, one ground of the intelligible masculinity of men. If women are allowed to question or to reject their maternity, then not only is the natural (sexed) basis of rights in jeopardy, but so is the natural basis of female identity, and, by implication, of masculine identity as well' (1992: 243; see also Secomb 1995). Poovey concludes that the abortion debate – and, I would argue, debates about women's reproductive authority in general – is about what it means to accept (or reject) 'the notion that there is a "natural" basis for individual identity and therefore for individual rights and sexual identity' (1992: 243).

The motherhood/contract opposition in neoclassical economics

The identification of woman with motherhood and motherhood with nature, and hence the binary constructions of culture/nature and motherhood/exchange, is also important within the discourse of neoclassical economics. It is particularly evident in the neoclassical model of the surrogate motherhood exchange. The introduction of the surrogate mother as a contracting agent is an obvious threat to the natural, virtuous mother, and hence, if the binary oppositions which support the identity of rational economic man are to be preserved, the surrogate mother must somehow be divested of her motherhood. The rewriting of the female body, necessary for its incorporation within the realm of masculine subjectivity, destroys the very feminine characteristics which give meaning to the economic sphere. Specifically, despite the transformation of the surrogate mother into a rational economic individual, she remains a woman, and, as a contracting woman, she is unnatural (see Pateman 1988: 217). This is one reason for the controversy and public attention which accompany exchanges of 'sexed body property' (Diprose 1996b: 254; see also Anleu 1992). A woman who profits from her womb is a mercenary mother who rejects her maternal instinct by contracting to part with her baby. She therefore threatens the figure of the nurturing/caring mother so essential for the retention of the culture/nature divide and its support of masculine subjectivity. As Anleu points out, critics of commercial surrogacy 'castigate these women for entering a contractual agreement to give up a baby, thereby violating assumed maternal instincts and abrogating "natural" motherhood. In contrast, many of these critics present surrogacy without payment as an appropriate and acceptable solution to infertility [arguing] that such an arrangement involves gift giving and the demonstration of love and sacrifice rather than rational self-interest' (1992: 32). The general condemnation of 'pregnancy for profit' is reflected in the most common legal regime imposed on the surrogacy market; namely, the prohibition of commercial but not altruistic surrogacy (National Bioethics Consultative Committee 1990). The surrogate mother, then, is the reverse side of the notion of maternal self-sacrifice which is constructed alongside the notion of fetal personhood and the right of the fetus to protection from the state (see Bordo 1993: 312n). She is the 'cold, selfish mother' prepared to contract away her natural identity, and hence antithetical to 'real' motherhood.

This vision of a calculating, avaricious mother who sells her own offspring for profit is kept at bay in a number of ways by representing the womb as rentable space. As already mentioned, such a metaphor operates to produce the object of the exchange as the service rather than the baby. Pateman, for example, argues that a woman 'who enters a surrogacy contract is not being paid for (bearing) a child; to make a contract of that kind *would* be tantamount to baby-selling' (1988: 212). The contract price, then, is the market-determined price which would be paid for storing an item in a house, which recompenses the owner for the disutility experienced from not being able to use the space themselves, and from having the item in the house. Judge Sorkow, the judge in the (original) Baby M case, stated this clearly in his decision: 'the money to be paid to the surrogate is not being paid for the surrender of the child to the father...The biological father pays the surrogate for her willingness to be impregnated and carry his child to term. At birth, the father does not purchase the child. It is his own biologically genetically related child. He cannot purchase what is already his' (quoted in Pateman 1988: 213). The surrogate mother, then, provides a service to men who desire biologically-related children (Posner 1989, 1992: 422), and this representation or construction of the exchange mitigates the threat to the binary opposition between motherhood and contract by eliminating the spectre of mothers selling their babies.

The metaphor of the womb-as-capital also reduces the threat to social order by facilitating the reconstruction of the surrogacy contract as a service provided by one woman to another – one who desperately wants a child but who cannot conceive or gestate one herself, the 'real mother', and one who is prepared to provide the services of her uterus for the sake of this other woman. The term 'surrogate mother', as well as 'contract pregnancy', contributes to this writing of the woman entering a contract as 'not a mother', since a surrogate mother is a substitute mother or a representative of a mother, not really a mother at all, or rather, not a 'real' mother at all. Indeed, the term arose from the use of an inanimate object to study the effect of newborn monkeys being separated from their real mothers. Posner urges his readers not to forget that 'the surrogates are not the only women in the picture' (1989: 27). In the context of the Baby M case, he argued that the 'purpose of the contract was not to extinguish a mother's rights but to induce a woman to become a mother for the sake of another woman' (1992: 426). He points out that occasionally a surrogate mother feels 'intense regret at having to give up "her" child' (ibid: 424), a statement in which Posner simultaneously relieves the contracting woman of any parental connection and therefore puts her motherhood into question, as well as supports the neoclassical understanding of the contract, specifically, the commissioning party's contractual 'ownership' of the product. Posner also argues that the surrogate mother is a 'surrogate' for the father's wife. She acts as a marital corrective since 'under modern permissive divorce law [a husband] is always free to "walk", and seek a fertile woman to marry' (1989: 27). The father's wife, however, becomes a mother only after a separate (adoption) contract is enacted. As Singer points out, Mrs Stern's claim to maternity was entirely dependent upon Mr Stern's acceptance of paternity (1989: 60–1). But although Mrs Stern had no contractual claim to Baby M, she is vitally important as the person in the position of the 'real mother'. She is the 'real mother' because the womb-as-capital is employed in her service, and she is the one with the 'natural' desire to nurture a child.

Thus the term 'surrogate mother' installs at centre stage the 'normal' mother, a woman who does not reject motherhood, but rather desires a child – the wife of the commissioning male – rather than the mercenary mother. This covers over the gestating mother's rejection of motherhood (in favour of the contracted price, or the utility benefit) which is actually at the heart of the surrogacy contract, as well as the tenuous grasp which the wife of the commissioning male actually has on the child. That the surrogate mother is not a 'real mother' is even clearer in the case of gestational surrogacy, in which the commissioning party consists of both a male and a female. Nearly as famous as the Baby M case, at least in the USA, is the case of Baby Johnson, in which Anna Johnson, a black woman, was employed for gestational surrogacy by a white couple. Six months into the pregnancy Anna Johnson filed suit for parental rights to the child-to-be. A blood test was used to establish the fact that she was not genetically related to the child, and hence that she was not the mother and had no custody rights. Although this seems to be in contradiction to the finding in the Baby M case (that the genetic relationship between Mary Beth Whitehead and Baby M did not constitute her as the mother), in fact, both cases come to the same conclusion: that the intention to procreate is sufficient to establish the identity of the 'natural mother' (see Douglas, 1994; Morgan, 1994). The term 'surrogate', then, or contract pregnancy in general, depends on the existence of a 'real', other, mother.

The motherhood status of the surrogate mother is further undermined by locating the source of the new life within the commissioning male. The male intention to parent (an act of will) and the concomitant surrogacy contract is credited with the creation of the child: 'But for the intention to parent', the argument goes, 'the child would never have existed' (Mykitiuk 1994: 86). Posner concurs: 'no contract, no child' (1992: 426). He also argues, in discussing the Baby M case, that 'What is at stake is an infertile woman's right to compensate a fertile woman for the cost...of assisting the former to overcome the consequences of her infertility' (ibid: 424). But the other woman was not a party to the contract, and, in Posner's own words, no contract, no child. The productive energy, then, is not that of the 'other woman' but of the man (see also Roof 1992; Secomb 1995). Thus the pregnancy is subject to or controlled by contract, eliminating the 'maternal instinct' of the contracting agent while elevating the maternal instinct of the wife of the commissioning party, crediting the contract and hence the father with generative or reproductive power, and, most importantly, maintaining the boundaries between the mother and contract, nature and culture, man and not-man. This idea of paternal or masculine procreative force and the concomitant repression of the mother is a major myth in phallocentric cultures (see Gatens 1991a, Lake 1992). It also plays an important but disavowed role in economics, as Feiner (1995) identified, and is played out in the story of Robinson Crusoe (Hewitson 1994).

It is therefore evident that the metaphor of the uterus as rentable space not only acts as the mechanism by which surrogate motherhood is incorporated in the neoclassical framework as a rational contracting agent, but is also the central means by which the threat to the binary opposition of motherhood and culture posed by this incorporation is mitigated. The metaphor constructs the surrogate mother as a contracting agent and as a non-mother, thereby disavowing the problem of sexual difference, and allowing the unproblematised retention of the fantasy of the universal individual. This is important because pregnancy is 'a site of rupture which threatens the humanistic rational all-knowing world view which is founded on [a] dichotomous organisation that separates man from animal, reason from non-reason, culture from nature, and the social from the biological' (Secomb 1995: 28). The conversion of a pregnancy into two distinct individuals, one of whom's temporary abode is the other's capital, resolves this threat. Thus the surrogate mother is rendered an 'embryo carrier', an 'incubator', a 'biological entrepreneur', a 'manufacturing plant', a 'gestator', a 'receptacle', 'a kind of hatchery', a 'surrogate uterus', 'a uterine hostess', in short, a 'rented womb', and anything but a mother. The metaphor of the womb-as-capital, then, permits the extension of the neoclassical discourse into the realm of nature – pregnancy and motherhood – yet without endangering its coherence as a discourse describing exchange relations between disembodied autonomous contracting agents.

Conclusion

In this chapter I have used the surrogate motherhood exchange as a case-study of the sexed construction of exchange in neoclassical economics. Neoclassical economists would deny that the contracting agent is a masculine figure, and the surrogate motherhood exchange, in which a female agent and a female body appears to play an irreducible role, may at first glance give credence to this denial. However, the argument is not that women cannot or do not enter economic exchanges – no-one would make such an absurd claim. Rather, my poststructuralist reading of the discourse of neoclassical economics through the surrogate motherhood exchange reveals that exchange is constructed within the neoclassical paradigm as one between two autonomous individuals. I have pointed to the ways in which the discourse of neoclassical economics supports, and indeed is premised upon, a phallocentric construction of sexual difference (the one-sex model), which (symbolically) forces women to enter the economic sphere with the specificity of their bodies, and their associated meanings, erased. This insight has some important implications. It indicates that surrogate motherhood poses something of a double bind for women. On the one hand, if surrogate motherhood contracts are declared illegal or unenforceable, women are excluded from the realm of exchange by virtue of their particular (gestational) embodiment. They are not allowed to be individuals who own their own bodies and have the right to dispose of the services of that body as they see fit, because of that particular body and that particular service. In short, the pregnant body is excluded from the realm of contract.

On the other hand, if such contracts are legal and enforceable and the one-sex model of sexual difference is thereby reproduced, then what is excluded from the realm of exchange is again the female body and its most infamous capacity, the simultaneous one-ness and two-ness of that female body in its reproductive mode. In this case, the pregnant body is excluded on a symbolic level, and woman is included in the realm of contract only insofar as she becomes the 'same' as man. The pregnant body – which under a different discourse is both one and two, and hence not separable, both the same as and different from itself, and hence not an individual – is now a rentable space.[6] Femininity is reinstated as maternal, natural and outside the realm of instrumental rationality, and masculinity retained as independent, rational and social; in short, real woman must remain the 'other' of the contracting agent. This ensures that the female body is maintained, within a series of binary oppositions, as the unacknowledged foundation of the economic and social spheres. Difference continues to be excluded from neoclassical economics, and racial and sexual others are incorporated into the realm of the social, political and economic only if they take up white masculine subject positions.

It should again be stressed that surrogate motherhood is not a special case in which the specificity of women's bodies is eliminated from the scene of exchange. It is a case of 'the exception proving the rule'. The surrogate motherhood contract involves the exchange of, using Diprose's term, 'sexed body property' (1996b: 254), and this is precisely what is exchanged in many other forms of implicit or explicit contracting as well. If bodies are always sexed bodies, then the employment contract, for example, is also for the exchange of sexed body property. Women are positioned as men in entering the social contract, whether as surrogate mothers or as workers of other kinds, in that they participate in the fantasy of sexually indifferent or neutral bodies owned by minds which are the essence of personhood. Hence many feminist economic approaches, as well as sex discrimination and equal opportunity laws which follow as remedial strategies from the gender approach, and which are informed by assumptions of disembodiment, are problematic. They fail to recognize, and hence begin to shift the meaning of, difference at the level of embodiment.

Finally, the analysis of this chapter has also undermined the claim by neoclassical economists that their analyses are descriptive and not productive of reality. Discourses, even those which are premised upon disembodied individualism, produce meanings beyond the conscious intentions of their authors. Specifically, the neoclassical economist implies that his or her analysis is independent of questions of sexual difference and the production of subjectivity by invoking a pre-existing, universal individual, the contracting agent. However, I have argued, using a feminist poststructuralist reading of the surrogate motherhood exchange, that this is not the case. Sexual difference is of key significance when neoclassical economics produces sexed body exchanges in particular ways. I suggest that neoclassical economics cannot deny its integral role in both producing and supporting phallocentric constructions of that difference. However, by delineating the binary opposition of maternity and contract within neoclassical economics and its productive effects, I am not suggesting that the paradigm of autonomous and disembodied individuals interacting in markets should, or indeed, could, be replaced with a different central figure. Above all, I do not advocate the mother–child relation as the paradigmatic relation to which all others should conform, as the sociologist Virginia Held, (provisionally) in her paper 'Mothering versus Contract', and some feminist economists, have done. Held advocates this point of view on the basis that, before the social contract, men were children and hence the mother–child relation could logically be seen as the founding relation of society (ibid: 288–9). It is nevertheless evident that a sexual relation preceded men's births and childhoods. It is the status of the sexual relation with which this chapter is concerned, that is, the issue of sexual difference as produced within neoclassical economics – the difference between procreative man and reproductive woman – and hence the disavowal of the sexed body as a production of discourse within neoclassical economics.

Notes

1 I would like to thank John King, Marilyn Lake, Allison Craven, and especially Gregory Moore, for their very useful comments on work upon which this chapter is based.
2 The terms 'postmodernism' and 'poststructuralism' are terms which have been used interchangeably to refer to the philosophical project within which this chapter works (see Huyssen, 1990: 258–67; Milner, 1991: 110–6; Appleby et al., 1996: 385–92; Amariglio, 1998). However, these terms can also connote quite different concerns. Postmodernism is often associated with the fields of architecture, literature, photography, film, painting, video, dance and music (Hutcheon, 1989: 1), while poststructuralism is associated with knowledge production, subjectivity and philosophy. In this use of the terms, 'Postmodernism is to art what poststructuralism is to philosophy and social theory' (Ryan, 1988: 559). In other works, poststructuralist theory is treated as a subset of postmodern theory, and postmodern theorists are viewed as extending poststructuralist insights in the realm of philosophy to new areas within social theory (see, for example, Best and Kellner, 1991: ch. 1). The term 'postmodernity', on the other hand, is also used to indicate both the general terrain of aesthetics and of knowledge production (see, for example, Seidman 1994; Grosz, 1986f: 10). In this chapter, as in Australian writings in general, the term 'poststructuralism' is used to denote theoretical writings which take as given the productivity of language and which are concerned with questions of subjectivity, truth and knowledge, keeping in mind that, in the United States, the term 'postmodernism' also covers this terrain. Note, however, that exceptions to this geographic divide exist. For example, Kirby (1994), an Australian author working in the United States, has written within an Australian text that 'As an intellectual phenomenon, postmodernism is a critique of Reason that examines the status of what constitutes knowledge and the "knowing subject"' (1994: 120), while the American feminists Butler and Scott write that '"post-structuralism" indicates a field of critical practices that…interrogate the formative and exclusionary power of dis-course in the construction of sexual difference' (1992b: xiii).
3 On liberal feminism, see Tapper (1986). On 'object relations' feminism, see Chodorow (1978). On 'constructionist' feminism, see Ferber and Nelson (1993) and Grosz (1994a: 17). On the sex/gender distinction, its importance to feminist theorizing, and its limitations, see Gatens (1983), Eisenstein (1984), Edwards (1989), Butler (1990), Sullivan (1990), Threadgold (1990) and Grosz (1994b).

4   This is a common criticism of economics, although it rarely constitutes the whole of a feminist economist's concerns. See, for example, Reagan (1975), Jones and Lovejoy (1980), Ferber and Nelson (1993) and Hyman (1994).
5   Note, however, that sanctified motherhood is, in particular in the USA and Australia, an ideal constructed especially around white middle-class women. That is, not all women are 'good mothers'. This is shown by the history of appropriation of the children of non-white women (see, for example, Collins, 1994; Lake, 1994).
6   The neoclassical version of the surrogate motherhood contract must, for its own coherence, render the surrogate mother a passive supplier of a service. On another reading, the surrogate mother is literally the contracting agent: her contracting uterus delivers the baby and fulfills the contract. Still another feminist discourse of the pregnant body poses it as different in kind to that of the contracting 'individual'. Pateman (1988), Anderson (1990) and Shanley (1993), for example, argue that the very selfhood of the pregnant woman is undermined when the labor of pregnancy is viewed in the same light as other types of labor, since the fetus is not alienated in the same way as other products of work.

References

Amariglio, J. (1998) 'Poststructuralism', in J. Davis, D. Wade Hands and U. Maki (eds) *Handbook of Economic Methodology*, Aldershot: Elgar.
Anderson, Elizabeth S. (1990) 'Is Women's Labor a Commodity?', *Philosophy and Public Affairs* 19: 71–92.
Anleu, S.R. (1992) 'Surrogacy: For Love But Not For Money?', *Gender and Society* 6(1):30–48.
Appleby, J., Covington, E., Hoyt, D., Latham, M. and Sneider, A. (eds) (1996) *Knowledge and Postmodernism in Historical Perspective*, New York: Routledge.
Bergmann, B.R. (1981) 'The Economic Risks of Being a Housewife', *American Economic Review* 71(2):81–6.
—— (1989) 'Does the Market for Women's Labor Need Fixing?', *Journal of Economic Perspectives* 3(1):43–60.
Best, S. and D. Kellner (1991) *Postmodern Theory: Critical Interrogations*, Houndmills: Macmillan.
Bordo, S. (1993) *Unbearable Weight*, Berkeley: University. of California Press.
Butler, J. (1990) *Gender Trouble*, New York: Routledge.
Butler, J. and J.W. Scott (1992) 'Introduction', in J. Butler and J.W. Scott (eds) *Feminists Theorize the Political*, New York: Routledge, xiii–xvii.
Chodorow, N. (1978) *The Reproduction of Mothering*, Berkeley: University of California Press.
Cohen, M. (1982) 'The Problem of Studying "Economic Man"' in A. Miles and G. Finn (eds) *Feminism: From Pressure to Politics* Montreal: Black Rose Books,147–59.
Collins, P.H. (1994) 'Shifting the Center: Race, Class, and Feminist Theorizing About Motherhood' in D. Bassin, M. Honey and M.M. Kaplan (eds) *Representations of Motherhood*, New Haven: Yale University Press, 56–74.
Cornell, D. (1991) *Beyond Accommodation*, New York: Routledge.
Culler, J. (1983) *On Deconstruction*, London: Routledge and Kegan Paul.

Dallery, A.B. (1994) 'The Politics of Writing (the) Body: Écriture Féminine' in A.C. Herrmann and A.J. Stewart (eds) *Theorizing Feminism*, Boulder: Westview, 288–300.

Diprose, R. (1992) 'The Body which Biomedical Ethics Forgets' in S. Darling (ed.) *Cross Currents*, Adelaide: Flinders University Press, 147–62.

—— (1994) *The Bodies of Women*. London: Routledge.

—— (1996a) 'The Gift, Sexed Body Property and the Law' in P. Cheah, D. Fraser and J. Grbich (eds) *Thinking Through the Body of the Law*, St Leonards: Allen and Unwin, 120–35.

—— (1996b) 'Giving Corporeality Against the Law', *Australian Feminist Studies* 11(24): 253–62.

Dodds, S. and K. Jones. (1992) 'Surrogacy and the Body as Property' in S. Darling (ed.) *Cross Currents*, Adelaide: Flinders University Press, 119–33.

Douglas, G. (1994) 'The Intention to be a Parent and the Making of Mothers', *Modern Law Review* 57 (July): 636–41.

Edwards, A. (1989) 'The Sex/Gender Distinction: Has it Outlived its Usefulness?', *Australian Feminist Studies* 10 (Summer): 1–12.

Eisenstein, H. (1984) *Contemporary Feminist Thought*, London: Unwin Paperbacks.

Eisenstein, Z.R. (1988) *The Female Body and the Law*, Berkeley: University of California Press.

England, P. (1993) 'The Separative Self: Androcentric Bias in Neoclassical Economics' in M.A. Ferber and J.A. Nelson (eds) *Beyond Economic Man*, Chicago: University of Chicago Press, 37–53.

Feiner, S.F. (1995) 'Reading Neoclassical Economics: Toward an Erotic Economy of Sharing' in E. Kuiper and J. Sap (eds) *Out of the Margin*, London: Routledge, 151–66.

Ferber, M.A. and J.A. Nelson. (1993) 'Introduction: The Social Construction of Economics and the Social Construction of Gender' in M.A. Ferber and J.A. Nelson (eds) *Beyond Economic Man*, Chicago: University of Chicago Press, 1–22.

Folbre, N. and M. Abel. (1989) 'Women's Work and Women's Households: Gender Bias in the US Statistics', *Social Research* 56(3):545–70.

Foucault, M. (1981) *The History of Sexuality*, vol. 1, trans. R. Hurley. London: Penguin.

Franklin, S. (1991) 'Fetal Fascinations: New Dimensions to the Medical-Scientific Construction of Fetal Personhood' in S. Franklin, C. Lury and J. Stacey (eds) *Off-Centre*, London: Harper Collins Academic, 190–205.

Gatens, M. (1983) 'A Critique of the Sex/Gender Distinction', *Intervention* 17: 143–60.

—— (1988) 'Towards a Feminist Philosophy of the Body' in B. Caine, E.A. Grosz and M. de Lepervanche (eds) *Crossing Boundaries*, Sydney: Allen and Unwin, 59–70.

—— (1991a) 'Corporeal Representation in/and the Body Politic' in R. Diprose and R. Ferrell (eds) *Cartographies*, Sydney: Allen and Unwin, 79–87.

—— (1991b) *Feminism and Philosophy*, Cambridge: Polity.

Grosz, E.A (1986) 'Introduction', in E.A. Grosz, T. Threadgold, D. Kelly, A. Cholodenko and E. Colless (eds) *Futur*fall: Excursions into Post–Modernity*, Sydney: Power Institute of Fine Arts, University of Sydney, 7–17.

—— (1989) *Sexual Subversions*, Sydney: Allen and Unwin.
—— (1994a) 'Theorising Corporeality: Bodies, Sexuality and the Feminist Academy', *Melbourne Journal of Politics* 22: 3–29.
—— (1994b) 'Sexual Difference and the Problem of Essentialism' in N. Schor and E. Weed (eds) *The Essential Difference*, Bloomington: Indiana University Press, 82–97.
Held, V. (1990) 'Mothering Versus Contract' in J.J. Mansbridge (ed.) *Beyond Self-Interest*, Chicago: University of Chicago Press, 287–304.
Hewitson, G. (1994) 'Deconstructing Robinson Crusoe: A Feminist Interrogation of "Rational Economic Man"', *Australian Feminist Studies* 20 (Summer): 131–49.
—— (1997) 'The Market for Surrogate Motherhood Contracts', *Economic Record* 73(222): 212–24.
—— (1999) *Feminist Economics: Interogating the Masculinity of Rational Economic Man*, Cheltenham, UK and Northhampton, MA: Edward Elgar.
Hutcheon, L. (1989) *The Politics of Postmodernism*, London: Routledge.
Huyssen, A. (1990) 'Mapping the Postmodern', in L.J. Nicholson (ed.) *Feminism/Postmodernism*, New York: Routledge, 234–77.
Hyman, P. (1994) 'Feminist Critiques of Orthodox Economics: A Survey', *New Zealand Economic Papers* 28(1):53–80.
Ince, S. (1984) 'Inside the Surrogate Industry' in R. Arditti, R.D. Klein and S. Minden (eds) *Test-Tube Women*, Boston: Pandora, 99–116.
Irigaray, L. (1985) *This Sex Which is Not One*, trans. C. Porter. Ithaca: Cornell University Press.
Jones, J.M. and F.H. Lovejoy (1980) 'Discrimination Against Women Academics in Australian Universities', *Signs* 5(3):518–26.
Karpin, I. (1994) 'Reimagining Maternal Selfhood: Transgressing Body Boundaries and the Law', *Australian Feminist Law Journal* 2 (March): 36–62.
Keane, N. and D.L. Breo (1981) *The Surrogate Mother*, New York: Everest House.
Kirby, V. (1994) 'Viral Identities: Feminisms and Postmodernisms', in N. Grieve and A. Burns (eds) *Australian Women: Contemporary Feminist Thought*, Melbourne: Oxford University Press, 120–32.
Lake, M. (1992) 'Mission Impossible: How Men Gave Birth to the Australian Nation-Nationalism, Gender and Other Seminal Acts', *Gender and History* 4(3):305–22.
—— (1994) 'Between Old World "Barbarism" and Stone Age "Primitivism": The Double Difference of the White Australian Feminist' in N. Grieve and A. Burns (eds) *Australian Women*, Melbourne: Oxford University Press, 80–91.
Laqueur, T.W. (1990) *Making Sex*, Cambridge: Harvard University Press.
Lloyd, G. (1984) *The Man of Reason*, London: Methuen.
Milner, A. (1991) *Contemporary Cultural Theory: An Introduction*, Sydney: Allen and Unwin.
Morgan, D. (1994) 'A Surrogacy Issue: Who is the Other Mother?', *International Journal of Law and the Family* 8: 386–412.
Mykitiuk, R. (1994) 'Fragmenting the Body', *Australian Feminist Law Journal* 2 (March): 63–98.
National Bioethics Consultative Committee (1990) *Surrogacy, Report 1*, Canberra: Commonwealth of Australia.
Nelson, J.A. (1996) *Feminism, Objectivity and Economics*, London: Routledge.

Pateman, C. (1988) *The Sexual Contract*, Cambridge: Polity.
Pateman, C. and M.L. Shanley (eds) (1990) *Feminist Interpretations and Political Theory*, Cambridge: Polity.
Petchesky, R.P. (1990) *Abortion and Women's Choice*, revised edn. Boston: Northeastern University Press.
—— (1994) 'Fetal Images: The Power of Visual Culture in the Politics of Reproduction' in A.C. Herrmann and A.J. Stewart (eds) *Theorizing Feminism*, Boulder: Westview, 401–23.
Poovey, M. (1992) 'The Abortion Question and the Death of Man' in J. Butler and J.W. Scott (eds) *Feminists Theorize the Political*, New York: Routledge, 239–56.
Posner, R. (1989) 'The Ethics and Economics of Enforcing Contracts of Surrogate Motherhood', *Journal of Contemporary Health Law and Policy* 5(1):21–31.
—— (1992) *Sex and Reason*, Cambridge: Harvard University Press.
Pujol, M.A. (1992) *Feminism and Anti-Feminism in Early Economic Thought*, Aldershot: Elgar.
Roof, J. (1992) 'The Ideology of Fair Use: Xeroxing and Reproductive Rights', *Hypatia* 7(2):63–73.
Ryan, M. (1988) 'Postmodern Politics'. *Theory Culture and Society* 5(2–3): 559–76.
Rylance, R. (ed.) (1987) *Debating Texts: Readings in 20th Century Literary Theory and Method*, Toronto: University of Toronto Press.
Secomb, L. (1995) 'IVF: Reproducing the "Proper [Family] of Man"', *Australian Feminist Law Journal* 4 (March): 19–38.
Seidman, S. (1994) 'Introduction', in S. Seidman (ed.) *The Postmodern Turn: New Perspectives on Social Theory*, Cambridge: Cambridge University Press, 1–23.
Shanley, M.L. (1993) '"Surrogate Mothering" and Women's Freedom: A Critique of Contracts for Human Reproduction', *Signs* 18(3):618–39.
Singer, L. (1989) 'Bodies-Pleasures-Powers', *differences* 1(1):45–65.
Sullivan, B. (1990) 'Sex Equality and the Australian Body Politic' in S. Watson (ed.) *Playing the State*, Sydney: Allen and Unwin, 173–90.
Tapper, M. (1986) 'Can a Feminist Be a Liberal?', *Australasian Journal of Philosophy* 64 (June): S37–47.
Threadgold, T. 1990. 'Introduction' in T. Threadgold and A. Cranny-Francis (eds) *Feminine/Masculine and Representation*, Sydney: Allen and Unwin, 1–35.
Waring, M. (1988) *If Women Counted: A New Feminist Economics*, New York: HarperCollins.
Young, A. (1993) 'Decapitation or Feticide: The Fetal Laws of the Universal Subject', *Women: A Cultural Review* 4(3):288–94.
Young, I.M. (1990) *Throwing Like a Girl and Other Essays in Feminist Philosophy and Social Theory*, Bloomington: Indiana University Press.

11
COMMENT ON CHARUSHEELA AND HEWITSON

Brian Cooper

Hewitson and Charusheela employ feminist poststructural and postcolonial theory to explore how economists, in theory and practice, address basic issues of equality and difference, and subjectivity and agency. They examine the tools and assumptions of economics to raise questions about the status of subjects and agents in economics: who are they and what are their characteristics? What kind of knowledge do they produce and what kind of knowledge do they exclude? How do they help us construct (describe and change) real life? Their chapters provide some answers to these questions. They demonstrate in particular how elements of mainstream economic theories of choice and exchange work to produce specific, not necessarily consistent, gendered notions of subjectivity and agency. They also indicate how these theories can simultaneously exclude sexual and cultural differences, and 'explain' the obvious differences in economic outcomes between groups.

Both papers should be required reading for our rethinking of subjectivity and agency in economics. Yet, even while they indicate limits to and aporia in the body of neoclassical economics, Charusheela and Hewitson tend to reduce its heterogeneity to homogeneity. As a consequence, they neglect what I feel are obvious examples of mainstream debates about the economics of the family which involve questions about subjectivity, and agency in theory and practice, and concerns expressed by mainstream economists about the ability of their tools to address questions of difference. I shall draw on my own particular research and teaching biases – the history of economics, and the economics of the family – to try to extend their analyses. Viewed in historical perspective, there are points in the past, most notably with Malthus, when Anglo-American political economy has been preoccupied with reproduction and family, sexed female and male bodies, as well as ethnocentrism and relativism, and the trace of these concerns remains in present-day theory.

Economists research, but also educate and persuade. We not only describe the world, but tailor it and its subjects to make them fit our descriptions. This tug and pull between description and prescription is itself imbricated in a world transformed by social, political and technological change. One use of history, then, is to point us toward questions raised by economists in the past that are similar to those about subjectivity and agency raised by Charusheela and Hewitson. Classification is critical in this respect: nineteenth century political economists assumed that a clear delineation of different types of people was required for the analyst to determine who was fit to be an economic (and political) subject and agent. Education is critical, too: classical political economists wished to school individuals and groups, especially the middle classes, in the principles of economics in order to change their behavior. Then as now, although more openly than we acknowledge today, political economists wished to make real economic subjects behave more like ideal subjects as part of their efforts at political reform.[1] They too lived in a period of continuity and change, when their theories and prescriptions seemed both apt and lacking. They too needed to make sense out of their world, and create new meanings, new understandings, and new possibilities for subjectivity and agency.

Conceiving families: surrogate motherhood and neoclassical theories of exchange

Charusheela calls for case studies that interweave the theoretical and the empirical, and that consider the specific historical, social, institutional, political, and cultural contexts of the economic agent. Hewitson eloquently wields feminist poststructural theory to undertake such a study in her examination of the meanings of surrogate birth arrangements in the USA. Hewitson writes that 'Meaning is created between texts rather than between texts and the real world, and hence neoclassical economics must be understood as intertextual' (p. 221). This restates a standard poststructuralist creed. Yet texts certainly belong to the real world, and are cited and employed by participants in real world economic and legal debates. Hewitson argues as much when she asserts that 'neoclassical theory is a discourse which actively produces its objects as well as its subjects of knowledge, rather than being a knowledge in relation to which a 'real world' of men and women, or masculinity or femininity has a separate existence' (p. 223). The crux of her essay reminds us that, in real life at least, the economic agent has a body. She argues, however, that the standard mainstream theoretical accounts and legal conceptions of a surrogate mother relationship erase the surrogate's body through her transformation, by means of the surrogate contract, into 'economic man'. Her body is desexed by the transformation of her womb into capital, with the exchange based on services derived from this capital. If the sexed body is absent, so too is the body itself, which is detached from the personhood (identity) of the agent. The woman is now equivalent to 'economic man' in her ability to contract out her capital services (she is not actually selling the baby that results from this process), and in her ability to maximize her utility on the basis of the sale of these services.

As Hewitson herself notes, surrogate contracts *are* often written in such a way as to recognize the body of the surrogate, and not just the womb itself. Strictures against drinking alcohol, smoking, and other drug use by surrogates are common. As Hewitson points out, however, when the debate about the surrogate relationship is restricted to the realm of contract it tends to elide the sexed body of the surrogate. It elides as well other dimensions of 'difference' that are the norm in the surrogate relationship: the surrogate is typically less educated, less well-off, and a member of a racial minority. Yet, while the legal framework on surrogacy in the USA smooths over questions of 'difference', it is not uniform, but an evolving patchwork that varies state by state, court ruling by court ruling. True, courts have consistently upheld contracts and ruled against attempts by surrogates to gain custody rights not specifically spelled out in the agreements. But courts' majority and dissenting opinions have varied widely, with some justices expressing uneasiness at the idea of complete enforceability of contracts (Grayson 1998: 534). Indeed, custodial parents have broken contracts (in and out of court) when surrogates have, contrary to contract, not kept healthy habits, or when the contract was not carefully written to take the health status of the surrogate into account and unhealthy issue resulted, or when the resulting offspring have turned out, for whatever reason, as 'goods' not to the parents' liking.

The unregulated surrogate contract model, with its transformation of the surrogate into an 'economic man', and its reliance on the court system to adjudicate disputes based more or less on a market model of the exchange of goods and services, is a peculiarly (though not exclusively) American one. Changes in reproductive technologies in general are only loosely regulated in the USA. These changes include the not-too distant prospects of human cloning and the artificial womb, two technologies which would, on the face of it, take the issue of sexual difference out of reproduction. The USA does have a presidential board, the National Bioethics Advisory Commission, as well as an informal network of doctors, lawyers and ethicists whom physicians and fertility clinics consult on biomedical issues. But their advice does not have the teeth of law. The result has been a set of ad hoc decisions by individual doctors and clinics, and inconsistent court rulings and state and federal legislation. The situation in other countries is likewise a patchwork.

Some nations rely on national legislation, others on national boards (England has the Human Fertilisation and Embryology Authority), which not only evaluate the market and moral dimensions of new reproductive technologies, and advise on their use, but can restrict or ban them altogether.

One such technology already in use in the USA, but banned in England, removes sperm from incapacitated men prior to or just after death, for future procreative use. This is sometimes done against the express desires and certainly without the conscious consent of the 'donors'. Here it is the sexed bodies of men that are involved in what has been dubbed 'procreation without permission'. The notion of a specifically male possessive individualism is violated in the name of (potential) future procreation.

Sexed bodies that willingly procreate without social and moral approbation have figured prominently in past debates in political economy. Malthus asserted the 'natural' importance of bodies: the bodies of women and men, both (albeit differently) sexed bodies, constituted one half of the problematic of his population principles. The passion for sex, and the biological capacity of humans (women) to reproduce, both universal givens, drove the model. For Malthus, people were 'compound beings', composed of mind and body, reason and passion, and neither element predominated, much less erased the other.

Malthus's work singled out the importance of family formation and behavior for economic performance and well-being. New reproductive technologies contribute to an increasingly fragmented set of understandings of what family is, who constitutes its members, and what functions they play (Grayson 1998). Sexed bodies also come into play in the consideration of what is 'natural', a concept that Hewitson employs to differentiate between the 'natural' mother and the surrogate. The former has a legitimate claim to a child on the basis of the father's 'natural' position as a male fulfilling a contract, and on the basis of the surrogate's 'unnatural' position as a mother involved in the same contract, and her 'unnatural' willingness to give up the baby, contrary to 'natural' maternal instincts (p. 235). Thus we could say that the award of the child to the father (and 'natural' mother) in the fulfillment of the contract both accords with 'natural' rights, and is 'naturalized' by the transformation of the surrogate into 'economic man'.

Yet, I think the term 'normal', rather than 'natural', is more apt here. Normal bridges the fact/value distinction and had supplanted (although not completely) 'natural' as the standard of what is good and correct in social relations by the mid-nineteenth century (Hacking 1990: 160–4). The Baby M and Baby Johnson cases, both of which Hewitson cites, are not symmetric, but involve different technologies of reproduction. In the former, the surrogate contributed both ovum and womb; in the latter, the surrogate contributed the womb, and the genetic mother the ovum. Thus, in the Baby Johnson case there were in fact two 'natural' mothers who, by the logic of those who wish to counterpoise a distinction between the natural and the social, are also 'unnatural' mothers: both the genetic mother and the gestational mother are contracting mothers. What more likely underlay the courts' decisions to award Baby Johnson to the genetic mother was the 'normal' and normative assumption that courts have held in many permutations of custody cases: the preservation of the two-parent, heterosexual family should trump all other considerations.[2]

The normative work which separates motherhood from paid labor in economic theory has itself been long, hard labor, involving a seesaw in which family formation and procreation have been treated as both private and public acts. Defining the proper boundary between private and public for 'family' has been uncertain, as has the definition of 'family' itself. For much of the eighteenth century, the dictum 'be fruitful and multiply' ruled, and the bodies of the laboring poor – women, men, and children alike – constituted a nation's strength. Malthus's analysis, in which instead strong individual bodies added up to national weakness, helped articulate and pave the way for the ideology of separate spheres and the creation of 'domestic woman' and 'economic man' (Valenze 1995). But, as Charusheela points out, this process, defining who was and who was not economic man, did not involve a simple, binary opposition between men and women, where the (absence of) the female body becomes the ground for the establishment of the masculinity and presumed universality of the economic subject (Armstrong 1987). James Mill famously defined women, children, and idiots as classes whose economic and political interests could be represented by adult males of the family. Critics pointed out that this not only represented an arbitrary carving out of exceptions to the rule of equality, but that, even if one were to grant these exceptions, whole subgroups within these classes were bereft of adult males to represent them.

While it has been easy to note the ways in which women and non-white males have been (and continue to be) seen as falling short of the ideals of economic man, it is conceivable that they will achieve full equality.[3] Children, however, represent another sort of liminal class altogether. If they don't exactly come into being as fully formed economic creatures, in present-day economic theories of consumer choice they soon come to have tastes and preferences just as consistent and ordered as those of adults. Unlike much mainstream (Ricardian and Malthusian) nineteenth century political economy, for which political reform was predicated upon mass education in the principles of economics, and which in the hands of writers like the Edgeworths (Maria and Richard Lovell) and Harriet Martineau, presumed, insisted even, that anyone – women, men, and children – could and should become a Smithian 'economist' (Cooper 1997), the economic education of children has only recently become visible in present-day economic theories of the family, where children are not so much 'economists in novo' as physical property, or intellectual property, or consumption goods, or investment goods. And, depending on their age and geopolitical location, children are endowed either with limited rights and responsibilities or the rights and responsibilities (hence a rationality) identical to those of an adult.[4]

Who are economic subjects and agents, and what do they do?

In the view of the nineteenth-century reformers just mentioned, education was necessary for commercial civilization because it generated and cultivated desire. Charusheela discusses how desires translate into action in mainstream economic theory, and how this translation, through the concepts of choice in neoclassical theory, underlines how 'both ethnocentrism and relativism are historical products of the same underlying conception of human agency' which developed in the Enlightenment (p. 197). These viewpoints, she asserts, make it difficult for Western feminists to conceive of, much less assess, non-Western agents, and to reconcile the goals of autonomy (the ability to make choices) and equality (of outcomes). While applauding the productive tension within Western feminism which has yielded 'the capacity for a sympathetic and complex understanding of feminist agency which leads to divergent conclusions and decisions', Charusheela maintains that this capacity 'has been harder to maintain as cultural and historical difference widen' (p. 199). As a result, ethical judgement of agents' behaviors becomes problematic, as does any basis for reform.

As Charusheela notes, notions of choice in mainstream economic theory build upon the supposed dichotomy and conflict between insatiable desires and scarce resources. Agents know their desires and their constraints, and they act. The analyst observes these actions. Once an action is taken, however, the dichotomy between desires and constraints breaks down for the observer. *Ex post* 'there is no *intrinsic* mechanism by which we can decide what component of the agent's action reflects desire, and what component reflects constraint' (p. 201). Charusheela uses the example of veiling to illustrate this breakdown: is this action an example of constraint, choice, or both?

Present-day economists have a ready answer to the questions of what role women's and men's fashions play in the (economic) regulation of desire and self. These are non-pecuniary costs and benefits, amenable to calculation by the agent, but not the analyst. Yet it is true, as Charusheela notes, that 'The problem with the theory is that there is no internal mechanism…which tells us how to divide the terrain of agent action into constraint on choice, socialized false choices, and true freedom and choice' (p. 204). The theory generates both relativist and ethnocentric viewpoints. The relativist position considers the choice, if it is a choice, as free, and (based on the assumption of individual autonomy) true, and hence we have no grounds to question this choice and its consequences; in the ethnocentric viewpoint the choice is deemed a false choice, made against one's own interests, and represents internalized oppression. The latter category provides choice theory its continuity with Enlightenment notions of agency because the existence of a margin consisting of individuals and whole groups who do not fit the criteria of free agency demarcates and defines those who do exercise free choice.

I think Charusheela is correct in her analysis of the consequences entailed by the ideal version of the choice framework, and how these are tied to the assumptions of a particular model of agency derived from Enlightenment notions of subjectivity. If we assume that choice is rational and consistent with preferences, then we have no method to account for agency that leads to choices that put a person or group at persistent economic disadvantage. Again, we have to fall back on the unobservable category of psychic costs or benefits. Yet she fails to mention that numerous critics within and without mainstream economics have raised the same questions about agency in the model of choice under constraint, that is, whether there really is any choice and agency involved at all. Critics have asked whether choice is simply a predetermined, mechanical procedure, whether the choice framework is an observation about what most people do most of the time, an approximation of the real that does not necessarily hold in every case, or simply an 'as if' condition convenient for theoretical and empirical analysis.[5] These same questions, for instance, arose in the context of the debate engendered by Gary Becker's work in the new home economics in the 1970s. His theories hinge on the interlocking nature of choice and constraint, and presented major difficulties, in theory, for those who wished to see improvement in the economic status of women. Becker's model of altruism (benevolent dictatorship), specialization and comparative advantage within the family implied that women, even those in the West, were caught in a vicious circle (Becker 1981, 1991). Women, through the combined effects of biology, socialization, and the exercise of their own rational agency, would persist in their choices to specialize in non-market activities (the economically efficient choice within the parameters set by the model), thus 'choosing' to work less and get paid less, relative to men, in the market. The model is most emphatically a two-sex model, with the sexual division of labor depending on sexual difference, what Becker calls the 'heavy biological burden' of women in pregnancy and child care. And the same charge that Charusheela levels at Western feminists – that they construct non-Western women's agency as a set of socially conditioned 'wrong' choices, or choices which the analyst was not supposed to judge, and which, in either case, leave women apparently frozen in time, unable to change, and without 'real' agency – is a construction that feminists still fight in court battles and in the theoretical and empirical literature of the West. Becker himself has questioned the outcome dictated by the logic of his model because it doesn't square with the facts of the steady influx of women into the paid labor market in the West.

Facts are not always friendly to economic theories. 'Economic man', as a representative of what Charusheela calls the 'true Enlightenment self', is best described as contested territory, originally mapped out in the analyses of sameness and difference that marked economics at its putative birth in the late eighteenth century as an inquiry into the wealth (and poverty) of nations. While users of stages of growth theories typically employed comparative, historical methods of analyses and identified commercial civilization as the endpoint of humanity, the only stage that allowed the true flowering of human nature (and true economic subjectivity and agency, with its prudence, foresight, and rational probabilities), they nevertheless presumed a universal human substrate – egotistical drives – common to all, savages, barbarians and civilized peoples. Different types of people, characterized by different psychological expressions of underlying human drives, were associated with the different stages of growth and, within each society, different groups such as landlords, capitalists and workers. The problem for the analyst was to discern how differences between peoples arose and persisted. They typically located causes of differences in the environment and in institutional arrangements – the evolution of property and its security were key factors, as well as the changes entailed by the progressive accumulation of capital. But the framework did not necessarily guarantee smooth narratives of progress, even for the history of Europe. Smith asserted that the history of the growth of towns, which, in the 'natural order of things', should have been stimulated by the growth of agriculture, demonstrated the exact opposite, and that in fact this relationship had

> in all the modern states of Europe, been, in many respects, entirely inverted. The foreign commerce of some of their cities has introduced all their finer manufactures...and manufactures and foreign commerce, together, have given birth to the principal improvements in agriculture.
> (Smith 1976; III, i. 9)

That is, 'the natural progress of opulence', in *Wealth of Nations* was 'unnatural' according to Smith's own model of the relationship between the psychology and the behavior of capitalists and agriculturalists, and the development of commercial society.

Classical political economists also realized that the same concept of subjectivity and agency generated both the relativist and universalist (ethnocentric) positions. They vigorously debated the merits of each, and often leavened their observations and representations with moral relativism and ethical judgments simultaneously. In *How to Observe. Morals and Manners* (1838), for example, Martineau relied on Smithian concepts of sympathy tempered by reason, impartial spectatorship, and viewing without prejudice to assert that a traveler should not judge horrific practices, such as the exposure of the elderly and infants, he (her choice of pronoun) might observe in other lands. Rather, these horrors, which, she noted, had commonly occurred in Europe in earlier periods, had to be understood within specific historical and cultural contexts. For Martineau, these practices were the result of ignorance, not wickedness. She denied, then affirmed, that there were universal principles of ethical behavior, and believed that these practices would change in time because all people had an underlying basic humanity, consistent (but not identical) with the revealed truth of Christian religion. Here are relativism and ethnocentrism, all together in the course of a few paragraphs. But out of this inconsistent amalgam rises at least the possibility that all peoples could change their own cultural practices for the better (or worse), without Western meddling.

The increasing frequency and strangeness of encounters by scientists, commercial travelers, and missionaries with overseas others from the eighteenth to the mid-nineteenth centuries led Europeans to reconsider Enlightenment notions of humanity, and associated egalitarian ideals (Raby 1997). Travel data provided critical evidence and analytical frameworks for political economists such as Smith (Hunt 1993). Indeed, the work of political economists (especially Malthus) on desire and its manifestations, and on the concept of value, helped other social analysts put all these data into order in the first half of the nineteenth century, served as a proto-anthropology, and was crucial to the development of the English concept of culture (hence, difference) itself (Stocking 1987; Herbert 1991).[6] The travel data led some writers on political economy however, like Martineau, to refashion their tools. Her inability to reconcile facts she observed during her travels – the economic and political subjugation of women and slaves in America – with her views on Ricardian and Malthusian political economy led her to rethink the methods for social analysis: *How to Observe* has been cited as the first methodological treatise in sociology and anthropology.

Political economists could change when confronted with new facts. The subjects of their theories could change, too. Travels and travelers' tales led some British to question their own identity and sense of difference from others – one could go 'native'.⁷ For the English, and later, the British, the bodies and attributes against which they defined their own sense of individual and national identity belonged as much, if not more, to their European competitors, such as France, as to Charusheela's 'non-West'. The epithets 'slavish', 'naked', 'thievish', and so on, were first applied by the English to the Irish in their colonial wars in the seventeenth century, and were later applied by travelers to other overseas peoples (Hunt 1993). The reciprocal (if unequal) relationship between the identity of 'economic man' and others holds for the case of later British encounters in the Americas. For the British who, enticed by commercial prospectuses promising huge returns on shares in North and South American mines and railroads in the nineteenth century, lost fortunes in the failure of speculative overseas investments, the experience could lead them to believe that they were just as irrational as the natives.

The example of the Irish and the Americans, colonial subjects, does not vitiate the importance of the distinction between West and non-West in defining Western economic subjectivity and agency. But they indicate that a distinction between Western and non-Western subjects, defined as the difference between rationality and irrationality, is not so clear. Like their domestic 'marginal' counterparts among the Irish and in the lower classes in Britain, overseas (post)colonial subjects talked back. They used encounters with European explorers and commercial travelers, and, later, tourists, as well as Western literature to rethink their own sense of identity (Pratt 1992; Grewal 1996). As Charusheela writes elsewhere, the definition of the postcolonial subject, a negotiated position between margin and center, applies as much to the Western subject as to the non-Western (Charusheela 1999).

Conclusion: what should we do?

It is true, the ideal neoclassical subject lacks, in theory, all aspects of difference – sex, gender, class, race, religion, nation. And, as Hewitson notes, it is difficult to transform others into liberal individuals, in theory, and in practice, too. But it is hard to transform any subject, including the real ones of the West, into an economic subject in part because domestic and overseas subjects are not mute. Yet, if our subjects are all too ready to give voice to what they perceive as the inadequacies of our tools, we are not deaf. We participate in an ongoing, never finished (therefore endlessly fruitful) effort to teach people how to regulate their behavior, but we are students, too. We can and should construct histories of economic analyses along the lines of how analysts and their subjects have tried to reconcile the theoretical assumptions of sameness with the empirical realities of difference.⁸ In doing so, we can reach out to other disciplines, like history, political science, and anthropology, for tools, and evidence on how to observe and represent both similarity and difference.

This has already occurred. Mainstream economists have moved beyond Becker's models of the family, for example, and are even willing to look beyond mainstream bargaining models of the family, with all their limitations (Agarwal 1997), to other disciplines. The most recent push for the education of children in India by mainstream economists was spurred by the research done by a political scientist, Myron Weiner (Weiner 1991). Weiner used techniques from his own discipline, as well as from anthropology, and placed his data in comparative historical perspective. His work indicated that educational reforms and increasing literacy often preceded rather than followed higher incomes, and implied that policy makers in India should not hesitate to increase investments in education, including educating parents on the value of educating their children. This has led feminists, mainstream economists, nongovernment agencies, and government officials all to line up, for various reasons, in support of increased educational opportunities for children. I think we can all agree that increasing the choice set (hence changing the constraints) of parents and children is good: the devil is in the details. Of course, education is social control, and raises moral issues, but this seems to address Charusheela's concerns about theory, policy, and ethics.

There are other instances when mainstream theory openly acknowledges 'difference' in its theories and allows breaches in the margins of the discipline: theories of discrimination; game theory, which some practitioners assert allows them to represent many 'economic men' rather than one representative, economic subject; macroeconomic growth theory which allows for different 'national' models of growth, and which explores the cultural bases for convergence or lack thereof, in per capita income; and the recent rage for basic economic education, which forces us to rethink the who, what, and how of economic instruction in the West. These all represent opportunities for us to participate in and change the conversations of mainstream economics, if we choose to do so.

Notes

1 While it is true that in the period from Smith to J.S. Mill, 'classical political economy' had little systematic to say about economic subjectivity (Oakely 1994; Levine 1998a and 1998b), and critics like Macaulay made hay out of this perceived lack (asserting that political economists assumed the very elements of human nature they needed to study), champions and detractors of political economy were involved in vigorous, ongoing debates about the outlines of ideal economic subjectivity.
2 The trial judge in the Baby Johnson case opined that the idea that the infant had two natural mothers was 'ripe for crazy-making' (quoted in Grayson 1998: 531), and based his award of the infant on the evidence of genetic (as opposed to gestational) parenthood as proof of a parent–child relationship, a decision upheld by the appellate court. The California Supreme Court upheld the award on the basis of the genetic parents' intent in contract. The collision

between the concept of natural and normal has occurred in divorce cases as well, where, with respect to fatherhood, a child cannot have two natural fathers: the courts in the USA have consistently presumed a man's 'fatherhood' of his wife's, the mother's, children. Courts have ruled inadmissible DNA evidence which could disprove 'natural' fatherhood in custody and support cases, citing such evidence as too disruptive and painful in the already difficult process of splitting up the two-parent (heterosexual) family. Here the courts have deferred to a norm of 'natural' fatherhood determined using older technologies and evidence (blood tests and blood types), and have chosen to ignore methods which can establish a 'truer' (genetic) determination of the 'natural'.
3   In the USA, the experience of two other marginal groups is instructive. The deinstitutionalization of the mentally retarded, and the accompanying expenditure on support services since the 1970s has done much to bring them into the mainstream, including the economic mainstream, of American life. The deinstitutionalization of the mentally ill, begun in the 1950s, on the other hand, has been a dismal failure.
4   Think of the different legal ages for voting, drinking alcohol, driving, military service, and marriage in the USA For reasons of space, I will not go into the questions raised by the extension of the privileges of 'possessive individualism' to embryos and fetuses.
5   The choice framework that Charusheela describes is a staple of undergraduate instruction in economics in the USA, and students often resist its assumptions and implications because they are not 'real'. Economists prefer the revealed preference model: agents know themselves, know their preferences, and know all this prior to the analysis. But once we acknowledge that preferences are endogenous, may be unstable, and are amenable to analysis, as mainstream economists have begun to do (Becker 1996), then this theory itself begins to break down.
6   The Belgian statistician Adolphe Quetelet, the inventor of 'average man', for example, used Malthus's population principles and the idea of the regulation of sexual desire to statistically define and rank the relative degree of civilization of nations: the lower the fertility and (as a result) mortality rates, the more civilized the country, and vice versa (Cooper and Murphy, 2000).
7   The self-interest of commercial travelers could all too easily degenerate into an all-consuming desire for travel. Robinson Crusoe is warned by his father that he should give up his wandering propensities and instead embrace the middle station of life, with the stability which later writers on political economy emphasized as necessary to produce economic subjectivity and economic agency.
8   We need to be careful though: Charusheela appears at one point to suggest that we replace one master narrative, a neoclassical theory of agency, with another, 'a feminist economics theory' of agency (Note 30).

References

Agarwal, B. (1997) '"Bargaining" and Gender Relations: Within and Beyond the Household', *Feminist Economics* 3,1: 1–51.

Armstrong, N. (1987) *Desire and Domestic Fiction: A Political History of the Novel*, New York: Oxford University Press.

Becker, G. (1981) *A Treatise on the Family*, Cambridge, MA: Harvard University Press.

—— (1991) *A Treatise on the Family: Enlarged Edition*, Cambridge, MA: Harvard University Press.

—— (1996) *Accounting for Tastes*, Cambridge, MA: Harvard University Press.

Charusheela, S. (1999) 'Economic Analysis, Political Activism and the Post-Colonial Condition', paper presented at the panel on Postcolonial Thought and the Politics of Economy and Economics, Union for Radical Political Economics at the Allied Social Sciences Conference, New York, January. Paper available from author.

Cooper, B. (1997) 'Family Troubles', in Heather Boushey, Ellen Mutari and William Fraher IV (eds) *Gender and Political Economy: Incorporating Diversity into Theory and Policy*, New York: M.E. Sharpe.

Cooper, B. and Murphy, M.S. (2000) 'Death of the Author at the Birth of Social Science: The Cases of Harriet Martineau and Adolphe Quetelet', *Studies in History and Philosophy of Science*, 31, 1: 1–36.

Grayson, D.R. (1998) 'Mediating Intimacy: Black Surrogate Mothers and the Law', *Critical Inquiry* 24, 2: 525–46.

Grewal, I. (1996) *Home and Harem: Nation, Gender, Empire, and the Cultures of Travel*, Durham: Duke University Press.

Hacking, I. (1990) *The Taming of Chance*, Cambridge: Cambridge University Press.

Herbert, C. (1991) *Culture and Anomie: Ethnographic Imagination in the Nineteenth Century*, Chicago: University of Chicago Press.

Hunt, M. (1993). 'The Commercial Gaze', *Journal of British Studies* 32, 4: 333–57.

Levine, D. P. (1998a) 'The Self and its Interests in Classical Political Economy', *The European Journal of the History of Economic Thought* 5, 1: 36–59.

—— (1998b) *Subjectivity in Political Economy: Essays on Wanting and Choosing*, New York: Routledge.

Martineau, H. (1838) *How to Observe. Morals and Manners*, London: C. Knight and Co.

Oakley, A. (1994) *Classical Economic Man: Human Agency and Methodology in the Political Economy of Adam Smith and John Stuart Mill*, Aldershot: Edward Elgar.

Pratt, M.L. (1992) *Imperial Eyes: Travel Writing and Transculturation*, New York: Routledge Press.

Raby, P. (1997) *Bright Paradise: Victorian Scientific Travellers*, Princeton: Princeton University Press.

Smith, A. (1976) *An Inquiry into the Nature and the Causes of the Wealth of Nations* (1776) (eds) R.H. Campbell, A.S. Skinner, and W.B. Todd,. Oxford: Clarendon Press.

Stocking, G.W., Jr. (1987) *Victorian Anthropology*, New York: Free Press.

Valenze, D. (1995) *The First Industrial Woman*, New York: Oxford University Press.

Weiner, M. (1991) *The Child and the State in India: Child Labor and Education Policy in Comparative Perspective*, Princeton: Princeton University Press.

PART V

FEMINIST/POSTMODERN ECONOMICS

12
THE TROUBLE WITH WOMEN AND ECONOMICS
A postmodern perspective on Charlotte Perkins Gilman

Ulla Grapard

The postmodern commitment to the idea that knowledge is socially constructed encourages attention to the specific arguments that – at different points in time – have been considered valuable contributions to the developing body of knowledge in a given field. Especially in disciplines that make claim to be scientific, and here we must include economics, we want to understand what makes arguments 'scientific' and 'true' to the community of knowers. To gain an understanding of what has been included in the canon, and why, it may be useful to look at work that has been excluded and try to understand what distinguishes the accepted from the rejected. Hence we want to seek out practitioners whose ideas and intellectual contributions have not made it into the corpus of the official history of ideas of the discipline. Charlotte Perkins Gilman's *Women and Economics* (1898) is a text that has been excluded from the canon in economics, and this chapter will examine some of the reasons for this neglect from a feminist, postmodernist perspective.

Feminist and postmodern perspectives on women and economics

For the last 30 years, feminist scholarship has been pointing out the social, historical and political construction of what is taught as knowledge. Lost or ignored voices of women from all academic disciplines have been painstakingly recovered and included, in varying degrees, in the curriculum. As this feminist project advances, epistemological issues have become more central. One reason for this is the realization that adding women's voices does not automatically guarantee a feminist agenda. Women scientists are not necessarily more likely to be skeptical of the scientific practices, nor are women economists necessarily critical of the methods and philosophical underpinnings of their field. Most feminist scholars will agree that to advance the feminist agenda, it becomes necessary to understand and address problems concerning the exercise of power, the hegemony of knowledge formation and the modernist discursive practices of the various disciplines. It becomes a question of how to transform knowledge production so that ideas, which could not even be thought and expressed within the disciplinary boundaries in an earlier time, become possible.

The feminist process of opening up the disciplines to scrutiny has found much in common with postmodern and poststructuralist methods of uncovering the hidden and unspoken foundations of disciplinary practices. Foucault (1973) uses what he calls genealogical and archeological methods of analysis to show how the modern human sciences – including economics – emerge, starting in the sixteenth century, as new forms of legitimate knowledge produced within particular *regimes of truth* in Western culture. Foucault is not trying to document the development of scientific truth or to describe the progress of knowledge toward an objectivity. In the postmodern era, that tends to be a meaningless statement except as a discursive artifact. Rather, he says, it is an inquiry 'whose aim it is to discover on what basis knowledge and theory became possible; within what space of order knowledge was constituted...' (1973, xxiii). His early work describes and analyzes what he calls the *episteme* and the possibilities for its existence; his later works develop more fully his ideas about knowledge as power, and power as knowledge.[1] As one of the first to pose the question of power in terms of discourse, Foucault's work adds a political dimension to the insights provided by the works of Saussure and Derrida in the fields of linguistics and literary criticism. Although their theories have not been developed with a view to feminist praxis, they have often influenced and paralleled feminist work on the social construction of gender and women's exclusion from knowledge production.

Feminist theory in the humanities and the social sciences has made much progress by showing that the dichotomous structures of discourse, through which meaning is created, are profoundly gendered. The focus on difference and hierarchically constructed pairs of opposites – so central to the deconstruction of all sorts of texts – has been adapted by feminists. They have used it in analyses of the fundamental and pervasive discursive formations that have constructed the category *Women* as the Other, as non-Man. The superior, masculine self is positioned in contrast to the inferior, feminine self; the public domain of the independent male citizen finds its counterpart in the domestic, dependent, female non-citizen; the rationality of the mind of the thinking male is constructed in opposition to the emotional, intuitive, female mind. The list goes on and on. What historian Joan Scott says about political history holds equally well for economic history:

> Political history has, in a sense, been enacted on the field of gender. It is a field that seems fixed yet whose meaning is contested and in flux. If we treat the opposition between male and female as problematic rather than known, as something contextually defined, repeatedly constructed, then we must constantly ask not only what is at stake in proclamations and debates that invoke gender to explain or justify their positions but also how implicit understandings of gender are being invoked and reinscribed.
>
> (Scott 1988:49)

Does this postmodern insistence that identity and subject position are slippery concepts present a problem for feminists? If the category *Women* is thus textually and discursively constructed, does that mean that *Women*/women do not exist? Or that we cannot talk about women having a collective voice, or that female agency disappears?

These questions have led to frictions within the feminist scholarly community because legitimate questions about alliances and political institutions make it problematic to start questioning the boundaries of categories that seem to have served well to mobilize a feminist agenda. The notion that political agency becomes impossible if we start to question the categories in the name of which change is demanded brings out the tension between some feminists and the postmodern project. Bordo, for example speaks for a number of feminists when she finds it curious that it is precisely at the moment when women's voices are beginning to be heard in the academy that 'we' are asked to deconstruct and give up that category (Bordo 1990:153). Hartsock is also critical of the theories presented by postmodern thinkers such as Foucault, Derrida, Rorty, and Lyotard because, as she says, in spite of their 'efforts to avoid the problems of European modernism of the eighteenth and nineteenth centuries, at best [they] manage to criticize these theories without putting anything in their place' (Hartsock 1990:159). She finds that postmodern perspectives make it difficult to talk about the actual lives of women in terms of subordination and domination. As a result, such ideas tend to impede the efforts of those who have been systematically excluded and marginalized and who are engaged in developing systematic changes in society.

Even as some feminists may worry about giving up what seems a useful category, i.e., *Women*, they really cannot avoid confronting the postmodern dilemma of the decentered and unstable subject. The question of who 'we' are in any given political, historical context must be dealt with when tensions surrounding gender, class, race, ethnicity, geography, and other categories open up and split apart the notion of universal, timeless, womanhood.[2]

In her book, *Only Paradoxes to Offer*, Joan Scott grapples with this tension as it constructs the historical context of French femininsts' long fight for equality. She claims that a paradox is inherent in a modernist, feminist discourse which takes for granted the march of progress, the autonomy of the individual, and the need to choose between equality and difference – without questioning the terms of that historical discourse.

> When exclusion was legitimated by reference to the different biologies of women and men, 'sexual difference' was established not only as a natural fact, but also as an ontological basis for social and political differentiation. Women thus came into existence through the discourse of sexual difference. Feminism was a protest against women's political exclusion; its goal was to eliminate 'sexual difference' in politics, but it had to make its claim on behalf of 'women' (who were discursively produced through 'sexual difference'). To the extent that it acted for 'women', feminism produced the 'sexual difference' it sought to eliminate. This paradox – the need to both accept *and* to refuse 'sexual difference' – was the constitutive condition of feminism as a political movement throughout its long history.
>
> (Scott 1996:3–4)

As I want to show, this paradox is also at the center of Gilman's text. Written at the turn of the century, *Women and Economics* is clearly an example of a modernist text. When Gilman formulates her claims for women's equality and emancipation in the language and theories of evolutionary biology, she adopts a discursive strategy that, in the post-Darwinian era, is most likely to 'ring true' both to Gilman and other progressive social scientists. Based on her theoretical analysis, she argues for women's and men's equality on the basis of a shared human identity; at the same time, however, the story of the evolution of social relations is filtered through a vision of men's and women's different natures. Furthermore, while she produces an analysis that in many ways conforms to the prevailing regime of truth, her feminist discourse presents an even greater challenge, and Gilman's work will be ignored by the formal economics discipline in the same way that many other women's work has been systematically neglected and excluded from the cannon.

Because feminists and postmodernists stress that all knowledge is situated, they share the view that all knowledge is produced within communities of knowledge makers. The form, content, and assumptions of what Kuhn calls a 'normal science', will relate in complex and contradictory ways to the dynamics (conscious and unconscious) of any scientific community.[3] The hierarchical power relations within that community and its relation to the rest of society will have a profound impact on *what* will count as valuable and 'true' knowledge, and on *who* will be allowed inside the community of knowledge makers.

I will argue that the methodology informing Gilman's work is at the cutting edge of fin-de-siècle social science inquiries. Although her arguments are built on as solid a foundation of evolutionary theories and logic as those of her scholarly (male) contemporaries, modern economists are likely to claim that her invisibility in the dismal science is due to her lack of academic credentials[4] and to the obsolescence of her theoretical framework. But a more compelling reason for the neglect of her work by the scholarly community, I believe, stems from the very feminist and radical proposals for social change that are the logical consequences of her evolutionary analysis of gender relations. More than others who have written about the family in an economic context, Gilman pays attention to the actual labor that is being performed in the household. She makes the crucial distinctions between a mother's love and a mother's labor that most commentators, even today, fail to consider. Indeed, one could argue that her scientific agenda permits her to avoid the self-serving sentimentality characterizing much social and economic discourse on gender and the family.

The focus in this discussion, however, will be on Gilman's evolutionary theory. The radical , feminist contributions will not be dealt with in much detail. Interested readers may want to turn to Gilman's text.

Knowledge claims and the discourse on women in mainstream economic thinking

Neoclassical or mainstream economics has a recognized 'hard core' (Lakatos 1976) of knowledge which encompasses assumptions concerning the proper domain for economic investigation, causality among economic forces, and human nature. Both classical and neoclassical assumptions and models have historically been contested by a number of heterodox schools of thought. A critical perspective on the knowledge claims of neoclassical economics emphasizes how unequal power among potential participants in the economic discourse leads to very unequal abilities to influence what will count as knowledge, progress and economics.[5]

Questions of gender have long been ignored within mainstream economics, and the few texts generated from marginalized discourses have not been very powerful in determining how economics as a discipline could approach the economics of gender theoretically. The exclusion of gender issues follows from economists' general adherence to the theoretical split between the public and the private spheres which underlies the philosophical structure of Western liberal democratic society. This means that interactions in markets and through legally binding contracts define what constitutes economic relation to the scholarly economic community. If economics only deals with activities of exchange in the public sphere, gender relations and the business of the household, which belong in the domestic sphere, is thus by definition outside the proper domain of economic inquiry.

The 'trouble' with women and economics starts from a classical, liberal tradition which exclusively recognizes women's roles as wives and mothers so that their primary activities are confined to the domestic sphere. Women acting outside the domestic sphere are viewed with a great deal of suspicion and horror.[6] One result of this naturalized, gendered dichotomy has been that explicit considerations of female agency have been excluded from mainstream economics. By definition, women have been absent from disciplinary discourse, both as subjects and objects of inquiry. One of the promises of the newly emerging field of feminist economics is that it enables us to go beyond an ahistorical view of gender relations while it offers us insights into the place of gender in economic discourse.[7]

Work by women economists on household production and use of time predates by several decades Gary Becker's work on these issue, but until he presented his theoretical work on 'The New Home Economics',[8] the economic aspects of families and domestic life were ignored by mainstream practitioners.[9] Becker is able to mold economic analysis to fit the prescribed form by assuming strictly complementary roles for men and women in marriage. Men have comparative advantage in the labor market, and women in child bearing, child rearing, cooking, cleaning and the management of household affairs. The model makes perfect sense as a representation of the 'Ozzie and Harriett' family presented on American television in the 1960s.[10] Decision making within the household is modeled as a neoclassical constrained optimization exercise where the husband, a 'benevolent dictator', altruistically incorporates other family members' utility into his own. In Becker's model there is no analytical method to deal with issues of conflict or unequal power.[11]

Becker's neoclassical approach rests on an essentialist vision of women and gender roles in which 'women' and 'men' have stable identities defined and constrained by their unchangeable biology. These identities conform to a 'natural order' so that patriarchal domestic relations are seen as an optimal, efficient social arrangement. For those with stakes in preserving the status quo, existing gender roles could thus be explained as the outcome of natural forces or tendencies operating on men and women in different but equally necessary ways. The argument invariably rests on assumptions about the biological origin of male superiority in terms of men's bread-winning abilities and the *natural* division of labor which takes man the hunter away from the home while women's child bearing responsibilities make the closer range of the home her natural sphere. In the neoclassical world, it thus appears that Nature has prescribed a naturally superior role for men as decision makers and providers in the family.[12]

The question of what *Nature* dictates, however, can be answered in a very different way if women's subordination isn't assumed *a priori* as a natural consequence of child bearing. Women's position of biological inferiority is strongly contested by Charlotte Perkins Gilman's analysis in *Women and Economics*, where she turns the usual assumption on its head. While she relies to some extent on essentialist notions of men's and women's *natures* when she addresses the issues of the family and the sexual division of labor, she argues, in contrast to other essentialist versions, that women actually have a *superior* nature because of the necessity to provide materially for their offspring. Gilman doesn't consider the human mother's necessity to find her own food supply to be problematic in the least, since other animals manage just fine. Were it not for man's individualistic nature, and the evolutionary need to develop in him a social consciousness, women would not have been in subordinate positions for so many years, she argues.

Women and economics

Not surprisingly, the contributions to economics of first-wave feminists like Charlotte Perkins Gilman have long been overlooked.[13] Gilman's book *Women and Economics* was not viewed as a serious scholarly work by professional economists even though she was renowned and much in demand outside the academy.[14] The book was reprinted nine times and translated into Danish, Italian, Dutch, German, and Russian. Gilman traveled widely in the USA and England where she was invited to give lectures in the aftermath of the book's publication.[15] That she was not the only forgotten woman economist and feminist activist is documented in an important new literature.[16] Such a systematic, consistent erasure of women's voices is not likely to have occurred by accident.

Gilman's text is one of the most interesting contributions to the theoretical analysis of the historical evolution of the economic relations between men and women. Although she doesn't mention it directly in connection with the writing of her book, Gilman had read J.S. Mill, and she mentions reading Marx and several contemporary social scientists.[17] She claims to be particularly influenced by the 'gynaecocentric theory', put forth in the 1888 article, 'Our Better Halves' by Lester Ward, one of the founders of American sociology.

In the case of Gilman, two factors are particularly relevant to the process which placed her outside the discipline of economics. First, she challenged accepted gender roles and sanctified domestic relations. Her proposal to socialize much of the work women perform in the home, work that has traditionally been romanticized and sentimentalized as being 'priceless' and done for 'love', and not for money, went against the opinions of the most prestigious male economists of the day.[18] Pulling the veil from the domestic economy to demystify the warping effects of women's economic dependence was not likely to be popular with those who had a substantial stake in the status quo. Gilman did not, however, hold individual men (or men as a group) responsible for the institutional arrangements which subordinated women. 'It was an essential step in our racial progress, a means to an end' she says.[19] She argued that the 'morbid sex distinction' characteristic of gender relations, and the corresponding sexual division of labor caused both men and women to suffer from an exclusive emphasis on male pleasure. The radical implications of her advocacy of paid employment and economic independence for women was obviously threatening to the existing social order since the reproduction of that order required the distribution of economic privileges through gendered institutions.

Second, she did not belong to the established community of scholars 'authorized' to produce economic knowledge.[20] She had neither the formal training nor the diplomas that are the *sine qua non* of academic legitimacy. Few women of her generation received higher education, and those who did were more often than not excluded from academic jobs. Gilman's father, who made a living as a writer and librarian, left the mother solely responsible for the two young children early in the marriage, and although for many years there was no divorce, he seems to have sent very little money to support them. Gilman's brother was sent to college, but there was no money for her to continue her formal education to obtain a college degree. Because the extended family was widely engaged with public intellectual and spiritual matters, Gilman had much guidance as she pursued an education on her own.[21] However, despite the fact that her theoretical explanation of the evolutionary forces bearing on the sexual division of labor was very much in line with the demands of academic discourse at the turn of the century, her exclusion from the academic community was not surprising. She was well-read, intellectual and political enough, and also close enough to academic renegades such as Edward Ross (student of Richard Ely's at Chicago), and John Dewey, but feminist issues seemed to her so critically important yet so alien to many academics and left-wing males that the women's movement occupied most of Gilman's time (Hill 1980: 248).[22] A close reading of *Women and Economics* will show how a feminist text, even when it conforms to the standards and conventions for knowledge claims of its time, still can be subversive and thus court the danger of being deemed improper or irrelevant to the concerns of the discipline for a very long time.

Next I want to examine how Gilman's theory of sexual inequality and her suggestions for change fit into the economic tradition of knowledge creation. In *Women and Economics* Gilman sets out to make sense of a long history of oppressive gender roles that have produced hierarchical, non-egalitarian sexual and economic relations between women and men. Gilman's argument relies on Darwinian evolutionary metaphors (the evolutionary theories that inform most intellectual and social debate at the turn of the century), but her feminist Social Darwinism rejects the economistic *laissez-faire* ideology associated with Herbert Spencer. Instead she builds her theoretical analysis on Lester Ward's dualistic notion of a separation between biological and social forces.[23] This theory distinguishes sharply between the purposeless evolutionary changes occurring through natural selection in the biological and physical realm and the mental, human evolution modified by purposeful action. The distinction between the *genetic* and the *telic* causes of motion leads Ward and Gilman to reject the Spencerian argument, which holds that the efficiency of the 'survival of the fittest' is best served by non-intervention by policy makers. Ward's theory of evolution in contrast embraces the idea of a legitimate role for moral reasoning and political action in social science.[24]

The text: *Women and Economics*

When Gilman writes about the economic relations between men and women she argues on the basis of an evolutionary model of social development that is prevalent in social discourse at the end of the nineteenth century. *Women and Economics* is praised by *The Nation* as 'the most significant utterance on the subject [on women] since Mill's Subjection of Women'.[25] Gilman considers herself both a socialist and a feminist, but she is unable – or unwilling – to identify herself with the interpretations commonly given to those terms:

> Among the various unnecessary burdens of my life is that I have been discredited by conservative persons as a Socialist, while to the orthodox Socialists themselves I was quite outside the ranks.

> Similarly the antisufffrage masses had me blankly marked 'Suffragist', while the suffragists thought me a doubtful if not dangerous ally on account of my theory of the need of economic independence of women.
>
> ([1935]1990:198)

Although put off by the confrontational class politics of Marx, she advocates an evolutionary socialist program that is, in terms of gender analysis, as radical as any in the Marxists tradition.[26] She calls for a total re-evaluation of women's positions as productive workers, as caretakers of families, and as producers of labor power. She questions the cultural idea of women's 'nature' and examines women's household work from a hitherto unexplored perspective.

Gilman sees the middle-class household at the turn of the century as a place where men, women and children lead stifling lives. The home is marked by inefficiency, waste and sometimes damaging child rearing practices because it forces all women, irrespective of interest and talent, to focus exclusively on their prescribed tasks as wives and mothers. Economic dependence reduces women to weak and frail human beings. Gilman goes beyond J.S. Mill and his demand for women's emancipation on the basis of equal citizenship rights to challenge a cultural definition of human (male and female) nature. As she struggles with Scott's paradox mentioned earlier, Gilman argues that women and men have different natures, yet she carefully calls attention to the vast areas of human activity where she does not think sexual distinction has any 'natural' role to play. It is as if she actually turns her concept of nature into a historically contingent construction.

She is revolutionary in her insight that we construct a masculine and a feminine role as if the two genders were the obvious and inevitable extensions of biological difference. She uses conventional views of male and female 'original' characteristics in order to present a subversive story of evolutionary forces operating on men and women in such a way as to render obsolete and counterproductive the kinds of extreme sexual distinctions that others use to justify the status quo. In conformity with her contemporaries, she argues that men's and women's behavior are governed by different energies, and that originally men have a natural tendency to spend and disperse their energy while women tend to conserve and save energy. But because circumstances change as cumulative change in technology and in human social relations take place, behaviors that are useful in one context can become dysfunctional in another set of circumstances. By identifying the changes in circumstances that have come about through evolutionary forces, she will argue that corresponding changes in men's and women's roles are desirable and inevitable.

I realize that it may be problematic that I seem to be attributing subversive intentions to Gilman's text. Did she really use evolutionary theory as a foil for her feminism? Or did she really believe that Victorian women were parasitic brakes on the progress of modernity? On the one hand, I do not think we can know for sure how Gilman herself saw her project, what her 'true' opinions were. On the other, I do not think that it matters for our purposes. It is precisely here that the postmodernist approach of Foucault and Joan Scott's analysis of the paradox of feminist history, which I discuss in the introduction, come into play. When I say that Gilman 'sets tasks' and 'needs to explain', I am talking about an imperative that flows from the construction of a particular discourse, not from what some would think of as Gilman's 'true vision'.

My point is not to present Gilman as a postmodern theorist – quite the contrary. I believe she constructs a clearly modernist argument, but I also think that this discourse is an attempt to get beyond the paradox just mentioned, and to open up possibilities for female agency. In her many public appearances and in her autobiography she is clear on the political aim of her work, yet she finds the suffragettes' exclusive emphasis on the vote insufficient. Their discourse positions women either in terms of equality, where women's individual, natural rights are claimed to be the same as men's, or in terms of difference, where women's particular nature confers upon them the moral high ground. Gilman, in *Women and Economics*, struggles with these options and seems to refuse to commit herself fully to either side of this dilemma.

The task Gilman sets for herself in developing an evolutionary theory of the economic relation between men and women is as follows. She needs to explain how gender inequality arises, i.e., she needs to look for *origins*. She also needs to explain how this happens through a process of natural selection and how it may have been 'optimal' from an evolutionary perspective at a certain time. If she wants to argue that female inferiority is unnatural or inefficient, she needs to identify the yardstick with which she measures outcomes. Her argument is a teleological argument whether equality in itself is seen as a measure of virtue or whether the point of view is concerned with the continued survival of the human species. Finally she needs to show that although women's subordination may have been optimal or served a purpose at some point in the evolutionary scheme, it has now become imbalanced or inefficient as a result of historical, evolutionary developments. Demonstrating the inefficiencies of the status quo, then, will provide Gilman with the justification for the radical changes she envisions. She must therefore explain which evolutionary forces will presently provide the incentive and rationale for people to change their way of doing things. If gender relations and the kinds of tasks men and women have traditionally performed are put into questions, she must show that the gendered ordering of the social and physical world no longer serves the purposes of progress (since that is her goal), and she must show how and why radical changes will redress the problems and imbalances she identifies in the current social order.

Gilman proceeds to construct her model of the evolution of the economic relations of gender in a scientific and rigorous way. In the following, the lines of her argument will be drawn out from the text, and her use of the tools and assumptions of scientific and evolutionary theory will be discussed.

Origins

Gilman is guided by the insight that in addition to being affected by the material environment and the consequences of their own actions, human beings are also 'affected by each other to a degree beyond what is found among even the most gregarious of animals' ([1898]1966: 2). A peculiar economic condition, however, 'unparalleled in the organic world' is affecting the human race:

> We are the only animal species in which the female depends on the male for food, the only animal species in which the sex relation is also an economic relation.
>
> (p.55)

Even if certain female animals depend on a mate for feeding at certain times of the reproductive cycle, only with humans does such dependency continue throughout the female's lifetime. Tradition has made it easy for us to assume our own arrangement is 'natural' and to assume that other animals do the same thing (p. 6).

In an argument that sets her apart from almost every other thinker dealing with the question of gender inequality, Gilman does not trace the origin to women's childbearing. Instead of attributing female subordination and the concomitant sexual division of labor to women's role in reproduction, she argues that it was to spare himself the continual fight for sexual access with 'his hairy rivals' that the human male enslaved the female. There is little moral judgment in her statement that

> There seems to have come a time when it occurred to the dawning intelligence of the amiable savage that it was cheaper and easier to fight a little female, and have it done with, than to fight a big male every time.
>
> (p. 60)

In Gilman's scheme, it was this enslavement by the male, not an inherent inability to procure food for herself and her off-spring, that lead to female dependency. Comparing humans with other species, Gilman rejects the notion that humans are totally different from other animals; in fact she is making many of her points by drawing on analogies with spiders, horses, bees, drones, and aphids.[27] To emphasize the evolutionary importance of females – and unimportance of males – in reproduction, she points to the evolution of the species which is characterized by 'long series of practical experiments in males, – very tiny, transient, and inferior devices at first, but gradually developed into fuller and fuller equality with the female' (p. 130). Similarly she says that 'with the carnivora, if the young are to lose one parent, it might far better be the father: the mother is quite competent to take care of them herself' (p. 6).

Gilman's use of evolutionary, biological 'data' allows her to propose an interpretation of the relative importance of males and females as providers and reproducers that finds much support in modern anthropology.[28] This is in sharp contrast to the conventional emphasis on 'man the hunter' and the aggressive, dominant behavior of alpha-male baboons.

Different natures and energies

Understanding Gilman's arguments requires close scrutiny of her text to discover the assumptions about biologically coded human sexual differences that are behind the story of female subordination. She proposes that the fundamental differences (sex distinctions) between men and women have been exaggerated to the detriment of human development over time. From the beginning, different behaviors reflect male and female types of energy:

> While the male savage was still a mere hunter and fighter, expressing masculine energy, the katabolic force, along its essential line, expanding, scattering, the female savage worked out in equally natural ways the conserving force of female energy.
> (p. 126)

When males render females subordinate, they must take on the burden of providing for the female and offspring. The disciplining of male energy that arises from this obligation is beneficial: struggling under the necessity for constructive labor, male energy causes labor to progress and vary more than it would have done in female hands.

> Male energy made to expend itself in performing female functions is what has brought our industries to their present development. Without the economic dependence of the female, the male would still be merely the hunter and fighter, the killer, the destroyer; and she would continue to be the industrious mother without change or progress.
>
> (p. 132)

It appears from this passage that industry and modern progress initially comes about as a side effect of women's subordination. It is necessary to discipline the wild spending of male energy because women as mothers already posses the social consciousness without which further progress is impossible. By obligating men to take care of their families, male energy which at first is 'purely individualistic' is harnessed for the 'upbuilding of the world' (p. 133). Women were originally, in their roles as mothers, motivated by a desire to serve their young and thus had an impetus to develop the first arts and crafts 'whereby we live'. But men have had to gradually enlarge their social sphere, and to make man a proper social being, he has had to care first for his own narrow family. Inducing him to do so, however, takes more than necessity. He must also be given pleasure. The extreme emphasis on sexual energy is the price women end up paying, in the name of human progress.

The morbid excess of sex distinction

Gilman argues that there are two separate, and often conflicting, evolutionary forces operating on the human species: natural selection which favors traits leading to self-preservation, and sexual selection which operates on humans to propagate the species. Self-preservation means the ability to feed oneself, race-preservation hinges on the ability to attract a mate. In human evolution, women have become enslaved to domesticity, and they have become unable to assure their own self-preservation. Their dependency on males has required an emphasis on 'feminine' attractiveness in looks and demeanor in order to secure their survival and the survival of their children.

> Where the female finds her economic environment in the male, and her economic advantage is directly conditioned upon the sex relation, the force of natural selection is added to the force of sexual selection, and both together operate to develop sex-activity.
>
> (p.58)

Exploring the status of the modern woman, Gilman says that her status in the modern family is neither that of a partner (she lacks control in exchange) nor that of an employee since there seems to be no connection between her reward in the form of increased consumption possibilities and the value of the labor she contributes to the household.[29]

> Her living, all that she gets, – food, clothing, ornaments, amusements, luxuries, – these bear no relation to her power to produce wealth, to her services in the house, or to her motherhood. These things bear relation only to the man she marries, the man she depends on, – to how much he has and how much he is willing to give her. The women whose splendid extravagance dazzles the world, whose economic goods are the greatest, are often neither houseworkers nor mothers, but simply the women who hold most power over the men who have the most money.
> (pp. 22–3)

Although our culture prefers to think that it is motherhood that keeps women on their toes from morning till night, and that it is in their capacity as mothers that they are maintained by men, Gilman argues to the contrary that it is 'house service; not child service' that keeps women busy (p.20). But the excessive sex distinction, she claims, has come to pervade all human relations and influence our child-rearing practices as well, as the following illustrates:

> One of the first things we force upon the child's dawning consciousness is the fact that he is a boy or that she is a girl, and that, therefore, each must regard everything from a different point of view.
> (p.54)

And, although most human activity 'to teach, to rule, to make, to decorate, to distribute' are along the lines of self-preservation,

> We have differentiated our industries, our responsibilities, our very virtues, along sex lines.
> (p.41)

> [S]o inordinate is the sex-distinction in the human race that the whole field of human progress has been considered a masculine prerogative. What could more absolutely prove the excessive sex-distinction of the human race?
> (p. 52)

The consequences of female dependency is this extreme gender polarization and androcentrism.[30] The subordination of women has enabled men to catch up and advance morally so that at the turn of the century they are socially conscious and capable of applying themselves and working for a common good beyond the individualistic household. In contrast, the lack of development and specialization on the part of women, who, because of the excessive sex-distinction, have been confined to the domestic sphere, is now proving to be a hindrance to further, overall human progress.

Gilman provides concrete examples of the inadequacy of most middle-class women's preparation to do a good job as cooks, cleaners and educators of children. Because they are barred from exploring the world of the public sphere and from getting an education on an equal footing with men, women know little about nutrition and thus fall victim to unscrupulous sellers of adulterated food supplies. The inefficiency of this is costly:

> Each mother slowly acquires some knowledge of her business by practicing it upon the lives and health of her family and by observing its effect on the survivors.
>
> (p.229)

This 'Cupid-in the-kitchen' arrangement can clearly be improved upon, she thinks, by professionalizing the task of cooking. Not only will it be safer and cheaper, but it will also free women from much time-consuming domestic labor so that they can become educated and eventually find the sort of paid employment that will allow them to achieve economic independence. Gilman develops similar arguments in favor of professional involvement in other household tasks and in the care of young children.

Her justification for change is thus not only based on notions of fairness and on the possibility for greater happiness for women. She is particularly interested in human progress through productive efficiency both in industry and in the household, as well as in the greater development of social consciousness. According to Gilman, female dependency has been injurious to progress because it has made men's labor and skills advance through specialization while women's labor has remained more generalized, at a lower stage of development.

In the name of progress

Underlying Gilman's argument is her goal of progress for humanity. That goal is widely shared by social scientists of her time, but what progress means to them may vary. Gilman's definition is quite general:

> According to the general law of organic evolution, it may be defined as follows: such progress in the individual and his social relations as shall maintain him in health and happiness and increase the organic development of society.
>
> (p.208)

Furthermore, she argues that it is the *duty* of society to progress and that all social institutions are to be measured by the extent to which they further 'race development'. To make sure that we do not confuse duty with pleasure – Gilman is, after all, a child of the Victorian era – she emphasizes that our 'enjoyment of a thing does not prove that it is right' and that 'our belief that a thing is "natural" does not prove that it is right' (p. 209).

The discourse of evolutionary change embodies notions of the betterment of the human race through natural selection. While Gilman's understanding of the fundamental principles of natural selection may be less than perfect, she isn't different from her contemporaries in this respect. Even Darwin's work contains Lamarckian ideas.[31] The belief that 'life means progress' is a modernist conviction she shares with a large segment of the scholarly establishment of her time. Gilman portrays the moral good of the eradication of inequality as being at the same time highly desirable for individual women and in accordance with her notion of progress in economic welfare for the human race:

> While the sexuo-economic relation makes the family the centre of industrial activity, no higher collectivity than we have to-day is possible. But, as women become free…so becomes possible the full social combination of individuals in collective industry. With such freedom, such independence, such wider union, becomes possible also a union between man and woman such as the world has long dreamed of in vain.
>
> (p. 145)

It is questionable how persuasive her deterministic vision really is. With her writing, doesn't she perhaps hope to convince women and workers to become engaged in the political struggle for human progress? Isn't she leaving the door open for political action in the same way that Marx encourages the workers of the world to unite and engage in a revolutionary class struggle even though, according to his analysis, capitalism invariably will collapse under the burden of its internal contradictions?

Winds of change

Gilman's evolutionary tale identifies the origin and the evolutionary consequences of women's subordination. She provides examples, which come out of the joint historical development of gender relations and economic structures, indicating the need for change. To complete the story, she needs to identify some of the signs that make her optimistic that evolutionary forces are working in the right direction. She finds such signs in two social movements:

> The time has come when we are open to deeper and wider impulses than the sex-instinct; the social instincts are strong enough to come into full use at last. This is shown by the twin struggles that convulse the world to-day – in sex and economics – the 'woman's movement' and the 'labor movement'.
>
> (p.138)

And she emphasizes that such change is not a thing to prophesy and plead for:

> The same great force of social evolution which brought us into the old relation – to our great sorrow and pain – is bringing us out, with equal difficulty and distress. The time has come when it is better for the world that women be economically independent, and therefore they are becoming so.
>
> (p.316)

Conclusion

In this chapter, I have analyzed Gilman's text from a postmodernist perspective. Foucault's theories have been useful in discussing issues of power, knowledge and disciplinary exclusion in economics, and feminist theoretical advances, in particular as articulated by Joan Scott, inform much of my analysis of the tensions in Gilman's modernism.

Gilman's text sets out to construct an argument for women's emancipation in terms that could be expected to be convincing to an educated, scholarly audience. She formulates a theory about gender relations that overturns the conventional wisdom. Framing her arguments in the scientific discourse of her time and enriching her story with experiential knowledge allows her to instrumentalize the very concept of gender and make it the focus of her analysis. Her discussion of men's and women's roles in terms of energies and equilibrating forces testifies to her commitment (shared by all her learned contemporaries) to the applicability of the second law of thermodynamics to social phenomena.[32]

Gilman's use of evolutionary theory rejects the Social Darwinism associated with Herbert Spencer. She does not espouse a biological, *laissez-faire* determinism that argues against a positive role for social action and government intervention. Gilman's analysis emphasizes the extent to which humans are shaped by social forces. Individual and collective action to change the conventional organization of gender roles emerges as the necessary path to achieve the common good.

The social evolution that 'necessitates' women's subordination to men starts from an original position where the responsibility for feeding and taking care of children makes women socially conscious and industrious. In contrast, men's individualistic pursuits make them less advanced in terms of human (race) development. When enslavement prevents women from procuring their own food supply, men, by necessity, become responsible for providing for wife and children. Men are therefore forced over time to reach a level of social evolution where they are less individualistic and more social in their desires. Meanwhile, a woman's inferior position in the home forces her to be less specialized and less productive than she would have been, had she been allowed to become educated and employed in a line of work of her own choosing.

She is an extraordinarily innovative thinker when she discusses motherhood, child rearing practices and the job of the middle-class housewife. More than most of her contemporaries, Gilman is in a position to talk about women's actual lives from the inside, and she argues persuasively against the essentialist notions that are so prevalent even today. Gilman does not confuse the issues of maternal love with the unpaid drudgery that maintains the household. She knows that a child needs much more than maternal love to grow and thrive. She also knows that romantic, sentimental reasons tie us to replicating in every kitchen and every laundry room tasks that could be done more efficiently, on a bigger scale, elsewhere. And she is convinced that as long as women do not have the education and training to make choices, their contribution to overall welfare will be less than it would otherwise be.

Gilman theorizes female subordination in a radically new way by making the 'invisible visible'.[33] For a long time her work has been ignored by economists and other social scientists. As Ann Lane, historian and Gilman biographer, remarks:

> To deny the power of Gilman's extraordinary insight required the denial of the body of her work as serious or useful or worthy of attention, and so a new layer of invisibility was imposed in an effort to deny the discovery. That disowning of Gilman's work has until now been successful.
>
> (1990: 301)

In this chapter I suggest that the reason for the *disowning* has less to do with her modernist methodology, or her 'pseudo-science', as Degler (1966) puts it, than it has to do with the radical feminist challenges with which her work confronts us.

It may well be that the story of Charlotte Perkins Gilman should be read as a morality tale for our own times. Working within neoclassical economics, many liberal feminists have uncritically absorbed the methodological stand of their non-feminist colleagues. Many have been told by teachers and advisers to stay clear of controversial political issues if they want to establish themselves in the profession. But – as I have argued here and as much of the work in feminist economics has shown – a conformist methodology or research agenda has not historically been a guarantee for inclusion.

Notes

1 See, for example, Foucault (1980).
2 Denise Riley (1988) provides a good introduction to this dilemma.
3 See Kuhn (1970).
4 *Women and Economics* was widely read, and this allowed Gilman to continue making a living by giving lectures throughout the USA and abroad. Gilman never received the kind of systematic education that would lead to a university degree.
5 See Strassmann (1993a, 1993b).
6 Feminist scholarship analyzing the split between the private and the public sphere has come from several disciplines. The following are some of the contributions from political science: Elshtain (1981); Kerber (1980); Pateman (1988). From economics: Grapard (1992); Jennings (1993); Pujol (1992). From philosophy and the history of science: Bordo (1987); Harding (1986); Longino (1990).
7 See Pujol (1992); Ferber and Nelson, eds (1993).
8 This term is used by Ferber and Birnbaum (1977).
9 Margaret Reid's work was particularly important and ground breaking, yet her contribution was not acknowledged by Becker or other economists whose work benefited from her insights until much later. In 1931, Reid earned a Ph.D. from the University of Chicago with her thesis *Household Production* which was publish in 1934. (Yun-Ae Yi 1996).
10 The ahistorical view of gender relations in popular culture generally is made obvious when we realize that the same household model also holds for the Stone Age household of the Flintstones as well as for the futuristic household of the Jetsons!
11 Later neoclassical economists have developed game theoretic bargaining models to address the shortcoming of Becker's marriage model. See Manser and Brown (1990); McElroy and Horney (1981); McElroy (1990); Lundberg and Pollack (1993). For a critical discussion of the value of bargaining models, see Seiz (1991) and Wooley (1993).
12 Although there are exceptions within the mainstream (e.g. Frank 1988) economists have not considered changing their ideas regarding the behav-

ioral characteristics of homo economicus much since the time of the social contract theorists and Adam Smith. The separation of public and private spheres has meant that women were not considered economic agents with the same motivations as men. While self-interested behavior is thought to prevail in the market place, altruism, in Becker's model, is assumed to govern decision making in the household.

13 A review of Gilman's *The Home, its Work and its Influence* (1903) appeared in the *Journal of Political Economy* (Hill 1904); very recently, economists have rediscovered and examined the economic content of *Women and Economics*. See O'Donnell (1988) and Dimand (1995).
14 The historian Carl Degler was instrumental in getting this work reissued in 1966. Economists have until now paid little attention to Gilman's work although she was widely read and admired in the first decades of the twentieth century. See Dimand (1995).
15 Lane (1990: 209)
16 See Pujol (1992) and Thompson (1973). Of particular note, Dimand, Dimand, and Forget (eds) (1995) constitute a major collaborative initiative to rediscover and document contributions by women whose work has been systematically excluded from consideration by 'malestream' economists. It is astounding to realize the extent of ill-will toward women economists. Even those who made significant contributions to the literature (measured in terms of articles published in prestigious economics journals) have been dropped from the discipline's collective memory.
17 See Hill (1980: 119) and Lane (1990: 203).
18 See Pujol (1995).
19 Gilman (1966: 128).
20 Egan (1989) makes the argument that Gilman should be included in the philosophical canon because her writing exhibits several of the assumptions held especially by the American pragmatists. Upin (1993) similarly argues that Gilman takes pragmatism beyond Dewey's instrumentalism.
21 She was the great-granddaughter of the famed religious leader Lyman Beecher, and grand-niece of the influential female Beecher rebels, Catherine Beecher, Harriet Beecher Stowe, and Isabell Beecher Hooker (Hill 1980:5)
22 Dewey, who personally knew Gilman, wrote to a colleague who criticizes some of Gilman's writings: ' In your natural disgust with part of Mrs Gilman's work you overlook what is sound, the plea for the economic independence of women.... If she were a man, she would have had a better technical training and become a specialist and won a great reputation and praise. In short she is the one-sided type that is extremely common among men, practically every scientific specialist, every university professor – including myself....You aren't much used to it in women and so jump on Mrs Gilman...' Quoted in Upin (1993: 41).
23 Lester Ward, one of the founding fathers of American Sociology, was strongly opposed to the Social Darwinist doctrine of Spencer's which advocated the careful elimination of the unfit and dependent through eugenic means. He said that it represented 'the most complete example of the oligocentric worldview which is coming to prevail in the higher classes of society and would center the entire attention of the whole world upon an almost infinitesimal fraction of the human race and ignore the rest' (Hofstadter, 1945: 65)
24 This point is made in Palmeri (1983).
25 See Degler's Introduction to the 1966 re-issue of *Women and Economics*, xiii.

26 In her autobiography she writes: 'This first visit to England was made to attend the International Socialist and Labor Congress of 1896. It was intended that I should go as a Socialist, to which end they sent me the membership card; but when I read that card utterly refused to sign it; sharply disagreeing with both theory and method as advanced by the followers of Marx' (Gilman, 1990:198).
27 See Egan (1989) for a fuller discussion of Gilman's use of evolutionary language and its relation to the melioristic process through which equality between males and females must come about.
28 See Haraway (1989) and Hrdy (1981). It is now understood that women are responsible for the greatest share of the food supply in earlier societies of hunters and gatherers. Women's reproductive strategies are also found to be much more complex than earlier assumptions about the passive female would have us believe.
29 See Dimand (1995).
30 Bem (1993) offers a contemporary analysis of gendered lenses and the relationship between gender polarization and androcentrism in terms that Gilman would have found congenial. Bem is much more skeptical of the lens of biological essentialism, however. Based on modern biological insights, she finds even less solid ground than Gilman on which to make pronouncements on human nature.
31 See Palmeri's (1983: 104) discussion of Neo-Lamarckian influences in Darwin's work and in the social sciences at the turn of the century.
32 See Mirowski (1988) for discussions of the impact of physics on economic rhetoric and methodology. See in particular chapter 6, 'The Role of Conservation Principles in Twentieth-Century Economic Theory'.
33 Lane (1990: 301).

References

Bem, Sandra Lipsitz (1993) *The Lenses of Gender*, New Haven: Yale University Press.

Bordo, Susan (1987) *The Flight to Objectivity: Essays on Cartesianism and Culture*, Albany: State University of New York Press.

—— (1990) 'Feminism, Postmodernism, and Gender-Scepticism', in Linda J. Nicholson (ed.) *Feminism/Postmodernism*, New York: Routledge, Chapman and Hill.

Degler, Carl (1966) 'Introduction', in Charlotte Perkins Gilman, *Women and Economics. The Economic Factor Between Men and Women as a Factor in Social Evolution*, New York: Harper and Row Publishers.

Dimand, Mary Ann (1995) 'The Economics of Charlotte Perkins Gilman', in Mary Ann Dimand, Robert W. Dimand, and Evelyn L. Forget (eds) *Women of Value. Feminist Essays on the History of Women in Economics*, Aldershot: Edward Elgar.

Dimand, Mary Ann, Robert W. Dimand, and Evelyn L. Forget (eds) (1995) *Women of Value. Feminist Essays on the History of Women in Economics*, Aldershot: Edward Elgar.

Egan, Maureen L. (1989) 'Evolutionary Theory in the Social Philosophy of Charlotte Perkins Gilman', *Hypatia* 4(1):102–119.

Elshtain, Jean Bethke (1981) *Public Man, Private Woman*, Princeton: Princeton University Press.
Ferber, Marianne A. and Bonnie G. Birnbaum (1977) 'The New Home Economics: Retrospect and Prospects', *Journal of Consumer Research* 4(4):19–28.
Folbre, Nancy (1982) 'Exploitation Comes Home: A Critique of the Marxian theory of Family Labor', *Cambridge Journal of Economics* (6):317–329.
Foucault, Michel (1973) *The Order of Things: An Archaeology of the Human Sciences,*, New York: Pantheon Books.
—— (1980) *Power/Knowledge*, (ed.) Colin Gordon, New York: Pantheon Books.
Frank, Robert H. (1988) *Passions Within Reasons*, New York: W. W. Norton.
Keller, Evelyn Fox (1985) *Reflections on Gender and Science*, New Haven: Yale University Press.
Gilman, Charlotte Perkins ([1898]1966) *Women and Economics. The Economic Factor Between Men and Women as a Factor in Social Evolution*, New York: Harper and Row.
—— ([1935]1990) *The Living of Charlotte Perkins Gilman: An Autobiography*, New York: Harper and Row.
Haraway, Donna Jeanne (1989) *Primate Vision: Gender, Race and Nature in the World of Modern Science*, New York: Routledge.
Harding, Sandra (1986) *The Science Question in Feminism*, Ithaca: Cornell University Press.
Hartsock, Nancy (1990) 'Foucault on Power: A Theory for Women?', in Linda J. Nicholson (ed.) *Feminism/Postmodernism*, New York: Routledge, Chapman and Hill.
Hartmann, Heidi I. (1979) 'The Unhappy Marriage Between Marxism and Feminism: Towards a More Progressive Union', *Capital and Class* (8):1–33.
Hill, Caroline (1904) 'The Economic Value of the Home', *Journal of Political Economy*12(3):408–19.
Hill, Mary A. (1980) *Charlotte Perkins Gilman. The Making of a Radical Feminist, 1860–1896*, Philadelphia: Temple University Press.
Hofstadter, Richard (1945) *Social Darwinism in American Thought. 1860–1915*, Philadelphia: University of Pennsylvania Press.
Hrdy, Sarah Blaffer (1981) *The Woman that Never Evolved*, Cambridge: Harvard University Press.
Jennings, Ann L. (1993) 'Public or Private? Institutional Economics and Feminism', in Marianne A. Ferber and Julie A. Nelson (eds) *Beyond Economic Man: Feminist Theory and Economics*, Chicago: University of Chicago Press: 111–129.
Kerber, Linda K. (1980) *Women of the the Republic: Intellect and Ideology in Revolutionary America*, Chapel Hill: University of North Carolina Press.
Kuhn, Thomas S. (1970) *The Structure of Scientific Revolutions*, Chicago: University of Chicago Press.
Lakatos, Imre (1976) *Proofs and Refutations: The Logic of Mathematical Discovery*, Cambridge: Cambridge University Press.
Lane, Ann J. (1990) *To Herland and Beyond. The Life and Work of Charlotte Perkins Gilman*, New York: Meridian Books.
Longino, Helen (1990) *Science as Social Knowledge: Values and Objectivity in Scientific Inquiry*, Princeton: Princeton University Press.

Lundberg, Shelly and Robert Pollack (1993), 'Separate Spheres Bargaining and the Marriage Market', *Journal of Political Economy*, 100(6) : 988–1010.

McElroy, Marjorie B and Horney, Mary Jean (1981) 'Nash-Bargaining Household Decisions: Toward a Generalization of the Theory of Demand', *International Economic Review* (22) 2: 333–49.

McElroy, Marjorie B. (1990) 'The Empirical Content of Nash-Bargained Household Behavior', *The Journal of Human Resources* 25 (4): 559–83.

Manser, Marilyn and Brown, Murray (1980) 'Marriage and Household Decisionmaking: A Bargaining Analysis', *International Economic Review* 21(1):31–44.

Mill, John Stuart ([1869]1986) *The Subjection of Women*, in Mary Wollstonecraft, *A Vindication of the Rights of Women*, and John Stuart Mill, *The Subjection of Women*, Vermont: Charles E. Tuttle Co., Inc. Everyman's Library.

Mirowski, Philip (1988) *Against Mechanism. Protecting Economic From Science*, New Jersey: Rowman and Littlefield.

O'Donnell, Margaret G. (1988) 'Charlotte Perkins Gilman's Economic Interpretation of the Role of Women at the Turn of the Century', *Social Science Quarterly* 69(1):177–92

Palmeri, Ann (1983) 'Charlotte Perkins Gilman: Forerunner of a Feminist Social Science', in Sandra Harding and Merrill B. Hintakka (eds) *Discovering Reality*, Dordrecht: D. Reidel.

Pateman, Carole (1988) *The Sexual Contract*, Stanford: Stanford University Press.

Pujol, Michèle (1992) *Feminism and Anti-Feminism in Early Economic Thought*, Aldershot: Edward Elgar.

—— (1995) 'Feminism, Anti-Feminism and Early Neo-classical Economics', in Edith Kuiper *et al.* (eds) *Out of the Margin: Feminist Perspectives on Economic Theory*, London: Routledge.

Riley, Denise (1988) *Am I that Name? Feminism and the Category of 'Women' in History*, London: Macmillan.

Scott, Joan W. (1988) *Gender and the Politics of History*. New York: Columbia University Press.

—— (1996) *Only Paradoxes to Offer: French Feminists and the Rights of Man*, Cambridge: Harvard University Press.

Seiz, Janet A. (1991) 'The Bargaining Approach and Feminist Methodology', *Review of Radical Political Economy*, 23(1 and 2): 22–9.

Strassmann, Diana, (1993) 'Not a Free Market: The Rhetoric of Disciplinary Authority in Economics' in Marianne A. Ferber and Julie A. Nelson (eds) *Beyond Economic Man: Feminist Theory and Economics*, Chicago: University of Chicago Press.

—— (1993a) 'The Stories of Economics and the Power of the Storyteller', *History of Political Economy* 25(1):147–65.

Thompson, Dorothy Lampen (1973) *Adam Smith's Daughters*, New York: Exposition University Press.

Upin, Jane S. (1993) 'Charlotte Perkins Gilman: Instrumentalism Beyond Dewey', *Hypatia* 8(2):38–63.

Veblen, Thorstein ([1899]1953) *The Theory of the Leisure Class*, Mentor Book, New York: New American Library.

Wooley, Frances R. (1993), 'The Feminist Challenge to Neoclassical Economics', *Cambridge Journal of Economics*, 17: 485–500.

Yi, Yun-Ae (1996) 'Margaret Reid: Life and Achievements', *Feminist Economics* 2(3):17–36.

13
FEMINIST ECONOMICS: OBJECTIVE, ACTIVIST, *AND* POSTMODERN?

Julie A. Nelson

> Why, sometimes I've believed as many as six impossible things before breakfast.
> The White Queen in Lewis Carroll (1872)
> *Through the Looking Glass*

What would the discipline of economics be based on, and what would it do, if it were to be thoroughly permeated and transformed by feminist concerns and insights? To many people, the idea of a thorough-going intellectual project joining feminism and the social science discipline of economics seems to be misguided. The sources of this pessimism, however, can vary widely.

Consider the concerns of a practicing economist steeped in the modernist scientific tradition. Such an economist will worry about economics losing its 'objectivity' if the agenda of a political and social movement such as feminism is injected into the core of the discipline. While feminism might appropriately affect the topics chosen for economic analysis, a modernist argues, any revision of core assumptions would compromise the discipline's claims to scientific objectivity. None of the economists authoring chapters in this volume are likely to espouse such a view. In our home departments, however, the modernist approach is rife among our colleagues, and fear of loss of scientific rigor is behind much of the dismissal of both feminism and postmodernism.

Consider, as a second criticism, the doubts that might be expressed by a feminist activist. To be more precise, feminist economist Barbara Bergmann has vociferously objected to feminists wasting their energies on theorizing, and particularly on 'postmodern academic trash' (Bergmann, 1997). Bergmann believes that theoretical discussions draw needed energies away from concrete action for social change. She is not alone, among feminist academics, if she also worries that works with 'postmodern' or 'deconstruction' in the title will actually threaten rather than reinforce the kinds of thinking necessary to promote feminist social progress (e.g. Bordo, 1990).

Which brings us to the doubts that might be expressed about this project by a thorough-going deconstructivist. A postmodernist may not only heap doubt on the modernist's notion of 'objectivity' (as a false universalism), but also on the concepts of 'woman' (as an 'essentialist' category – see examples discussed in Bordo, 1990) and perhaps the notion that there can be beneficial social 'progress' as well. Neither concerns for science nor activism carry much weight, and neither economics nor feminism are seen as more than areas for discursive play.

While these are obviously oversimplifications of these positions, they capture some key distinguishing elements. As a person who is, all at the same time, a practicing economist, a feminist concerned about oppression, and a post-modernist (in the 'after-modernist' sense of recognizing the social construction of the disciplines, though not necessarily in the sense most popular among literary theorists), I take all these objections seriously. Yet I believe that such an intellectual overhaul of economics by feminists is yielding, and will continue to yield, much fruit.

This chapter argues that a revamped, feminist discipline of economics is objective, more useful in forwarding social change, *and* postmodern. How can it be all three at the same time? My first argument is that there is room in the notion of objectivity for social commitments like feminism. In fact, the argument will be that scientific objectivity not only permits feminism, but requires it. Then, I will argue that this feminist economics can be useful to feminists in forwarding social change. In fact, the argument will be that a feminist economics is more useful in understanding any real-world economic problem, whether related to feminist issues or not. Last, I will show that this way of thinking about gender and about economics offers an alternative to both extremes of modernism and extremes of deconstructionism.[1]

These goals will be pursued subject to some specific limitations. The conceptions of gender, science, and economics that are dealt with here are those that have grown out of the dominant post-Enlightenment, Euro-American traditions. Other traditions are ignored.[2] The focus will also be on envisioning an alternative economics. The substantial questions of power that affect the actual implementation of an alternative, because of limitations in space, are grossly neglected.

What is objectivity?

Objectivity, many economists will tell you, has to do with detachment. An objective study is one in which the economist keeps his or her own interests and concerns from influencing the results. The economist puts his or her emotions, social and political commitments, and experiences aside, in order to address the research question with neutrality. Objectivity can be gained by the individual researcher if he or she follows the rules of scientific procedure – the rules of logical proof and, if not, in economics, controlled experimentation, at least of replicable empirics. Most economists are, in their day-to-day work if not in their more philosophical musings, holders of this 'modernist' creed. To fail to pursue such detachment, it is believed, is to flirt with unscientific subjectivity, relativism, and contamination. If sometimes the social, political, racial, gender, or economic environment of the researcher influences the content of the scientific theory, these deviations are assumed to be in the direction of irrationality and are labeled 'bad science'.

Feminist theorists, meanwhile, have pointed out the gendered nature of the objectivity/subjectivity dualism – and of many other dualisms underlying the definition of contemporary economics, as illustrated in Table 13.1. Historically and socially the ideals of objectivity, separation, logical consistency, individual accomplishment, and the image of the scientist have been associated with masculinity. In contrast, subjectivity, connection, 'intuitive' understanding, cooperativeness, and the image of nature have been linked to femininity. These ties have been most notably pointed out in terms of the history of science by Evelyn Fox Keller (1985), Sandra Harding (1986), and Susan Bordo (1987). Pointing out those associations, however, does not in itself give a road map to what feminist activists should do.

One possibility is to take the definition of science as given by modernism, and encourage women to enter the field by overcoming sex-stereotyped cultural conditioning. That is, the notion is to encourage women to 'be more objective' than is socially expected, which is also to say, given the historical and cultural patterns, to 'be more like the boys'. This plan has the advantages of explicitly recognizing that gender associations are social rather than biological, and of seeking to put women into positions of power and prestige, but it puts all the onus for change on girls and women and all the attention on women's perceived deficiencies. Another possibility is to take as given and as valuable women's experiences in living lives defined by the feminine side of the dualisms (subjective, connected, closer to nature, etc.), and seek to change the definition of science. This approach is fraught with dangers, however. The first reaction of many economists to the idea of a 'feminist economics' is to envision a 'feminine' economics in which, for example, subjectivity replaces objectivity or the notion of altruism replaces self-interest, and/or a 'female' science, for which women are exclusively (and biologically) suited. Many women economists are rightly fearful of any mention of sex or gender issues in science that, because it reinforces their colleagues view of them as 'different', could jeopardize their hard-earned and often still tenuous places within the male-controlled hierarchies of the discipline.

Table 13.1 The contemporary definition of economics

	Core	Margin
Domain:		
	public (market and government)	private (family)
	individual agents	society, institutions
	efficiency	equity
Methods:		
	rigorous	intuitive
	precise	vague
	objective	subjective
	scientific	non-scientific
	detached	committed
	mathematical	verbal
	formal	informal
	general	particular
Key assumptions:		
	individual	social
	self-interested	other-interested
	autonomous	dependent
	rational	emotional
	acts by choice	acts by nature
Gender/sex associations:		
	masculine	feminine
	men	women

Source: Nelson (1996)

Modernists defend the objectivity side of the objectivity/subjectivity dualism; feminists point out the gendered nature of the dualism and question its meaning for men, women, and science; meanwhile, postmodern literary theories (as explained in Rossetti, Chapter 14) seek to dismantle all claims to objectivity and universal, timeless knowledge. Each side of a dualism (such as science/non-science or male/female), according to such theories, maintains its meaning only in relation to the opposite concept. The concepts themselves have no essential meaning. In postmodern literary thought, language does not convey meaning but rather creates it through such binary oppositions. As there is no meaning outside of language, there are no objects or ideas that are fundamental, eternal or universally true. Language reflects the time, place, and worldview of the community. To 'deconstruct' a text is to show how a particular discourse poses as universal and objective – to show how the subordinate sides of the dualisms are implicit in the argument and how dominance is created. Once a text which has been purported to expound on subjects universal and objective has been exposed in all its particularity and subjectivity, however, the contribution of deconstruction ends. Such deconstruction does not offer a new way of evaluating the adequacy of knowledge claims; it offers only 'endless deferral or play' (Poovey, 1988). There is no conception of progress towards more reliable knowledge. Once one game – say, exposing the modernist beliefs underlying neoclassical economics – starts to become less fun, one can simply invent a new game. Perhaps one can turn to exposing *postmodern* beliefs in neoclassical economics – like showing how neoclassic theory proliferates a postmodern fragmented body (Amariglio and Ruccio, Chapter 6) or how game theory contributes to postmodernism (Hargreaves Heap, Chapter 17). If one would like to call this process decadent, that is likely a label to which the participants would thrill. The economist interested in reliable knowledge, and the feminist interested in social justice, however, are unlikely to find the extremes of deconstructionist criticism an appealing road.

Consider, instead, an approach to understanding science and the pursuit of objectivity which puts together aspects of all these concerns. Learning from deconstructionism, it pays attention to the socially constructed nature of language and searches out the meanings hidden in binary dualisms like those in Table 13.1. As a feminist approach, it seeks to address questions relating to sex, gender and science. As an approach designed by a practicing economist, it retains the idea that gathering knowledge which is in some sense objective (or reliable) is a desirable goal.

Start by thinking about how one learns the language of one's culture, and how to think in its terms. George Lakoff and Mark Johnson (1980) have argued that language and cognition are based in large part on the metaphorical elaboration of bodily experiences. For example, onto the physical experience of the relationship 'up–down' are mapped many other relationships. In English, happy is 'feeling up', while sad is 'down in the dumps'. Being in control is 'having the upper hand', while being subject to control is 'being under someone's thumb'. More to the point, men and masculinity are commonly regarded as 'up' or superior or central, and women and femininity as 'down' or inferior or marginal (as seen in Figure 13.1). Feminists would obviously like to break the cognitive association of men with superiority and women with inferiority.

What is to be done with the masculine/feminine dualism itself is more open to debate. A fundamental insight of feminist theory is that gender assignments are not reflective of biological sex difference, but are culturally created. Characteristics such as softness or emotion, for example, have not become feminine-identified in the dominant Western culture because all women are by nature or 'in essence' soft or emotional; rather,

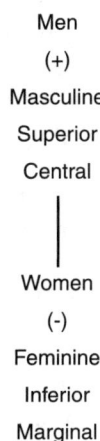

Figure 13.1 The hierarchical dualism

women are associated with softness and emotion on a cultural plane – women and the characteristics share the same culturally defined cognitive category of 'feminine'. The cultural variation in such assignments (or even intra-cultural variation – for example, in the USA black women are less likely than white women to be associated with softness) should serve as a constant warning against biological essentialism. To say, then, that 'science is considered masculine' is to say that it reflects social beliefs about masculinity, not that it reflects some special properties brought to it by the maleness of its traditional practitioners.

Some feminist scholars have claimed that sexism will only stop if gender as a concept is itself erased – i.e. masculine and feminine become meaningless concepts, and science becomes completely gender-neutral. A different approach is taken here. Think, instead, of gender as simply the metaphorical association of various concepts with the biological differentiation of the sexes – sometimes a fairly close association, sometimes so distant an association as to be apparently arbitrary. That such assignment of gender associations is in actuality an important means of mental organization for many people is empirically observable in psychological surveys (for example, Bem 1981) and in languages in which grammatical gender is related to sex differentiation. Such evidence leads me to suspect that attempts to banish gender outright will most likely only force it underground.

If the hierarchical structure of the masculine/feminine dualism comes from, as in Lakoff and Johnson's argument, a mapping of concepts onto the particular physical experience of up/down, then an alternative to simply trying to erase the dualism (as some feminists argue should be done) or explode the dualism (in the deconstructionist solution) is to try to link it with a different bodily experience – to use a different metaphor. Instead of thinking of masculinity–good and femininity–bad as two poles in a single dimension of movement, try thinking about movement in two dimensions, right/left as well as up/down. Let up/down represent value differences, while right/left represents gender differences, as in the 'gender/value compass' (Figure 13.2).

The gender associations come from cultural usage. Value judgments play an explicit role in determining what goes in the top quadrants vs. the bottom quadrants, and the term directly below each top spot should represent a perversion of the top term, when unbalanced by the other positive term. The diagonals represent a logical relationship of lack. The top two quadrants together give a positive complementarity, and the two bottom quadrants, a negative complementarity.

As an illustration of the compass in use, and also of the force of gender ideology is the creation of language, consider the dualism of virile (meaning 'manly vigor') vs. emasculated. Clearly the term 'virile' belongs in the M+ quadrant, while the term 'emasculated', denoting lack of virility, belongs in the F– quadrant. These terms are in common usage, and the usual masculine–positive/feminine–negative relationship is easily completed. But doesn't womanhood mean something more than just a lack of manhood? A diligent search of an English dictionary revealed the word 'muliebrity', as meaning 'womanliness' or the 'feminine correlative of virility'. While not a commonly used word in a culture where woman are not supposed to have strength, it obviously fills the F+ cell. By analogy to 'emasculated', one would think that 'effeminated' might be the word for a lack of womanly vigor. But, in fact, the term

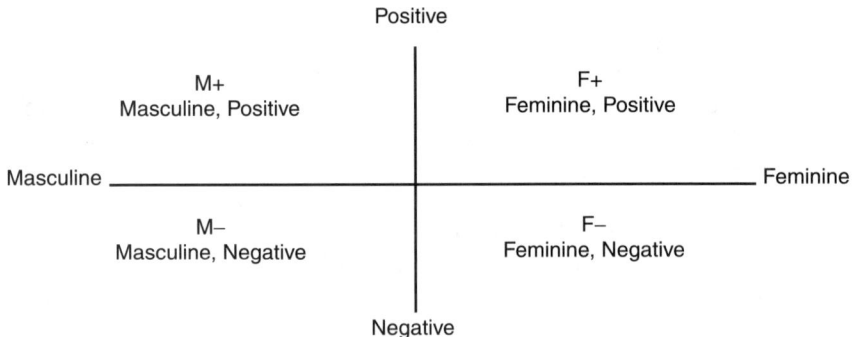

Figure 13.2 The gender/value compass
Source: Nelson (1992a, b)

effeminate denotes an excess of (presumably negative) womanly traits, and there is no word in the English language for the failing of insufficient womanliness.

This example demonstrates the purpose of the diagram, which is to break apart dualisms that perhaps are unexamined, while highlighting the gaps in language and understanding which simple dualistic thinking has spawned. The purpose is *not* to 'define' any terms, nor to attempt to permanently structure our understanding of them. The diagram is a tool that is useful in some contexts and not useful in others, and should hence be used or disregarded as appropriate. Certainly there are cases where a greater multiplicity of dimensions is necessary, or finer (or continuous) gradations, or even a move away from the idea of dimensions at all to a less linear or analytical understanding. The compass should be thought of as a starting point, not an ending point. I believe it is true, however, that many times when we think we have moved into a deeper and more complex understanding, we are actually still bound by the type of dualism which this rather simple 'compass' is designed to break up. I will explore this using the example of the modernist/postmodernist dualism below.

Now to the question of what this means for objectivity. As noted above, a considerable feminist literature has argued that the image of the human self as fundamentally detached from nature and from other humans reflects a particularly masculine viewpoint. A feminine angle is more characterized by a view of the human self as part of nature and embedded in networks of social relations. Fitting this into a gender/value compass gives detachment or separation on the left, attachment or connection on the right. Catherine Keller, in her book *From a Broken Web: Separation, Sexism, and Self* (1986), suggests terms that fit well into the negative quadrants. The masculine-associated tendency to detachment, if unmitigated by connection, gives rise to the 'separative' self, one led to build myths of autonomy and detachment. Not actually able to exist on his own, however, his apparent independence from others and from nature is supported by the invisible work of the corresponding 'soluble' self – the self-denying wife, who dissolves her identity into his, and who raises the children, writes the holiday greeting cards and cooks the dinner. This perverse complementarity of stereotyped roles and self-defeating myths stands in contrast to the definition of selfhood suggested by the positive quadrants in Figure 13.3.

The person who has no need of myths, or of relations of domination and submission, to support his or her self image is one who can draw from the positive aspects of both separation and connection, who recognizes him or herself as both an individual and as embedded in relationships.

Science has been socially constructed along a distinctly masculinist

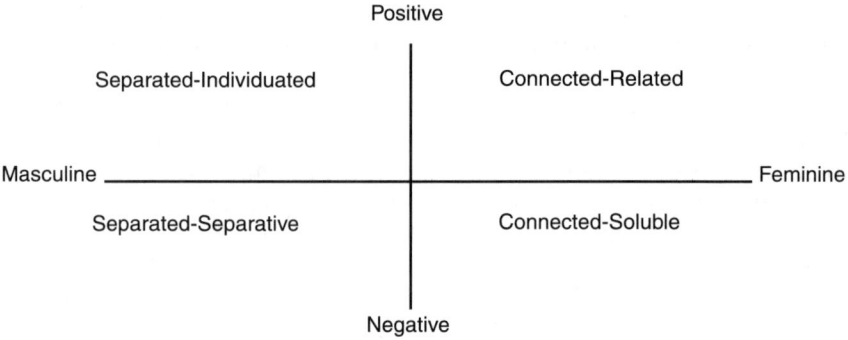

Figure 13.3 Separation and connection

line. The definition of objectivity held by modernists, which depends crucially on the notion of detachment, has been termed 'weak objectivity' by Sandra Harding (1995), or 'objectivism' by Evelyn Fox Keller (1985). Keller points out its emotional foundation. 'The scientist is not the purely dispassionate observer he idealizes', she has written, 'but a sentient being for whom the very ambition for objectivity carries with it a wealth of subjective meanings' (1985: 96). Objectivism does not describe the 'hard reality' of the situation of the scientist, but is rather an emotionally potent romance rooted in masculine anxiety about connection. Objectivism, in terms of the gender/value compass, is an M− term. A rejection of objectivism does not imply that one must reject the goal of reliable knowledge, and overwhelmed by awareness of connection or situatedness, revert to a radical relativism (in the F− quadrant). Keller suggests, as an alternative to objectivism, a concept of 'dynamic objectivity' in which the very real connections between the researcher and the object of study, or of mind and nature, are not only recognized but actively drawn on as a resource. Harding argues that the quest for reliable knowledge is enhanced, not damaged, by reflection on and critical examination of previously ignored cultural influences. Harding's 'strong objectivity' thus requires a recognition of both the M+ and F+.

But what is to guarantee that the resulting work is reliable? First, in contrast to some deconstructionist works which see all of reality as merely a text, it is recognized that there is something 'out there' (called 'nature', for short) to which theories must in some sense be responsive. Second, the pursuit of objectivity can be seen as an activity of a community in mutual conversation and debate. Helen Longino has written,

> The objectivity of individuals...consists in their participation in the collective give-and-take of critical discussion and not in some

special relation (of detachment, hardheadedness) they may bear to their observations. Thus understood, objectivity is dependent on the depth and scope of the transformative interrogation that occurs in any given scientific community. This communitywide process ensures (or can ensure) that the hypotheses ultimately accepted as supported by some set of data do not reflect a single individual's idiosyncratic assumptions about the natural world. To say that a theory...was accepted on the basis of objective methods...[is] to say...that it reflects the critically achieved consensus of the scientific community.

(1990: 79)

While it is acknowledged that nature can never be directly known, but is always interpreted within the limitations of human cognition and language, the requirements of responsiveness to nature as well as community acceptance prevent someone from deciding to just believe anything she or he wants. The commitment to expanding the 'depth and scope' of the scientific community, so that acceptance of a theory does not depend on the idiosyncrasies or ideologies of a particular group, means that feminism is necessary for the objectivity of economics. The antidote to inappropriate subjectivism and personal whim comes not from purity in method, but from comparison and dialog among various views within an *open* community of scholars. If a group is predominantly male and male-controlled, certain biases will be endemic. The feminist-advocated inclusion of women in economics – as well as the inclusion of people of various races, classes and ethnicities – opens up the scholar community and can lead to more reliable knowledge.[3]

Economics and social change

A feminist economics would be one freed from masculine biases. Instead of allowing masculine, separative ideology to define the discipline, the criteria for judging good practice would be drawn from both of the positive quadrants of the gender/value compass. The primary characteristics of a feminist economics can be distinguished from those characterizing contemporary mainstream economics in the USA, in three areas: definition, methods, *and purpose*.

Contemporary economics is largely defined around the rational choice model. Even macroeconomists are now expected to base their work on theories of the individual, rational agent. 'Economic man' is of course the very image of the separative self – completely autonomous, independent of all natural needs and social influences. Yet this is not the only definition of economics. Older definitions of economics, and ones more commonly held by the person-in-the-street, are of economics as being about material goods, or as being about markets. None of these definitions is particularly appealing for feminists. One can say very little about oppressive social institutions from within an individualistic rational choice model. One can say nothing about caring services if the definition is based on physical goods, or about non-market work if the definition is about markets. A definition that would be more helpful can be found by thinking beyond the usual 'man'/nature dualism. Instead of posing a dilemma between human choice and material nature as core concepts, one can think of economics as the study of humans in interaction with the world which supports us – of economics as the study of the organization of the processes which provision human life. This definition would put activities traditionally allocated to females (and then ignored) such as child care, basic nutrition, and basic health care, as well as some masculine-associated and market-oriented provisioning activities, right at the core of the discipline.

What about economic method? While some marginal space remains in current mainstream economics for studies of a qualitative or historical nature, it is clear from the design of graduate programs, from the acceptance policies of prestigious journals, and from the funding decisions of major research bodies that the high prestige part of current economic practice is in the development of formal mathematical models. Formal mathematics is very appealing to the researcher who disdains any taint of connection or feminine squishiness. A formal proof or derivation is unambiguously hard, logical, and precise, and requires no contact with the world beyond that of a pencil on paper. No trace can be found in it of feminine-identified softness, illogic, vagueness, or submersion in experience. But are these the only alternatives? The gender/value compass suggests that this focus on masculine virtues and feminine vices leaves out important characteristics on the opposite diagonal. An overenthusiastic focus on achieving hardness, logic, precision, and detachment (M+ terms) can bring along with it rigidity, an overly narrow focus, thinness and a situation of being out of touch with reality (M− terms). In addition to being hard, logical, and precise, and reflective, can we not also envision an economics that is flexible, attentive to context, rich, and engaged (the F+ terms)? A feminist economics, while not disdaining the use of mathematical models of rational choice in contexts in which they might be appropriate, would require that other research methods also be taught and practiced. If, as in many cases, the phenomena being studied are not reducible to terms that can be manipulated using formal logic, the analysis must precede using a richer, verbal reasoning – without apologies. If standard sources such as government statistics and machine-coded surveys do not get at the information needed, a feminist economics would require that other tools – including the case studies, open-ended questioning, and ethnographic methods much disdained by 'hard' (read:

rigid) scientists – be applied. Instead of a research program narrowed to the circle of illumination falling from the streetlamp of the rational choice model and formal methods, a feminist economics would require research which goes to where the issues of provisioning lie, and which only then selects from among numerous illuminating techniques the one the most helpful and appropriate.

What about the purpose of a feminist economics? The idea of scientific research having a purpose or telos is sometimes an awkward one for mainstream researchers. Sometimes the discussions suggest that science is its own reward: one works for the beauty of knowing, driven only by the requirements of pure reason. Perhaps this emphasis on aesthetic sensibilities might be the nearest commonality between certain mainstream researchers and certain deconstructionists, although the latter's tastes run along somewhat different lines. To other mainstream researchers, the 'dictates' of logic provide their own moral justification.[4] At other times, it is argued that highly abstract formal reasoning is justified because it may, eventually, at some point very far down the road, be related to something useful.[5] And let's not forget the purely self-interested motivations: doing academics along accepted lines (whatever they may be) can yield one publications and a steady income. Meanwhile other economic problems related to hunger, disease, infant mortality, war, sexism and racism, or economic depression, if they cannot be stated in formal terms, go unstudied. While in a world with unlimited resources, pursuit of extended chains of logic would be costless, in the real world one must ask of science not only 'Does it follow the rules?' but, also, 'Is it responsible?' In terms of a gender/value compass, the separation/connection dualism played out for the question of the purpose of economics is shown in Figure 13.4.

A feminist economics would be concerned with understanding the underlying causes of the problem being studied, and so avoid recommending shallow and ultimately unsuccessful remedies. But it would also keep applied problems at the center of concern, to avoid spinning off into theoretical irrelevancies.

Labor economics, family issues, and the policies affecting women in these areas have long been, and continue to be, major concerns of feminist economists. While substantial contributions have been made in these areas by feminists using standard neoclassical tools,[6] in the last few years contributions using broader ideas of definition and method have mushroomed not only on these topics but on others as well. Theoretical, empirical, and policy-oriented work on macroeconomics, econometrics, and economic restructuring, for example, have joined work on discrimination and welfare, in such outlets as the journal *Feminist Economics* (the journal of the International Association for Feminist Economics), and volumes like *Out of the Margin* (Kuiper and Sap, 1995), and *The Strategic Silence* (Bakker, ed., 1994).

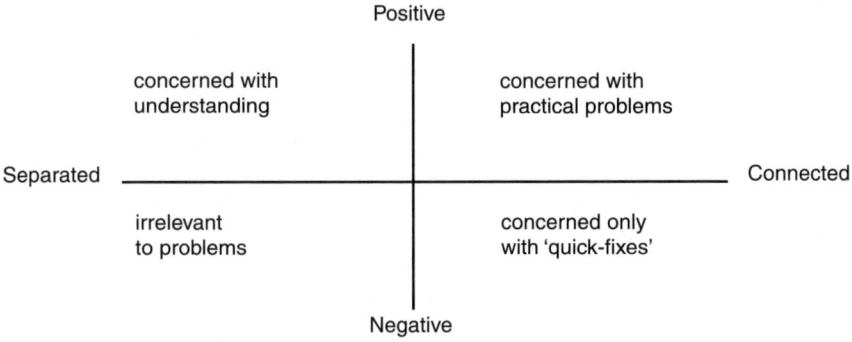

Figure 13.4 Detachment and engagement

Putting economic problems rather than conventional, detached, methods at the core of the discipline radically reorders the priorities for research. Consider macroeconomics. The exclusion of household labor from national income accounts is a well-known example of masculine bias, but a feminist re-visioning of macroeconomics can take in much broader issues. For example, the notion of 'expectations' has always played a role in macroeconomics (e.g. in long-term interest rates and futures markets) and recently was the target of even more theoretical attention, in the 'rational expectations' debate. The norms of detached economics, however, require that in the study of expectations, economists borrow only from the 'hard' disciplines of mathematics and statistics, and not from the 'soft' disciplines of psychology and sociology. How do people come to form expectations about the future? The answer of current macroeconomists to all these questions seems to be the rather unscientific one of 'We don't know, and we don't care'. The norms of detached economics also dictate that progress is to be made by formal modeling and testing; data gathering (sometimes referred to as 'touching' the data) is taken to be of low status, and within the area of data gathering the use of one-on-one survey techniques is the lowest of the low. Thus Alan Blinder, who has been using surveys to research the causes of price stickiness, included in an article a section entitled 'getting economists to pay attention' (1991: 92). Thus Larry Summers's (1991) advocacy of informal, pragmatic empirical analysis over highly formal econometric testing ('very much in the same spirit as the attack on modernism in McCloskey's...*The Rhetoric of Economics*', p. 130) was less than enthusiastically received. While Blinder and Summers and other economists who criticize the discipline's over-concern with detachment and formal technique are not explicitly feminist, there are obvious areas of overlap. Barbara Bergmann (1987) has raised very similar criticism about the methodology of macroeconomics in regard to its inability to address real-world problems.

Bergmann, while a feminist (and perhaps the profession's best-known one), does not see much use for feminist theorizing, however, as was mentioned in the introduction. Does feminist theoretical analysis contribute anything beyond what we can get from common sense? I believe so. The feminist analysis suggests that the preference in the discipline for overly detached analysis is not merely accidental, but is rather the product of an ingrown and exclusive community, whose masculinist biases have heretofore remained unnoticed. The feminist analysis suggests that changing such a long-held and emotionally rooted preference will require not just rational arguments – no matter how prestigious the speaker – and tinkering here and there, but a radical rethinking and even re-feeling of the relation of gender to value, and a re-thinking of the dualisms underlying our current conceptions of science. A feminist macroeconomics would be set free from the harmful neglect of and disdain for 'connected' methods of research. While that sort of change obviously does not by itself rid the world of problems, getting the questions right and the methods adequate can be a substantial first step.

Is this 'postmodern'?

I have sought to show that a feminist economics can encompass both 'strong objectivity' and a commitment to social responsibility. But the third objective I have set out is to show that the alternative I propose is also 'postmodern'. Whether I succeed, of course, depends on what one thinks of as 'postmodern'.

I believe my gender/value compass is a useful tool for examining and getting past the *simple* binary logic characteristic of modernist thinking, and so I claim it as post-modernist in that sense. Obviously, it does not completely overcome dualisms, since it multiplies them and makes them more complex, rather than eliminating them. I believe (though many readers of this volume may disagree) that binary oppositions are basic conceptual building blocks, that cannot be directly avoided. Rather, we can recognize that while unidimensional dualisms (e.g., up/down) are fundamental, we all learn at an early age to handle more than one dimension at a time. Moving through space, for example, we can deal with up/down as well as left/right and forward/back. Even though we might in some contexts draw on metaphorically constructed links between up-right-forward(-good) and down-left-back(-bad), we certainly do not use these all the time, or we would never be able to order our movements. Moving spatially, we can deal with the fact that 'up' and 'left' are related, but the relation is not oppositional. Rather than explode dualisms as a building block of cognition, my solution is to build up our cognitive sophistication in their use.

One can argue, in fact (like Sheila Dow, Chapter 2), that much of the modernism/postmodernism debate takes place very much within dualistic thinking. Table 13.2 illustrates some crude categorizations of frequent issues of debate, when postmodernism is taken at its extreme. One may even point out that the debate can be on the binary point, 'binary/non-binary'!

My arguments are for notions of 'relational selves', rather than either the extreme of purely unitary or the extreme of purely fragmented selves, and for a concept of 'situated knowledge' rather than either of the extremes of mind-of-God knowledge or no knowledge. These are the sorts of 'positive complementarities' I referred to in my exposition of the compass diagram.

As another example of a use of the 'compass' in this context, consider the claim that modernist thought is 'universalizing' (bad) while postmodernist thought favors 'difference' (good). The compass in Figure 13.5 puts the modernist pull towards unifying and totalizing on the left and the postmodern pull towards fragmentation and multiplicity on the right.

The modernist believes, for example, that people can be grouped – can be placed with others, cognitively – on the basis of some similarities (e.g., gender). The extreme form of a modernist approach to identity, however, is an emphasis on similarities without respect to differences. The notion that all people are 'rational economic man' is one such extreme modernist position. Another is the consideration of 'Woman' as a universal category, even as the traits of this supposed creature tend to look rather

Table 13.2 Extremist binary oppositions in the modernism/postmodernism debate

Modernism	Postmodernism
centred	all over the place
universalism	fragmentation
all externally constructed	all socially constructed
matter	discourse
perfectible knowledge	no knowledge
Progress	no place to go

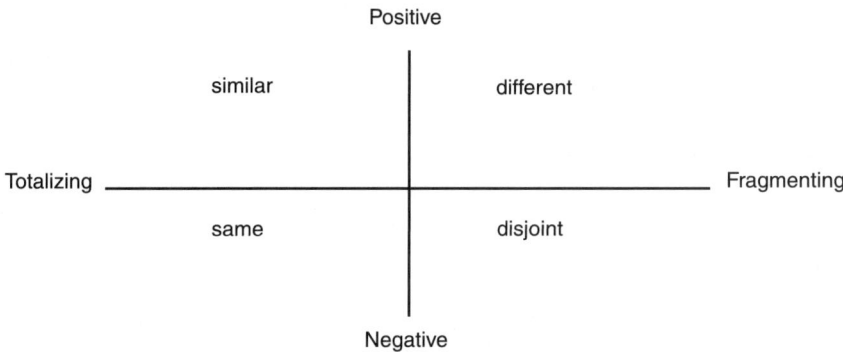

Figure 13.5 Unity and multiplicity

Euro-American, etc. The postmodernist, fragmenting approach emphasizes difference and warns against such false universalisms. To argue that difference is 'good' while universalizing is 'bad', however, ignores the negative quadrant on the right-hand side. Radical fragmentation means that every person must be judged as completely unique in all ways. Endless variation and multiplicity means that *no* generalizations can be made. One may not be allowed to speak of 'women', even as a somewhat indistinctly defined group based on physical and/or cultural similarities (Bordo, 1990). This creates problems for the feminist project.

The modernist/postmodernist simple binaries (illustrated in Table 13.2) arise from thinking of the fragmenting and unifying modes of thought as *alternatives* between which one must choose. I suggest, rather, that they are better perceived of as modes that coexist in creative tension. Recognizing the legitimacy of each, we can more adequately deal with people as being both individual and connected, both distinct and similar.

One may also look at recent debates on multiculturalism in the light of this more dialectical understanding. Pro-mulitculturalist scholars tend to use positive sounding words like 'diversity' and 'multiculturalism' to describe the advantages of multiplicity (the fragmenting-positive quadrant in the compass), and negative words like 'mass culture', 'uniformity', or 'homogeneity' (totalizing-negative) to describe what they envision their opponents to be backing.[7] The anti-multiculturalists, not surprisingly, choose to focus on the other pair of diagonally-related quadrants. Positive words like 'unity' or 'solidarity' are used to describe the advantages of emphasizing similarity (totalizing-positive), while pejorative terms like 'partisan', 'factional', or 'schism' describe what they are opposing (fragmenting-negative). Each side has downplayed the dangers (negative quadrant) of its own position. I suggest that what is needed is not more debate along these rather tired lines, but rather a pragmatic approach that weighs both the advantages and dangers of pulling towards either side, on a case-by-case basis. Cultural diversity and individual freedom existing within an atmosphere of larger-scale social solidarity may be the positive complementarity we can all seek.

It should be remembered, however, that there also exists the possibility of a negative complementarity, in which the worst of each side is taken instead of the best. A chaotic, factionalized society in which each faction militantly imposes internal uniformity, for example, could be a worst-case outcome, thinking in terms of the multiculturalism debate. I would also argue that some of the contributions to this volume might be heading towards a negative complementarity in what they take from neoclassical economics and what they take from postmodernist thought. Jack Amariglio and David Ruccio take the mind/body dualism and convert the 'body' to 'desires'. In this case, corporeality disappears and the so called 'postmodern body' collapses back into just another bit of mind. Philip Mirowski's chapter takes the self-interest/altruism dualism, defines altruism as 'selflessness', but then redefines it as just another 'taste' so that it collapses back into self-interest.[8] The reader may decide if these constitute progress.

It should also be remembered that the 'compass' is simply a provisional tool, helpful in exploding some binaries and pushing us out of some lazy patterns of thinking, but never intended to be definitional of the concepts included, nor universally applicable to any problem of thought and language.

Conclusion

I have argued in this paper that feminist economics can search for reliable knowledge, be useful in making progress towards positive social change, and not depend on modernist thinking. It can be defined by the subject of the provisioning of human life, chooses its methods from the broadest range of options, and is committed to understanding real economic phenomena. Using the insights of feminist theory concerning the overvaluation of detachment over connection, it redefines all of economics (not only the areas thought of as being of particular concern to women) in a practical and useful way. It is 'postmodern' in rejecting much of the modernist notions of science, but does not fall prey to the extremes of dualistic modernist/postmodernist thinking.

Feminist economics *can* be objective, activist, and postmodern. It may take some mental calisthenics, however, to break the habits of thinking that keep us from seeing all our options. I recommend starting with thinking only one or two impossible things before breakfast.

Notes

1 For a fuller exposition, see Nelson (1996). For an introduction to feminist social constructionism, see Ferber and Nelson (1993).
2 The dominant tradition in economics is the 'neoclassical' school, in the broad sense. Feminists have also begun analysis of other schools, for example institutionalist economics (Jennings, 1993), socialist economics (Folbre, 1993) and 'humanistic' economics (Nelson, 1993).
3 Gary Becker's (1981) theories of the family, for example, could not long maintain a pretense of objectivity in the economics I envision.
4 See Debreu's language of 'Mathematics... is a forbidding *master*. It ceaselessly asks...' (1991: 4, emphasis added) and Katzner '*...one has no choice* but to follow the accompanying formalizations to their logical ends' (1991: 22, emphasis added).
5 See Katzner (1991), on working out the general equilibrium model 'so that its viability and usefulness can eventually be appraised' (1991: 20).
6 See, for example, Blau and Ferber (1992) and the references therein.
7 Some of the example terms are drawn from a discussion in Zelizer, 1999.
8 For a discussion of problems with the notion of 'selflessness' as a virtue, see Nelson, 1996, Chapter 9.

References

Bakker, Isabella, (ed.) (1994) *The Strategic Silence: Gender and Economic Policy*, London: Zed Books.
Becker, Gary S. (1981) *A Treatise on the Family*, Cambridge: Harvard University Press.
Bem, Sandra Lipsitz (1981) 'Gender Schema Theory: A Cognitive Account of Sex Typing', *Psychological Review*, 88(4): 354–64.
Bergmann, Barbara R. (1987) '"Measurement" or Finding Things Out in Economics', *Journal of Economic Education* 18(2): 191–203.
—— (1997) Posting on FEMECON-L listserver, August 13, 1997.
Blau, Francine D. and Marianne A. Ferber (1992) *The Economics of Women, Men, and Work*, Englewood Cliffs: Prentice-Hall.
Blinder, Alan S. (1991) 'Why Are Prices Sticky? Preliminary Results from an Interview Study', *AEA Papers and Proceedings*, 81(2): 89–100.
Bordo, Susan (1987) *The Flight to Objectivity: Essays on Cartesianism and Culture*, Albany: State University of New York Press.
—— (1990) 'Feminism, Postmodernism, and Gender-Scepticism', in Linda J. Nicholson, (ed.) *Feminism/Postmodernism*, New York: Routledge, 133–56.
Debreu, Gerard (1991) 'The Mathematization of Economic Theory', *American Economic Review* 81 (March): 1–7.
Ferber, Marianne A. and Julie A. Nelson (1993) 'The Social Construction of Economics and the Social Construction of Gender', in Marianne A. Ferber and Julie A. Nelson, (eds) *Beyond Economic Man: Feminist Theory and Economics*, Chicago: University of Chicago Press, 1–22.
Folbre, Nancy (1993) 'Socialism, Feminist and Scientific', in Marianne A. Ferber and Julie A. Nelson, (eds) *Beyond Economic Man: Feminist Theory and Economics*, Chicago: University of Chicago Press, 94–110.

Harding, Sandra (1986) *The Science Question in Feminism*, Ithaca: Cornell University Press.
—— (1995) 'Can Feminist Thought Make Economics More Objective?' *Feminist Economics* 1(1): 7–32.
Jennings, Ann L. (1993) 'Public or Private? Institutional Economics and Feminism', in Marianne A. Ferber and Julie A. Nelson, (eds) *Beyond Economic Man: Feminist Theory and Economics*, Chicago: University of Chicago Press, 1993, 111–129.
Katzner, Donald W. (1991) 'In Defense of Formalization in Economics', *Methodus: Bulletin of the International Network for Economic Method* 3(1): 17:24.
Keller, Catherine (1986) *From a Broken Web: Separation, Sexism, and Self*, Boston: Beacon Press.
Keller, Evelyn Fox (1985) *Reflections on Gender and Science*, New Haven: Yale University Press.
Kuiper, Edith and Jolande Sap (1995) *Out of the Margin: Feminist Perspectives on Economics*, New York: Routledge.
Lakoff, George and Johnson, Mark (1980) *Metaphors We Live By*, Chicago: University of Chicago Press.
Longino, Helen (1990) *Science as Social Knowledge: Values and Objectivity in Scientific Inquiry*, Princeton: Princeton University Press.
Nelson, Julie A. (1992a) 'Thinking About Gender', *Hypatia* 7(3): 138–54.
—— (1992b) 'Gender, Metaphor, and the Definition of Economics', *Economics and Philosophy* 8: 103–25.
—— (1993) 'Gender and Economic Ideologies', *Review of Social Economy* 51(3), Fall, 287–301.
—— (1996) *Feminism, Objectivity, and Economics*, New York: Routledge.
Poovey, Mary (1988) 'Feminism and Deconstruction', *Feminist Studies* 14:51–65.
Summers, Lawrence H. (1991) 'The Scientific Illusion in Empirical Macroeconomics', *Scandinavian Journal of Economics* 93(2): 129–48.
Zelizer, Viviana (1999) 'Multiple Markets: Multiple Cultures', in Neil Smelser and Jeffrey Alexander (eds) *Diversity and Its Discontents: Cultural Conflict and Common Ground in Contemporary American Society*, Princeton: Princeton University Press, 193–212.

14
POSTMODERNISM AND FEMINIST ECONOMICS

Jane Rossetti

The increasing presence of women in academic economics in the past several decades has had a clear impact on the practice of economics. As more women join the ranks of economists, research in the discipline has been extended and deepened in particular ways. As Rebecca Blank put it

> Certainly, female scholars have done a great deal of research on gender-related issues that in all likelihood would not have been as thoroughly explored if only men were in the field. Much of the literature on issues of family, children, and women in the economy has been written because of the interests and presence of women scholars in the profession.
>
> (Blank, 1993: 119)

Blank's list should also include issues of taxation, national account keeping (see Waring 1988 for more references), women in development, and volunteer work. Discrimination, occupational segregation, differential rates of unemployment, and differential rates of labor force participation all fall under the rubric 'women in the economy' and have an extensive literature. As more women enter the discipline, their personal experiences broaden the field, which pushes research further and deeper into particular topics and makes women more visible as objects of analysis.

However, this extension of the realm is not where feminist thought in economics will leave its biggest mark. The bigger mark is being made in a feminist approach to the *analysis*, not the object thereof. For example, the models of discrimination in the labor market may use neoclassical economic analysis, specifying a taste for discrimination in order to incorporate discrimination into the neoclassical model, à la Gary Becker. Feminist economic analysis does more than focus on women using established tools, categories, or methods. It is creating its own categories and approaches to analysis.

The creation of a feminist discourse in economics has begun.[1] This discourse is closely connected to postmodern theory, and is what I wish to explore below. What I will do is briefly present elements of postmodern theory, especially of deconstruction; set out what I perceive as feminist criticisms of economics; show how the two are related; and evaluate what postmodernism has to offer feminist economics.

The rudiments: from modernism to deconstruction

The development of neoclassical economics has been a modernist undertaking from its very inception. The degree of self-consciousness in the aspiration to certainty, objectivity, and universality varies from writer to writer, but the desire to reduce complex economic behavior to the working out of very simple, enduring, and universal laws of behavior is never far from the surface. Menger, one of the three founders of neo-classical thought, was explicit:

> In what follows I have endeavored to reduce the complex phenomena of human economic activity to the simplest elements that can still be subjected to accurate observation, to apply to these elements the measure corrreponding to their nature, and constantly adhering to this measure, to investigate the manner in which the more complex economic phenomena evolve from their elements acording to definite principles.
> (1981: 46–7)

Keynes relied on a 'fundamental psychological law' (1964: 96) in constructing his consumption function. Most, if not all, introductory textbooks begin with a section on 'Economics as a social science' and explain how economics can still be a science, even without a laboratory. Philip Mirowski[2] has written on the relationship between economic thought and physics. Deirdre McCloskey has contributed significantly to the literature examining the relationship between economics and modernism.[3]

Economists were not the only social scientists patterning their research after the biological and physical sciences of the late nineteenth and twentieth centuries. The positivist search for underlying, universal, and *true* laws of human behavior included sociologists, anthropologists, political scientists, and others. The immediate post-war period represented the apotheosis of the modernist theories in all these disciplines, (exemplified perhaps by the appearance of the first edition of Samuelson's textbook) as well as in art, architecture, and music.

Postmodernism challenged the certainty, the 'scientificness', the possibility of finding 'Truth', the bedrock on which modernism rested. The challenge to modernism's universality, appropriately enough, took on different forms in different disciplines. In philosophy, linguistics, and literary theory this took the specific form of post-*structuralism*, in response to structuralist theories which had (in broad terms) characterized these disciplines in their modernist period.

The structuralist theories in these disciplines can all be characterized by heavy reliance on formal models and the attempt to forge universal and timeless assertions about the human mind, human nature, or human social life. 'In a word, structuralist theories are grand theories'.[4] These are the theories of Althusser, Parsons, Chomsky, and Levi-Strauss. They stand in contrast to the 'poststructuralist' theories which, in various ways, stress particularity, specificity, context, and perspective in both creating and understanding, for example, culture or language or economies. Deconstruction is a particular manifestation of a poststructural perspective, with its historical origins in linguistics and literary criticism. The philosopher Jacques Derrida and the literary critic Paul De Man are two influential figures who have articulated and advanced the principles of deconstructionism.

Deconstructivists claim that language cannot objectively convey the essence of an object or an idea. This is so because objects, or ideas, do not have an essence, that is, essential, fundamental, universally true characteristics. Rather, objects have characteristics *attributed* to them. The types of characteristics ascribed will depend on the community's needs and values. Language does not convey an essential meaning, but rather creates that meaning. Without language, we would not have words to describe the objects; nor would we have the categories words express (e.g. texture, weight, value) in which to place (figuratively) the objects. Without language we could not interpret the characteristics or meaning of an object, for we wouldn't know what types of characteristics need to be expressed or contemplated. Language does not express a previously inarticulable thought, it is not a veil. It is not a means of cleanly and objectively conveying pre-existing thoughts. It creates the system that allows us to have those thoughts. Without language we could not think. Language gives us the words and the categories to identify objects and subjects, and think about how they can relate to or interact with each other. Language creates the meanings.

Try to imagine yourself without language. Contemplate some object in your mind. How would you understand this object? If postmodern theory is correct, you cannot. You might hold it, physically, but you couldn't then say to yourself 'Aha! It's heavy!' or rough or silky or tasty or inanimate, or anything else, because you would not have the words for it. You would be left hefting and touching and tasting and waiting to see what the object might do on its own, but you couldn't think about the process or the object. You cannot *think* about the object. To think about it, you need words. Once you have 'heavy' you can think 'Aha! The rock is heavy!'

Yet these words ('silky' 'heavy' 'tasty') cannot convey the object's essence, since it doesn't have one before you can think about what it might be. The words *create* the essence, allow you to categorize the object in n-many ways. But this isn't completely correct either. Words give us categories in which we can attribute characteristics (e.g. weight, as a category allows us to attribute lightness, heaviness); but this does not create a universal, timeless, meaning for the word or object it represents, since the characteristics themselves have no essential, eternal, objective meaning, for the same reasons the object does not. The categories themselves are not inevitable. For example, if we grew up in zero-gravity, there probably wouldn't be a category weight, and the 'essence' of a rock would have nothing to do with its heaviness. Words can't convey an essence, since there is no essence to convey, and if there were an essence, we would have no way to affirm it.

Without an essence, the words themselves have no fixed meaning. They only function in opposition to other words – 'silk' on its own tells us nothing. We can only grasp its meaning in opposition to other words and categories: not rough, not prickly, not sharp. And of course 'rough' can't stand on its own. Language is a web of meanings: any word in itself conveys nothing, only in opposition to other words (themselves empty of independent meaning) can any meaning arise. Language then is based on a system of contrary, opposite, comparable, meanings, none of which are independent. Language, and the thoughts we can have in that language, reflects a particular time and place and view of the world.

Objects or concepts gain meaning only from being enmeshed in a system of language, categories, and opposites. Objects have no essence; language cannot *convey* them, but rather *creates* them through a series of specific and contingent categories. Since there is no objective presence to convey, the attributes chosen necessarily reflect a subjective, value-laden, world view. There is no high ground from which to cast magisterial judgements. Language and meaning are inherently subjective: arguments made in language have their own perspective built in and can never attain objective status. Language reflects the values of the community in what it allows us to express, or keeps us from expressing.[5] Meaning is subjective, particular to place, history, and presenter. And we have no means of escaping the shifting web of meanings, and no way to ascertain or evaluate the 'truth' or 'reality' of any claim.

What such thinkers as Stanley Fish, Richard Rorty, and Deirdre McCloskey have in common is the belief that, first, we do in fact hold beliefs; that is, we have adopted positions even though we accept that those positions are not grounded in some universal eternal truth. Second, they argue that not all beliefs are equally valid, not all interpretations are equally good. Meanings are constrained by the interpretive community, or the marketplace of ideas.[6] While the standards of meaning and valuation are subjective (or contingent, or based on a particular perspective), they are not arbitrary. This is not a case of 'anything goes'. The quality of a model, or a narrative, or a translation, cannot be judged by how close it comes to reflecting or encapsulating its True version, for there is no True version. Nontheless, it can be judged against qualities *esteemed* by the relevant communities, e.g. parsimony, elegance, high R-squared. This stance stops any descent into complete relativism and its suspected perils.[7] It also allows meanings and valued characteristics to change over time, as standards and communities themselves change.

One implication of poststructural thought is that both the speaker and the objects of speech are decentered. The speaker herself (as the object itself, above) has no essence, no self, outside the community and language. The subject is decentered in two senses: she no longer sees the object as divorced from herself, for they are connected by the unavoidable language and interpretation, and the subject loses a center herself – she has no core outside the community of meaning. Meanings, subjects and objects all shift together, around, and with each other. The boundaries of the object are now permeable, allowing new qualities and juxtapositions into themselves. For example, the boundary of 'the economy' is no longer seen as an ahistorical universal entity, but as a created and enforced boundary of thought, not fact.

Meaning comes out of categorization and opposites, and in Western thought hierarchies express these dualisms. Thus rational dominates irrational, thought/emotion, objective/subjective, and so on. These hierarchies reflect interpretive common values, not inherent superiorities. They reflect the power the dominant community has in enmeshing and even rendering invisible the second set of these categories. They appear universal and without context when, as Fish would say, the context is so shared as to be invisible. To the extent that the unprivileged categories are marginalized, written out of the text by virtue of being not written into the text, the dominant community uses its power, here the power of bounding the discourse, to continue to silence the unprivileged. Thus the link to the political content of deconstruction.[8]

Deconstructive readings make these categories visible – bring them into the light. Such readings reveal the categorizations, the construction of the argument, the hierarchies and their implicit value structure. They point out what is missing, invisible: the empty space, the invisible categories, occupied by women or people of color, or nature, are shown to be implicit in the privileged position occupied in the texts by men or whites or industry. Since language works as a system of oppositions, the opposite or subordinate is implicitly present even in analysis or theory concerned only with the dominant categories. When the text claims, or assumes, universality, a deconstructive reading brings to light the places in the text where the omitted categories are necessary to the argument, and presumed by it. They show the relation between these two sets of categories, and show the dominance as imposed, not natural or inevitable. They show how the discourse that appears to be universal, is in fact very particular. Deconstructive readings take apart the 'universal', the enthroned hierarchies by showing how the 'other' is implicit in the text, and how the text reveals the mutual dependence, not the dominance, of one over the other. One set of characteristics cannot logically be subordinate to another which requires the first for its very existence. The meaning in the text which strove for universality is undermined. In its place one is shown how the meaning depends on particular perspectives.

This is not to say that a better or truer meaning is found, in an absolute sense, since there is not an absolute sense of anything any longer. A new meaning is created – any decoding is another encoding. If the argument were to stop here, we would be left with a *reductio ad absurdum*. We could analyze the metaphors, the rhetoric, the means of persuasion, the empty self-referential definitions and leaps and gaps in logic and end with a destroyed text, an annihilated argument, perhaps a sense of accomplishment at their destruction, and no where else to go.

But if we take seriously these insights about constructed knowledge and the power of community to confer or deny acceptability of theory and the accompanying heuristics, the function of language of creating and limiting what can and should be discussed, we arrive at a different kind of postmodern argument, a much more powerful one. It is this line of argument that connects with contemporary feminist economic thought.

Since there isn't a True eternal meaning to be found, there are competing, contingent, particular, meanings which communities regard as true. The one which 'wins' will depend on, among other factors, the relative power of those making the respective readings and those evaluating them. So postmodernist thought leads to contending meanings and consideration of power issues in resolving them. While the implications for debate within the academy are fairly obvious by this point, the implications for the 'real world' are perhaps in the long run even more important. For no longer are just the terms of evaluation up for debate but the very definition of the field and its 'actors' themselves. When we are brought face to face with the knowledge that the 'economy' is constructed, we are given the opportunity to redefine its own limits: to include day care and school lunches as central parts of an economic theory that privileges humanity rather than efficiency.

Postmodern thought denies the possibility of objective knowledge, it trumpets the subjective (socially constructed) nature of categories, hierarchical organization, and meaning. It claims readings and arguments and texts cannot be universal, but are necessarily subjective and particular, contingent to history, class, race, gender, sexual orientation...and opens wide the doors to disputes over standards, meanings, and approaches. By revealing the particular perspective behind theses and methods of analysis it allows the dominant ones (e.g., modernism, falsificationism) to be challenged not on positive (in the economic sense) grounds, but in their very construction. It also argues that the new constructions will be built on some new, but not universal, basis. They can claim no objective superiority, but are inevitably subject to the same types of criticisms as can be leveled at their precursors. Deconstructive readings reveal the 'high ground' of modernist theory to have been, in fact, quicksand, but cannot provide *terra firma* for modernism's replacement. But at least it invites all to play the game of contestation.

Feminist economics

Feminist economics may not yet have a firmly established new paradigm or scientific research program. It is, afer all, rooted in feminism, which is itself contested. While there appears to be agreement on a number of areas or topics which should be further investigated, there is not, yet, an agreement on exactly how to go about the investigation. How would feminist economics analyze the determination of women's wages? What methods would be appropriate? What categorizations can go unchallenged? But if the first step in creating a feminist economics is in criticizing the failure of the old economics in order to clear space for the new, then feminist economics is well on its way. Feminist critiques of economic paradigms (here I mean neo-classical and Marxist) are a wonderful, albeit not always self-conscious, example of deconstructive criticism at work. I don't mean to detract from these criticisms, or label them derivative, but to show how feminist critiques exemplify postmodern thinking. Let me trace out the similarities.

1 Feminist critiques[9] begin with the recognition of dualisms and hierarchy found in the assumptions of economic theory and analysis:

> post-Enlightenment Western philosophy is rooted in a deeply gendered web of conceptual dualisms: objectivity vs. subjectivity, reason vs. emotion, culture vs. nature, positive vs. normative, mind vs. body, public vs. private, quantitative vs. qualitative, etc. Modern science identifies masculinity with the first term of each pair, femininity with the second.
>
> (Williams, 1992: 1)

> we critically examine the logic and consistency of a set of basic assumptions that have divided the economist's world into two parts, variously designated public and private, market and

household, economic and non economic, self-interested and altruistic, male and female.
(Folbre and Hartmann, 1988: 185)

Folbre and Hartmann continue, observing 'Within both the neoclassical and Marxian traditions predominantly male economists have assumed that individual self-interest motivates men's decisions in the capitalist marketplace, but does not motivate men or women in the private sphere of the home' (1988: 185) and 'Contemporary neoclassical economists ... continue to treat the "female realm" separately from the "male realm" of individualism'(188). In Marxian analysis 'Class interest has traditionally been defined largely in terms of the interests of working-class men' (191). The male, market, public sphere is granted primacy over the female, private, household sphere. The former is the primary domain of analysis. How the latter is treated is discussed below.

2 The feminist critics then point out what is *omitted* or not valued here: family, the work or value of child-bearing, decision-making inside the household. A notable example is in Seiz's well documented passage (1992: 286–7) on the omissions of economic theory: household production, volunteer work, conflict within families over allocation of labor or income. More is missing, Seiz points out, than just the topics:

> And discussions of economic policies regarding, for example, taxation, government expenditure, economic development, and international trade only rarely ask what effects policy choices will have on women and on gender relations.
> (Seiz, 1992: 286)

> Within the neoclassical tradition, the assumption of a joint utility function has obscured the possibility of conflicts between individuals in the family. Within the Marxian tradition, the assumption that class interests are primary has obscured the possibility of conflicts between individuals within the same class. By virtue of their association with this distinctly non-self-interested and therefore 'non economic' domain, women themselves came to be portrayed as relatively 'non economic' creatures.
> (Folbre and Hartmann, 1988: 185)

Folbre and Hartmann, citing Hartsock, continue that this notion of individualism 'could be asserted only if family life, and specifically child rearing, were bracketed and excluded from analysis' (1988: 187) and that 'The possibility that there might be unequal distribution of the products of home production or that independent access to market income might affect the allocation of goods and leisure within the home is simply never entertained' (189). Further,

> Marxist economists confine the concept of exploitation to the capitalist firm and use the rhetoric of class solidarity to avoid the possibility of exploitation in the home.... Marx's analysis of capitalism sidestepped the issues of household production and childrearing.... While Marxist economists discuss housework and the role of the family in capital accumulation, they tend to minimize potential conflicts between men and women in the home and workplace.... The actual labor process of housework is ignored.
> (Folbre and Hartmann, 1988: 191)

Other Marxian analyses 'bypass the opportunity to explore inequality in the allocation of time and goods between men and women within peasant households' or presume 'no differences between men and women in the economic consequences of children' (191). Seiz adds: 'I note that while Marxists have begun to do interesting work on the labor market and workplace with the bargaining approach, they have not systematically examined what difference gender makes to workers' bargaining power in that context' (1991: 24).

Waller and Jennings offer this observation:

> The tendency to ignore women is not just an oversight and the tendency to slip unknowingly into dualistic constructions not just an error in terminology; it is the result of the fact that our language, itself a cultural artifact, constrains our intellectual constructions and contains within its structure our cultural values and prejudices. The cultural character of knowledge stops us from addressing certain questions because these questions do not exist as possible areas of inquiry within the culture.
> (1990: 618)

Certain omissions are striking. Cynthia Wood opens her essay with:

> It is by now a central tenet of feminist economics that unpaid domestic labor (hoursework or household production) is not accorded the status of an economic activity in mainstream economic theory, nor is it incorporated in any meaningful way into mainstream economic analysis.
> (1997: 47)

Similar points are made by Bina Agarwal (1997) and Elizabeth Katz (1997).

3 The next step is to show the relation between the spoken and the unspoken: the importance of the 'female side' in allowing the 'male side' to exist. The 'other' is shown or argued to be required for the first to be possible. 'The presumption of fixed opposition conceals the hierarchical *interdependence* of these terms and the extent to which they depend on one another for their meanings' (Williams, 1992: 1–2, emphasis added). England (1990: 167) in discussing the rational/emotional opposition states: 'In reality, there is much more commingling of the realms of emotion and cognition. Indeed, the radical/cultural feminist position is that they are inconceivable and unfruitful without each other, so the conceptual separation is artificial'. Folbre and Hartmann trace the neoclassical self-interested agent from seventeenth century political theory (Locke, Hobbes) in which 'individualism inheres in the concept of man as proprietor of his own person or capacities, owing nothing to society for them' (1988: 186). This ignores activity outside of the individual, isolated man, 'the years of nurturance, provision, and protection that men...require' (187). Citing Adam Smith's comment regarding the lack of benevolence of the butcher, *et. al.* Folbre and Hartmann observe 'But Smith never pointed out that these purveyors do not in fact make dinner' (187).

Wood takes this observation in another direction, away from the female/male to the first/third world women, and the definition of 'production'. The system of accounts to which she refers 'include certain nonmonetary activities in the third world as economic because they are monetary activities in the first world' (1997: 62). The first world is the source of the definition for production in the 'other', the third world; the latter has no autonomous definition, but relies on the former for its provision.

4 This recognition of mutual dependence but partial silence, challenges the fundamental organization of the models under investigation: the categorization is shown to be based on 'false dichotomies' (England and Kilbourne, 1990: 167) and the supposed universality revealed to be based on one world view, here from a male perspective of a particular time and place. The self-interested individual is shown to be a very particular form of being. The privileging of the particular is articulated by analyzing the choices made, implicitly, in the construction of the model. 'Elaborating a theoretical argument, developing and testing a hypothesis, and interpreting empirical results require the researcher to make a number of choices...' 'tacit assumptions and silences' can be analyzed (Seiz, 1992: 289). In this vein, the primacy of the self-interested, rational actor is challenged.

> Feminist historians and philosophers have argued persuasively that modern Western concepts of 'rationality' and 'individuality' have been fashioned to conform with the particular emotional

needs and self-images of men (or more precisely, of men who are privileged by class and race as well as gender).... A feminist analysis would view this (economic man) as a seriously distorted portrayal of human actors because it neglects the imbeddedness of individuals (both female and male) in social relationships that shape both our actions and our wants.

(Seiz, 1992: 295)

Choice, too, is identified as an androcentric result:

One might argue that the options facing women are so limited, and so different from those faced by men, that to put the emphasis on 'choice' is extremely misleading.

(Seiz, 1992: 297)

As Folbre and Hartmann sum it up: 'The economic individualism so central to neoclassical economic theory could better be termed male individualism' (1988: 186). Jehlen puts this as follows:

As a critical term 'gender' invokes women only insofar as in its absence they are essentially invisible.... Uncovering the contingencies of gender at the heart of even the most apparently universal writing has been a way of challenging the view that men embody the transcendent human norm.

(1990: 265)

This leads to a recognition of the lack of an objective basis for the analysis, the presence of values not accounted for or admitted. Seiz devotes a long section presenting issues of objectivity, subjectivity and 'the *social* nature of scientific activity' which have been raised by feminist critics not of economics but of the enterprise of 'science'. The feminist argument

brings the traditional boundaries between self-interest and altruism into question and suggests that they may be as overdrawn as the traditional boundaries between science and humanism, facts and values, public and private, reason and emotion, male and female.

(1988: 197)

England and Kilbourne argue that 'the four assumptions of rational choice theories harmonize more readily with a separative rather than with a connected model of self, and that this imbalance distorts the theories' (1990: 157). The separative self is associated with the male, not the female, so rational choice theories are built around men, not people. 'Thus the assumption of the utterly subjective nature of utility is one more example of basing models on a socially constructed specific of male psychology, while claiming that they rest on a constant of human nature' (1990: 164).[10]

More concretely, Wood points to the arbitrary division between what counts as production and what doesn't count, the result of a false dichotomy between economic and noneconomic activity.

> Grinding corn or plucking chickens are market activities in the first world; in third world economies, this work would count as nonmarket economic activity...But cooking the food for the evening meal is something women in the first world generally do as part of their unpaid domestic labor. It would not, therefore, be considered an economic activity when performed by a woman in the third world....
>
> (1997: 63)

5   This leads to a discussion of power and authority both within the discipline and in the policy-making world which looks to economics for advice. How and why are these categories and hierarchies established and maintained? The origins of the andro-centric categories underlying contemporary neo-classical economics are traced to Descartes, Locke, and Hobbes by the authors cited above, in their turn drawing heavily on non-economic feminist critiques of modernism itself. (See for example Sandra Harding's work.) These categories and their hierarchical relationship are maintained by the rules of the interpretive community, and especially those with power in it. Thomas Kuhn in *The Structure of Scientific Revolutions* points out that paradigms are supported by more than intellectual consistency and promise. They are maintained by those with a vested interest (lots of human capital) in them through the control of journals, funding, graduate programs, and so on. As Folbre and Hartmann put it, 'Some arguments persuade more than others partly because they deliver greater benefits to those who decide the outcome of the debate' (1988: 185).

It is important to note that the support of an existing paradigm does not depend on self-conscious defensive self-interest among its practicioners. Rather, those within it see themselves, in Lakatosian terms, as participating in a scientific research program, attempting to extend and deepen the scope of the correct theory. Within the context of such research, economists for example, evaluate arguments based on the dominant rules – utility maximizing, 'rational' individual agents. Authors of 'good' models (those which follow the rules in interesting ways) are rewarded with publication, tenure, grants, and Nobel prizes.

Whether one views this as an intellectual 'survival of the fittest' or as success in the 'marketplace of ideas' the outcome is the same. Orthodox authors succeed, reproduce, and maintain their collective hold on power and authority within the discipline.

The feminist heterdox challenge is to construct an alternative paradigm which shows both promise and achievement, and in so doing wins both converts and resources. Certain 'hard-core' assumptions are in place in feminist economics to sustain such a research program. For example, a broader conception of decision-making relying on interdependent, not autonomous, agents; explicit redefinition of what is considered work or production, and (of course) explicit recognition and investigation of the role of gender in all areas. Some of the positive and negative heuristics remain unsettled, notably *methodological* issues. It is already clear that a more pluralistic approach to methodological practice is an attribute of feminist economics, that a formal mathematical model is *not* a necessary component of 'good' feminist economic work, that actually talking to individual consumers, producers, mothers, and unemployed persons rather than compiling and analyzing statistics about them is an acceptable, even beneficial, method of research. Yet beyond an easy pluralism, difficult methodological issues remain, for example, can a formal mathematical model be 'good' feminist economics? Under what conditions? Since feminist economists come from neoclassical, Marxist, and institutional perspectives themselves, one should not expect any early or easy resolution to methodological questions.

6   The question of standards is inevitably raised. If categories and hierarchies are successfully redefined, economic analysis would begin from a different – non-androcentric – point, with perhaps a different end, and apply different standards. Julie Nelson, in one of the seminal articles on feminist economics (1992) has suggested what these standards might be. Since economics would be done differently, it isn't a great leap to suggest that economic policy might look different as a result.

> No one should be surprised that economic discourse is a prime terrain for political struggle. The theoretical, empirical, and methodological questions being sparked in economics, as a result of political conflicts outside the discipline, present exciting challenges for all economists, and the consequences of these debates will be far-reaching.
>
> (Seiz, 1992: 301)

> If...a first-world/third party criterion operates to define economic activity for policy-makers, then it is not surprising that policy targeting women's nonmarket work in the third world tends to focus only on domestic labor which is performed in the market

in the first world.... This is especially true when such policy is promulgated by international agencies such as the World Bank which are explicitly directed to address only 'productive' or economic activities. While these activities are certainly worthy of attention and policies directed at them are likely to contribute to the improvement of women's well-being, such exclusive attention suggests that their inclusion is premised on the continued marginalization of other domestic activities such as child care and cooking from policy consideration.

(Wood, 1997: 64)

Recognizing that objectivity is not to be had, Seiz raises issues of evaluation. 'How can feminists acknowledge the value-ladenness of inquiry and the fallibility of knowledge without embracing relativism or seeming to assess claims principally by their consistency with the political goals of feminism, disregarding other criteria?' (Seiz, 1992: 283). Her suggested solution is that feminist economists should maintain the code of civil conversation, 'be open to criticism, to confrontation with evidence, and to persuasion' (1992: 284). This is the solution offered (though not to questions of feminism, *per se*) by McCloskey in *The Rhetoric of Economics*, and more generally by Rorty in *The Consequences of Pragmatism*. Seiz adds that ' insisting that all inquiry is guided by values, and making those values explicit, should facilitate (not hinder) inquiry and theory-assessment' (1992: 284).

The Inevitable Conclusion: the seeds of its own destruction

The recognition that 'all inquiry is guided by values' and cannot hope to be objective and universal gives feminist economics a difficult problem, one recognized by the authors themselves, and common to all postmodern work. 'So to posit a unitary woman's standpoint is to engage in the same sort of false universalization that feminists have deplored in androcentric discourse' (Seiz, 1992: 282).

Thus to articulate 'women's' self-understanding homogenizes the ways of being and knowing of !Kung gatherers, Japanese peasants of the Meiji restoration, working class Chicanas in electronics factories in the Maquiladoras zone, and professional Black lesbians in Washington, D.C..... Black feminists, for example, have reminded their white sisters that race, nationality, sexuality, etc. construct the meaning/experience of gender – there is no unifying 'woman'.

(Williams, 1992: 8)

Williams argues that the construction of a feminist economics must 'engage these complexities, or run the real and present danger of remaining woefully incomplete' (8). Wood recognizes this problem in her own work, that trying to create better definitions of unpaid domestic labor is inevitably problematic when one must 'treat subsistence and domestic labor as separate categories in third world contexts, even when they occur in the same household, are both unpaid, and are done by the same woman simultaneously' (65). The dichotomy between economic and non-economic production is not easy to circumvent, nor render universal.

But the lesson of postmodernism is that these theories – any theories – are bound to be incomplete in the sense that no theory can ever be truly universal. Economists, including feminist economists, stand in different places and are bound to see different things, and to see the 'same' thing differently. Two important implications follow. First, lacking a universal True standard against which to judge one's perspective allows many perspectives legitimacy, and precludes any *final* arbitration as to relative merit. This results in the desire and the need to emphasize civil conversation and methodological pluralism.

Second, and more importantly, a postmodern understanding *necessarily* entails an incomplete theory. One of the crucial insights of postmodern theory is that one can never be outside some context, a language-driven web of meaning and opposition and value. One is constructed by and inhabits a particular time, place, and world. One's perspective, one's self, may well change over time, but only change, not cease to exist. One can never step outside *some* context (at least while alive). So any model or analysis or argument is built upon a specific, particular, non-universal and hence incomplete context or perspective (unless, perhaps, One is God). To attempt to construct a complete theory simultaneously and consistently incorporating all perspectives is to revert to a modernist view of the world, where we try to obliterate perspective and agree on where to stand, from where to base this one, privileged perspective. Only then can we all have the same view, and set about building theories and models to represent this view completely. Theoretical incompleteness is an inevitable result of the postmodern understanding of the world. Feminist economics can (and has) become more *inclusive* of differing perspectives (e.g. recognizing the differences that race plays for women of colour, or differences between the first and third worlds) but it cannot include *all* perspectives. What would feminist economics be if, for example, it included the perspective that gender doesn't matter? The quest for completeness is doomed. The arguments over the importance of categories chosen, the importance of those left out, will go on: 'And those arguments will never be 'resolved' since methodological choice always values, whether those be political, aesthetic, or career-driven pragmatic ones' (Seiz, 1992: 300).

From a postmodern perspective the unresolvability of those arguments is inescapable. On one hand, this allows ever-ongoing discussion and debate; new, interesting and compelling arguments challenging us to see the world anew over and over and over yet again. We are forced to re-evaluate, to listen, to clarify our own thoughts. These are admirable qualities in intellectual debate, and postmodernism holds our feet to their fire, a good thing.

On the other hand, it also carries the seeds of its own particular destruction/deconstruction. Because 'choice always values', those with other values will make other choices and point out the omissions and specific hierarchies which underlay one's own theories, e.g. feminist economics. Those who deconstruct one theory leave themselves open to the same critique of claims of universality and perspectival bias. While some omissions can be rectified (e.g. the women of color issue) those omissions which stem from the hard-core beliefs of feminist economics cannot be incorporated without destroying feminist economics itself. As neoclassical or Marxist or institutional theories can be deconstructed, so can feminist ones. Since authors always have a perspective, the theory cannot evade perspective. Authors have to stand somewhere in the social/linguistic web. Some assumption, some category, becomes foundational. All that is required is beginning with a specific point of view which differs from the fundamental perspective of feminist economic work. From that perspective, one can point out the omissions and hierarchies implicit in feminist economics, where the theory glides over a crucial (from the critic's perspective) missing category, or implicitly assumes a universality where none exists. This would be easier for someone *outside* a feminist perspective to do, than for one inside it. I do not propose to present a fully worked-out example, but only to present a straw-person case to illustrate the general point. One potential argument might run as follows:

'A core claim of feminist economics is that gender matters. Men and women, in general and on average, are socially constructed in opposition to each other and inhabit different worlds and have different perspectives. Qualities associated with the male half have been valued and those of the female half undervalued. Feminist economics sets out to not only recognize, but incorporate, the existence of different genders explicitly into economic analysis. Feminist economics, then, relies at its core on these two opposing categories of male and female. It places these constructed genders at the center, albeit without the old hierarchical relationship between the two, and proceeds therefrom. Therefore, such an argument might run, it privileges dichotomized gender over other potential categories of analysis.'

'However, we know gender is not an "essential" component of individuals, but a socially constructed one. What assumptions lurk behind this particular construction of a gendered world in feminist economics? Perhaps one can show it is implicitly a heterosexual world view, wherein two genders are necessary, even foundational. Maybe this explains feminist economic's early concern with the gender implications of intra-household bargaining and decision-making – an implicit assumption that households consist of two genders. If the world view were a homosexual one, this particular topic would be of no interest. Rather, one would expect the topic to be conflict resolution *between* households of different genders, or perhaps just of different sexes. In a gay world, indeed, would there be a *need* for constructed gender? If so, one suspects the gender identities would be radically different from those in our hetero-world. Feminist economic's emphasis on gender masks its assumption of a univeral heterosexuality in which two opposing and complementary genders are socially necessary, and hence *seem* universal. This silences the gay world.'

This type of criticism cannot be incorporated into even a pluralistic feminist economics, for it sets out to eradicate gendered differences, a core claim of feminist economics. A gay economics would (in this hypothetical example) dismantle feminist categories by destroying the illusion of the need/universal existence of distinct gendered identity. (What it would erect instead is an intriguing question.) Adherents of feminist economics could not in turn claim the gay view is *wrong*, that a gendered identity *is* a universal state of being. Feminist economics would be revealed to be as perspectively biased, as particular as that which it is striving to replace, albeit particular along a different line.

Postmodernism and feminist economics

I have tried to show that feminist critiques of neo-classical and Marxian economics follow a postmodern path in many ways, self-consciously or not. Both lead us to question the categories and hierarchies on which theory and analysis is based. Both question the universality and objectivity implicitly claimed by economic theory. Both lead us to questions of standards and values, and policy implications. They call for a re-contextualisation of theory, to show that far from discussing universal experiences, the non-feminist models present particular gendered experiences, raising up the male side of science, rationality and the market. Adding gender as a category complicates the analysis, but enriches it, by asking new and interesting questions. In these ways, postmodernism in general is an ally of feminist economics, by providing a theory of knowledge and language to support the feminist criticisms of other extant economics.

Deconstruction in particular can add more to feminist economics than it has so far, by providing more specific criticisms of non-feminist economics' crucial texts. Some beginning work has been done here[11] but much more remains. The benefit would be to annihilate the claims of universality in specific important texts, to undermine their status, and so strengthen the general claims of postmodernism with specific examples. The gentle criticism of neoclassical and Marxist analysis that they are incomplete and that benefits can be had by extending the analysis through the recognition of the gendered basis of the theory can be rendered more potent by taking apart treasured texts. So far, feminist critiques by and large have not shown how the theories undermine themselves, just that they are based on the particular (male), not universal (person). Deconstructive readings would make that point. They would illustrate how the 'other' gender, the second and subordinate category, is already present, allowing the dominant one to function as it does. Thus it isn't a question of adding to the analysis, but of bringing into the open what it already is. This second category does not have to be *added* to the analysis, it's already there. Deconstructive readings would show explicitly how this 'other' is treated.

This recognition is implicit in many of the works referred to above. However, making this point more explicitly would strengthen the argument that overt attention to gender is necessary, as well as nice. If feminist economists show explicitly how the gendered analysis does not omit the second sex, but depends on them in a particular way, the cry for a 'more inclusive' economics would be changed to one for a more honest one: one which recognizes the implicit role assigned to women, households, connected selves. Thus it is not a plea for enrichment, but for an overt recognition, and evaluation, of what is there already. Bringing consideration of the hitherto subordinate and overlooked into the discussion is shown to be necessary, not magnanimous on the part of those involved in the dominant discourse. That is one insight of deconstruction that has not been used to full advantage, a benefit of postmodern thought of which feminist critics of economics should take advantage.

Deconstruction is, then, a tool or strategy which should not be overlooked in a feminist critique of other economic theories. It is a powerful destructive weapon. But it is double-edged, for it eradicates the claim that feminist economics is objectively better or truer than what it strives to replace. The charge of 'perspectival bias' will be as correct a charge against feminist economics as against its androcentric predecessors. Since feminist economics has to stand somewhere to begin, it must incorporate some perspective of its own. It has to have some foundational beliefs, which open the door to charges of false universality and the silencing of some 'other' group. In a postmodern world, theories are bound to be incomplete, particular, and mutable. The hard-core assumptions of, for example, gender, are not on *terra firma*, nor can they be. So an overt embracing of postmodern thought and deconstructive strategies of criticism carries a non-negligible cost.

Yet a postmodern world offers a way of thinking in which charges of subjectivity rather than objectivity are no longer necessarily fatal. Arguments have to be – and are – put forth concerning how feminist economics offers a better approach to problems of production, consumption, markets, and public policy, than non-feminist economics. There are no longer tacit assumptions and implicit standards. Since any perspective is known to be a reflection of values, it must be explicitly acknowledged. So we see feminists self-consciously redefining the scope of the discipline, debating the definition of 'economics' and 'economy' to bring into the discussion heretofore ignored[12] aspects of providing for one's self and one's household outside of the market. We hear clear methodological debate,[13] rather than a reflexive practice of some received view of it. Even more startlingly perhaps, we are encouraged in a multiplicity of fora, to explicitly acknowledge our own perspectives, positions, and desired outcomes rather than cloaking them in 'disinterested' language. As in other disciplines, so too in economics, has the postmodern view opened up debate into previously unexplored, and occasionally unforeseen, territory. Feminist economics is the best example of this to date in economics.

The debate about the meaning and use of rationality in economic models is a wonderful example of how other parts of the discussion might progress. As we look more closely at the meanings we as economists have attached to the word, and uncover their masculine bias, we are forced to notice how the meaning of 'rationality' depends on its relation to a host of other assumptions within the theory. We have no choice but to see that when those assumptions shift, the meanings of the word shift, and appropriately enough, overtly take on an more relational tone and content. Far from allowing us to sit back and destroy texts and meanings, a deconstructive/postmodern questioning of assumption and meaning impels us to *give* meanings to the words we use and the ideas we explore and create; it forces us to recognize that meanings cannot be apart from the world and our places in it. A postmodernist understanding of the world does not turn us into effete connoisseurs of arcane texts. It forces us back *into* the world. One of the greatest benefits to be gained from a postmodern feminist economics is that it will remind us, as economists, that there is something more at stake here than closed systems of words and logic that can be analyzed or understood apart from the world, both inside and outside of the academy, in which we live, and through which we construct our models and understandings of the economy.

Notes

1 See Nelson (1992), Seiz (1992), Folbre and Hartmann (1988), Williams (1992), Jennings and Waller (1990), Strassman (1994), Waring (1988), just as a beginning.
2 See Mirowski (1989).
3 See McCloskey (1985) or (1994).
4 Billig, (1997:7).
5 See Nelson's discussion of the lack of a feminine equivalent for 'emasculate'. Language allows us to have certain thoughts, but not others. If the gender of woman is constructed as powerless, words ascribing power to women will be lacking.
6 See Fish (1980), or Richard Rorty (1982) for a full development of this argument.
7 That standards are *already* upheld by communities should be self-evident to anyone who has ever refereed an article or reviewed a book.
8 See Foucault (1980) or Bourdieu (1991).
9 Here I focus primarily on the work of Folbre and Hartmann, Nelson, and Seiz (1992), as the clearest examples. Most, if not all, of the other works cited herein contain elements of the same analysis. I restrict the field for manageability. I make the argument below in logical time: it reconstructs parts of the arguments of the critics to mirror the order of the deconstructive argument I made above, in order to make the similarities more clear. Readers who desire a fuller introduction to feminist economics should consult M.A. Ferber and Julie A. Nelson (eds) (1993) or Edith Kuiper and Jolande Sap (eds) (1995) *Out of the Margin: Feminist Perspectives on Economics*, London: Routledge.
10 See Williams (1992) for an analysis of how the feminist criticisms are themselves guilty of false universalization along racial lines.
11 For example, in the history of economic thought, see Michele Pujol (1992).
12 by contemporary economic thought. Earlier writers, especially the 'old home economics' school addressed these issues and provide beginning points for the current debate. See, for example, Hirschfeld (1996) and the issue of *Feminist Economics* devoted to Margaret Reid.
13 Diana Strassman, editorial in *Feminist Economics*, 3:2, and the references cited therein.

References

Agarwal, B. (1997) '"Bargaining" and Gender Relations: Within and Beyond the Household', *Feminist Economics*, 3:1, 1–51.
Barrett, N.S. (1983)'How the Study of Women has Restructured the Discipline of Economics', in Elizabeth Langland and Walter Gove, (eds) *A Feminist Perspective in the Academy: The Difference It Makes*, Chicago: University of Chicago Press.
Billig, M.S. (1997) *The Demise of Grand Theory*, unpublished manuscript.
Blank, R. M. (1992) 'A Female Perspective on Economic Man?' in Sue Rosenberg Zalk and Janice Gordon-Kelter, (eds) *Revolutions in Knowledge: Feminism in the Social Sciences*, Boulder, CO: Westview Press.
Blau, F. D. and Ferber, M. (1986)*The Economics of Women, Men and Work*, Englewood Cliffs, NJ: Prentice-Hall.
Bourdieu, P. (1991) *Language and Symbolic Power*, Cambridge: Harvard University Press.

Derrida, J. (1982) 'Difference' trans. Alan Bass, in *Margins of Philosophy*, Chicago: University of Chicago Press: 1–27.

Eagleton, T. (1983) *Literary Theory: An Introduction*, Minneapolis: University of Minnesota Press.

England, P. (1990) 'Feminist Critiques of the Separative Model of Self: Implications for Rational Choice Theory', *Rationality and Society*, 2 (2): 156–71.

England, P. and Kilbourne (1990) 'Markets, Marriages and Other Matters: The Problem of Power' in Roger Friedland and A. F. Robertson, (eds) *Beyond the Marketplace: Rethinking Economy and Society*, New York: Aldine de Gruyter, pp. 163–88.

Feiner, S.F. and Morgan, B. A. (1987) 'Women and Minorities in Introductory Economics Textbooks: 1974–1984', *Journal of Economic Education*, 18 (Fall) 376–92.

Feminist Economics (1996) Special issue devoted to Margaret Reid, 2(3) Fall.

Ferber, M.A. (1990) 'Gender and the Study of Economics', in Phillip Saunders and William Walstead (eds) *The Principles of Economics Course: A Handbook for Instructors*, New York: McGraw-Hill.

Ferber, M.A. and Julie Nelson, (eds) (1993) *Beyond Economic Man: Feminist Theory and Economics*, Chicago: University of Chicagor Press.

Ferber, M.A., and Teiman, M.L. (1981) 'The Oldest, the Most Established, the Most Quantitative of the Social Sciences – and the Most Dominated by Men: The Impact of Feminism on Economics', in Dale Spender, (ed.) *Men's Studies Modified: The Impact of Feminism on the Academic Disciplines*, New York: Pergamon Press.

Fish, S. (1980) *Is There a Text in this Class?* Cambridge, MA: Harvard University Press.

Folbre, N. and Hartmann, H. (1988) 'The Rhetoric of Self Interest and the Ideology of Gender', in Arjo Klamer, Donald N. McCloskey, and Robert M. Solow (eds) *The Consequences of Economic Rhetoric*, New York: Cambridge University Press.

Foucault, Michel (1980) *Power/Knowledge: Selected Interviews and Other Writings*, New York: Pantheon Books.

Hirschfeld, M. (1996) 'The "Old" Home Economics', unpublished manuscript.

Jehlen, M. (1990) 'Gender' in Frank Lentricchia and Thomas McLaughlin (eds) *Critical Terms for Literary Study*, Chicago: The University of Chicago Press.

Jennings, A. and Waller, W. (1990) 'Constructions of Social Hierarchy: The Family, Gender, and Power', *Journal of Economic Issues*, 24 (2) 623–32.

Katz, E. (1997) 'The Intra-Household Economics of Voice and Exit'. *Feminist Economics*, 3, 3, 25–46.

Keynes, J.M. (1964) *The General Theory*, New York: Harcourt Brace Jovanovich.

McCloskey, D. (1985) *The Rhetoric of Economics*, Madison Wisconsin: University of Wisconsin Press.

—— (1994) *Knowledge and Persuasion in Economics*, New York: Cambridge University Press.

Meagher, G. (1997) 'Recreating "Domestic Service": Institutional Cultures and the Evolution of Paid Housework', *Feminist Economics*, 3:2, 1–28.

Menger, C. (1981) *Principles of Economics*, trans. J. Dingwall and B. Hoselitz, New York: New York University Press,

Mirowski, P. (1989) *More Heat than Light*, New York: Cambridge University Press.
Nelson, J. (1992) 'Gender, Metaphor and the Definition of Economics', *Economics and Philosophy*, 8 (1) 103–125.
Peterson, J. (1990) 'The Challenge of Comparable Worth: An Institutionalist View', *Journal of Economic Issues*, 24 (2) 606–12.
Pujol, Michele A. (1992) *Feminism and Anti-Feminism in Early Economic Thought*, Hants: Edward Elgar.
Rorty, Richard (1982) *The Consequences of Pragmatism: Essays 1972–1980*, Minneapolis: University of Minnesota Press.
Rossetti, J. (1990) 'Deconstructing Robert Lucas' in Warren Samuels, (ed.) *Economics as Discourse*, Boston: Kluwer Academic Publishers.
Schabas, M. (1990) *A World Ruled by Number*, Princeton, NJ: Princeton University Press.
Sarup, M. (1988) *Post-Structuralism and Postmodernism*, 2nd edn, Athens: University of Georgia Press.
Seiz, J.A. (1991) 'The Bargaining Approach and Feminist Methodology', *Review of Radical Political Economy*, 23 (Spring/Summer): 22–9.
—— (1992) 'Gender and Economic Research', in Neil de Marchi, (ed.) *Post-Popperian Methodology of Economics: Recovering Practice*, Boston: Kluwer Academic.
Strassman, D. (1991) 'Feminism and Economic Knowledge' unpublished manuscript.
—— (1994) 'Feminist thought and Economics: Or, What Do the Visigoths Know?' *American Economic Review*, 84(2) May: 153–8.
Waller, W. and Jennings, A (1990) 'On the Possibility of a Feminist Economics: The Convergence of Institutional and Feminist Methodology', *Journal of Economic Issues*, 24(2): 613–22.
Waring, M. (1988) *If Women Counted: A New Feminist Economics*, San Francisco: Harper and Row.
Williams, R.M. (1993) 'Race, Deconstruction, and the Emergent Agenda of Feminist Economic Theory', in Marianne Ferber and Julie Nelson (eds) *Beyond Economic Man: Feminist Theory and Economics*, Chicago: Chicago University Press, pp. 144–53.
Wood, Cynthia A. (1997) 'The First World/Third Party Criterion: A Feminist Crique of Production Boundaries in Economics', *Feminist Economics*, 3:3, (Fall).
Zalk, S. R. and Gordon-Kelter, J. (1992) 'Feminism, Revolution, and Knowledge', in Sue Rosenberg Zalk and Janic Gordon-Kelter, (eds) *Revolutions in Knowledge: Feminism in the Social Sciences*, Boulder, CO: Westview Press.

15

NO MORE NICE GIRLS?

Feminism, economics, and postmodern encounters

Suzanne Bergeron

The question of postmodern feminist economics is, to paraphrase Judith Butler (1992), surely a question. Is there, after all, something we could call by that name? Does it refer to a particular theoretical position, a form of politics, or a set of stylistic conventions? Is this a label that an economist takes on for herself, or is it more often a name that she is called when she engages in a critique of the rational economic subject, a challenge to traditional epistemology, or a discursive analysis of economic literature?

There have been a multiplicity of perspectives on the relationship between postmodern ideas and feminist economics, which is not surprising given that postmodernism, feminism, and economics are each highly contested terms. Categorizing along conventional theoretical feminist lines, while problematic, introduces some of these different responses. Liberal feminists, who are concerned with integrating women into existing theories and institutions, have largely dismissed postmodernism as at best irrelevant to the 'real' work of feminist economics, and, at worst, distracting 'postmodern academic trash' (Bergmann 1997). While some feminist economists working in the Marxian tradition find compatibility with postmodern ideas in the working out of their analyses (e.g. Biewener 1999), others have expressed concern with the postmodern critique of grand theories (such as patriarchy and capitalism), arguing that it may deny the possibility of creating economic knowledge that can contribute to a politics of resistance. Those drawing on a radical/cultural feminist perspective that values 'female' characteristics of nurturing and connectedness over 'male' characteristics have, in some cases, contributed to a process of deconstructing the masculine biases of economic theory that shares some common ground with postmodern feminist economic analyses. Recent investigations of the gendered and socially constructed nature of economic discourse have, for instance, emphasized the importance of revaluing those economic knowledges and practices dismissed as 'feminine'. But postmodern feminism, with its focus on the plural, ever-changing definitions of gender difference, is often at odds with theories (such as radical feminism) that are based on fixed meanings of gender, so there are tensions here as well.

While some feminist economists are hesitant to embrace postmodernism, others find strong affinities between feminist economics and postmodern theory. Feminists employing postmodern critiques of knowledge and science, for example, have produced a body of literature that has exposed the gendered, hierarchical dualisms that inform mainstream economic analysis, as well as some of the effects of such gendered ways of thinking. This has cleared the space to begin to construct new theoretical perspectives and methodologies based on alternative notions of subjectivity and knowledge. That such approaches have gained currency in the field within the past decade is evidenced in the frequency of references to the edited collection *Beyond Economic Man* (Ferber and Nelson, 1993), the appearance of a growing number of articles in the journal *Feminist Economics* that exemplify postmodern thinking, and the frequent debates and discussions about postmodernism on the feminist economics listserv, femecon-l.

The essays by Ulla Grapard, Julie Nelson and Jane Rosetti in this volume each take up the postmodern project and its relationship to feminist economics in different ways, responding to and producing different sets of questions, reactions and readings. Jane Rosetti's deconstructive approach focuses on the gendered languages and meanings produced in the texts of economics, showing the ways that binary notions of masculine and feminine condition the methods, theories, and values of the profession. Here, postmodernism is presented as a set of ideas and tools that support and extend feminist work that is already being done. Feminist critics of neoclassical and Marxian economics, for instance, have long argued that what is presented as objective and universally applicable is in fact valid only for white, middle-class, North Atlantic men. They have also criticized the profession's cherished ideals, such as detachment, rationality and logic, as reflective of specifically masculine values. As postmodernism leads us to ask similar questions about the categories, values and standards on which modern sciences are based, it is, Rosetti argues, a natural ally of feminist economics.

Are we all postmodernists now? Rosetti may agree with feminist theorists such as Jane Flax (1990) who contend that feminism is on postmodern terrain, but given the continuing skepticism toward postmodern ideas in some feminist quarters, plus the special tensions feminist economists face working in a discipline dominated by modernist ideas of science and knowledge, it is not such an easy sell. For those who may still harbor a lingering attraction for Enlightenment ideals of rationality and objectivity, however, Rosetti makes the case that all inquiry is guided by values, and thus objectivity in the sense of 'mirroring nature' is not possible, anyway. All theories are incomplete, partial, and value-laden. A 'good' feminist analysis would thus not pretend to be value-free, but rather would state its values up front. It would also be willing to evaluate and rethink knowledge claims by being open to criticism, alternative viewpoints, and new evidence, in civil conversation with others. Arguing against those who have claimed that embracing postmodernism will derail feminist attempts at social change, Rosetti points out that the deconstructive approach does not mean 'discourse is all there is'. Instead, she contends, deconstruction allows for an analysis of the ways that economic meanings function as strategic instruments and effects of power in the world, opening up the space in feminist economics for new forms of critical engagement and action.

Julie Nelson's contribution, while it gets there by a different route, comes to similar conclusions. Nelson states that postmodernism brings feminist economics some good things, such as the ability to expose and deconstruct the gendered hierarchical dualisms that inform mainstream theory. And, like Rosetti, Nelson emphasizes the value ladenness of economic theory production, as well as the related idea that knowledge is produced and evaluated not by 'mirroring nature', but by a discourse community engaged in conversation and debate. But while Rosetti's postmodernism is drawn from literary currents, and the work of authors such as Jacques Derrida, Stanley Fish, and Deirdre McCloskey, Nelson's owes more to feminist critics of modern science such as Sandra Harding, Evelyn Fox Keller, and Susan Bordo. As many of these authors' own relationships to postmodernism are mixed or ambivalent, it is not surprising that Nelson is, too. A critical formulation of postmodern 'excesses' provides the backdrop here: if reality is just a text, if real bodies no longer exist, and if one may no longer speak of 'women' as a meaningful category, then there is no knowledge, no politics, and all we have is endless discursive play. It is against this imminent nihilism that Nelson attempts to recast the problems of authority and identity in feminist economics in ways that provide the comfort of objectivity (and thus grounds for understanding and solving real-world problems) without the rigidity of modernist disciplinary practices. Thus a feminist economics that is objective, activist, *and* postmodern.

The proliferation of postmodern approaches encompasses various contradictory tendencies, including some that might foster a flight from knowledge and politics in the ways that Nelson imagines. But is politically disabling relativism the only alternative to objectivity? Is questioning the Western Enlightenment notion of the centered subject the same thing as undermining any possibility for knowledge and agency? Does problematizing the category of women deny the possibility for feminist politics? While there are moments when Nelson's project interrogates this ground, at other points it retains key features of modern economics that it is seeking to deconstruct.

Nelson's attempt to authorize feminist economics with a privileged status of 'better science', for example, relies on a discourse of hierarchical distinctions and standards of judgment and normalcy that veers dangerously close to the all too familiar epistemological and disciplinary strategies of modern economics. Mainstream economics is characterized as having androcentric biases toward what is hard, logical, precise, detached, making it 'rigid' and 'out of touch with reality'. In contrast, feminist economics is portrayed as more balanced, combining mainstream 'masculine' methods, such as mathematical models and proofs, with such 'feminine' and devalued, connected forms of research as surveys, case studies, and ethnography. Here, following thinkers like Harding (1990), Nelson is utilizing feminist inquiry in an aim to produce a less perverse, or partial, economic knowledge, a perfectly reasonable goal from the perspective of feminist standpoint theory. However, here some of the language seems to assert (*contra* Harding's, and many others, view of the standpoint approach) that what this new feminist economics constitutes is a complete, general, methodologically adequate theory, one that could root out the 'underlying causes' of the economic problems under investigation, thus avoiding 'shallow and ultimately unsuccessful remedies, ' while focusing on the real 'applied problems' of the day to avoid 'spinning off into theoretical irrelevancies' (pp. 297). As Jane Rosetti notes in her contribution to this volume, such attempts at constructing a unified theory by marrying different perspectives and methodologies (in this case, taking the best from the masculine and feminine ones) reverts to a modernist view of the world, one that tries to obliterate perspective and agree on what constitutes 'good' economics. This is not simply a semantic issue, but one that has to do with power, and silencing. What is authorized and what is excluded in such attempts to judge as 'theoretically irrelevant' alternative perspectives and methodologies that lie outside the balanced union of rationalism and empiricism prescribed here, including some (if not most) of the essays contained in this volume? If this is the entry fee for the privilege of competing with mainstream, modernist economic theories for the authority to produce knowledge, one should figure in such costs.

Alongside such authoritatively prescriptive and normative moments, however, Nelson's feminist epistemological analysis simultaneously unhinges their possibility. Showing that the androcentric biases of modern economics are a foundational rather than a subordinate feature of its scientific procedures not only acknowledges the intimate gender dimensions of economic inquiry, it disrupts the privilege of modern economics by interrogating the knowledge claims and political stakes of all claims to authority. This recognition problematizes the idea that feminists could reach a general consensus as to the critical limits on what constitutes an adequate feminist economic theory, or for that matter, an adequate feminist activist politics. Feminist economics, then, would be better characterized as a diverse range of epistemological, theoretical, and emancipatory commitments coming into contact with each other through discussion, debate, struggle, agreement, and strategic alliances (a characterization of knowledge and action that Nelson alludes to, but does not emphasize, in the essay). It is within the context of such struggles and alliances that feminist economics creates its knowledges and practices. Julie Nelson's contributions (both here and elsewhere) offer a provocative invitation for feminist economists to rethink, and even, as she puts it, refeel these processes and our commitments.

The essay by Ulla Grapard offers another way of rethinking. Grapard utilizes Foucault's theories of power, knowledge and disciplinarity to provide a fascinating account of the exclusion of Charlotte Perkins Gilman's *Women and Economics* from the disciplinary canon. The analysis focuses on Gilman's discursive strategy through a close reading of the text, and locates a paradox, one common to many Enlightenment feminist works, at its heart. Gilman employs the evolutionary theories and languages that characterized the cutting-edge social science methods of the day to argue for the equality of women and men, while at the same time offering a history of gender relations that emphasizes the difference between the sexes. The paradox is that in advocating for 'women', Gilman's *Women and Economics* produces the very idea of sexual difference that it aims to eliminate. Further, while Gilman's proposals for social change, such as her advocacy of economic independence and paid employment for women, logically flowed from the same theories as those of her scholarly contemporaries in economics, they were ignored and dismissed, likely due to their feminist content. *Women and Economics* was highly regarded and widely read in other circles, but was overlooked by professional economists. Grapard's analysis suggests that even when feminists produce socially relevant work that conforms to the standard methodological and theoretical conventions of economic knowledge, their contributions can be dismissed as irrelevant and pushed to the boundaries of the discipline.

Grapard's discussion of the exclusion of Gilman's work from the canon troubles economics. It challenges the scientific claim that mainstream economics is the result of a free exchange in the marketplace of ideas. What counts as economic 'science' is instead shown to be inscribed in a system of power, through a set of disciplinary languages and practices that create knowledge and establish authority. Because Gilman was a woman, because she was not university trained, and especially because she challenged accepted gender roles, her work was regarded as irrelevant and placed outside the discipline of economics. As Grapard points out, there is an emerging literature aimed at recovering the work of feminist thinkers like Gilman who have been neglected by mainstream economists. Under the auspices of such a research program, it might be interesting also to document the influence of feminist economists such as Gilman on such 'alternative' economic knowledges as those produced within departments of home economics, state welfare agencies, and/or feminist activist organizations, which would provide a potentially useful narrative of economic knowledge production that could be compared and contrasted to the one undertaken here.

The analysis provided in Grapard's essay does not only challenge mainstream androcentric economics, however. It troubles feminist economics, too. As she suggests in her conclusion, the story of Gilman's reception in economics provides a lesson to which feminist economists should pay heed. Gilman put forth her argument in a form that one would expect to convince an educated, scholarly audience. She framed her arguments in the scientific discourse of the time. Yet her work was still dismissed by the academic economic community due to its feminist content. Today, many feminist economists are adopting conventional methodologies and discourses in their aim to establish themselves in the profession, and get feminist ideas a 'fair' hearing. But despite what one is told in graduate school, adopting a conformist methodology or research agenda is no guarantee for inclusion. Perhaps an alternative strategy would be one in which feminist economics stakes its claims in a more bold, confrontational manner. In the debates about what feminist economics is, and what is could be, the postmodern analyses found in the three essays by Rosetti, Nelson and Grapard discussed here help us to imagine what that might look like. By looking at the details of how the mainstream has kept us out, and suggesting new ways of thinking about knowledge, the economy, and politics, these essays help contribute to a feminist economics that is as disruptive as possible toward disciplinary conventions.

References

Bergmann, Barbara R. (1997) Posting on FEMECON-L listserver, August 13.
Biewener, Carole (1998) 'A Postmodern Encounter: Poststructuralist Feminism and the Decentering of Marxism', *Socialist Review* 27(1): 71–96.
Butler, Judith (1992) 'Contingent Foundations: Feminism and the Question of "Postmodernism"', in Judith Butler and Joan Scott, (eds) *Feminists Theorize the Political*, New York: Routledge, p. 3.
Ferber, Marianne and Julie Nelson, (eds) (1993) *Beyond Economic Man: Feminist Theory and Economics*, Chicago: University of Chicago Press.
Flax, Jane (1990) *Thinking Fragments: Psychoanalysis, Feminism, and Postmodernism in the Contemporary West*, Berkeley: University of California Press.

Harding, Sandra (1990) 'Feminism, Science, and Anti-Enlightenment Critiques', in *Feminism/Postmodernism* (ed.) Linda Nicholson, New York: Routledge, pp. 83–106.

PART VI

POSTMODERNISM, ECONOMIC RATIONALITY AND THE PROBLEM OF 'REPRESENTATION'

16
FROM MYTH TO METAPHOR
A semiological analysis of the Cambridge capital controversy

Stephen Cullenberg and Indraneel Dasgupta

Of all the major debates in the history of economic theory, probably the one most perplexing to a contemporary observer is the Cambridge capital controversy. While the debate raised passions on both sides to levels seldom witnessed in 'academic' discussions, at the end of it all one was left with the somewhat curious spectacle of both armies clutching their respective flags and claiming victory. Given the obviously unsettled nature of the debate, a natural question has been – why was there no decision? Why is it that issues perceived as 'scientific' by participants on both sides alike were left unresolved? Why couldn't the formal protocols of mathematics, logic and economic theory bring closure to this debate?

In recent years some attempts have been made to answer this question by analyzing the methodological underpinnings of the alternative positions in the debate. Adopting a Kuhnian framework, Sheila Dow (1980) has argued that the Cambridge (UK) Revolution did not succeed and instead remains the unresolved Cambridge Controversies because of a failure by post-Keynesian critics to launch an alternative paradigm defined in terms of models and tools quite distinct from those of the then ruling neoclassical paradigm. Thus, the Cambridge (UK) critique of orthodox economic theory failed to become an actual, but has rather remained a potential, 'scientific revolution' (in the Kuhnian sense) because the critics allowed their arguments to be translated into the formal framework specific to the neoclassical paradigm. Avi Cohen (1984) similarly argues that different conceptions of what constitutes an 'explanation' account for the lack of resolution of the Cambridge controversies. More specifically, while the post Keynesian methodology emphasizes causal mechanisms, the focus of neoclassical theory is on its predictive aspects. This fundamental difference is reflected in different conclusions about the implications of the UK critique for the neoclassical framework.

An entirely different approach has been suggested by Deirdre

McCloskey (1983, 1994). McCloskey makes the point that the controversy was essentially an argument about metaphors, and therefore amenable to literary analysis.

> The very violence of the combat suggests that it was about something beyond mathematics or facts. The combatants hurled mathematical reasoning and institutional facts at each other, but the important questions were those one would ask of a metaphor – is it illuminating, is it satisfying, is it apt? How do you know? How does it compare with other economic poetry? After some tactical retreats by Cambridge, Massachusetts, on points of ultimate metaphysics irrelevant to these important questions, mutual exhaustion set in, without decision. The reason there was no decision was that the important questions were literary, not mathematical or statistical.
>
> (1994: 428)

The distinction that McCloskey makes in her idea of rhetorical tetrad between 'fact' and 'logic' on the one hand and 'metaphor' and 'story' on the other, with the implicit assumption that tools of literary criticism can be profitably applied to the latter but not the former, gets problematic however once one recognizes that facts have to be stated, and logic expressed, within a matrix of meanings, i.e., within a language. Such an admission in turn legitimizes a study of the debate purely and entirely in terms of its language, i.e. a study of the debate as a series of overlapping texts distinguished by their strategies of meaning creation and persuasion.

This essay attempts such a (re)reading of the Cambridge debate. We develop McCloskey's theme further to argue that the debate was not simply about *metaphors* but also fundamentally about *myths*, and that this distinction is critical in analyzing the debate as a contestation over meanings, i.e. over alternative *significations*. Using tools developed first by Ferdinand de Saussure, and later by Roland Barthes and Stuart Hall, we reinterpret the debate in terms of alternative semiotic strategies.[1] Our primary interest lies in analyzing the ways in which a critique perceived as radically subversive by its champions is absorbed and integrated into a dominant meaning system. In other words, our focus is on strategies of *containment* of semiotic dissonance, i.e., on the *mode of disappearance* of the critique.[2] We attempt to do this by a selected textual analysis of some of the final comments and evaluations of the debate by four protagonists on the neoclassical side of the controversy: Samuelson (1975), Solow (1975), Stiglitz (1974) and Blaug (1975).

The main body of the paper consists of five sections. We start with a brief survey of the major issues raised in the debate, focusing largely on the 'technical' questions. In the subsequent section, we attempt a textual analysis of different responses on the neoclassical side to their critics' evaluation of the neoclassical research program in light of the issues raised in the earlier, 'technical' part of the controversy. In the third section, we develop the concepts and analytical categories that would allow us to specify the semiological processes at work in the debate. In particular, we develop the distinction between *myth* and the *metaphor*, identify the metaphorical elements in the debate and situate the interpretative divergence between the two sides within a context of *myth formation*. The fourth section identifies some rhetorical structures utilized in the neoclassical (re)interpretations of Cambridge (UK) criticisms as *significatory moves*. The last section situates alternative readings of mainstream economic discourse within different structures of reception and reproduction (decoding and encoding) of significations, i.e., within alternative semiological logics.

So, what was the Cambridge capital controversy about? A potted history

The theory of capital has played a central role in the history of economics beginning at least with Adam Smith, David Ricardo and Karl Marx. For Smith, Ricardo and Marx, capital played a central role in the distribution, accumulation and growth processes of a capitalist economy. Although each theorized capital differently, capital was seen as a part of the social relations of production and historical process of capitalist development. Workers and capitalists played distinct and asymmetric social roles in their theories, where capital hires labor but labor does not hire capital. Relative shares of wages and profits were a matter of the historical conditions of social and class struggle and not technologically determined. Power, ideology and persuasion were all important elements of the bargaining between labor and capital.

Beginning most clearly with J.B. Clark, the neoclassical approach to capital and distribution adopted what was known as the marginal productivity theory of income distribution. The marginal productivity theory of income distribution argued that in equilibrium the marginal product of all factors of production (including labor and capital) would be equal to the real value of their factor prices. Thus, in equilibrium the marginal product of labor would equal the real wage and the marginal product of capital would equal the real rate of the price of capital (alternatively referred to as the interest or profit rate). Some have inferred from this equilibrium result that factor prices are determined by their respective marginal productivities. Others have insisted that factor prices are better understood as a measure of marginal productivity. One inference that has often been made from this result is that factors of production receive the payments (whether wages or profits) each 'deserves' because each receives a factor payment equal to its contribution (marginal productivity) to the overall value of production. This is of course a problematic ethical inference and requires much more philosophical argument linking the idea of contribution to what one deserves than is often articulated, and certainly most economists today would not make such a straightforward connection between a claim of an equilibrium result and a claim of justice. Nevertheless, as Samuelson has put it, the capital and distribution theory based on this approach has served well the 'apologist for capital and for thrift' (1966: 577). And, certainly, the loose theory of justice implied by marginal productivity theory lurks as part of the folklore of economics even today.

These two alternative visions of capitalism and the role that capital, accumulation and distribution played in the growth process became the underlying issue of the Cambridge capital controversy, even though as we show below, the debate quickly became bogged down in technical issues of logic and economic theory. Joan Robinson in her 1953–54 article 'The Production Function and the Theory of Capital' began the Cambridge debate by questioning the equilibrium approach used by neoclassical economists when they considered the change over time and growth of an economy. She was critical of an approach to capital and accumulation that was not grounded in real, historical time and the actual social institutions of an economy. Robinson also offered a logical critique of the neoclassical aggregate Clarkian version of the production function, what she called the pseudo production function that underlay the neoclassical equilibrium vision of growth. She pointed out that in order to equate the marginal product of capital to the profit rate, as neoclassical theory requires in equilibrium, one needs to have a prior measure of the marginal product of capital. To know the marginal product of capital, however, one must have a measure of the magnitude of capital. But in order to know the magnitude of capital one must know the rate of profit in order to aggregate the heterogeneous bundle of capital goods used in production. Yet, to know the rate of profit requires that one know the marginal product of capital. As she put it 'The analysis showed that there is no meaning to be given to a 'quantity of capital' apart from the rate of profit, so that the contention that the 'marginal product of capital' determines the rate of profit is meaningless' (1970: 309). Thus, according to Robinson, the idea of an aggregate production function falters on the circular logic underlying the aggregate theory of capital, and so too does the neoclassical theory of growth, accumulation and distribution collapse.

In her analysis of the pseudo production function Robinson discovered that some techniques of production which 'become eligible at a higher rate of profit (with a correspondingly lower real wage rate) may be less labour-intensive (that is, may have a higher output per man employed) than that chosen at a higher wage rate, contrary to the rule of a "well-behaved" production function' in which a lower wage rate is always associated with a more labour-intensive technique' (1970: 309). Robinson called this the Ruth Cohen Curiosum. Piero Sraffa found separately later in his *Production of Commodities by Means of Commodities* (1960) that it was perfectly possible that the same technique of production would become eligible at several different rates of profit. It was from this insight that the intense debate over 'reswitching' and 'capital-reversing' took place several years later, roughly from 1965–7. Reswitching refers to the possibility that the same technique of production might be the most profitable one at several different rates of profit, even though another technique of production would be the most profitable one in between. Capital-reversal refers to the possibility that there is a positive relationship between the capital–labor ratio and the rate of profit when the switch from one technique to another is considered.[3] See Figure 16.1 for a graphic depiction of reswitching and capital reversal. The upper quadrant of Figure 16.1 depicts two techniques of production, a and b, in what is often called the factor–price space by neoclassical economists or alternatively, the wage–profit frontier by the Cambridge (UK) economists, a difference in appellation which is telling. Technique b is the one chosen when wage rates and the capital labor ratio are high, then at wage rate w_{ab} technique a is chosen at a lower capital labor ratio. Between r_{ab} and r_{ba} the capital labor ratio rises as does r. And, finally, after the wage rate falls to w_{ba} technique b is chosen again at a higher capital labor ratio. Thus we have both the reswitching of techniques of production, namely one technique, b, is chosen at both high and low wage rates while the other, a, is chosen at wages rates that fall in between, and capital reversal where the capital labor ratio rises as the wage rate falls.

The possibility of reswitching and capital-reversal violates several of the fundamental 'parables' of the neoclassical theory of capital and income distribution. Four of the most important parables are: (1) there is an inverse relationship between the rate of profit and the capital labor ratio, (2) there is an inverse relationship between steady state consumption per person and the rate of profit, (3) there is an inverse relationship between the rate of profit and the capital-output ratio, and (4) in competitive conditions the distribution of income between workers and capital can be determined by equating the marginal products of labor and capital to the wage and profit rates respectively.[4] These four parables can be shown to follow from a well-behaved production function, such as the Cobb–Douglas production function, given competitive conditions, and assuming a one good world with malleable or 'jelly' capital and output. The presumption held by many economists was that these parables

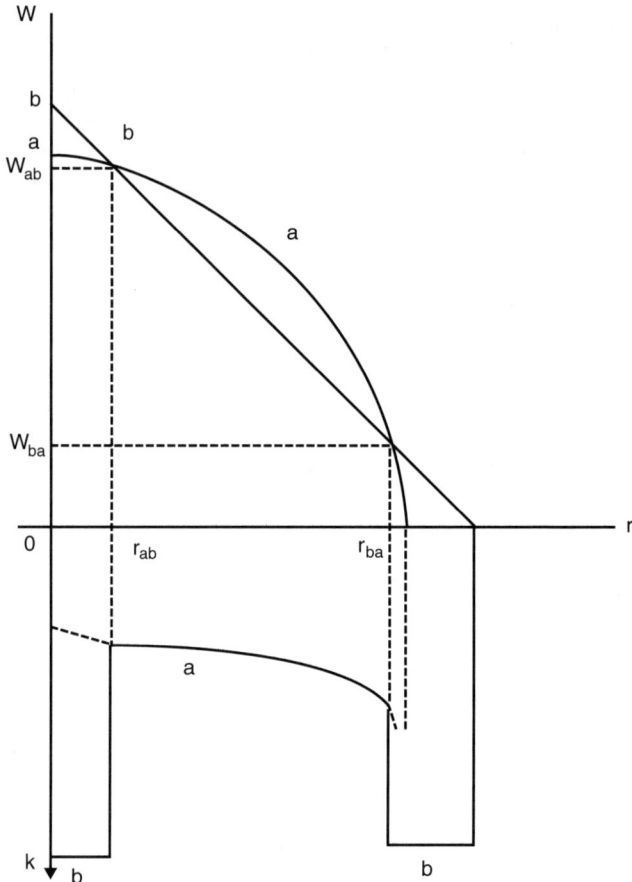

Figure 16.1 Reswitching and capital reversal

would also hold true in a world of heterogeneous capital and output. Robinson and Sraffa showed that in general this was not true.

The importance of these parables was that they provided a useful framework for the analysis of capital accumulation, growth and technical progress as Solow had done. Some argued that the aggregate version of the production function was no longer relevant as the general equilibrium approach of Arrow and Debreu had superceded it as the most sophisticated version of neoclassical theory. Nevertheless, the aggregate production function version was important because it provided the basis for empirical and econometric analyses of growth and distribution. Samuelson (1962) proposed the idea of a surrogate production function as a possible way to maintain the neoclassical parables of the jelly world in the face of heterogeneous capital. Samuelson's surrogate production function was built in essence around labor value prices. He assumed that the capital-labor ratio was uniform across techniques of production thus making the value of capital independent from the rate of profit. This, along with a few other technical assumptions, made the surrogate production function look just like a well-behaved production function that obeys the neoclassical parables. But as Garegnani quickly pointed out the surrogate production function was a special case and could not be readily generalized as Samuelson later admitted (1966).

The participants in Cambridge controversy continued debating these and other issues but the theoretical ground had been laid. Cambridge (UK) had successfully challenged some of the fundamental propositions theoretical of the aggregate version of the neoclassical production function and capital defended by Cambridge (MA). Yet, perhaps not unsurprisingly, neoclassical theorists seemed nonplussed by the Cambridge (UK) critique as they increasingly couched their theories in the micro framework of general equilibrium theory thought to be immune from the viruses of the aggregate production function. How and why this happened depended, as we suggest in the rest of this chapter, on the manner in which various semiological strategies of myth building and containment were constructed by the Cambridge (MA) school and their fellow travelers.

So, what does it all mean?

Trying to explain what the debate was all about, Harcourt insisted that 'There are fundamental issues at stake...divergent views concerning the nature of economic analysis and its relationship to the existing stages, classes and institutions of society are still central to the controversies' (1972: 244–5). Further, the Cambridge controversy raised the question whether profits are justified, and not simply how profits are determined (1972: 196). Even more fundamentally, 'it is the general methodology of neoclassical analysis, rather than any particular result, which is basically under attack' (1974: 398).

On the other side of the theoretical divide, we find a complete disavowal of the possibility of any such radical implication, even with regard to the analysis of distributional issues. Thus, for example, Stiglitz claims that 'the appropriateness of the marginal productivity theory as a theory of distribution of income among factors is completely unrelated to any of the controversies concerning double-switching, savings behavior, or the aggregation of capital' (1974: 302). In the same vein, after citing a litany of ills afflicting neoclassical analysis, Solow concludes that 'these are important limitations and deficiencies of neoclassical analysis in the general field we are talking about.…But the interesting thing about this list of shortcomings is that none of them has anything to do with reswitching' (1975: 51). Samuelson further argues that 'one who believes that class power can wrest great gains in absolute and relative income shares within a market system need not reject neoclassical constructs involving smooth marginal productivities and simple capital aggregates' (1975: 46).

As these quotes amply demonstrate, the various forms of the 'technical' questions in the capital controversy connote (signify) startlingly different meanings. For Harcourt, they imply a total critique of neoclassical theory. For Samuelson, Stiglitz and Solow however, they signify only their own irrelevance.

Metaphor, myth and all that

In its discussion of semiological phenomena, linguistic theory often employs a distinction between 'denotation' and 'connotation'. 'Denotation' may be used to distinguish those aspects of a sign that appear to be taken, in some semiological (language) community as its 'literal' meaning from the more associative meanings for the sign which it is possible to generate, i.e. its 'connotations'. The distinction is an analytic one, since in actual discourse most signs combine the denotative and the connotative. The word 'literal' itself is used here in the sense of *naturalized*, i.e. to refer to those codes or significations that are so widely distributed in a given semiotic community (culture), 'that they appear not to be constructed – the effect of an articulation between the sign and the referent, but to be "naturally" given' (Hall, 1993: 95). What these near universally consensualized meanings demonstrate is the degree of habituation produced by an achieved equivalence between the encoding and decoding sides of an exchange of meaning.

The denotative level of the sign is fixed by certain relatively limited, 'closed' codes. But its connotative level, though also bounded, is more open. At its connotative level, therefore, the sign is subject to relatively more active transformations. These transformations take advantage of the potential multiplicity of interpretations that a sign may be open to at its connotative level, i.e. these transformations exploit the polysemic values of a given denotation with respect to its corresponding connotation(s). Any constituted sign is potentially transformable into more than one connotative configuration. Signs appear to acquire their full significative value, i.e. appear to be open to articulation with wider ideological discourses and meanings at the (connotative) level of their *associative* meanings. This happens because here meanings are not apparently fixed in natural perception, and therefore their fluidity of interpretation and association can be more fully appropriated, exploited and transformed. It is thus at the connotative level of the sign that situational ideologies alter and transform signification[5] (i.e. the implication of a given denoted sign). 'At this level we can see more clearly the active intervention of ideologies in and on discourse: here, the sign is open to new accentuations and…enters fully into the struggle over meaning' (Hall, 1993: 97).

The transference from the denotative to the connotative levels of signification can be interpreted as the contextual transition from the *metaphor* to the *myth*. By 'metaphor' we understand a relatively uncontested meaning as a first-order signification. 'Myth', on the other hand is a higher-order signification, one in which the sign in the first system, that of the metaphor, becomes a mere signifier; 'as if myth shifted the formal system of a first signification sideways' (Barthes, 1972: 115).[6] Figure 16.2, as originally presented by Barthes (1972: 115), illustrates well the idea that in myth there are two semiological systems. One is a linguistic system, or what Barthes calls the language object (1972: 115) and the other system is myth itself which Barthes calls 'metalanguage, because it is a second language, in which one speaks about the first' (1972: 115).

The metaphorical is the denotative in the sense that the possibilities of alternative significations embedded in it are relatively less than those in its higher-order mythification. The myth is more than a mere collection or articulatory structure of metaphors since the signification of a myth, having been subjected to selective appropriation/transformation at every individual level of signification, is much more than the sum of the individual significations of its constituting signifiers (i.e., of its constituent metaphors) signified in isolation. The myth thus embodies the connotative. Note that the distinction is analytic-contextual: the metaphor in its turn can usually be analyzed as a lower-order myth, and conversely, the myth can be interpreted as the signifier (hence, the metaphor) in a higher-order semiological chain.

The Cambridge capital controversy started out as a contestation over metaphors, in particular the metaphor of the aggregate production function. Joan Robinson's original critique was aimed at the denotative signification of the notion/concept of an aggregate capital stock, and

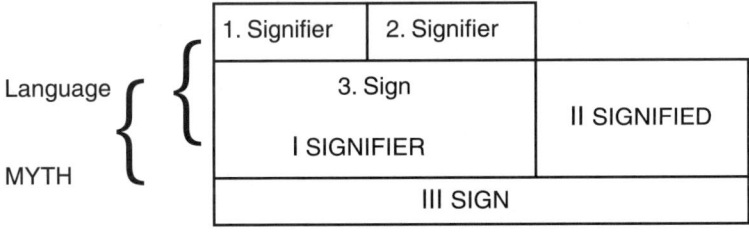

Figure 16.2 The semiology of myth

challenged in essence the 'literal' meaning of the metaphor within the neoclassical discourse (language community). Subsequent critiques of neoclassical 'parables' involving the aggregate production function and the marginal productivity theory of distribution, with their focus on the possibility of reswitching and capital-reversal, also involved challenging specific significations within a common semiological system (language community), where the rules of encoding and decoding (or the canons of 'natural logic') were being shared by all parties concerned. The repeated emphasis on the possibility of settling the 'purely logical' aspects of the question by both parties appears thus as a consequence of this alignment.[7] The debate over such questions was settled finally with Samuelson's acceptance in 1966 of the logical possibility of reswitching and capital-reversal, along with the illegitimacy of the aggregate production function as an analytical construct. Once we remember that the relative closure of the denotative level of the sign by commonly held codes of reading and interpretation (a common structure of formal logic in this case) limit sharply the possibilities of alternative consistent appropriations and transformations within the same discursive community, it is not surprising that the technical debate was settled in this manner.

The broader debate, however, raged on over what the 'settled technical questions' implied. As we have already seen, the opposing sides read diametrically opposite meanings into the implications of the very same issues on which they more or less agreed. In terms of our framework, what occurred was that the same metaphors, (i.e., the formal results agreed upon) acting now as mythical signifiers, were subjected to entirely different (contradictory) appropriations and transformations. In other words, the rules of signification under which meaning was being created were diverging, leading to the gradual development of two distinct language communities (discursive formations) defined by alternative myth-patterns. As the debate gradually changed from a contestation over metaphor to one over myth (i.e. from the denotative to the connotative) the once common language structure started getting differentiated until finally mutual exclusivity set in. The contestants stopped employing similar processes of decoding and encoding, and situational ideologies dramatically altered the nature of articulation between the sign and the referent, leading to incompatible readings of the 'associative' meanings of the debate.

Some rhetorical forms

Any specific strategy of mythification is by definition one of selective transformation and appropriation. The primary choice of one signification over another, perceived as a conscious intervention at the denotative level of the sign(s) has itself to be legitimized. Creation of such legitimacy is an act of persuasion (seduction), requiring *rhetoric*, i.e., tools of persuasion.[8] Faced with a challenge to its internal coherence, a language community might be expected to attempt to expand its own semiotic matrix in a manner that allows the incorporation (co-optation) of dissonance. Stiglitz, Solow, Blaug and Samuelson thus are all concerned with fashioning a rhetoric that can be utilized in the discursive construction of an 'immunizing' mythology.[9] We now turn to the investigation of some common rhetorical forms that they employ for this purpose.

The typology used in this section is based upon Barthes (1972: 148–55). The list of rhetorical forms discussed here is not meant to be exhaustive, and it might be possible to discern other organizing figures as well. We confine our attention to the most recurrent ones.

The inoculation

This is the device whereby one immunizes the contents of a meaning-system by means of a small inoculation of acknowledged dissonance, thus protecting it against generalized loss of coherence (subversion). Consider the following concession by Solow: 'the reswitching phenomenon does show that the extension of neoclassical theory to easy parables can be misleading' (1975: 51). The same device is used by Stiglitz to even greater effect: 'Thus, although reswitching has no implications for the validity of neoclassical distribution theory or for qualitative statements concerning the consequences of a given economy's increasing its level of consumption, it does mean that statements such as 'the reason that one economy has a lower interest rate than another is that the former economy has a higher capital-labor ratio' may be seriously questioned, for it is possible that a given economy have a lower interest rate than another and a higher interest rate than a third, but that the two comparison economies be identical in all physical respects' (1974: 897). A minimal indeterminacy (incoherence) is acknowledged by this tokenism, allowing one to co-opt, localize and absorb an otherwise potentially generalized dissonance.

Neither-norism

This consists in stating two opposites and balancing one by the other, reducing both to two binary opposite poles which balance each other only in as much as they are purely formal, relieved of all their specific (differential) weights. The specific reading intervenes between the signifier and the signified by removing precisely any notion of asymmetric importance and implanting a new equivalence. A classic use of this particular rhetorical strategy is by Blaug: 'Heterogeneous capital is no more difficult to measure than heterogeneous labour or heterogeneous output' (1975: 80). A somewhat more subtle use of this device is by Stiglitz: 'In more general models, there is a simultaneity of the determination of the values of the variables of interest in the short run and long run equilibria' (1974: 895). Coming at the conclusion of a discussion about whether the rate of profit is determined by the rate of growth and the savings rate (Cambridge, UK) or by the capital-labor ratio (Cambridge, MA), the above assertion is obviously meant to imply that both positions are equally simplistic and should be identically replaced by the one 'true' framework, i.e. a general equilibrium model. The entire debate is thus dismissed by imposing an equivalence of approximation errors by fiat. Another recurrent use of this particular rhetorical device is in equating the capital-reversal phenomenon with the Giffen good paradox, signifying the import of the first as being of no less triviality than that of the second (for example, by Solow 1975: 51).

Identification

By identification, we imply the reduction of any otherness to sameness. If suddenly however the other is revealed as irreducible (i.e., only partially appropriable), there emerges a figure for emergencies: *exoticism*. The Other is perceived as an innocuous spectacle, a curiosum, a clown (Barthes 1972: 152). Such a rhetorical device is applied, for example, by Stiglitz. 'If you accept (as most participants on both sides of the controversy do) the von Neumann (Sraffa; Samuelson; Solow *et al.*) dual price – interest rate inequalities and the assumption that at any prices the cost-minimizing techniques are chosen, you have accepted the full content of the (microeconomic) neoclassical analysis of steady states. Reswitching says something about what that does/does not imply for comparisons of steady states, but no more' (1974: 898). Thus, the technical conclusions of the debate are first reduced to (minor) theorems of neoclassical economics, and then further deprived of significatory content (meaning) to read as mere theoretical curiosum – say, a Giffen good. Differences are stripped of their significatory content in the same manner by Samuelson. 'I think there may well remain differences of opinion between some in Cambridge (UK) and some in Cambridge (MA) over whether non steady-state analysis can be meaningfully formulated and handled' (1975: 45). Surely, just an honest difference of opinion of minor import among reasonable economists?

The privation of history

Myth attempts to deprive the object of which it speaks of all history, or better, by positing the 'natural' as its source, removing all trace of origin or choice. Both Blaug and Solow argue that for the Cambridge (UK) critics, any notion of a downward-sloping demand function for capital, implying that the rate of interest or profit is an index of the scarcity of capital, signifies an argument for private property (Blaug), or a 'just' income distribution (Solow). But, they hasten to add, such a signification is illegitimate precisely on the grounds of neoclassical welfare theory and the 'natural' rules of the logic of supply–demand analysis. What this obfuscates is the historical role of such analysis in promoting scepticism about the possibility of changing income distribution in a competitive private-ownership economy through political action by organized labor, a point that is conceded by Samuelson: 'one who believes technology to be more like my 1966 reswitching example than like its orthodox contrast, will have a more sanguine view about how successful militant power by organized labor can be in causing egalitarian shifts in the distribution of income away from property even in the long run' (1975: 46).

The quantification of quality

By reducing quality to quantity, myth economizes cognition: it interprets much more cheaply. The justification for using aggregate neoclassical growth models is that they 'may do reasonably well in explaining long-term movements in certain macro variables' (Stiglitz, 1974: 901), i.e., a quantitative justification; further, the Cambridge critics of orthodoxy are brought to censure for their 'remarkable absence of attempts at empirical verification' by both Stiglitz and Blaug. The usefulness of the neoclassical aggregate growth model in a quantitative sense is however posited as a matter of faith, and not because of its empirical robustness. A qualitative question is thus reduced to one of spurious quantitative signification.[10]

In conclusion: what lay behind 'That's not the point at all'

Following Hall (1977, 1993), we identify three different positions from which decodings of neoclassical metaphors may be constructed in the context of the Cambridge capital controversy. We posit that there is no one-to-one correspondence between the two parts of the process of transference of a message (concept); i.e. decodings do not exist as some well-defined *function* (a one-to-one mapping) from the domain of encodings. This helps to deconstruct the common-sense meaning of 'misunderstanding' (a perennial complaint of the participants in the debate) in terms of a theory of *correspondence*, i.e. of *systematically distorted communication*.

When the decoder takes the connoted meaning and reads (decodes) the message in terms of the reference code in which it has been written (encoded), we might say that the decoder is operating within the *domi-*

nant code. This is the ideal-typical case of 'perfectly transparent communication.' Within this we can distinguish the positions produced by the *professional code.* The professional code decodes and then re-encodes a message which has already been signified in a hegemonic code (a dominant meaning system), applying criteria and transformational practices of its own, essentially those of a technico-practical nature. [11] The professional code serves to reproduce the dominant definitions by operating with displaced professional codings which foreground apparently neutral-technical questions. The interventions on the neoclassical side of the debate are essentially of this form.

Decoding may be said to be carried out within a *negotiated code* when the version decoded contains a mixture of adaptive and oppositional elements: it accepts the legitimacy of the hegemonic definitions with respect to the grand (abstract) significations while insisting on its right to make a more negotiated application to 'local conditions', i.e. on its right to make exceptions to the rule in specific (situated) contexts. Arguably, most 'misunderstandings' in the context of the capital controversy arose from the contradictions and disjunctures between hegemonic-dominant encodings and negotiated-corporate decodings. The Cambridge (UK) deconstruction of the neoclassical dominant-hegemonic meanings began as a negotiated-corporate decoding. As the debate progressed, however, it progressively turned into what can be termed the *oppositional code*. A subject may be said to be operating within the *oppositional code* when she decodes messages in a globally contrary way. The subject detotalizes the message in the preferred (hegemonic) code to retotalize it within some alternative (self-contained) framework of reference.

By the late 1960s and early 1970s, for most partisans of Cambridge (UK) and especially for Garegnani, Harcourt and Robinson, the negotiated corporate decoding had been displaced by a full-blown oppositional code. Hence the neoclassical cavil that for the Cambridge critics, neoclassical theory is (unfairly) read as (bourgeois) ideology, and in essence a justification for the political status quo. Or so the myth is told.

Notes

1   It might seem inappropriate to deploy a semiotic analysis in a volume dedicated to postmodernism in economics. While we recognize that semiotics, especially in Saussure, can be perceived as a structuralist approach to language, we also feel that semiotic tradition as developed by Barthes and Hall allows for a recognition of postmodern moments such as undecidability and uncertainty. In any case, the use of a semiotic approach in economics pushes the postmodern insight in ways that may be passé in cultural and literary studies, but for most economists, the idea that language is symbolic, and a system of arbitrary signs not linked naturally to the economy, is itself a transgressive and unsettling postmodern claim.

2 Dow also argues that containment exists in a Kuhnian sense as she points out that it is difficult to construct an alternative paradigm using the theoretical tools of an existing one. She notes that this 'mode of expression but itself points the way to containment of the critique. By noting the circumstances in which "anomalies" may arise, the critique indicates the assumptions that must be made to preclude these anamolies. As long as the practitioners of the orthodoxy find these assumptions acceptable, they will not perceive any crisis, no matter how unacceptable the assumptions are to the critics' (1980, 376). This is similar to the myth strategy of 'inoculation' as we develop later.
3 See Harcourt (1972) for more detail on these debates.
4 We should note that the possibility of reswitching between techniques of production is an example of a postmodern moment in an otherwise modernist economic theory. The indeterminacy of the choice of technique runs counter to the theoretical taste of neoclassical economists for closure and perhaps explain in part the urgency of this formal debate over capital theory.
5 This is not to argue that the denotative or 'literal' meaning is outside ideology. The distinction is rather between the different *levels* at which ideologies and discourses intersect. As Barthes (1974: 9) notes: 'Denotation is not the first among meanings, but pretends to be so; under this illusion, it is ultimately no more than the last of the connotations (the one that seems both to establish and to close the reading), the superior myth by which the text pretends to return to the nature of language, to language as nature.' Denotation distinguishes itself from other significations (connoted) by its singular function of effacing the traces of the ideological process by restoring its universality and 'objective' innocence. 'Far from being the objective term to which connotation is opposed as an ideological term, denotation is thus (since it naturalizes the very process of ideology) the *most ideological term* – ideological to the second degree.' (Baudrillard, 1988: 90.)
6 The 'sign' here is to be understood formally as the associative total of the signifier and the signified. The formal theory of the sign was first developed by Saussure (1959), who distinguished among the signifier (the word in his case), the signified (i.e. the mental image) and the referent and showed how any particular 'value' of the sign is constituted by structural relations with other signs. 'Metaphor' in our (and McCloskey's) usage, being defined by its specific significatory function, is a much broader term than that implied by the word in classical rhetoric.
7 Both parties appear to have implicitly maintained a belief in the possibility of perfect logical translation (at least with respect to the formal questions). For an especially lucid discussion of the problems associated with such an epistemological presupposition see Berlin (1981: 56–80).
8 By rhetoric here we mean a set of relatively fixed, regulated, recurring patterns according to which the different forms of the mythical signifier arrange themselves (Barthes, 1972: 150).
9 Reduction/displacement of cognitive dissonance obviously plays the same role in a global meaning system as that played by 'ad hoc' hypotheses in a Popperian analysis of (scientific) theories. For a discussion of the status of 'immunizing stratagems' in the Popperian framework, see Blaug (1992: 17–21).
10 At the same time, it is argued either that the 'true' version of neoclassical theory is one without any capital aggregate, i.e. a completely disaggregated general equilibrium framework (Samuelson) or that the theory could easily be generalized to include 'perverse' possibilities – just as the consumer's theory embraces Giffen goods (Solow). What emerges from the 1975 state-

ments of Samuelson and Solow is that it is impossible to derive empirical generalizations from 'true' neoclassical theory. There are no deductive propositions in the neoclassical theory of distribution as regards the sign of the relationship between factor intensity and relative factor prices that can be submitted to empirical refutation/corroboration. This holds because in the Samuelson case we can find empirical counterparts only at the aggregate level, and in the Solow case the proposed generalization leaves the sign indeterminate (Salanti, 1982).

11 The definition of a hegemonic viewpoint is (a) that it defines within its terms the mental horizon, the universe, of possible meanings of the relevant semiological system (formal economic theory in our case), and (b) that it carries with it the stamp of legitimacy – it appears coterminous with what is 'natural' about a sign system (the rational agent in economic discourse) (see Hall, 1993).

References

Barthes, R. (1972) *Mythologies*, trans. A. Lavers, New York: Noonday Press.
—— (1974) *S/Z*, New York: Hill and Wang.
Baudrillard, J. (1988) *Selected Writings*, Mark Poster (ed.) Stanford: Stanford University Press.
Berlin, I. (1981) *Concepts and Categories*, H. Hardy (ed.) London: Penguin.
Blaug, M. (1975) *The Cambridge Revolution: Success or Failure?* Institute of Economic Affairs, Great Britain.
—— (1992) *The Methodology of Economics*, 2nd edn, Cambridge: Cambridge University Press.
Cohen, A. J. (1984) 'The Methodological Resolution of the Cambridge Controversies', *Journal of Post Keynesian Economics* 6(4): 614–29.
Dow, S. C. (1980) 'Methodological Morality in the Cambridge Controversies', *Journal of Post Keynesian Economics* 2(3): 368–80.
Hall, S. (1977) 'Culture, the Media and the "Ideological Effect"', in J. Curran, M. Gurvitch and J. Woollacott (eds) *Mass Communication and Society*, London: Edward Arnold, 315–48.
—— (1993) 'Encoding and Decoding in Television Discourse', in S. During (ed.) *The Cultural Studies Reader*, London and New York: Routledge, 90–103.
Harcourt, G. C. (1972) *Some Cambridge Controversies in the Theory of Capital*, London: Cambridge University Press.
—— (1974) 'The Cambridge Controversies: The Afterglow', in M. Parkin and A. R. Nobay (eds) *Contemporary Issues In Economics*, Manchester: Manchester University Press, 305–34.
McCloskey, D. (1983) 'The Rhetoric of Economics', *Journal of Economic Literature*, 21(2), June: 481–517.
—— (1994) *Knowledge and Persuasion in Economics*, New York: Cambridge University Press.
Robinson, J. (1953–4) 'The Production Function and the Theory of Capital', *Review of Economic Studies* 21(2): 81–106.
—— (1970) 'Capital Theory Up to Date', *Canadian Journal of Economics*, May: 309–17.

Salanti, A. (1982) 'Neoclassical Tautologies and the Cambridge Controversies', *Journal of Post Keynesian Economics*, (Fall): 125–8.
Samuelson, P.A. (1962) 'Parable and Realism in Capital Theory: The Surrogate Production Function', *Review of Economic Studies*, xxix: 193–206.
—— (1966) 'A Summing Up', *Quarterly Journal of Economics*, (November): 568–83.
—— (1975) 'Steady-State and Transient Relations: A Reply on Reswitching',*Quarterly Journal of Economics*, 89 (February): 40–7.
Saussure, F. de (1959) *Course in General Linguistics*, New York: Philosophical Library.
Solow, R. (1975) 'Brief Comments', *Quarterly Journal of Economics*, 89 (February): 48–52.
Sraffa, P. (1960) *Production of Commodities by Means of Commodities: Prelude to a Critique of Economic Theory*, Cambridge: Cambridge University Press.
Stiglitz, J.E. (1974) 'The Cambridge–Cambridge Controversy in the Theory of Capital: A View From New Haven', *Journal of Political Economy*, (July/August): 893–903.

17
POSTMODERNITY, RATIONALITY AND JUSTICE

Shaun Hargreaves Heap

I suspect that most people who are interested in the relation between postmodern thought and economics are inclined to view it as a slow moving one-way street, largely because the postmodern spirit has taken a long time to reach economics. Indeed while a postmodern jouissance has been breaking out across the social sciences, economics has remained largely immune to the festivities. This paper focuses rather unusually, therefore, on a contribution which economics makes to postmodern thought.

Of course, I exaggerate slightly, as we all do from time to time to make a point. But before I explain exactly what form this exaggeration takes, some staging of the argument is called for. An enduring theme in postmodern writing is the illusion of modernity's certainties. The 'truth' always turns on close inspection to be just another 'narrative' or just another 'discourse'. To use Berman's (1983) evocative phrase describing the way in which modernity has come to undermine its own projects and so set the postmodern course, 'All that is solid melts into air'.[1] But what kind of an idea is this?

It is obviously an appealing one, if for no reason other than the fact that many previous certainties seem to be unravelling before our eyes. For instance, the ideological certainties of the Cold War were shaken by the collapse of the Berlin Wall. Likewise, the Enlightenment faith in human progress was further dented by the recrudesence of ethnic cleansing in Yugoslavia; and with the scare over global warming, even Science appears to have lost its magical power to understand and control key aspects of the natural world.

Nevertheless, the idea that 'all that is solid melts into air' is also problemmatic, not least because it appears to fail an important pragmatic test. The great virtue of Enlightenment thinking was that it gave clear advice on what to do when two 'narratives' conflict. One should set about discovering, depending on the nature of the claims being made by the narratives, which of them was true or ethically correct. This, of course, makes no sense to the postmodern because the standards of truth or ethical correctness have no greater status than the narratives they are called upon to judge. Apart from warning against Enlightenment's conceits in this matter, the characteristic postmodern response to such conflicts has been to encourage a sense of ironic tolerance. One might, so to speak, smile knowingly and exclaim 'c'est le differend' while experiencing the frisson of the situation. Such ironic distance may be entirely appropriate in some settings where no action is required, but what advice does the tradition of postmodernity offer its followers when the conflict applies to a choice that has to be made?[2]

To be specific, suppose that there is some resource that can be variously employed and that there are two ethical (political, ideological or some such) narratives which evaluate these various possible different uses. One can imagine either that there are two individuals or groups who subscribe to these respective ethical (or whatever) narratives and who must agree on the use of the resource. Alternatively, one can imagine that it is an individual who must decide on the use of the resource and he or she recognizes that there are two ethical standards that could be used for the task, but feels no special allegiance to one or the other. The question, then, is what would two people/groups decide to do if both held the postmodern insight that each ethical standard was just one among many narratives? Or in the case of the individual decision maker, what would an individual decide if he or she recognized that both ethical standards were simply narratives? In short, whichever way the choice is understood, does the postmodern tradition at least satisfy a simple pragmatic condition of providing advice to its follower(s) on what to do in such circumstances?

As a first thought, a negative answer seems the most likely. Since the conflicting ethical views can claim to be narratives and apparently the claim to be a narrative is all that can be made, what more could be said? After all, there are no metanarratives in a postmodern world. Furthermore, the critical and sometimes nihilistic quality of much postmodern writing encourages just such a suspicion (e.g. see Baudrillard, 1989). 'We are in a period when hope is not a very lucid idea' Baudrillard reminds us in his *Marxism Today* interview in January 1989, so why expect anything more? Thus postmodernity seems more concerned with puncturing the conceits of modernity than a project which offers conspicuous advice on how to choose between (or just cope with) conflicting narratives.[3] In fact, the postmodern discussion of such conflicts has tended to focus *not* on how they ought to be resolved, but rather on how their resolution embodies the power relations of a society (see, for instance, Foucault, 1976).

On further reflection, the postmodern tradition may have more to say through its appeal to the 'particular'. For example, it might be argued that such conflicts between narratives are always located in 'time and place' and one must appeal to the rules of that 'place' governing dispute resolution for the advice. Thus if one wants specifically postmodern advice, then imagine a conflict occurring within a postmodern community. The task is not impossible, but it is unlikely to yield general advice since the terms of the disputes within such a community are liable to influence the character of the rules for dispute resolution. Different communities will have different points of agreement, and with them, different rules for dispute resolution (see for instance, Mehta's chapter in this volume). This is the comforting general response, then, that avoids the charge of having nothing to say while actually saying nothing in particular. But what if there is no point of agreement, other than a shared postmodern belief that 'all ethical or truth claims are just narratives', what then? This is the difficult case where the postmodern idea itself has to do all the work (rather than relying on some contingent other source of agreement). This is the case addressed by this paper.

Of course, it is possible to question or wonder whether 'posties' should be or are concerned by the absence of any clearer advice in this difficult case? But it seems difficult to resist the pragmatic criterion that ideas should at least help agents to act even if we cannot any longer demand truth value or ethical correctness from them and we want to know how specifically postmodern ideas help in this regard. Likewise, it is clear that some 'posties' at least are concerned with this issue. For example, Lyotard's *The Differend* turns on precisely this type of conflict: 'a differend would be a case of conflict, between (at least) two parties, that cannot be equitably resolved for lack of a rule of judgement applicable to both arguments.' (1988: xi)

Thus this paper takes up the challenge of 'the differend' and it argues against a nihilistic view by suggesting that a belief in the idea 'that all truths or ethical claims are narratives' can entail advice on how to choose between such narratives. Thus it belongs at least to the Lyotard tradition of postmodernity and it aims to satisfy those outside this tradition who apply a pragmatic criterion to postmodern thought.

My argument begins with the thought that postmodern scepticism cashes in as a commitment to pluralism: that is, the positive valuing of a diversity of view in the minimal sense that one who is so committed would not want to reduce the number of available narratives or views in a society. The connection is straightforward in the sense that the absence of a reason for preferring one narrative to another is at the same time a reason for not excluding any from consideration. Rorty (1989) is perhaps the most obvious postmodern philosopher who has made this connection. For instance in his essay on the contingency of community, he expresses it in terms of an aestheticised culture where the goal is ever more various multicoloured artefacts:

An aesthetised culture would be one which would not insist we find the real wall behind the painted ones, the real touchstone of truth as opposed to touchstones which are merely artefacts. It would be a culture which, precisely by appreciating that all touchstones are such artefacts, would take as its goal the creation of ever more various and multicoloured artefacts.

(Rorty 1989)

Equally Lyotard (1988) seems to arrive at a similar connection and so I shall not defend this premise of my argument any further here. Instead, I plan to show how a commitment to pluralism does entail advice on how to choose between conflicting views in the sort of difficult cases where there are no relevant points of agreement between them.

To show that a commitment to pluralism does entail advice on what to do when two ideas are in this type of deep conflict, I draw on some economic analysis of the bargaining problem and so hope to demonstrate the somewhat unusual flow of influence between postmodernity and economics.

The bargaining problem refers to settings where two (or more) interests conflict and it is concerned with how those conflicts are resolved. The classic example is the division of a pie: the larger my share, the smaller yours is, and the more my interests are satisfied at your expense. At first glance, this looks a rather different problem from the one I have sketched above regarding conflicting narratives. However, what must be remembered is that 'interest' is understood broadly in mainstream economics and there is nothing to prevent thinking of people's interest as being constructed through their narratives (particularly the ethical narratives to which they show allegiance) with the result that what underpins a conflict of interest is actually a conflict of narrative. Likewise, there is no reason to tie the analysis to cutting pies. The same form of conflict arises whenever there are range of mutually exclusive actions under consideration and there are two or more perspectives which value each action differently.

The representation of a postmodern conflict of narrative: a defence of the bargaining framework

I have already suggested that it is helpful to make the problematic conflict between narratives concrete by focusing on two ethical or political theories that value the use of a resource in different ways. This conflict is in turn capable of being interpreted in two ways. It could be between two people/groups who each subscribe to one or other of the narratives, but who share a belief in the value of pluralism. Equally, it could be a conflict that an individual entertains between two equally appealing narratives and which he or she tries to resolve by appealing to a third principle, the commitment to pluralism. There is a further option. The narratives need not be anyone's as the point of the exercise could be merely to show logically that a commitment to pluralism in these circumstances is not contentless in the way that the idea of relativism is sometimes charged. In other words, this is a formal observation about what is entailed by an idea and for this purpose the narratives along with their entailment are abstract constructions and need belong to no one as such.

It does not matter which of these interpretations is used in developing the argument in this section. It only matters for the interpretation of the result in the next section where the implications will obviously depend on the setting. For convenience, I shall develop the argument here for the case where the conflict arises between two people/groups and skip further reference to the alternative interpretations.

As I intend to use the representation of a conflict found in the economists' bargaining theory, it is helpful to begin with a reminder of how conflicts are depicted in that theory. The typical conflict in that theory arises over the distribution of some resource between two agents, A and B, where each prefers more of the resource to less (i.e., the proverbial problem of how to 'divide the pie' between two hungry people). Each person's preferences over the possible allocations are represented by a cardinal utility function ($U_A(z)$ and $U_B(z)$, where 'z' is the allocation of the resource). Nothing deep or utilitarian should be read into the use of utility functions here. The utility function is just a mathematical device that assigns numbers ('utils', if one likes) to different allocations such that a more preferred outcome has a higher number than a less preferred outcome. Plainly a variety of sets of numbers (that is, functions) can be used for this purpose since, when outcome 'x' is preferred to 'y', the utility numbers associated with 'x' and 'y' could be any pair that preserves the ordering $u(x)>u(y)$. The requirement that the utility functions be cardinal goes slightly further. It means that the utility function not only captures the ordering of preferences, it also captures the intensity of the person's preference. (Mathematically, it restricts the possible set of utility functions to those that are linear transformations of each other. So whichever utility function is chosen to represent preferences, it will always be the case that the ratio of the utility gain from getting 'a' rather than nothing to the utility gain from getting 'b' is always the same.) Hence, there is *no* sense in which these utility numbers are interpersonally comparable. They are simply numbers that reflect each person's intensity of preference over the possible allocations of the resource.

If we suppose that in the event of a disagreement between the two agents over the allocation, so that no allocation is possible, the agents' respective utility levels are $[c_A, c_B]$, then, we can map the various possible allocations of the resource into a utility space given by Figure 17.1. The frontier represents the possible utility outcomes for each agent that come from the various allocations which exhaust the resource.

Thus in the bargaining framework, there is conflict of interest over the allocation of this resource in the sense that A would prefer the allocation yielding $[u_A^*, c_B]$, whereas B would prefer the allocation yielding $[u_B^*, c_A]$ and the task of bargaining theory is to explain how or why one point on the frontier between these extremes comes to be or should be selected.

There are two obvious ways in which this representation of a conflict of interest seems different from the postmodern conflict between 'narratives'. One concerns the language of interest rather than 'narrative'. I have already suggested that this is not obviously worrying as the economist's sense of interest is quite elastic. People have preferences and their interests are satisfied to the extent that those preferences are satisfied. Next to nothing is said about how those preferences arise. Indeed, it is often claimed that the agnosticism regarding the motives which lie behind preference is one of the advantages of the economic model. So there seems nothing in principle to preclude the interpretation that preferences here are constituted by 'narratives' and so the conflict between preference satisfaction translates as a conflict between competing 'narratives'.

An illustration may help to make explicit the scope that exists for connecting interest and narrative.

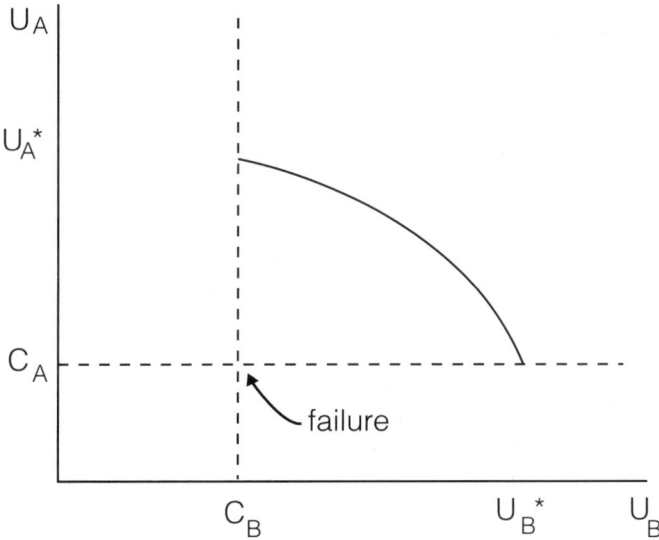

Figure 17.1 Conflict over a resource

Digression: a Utilitarian conflicts with a Rawlsian

Consider a simple conflict over the use of land between two neighbours in row/terrace houses who are in disagreement over the trees that neighbour A has grown on the border of their two yards/gardens. The trees are currently fully grown and have reached a height of 20 feet and they cast a considerable shadow over neighbour B's garden. Both neighbours agree that trees of 6 feet in height are acceptable as this height guarantees privacy to both parties. Beyond this height there is conflict because neighbour B dislikes the increasing shadow which is cast by progressively larger trees; whereas neighbour A likes the increasing majesty of ever larger trees. Thus there is a conflict, so to speak, over the last 14 feet of the trees: what proportion of this 14 feet should neighbour A control (and so preserve this height of the tree in excess of the agreed 6 feet) and what proportion should B control (and so cut the trees by this amount)? In what follows, let π denote A's share of this disputed 'resource' and $1-\pi$ stand for B's share.

Both neighbours recognize that there is a conflict here and both hold ethical beliefs about how such conflicts should be resolved, but their respective ethical theories are different. Neighbour A is a Utilitarian who believes that outcomes should be judged in conflictual settings according to the sum of the pleasures of the parties to the conflict. In fact A believes that each additional foot of control over the tree yields linear increments of pleasure to both parties, but he does not believe that each foot of control yields the same pleasure for each neighbour. Actually, A subscribes to the particular utilitarian doctrine that distinguishes between higher and lower pleasures and weighs the 'high' pleasure of enjoying the majesty of trees more highly than the lower pleasure of basking in light and sunshine. Specifically, A believes that 'high' pleasures are twice as intense as 'low' pleasures and his or her Utilitarian ethical preferences are represented by $U_A = 2(\pi) + (1-\pi)$. In other words, this function encodes A's ethically informed preferences over how best to resolve this dispute in the sense that A judges outcomes using this function and so a higher value for this function means that A's particular utilitarian preferences over outcomes are better satisfied than they would be by a lower value.

Neighbour B is a Rawlsian who believes that the outcomes in conflictual settings should be judged by the welfare of the poorest person. In this dispute B is the poorest and B believes that each extra foot of control over the height of the tree contributes to his or her preferences satisfaction at a diminishing rate. To be specific, suppose this diminishing effect is captured by the function $(1-\pi)^{1/2}$, then B's Rawlsian inspired preferences over how the dispute should be resolved is given by $U_B = (1-\pi)^{1/2}$.

Of course, the precise functional forms used here for representing each person's preferences have been chosen for their analytic simplicity to demonstrate a point and Figure 17.2 depicts the conflict in the manner of Figure 17.1. There is a conflict over the full 14 feet since U_A and U_B respectively increase and decrease monotonically with increases in π. Furthermore as U_A and U_B respectively reflect the influence of the Utilitarian and Rawlsian ethical narratives when applied to the dispute over the height of the tree, the conflict in Figure 17.2 can be interpreted as the representation of a conflict between ethical narratives.

The second and more problemmatic difference concerns the generality of the utility representation of 'narratives'. In order to use the bargaining model representation, one has to be able not only to say that 'narrative' helps construct a sense of individual interest but that various outcomes can be judged with respect to each narrative using the device of a utility function. In effect one has to be able to use utility numbers to capture how the various allocations are assessed by each narrative. The issue is: is this possible? And if it is possible in some settings, how special or general are those settings?

The illustration of the conflict between a Utilitarian and a Rawlsian plainly shows that such a substitution is possible, but it says nothing about the generality of such a move. Indeed those two ethical theories were chosen precisely because they are frequently represented using utility numbers, so they are poor examples for a general argument. Instead, my argument for generality comes in three parts. First I shall

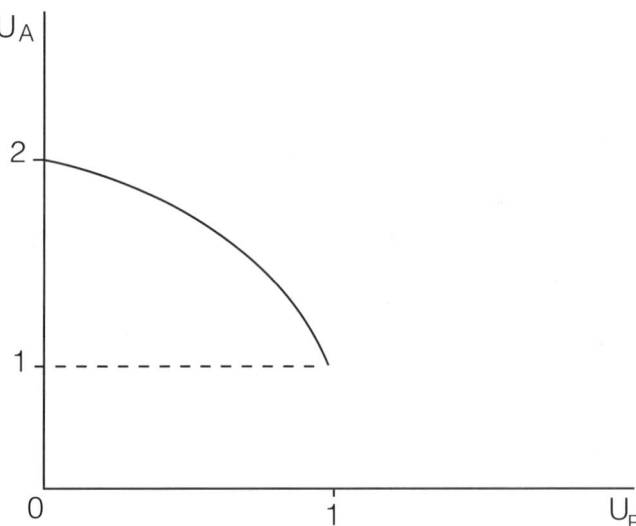

Figure 17.2 Conflict between a Utilitarian and a Rawlsian

argue that frequent postmodern invocation of a concept of power requires a coherent notion that people have interests, broadly understood as a coherent sense of engagement with any situation where there is conflict. Second, I shall suggest that while there are a variety of models of individual interest or engagement, the instrumental one which has people satisfying preferences is defensible in this context. Finally, I shall make a standard argument for the utilty representation of such preference-satisfying behaviour.

The first part of my argument turns on exploiting the postmodern (and specifically Foucauldian) idea that the prioritisation of one narrative over another encodes a power relation in society. The point here is that it is not obvious that talk of a power relation between individuals makes sense without a corresponding and coherent notion of individual interest or perspective or engagement. This is not to say that power relations are merely constituted in the relation between individuals since Foucault, like many others, argues powerfully that power has more systemic origins (e.g. through the part played by discourses). It is a question of knowing when power is at play in a relation between two individuals. What distinguishes the operation of power from other phenomena that affect social relations?

The mainstream social science answer to this question ties the concept in closely with that of individual interest: one person has power over another when their interests conflict and the conflict is resolved in a way which favours one rather than the other (see Lukes, 1974). This does not mean that interests have to be treated as exogenous. For instance, Lukes's third dimension of power is exercised through the capacity to influence how people perceive of their interests. But it does mean that the the use of the concept of power to bring closure to a situation of conflict depends on a coherent concept of individuals having something that it makes sense to talk of being more or less satisfied, like interests, even when those interests are socially constructed. Those interests can be broadly interpreted in the sense that they may arise from ethical beliefs as the Utilitarian/Rawlsian example shows. And again as that example shows, there is *no* necessary implication that an individual's interest is selfish. The point is that power is related to conflict and the idea of a conflict between individuals depends on being able to represent an individual's interest in or perspective on or attitude to that situation.

If it is accepted that postmoderns need a concept of individual interest broadly understood, the second part of my argument addresses whether individual interests in or more generally his or her engagement with the world can be identified as preference satisfaction. My first instinct is to answer no, since much of my recent research has been concerned with the inadequacy of the instrumental model of action: that is, the model which has agents acting so as to satisfy best their preferences (see Hargreaves Heap, 1989). There are two particular ways in which this model seems wrong or inadequate, at least when cast in the particular form found in economics texts, where it is the exclusive source of motivation (i.e. it sums up an individual's engagement with the world). I shall need to argue that neither is worrying in this context if the model of preference satisfaction is to be convincing (and the emphasis will have to be on 'in this context' if the humble pie is not to stick in my throat!).

Firstly the exclusively instrumental model fails to give agents a reflective capacity which would enable them to choose how to choose. This is sometimes put as a point about self esteem. People do not just act on preferences, they also like to feel that their preferences are worthy; and in this way people enjoy self esteem. Alternatively, it is sometimes conceived as an observation about autonomy as people only begin to feel autonomous when they are able not only to act on preferences but to choose which preferences to act upon (e.g., see Hirschman, 1984 and Hargreaves Heap, 1989).

Of course, this observation regarding how to model individual behaviour is not shared by all philosophers. Hume (1740) famously endorses the instrumental model by casting reason as the servant of the passions. Desires motivate someone to act, and reason's contribution is merely to guide the agent to those actions which best satisfy the person's desires on this account. In contrast, it is Kant who casts reason more ambitiously in the quest for autonomy. So the objection here is hardly decisive as it forms but one side in what is a major philosphical dispute between Hume and Kant (and on this occasion I find it convenient to side with Hume!). Perhaps the more telling line of argument in defence of the instrumental model is that, while the specific Kantian view of autonomy undercuts the preference-satisfying model (through the connection between autonomy, morality and the use of the categorical imperative), the common-sense version of the point qualifies rather than contradicts the model. In the more common-sense versions of the argument people originate change in their preferences through reflection, they do not simply act on them. So the criticism concedes that people have ends that they pursue, since otherwise it makes no sense to talk of people reflecting on those ends.

From this perspective, at a moment in time, the preferences could be taken as describing the interests of the person; and the problems really only arise over time when preferences can change as a result of reflection. Thus, so long as we are concerned only with interests at a particular moment in time, it seems possible to finesse the suggestion that some part of people's interests or engagement in a situation have been overlooked (i.e. their reflective activities). To make this argument more positively, the inclusion of a reflective capacity here would not alter the depiction of the problem that interests me. To see this, suppose one allowed for a reflective capacity that produced change in the ends that our parties pursued. The change in the ends will either modify the interaction so that the conflict is removed or modify the terms of the conflict, but not the fact of a conflict. In the former case, the inclusion of the reflective capacity simply dissolves the problem which has been set in a particular case rather than solving it in a general way. In the latter case, the problem remains albeit in a modified form; and so nothing has been gained in terms of solving the general problem by acknowledging that people also have a reflective engagement with the world.

Second, the instrumental model seems flawed when preferences are construed (as they standardly are in economics) as individual *qua* individual preferences in the sense of liberal individualism. The issue here differs from the Kantian one of whether preferences are truly owned, unless endorsed by the person's reflection. It concerns whether individual interest can be conceived independently of social context. This criticism gets made in a variety of ways ranging from the Wittgensteinian idea of a language game (and the impossibility of private languages, see Wittgenstein, 1953), to the anthropologists' idea that we use actions symbolically to communicate with others and this activity depends on shared rules (see Douglas, 1982), to the postmodern idea of the de-centred self, where the self cannot be identified independently of its significant 'others' (see Lacan, 1975). Even economics is groping to a similar conclusion in game theory, where the parsimony of modelling individuals as a set of individualistic preferences frequently yields indeterminacy (see Kreps, 1990). People can only act in such settings, it seems, when they draw on contextual social rules, thus making their actions (and hence in the logic of these models, their preferences) depend on something which is shared and socially contextual.

Again though, it is important to focus precisely on what damage these powerful lines of argument do to the instrumental model. They qualify it by casting doubt on the notion of preference as something that can be identified independently of social context. This is an important observation, but it need not damage the notion of acting on a preference per se. It simply means we must be careful in distinguishing actions and the objects of preference when they are socially contextual. Otherwise, for example, we are liable to make the sort of error that conflates winking and blinking. These are, of course, very different actions and would seem to involve different sorts of preferences, but their difference is only discernable once we are familiar with the social rules governing 'winking'.[4]

In short, once actions are appropriately distinguished, it is not obvious that this line of argument tells against people having preferences over actions. The fact that an individual has a preference for some sort of action only because the action has acquired meaning as a result of some shared social rule is again a point which addresses the origin of the preference and not the relevance of the model of action. All it means is that there is something more to the social interaction than two preference satisfiers colliding. Of course, in many circumstances, this something more, the sharing of social rules, may have further consequences for troubling conflicts as it may provide the key to a shared understanding regarding how these problems should be solved. But since I am expressly concerned with the difficult cases of conflict between postmoderns who share no other points of agreement that might be relevant to the conflict, this supplies a good reason for suppressing the influence of such social rules in this instance.

To summarise, there are good reasons for supposing that the instrumental model of people as preference satisfiers is partial. There is more to people's engagement with the world than this model allows. But there are equally good reasons for overlooking these other aspects here because in so far as they have the effect of removing the conflict altogether, the problem set simply disappears; and in so far as they merely modify the form the conflict takes, the general representation of the problem remains unaltered. I turn now to the last part of the argument in this section, the case for the utility representation of interest by focusing briefly on what are the minimal requirements for a model of action to enable talk about preferences being more or less satisfied.

It seems plausible in this respect to argue that actions must minimally satisfy the condition of transitivity (at least under conditions which concern us here of constant preferences, where preference is appropriately understood as socially contextual, and the subject of reflection, etc). Consider the alternative where a person makes intransitive choices. It is well known that such a person can be traded into poverty. To see this, suppose a person has the following intransitive choices: x is preferred to y; y is preferred to z; and z is preferred to x. This person would pay to swap x for y (since x is preferred to y), they would also pay to swap x for z (as z is preferred to x); and they would pay to swap z for y (because y is preferred to z). It does not matter where you begin in this sequence of trades, the person will pay at each stage and end up exactly where they started, ready to pay for the round trip again. And if there are people around who have transitive preferences, they are likely to take advantage of the person with intransitive preferences repeatedly in this way until that person has been traded into poverty! The difficulty then is how to reconcile this movement into poverty with the idea of the person having interests of any sort which they act upon since the person in poverty becomes unable to act on any interests. (Or to put this more generally, a person whose engagement with any situation leads to intransitive choices will undermine his or her ability to engage with any situation at all.) At best perhaps one could understand such a person as having an interest in not being able so to act. And perhaps it is not implausible to imagine people who identify their interests with a state of poverty in this way. But, surely, if this is the case, then there are simpler ways of getting to poverty than moving through a sequence of intransitive exchanges; so again it would be surprising to find intransitive choices.[5]

Once the condition of transitivity for sequences of repeated actions is accepted for sense to be attached to a person acting on their interests, it is well known that, with the addition of a further continuity condition on choices, choices can be represented via a utility function (see any intermediate economics text). I must confess that I have no good argument to offer for the continuity assumption except for the common one that everything has its price. Nothing is really so absolute or inviolable as to undermine the principle of continuity as even those who apparently hold the most absolute of beliefs can be found to trade-off some of the more marginal aspects of those beliefs if the terms are right. However, I make no claim to a decisive argument here. All I hope to have achieved is sufficient suspension of disbelief regarding the utility representation of interest/narratives to allow the next stage in the argument.

The commitment to pluralism

Interestingly Rawls (1992) has recently recast his theory of justice as a theory that applies to societies that are committed to pluralism – what he refers to as a 'reasonable pluralism'. Recall the two principles of this theory. The first provides for the full range of liberal freedoms that can be consistently enjoyed by all. The second is the difference (or maximin) principle. This is used to choose between different social arrangements that embody the first principle.

Much of his new argument is concerned with why people belonging to a reasonable pluralism will subscribe to the first principle. I am not especially interested in this argument here since it would not by itself help resolve the sort of conflict we are concerned with; whereas the second principle would appear to do this. Thus I focus on the old Theory of Justice argument for the second principle. This has two parts.

The first holds that agents with 'moral personalities' will seek arrangements that are impartial in their operation and this is used to licence the device of the 'veil of ignorance'. This seems fine to me and the condition of impartiality in the presence of disagreement seems to flow naturally from a commitment to pluralism. My doubts surface over whether reflection from behind the veil of ignorance will always deliver the second principle. The difficulty here is that an agreement on this principle seems to presume (at least) two other types of agreement. First it presumes that each person when they go behind the veil of ignorance will actually evaluate the outcome for each actual person under each possible arrangement in the same way. One can see why this must be the case, otherwise it would be perfectly possible for different people behind the veil of ignorance to rank social arrangements differently, even though they are using the same decision rule (for the simple reason that they see each arrangement differently). Second, it assumes that maximin is the decision rule which rational agents will employ when making decisions under this kind of uncertainty.

Of course, as a matter of fact, the variety of views in some pluralist societies may share these presumptions. Alternatively they may share other presumptions which yield a different result. There is nothing wrong with this per se. However, it would not be very satisfactory from the point of view of this paper because it would mean that whatever had been shown regarding the commitment to pluralism, it depended in part on some further types of agreement between the parties to the conflict. In which case, we would not have shown that this commitment to pluralism per se had content.

Another, and more fruitful, approach to what is entailed by the commitment to pluralism comes from O'Neill (1989a and 1989b). She suggests that a commitment to pluralism within a society generates principles of justice which must be universalisable. Thus having asked 'What does justice require of such a plurality?', she replies:

> At least we can claim that their [pluralists'] most basic principles must be ones that *could* be adopted by all. If they were not, at least some agents would have to be excluded from the plurality for whom the principle can hold, whose boundaries would have to be drawn more narrowly.
>
> (1989b:18)

In other words, unless a principle for action is universalisable, its use would undermine the plurality to which people are committed. The link with Kant's moral philosophy and the categorical imperative will be obvious, but it also runs deeper in a way that illumines why it should appeal to the postmodern frame of mind.

For Kant the crucial insight of reason is that it knows its own limits – this is why the books were titled 'critiques of reason'. Thus, he rejects the Cartesian enterprise of introspection because it exempts one's own life from radical doubt. Like all attempts to build knowledge on secure foundations, it begs questions about the justification of the foundation. And to answer the question by an appeal to some more 'fundamental' foundation (in the spirit of foundationalism) is to initiate a process of infinite regress as the same question is asked of these more 'fundamental' foundations, and so on. Instead, Kant is looking for how knowledge can be shared and constituted among a group of people, each with a different voice and each with a different view. His answer is weak in the sense that it does not tell us directly what knowledge consists of, but he does supply a negative constraint which any principle of knowledge must satisfy if it is to be shared by a community of people: any principle of thought must be capable of being followed by all if it is to be constitutive of knowledge in a group of rational agents.

In this way the categorical imperative is linked to a pervasive uncertainty regarding knowledge claims which should appeal to postmodernity. Again O'Neill puts the point in the following way:

> (Kant) denies not only that we have access to transcendent metaphysical truths, such as the claims of rational theology, but also that reason has intrinsic or transcendent vindication, or is given in consciousness. He does not deify reason. The only route by which we can vindicate certain ways of thinking and acting, and claim that those ways have authority, is by considering how we must discipline our thinking if we are to think or act at all. This disciplining leads us not to algorithms of reason, but to certain constraints on all thinking, communication and interaction among any plurality. In particular we are led to the principle of rejecting thought, act or communication that is guided by principles that others cannot adopt, and so to the Categorical Imperative.
>
> (1989a: 27)

This seems reasonable enough for 'knowledge' hounds, but it plausibly ought also to appeal to 'posties'. For instance, it is no coincidence that Lyotard (1988) places much of his ideas in dialogue with Kant and appears to substitute a similar maxim, of 'acting in such a way as not to make this the last word', in place of Kant's more famous categorical imperative. Indeed the point for Lyotard is to find some way out of the impasse of The Differend, the conflict between two narratives. The difficulty is that the usual forms of judgement in such circumstances are just further narratives making tendentious knowledge claims of their own; and they do an injustice to one or other of the conflicting narratives. So rather than judge, perhaps what is required is some procedural rule which will accommodate the difference rather than snuff it out. In short, we should be looking for rules that can be acted upon by all. Or to return to the pragmatic challenge with which this paper began. The argument can be couched in the following way. If the challenge is accepted by postmoderns then, without attempting to provide specific advice, one can argue that any advice must satisfy the constraint that it must be capable of being acted upon by all without creating a contradiction or an inconsistency. Otherwise it could not serve as a piece of advice in a community of postmoderns.

The burning question on either account of this matter is: does a condition of universalisability carry any bite for the bargaining problem? In particular, does it suggest a principle which agents should act upon?

At first sight the answer does not look very promising as one of the traditional criticisms of Kantian ethics is precisely that too many principles satisfy the condition of universalisability for it to be at all helpful. However, it does carry surprising bite under certain conditions. When the two agents literally agree about nothing, including the description of the problem itself, then there is only one principle which is universalisable and which is not sensitive to the arbitrary choice of units in each party's utility function. (Recall I have assumed that each party's evaluation of outcomes, inspired by their respective narratives, can be represented by a cardinal utility function. Such functions are arbitrary with respect to any linear transformation, and so we do not wish the outcome to be sensitive to the precise choice of units that any party employs in their utility function representation of their narratives.) The unique principle which universalises under these conditions is the principle of *equal relative concession* (typically known in the literature as the Kalai-Smorodinsky, 1975, principle). It selects the allocation of the resource that yields the utility pair $[u_a, u_b]$ on the bargaining frontier such that $(u_A - c_A)/(u_A^* - c_A) = (u_B - c_B)/(u_B^* - c_B)$

It can be shown diagrammatically in Figure 17.3 by constructing the ray from the conflict point to $[u_A^*, u_B^*]$, as this shows the points of equal relative concession, and observing where this intersects with the frontier. In the earlier illustration of conflict between Utilitarian and Rawlsian narratives, the minimum equal relative concession rule leads to $\pi = .62$: this means the trees would be lopped to a height of about 14.64 feet.

The first thing to note is that this rule satisfies the condition of universalisability since it requires every group to be treated in the same relative way. Thus any group's relative concession is matched by all other group's concessions and the application of the principle to one group does not preclude its application to another group. What is perhaps less obvious is why this is the only principle which is universalisable under the specified conditions.

The quick explanation is as follows (see Hargreaves Heap, 1994, for a full discussion). The assumption of cardinality with respect to each party's utility function, together with the requirement that the outcome should not be sensitive to arbitrary choice of units in each party's utility function means that we can represent the maximum and minimum utilities for each party by '1' and '0' respectively without any loss of generality. The condition that the parties must be able to disagree about everything including the description of the problem means that any

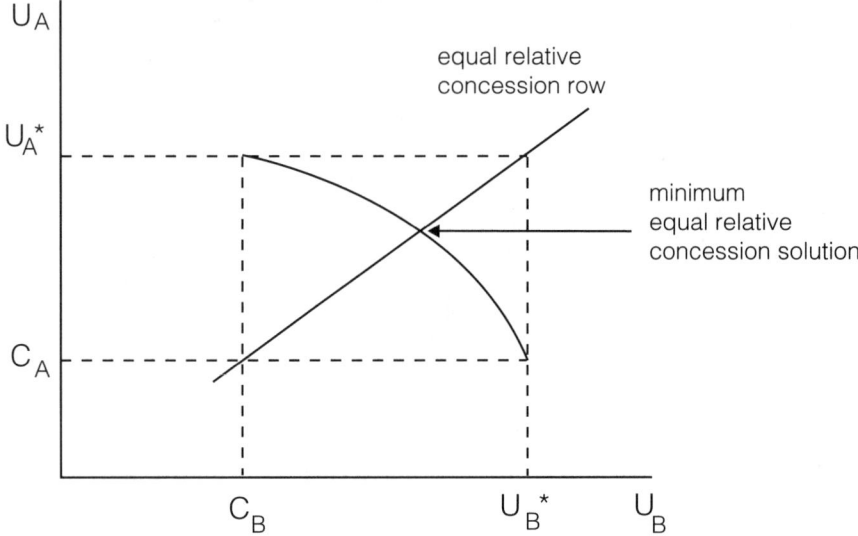

Figure 17.3 Equal relative concession

candidate rule must operate for each agent only on that agent's utility information. The reason is that if the rule operates for agent A on the utility information of both A and B (and likewise when applied by B), then the rule will only generate consistent actions for both agents when they share the same utility description of the problem (i.e. how different allocations generate utility for A and B). In comparison when the rule for A operates only on A's utility information and B's operates on B's utility information, then it does not matter if, for instance, A does not share B's view of how the allocation affects B's utility because this view does not affect the application of the rule. Thus a rule must select a fraction for each agent when it operates on that agent's (0,1) utility interval. Hence, admissable rules select fractions individually and the condition of universalisability means that any fraction selected must be capable of being selected for all agents. Thus we are looking for equal fractions; and this is exactly what the equal relative concession principle requires.[6]

In other words, the commitment to pluralism under conditions of what otherwise amounts to complete disagreement entails a commitment to a shared principle of justice (equal relative concession). Of course, in many actual pluralist societies, the disagreements may be less far reaching; with the result that the agreement occurs around a different principle of justice (again see the Mehta paper in this volume). But this is not the point of this paper. I have been concerned to show that a shared commitment to pluralism per se does offer advice over how to reconcile a conflict.

Conclusion

The neoclassical economic model of action is strangely lacking in both reflection and a social and historical context. In many circumstances, this lack of flesh and blood is a handicap for neoclassical economics. Indeed, one might suppose that this is so for most circumstances since most interesting problems in life appear for reflective agents who share a particular social and historical context. I have argued, however, and this seems ironic if the argument has been persuasive, that the one set of circumstances where reflection and a shared social and historical context cannot matter for social interaction is that which is imagined in an extreme form of a postmodern conflict: that is, a conflict where the narratives or the parties agree about next to nothing except that 'all that is solid melts into air'. In other words, the one time when it might be appropriate to use the neoclassical model without qualification is for studying the pure problem of conflict in conditions of extreme disagreement.

Thus I have justified the use of some neoclassical economics to explore what might be entailed pragmatically for action in the face of conflicting 'narratives' by the proposition that 'everything is relative or just another narrative'. Strictly speaking, I have had to interpret this proposition as implying a shared respect for pluralism, in the sense that a diversity of views is positively valued, but once this is in place, I hope to have shown that postmodern tilt at modernity's certainties need not be nihilistic and it can amount to more than 'playfulness'.

This paper was prepared for the UC Riverside Postmodernism, Economics and Knowledge Conference (3–5 March 1995). It has benefitted from a large number of comments from others at the conference and, in particular, from the detailed comments of Stephen Cullenberg, Jane Rossetti and David Ruccio.

Notes

1 The phrase is 'borrowed', of course, from Marx.
2 The continuity between some critical currents of modernity and postmodernity is worth recalling in this context (see Berman, 1983) because it is not as if modernity actually offers such pragmatic advice. The difficulty with recognizing such continuity is, of course, how to distinguish one from the other. On this, it seems to me that postmodernity is best distinguished not by an appreciation of modernity's difficulties (because modernity is not blind to them) but by a fresh approach to them that is also different from, for instance,

the tack taken by MacIntyre (1982) who uses these difficulties to argue for an engagement with a pre-modern tradition.

3   I make this point in terms of pragmatic failure. It is sometimes made as a point concerning the incoherence of relativism which is revealed once the doctrine of relativism is applied to itself.

In some respects this last way of putting it is certainly ironic, if not unfair, since it is actually precisely this argument which posties (i.e. Lyotard, 1988) like to use against claims to truth. Either such claims must use an external standard, in which case they can only be claims relative to this standard and are prone to a problem of infinite regress as one asks what justifies the use of this standard and so on, or their claims are made self referentially, in which case they are always liable to a paradox of self reference. The object of postmodern thought from this perspective is to open up some space between the two extremes of objectivity and relativism; and this paper can be cast in that vein.

4   This point is also important for a later argument regarding transitivity of choice because it can help explain why apparently intransitive choices need not be so. Thus much of the evidence on intransitive choice is often dismissed because actions which are taken to be the same (like the movement of an eyelid) and which reveal the supposed intransitivity reveal nothing of the sort once a careful individuation of the circumstances exposes them as different actions (like blinking and winking).

5   An alternative way of making this argument might be to ask, for example, what must be minimally assumed of the 'I' when Fish (1993) says 'I do it because I like the way I feel when I'm doing it'.

The point of asking this question in this context is that Fish is offering a response to the question of how the activity of literary criticism can be justified; and he eschews the more usual justifications with typical postmodern flourish. They are not reasons that are external to the activity of the various communities of literary critics. So his explanation is of course another way of saying that he belongs to a community with rules which supply the reasons (his particular forms of liking) for this type of activity; and so it is circular. But as he says 'that is the only way a justification gets off the ground.... Justification never starts from scratch, but can only ever begin if everything it seeks to demonstrate is already taken for granted'.

6   Strictly speaking, any pair of outcomes on the ray in Figure 17.3 shows points of equal relative concession and the parties must agree to the equivalent of the Pareto principle if the intersection point with the frontier is to be selected.

References

Baudrillard, J. (1989) *America*, London: Verso.
Berman, M. (1983) *All That Is Solid Melts Into Air*, New York: Simon and Schuster.
Douglas, M. (1982) *Cultural Bias*, London: Royal Anthropological Society.
Fish, S. (1993) 'Why Literary Criticism is Like Virtue', *London Review of Books*, 10 June, 11–16.
Foucault, M. (1976) *Power/Knowledge: Selected Interviews and Other Writings 1972–77*, C. Gordon (ed.), New York: Random House.
Hargreaves Heap, S. (1989) *Rationality in Economics*, Basil Blackwell: Oxford.
—— (1994) 'Conflict Resolution in Deeply Divided (or Postmodern) Societies', UEA Discussion Paper.

Hirschman, A. (1984) 'Against Parsimony: Three Easy Ways of Complicating Some Categories of Economic Discourse', *American Economic Review, Papers and Proceedings*, 89–96.

Hume, D. (1740) *Treatise on Human Nature*, L. Selby-Bigge (ed.), Oxford: Clarendon Press, 1978.

Kalai, E. and Smorodinsky, M. (1975) 'Other Solutions to Nash's Bargaining Problem', *Econometrica*, 43, 513–18.

Kreps, D. (1990) *Game Theory and Economic Modelling*, Oxford: Clarendon Press.

Lacan, J. (1975) *Language of the Self*, New York: Delta.

Lukes, S. (1974) *Power: a Radical View*, London: Macmillan.

Lyotard, J-F. (1988) *The Differend: Phrases in Dispute*, Manchester: Manchester University Press.

MacIntyre, A. (1982) *After Virtue*, London: Duckworth.

O'Neill, O. (1989a) *Constructions of Reason: Explorations of Kant's Practical Philosophy*, Cambridge: Cambridge University Press.

—— (1989b) *Justice, Gender and International Boundaries*, WIDER Working Paper 68.

Rawls, J. (1992) *Political Liberalism*, Cambridge: Harvard University Press.

Rorty, R. (1989) *Contingency, Irony and Solidarity*, Cambridge: Cambridge University Press.

Wittgenstein, L. (1953) *Philosophical Investigations*, Oxford: Basil Blackwell.

18

A DISORDERLY HOUSEHOLD – VOICING THE NOISE

Judith Mehta

First words

Hitherto, the discipline of our discipline has been well equipped for dealing with a certain amount of noise (or, as defined here, disordered information). Where practitioners are concerned, the language of methodological individualism has ensured that those given voice do not meander too far from orthodox assumptions and practices; there simply has been no other language in which to talk or to do economics. As for the economic agents of the household, the error term provides the discipline with a discreet sponge for soaking up any random deviations in their behaviour – 'white noise' – so that models are tidy and economical in appearance. Economics is, moreover, a moralistic discipline, eliciting conformity to its maxims with a carrot and stick; in this respect, the champions of rational choice theory are both our exemplars and our masters. It is within their gift to grant dispensation to repudiate short-run utility-maximisation provided agents have long-run utility-maximising reasons for doing so; but truancy lies beyond the bounds of acceptable behaviour. Agents who act suboptimally reap lower payoffs, and herein lies the incentive for their foolishness to be displaced by orthodox calculations of strategic advantage. Marshalled and policed by the tools of scientific method, the marginalised, the suppressed, or the merely flagellated of the household could, until recently, take comfort from knowing that the judicial process to which they had fallen victim was administered with the impartiality of an invisible hand.

But economics is no longer master in its own house. Other voices clamour for attention and threaten to upset the modern project of a well-regulated household. I suggest this follows the appearance of a new language: postmodernism, the new rhetoric or social constructivism – call it what you will. But within this new self-consciousness is a transformation of the economic imagination with the potential to convert noise into voice. The process is not a clean and tidy one, nor is it given to recognising property rights:

> Language gives one to think but it also steals, spirits away from us, whispers to us [elle nous souffle], and withdraws the responsibility that it seems to inaugurate; it carries off the property of our own thoughts even before we have appropriated them.
>
> (Derrida, 1992:80)

This essay reflects upon the terms of the economic imagination as they are beginning to emerge, but it is attentive to the Hegelian suspicion that truth (or, what I shall call, understanding) *"is not a minted coin that can be given and pocketed ready-made"* (Hegel, [1807] 1977: 22); the re/production and transformation of understanding invokes a multiplicity of voices, past, present and future, and from all parts of the household. These voices challenge the modern notion of the subject prevalent in economics and its model of rational choice and, if heeded, may be saying that it is beyond the agency of economists by themselves to bring about a transformation of the discipline. I suggest it is intrinisic to a discipline constructed on exclusions and enforced silences that it will interpellate itself; all that is needed is a language – or a form of re/presentation – in which the noise can be voiced. Exclusion and re/presentation in the construction of economic knowledge therefore constitute the two central, but interwoven, themes of this essay. At issue are those elements of behaviour which rational choice theory would exclude from its narrational framework, how to re/present them while respecting their complexity, and their impact on our understanding of behaviour.

Exclusion, as Foucault (1984) argues, is the condition of a discourse: by placing boundaries between what is inside it and what is outside it, a discourse constitutes its objects. Thus, he observes that madness is constitutive of sanity, and criminality constitutive of legality (1971; 1977). Similarly, notions of 'unreasonable behaviour' are inescapably implicated in the orthodox economic construction of rational behaviour. In this sense, noise is the means by which the economic discourse constitutes itself. But it is a characteristic of any discipline founded on notions of exclusion that elements which lie outside the discourse retain a claim on those within it. On my interpretation, the Freudian notion of 'the return of the repressed' is a paradigm of the way in which elements which have been excluded return to challenge an organisation of knowledge which would condemn them to silence. Such is the case when certain ontological assumptions about the nature of human subjectivity are disappointed in behaviour; exclusions return to haunt the discipline in the form of the problems and paradoxes which have surfaced in rational choice theory. *'Ça vient de partir. – Ça revient de partir. – Ça vient de repartir'* says Derrida (1987: 382), in a rephrasing of the Freudian compulsion to repeat. It is in this sense that the critique of orthodox economics emanates from *within* the household and is reflexive; it is only the language of that critique which comes from without.

My strategy, then, is to interrupt our discourse on the discourse by staging a forum in which the noise of many narratives can come to voice. I shall report excerpts from transcripts of conversations with and between people as they engage in bargaining problems. For present purposes, the extent to which behaviour conforms to the predictions of rational choice theory is treated implicitly. To privilege the voice of rational choice theory in this performance would harm my purpose in two ways. First, it would suggest that it is the assumptions of the theory which constitute the object of investigation rather than the behaviour itself; and second, it would permit rational choice theory to impose a closure on the subject of bargaining behaviour. In defence of the conversational method itself, let me point out that Arjo Klamer (1984) has already demonstrated that it can alert us to the problems of communication in economic discourse and the frictions between diverse styles of argument. But why limit ourselves to what can be gained from listening in to conversations between economists? And why exclude the economic agents of the household from a conversation about what goes on in the bargaining process? Indeed, Ariel Rubinstein (1991) observes that language plays a crucial role in resolving conflicts, a role which game theory has so far been unable to capture. This is because representation in economics is focused on outcomes, constructed in mathematical terms; as long as we ignore the rhetorical enuciation of our subjects as these outcomes are being negotiated, we cannot fully understand their meaning, let alone how they are reached. The conversational method therefore offers us the potential to open up a new theoretical space, one in which we are sensitive to both regularities and differences in behaviour, and to the negotiation of frictions between the actors themselves and competing narrational frameworks. In other words, it may permit an open-ended giving-taking of understanding (a *circulation*) in which we can observe how the rhetorical enunciation of the actors folds back on their discourse, at the same time as allowing that discourse to fold back on its own.

The unfairness of representation: an agenda

The experiment reported below constitutes just one element in a larger research program designed to investigate bargaining behaviour. This program is motivated by the observation that the grand narrative of rational choice theory often sits uneasily alongside the narratives of the actors. The vehicle for my concerns is the orthodox response to Nash's (1953) 'demand game', a game which confronts the discipline with an embarrassment of riches in the form of multiple Nash equilibria. The problem for the theorist is that any pair of strategies leading to a Nash equilibrium can be understood as a rational choice; but the analysis is unable to discriminate between equilibria, or to explain how real people are able to reach an agreement when they do so. The orthodox approach to the dilemma lies in a project of refinements of the Nash equilibrium concept. Thus, for this and many similar problems, resolution is understood to be a matter of determining the criteria by which certain equilibria can be categorized as 'intuitively unreasonable' and so excluded from the feasible set.[1]

In an earlier essay (Mehta, 1993), I argued that this approach was inappropriate at the positive level and, in so doing, identified an agenda for future work with bargainers. I suggested that models of the Rubinstein (1982) type, which rely upon the subgame-perfect refinement, appeal to the orthodox theorist because they generate a unique solution. But they are products of the presuppositions and predispositions of a discourse which celebrates uniqueness in the context of a normative project rather than having anything to do with the real world and the rich institutional setting in which behaviour takes place. As such, they contribute little to our understanding of real bargaining behaviour. Moreover, a challenging gap exists between accounts of behaviour framed by rational choice theory, and experimental evidence of how people actually do behave in a bargaining situation. Thus, we find that a number of social or institutional factors which have hitherto been regarded as irrelevant to players in the world defined by rational choice theory would appear to explain (i) why bargaining games that are structurally equivalent in game-theoretic terms do not always yield identical behaviour; (ii) why bargainers may settle for outcomes that 'fall short' of Pareto-optimality; and (iii) how players can discriminate and choose between multiple Nash equilibria.[2] Indeed, Roth *et al.* are led to conclude from their experimental work that:

> sociological factors – that is, factors unrelated to what we normally consider to be the 'economic' parameters of a game – can decisively influence the outcome of bargaining.
> (Roth *et al.* 1981: 176)

Since these factors enter systematically into behaviour, they cannot be consigned to the error term; yet there is no obvious way of appropriating so-called sociological factors which preserves the unity and order of the orthodox economic program. As an example, consider the notion of 'fairness'. Using experimental techniques, it would seem to be a straightforward matter to determine the contexts in which fairness is relevant to bargainers and what exactly is meant by 'a fair solution'. By excluding 'unfair solutions', at least some of the indeterminacy generated by standard theory could be eliminated. But under the auspices of deconstruction, I have argued that these elements remain intractable to the functional forms which characterise orthodox economics because they are not fixed and commensurable as the discourse requires. Thus, 'the fair solution' does not have some singular, objective meaning or exteriority such that a determinate value can be assigned to it. The meaning of 'the fair solution' is not fixed and univocal, but situational in that its precise meaning for two bargainers shifts according to its negotiated difference from 'unfair solutions' in a given bargaining situation. By similar argument, a bargainer's sense of self (whether they see themselves as a friend or rival in bargaining, for example), is wholly indeterminate. And if there is no univocal meaning with which to represent fairness, nor a unitary identity with which to represent the bargainer, then there is no continuity or stability which can be captured by a single model of bargaining behaviour.

Yet the complexity of some behaviours – their refusal to submit to orthodox functional forms – is not the only reason why they are excluded from representation. We must also recognise the part played by the taxonomies of the dominant discourse in conditioning representation in order to comprehend why it is that behaviour which conforms to the axioms of rational choice theory is privileged, while non-instrumentally-rational behaviours are rendered voiceless. One of the sources of Foucault's argument about the part played by exclusion in a discourse is the work of Martin Heidegger. In an essay (originally written in the 1930s), Heidegger observes:

> Nature and history become the objects of a representing that explains...Only that which becomes object *is* – is considered to be in being.
>
> (Heidegger, 1977: 127)

In these terms, he conceives of the modern age as 'the age of the world picture', that is, the age in which phenomena must be represented as objects in order to have voice. By implication, the not-object is silent in explanation. Thus, non-instrumentally-rational behaviours fail in their representations because they lie outside the organising assumptions of rational choice theory: because they are not represented they cannot exist, and so they must be constituted in annulment, that is, in exclusion. The challenge for a new agenda in economics then becomes clear. New forms of re/presentation must be found that give voice to those elements of behaviour which are unpresentable in orthodox models. This approach could take many different directions, each of which has validity if it deepens understanding.

Yet, as we will observe, bargainers themselves play with notions of exclusion; they attempt to bring order to their situation through a negotiation of the criteria by which competing demands for a share of the pie can be categorised as either 'reasonable' or 'unreasonable', 'fair' or 'unfair'. A discourse which recognises and engages with these negotiations necessarily radicalises the gap between oppositions. It doesn't seek to diminish that gap by focusing on either the unity or plurality of bargaining solutions and their supporting narrational frameworks, but listens to the voices of actors (their *petits récits*) as meaning and identity are constituted in the bargaining game. In this sense, I advocate a decentering of orthodox concerns for the outcome of bargaining. But let me emphasize that this is *not* to exclude modern theory's narrational framework – which would be to repeat the original act of imperialism – but to engage with the dissonance between narratives. While it is beyond such an approach to elicit the fixed and universal forms of understanding which modernity desires, it may enable us to attest to a richness and variety in behaviour which is otherwise unpresentable. Then,

> The postmodern would be that which, in the modern, puts forward the unpresentable in presentation itself;...that which searches for new presentations, not in order to enjoy them but in order to impart a stronger sense of the unpresentable.
> (Lyotard, 1984: 81)

In this sense, orthodox economic theory remains very much a part of a transformed economic imagination, but open to interpellation by its exclusions.

Games people played: the experiment

The conversations reported below took place with and between people as they engaged in a one-shot simultaneous-move bargaining problem preceded by one round of 'cheap talk'. Twenty-four volunteers were recruited from the population of students at the University of East Anglia. None of the subjects had participated in any previous experiments with bargaining games, and subjects were told nothing about the nature of the experiment before they took part. The experiment took place over six separate sessions. For each of these sessions, four subjects were randomly divided into two teams of two players each. Each team occupied a separate room, together with an organiser who read through a set of instructions and tape-recorded the event.[3] Neither team met the other team either before or after the experiment, and members of the same team had not previously met each other. Within each session, the two teams had to bargain over the distribution of £16 between them, with any gains being divided equally between team members. Subjects were explicitly instructed to think of the game as a bargaining problem; they were given the example of the problem faced by the buyer and seller of a house who each want to get the best possible terms for themselves, and they were instructed to *'try and get as much as you can for your team'*. This instruction was given to reinforce the incentive structure of the game as it is understood by standard theory; the significance of any notions of fairness would then be strengthened if indeed 'fair play' was a component of behaviour.

This experiment differed from conventional experiments in economics in two respects. First, it is usual for experiments to be conducted with large numbers of people playing as individuals, the aim being to acquire a substantial dataset describing outcomes. The idiosyncratic thought processes of the bargaining subjects are generally of little interest. But in this experiment, I am more concerned with process than with outcome. When people are part of a team of two, it is necessary for them to verbalise their understanding of the situation so that they might act together. So by using teams rather than individuals, it becomes possible to witness the formation of meaning and identity by the players and the negotiation of any differences.

Second, many of the usual features of a real-world bargaining situation are absent in the experimental environment; for example, in this experiment, people without the history of a relationship find themselves playing either in the same team or in competing teams. But by simplifying the context in which bargaining takes place, we can focus more clearly on the ways in which the actors constitute the meaning of the situation and their identities within it. Two elements of context were introduced to the game, both of which were matters of common knowledge, but both of which would be regarded as irrelevant to behaviour on the orthodox account.[4] The intention was to see if, and how, players would draw on these features to help them coordinate their strategies. First, for each pair of teams, one team was randomly designated 'the Buyer', and the other 'the Seller'; and second, each team was randomly dealt four playing cards from a set of 4 aces and 4 twos. Each team could determine the other team's cards from their own hand; for example, a team holding 3 aces and 1 two would know that the other team held 1 ace and 3 twos.

All the players received identical instructions. They were told that for the Buyer team, a full set of 4 aces was 'worth' £16, but all other sets of cards were 'worth' nothing. At the end of the game, a Buyer team holding all 4 aces could exchange their cards for £16 from the organisers. A Buyer team holding less than 4 aces could try to buy the remaining aces from the Seller team. If the teams reached an agreement, the Buyer team would receive the £16, less the amount they had agreed to pay the

Seller team for their aces, and the Seller team would receive the agreed selling price. A Seller team, on the other hand, could obtain nothing for their cards from the organisers, even if they held the full set of 4 aces; but a Seller team could try to sell any aces they held to the Buyer team.

Bargaining between teams was enacted anonymously as follows. Each team was instructed to send a preliminary non-binding message to the other team prior to making their final demand. The Buyer team was instructed to complete the statement: *PRELIMINARY OFFER: We are willing to pay a total of…to buy the Seller's aces*, by specifying an amount of money. At the same time, the Seller team was instructed to complete the statement: *PRELIMINARY OFFER: We are willing to accept a total of…from the Buyer in return for our aces*, by specifying an amount of money. When both teams had completed these statements, each team's message statement was transmitted to the other team by the organisers by telephone. Each team was asked to discuss the final and binding offer they wanted to make and then to complete a further statement. The Buyer team was instructed to complete the statement: *FINAL OFFER: We are willing to pay a total of…to buy the Seller's aces*, by specifying an amount of money. The Seller team was instructed to complete the statement: *FINAL OFFER: We are willing to accept a total of…from the Buyer in return for our aces*, by specifying an amount of money. When both teams had completed these statements, their responses were collated by the organisers by telephone. The pair of teams was deemed to have reached an agreement if the amount the Buyer team was willing to pay for the Seller team's aces was greater than or equal to the amount the Seller team was willing to accept. In this case, both teams were paid the agreed amounts in cash, with each team member receiving a half share of their team's gain. But if the amount the Buyer team was willing to pay was less than the amount the Seller team was willing to accept, then the players were deemed to have failed to reach an agreement; in this case, neither team received anything.

Representing behaviour

How would we expect people to behave in this experiment, and what did they actually do? The next section represents a response to these questions. Rational choice theory's narrative appears in a column on the left, the players' own narratives appear on the right. I do not deny my organizing role in these narratives – the reader will be aware that they are marked by my own taxonomy of what is salient and what is not. The narrative of rational choice theory is, of course, my own characterization of it. As for the narratives of the players, these are distilled from several hours of tape-recorded conversations. The transcripts were combed for statements which shed light on behaviour in any respect or provide answers to four specific questions: is behaviour affected by the distribution of cards between teams? Is 'cheap talk' treated seriously? Do notions of fairness enter into play? And, is player identity a matter of concern? My eidetic interventions on these issues appear in boxed text. The result is not representative of bargaining behaviour, but a representation of how these 24 subjects bargained. As such, it can be treated as a comment on rational choice theory, and a guide to areas of behaviour which call for further investigation. But more importantly for present purposes, it points to what is at stake in the act of representation.

The following information will be of help in following players' narratives. Subjects were promised that their anonymity would be preserved in reporting behaviour; hence, each player has been assigned an individual code which identifies the session in which they participated. Thus, for Session 1, the Buyers are B1 and B2 and the Sellers are S1 and S2; for Session 2, the Buyers are B3 and B4 and the Sellers S3 and S4, and so on. The effect of these codes is to disembody player voices. Of course, this feature of the representation is congruent with the orthodox approach which sees 'rational' players as constituted by well-behaved sets of preferences and otherwise undifferentiated. But recall that the teams themselves face a disembodied 'other'. In this setting of relative anonymity, we may be able to discern whether, and in what respect, player identity is a matter of concern.

Of course, in conversation, people do not always speak grammatically, nor do they always finish sentences. In some instances, the meaning of a statement is conveyed or reinforced by gesture or intonation, and agreement or disagreement is signalled by a nod or shake of the head. Within the constraints of the written word, every attempt has been made to report comments as accurately as possible, not to dislocate comments from the context in which they were made, and to use punctuation such that the spirit of the comment is retained. Contextual information which is not otherwise obvious (such as which stage of the game is in the process of being played, or is under discussion) is contained within square brackets. And any interventions by the session organiser are clearly marked.

Table 18.1 summarises the quantifiable information pertaining to each session. From this table, it can be seen that there were three different deals of the cards, and that each deal of the cards was held by two teams.[5] For clarity, the offers made by both the Buyer team and the Seller team are expressed in the table in terms of the amount of the pie which each team demanded for themselves; thus, for a pair of Buyers and Sellers to reach an agreement, final demands must sum to £16 or less.[6]

Table 18.1 Summary of results

SESSION NUMBER	BUYERS	SELLERS	AGREEMENT
1	Players: B1 and B2. Dealt 1 ace + 3 twos Message: demand £8.00 Final offer: demand £8.00	Players: S1 and S2. Dealt 3 aces + 1 two Message: demand £8.00 Final offer: demand £8.00	YES
5	Players: B9 and B10. Dealt 1 ace + 3 twos Message: demand £12.00 Final offer: demand £8.00	Players: S9 and S10 Dealt 3 aces + 1 two Message: demand £12.00 Final offer: demand £8.00	YES
2	Players: B3 and B4. Dealt 2 aces + 2 twos Message: demand £10.00 Final offer: demand £8.00	Players: S3 and S4. Dealt 2 aces + 2 twos Message: demand £8.00 Final offer: demand £8.00	YES
4	Players: B7 and B8. Dealt 2 aces + 2 twos Message: demand £11.00 Final offer: demand £10.00	Players: S7 and S8. Dealt 2 aces + 2 twos Message: demand £7.00 Final offer: demand £7.00	NO
3	Players: B5 and B6. Dealt 3 aces + 1 two Message: demand £10.00 Final offer: demand £8.00	Players: S5 and S6. Dealt 1 ace + 3 twos Message: demand £10.00 Final offer: demand £8.00	YES
6	Players: B11 and B12. Dealt 3 aces + 1 two Message: demand £11.00 Final offer: demand £9.00	Players: S11 and S12. Dealt 1 ace + 3 twos Message: demand £8.00 Final offer: demand £8.00	NO

V. The narrative of rational choice theory.

Let us consider what we would expect the players to do from the point of view of standard game theory.

First, recall that the distribution of cards between the pair of teams is irrelevant to rational players; this is merely a presentational feature of the game.

V. Conversations with and between bargainers.

B1: We've got £16 in total. So half of it for two, that's £4 per ace.
B2: That would be very reasonable.
B1: ... so shall we put half, then?
B2: You reckon?
B1: OK.

S3: Right; so 2 aces each, and if 4 are worth 16, then these are worth £8.
S4: So we ask for £8, and then everyone gets the same amount.
S3: Yes. £8 each. Seems fair enough.

B7: So the more aces you get, the better it is really.
B8: I don't know really. It's always the same because you need to get all of them. It doesn't matter how many you start off with - if you start off with zero, if you start off with 3: it doesn't do you any favours.

Org: [After the experiment.] Did you think the distribution of the aces was significant?
S7: Yes, I think so.
S8: Yes.
Org: So if you'd had 1 ace, what would you have done?
S7: Put the price up probably.
S8: Yes, probably, because, I mean, in a way, we've got the scarce commodity so I suppose it's worth more.
Org: So with 3 aces, you'd have asked for less?
S8: Probably about half, in fact.
S7: Yes.
S8: Probably, don't you think?
S7: Yes.

S9: My feeling is that each of the aces are worth £4 to the other team and therefore they should be prepared to pay £4 for each of them because they will make a profit at the end of the day because they will have 4.
S10: Yes.
S9: So I propose that the preliminary thing should be £12.
S10: Yes, right, I agree, seems fair enough.

S5: [After the experiment.] I was just wondering: what's the point of the cards?
Org: Well, that's one of the things we're interested in ... your feeling would be they're of no significance?
S5: No.
S6: No, I didn't even think about it really.

As far as B8, S5 and S6 are concerned, the cards are irrelevant; but other players find them to be significant. In particular, the comments of S3, S4, B7, S7, S8, S9 and S10 provide tentative support for a hypothesis derived from the work of Thomas Schelling (1960), namely that players look to the distribution of the aces for clues to the 'focal point' (that is, the solution on which the players' expectations can converge).

B1: They're probably going through the same thing as we are, thinking what are we going to do - because they haven't got a clue.

B1 appears to be reasoning along the lines described by the common knowledge assumption.

Similarly, the asymmetric labels (Buyer and Seller) assigned to each team make no difference to each team's real bargaining power; in this respect, the players remain undifferentiated.

> There are no comments in any of the transcripts which suggest players are influenced by the asymmetric labels (Buyer and Seller) assigned to them.

All six games share a common mathematical structure. There is a family of pure-strategy Nash equilibria: for any value of x in the range $0 \leq \pi \leq £16$, any pair of strategies such that one team demands x and the other team demands $£16 - x$ constitutes a Nash equilibrium. Each team of the pair can be expected to differ only in terms of their preferences over the different outcomes. (Different teams, or individuals within teams, may of course have different utility-of-wealth functions, and so in this sense there will be a difference between games. But since the cards are dealt at random, there can be no systematic difference between the utility functions of players according to the number of aces they hold.) The distribution of cards, and the designation of teams as either Buyers or Sellers, are therefore merely presentational devices.

Second, some game theorists would suggest that preplay communication which doesn't directly affect payoffs will have zero effect on behaviour in the final and binding stage of the game. The rationale for this view is that, in the absence of an external enforcement mechanism or a commitment to the promised course of action, teams comprised of players who are equally rational both know that neither team has

B11: [Mulling over the fact that the teams failed to reach an agreement.] We're not poor enough. We should play this game at the end of term.
B12: I still haven't paid my tuition fees; I've still got loads of money in my account.

S11: Mmmm. Should we overstate or understate the preliminary offer?
S12: In the preliminary, if we say we'd accept 6, they'll think, great. They'll put 6 then, won't they, and we can't really up that price.
S11: Alright. ... Let's just go straight out and say, we know what we're all doing here ...
S12: Yes.
S11: ... and we put down 8 and they'll think, aha, they're playing it fair, let's play it fair: we'll all be better off.

> *S11 and S12 are using the message to signal otherwise private information about their identities, that is, that they are 'fair' players. They anticipate that, once shared, this information will lead to a convergence of expectations on, what they perceive to be, the fair solution: equal division of the pie.*

any reason to carry out that action. As a result, it is predicted that rational agents will simply ignore messages and act as if they hadn't been sent; in other words, messages will be mere 'babble'. It is on these grounds that Farrell (1987) suggests there is certainly an equilibrium in which messages do not affect behaviour in the game (that is, a 'babbling equilibrium'). He points out that if everyone believes that cheap...

S12: ... rather than trying to get an extra pound each. I mean, if we just put 8 - I can't think we deserve any more.
S11: No.
S12: Cos, I mean, we need them to get anything and they need us to get anything.
S11: We've got no reason to hold a grudge against them.
S12: No, it's not as though we're dealing with old rivals.
S11: Right - run round the corner and bonk us!

> *S11 and S12's demand for a fair share of the pie is grounded in their construction of the other team's identity: these are not 'old rivals'.*

... talk will be ignored, then it is optimal for each player to send a message which is uncorrelated with their final action, and then everyone's scepticism about the role of messages is warranted.

If this is indeed the case, then for the game being played in the experiment we would expect the preliminary demands stated in messages to be randomly distributed. Moreover, we have no grounds for expecting final demands to be other than randomly distributed; nor have we grounds for expecting the final demands of the pair of teams to be correlated. Indeed, if final demands are chosen at random as rational choice theory implies, we would expect 52.3% of pairs of teams to reach an agreement.[7]

Org: [After the experiment.] Did you expect that message to have any effect on how they would behave in the final round?
S5: Oh yes.
S6: Yes, I think so. Yes, I think that if we'd asked for 8 and they'd asked for 6, we'd probably have ended up with less than 8.
S5: Yes.
Org: So you think that by asking for more, you're likely to end up with more?
S5: Yes.

Org: [After the experiment.] Did you believe the message from the other team?
B1: Yes.
B2: We have no reason not to.
Org: [After the experiment.] Did you believe the message from the other team? They said they'd

Yet casual observation suggests that real people frequently do engage in cheap talk before final actions are taken; are they really exchanging meaningless babble, or is there some means by which non-binding messages can help them to coordinate their strategies? Several theorists claim there can be equilibria in which cheap talk is taken seriously.

accept a total of £10: did you believe that message?
B5: No, I thought they'd come down.
B6: Yes, I smiled when you said it because it was exactly what I expected.
Org: Did you expect your message to influence the other team?
B5: Only as much as their's influenced us.
B6: I think our message said that we weren't going to be done out: we were going for equal shift, or more for us; we weren't going to play around really.
B5: Yes.

B11: You must try to squeeze it below 8; you must give them the impression that we are willing to risk all.
B12: Yes, that's an idea - but we *are* willing to pay them up to 8?
B11: Yes. The thing is, you want to trick them that we are *not* willing to go up to 8.
B12: So let's put 4.
B11: You put 4 or 5?
B12: Let's make it 5.
B11: Yes, 5. Yes, that'll do.

Org: [After the experiment.] Did you believe the message from the other team?
B7: No ... well, I thought maybe they'd be open to change a bit.
B8: I mean, you always, like, if you're in a bargaining decision, you always start higher than you want, or lower than you're willing to pay.

B7: That's what the word 'bargaining' means really.
Org: Did you expect your message to influence the other team?
B8: Yes.
B7: Yes: I think it gives the message that we're prepared to pay a bit higher. But obviously, we're saying, we'll come down. I think that's usual.
Org: So there was a coded message in your message?
B8: Yes.

Notice that 13 players make comments which suggest they are treating cheap talk seriously. B1 and B2 trust in the truth of the message of intent sent to them. In contrast, S5, S6, B5, B6, B11, B12, B7 and B8 view the message as embodying information to be interpreted rather than taken at face value.

Within the literature, there is a class of models which assumes some distribution of player types, and that each player has private information about their own type (see, for example, Crawford and Sobel, 1982; Farrell and Gibbons, 1989). These models typically generate several equilibria, at least one of which could not be supported in the absence of talk. Three conditions are required for messages to be informative: (i) a Sender can be typed according to their preferences over the Receiver's final actions; (ii) a Receiver prefers different final actions depending on the Sender's type; and (iii) the Receiver's preferences over final actions are not completely opposed to the Sender's preferences. It can be shown that if these conditions are satisfied, and contingent upon the combination of player types, there can be an equilibrium in which different player types have an incentive to send different messages. The finding that cheap talk can matter is an interesting one, although it is not clear how the players in this experiment

B8: [Mulling over message received.] It just makes it so much harder not being able to see who you're dealing with. Because if you were actually in a normal bargaining situation, you'd be looking at them. You could see their expression ...
B7: How serious they are.
B8: Yes. ...
Org: [After the experiment.] Did the problem remind you of any real-world situation?
B7: Not really. Most situations, you're not that far removed from people you're dealing with. I used to work in a market selling things. You look at the person and you think how much they're going to pay. It's all to do with their personality and their appearance as to how much you think you can sell something for.

B5: It's tough because you don't know what the other people are like.

could be 'typed'. Recall that our players have been instructed to try and get as much money as they can for their team, and that this instruction is common knowledge. If both teams believe that the behaviour of the other is indeed motivated by the maximisation of monetary gain, then the preferences of both over outcomes are transparent and identical: each team prefers the largest possible share of the pie.

> The comments of B8, B7 and B5 show that they are finding coordination difficult in the absence of visual clues to player types.

Alternative models have been developed for situations in which there is *no* private information and the players are assumed to be identical. Arguably, these situations are closer to the one described by the experiment. Farrell (1987), for example, addresses a problem which, in some respects, is analagous to the bargaining problem of this experiment; that is, how 2 players who are initially symmetric are able to achieve asymmetric coordination.[8] The vehicle for Farrell's investigation is a model of an 'entry game', where each of two identical firms makes an initial announcement about their entry plans for a natural monopoly market ('in' or 'out'), followed either by entry to the market or staying out. The parameters of the game are such that it is in each firm's interest to stay out if the other firm enters. Farrell finds there is at least one equilibrium to this game where the information contained in the announcement is treated seriously. For the purpose of this essay, it is sufficient to note that a crucial element of the model is the assumption that where initial plans would constitute a Nash

B1: [Debating whether to revise plans that if actually played would lead to agreement.] So shall we stick with that, £8?
B2: Yes, there's no point in reducing it, because if they increase, then we don't know how much they're going to increase it by.
B1: No.

equilibrium if actually played, these plans will be followed in the final stage of the game on the grounds that the equilibrium has become 'focal'. However, the theoretical grounds for the assumption remain undeveloped. While intuitively it may seem obvious that an announced Nash equilibrium would be played in the final stage of the game, there is nothing in the logic of orthodox game theory to support the assumption. We can only assume that Farrell's argument involves an appeal to players' intuitions about 'prominent' (or 'salient') strategies along the lines of Schelling's (1960) theory of focal points. But to support this notion, we would have to deviate significantly from the assumptions of standard game theory.[9]

Org: [After the experiment.] Did you expect your message to affect what they would do in the final round?
S1: If the amounts had been different, then I probably would have done. The fact that they were the same meant that I think we'd all come to the same conclusion really.

Farrell's assumption appears to be applicable in this experiment. Notice that the preliminary demands of B1, and B2, and S1 and S2 (each team demands £8 as their share of the pie) would constitute a Nash equilibrium if actually played in the final stage of the game; as such, the equilibrium has become focal.

It remains for us to consider whether there is a role for 'fairness' in the game being played. Güth, Schmittberger and Schwarze (1982) undertook a controlled investigation of a (one-stage) ultimatum game.[10] Their key finding is that behaviour deviates significantly from the game-theoretic prediction according to which Player 1 offers all but the smallest possible positive amount to Player 2, which Player 2 accepts on the grounds that a small amount is better than the zero which would result if the offer is turned down (see Rubinstein, 1982).

Org: [After the experiment.] Suppose you've got a situation between an employer and striking workers ...
B5: Yes, you know it's not an all or nothing situation, that if an employer gives too much they'll be back at work, but if he doesn't give enough, they might be out another week. But you know that there's going to be a result at some point. And you also know your employer is in a stronger position than the worker because he's a weekly worker and he knows he's not going to get any wages on Friday:

his bargaining power has immediately gone down because the employer knows he's more desperate and so can usually hold out longer than the employee. But here [the experiment]: it was equalised ... it makes you be fairer than you would be in a real situation.

B6: ... in business, I'd never be that fair [compared to the experiment]; you're always trying to get more for yourself.

B5 displays an intuitive grasp of the mechanisms at work in bargaining between employer and employee as formalised in models of behaviour following Rubinstein (1982). However, in the current setting, both B5 and B6 reject this instrumentally rational approach to bargaining in favour of a 'fair' approach. For both players, it appears that the context in which bargaining takes place determines whether or not rules of fairness apply.

Instead, subjects frequently settle on what they consider to be a fair or justified amount. Güth *et al.* also find that if player roles (first and second mover) are assigned by chance, then the more fortunate subjects are often reluctant to exploit their 'unjustified' strategic advantage. Moreover, some subjects are prepared to pay to avoid unfair allocations.

B9: I think we've got to show ...
B10: ... that we're serious about this? No, I don't agree with that at all. Because if you say to them, you give us all your cards, we're only going to give you 2 quid for them, they'll say, stuff you, that on an ethical basis that is not right, and I would rather have no money than put my principles ...

B10 voices the belief that the other team might forfeit any gains rather than accept an 'unethical' share of the pie. B9 is thus persuaded of the merit of offering the Sellers £4 (rather than £2) at the preliminary stage. In fact, the teams settle on £8 each at the final stage. But the demands of B9 and B10 appear to be grounded in pragmatism rather than a preference for fairness.

Kahneman, Knetsch and Thaler (1986) generated a similar set of findings in their investigation of the behaviour of firms. They conclude that *'the characteristics of transactors affect the environment in which profit-maximising firms operate and alter the behaviour of these firms in predictable ways'*. Factors which enter into the calcus may include the history of relations between firm and individual. Where, as a

S11: [On hearing that the teams have failed to reach an agreement: this team demanded £8, but the Buyers demanded £9.] The fools!
S12: The donkeys!
S11: ... Probably got a fascist mentality.
S12: I mean, £7!
S11: I just don't understand why they didn't go half and half ... I'd just go for 8 quid; it's the only fair thing, especially considering the

consequence rules of fairness are applied, they can induce wage stickiness or asymmetric price rigidities. The implication of these findings is that standard theory is mistaken in assuming that fairness is irrelevant to economic analysis. We should therefore be alert to the possibility that, in this experiment, a preference for fairness may enter in to the objective functions the players seek to maximise.

situation: you know we're just 4 people dragged in. You think, oh well, let's just share the money.
S12: Exactly. ...
S11: ... sending a message of 8 wasn't just a message of, that's what we want. It's also saying, you know, let's just split the money. Wasn't it?
S12: Right.
S11: That's what we decided.

> S11 and S12, and B11 and B12, have clearly failed in their negotiations. Both teams treated messages seriously; but the coded information they sent was not as transparent as they perceived it to be.

However, Binmore, Shaked and Sutton (1985) remain unconvinced that 'fair play' is of any consequence in bargaining behaviour. They claim that subjects' convictions about fairness or distributive justice are ephemeral; they are merely features of inexperienced play which are easily displaced by calculations of strategic advantage once players are fully cognisant of the structure of the game. In support of this claim, Binmore *et al.* point to the results of their own experiment with a two-stage ultimatum game in which a tendency to play as 'fairmen' in one game is replaced by a strong tendency to play as 'gamesmen' in a second game. On their view, players who display a tendency to make fair demands in the first game are simply choosing 'equal division' because it is an 'obvious' and 'acceptable' compromise in the face of a new problem.

Of course, the game being played in the experiment reported here is a one-shot demand game. But Binmore *et al.*'s finding does suggest that any tendency towards equal division (£8-£8) should be treated as a trivial and

S1: But they're thinking the same thing; we're both trying to get as much money for our team as possible. So if they're thinking, we want to get as much money but so do they, then I think the only fair offer is 8, and hope that they come to the same logical decision.
S2: Yes, I'm game.
S1: Yes, I think 8. You couldn't go any higher; and any less ... what do you think?
S2: Yes, I think we should go for that. [Completing message statement.] ... Does this mean we're not good capitalists, trying to be fair?
S1: [After the experiment.] Well, we both played it cooperatively ...
S2: ... fairly.
Org: What's your sense of 'fair'?
S1: Well, that both of us had something that was worth nothing without cooperation. So that means, equal cooperation..
Org: So you felt the 50-50 split was fair?
S1: Yes.

Org: What did you think about the result? [£8-£8 split.]
S3: Fair.
S4: Obvious.

unremarkable result, devoid of any ethical considerations on the part of the players, and a result which we would not expect the players to repeat.

Org: In what sense, obvious?
S3: If you think about it, the purpose of it is that everyone should get 8 - well, £4 each. ... it was obvious that £8 for each side was the only obvious outcome.
S4: It's a case of compromise.
S3: ... because everyone benefits instead of no-one benefitting.

> *In other words, Binmore et al. see any manifestation of 'fair' play in a one-shot game as mere noise and not representative of the behaviour of rational players. Certainly, equal division constitutes an 'obvious' solution for several of the players in this experiment. Yet it is a solution that is grounded in principles of fairness, and one that at least some players claim they would pursue again if the game was to be repeated.*

The small sample size does restrict the degree of significance which can be attached to any findings in this experiment. But the quantifiable results can be summarised, as follows:

- 4 of the 6 pairs of teams reached an agreement about the division of the pie;
- of these 4 pairs, the declared preliminary plans of only 1 pair constituted a Nash equilibrium, and these plans were indeed followed in the final and binding stage of the game;
- all 4 pairs who reached an agreement settled on an equal division of the pie;
- 9 of the 12 teams chose as their final demand the strategy which if chosen by both would yield an equal division of the pie (£8-£8);
- the mean preliminary demand of teams subset according to the number of aces held is:

B3: We've got 2 and we've got to get 2.
B4: Yes.
B3: The easiest way is so that they get 8 and we get 8.
B4: We're supposed to be maximising the amount of money. ... They're bound to put something higher, and we're bound to put something lower.
B3: If it was me, I'd put 8 to get it over and done quick.
B4: Oh, I don't know. [Waiting for final result.]
B3: Not very aggressive, really, are we?
B4: Well, I'm not like that.
Org: [After the experiment.] What do you mean by 'fair'?
B4: Everyone gets the same. We started off with the same: we had 2 aces and they had 2 aces; so it's only fair.
Org: Supposing you'd got 3 aces; then what would have been 'fair'?

- 1 ace: £9.50; 2 aces: £9.00;
- 3 aces: £10.25;
- the mean final demand of teams subset according to the number of aces held is: 1 ace: £8.00;
- 2 aces: £8.25; 3 aces: £8.25.

Thus, notice there is a tendency for both preliminary and final demands to rise with the number of aces held.[11]

B3: Probably have ended up with the same result.
Org: Suppose we ran the experiment again: would you do anything different?
B3: No.
Org: [Players have settled on an equal division of the pie.] If we ran the experiment again, would you behave any differently?
B5: No, I think I'd have done exactly the same. ... you'd be daft, don't you think, to do anything differently?

The last word

In the above representation neither rational choice theory nor the players are privileged with the last word on bargaining behaviour. Indeed, even within each narrative, there are several smaller narratives jostling for attention in the struggle to give meaning to behaviour.[12] This observation unsettles my confidence as the organising authority of the text: perhaps there should be more columns, less text, more text, but which text? It also becomes impossible to situate a 'Conclusion' at the end of the text, as the modern convention dictates; any conclusion about bargaining behaviour must be authorised by the narratives themselves and thus necessarily occupies their interstices. So let my last words, like the rest of my words, be an appropriation:

> This text, then, is also the piece, *perhaps* a piece of counterfeit money, that is, a machine for provoking events.
> (Derrida, 1992: 96)

Acknowledgements

I wish to thank Chris Starmer and Robert Sugden for their theoretical and organisational help with the experiment. Participants in the conference at Riverside provided invaluable comments on a first draft of this essay. No one is responsible for the result.

Notes

1   For example, James Friedman (1991: 44) states: 'It is easy to invent examples of games having multiple equilibria certain of which are intuitively unreason-

able. The basic thrust of refinements is the attempt to delineate criteria that can be used to separate the *reasonable* from the *unreasonable* equilibria'.
2 For example, an early paper by Morgan and Sawyer (1967) reports that the outcome of bargaining is significantly affected by whether the players are 'friends' or 'non-friends'. Friends, though they *prefer* equality, will accept an unequal solution when one believes the other might want it; non-friends appear less willing to accept anything but equal solutions. More recently, Kahneman *et al.* (1986) find that maxims of 'fairness' can enter into play which take their cue from the social environment and the interactions among transacting agents. For example, a player is prepared to accept a smaller amount when bargaining with a partner regarded as 'non-greedy', and will pursue a larger amount when bargaining with a partner regarded as 'greedy'. And Mehta *et al.* (1992) find people draw on common knowledge of social rules and conventions to help them identify the one solution on which their expectations can converge.
3 The complete set of instructions is available on application to the author.
4 On the orthodox view, the only features of the game which are relevant to rational players are the utility payoffs and the structure of the payoff matrix itself.
5 Card deals were randomly assigned, but deals in which the Buyer team received all 4 aces were excluded. Given the objectives of the experiment, this particular game would have been of no interest since it would not have faced the players with a coordination problem.
6 But note that throughout the conversations, Buyers are discussing the amount they are willing to offer the Sellers for their aces.
7 The expected proportion of the sample (of 6 teams) who would coordinate if their demands are chosen at random can be calculated as follows. First, we assume that a team comprised of rational players will not demand zero since they have nothing to lose by making a positive demand and might gain by doing so; by implication, we would expect no rational team to demand £16. We assume the universe of possible demands ranges from £0.50 to £15.50 in intervals of 50 pence; this seems a reasonable assumption given that in previous similar experiments, all players expressed their demands in multiples of 50 pence. If teams choose from 31 potential demands, then:

P[1st demand = £0.50 *and* 2nd demand £15.50] = $1/31 \times 31/31$
P[2nd demand = £1.00 *and* 2nd demand £ £15.00] = $1/31 \times 30/31$
and so on. Hence, the probability of coordination, assuming random demands, is:
$(1/31 \times 31/31) + (1/31 \times 30/31) + \ldots + (1/31 \times 1/31) = 0.523$.

8 In earlier experiments with bargaining problems, the author and her colleagues found that a significant number of initially symmetric players were indeed able to achieve asymmetric coordination (Mehta *et al.* 1994b).
9 For a development of the line of argument required to sustain the 'focal points' assumption, see Mehta *et al*, 1994a and 1994b.
10 This is a bargaining game in which Player 1 declares the amount a_1 of the pie of size c which they claim for themselves. The difference between c and a_1 is the amount which Player 1 wants to leave for Player 2. Player 2 must then decide whether to accept Player 1's proposal or not. If Player 2 accepts, Player 1 receives a_1 and Player 2 receives $c - a_1$; otherwise, both players receive zero.

11 The reader may be interested in the results of a very similar experiment conducted prior to the current experiment. The only difference between experiments was that the earlier one was conducted with a sample of 98 subjects playing as individuals rather than as teams of two. The results (to be discussed in a separate essay) can be summarised as follows:

- 44 (90%) pairs of subjects reached an agreement about the division of the pie;
- the declared preliminary plans of 12 pairs constituted a Nash equilibrium, and all 12 of these pairs followed their preliminary plans in the final and binding stage of the game (in line with Farrell's expectation);
- 51 (52%) subjects chose as their final demand the strategy which if followed by both would yield an equal division of the pie (£8-£8);
- the mean preliminary demand of subjects subset according to the number of aces held is: 1 ace: £7.30; 2 aces: £8.74; 3 aces: £9.70;
- the mean final demand of subjects subset according to the number of aces held is: 1 ace: £6.78; 2 aces: £7.83; 3 aces: £8.60.

These results suggest that, contrary to the orthodox game-theoretic view, players' demands, both at the message stage and the final stage, are strongly influenced by the number of aces held: the more aces a player holds, the higher are preliminary and final demands. This finding is supported by regression analysis, which also suggests that the asymmetric labelling of players as Buyer or Seller exerts a minor influence at the message stage, but is insignificant at the final stage. Thus:

(i) PREDEM = 6.303 + 1.210 DEAL − .070 LABEL
(10.116) (5.270) (.214)
where $R^2 = .23$ and Adjusted $R^2 = .21$

(ii) FINDEM = 6.061 + .447 EGOPRDEM − .264 OTHPRDEM + .080 LABEL
(9.633) (10.551) (6.225) (.549)
where $R^2 = .69$ and Adjusted $R^2 = .68$

Note that DEAL (number of aces held) is dropped from the second equation since it enters through players' preliminary demands (EGOPRDEM being the player's own preliminary demand, and OTHPRDEM their partner's preliminary demand).

12 In a verbal presentation of this essay, the two columns of text are spoken simultaneously. The reader may wish to try this 'reading' of the text for themselves. The cacophony which results is symptomatic of the problem of representation.

References

Binmore, K., Shaked, A. and Sutton, J. (1985) 'Testing Noncooperative Bargaining Theory: A Preliminary Study', *American Economic Review*, 75(5).

Crawford, V. and Sobel, J. (1982) 'Strategic Information Transmission', *Econometrica*, 50.

Derrida, J. (1987) *The Truth in Painting*, Chicago and London: University of Chicago Press.

—— (1992) *Given Time: I. Counterfeit Money*, Chicago and London: University of Chicago Press.

Farrell, J. (1987) 'Cheap Talk, Coordination, and Entry', *Rand Journal of Economics*, 18(1)

Farrell, J. and Gibbons, R. (1989) 'Cheap Talk Can Matter in Bargaining', *Journal of Economic Theory*, 48.

Foucault, M. (1971) *Madness and Civilization*, London: Routledge.

—— (1977) *Discipline and Punish*, London: Penguin.

—— (1984) 'On Power', reprinted in Kritzman L D, (ed), *Michel Foucault: Politics, Philosophy, Culture: Interviews and Other Writings 1977–1984*, New York and London: Routledge, Chapman and Hall, 1990.

Friedman, J. (1991) *Game Theory with Applications to Economics*, Oxford: Oxford University Press.

Güth, W., Schmittberger, R. and Schwarze, B. (1982) 'An Experimental Analysis of Ultimatum Bargaining', *Journal of Economic Behaviour and Organization*, 3.

Hegel, G. W. F. (1807) *Phenomenology of Spirit*, Oxford: Oxford University Press, 1977.

Heidegger, M. (1977) 'The Age of the World Picture', in *The Question Concerning Technology, and Other Essays*, New York and London: Harper and Row.

Kahneman, D., Knetsch, J. and Thaler, R. (1986) 'Fairness and the Assumptions of Economics', *Journal of Business*, 59(4) pt 2.

Klamer, A. (1984) *The New Classical Macroeconomics*, Sussex: Wheatsheaf Books.

Lyotard, J–F. (1984) *The Postmodern Condition: A Report on Knowledge*, Manchester: Manchester University Press.

Mehta, J. (1993) 'Meaning in the Context of Bargaining Games – Narratives in Opposition', in W. Henderson, T. Dudley-Evans and R. Backhouse (eds) *Economics and Language*, London and New York: Routledge.

Mehta, J. Starmer, C. and Sugden, R. (1992) 'An Experimental Investigation of Focal Points in Coordination and Bargaining: Some Preliminary Results', in Geweke J, (ed.) *Decision Making Under Risk and Uncertainty: New Models and Empirical Findings*, Dordrecht, Boston, London: Kluwer Academic Publishers.

—— (1994a) 'Focal Points in Pure Coordination Games: An Experimental Investigation', *Theory and Decision*, 36.

—— (1994b) 'The Nature of Salience: An Experimental Investigation of Pure Coordination Games', *American Economic Review*, 84(3).

Morgan, W. and Sawyer, J. (1967) 'Bargaining, Expectations, and the Preference for Equality Over Equity', *Journal of Personality and Social Psychology*, .6(2).

Nash, J. (1953) 'Two-Person Cooperative Games', *Econometrica*, 21.

Roth, A., Malouf, M. and Murnighan, J. (1981) 'Sociological Versus Strategic Factors in Bargaining', *Journal of Economic Behaviour and Organization*, 2.

Rubinstein, A. (1982) 'Perfect Equilibrium in a Bargaining Model', *Econometrica*, 50(1).

—— (1991) 'Comments on the Interpretation of Game Theory', *Econometrica*, 59(4).

Schelling, T. (1960) *The Strategy of Conflict*, Cambridge, MA: Harvard University Press.

19

POSTMODERN ENCOUNTERS

Henry Krips

The postmodern, David Harvey suggests, 'swims, even wallows, in the fragmentary and the chaotic currents of change as if that is all there is' (1989: 44). In particular, it 'insists upon the plurality of "power discourse" formations (Foucault), or of "language games" (Lyotard)'. More generally, it rejects any 'metalanguage, meta-narrative, or meta-theory through which all things can be connected or represented. Universal and eternal truths [and facts] if they exist at all, cannot be specified' (45).

Many of these postmodernist principles are underwritten by the philosophy of poststructuralism. In its deconstructive (Derridean) mode, this philosophy sets out to critique certain key oppositions such as text/context and the related opposition between language as code (langue) and as concrete utterances (parole). Indeed, by emphasizing the intertextual dimension of all discourse, poststructuralism undermines the whole notion of 'context' as a self-contained network of mutually interdefining linguistic terms (what Donald Davidson calls 'the very idea of a conceptual scheme'). In its Foucaultian form, poststructuralism also seeks to expose the strategic (and sometimes overtly political) intentions which sustain the apparent integrity of individual networks of terms. And finally, by showing that 'facts' are always and already linguistically mediated, it critiques the orthodox, Sassurean view that language expresses a domain of extra-linguistic facts.

The three essays in this volume upon which I shall comment, each take up some facet of the postmodern. However, each in its own way stops short of implementing a thoroughgoing postmodern analysis. This, I shall argue, indicates an inherent limitation of postmodern analysis rather than particular flaws in the essays. The limitation in question is that for an analysis of a particular discourse to be finite it must arrest the moment of poststructuralist critique at some point. To be specific, it must take for granted that certain propositions have a fixed identity within the discourse. In particular, it must accept them as 'facts', their meanings fixed by the discourse, rather than uncovering their polysemic nature by positioning them in a potentially endless field of other discursive settings. As Slavoj Žižek makes the point: 'the metonymical slippage must always be supported by a metaphoric cut' (1989: 154).

From a properly poststructuralist point of view, of course, such limitations upon poststructuralist critique must be taken as merely strategic, dictated by the requirement of finitude. I take my task here to be the constructive one of indicating possible directions in which such critique may be extended in particular cases, extensions which must nonetheless be halted at some point if the dialectic between structure and poststructure is to be finite in extent.

Cullenberg and Dasgupta

Cullenberg and Dasgupta seek to critically extend McCloskey's claim that the Cambridge capital controversy was rhetorical in nature, about 'something beyond mathematics or facts' p. 338). Specifically, they criticize McCloskey's restrictive distinction between 'fact' and 'logic' on the one hand and 'rhetoric' on the other. There are, they argue, no purely 'factual' or 'logical' issues which are not rhetorical as well. In particular, they claim that 'once one recognizes that facts have to be stated, and logic expressed, within a matrix of meanings, i.e. within a language' then one realizes that it is legitimate to study the Cambridge capital controversy (or indeed any other controversy) 'purely and entirely in terms of its language' (p. 338). In taking such a position they align themselves with a famous poststructuralist position, one which Alan Sokal has criticized recently, namely that 'there is nothing outside the text' (Derrida 1976: 158). In asserting this Derrida does not mean that there are no facts as such, however, but rather that all knowledge of which one speaks/writes is mediated by language and not merely a reflection of an extra-discursively constituted domain of facts.

Upon closer examination however, it would appear that Cullenberg and Dasgupta fail to consistently implement a poststructuralist perspective. Consider their claim that as the Cambridge capital controversy unfolded, the Cambridge (UK) group came to operate 'within an oppositional code' (p. 350), meaning that they translated the messages at the root of the controversy (namely neoclassical descriptions of double-switching and the aggregate production function) into an 'alternative (self-contained) frame of reference' (p. 350). By making this claim, Cullenberg and Dasgupta appear to transgress a fundamental poststructuralist principle, namely that, because it always and already risks subversion by its own context, no 'framework' is 'self-contained' or, as Derrida puts it trenchantly, 'no context permits saturation' (1979: 81).

By talking about 'alternative' – indeed rival – 'frames of reference', Cullenberg and Dasgupta apparently contradict another poststructuralist principle, namely that all oppositions are candidates for deconstruction, and in particular that what appears to be a 'rival' framework always and already carries at its heart an element of that which it 'opposes'. They also, it seems, contradict the poststructuralist axiom that all knowledge is textually mediated. In particular, by asserting that one group involved in the Cambridge controversy – Garegnani, Harcourt and Robinson – operated within a heterogeneous linguistic code, they seem to engage with a domain of pure 'facts', namely facts about certain speakers and the language they used. A more thoroughgoing poststructuralist analysis would reanalyze 'Garegnani', 'Harcourt' and 'Robinson' not as proper names belonging to real individuals but rather as constructs associated with corresponding signifiers, or, more specifically, with certain discursively constituted positions whose relation to real people is properly speaking outside the terms of the debate. It would also deconstruct the opposition between what Cullenberg and Dasgupta refer to as 'alternative frameworks', as well as between the Cambridge (UK) group's framework and context. The domain of linguistic facts which Cullenberg and Dasgupta take for granted might also be deconstructed, by showing how such 'facts' are strategically constructed to suit the terms of the local debate in which they are involved.

I am indicating Cullenberg and Dasgupta's 'failures' to implement a totally poststructuralist analysis not as a criticism of their work, however. On the contrary, as I indicated in the introduction, in any finite analysis the moment of poststructuralist critique must be arrested at some point. Instead, my intention is to indicate possible ways in which such critique might be continued. The question of whether and in what direction it should be continued is, then, a matter to be decided in relation to the local purposes of whoever continues the analysis.

Hargreaves Heap

Heap's essay argues for an extension of economic orthodoxy to an area of economic behaviour which he calls 'the post-modern'. He considers what he calls 'an extreme form of a postmodern conflict' in which not only do 'the parties agree about nothing' but also their disagreement is irreconcilable because they recognize no extra-discursive 'fact of the matter' which would settle their dispute (p. 371). In such situations, it seems, the parties can only 'smile knowingly and exclaim 'c'est le differend' (p. 340). Heap argues that although a situation of radical disagreement may seem to be the very worst-case scenario for neoclassical economics, it is (ironically) 'the one time when it might seem appropriate to use the neoclassical model' (p. 371). His argument to this effect depends upon a particular way of explicating the Kantean principle of universalizability, namely in terms of the Kalai-Smorodinsky principle 'that any group's relative concession is matched by all other groups' concessions' (p. 369).

Rather than discussing the validity of Heap's specific gloss of the universalizability principle, I focus upon the relation of his essay to Cullenberg and Dasgupta's. Heap's argument illustrates perfectly Cullenberg and Dasgupta's contention that neoclassical economics is capable of comprehending even the apparently most recalcitrant empirical situations. In particular, he shows how neoclassical economics can deal with what he calls 'postmodern conflicts' in which the economic agents themselves, rather than the theorists who describe their behavior, recognize that, in Berman's words, all that is solid melts into air, and, in particular, that there is no extra-discursive truth which will settle disagreements. In short, Heap, unlike Cullenberg and Dasgupta, concerns himself with the postmodern at a substantive rather than methodological level. That is, his concern is to theorize the world of postmodern economic agents within a neoclassical framework rather than, as Cullenberg and Dasgupta do, retheorize the world of economists in terms of a poststructuralist theoretical framework.

As in the case of Cullenberg and Dasgupta's analysis, the terms of Heap's analysis can be deconstructed. In particular, it can be argued that in his efforts to preserve the neoclassical metalinguistic framework, Heaps has impoverished the object language concept of the postmodern. 'Postmodern agents', according to Heap, are individuals who, because they recognize no facts of the matter, engage in irreconcilable disagreements, to which they respond by 'smiling knowingly'. A richer concept of the postmodern would construe postmodern agents along different lines as individuals who, refusing to recognize any distinction between language and metalanguage, go outside the framework within which a decision is reached rather than attempting to reach a decision within such a framework. Such postmodern agents, unlike Heap's 'knowing smilers', stretch the resources of neoclassical economics – which brings us neatly to the third of the essays to be considered here.

Mehta

Mehta's essay is in some respects the antithesis of Heap's. Rather than attempting to extend neoclassical thought to the postmodern, she concerns herself with situations in which the symbolic grid of neoclassical economic theory fails to take a grip. In particular, she considers situations of people coming to agreement when they play Nash's 'demand game', situations in which, because of the existence of multiple Nash equilibria, there is no unique solution to the problem of rational choice. Because, as Mehta puts it, 'there simply has been no other language [no language other than rational choice theory] in which to talk or do economics', such situations constitute what she calls 'white noise' (p. 374). That is, because the language of economics can offer no account of the strategies and discourses by which people in fact come to decisions in such situations, their description from an economic point of view counts merely as static.

Mehta then asks how such truant situations can be represented. She suggests describing them in terms of 'other voices' within the household but from outside the frame of traditional economics (p. 374). In particular, her strategy is to 'interrupt our [economists'] discourse' by 'report[ing] excerpts from transcripts of conversations with and between people as they engage in bargaining problems' (p. 376). In short she reports/constructs a sort of folk economic discourse which falls outside the decoding/encoding strategies of official discourse (what Cullenberg and Dasgupta call 'the negotiated code'). It is the dissonance between these voices and neoclassical theory which, then, constitutes the site of action of the new postmodern sensibility – what Mehta calls a 'new self-consciousness' (p. 374). Like Heap, Mehta considers what may be classified as a postmodern economic situation. But, whereas for Heap the postmodern is characterized by radical disagreement, for Mehta (and here she cites Lyotard) it is characterized by 'that which in the modern, puts forward the unpresentable in presentation itself...that which searches for new presentations, not in order to enjoy them but in order to import a strong sense of the unpresentable' (p. 375). In short, the postmodern is associated with phenomena which are excluded by the dominant discourses of the 'modern' understood as the official and the contemporary. A tension is apparent within Mehta's remarks at this point. For her, we have seen, the vehicles which trail the postmodern into the economic sphere are 'other' voices, the 'native' voices of the economic agents themselves rather than of the economists who describe their behaviour. Which is not to say that she privileges the native voices as the sites of a postmodern sensibility – 'neither rational choice theory nor the players are privileged with the last word on bargaining behaviour' (p. 395). On the contrary, she says, 'any conclusion...necessarily occupies their [the voices'] interstices' (p. 395).

Despite the latter qualification, at this point in her argument Mehta seems to be straying from the letter of Lyotard's principle that the postmodern inhabits the space outside the discursive as such, the space of white noise where, losing its sense, the voice disintegrates into noise and the signifier metamorphoses into the letter. To conceptualize such noise in terms of a dissonance with 'other voices', as Mehta does, is to be unduly restrictive. Instead, and here I follow Lyotard, the postmodern is the site of what Lacan calls 'the Real': an inchoate 'rupture between perception and consciousness' when we know something exists without knowing what it is, that is, without its falling under some form of knowledge (Lacan 1978: 56).

How, then, as economists can we take into account the Real in this generalized sense? I suggest that it is by focusing upon the paradoxes, the monsters, the anomalies which constitute the white noise at the edges of neoclassical theory. On particular occasions, Mehta suggests, such a focus may be enabled by foregrounding other dissonant voices within the household (economy). However, one must resist the temptation to generalize this special case and conclude that white noise is always constituted through the advent of 'other' voices. On the contrary, Lyotard's principle allows that white noise may be constituted simply by interruptions to the voice, a static which speaks in no voice at all.

In general terms, this means that the postmodern in Mehta's transcriptions resides not, as she claims, in the dissonance between her informants' voices, her own voice, and the otherwise deafening roar of neoclassical theory. Instead, it is to be found in those limits to the modern discourse of neoclassical theory which, in the local context of her paper, the dissonance between those various voices foregrounds. In short, the postmodern subsists not in a heteroglossia of 'other' voices but rather in those strange liminal moments when the ideologically constituted integrity of the voice disintegrates into white noise, and we lose our grip upon reality, and confront the Real. Mehta's work, as well as the essays by Heap, and Cullenberg and Dasgupta, lead us to encounters with this twilight zone.

References

Derrida, Jacques (1976) *Of Grammatology*, trans. Gayatri Chakravorty Spivak, Baltimore: Johns Hopkins Press.

—— (1979) 'Living On', in Harold Bloom *et al.* (eds) *Deconstruction and Criticism*, London: Routledge.

Harvey, David (1989) *The Condition of Postmodernity*, Oxford: Blackwell.

Lacan, Jacques (1978) *The Four Fundamental Concepts of Psychoanalysis*, trans. Alan Sheridan, (ed.) Jacques-Alain Miller, New York: Norton.

Zizek, Slavoj (1989) *The Sublime Object of Ideology*, London: Verso.

PART VII

IS THERE A (POSTMODERN) ALTERNATIVE IN ECONOMICS?

From markets to gifts

20
DECENTERING THE MARKET METAPHOR IN INTERNATIONAL ECONOMICS

William Milberg

Fredric Jameson writes that the term 'the market' has always had a dual meaning, being 'at one and the same time an ideology and a set of practical institutional problems'.[1] In this paper I argue that the 'metanarrative' of economics – the beneficence of the free market – is built on a central metaphor of 'the economy as market system' that is as ideological as it is practical. I focus on the field of international economics, where the centrality of the market metaphor has narrowed the scope of the analysis of the international economy to such an extent that economics has been unable to recognize certain important trends, much less theorize them. The exclusive focus on markets has precluded a rigorous treatment of new developments in the organization of business and the production process and in the role of the state in international transactions.

The metaphors of 'economy as market system' and 'economy as equilibrium state' that characterize modern economics are particularly inappropriate as the basis for a description of contemporary international economic relations. While international economic theory is still today largely an application of general equilibrium analysis, trends in the international integration of production are moving a growing share of international transactions outside the confines of 'the market' and into the realm of non-arm's-length transactions, in which the two parties in the exchange either have common ownership or some other contractual relation, or that involve the state as buyer or seller. Moreover, there is a growing list of international corporate alliances, in which corporations from different nations share services and information. The 'competition' that underpins 'general competitive analysis' thus has a diminishing role in international economics. Not surprisingly, then, the equilibria that gird the notion of 'the international market' as the constitutive metaphor for international economists have also diminished in relevance. Large and persistent trade imbalances, recurring balance of payments crises, and considerable (though unevenly distributed) excess capacity are increasingly the norm. The metaphor of the market economy and the related concept of equilibrium are no longer relevant to a large portion of international economic relations.

The conception of science that has dominated economics since the 1870s has asserted that market exchange constitutes the full scope of economic thought.[2] The continued dominance of the market metaphor in a world in which its applicability is in doubt, is due in part to the inevitably slow pace at which the Lakatosian core is overturned in any science. But the result of this reduction of 'economy' to 'market' is that modern international economics lacks a serious treatment of the firm and the state, the two institutions that today are extending the scope of non-arm's-length transactions in the international economic relations. In its insistence on a binary demarcation between market and non-market, economics presents the former as both pure and universal. The limits of this dichotomy for the analysis of the family have been the focus of numerous studies.[3] In this essay, I emphasize the weakness of this binary opposition for a sphere much closer to traditional economic analysis, that of international trade and finance.

Postmodernism and markets

The metanarrative

Postmodernist thinking in economics has developed along two main lines. The first is a critique of claims to objectivity. The second is a criticism of the economics conception of a unified and rational subject.[4] I want to emphasize the way these two lines of criticism are linked. The critique of objectivity has largely been driven by a reconceptualization of economics as discourse, in which truth claims are viewed as efforts to persuade using metaphors and other rhetorical figures.

The critique of the notion of subjectivity in economics focuses on the static, asocial and homogeneous nature of 'homo economicus'. The concept has been attacked by Marxists, feminists, Post Keynesians, institutionalists and others for decades. The postmodernist attack has been on the assumed exogeneity of the process of subjectivity and the stasis of the subject as a social being. That is, the notion is based on the idea that individual identity already exists prior to any interaction with 'the economy', and that it doesn't change with such interaction. Preferences are 'exogenous' and fixed. The postmodern notion of subjectivity insists not only on the endogeneity of 'preferences', but on the ongoing nature of the process of subjectivity, whereby identity is created and recreated through individual choices, structures of constraint and social change.

Postmodern critiques of objectivity and economic subjectivity are linked. Both are attacks on the modernism of knowledge in economics. In his well-known essay, *The Postmodern Condition: A Report on Knowledge*, Lyotard (1984) identifies the 'metanarrative' or 'grand narrative' as key to the legitimation of modern knowledge, and in particular its foundationalist claims.[5] Metanarrative is narrative that purports to capture the totality of a given field and thus that serves to structure its knowledge, for example the notion of history as the story of the progress of mankind. For Lyotard, such narratives are exclusionary and presume universality. Postmodernism, by contrast, rejects the metanarrative as the basis of knowledge. According to Lyotard:

> In contemporary society and culture – postindustrial society, postmodern culture – the question of the legitimation of knowledge is formulated in different terms. The grand narrative has lost its credibility, regardless of what mode of unification it uses, regardless of whether it is a speculative narrative or a narrative of emancipation.
>
> (1984: 37)

'The beneficent role of the free market' is truly the metanarrative of economics. Its status derives from its purported naturalness and thus universality – the narrative is relevant across all time and space – as well as its emancipatory theme. In economic thought – from Smith's 'society of perfect liberty' to Samuelson's 'first fundamental theorem of welfare economics' (i.e. that general equilibrium is Pareto optimal) – the market represents the locus of attainment of both individual freedom and maximum social welfare. The market has served as *the* organizing construct for economic thought. Market competition and market forces are the foundation of the economic notions of equilibrium, welfare, agency, economic policy and scientific legitimacy. Market analysis demarcates economic from non-economic thought. That which can be subjected to market analysis – be it recognizable markets or spheres in which interaction is like ('as if') a market – is contained within the proper scope of economics. Polanyi (1957: 270) referred to this conflation of market with economy as the 'economistic fallacy'. According to this binary approach, non-market phenomena are distinct and non-economic. What if we attempt to explode, or at least reverse, this binary dissection of society? To do so, we must begin by exploring the metaphoric power of the notion of markets.

Economic metaphors

The idea of 'the economy as market system' functions as a metaphor in the metanarrative of economic knowledge. What makes the market a metaphor? According to Webster, a metaphor is an 'implied comparison, in which a word or phrase ordinarily and primarily used of one thing is applied to another (e.g., screaming headlines, 'all the world's a stage'). [6] Thus, a metaphor is a figure of speech that makes meaning by substituting for one thing something it doesn't typically resemble. A figure is any non-literal way of describing or referring to something. What distinguishes different types of figures from each other is the way they make meaning – by analogy, or by contiguity, social consensus, or resemblance (i.e. metaphor). All language is figural in that the relation between the word (or image) and the concept it represents is fundamentally arbitrary. There is no reason, for example that we call a tree 'a tree' in English or 'un arbre' in French. There is no *natural* relation between the word and the thing, or what Saussure call the signifier and the signified. According to Saussure:

> The bond between the signifier and the signified is arbitrary...The term [arbitrary] should not imply that the choice of the signifier is left entirely to the speaker (we shall see below that the individual does not have the power to change a sign in any way once it has become established in the linguistic community); I mean that it is unmotivated, i.e. arbitrary in that it actually has no natural connection with the signified.
> ([1915]1966: 67, 69)

As language is inherently figural, so must be any interpretation or theory. If all language is non-literal, why do we make the distinction between literal and figurative? The figurative trumpets its figurativeness. To say that the market is a metaphor is not to suggest that all other economic terms should be understood literally. It is instead to highlight its status as a construct of the discipline. Markets are a social construct in two senses. First, markets don't exist in nature but take particular forms depending on culture and history. Second, markets have no reality beyond our conceptualization of them, that is, our knowledge of markets and market forces is framed by out narratives about how markets work. Thus, the issue is not that representation through metaphor is unscientific. It is that the centrality and primacy of the metaphor of 'economy as market system' is a particular and for many purposes narrow focus for the study of the global economy.

The power of market analysis

Market analysis has been central to the grand narrative of economics for centuries because it gives a sense of order to the perception of an otherwise chaotic social existence, providing what Adam Smith termed an essential component of any science, 'to allay the tumult of the imagination.'[7] But economics moves from the status of mere 'political economy' to that of true 'economic science' at the point when the analysis of market exchange comprises the *full scope* of economics. Thus modern economics is synonymous with the analysis of market exchange, whereas classical economics sought to uncover the natural laws of value and distribution around which market outcomes were said to fluctuate.

The power of market analysis comes from its two basic, and connected premises: the anonymity of market relations and the autonomy of markets themselves. The anonymity of market relations implies that the buyer and seller in the market are independent, as are their respective motives. These transactors in the market are said to act exclusively in their own self-interest. Rivalry characterizes the relation among suppliers, and supplier–demander relations are based on the complete independence of the two sides of the market. Thus market transactions are termed 'arm's-length' transactions.

The impersonalness of the market also requires that the actors – their preferences, technologies and endowments – are *given* to the economic problem of market analysis, as opposed to being endogenous to any process of market interaction. This has two important implications. First, it implies that the production process is largely given and can be neglected.[8] Second, it roots market dynamics in nature, rendering them autonomous and determined by the natural 'laws' of supply and demand. The impersonal and natural characteristics of markets together make analysis of market interaction – economics – scientific. Even if we understand the problem of modern economics to be the analysis of given but socially constructed conditions, we still must retain the independence of market from other social forces. When markets are viewed as embedded in a broader social structure, economic science becomes indistinguishable from economic anthropology and economic sociology. But efforts to reconstruct economics with a notion of markets and other institutions as more broadly embedded have met enormous resistance from economists. According to Barber (1995: 388), 'the career of the concept of embeddedness can be seen as one long struggle to overcome, to correct, the common tendency among economists and others to…the absolutization of the market'.[9]

With markets at the center of economics, the result of the working-out of market 'forces' – that is, the attainment of market equilibrium – becomes the focus of all economic analysis. Model assumptions are unapologetically adopted simply on the grounds that they are necessary if the model is to exhibit a stable equilibrium. Equilibrium represents closure, as in any classic realist literary text. According to Belsey (1980: 80), 'the movement of the classic realist narrative towards closure ensures the reinstatement of order, sometimes a new order, sometimes the old restored, but always intelligible because familiar.' Belsey's (1980) description is of fiction, but it is surprisingly relevant to contemporary economic narratives about the economy.[10]

When there is less than arm's length between buyer and seller, market forces break down. Market analysis, that is, modern economic tools, are rendered inadequate. For one, it is difficult to prove the stability of a market equilibrium when supply and demand are interdependent, a point already noted in the nineteenth-century with Marshall's depiction of downsloping supply and demand curves. Second, the individual freedom said to be realized in market exchange is compromised when supply determines demand (or vice versa). If preferences, for example, are driven by cultural conditions including market structure and workplace organization, then the subjectivity of preferences can no longer provide adequate philosophical foundations for economics.[11]

Markets and the international economy

There has recently been a growing awareness of the limited scope of the market, especially in light of new research on the household and the firm.[12] According to Auerbach (1988) 'Of the enormous number of transactions in an economy, only a tiny fraction of them take place in what may literally be described as a market.' Klamer and McCloskey (1995), drawing on Hirschman's (1970) three forms of economic signaling (exit, voice, and loyalty) estimate that about 25 per cent of GDP is 'persuasion', that is, not related to anonymous market interaction. Feminist economists have also rejected the centrality of market forces in the study of economy. Nelson (1993) for example, rejects both the neoclassical emphasis on markets as a locus of free choice and the classical focus on natural laws of distribution of income and wealth. She argues instead for a focus on:

> the provisioning of human life, that is on the commodities and processes necessary to human survival...Such a study of economics need not rule out studies of exchange, but it does displace them from the core of economics. When human survival – including survival through childhood – is made the core of economic inquiry, nonmaterial services, such as child care and supervision, as well as attendance to health concerns and the transmission of skills, becomes just as central as food and shelter.
> (Nelson, 1993: 32–33)

Despite these developments, the market metaphor continues to predominate in theories of international trade.

In the neoclassical tradition, international trade is an application of general equilibrium analysis. Capital and labor are 'endowed' on a country, individual consumer preferences and technological knowledge given exogenously, and the direction of trade and the gains from trade are determined as the result of equilibrium prices and trade quantities (i.e. exports and imports) that derive from the logic of firm and consumer optimization in the transition from a state of 'autarky' to one of 'free trade' under conditions of perfect competition and constant returns to scale.[13]

'Pure' trade models assume the absence of capital flows. As a result, balanced trade (that is, exports equal imports for all countries) is an equilibrium condition. In standard macroeconomic models, the trade balance is determined by private and public saving and investment. Comparative advantage determines which commodities each country exports and imports. Free trade in goods not only brings efficient resource allocation and maximum social welfare for all nations, but also equalizes factor prices (wage and profit rates) globally, thus rendering international factor mobility unnecessary for the attainment of efficiency.

Constructing comparative advantage

'[W]hen they affirm a law', writes McCloskey (1985: 57, 58), 'scientists are trying to persuade other scientists...Proofs of the law of demand are mostly literary.' So it is with comparative advantage. Like the law of demand, the principle of comparative advantage is based on a very particular construction, and its proof relies even more heavily on introspection and analogy than does the law of demand. In fact, while the law of comparative advantage is commonly referred to as the most widely accepted principle among economists, it has never been formally generalized. It is fairly simple to extend Ricardo's well-known example of English and Portuguese wine and cloth production and trade to the case of many countries and two commodities or many commodities and two countries. But it has never been shown that the principle yields a deterministic result in the case of many countries and commodities. The most developed attempt of this case is Jones (1961). But in order to get a deterministic result he assumes that the number of countries and commodities are the same and that each country specializes in the production of, and thus exports, a different commodity. Deardorff's (1980) proof of 'the general validity of the law of comparative advantage' ultimately abandons the goal of determinism and settles for a probabilistic relation between relatively high (low) productivity in a sector and exports (imports). This uncertainty and openness belies the determinism and symmetry implied by the principle of comparative advantage. The simple techniques adopted for market closure – for example, assuming a limited number of goods and countries, full employment, balanced trade

– hardly support economists' claims of the universal relevance of comparative advantage in the determination of the international division of labor. In sum, the principle of comparative advantage is a much more delicate construction than the textbooks indicate, and the rise of a 'New International Economics' (see below) reflects the fragmentation of knowledge to which this fragility leads.

The principle of comparative advantage dates to the classicals, but it is with the neoclassical conception of markets that comparative advantage becomes determined by natural endowments, thus leaving the determination of trade flows to 'nature'. As with the binary opposition between market and non-market spheres, the natural/social demarcation is artificial and problematic. What if, for example, trade itself leads to changes in labor skills or technological capabilities? Then the traditional link between trade and factor endowments would be reversed. The assertion of a natural basis for trade ultimately has a double edge for neoclassical economics. On the one hand, it anchors economic outcomes in the natural realm, thus bestowing on the process a status akin to that analyzed by the natural sciences. On the other hand, by positing the determination as outside of the market proper, the narrative of international trade leaves its determinants outside the realm of the economic sphere. Thus defining 'the natural' is also to demarcate a distinct social sphere, and to circumscribe a proper scope of economic analysis.[14]

While the law of comparative advantage – in both its classical and neoclassical versions – can be seen as a delicate construction, it is the particularity of its conception of the firm and the state that identify it so completely with the constitutive metaphor of the economy as strictly a set of markets. Both classical and neoclassical trade theories are based on a conception of an industry as consisting usually of a single firm, in effect a metaphorical 'national firm'. In such a world, intra-industry trade (trade in similar products between two nations) is a logical impossibility, since by definition no two nations have a comparative advantage in the same sector. Multifirm industries are at most contained of identical firms, precluding any heterogeneity in firm response to similar market forces.[15] Moreover, intra-firm trade is ruled out by construction: there is no rationale for a single 'firm' to operate in two countries, since international factor movements are seen as unnecessary to bring about an optimal result. Foreign direct investment then has no role in the determination of trade flows. Also, the role of the state in raising national welfare is limited to a single and narrow case of market failure. A nation with market power (that is, facing less than perfectly elastic demand) can impose an 'optimal tariff', altering relative prices to raise its export revenues and its national welfare.

The neoclassical reconstruction

In the late 1970s, international economists began exploring the implications of relaxing the assumptions of perfect competition and constant returns to scale and of replacing 'rational economic man' with 'game-playing man', that is introducing strategic behavior on the part of individual agents. This was motivated in part by the desire to explain the observed importance of intra-industry trade and the apparent success of some trade-orientated industrial policies, such as in Japan and South Korea. While these models invariably assume full employment and balanced trade, they also attribute trade to factors other than comparative advantage. As a result, commercial policy (e.g., subsidies and tariffs) can be shown to be welfare enhancing for a given nation under certain conditions.[16]

The pro-interventionist conclusions of much of the new international economics have proven to be too contentious in a profession whose broad adherence to the principle of free trade has been one of its hallmarks. Paul Krugman, the founder of this 'new international economics', has himself backed away from the policy conclusions of these optimization models, arguing that they are too sensitive to particular assumptions and that their application to actual policy would require an unrealistic ability for disinterested fine tuning on the part of the state.[17] Krugman's retreat from these heretical conclusions reveals a discrepancy between the rigor with which market dynamics are analyzed and the looseness in the treatment in the notion of the state. Market dynamics based on rational-agent optimization are painstakingly constructed both mathematically and verbally. Conclusions about the capacities and nature of the state, on the other hand, are drawn almost whimsically, and based on casual observation and even stereotype. Such an asymmetry in the treatment of markets and states is only acceptable because the dominant and central metaphor of economic discourse is 'the economy as market system'.[18] Why is the state treated so cavalierly, the market so 'scientifically'? Non-market institutions are notoriously difficult to interpret through the lens of the market. And while neoclassical economists have largely agreed that this metaphorical transfer is acceptable when it comes to the study of the firm (see below), no such agreement exists about the conceptualization of the state. Moreover, 'policy relevance' has emerged as an important criterion of professional significance. Rendering the variations of the market metaphor policy relevant has required a flexibility in the representation of the role of the state and state-market relations. To put it more strongly, policy relevance requires flexibility in the treatment of policy as a necessary antidote to the sterility of the treatment of the market.[19]

Firms and states in international transactions

In the theory of international trade, both old and new, all transactions are market transactions. Firms face perfectly competitive factor markets domestically and either perfect or imperfect competition in international product markets. Entirely overlooked in this conception is the significant volume of international transactions that take place within the firm, with the heavy involvement of the state, or even between firms cooperating with each other. Simply put, the scope of transactions in the international economy is much broader than the theory of international trade would lead us to believe. Today's international economic relations are characterized by considerable amounts of non-arm's-length transactions. These take the form of intra-firm trade, inter-corporate joint ventures and alliances, special arrangements between buyers and sellers (suppliers), and state-negotiated trade. The scope of this array of forms of non-arm's-length transactions is so broad that the relevance of the market cum locus of arm's-length transactions is greatly diminished. The dominance of the market metaphor in the discourse of international economics has made it difficult for economists to even identify certain trends (for example, in intra-firm trade), much less theorize them. As a result, this task has fallen increasingly to experts in management and political science.[20]

Intra-firm trade

Intra-firm trade is the international trade of goods or services within a single firm. Since the firm in this case is, by definition, a transnational corporation (TNC), the large share of intra-firm trade in overall international trade is a relatively recent phenomenon. Moreover, it is neglected in both the old and new international economics, because neither even has a theory of the transnational corporation.[21] While transnational corporations have existed for over 300 years, their prominence has risen steadily over the past twenty-five years. By the late 1990s there were about 53,000 parent transnational corporations, compared to only 7,000 in 1970. These corporations controlled over 448,000 foreign affiliates. The world stock of outward foreign direct investment reached $3.5 trillion in 1997, up from $2.1 trillion in 1993 and $282 million in 1975. The share of foreign direct investment in world gross capital formation rose by two-thirds between the early 1980s and the early 1990s; for developing countries, the increase was by three-quarters. Other indicators of international production by firms have risen accordingly. Between 1975 and 1992, the number of employees of transnational corporations almost doubled from 40 to 73 million employees, and since 1985 almost all the expansion was accounted for by employment in affiliates. Between 1986 and 1995, sales of foreign affiliates of transnational corporations grew by almost 15 per cent per annum, compared with only 2 per cent in the first half of the 1980s. Assets of foreign affiliates grew almost 20 per cent per annum since the mid-1980s.[22]

On average, transnational corporations today have many more foreign subsidiaries and affiliates than they did twenty-five years ago. More important, the organization of the transnational corporation has changed quite drastically over this period. The typical transnational corporation in the 1960s had subsidiaries that either produced the product for shipment to the home country, or it served as a marketing branch in the host country. Today, the transnational corporation has widened its geographic coverage and deepened the nature of the links among affiliates. The widening of the geographic coverage was already noted by Vernon (1979). The trend has continued since, and taken the form of both horizontal and vertical integration. A stylized example is depicted in Figure 20.1, which illustrates how the expansion of the transnational corporation may involve the establishment of foreign affiliates through direct investment, or develop foreign linkages through licensing, subcontracting or joint venture.

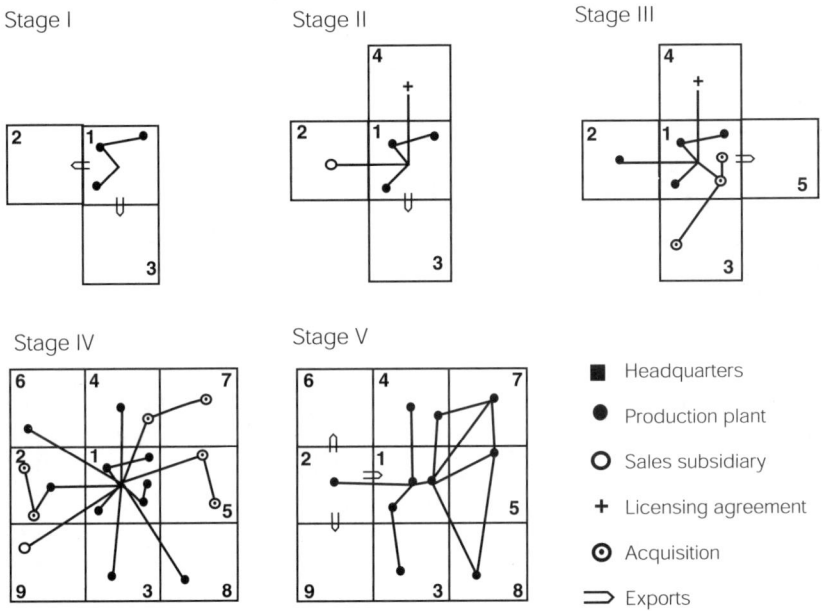

Figure 20.1 Organization and location of a transnational corporation: hypothetical case

Source: Dicken (1992: 211)

To ignore intra-firm trade, then, in a discussion of the theory of international trade or in the formulation of trade policy, is to ignore a major share of world transactions. Table 20.1 gives the share of intra-firm trade in total trade of the USA, Japan and Sweden. For the USA, in 1993, 36 per cent of exports and 43 per cent of imports were intra-firm. The figures for manufacturing alone are even higher in most cases.

Intra-firm trade has considerable consequences for the US balance of trade. According to a study of the 1980s, the US balance on intra-firm trade in 1982 was in deficit of $25.9 billion. This consisted of a surplus of $4.6 billion for US-based transnational corporations and a $30.6 billion deficit of foreign based transnational corporations. Consider the politically sensitive case of US–Japanese trade. About two-thirds of US imports from Japan are intra-firm trade by Japanese transnational corporations. And even US exports to Japan are dominated by intra-firm trade by Japanese transnational corporations.[23]

Intra-firm trade is likely to increase in the future as firms become increasingly multinational. But the particular form of this multinationalization is quite important. Transnational corporations may 'widen' their degree of integration by replicating existing affiliates in other countries. Transnational corporations are said to 'deepen' their international integration when they integrate more sophisticated aspects of operations

Table 20.1 Intra-firm trade, USA, Japan, and Sweden, selected years (percentages)

USA	1977	1982	1983	1989	1992	1993
Share of intra-firm exports in total exports	36	33	34.2	36	37.2	36
Share of intra-firm imports in total imports	40	37	36.8	42.8	42.5	43
Japan	1977	1982	1983	1989	1992	1993
Share of intra-firm exports in total exports	n.a.	n.a.	22.5	24.5	26.9	25
Share of intra-firm imports in total imports	n.a.	n.a.	15.1	15.3	14.8	14
Sweden[1]			1986			1994
Share of intra-firm exports in total exports			38			38
Share of intra-firm imports in total imports			3			9

Source: United Nations Centre for Transnational Corporations (1988), United Nations (1994) and (1996).

Note:
[1] Data covering only manufacturing

among affiliates. While transnational corporations have increasingly integrated in both ways, the recent trend is for transnational corporations to integrate with foreign affiliates at even the most sophisticated levels of the firm's operations. This has been termed a 'deepening of the functional integration' of transnational corporations.[24]

The process of deepening functional integration of the transnational corporation is illustrated in Figure 20.2. In case (a), interaction between parent and affiliates is limited to one or two functions. Case (b) is the much broader functional integration of international production. Also, the integration takes place even in the firm's most sophisticated functions. Note that Figure 20.2 depicts, for simplicity, a transnational corporation with only a single foreign affiliate. Note also that in the case of both widening and deepening, the transnational corporations arm's-length exports may not rise. But non-arm's-length transactions are likely to be rising, as the firm's functions have been integrated at increasingly higher levels of the value chain. Thus while world trade has grown steadily but slowly relative to GDP over the past 25 years, reaching their 1913 level only in the late 1970s, the share of intermediate goods in total trade rose more rapidly.[25]

With deepening international integration of production, the national identity of a transnational corporation has become increasingly difficult to pinpoint and, in many respects, less important, rendering the 'national firms' of trade theory even more inappropriate as characterizations of contemporary production units. Also, it raises thorny questions for national economic policy by distinguishing a nation's assets from its property owners.[26]

Interfirm collaboration

While transnational corporation integration raises the level of intra-firm trade, there are a growing number of cooperative arrangements among otherwise rival corporations that represent non-arm's-length transactions that are not captured by the intra-firm trade statistics. These intercorporate alliances range in nature from the sharing of technological information, to the sharing of marketing, distribution or after-sales servicing functions, to agreement on joint production. The intercorporate sharing of technological information is particularly common, with over 8,000 cases of inter-firm technology agreements recorded between 1980 and 1996. In 1996 alone, 650 of these agreements were made.[27] These are motivated by the desire of firms to share in the cost and risk of new high-tech product development (e.g. biotech, new materials technology, semiconductors). For example, three major transnational corporations in the semiconductor industry, IBM, Toshiba and Siemens, signed an agreement in 1992 to 'share the huge costs involved in designing the new

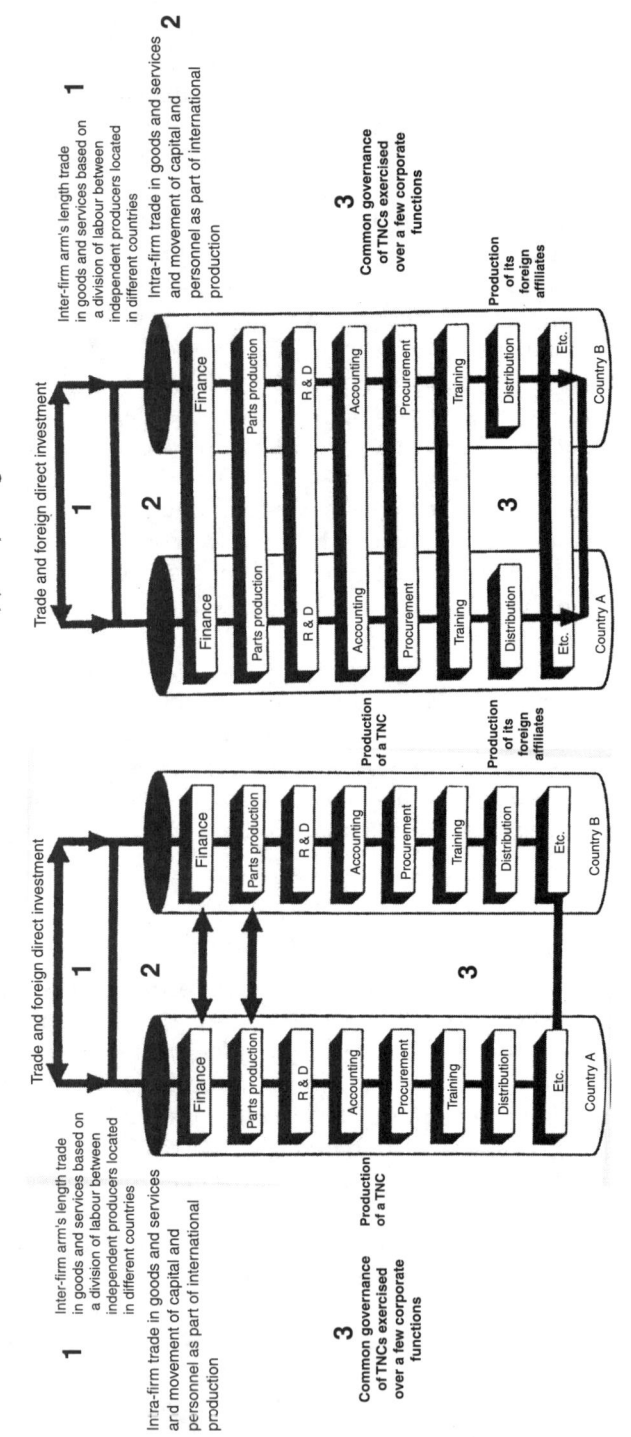

Figure 20.2 Varieties of international intra-firm integration of production
Source: United Nations 1993: 162–3

[256 megabyte] chip and its fabrication process (estimated at $1 billion) and the risk associated with it.'[28] In other industries, such as automobiles, chemicals, food and beverages, consumer electronics and even services, the alliances are motivated by the desire for market access. In the airline industry, for example, there is a growing web of shared use of computer reservation systems. The links are shown in Figure 20.3. According to the United Nations:

> Given the cost of establishing and operating such systems and providing the related services, an increasing number of airlines pool these resources and engage in CRS-alliances [computer reservation systems]. These are often cemented by equity stakes from the partner airlines. International airlines establish technical assistance links, code-sharing and other forms of commercial alliances mainly for some complementary strategies: to get access to foreign markets through the marketing and distribution networks of their partners; to capitalize CRS software and services; and to adopt/adapt advanced technology in order to reduce the development time and costs involved in changing their own computer networks.
> (1993: 146)

The role of the state

In addition to intra-firm trade and intercorporate alliances, the state's role as an agent in non-arm's length international trade is considerable. In the USA, for example, the Export-Import Bank, an agency of the US government, supplies loans, loan guarantees and insurance to foreign countries to facilitate the purchase of American products, ranging from aircraft to printing presses to hearing aids. Exports supported by the Export-Import Bank rose from about $6 billion in 1989 to $15 billion in 1994.[29]

Another steady and direct source of US government intervention in international trade is the shipment of agricultural products to developing countries under Titles I, II and III of PL480. Since 1970, these shipments have averaged well over $1 billion dollars per year, providing an important vent for agricultural surplus and bolstering US agricultural exports in their position as the largest export sector of the US economy.

Less direct, but equally important, is the US government role in the sale of military equipment. These sales currently account for about 5 per cent of US exports and totaled $134 billion in the 1980s. While they are officially sales of private corporations, these sales – ranging from weapons to aircraft – are heavily promoted by the government.[30] Speaking to arms exporters in 1993, former Secretary of Commerce

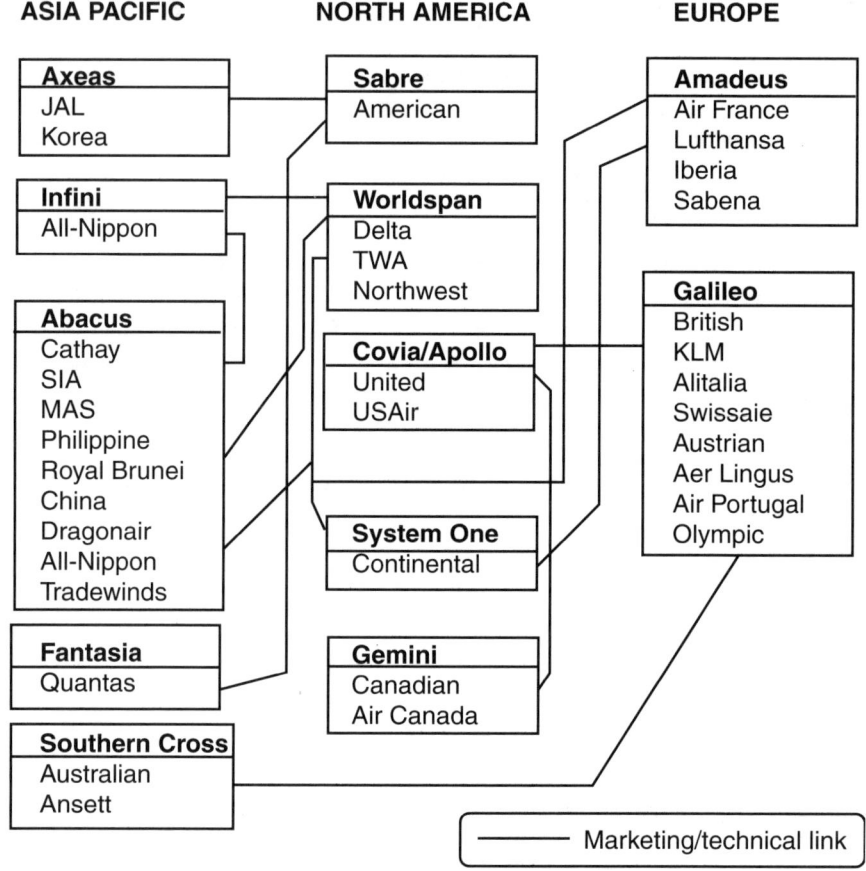

Figure 20.3 Alliances among airline computer reservation systems
Source: United Nations 1993: 145

Ronald Brown stated, 'The president is committed to moving beyond the arm's-length relationship that has too long existed between private and public sectors...We will work with you to help you find buyers for your products in the world marketplace, and then we will work to help you close the deal.' Of course the close government involvement in arms exports has a long tradition in the USA (Hartung 1994).

The stability of international equilibrium

The stability of equilibrium in international exchange is manifested in the two central and complementary features of the theory: balanced trade and automatic adjustment in the balance of payments. Table 20.2

shows the cumulative trade balances of a selection of countries, industrialized and industrializing. Not only is the volume of the imbalances relatively large, but the imbalances have persisted over considerable periods of time, up to eleven years in some cases. It is difficult to make a case for the existence of an automatic adjustment mechanism in such a context.

Of course, by accounting conventions, capital flow imbalances must offset the trade imbalances each year. But these do not come 'naturally', since they often require considerable state intervention in the form of official reserve flows and foreign exchange market intervention. Moreover, even such a non-market institution can be inadequate to stem a 'balance of payments crisis' which inevitably requires drastic state intervention.[31] International economic relations could just as well be said to be dominated by persistent imbalances than by tendencies toward balance. Thus a decentering of the market in the analysis of the international economy would also bring into question the stability of the international equilibrium that reinforces the logic of the metaphor.

Table 20.2 Cumulative current account balance, selected countries

Country	Cumulative account balance		Consecutive years with same sign		Cumulative current account balance (% of end-period GDP)	
	1970–1980	1985–1995	1970–1980	1985–1995	1970–1980	1985–1995
Australia	-20,668	-132,275	7*	11*	10	41
Austria	-7,780	-6,140	11*	4*	7	4
Canada	-22,115	-179,676	7*	11*	6	31
Germany [1]	20,304	173,341	8	6	2	12
Ireland	-7,592	2,933	11*	6	26	5**
Italy	-6,651	-37,775	4	6	1	4
Japan	20,512	948,084	3	11*	1	39
Netherlands	13,338	92,379	8	11*	7	34
United Kingdom	-2,244	-162,570	5	10*	0	17
United States [2]	3,823	-1,233,324	4	11*	0	19**

Source: OECD (1996)

Notes:
* indicates the series of consecutive surpluses or deficits indicates the final year
[1] Series begins in 1971
[2] Series begins in 1973
** indicates a sign change between the two periods

International economics with decentered markets

'Where, after the metanarratives, can legitimacy reside?' asks Lyotard (1984: xxv). Similarly, a 'postmodern economics' must address the question of what economics might look like once its principal metanarrative is dislodged. I have argued that the exclusive focus on the metaphor of market relations in the grand narrative of international economics has resulted in a blindness to the question of the organization of production, and that it is precisely the radical reorganization of business and the production process that characterizes contemporary international economics.[32] A focus on exogenously given atomistic agents interacting in autonomous markets can shed very little light on the question of the organization of production within the firm and thus on non-arm's-length international transactions. It is not even clear that such a system – that is, a perfectly competitive, free-market system – is sustainable over time. The history of modern capitalism is one of evolving business organizations and market structures. For example, the rise of oligopoly as a dominant market structure in the United States in the 1890s was arguably a necessity for firms' survival.[33] Thus even the interpretation of arm's-length transactions will be different if the conception of the transactors changes.

Economists have traditionally addressed the question of organization – that is, the question of why the firm exists at all – by hypothesizing a prohibitively high level of transactions costs in certain types of markets. The firm is the mechanism by which such costs can be avoided.[34] This tradition has been extended to the analysis of the transnational corporation, with an emphasis on the firms as a means of internalizing advantages that would be lost (or simply not be as profitable) if left to the market for export.[35] The transactions-cost approach has been integrated only with much difficulty into a neoclassical mold. Neoclassical economists have attempted to recoup this conception by considering intra-firm interactions *as if* they were occurring in markets.[36] A similar approach has been used to analyze commercial policy, with policy outcomes viewed as the result of the interaction of the supply and demand for trade protection.[37]

There are at least two objections to this effort to recoup the interpretation of non-market transactions within the metaphors of the market. First, it reduces all interagent communication to the category of price signals. This may be fine in the confines of that idealized institution known as a 'market', but within firms, households and states, there exists a wide range of non-price relationships. Hirschman's 'exit, voice, and loyalty' captures some of the possibilities. The exclusive focus on price competition is inappropriate even for the analysis of interfirm relations. When the scope is broadened to other forms of competition, in areas such as technological innovation, product quality, marketing, and after-sales service, then a range of organizational forms of organizing production become thinkable. A growing body of empirical studies of international trade show the dominance of non-price over pure price competition.[38]

The second problem with the Coasian tradition is that the firm and market are viewed as alternatives. This ignores that the two serve different functions. Production takes place within firms, not markets. And it is firms that establish a market, or even extend the scope of an existing market. As firms expand internationally, markets are transformed – they do not disappear.[39] The point is not to deny that the market metaphor *could* be reintroduced to 'explain' the firm, but to emphasize that such an analytical move is to exclude other important forms of knowledge and to further reify the notion of the market. The atomism of agents implied by such a conception removes the possibility of a serious treatment of internal organizational dynamics.[40] Such phenomena as intra-firm trade, market-seeking foreign direct investment, and industrial policy, to name a few, become difficult to conceptualize, and thus analyze, when only arm's-length transactions are considered. Endogenous changes in productivity, innovations in process and product, dynamics of industrial relations that influence productivity and location are all largely ignored when internal organizational dynamics are not part of the narrative of economics.

Could an international economics exist without market analysis at its center? Such an economics would give a prominent role to the organization of business, and consider arm's-length transactions as one of a number of possible forms of international transactions. Replacing a focus on markets and equilibria with one on business organization is not the substitution of one centered, unified concept ('the market') with another ('the business organization'). Business organization is not an ideal type but an evolving process that varies over time and over space. Chandler (1977, 1990) has shown in much detail how the dynamics of capitalism – from industrial revolution to the golden age of 1945–73 – can be related closely to the evolution of business organization. And a number of recent studies have argued that international competition can be viewed as a struggle among alternative organizational forms, characterized as 'American', 'Japanese' and 'German' (with considerable variety in each type).[41]

The existence of the firm has always been problematic for neoclassical economics because it is conceived simply as an alternative to the market, which is presupposed to be the most efficient mode for transactions. A postmodern theory of international trade must, at the very least, question the metanarrative of 'the beneficence of the free market' by problematizing the naturalized market metaphor and the essential dualisms on which it rests: market/non-market, social/natural, and market/firm. Firms both create and destroy markets. 'Market forces' or 'the forces of international competition' may loom large in popular debates over globalization and social policy, but these notions must be denaturalized in a way that captures their institutional embeddedness and their ideological thrust. New technologies in communication, design, data management and communication have made possible the international integration of the firm at the deepest levels of its functioning. As a result, the dynamics of international business (both inter- and intra-firm) can be seen as more important than 'market forces' in the determination of the international division of labor, income and wealth. The firm, the state and the household are just a few institutions whose dynamics can be theorized when the market metaphor is decentered, and ceases to serve as the only metaphor available to economists.

To put into question 'the market' as central metaphor in the metanarrative of economics is also to question the status of that metanarrative. The story of the beneficence of the free market has driven knowledge in the field of international economics for over 100 years. The role of postmodernism in international economics is to end the era of the exclusionary metanarrative and to insist on the sociality of both 'the global economy' and the discourse that creates our knowledge of it.

Acknowledgements

I would like to thank Jack Amariglio, Suzanne Bergeron, Peter Gray, David Gold, Hedy Kalikoff, Deirdre McCloskey, Phil Mirowski, Lois Woestman and the participants in the conference on 'Postmodernism, Knowledge and Economics' held at the University of California at Riverside for comments on a previous draft. I am especially grateful to Stephen Cullenberg for his constructive criticism on the first draft and his patience in waiting for the second.

Notes

1 Jameson (1990: 260).
2 See, for example, the classic definitions of economics by Leon Walras and Lionel Robbins.
3 See Elson (1991), for an application to stabilization policy.
4 On the issue of objectivity, see the pathbreaking work by McCloskey (1985) and Mirowski (1989). On the question of the economic subject, see Amariglio (1988) and Ferber and Nelson (1993).
5 See also Best and Kellner (1991: 164–7)
6 On the use of metaphors in economics, see Klamer and Leonard (1994) and McCloskey (1995).
7 Smith (1980: 39).
8 See Sawyer (1992: 38).
9 See Woestman (1997) for an anthropological view of debates over embededness. Even among feminist economists there is disagreement. See Weisskopf and Folbre (1996).

10 See Milberg (1988).
11 Schor (1998) shows in detail the cultural contingency of preferences in contemporary American society.
12 On the importance of household production, see Folbre (1994). On the role of intrafirm transactions, see Auerbach (1988).
13 For those interested in the question of subjectivity, it is worth noting that the individual agent in international trade theory is such a unified construct that he/she represents the nation! The social welfare function of international trade theory is typically represented by a single mapping of indifference curves, called social indifference curves. This concept of national welfare obviously denies difference along the lines of class, race, or gender. More simply, it assumes that when there are winners and losers as the result of the opening to trade, that the winners compensate the losers, bringing a Pareto superior state.
14 See Milberg (1993).
15 See Luria (1996) for an empirical study of precisely such heterogeneity of response.
16 See Krugman (1986) for a survey treatment.
17 See Krugman (1992).
18 For a detailed empirical analysis of the rhetoric of policy relevance in international economics, see Milberg (1996).
19 Milberg (1996).
20 See, for example, Encarnation (1992) and Cowhey and Aranson (1993).
21 See Markusen (1995: 191) regarding the absence of the transnational corporation in the new international economics.
22 See UNCTAD (1998: 23).
23 Cowhey and Aronson (1993: 42)
24 United Nations (1993).
25 For figures on the ratio of imported to domestic inputs for industrialized countries, see Milberg (1998). This phenomenon has now been widely acknowledged in the mainstream literature. Note that in contrast to the UN terminology of the 'international integration of production' that I have adopted here, Feenstra (1998) refers to it as the 'disintegration of production'. Krugman's (1995) term is the 'slicing up of the value chain'.
26 See the debate between Reich (1990) and Tyson (1991).
27 United Nations (1993: 143).
28 United Nations (1993:143).
29 Export-Import Bank of the Unites States (1993, 1994).
30 See Hartung (1994).
31 See Godley and Milberg (1994).
32 Again, this focus is not unique to international economics. According to some, neoclassical economics generally lacks a theory of the firm. See Best (1992).
33 See Eichner (1969: xi).
34 Coase (1937) and Williamson (1975).
35 Hymer (1976) and Dunning (1993).
36 See Alchian (1950) and Alchian and Demsetz (1972).
37 See Baldwin (1982).
38 See Fagerberg (1996).
39 See Sawyer (1992).
40 See Sawyer (1992: 32).
41 For example Best (1990), Ohmae (1985), Dunning (1993), Porter (1990), Cowhey and Aronson (1993).

References

Alchian, Armen (1950) 'Uncertainty, Evolution and Economic Theory', *Journal of Political Economy*, 58 (June) 211–21.
Alchian, Armen and Demsetz, Harold (1972) 'Production, Information Costs, and Economic Organization', *American Economic Review*, 62 (52): 777–95.
Amariglio, Jack (1988)'The Body, Economic Discourse and Power: An Economist's Introduction to Foucault', *History of Political Economy*, 20(4).
Auerbach, Paul (1988) *Competition: the Economics of Industrial Change*, New York: Basil Blackwell.
Baldwin, R. (1982) 'The Political Economy of Protectionism', Chapter 10 in J.Bhagwati, (ed.) *Import Competition and Response*, Chicago: University of Chicago Press.
Barber, Bernard (1995) 'All Economies are "Embedded": The Career of a Concept and Beyond', *Social Research*, 62(2) Summer.
Belsey, Catherine (1980) *Critical Practice*, London: Methuen.
Best, Michael (1990) *The New Competition: Institutions of Industrial Restructuring*, Cambridge: Harvard University Press.
—— (1992) 'The Firm and the Market: The dynamic Perspectives of Schumpeter and Penrose', *Social Concept*, 6(2) June: 3–24.
Best, Steven and Kellner, D. (1991) *Postmodern Theory: Critical Interrogations*, New York: Guilford Press.
Chandler, Alfred (1977) *The Visible Hand: The Managerial Revolution in American Business*, Cambridge: Harvard University Press.
—— (1990) *Scale and Scope: the Dynamics of Industrial Capitalism*, Cambridge: Harvard University Press.
Coase, Ronald (1937) 'The Nature of the Firm', *Economica*, 4, November.
Cowhey, Peter and Aronson, Jonathan (1993) *Managing the World Economy: The Consequences of Corporate Alliances*, New York: Council on Foreign Relations Press.
Deardorff, Alan (1980) 'The General Validity of the Law of Comparative Advantage', *Journal of Political Economy*, 88(5): 941–57.
Dicken, Peter (1992) *Global Shift: the Internationalization of Economic Activity*, 2nd edn, New York: The Guilford Press.
Dunning, John (1993) *Multinational Enterprise and the Global Economy*, Wokingham: Addison-Wesley.
Eichner, Alfred (1969) *The Emergence of Oligopoly*, Baltimore: Johns Hopkins University Press.
Elson, (1991) *Male Bias in the Development Process*, New York: Manchester University Press.
Encarnation, Dennis (1992) *Rivals Beyond Trade: America and Japan in Global Competition*, Ithaca: Cornell University Press.
Export-Import Bank of the United States (1993) *Annual Report*, Washington.
—— (1994) *Annual Report*, Washington.
Fagerberg, Jan (1996) 'Technology and Competitiveness', *Oxford Review of Economic Policy* 12 (3): 39–51.
Feenstra, (1998) 'Integration of Trade and Disintegration of Production in the Global Economy', *Journal of Economic Perspectives*, 12 (4) Fall: 31–50.

Ferber, Marianne, and Nelson, Julie (eds) (1993) *Beyond Economic Man: Feminist Theory and Economics*, Chicago: University of Chicago Press.
Folbre, Nancy (1994) *Who Pays for the Kids? Gender and the Structure of Constraint*, New York: Routledge.
Godley, Wynn and Milberg, William (1994) 'US Trade Deficits: The Recovery's Dark Side', *Challenge Magazine*, November/December.
Hartung, William (1994) *And Weapons for All*, New York: Harper Collins,.
Hipple, Steb, 'Multinational Companies and International Trade: The Impact of Intrafirm Shipments on US Foreign Trade 1977–82' (1990) *Journal of International Business Studies*, 21, Third Quarter.
Hirschman, Albert (1970) *Exit, Voice and Loyalty: Responses to Decline in Firms, Organizations and States*, Cambridge: Harvard University Press.
Hymer, Stephen (1976) *The International Operations of National Firms: A Study of Direct Foreign Investment*, Cambridge: MIT Press.
Jameson, Frederic (1990) 'Postmodernism and the Market', in *Postmodernism, or the Cultural Logic of Late Capitalism*, Chapel Hill: Duke University Press,
Jones, Ronald (1961) 'Comparative Advantage and the Theory of Tariffs: A Multi-Country, Multi-Commodity Model', *Review of Economic Studies*, June.
Klamer, Arjo and Leonard, Thomas (1994) *Natural Images in Economic Thought*, (ed.) Philip Mirowski, Cambridge: Cambridge University Press.
Klamer, Arjo and McCloskey, Deirdre (1995) 'One Quarter of GDP is Persuasion', *American Economic Review*, 85(2) May.
Krugman, Paul (ed.) (1986) *Strategic Trade Policy and the New International Economics*, Cambridge: MIT Press.
—— (1992) 'Does the New Trade Theory Require a New Trade Policy?' *The World Economy*, 15(4): 424–41, July.
—— (1995) 'Growing World Trade: Causes and Consequences', *Brookings Papers on Economic Activity*, 1 (Spring): 327–78.
Luria, Dan (1996) 'Why Markets Tolerate Mediocre Manufacturing', *Challenge Magazine*, July/August: 11–16.
Lyotard, Jean-Francois (1984) *The Postmodern Condition: A Report on Knowledge*, Minneapolis: University of Minnesota Press.
McCloskey, Donald (1985) *The Rhetoric of Economics*, Madison: University of Wisconsin Press.
—— (1995) 'Metaphors Economists Live By', *Social Research*, 62(2) Summer.
Markusen, James (1995) 'The Boundaries of Multinational Enterprise and the Theory of International Trade', *Journal of Economic Perspectives*, 9(2) Spring.
Milberg, William (1988) 'The Language of Economics: Deconstructing the Neoclassical Text', *Social Concept*, 4(2).
—— (1993) 'Natural Order and Postmodernism in Economic Thought', *Social Research*, 60.
—— (1994) 'Is Absolute Advantage Passé?: Toward a Post Keynesian/Marxian Theory of International Trade', in M. Glick, (ed.) *Competition, Technology and Money: Classical and Post Keynesian Perspectives*, Aldershot: Edward Elgar,
—— (1996) 'The Rhetoric of Policy Relevance in International Economics', *Journal of Economic Methodology*, 3 (2) December: 237–59.

—— (1998) 'Technological Change, Social Policy and International Competitiveness', Working Paper No. 7, Center for Economic Policy Analysis, New School University.
Mirowski, Philip (1989) *More Heat than Light: Economics as Social Physics and Physics as Nature's Economics*, New York: Cambridge University Press.
Nelson, Julie (1993) 'The Study of Choice or the Study of Provisioning?' in Ferber, M. and J. Nelson (eds) *Beyond Economic Man: Feminist Theory and Economics*, Chicago; University of Chicago Press.
Ohmae, Kenichi (1985) *Triad Power*, New York: The Free Press.
Polanyi, K. (1957) 'The Economy as Instituted Process', in Polanyi, K. C., Arensberg, and H. Pearson (eds) *Trade and Market in the Early Empires: Economies in History and Theory*, New York: The Free Press, pp. 243–69.
Porter, Michael (1990) *The Competitive Advantage of Nations*, New York: The Free Press.
Reich, Robert (1990) 'Who is Us?', *Harvard Business Review*, 90(1) January/February.
Robbins, Lionel (1932) *An Essay on the Nature and Significance of Economic Science*, London: Macmillan & Co.
Saussure, Ferdinand de ([1915]1966) *Course in General Linguistics*, New York: McGraw-Hill.
Sawyer, Malcolm (1992) 'The Nature and Role of Markets', *Social Concept*, 6 (2).
Schor, (1998) *The Overspent American: Upscaling, Downshifting and the New Consumer*, New York: Basic Books.
Smith, Adam (1980) 'The History of Astronomy', in *Essays in Philosophical Subjects*, Oxford: Clarendon Press.
Tyson, Laura (1991) 'They are Not US: Why American Ownership Still Matters', *The American Prospect*, Winter.
United Nations (1993) *World Investment Report*, UN Center on Transnational Corporations, New York.
United Nations Conference on Trade and Development (1994) *World Investment Report*, Geneva.
—— (1996) *World Investment Report*, Geneva.
—— (1998) *World Investment Report*, Geneva.
Vernon, Raymond (1979) 'The Product Cycle Hypothesis in a New International Environment, *Oxford Bulletin of Economic Statistics*, 41, November.
Walras, Leon (1969) *Elements of Pure Economics; Or, The Theory of Social Wealth*, trans. William Jaffé, New York: A. M. Kelley.
Weisskopf, T. and Folbre, N. (1996) 'Debating Markets', *Feminist Economics*, 2(1): 69–86.
Williamson, Oliver (1975) *Markets and Hierarchies, Analysis and Antitrust Implications: A Study in the Economics of Internal Organization*, New York: The Free Press.
Woestman, L., (1999) 'Mesmerized by the Market', mimeo, Department of Anthropology, New School University, New York.

21

REFUSING THE GIFT

Philip Mirowski

These English psychologists – what do they really want? One always discovers them voluntarily or involuntarily at the same task, namely at dragging the *partie honteuse* of our inner world into the foreground and seeking the truly effective and directing agent, that which has been decisive in its evolution, in just that place where the intellectual pride of man would least *desire* to find it...what is it that really always drives these psychologists in just this direction? Is it a secret, malicious, vulgar, perhaps self-deceiving instinct for belittling man? Or possibly a pessimistic suspicion, the mistrustfulness of the disappointed idealists grown spiteful and gloomy? Or a petty subterranean hostility and rancor toward Christianity (and Plato) that has not even crossed the threshold of consciousness?...The way they have bungled their moral genealogy comes to light at the very beginning, where the task is to investigate the origin of the concept and judgment 'good'...One sees straightaway that this primary derivation already contains all the typical traits of the idiosyncrasy of the English psychologists – we have 'utility' 'forgetting,' 'habit,' and finally 'error,' all as a basis of an evaluation of which the higher man has hitherto been proud as though it were a kind of prerogative of man as such. This pride has to be humbled, this evaluation disvalued: has that end been achieved?
(Friedrich Nietzsche, 1967: 24–5)

These neoclassical economists – what do they really want? There have been times – and it may have also happened to you – when they say something whose audacity and sheer philistinism just takes my breath away. And I don't mean those quotidian sources of garden-variety outrage, like when they claim that toxic waste should rightfully be dumped in the third world because life is cheaper there, or that it is useless for the government to mandate seatbelts in passenger autos because people just end up driving more recklessly to 'compensate'. No, if you happen to be in this business, you rapidly grow inured to a certain level of humdrum apologetics for corporate rapacity; economists apparently unconsciously extrude these gems in prescient advance of their clients' needs. Rather, what I intend here is closer to what Nietzsche meant when describing the utilitarians: The production of moral genealogies whose whole purpose seems to debase any little piety or sympathy left in our fragmented infoculture. Economists revel in their capacity to be 'more hard-boiled than thou': no one will ever catch them succumbing to smarmy sentimentality (will they?). Examples could easily be multiplied, but here we shall restrict ourselves to surveying how neoclassical economists talk about 'gifts.'

I choose an article from the recent *American Economic Review* (*AER*) which, by its very triviality, elevates the problem into heightened contrast. The topic is an article by Joel Waldfogel called, 'The Deadweight Loss of Christmas.' Any well-trained economist will be able to reconstruct the argument from the bare title alone. Briefly, it is a dogma amongst neoclassicals that any transfer of resources which was not 'chosen' by the recipient through the market will generally be inefficient, by some optimality criteria which we can thankfully ignore for our present purposes. The fact that people give gifts rather than cash equivalents at Christmas fits this paradigm; and Waldfogel proceeds to retail a little 'empiricism lite' in order to offer up his result that 'holiday gift-giving destroys between 10 per cent and a third of the value of the gifts'. His sense of timing meshing closely with his comic genius, he proceeds to hammer his punchline: 'a conservative estimate of the deadweight loss of Christmas is a tenth as large as estimates of the deadweight loss of income taxation', another institution of modern life which conventionally does not meet with the approval of the neoclassical economist. We could also go into detail about the ceremonial function of the attendant regression analysis, as well as his witty synecdoche comparing gift giving to risk aversion, but all this would merely distract us from the primary question.

What is it that we want from neoclassical economists? You might say that this was all a *jeu d'esprit*, the kind of economist's joke one has to endure at American Economics Association (AEA) conventions; but I don't think so. The reader should stop and consider that that the *AER* (unlike, say, the *Journal of Political Economy*) has never betrayed a penchant for the tongue-in-cheek article – ; but then I first heard about this argument on CNN around Christmas time 1993. The media moguls themselves didn't quite know how to treat it on TV – they opted for one part, 'There go those frisky madcap economists again...', and one part, 'Isn't this wicked but true?' In other words, they were suspended somewhere between easy irony and a wry admiration for the iconoclastic cheek of the man. The *Chicago Tribune* actually wrote an editorial on the article – but you might aver, the *Trib* is not a serious newspaper. And then again, as if to telegraph the point that this is not 'simply' or 'merely' a joke, just as I sat down to write this, I discovered in the Christmas edition of the *New York Times* business page a reprise of the story (Herring, 1994). That puckish Joel Waldfogel is at it again! Estimating the differential 'yield' from different classes of gift-givers! The fellow clearly has got what it takes to succeed at Yale; take it from me, I spent some time there.

> If Jacques Derrida can start from a post card as a pretext to discuss everyone from Plato to Austin, maybe I can start with Joel Waldfogel to discuss everyone from Mauss to Derrida. You see I am not offended by this tr[o]ipe; on the contrary, this offal enfolds a pearl of great price, though we may have to reach for the gas masks while we peruse the entrails to read the portents. Much has to be digested to appreciate the fact that our culture is amused by the *likes* of Joel Waldfogel – that he and people like him are one of the primary reasons why neoclassical economics has vanquished all rivals and has become the icon of rational self-knowledge for academics and businessmen alike. By bequeathing people a stark yet seemingly paradoxical image of what they want, neoclassical economics can get what it wants, which is to subsume or displace all other academic social theory in the name of unified science. To accomplish this task, it is not enough to brandish point set topology and subgame perfect Nash equilibria, though that helps. Neoclassicism must also undermine every possible rival account of exchange by ruthlessly exposing its vulnerability to self-contradiction. It is characteristic of these rival accounts that they are usually 'non-economic': that is, they arise outside of formal academic economics and set themselves apart from it; they would like to oppose technocrats with technocrits. People favorably inclined to postmodernism and critical theory are especially prone to make these sorts of arguments: economic anthropologists, literary critics, French poststructuralists, science studies scholars, feminist social theorists, and the like.
>
> My argument, in a nutshell, is this. The concept of 'the gift' has been constitutive to any number of anti-neoclassical social theories in the twentieth century, but *all* the traditions that have relied upon it to explicate various forms of exchange have been ultimately vanquished *qua* social theory. (Do I really mean *all*? Yes, I do, though this is ultimately a historical question.) The reason is that the modern concept of 'the gift' is itself incoherent, the weak link in

> the quest to define the 'non-economic.' From this we may extrapolate that all further attempts to capitalize on the gift will go the way of their predecessors, and worse, attempts to base social theory upon it actually serve to strengthen the neoclassical orthodoxy.
>
> My own little *bricolage* points towards an attempt to circumvent the impasse, if not actually transcend it, and not just gesture towards it ineffectually, as I shall accuse Jacques Derrida of doing in his recent *Given Time I: Counterfeit Money* (1992). The resolution will be sought in a reconfiguration of the theory of value.

No More Free Lunch

> Now the gift, *if there is any*, would no doubt be related to economy. One cannot treat the gift, this goes without saying, without treating the relation to the economy, even the money economy. But is it not the gift, if there is any, also that which interrupts the money economy? That which, in suspending economic calculation, no longer gives rise to exchange? That which opens the circle so as to defy reciprocity or symmetry the common measure, and so as to turn aside the return in view of the no-return?…Not that it remains foreign to the circle, but it must *keep* a relation of foreigness to the circle, a relation without relation of familiar foreigness. It is perhaps in this sense that the gift is impossible.
>
> (Derrida, 1992: 7)

> *The Setting*: A blow-dried citizen from Generation X strides up to an ATM machine in some warm climate, probably California, to judge by the withered sleazy stucco of the surrounding building and the cloudless sky. He is stopped by an obvious bum, propping up a plastic shopping bag and searching endlessly for something secreted on his person. As the technonerd fearlessly raises his plastic card to the black slot, the bum says, in a slightly aggressive tone: 'Spare change?'
>
> Mr.X: 'Look, my man, if I give you a dollar, your income will go up, so average spending will rise without any offsetting rise in production. That will push inflation up, devaluing our currency after worsening our trade deficit, not to mention shifting the tax burden onto the more productive sectors of society. The dollar becomes

> worthless, and more people are thrown out of work. So I'd like to help ya, guy, but don't you think things are bad enough already?'
>
> Bum: 'Wha??'
>
> ATM Door: Bzzzzzz...Click

The utility of futility

There is a trope which is emblematic of neoclassical economics, which we might call the 'Futility Thesis'. In all its various manifestations, the common denominator is some assertion that the world is so structured and interlinked that anything one might wish to accomplish will be offset – usually in some unexpected or unanticipated manner – returning you to the original situation. For those remaining *au fait* with such matters, names such as Ricardian Equivalence, the Coase theorem, the Modigliani–Miller Theorem, The Regulatory Capture thesis, and a whole host of other doctrines will come to mind. There is a long tradition of such arguments in economics, dating back at least to Malthus's assertion that poor relief will only confirm the poor in their status. While many of these arguments are actually disguised restatements of some principle of arbitrage, there is a more restrictive class of futility theses that should warrant more sustained analysis. In this class of *topoi*, one essentially asserts that gifts are impossible.

Let me cite just a few incidents from the postwar economic orthodoxy, although there are many more to choose from. One exemplary instance is a paper by Robert Sugden (1982), where he argues that the neoclassical case for governmental supplement to philanthropic provision of public goods is based upon a logical inconsistency between the postulates of publicness, utility maximization, and Nash conjectures. His argument is basically a restatement of the Futility Thesis, but tempered in its harshness by his assertion that people in fact do not seem to conform to the empirical predictions of the model. The tension is purposely left unresolved in this paper: theory says gifts are impossible, but people seem to act contrary to this knowledge; hence (it is hinted) some revision of theory is needed, which will perhaps restore the actors to the vaunted status of rational choosers. If the hoped-for revision of the theory also manages to reinstate the assertion that governmental activity is ineffectual in some larger frame, well, that would be okay with Sugden, too.

Another instance is Gary Becker's *Treatise on the Family* (1981), a compendium of his papers from the previous decade. As is characteristic of Becker, he is much more interested in showing that simple Marshallian stories can be used to 'analyze' seemingly non-economic phenomena, thus flexing the imperialistic muscle of neoclassicism, rather than looking more closely at his own theory; in this case, he contradicts himself in the space of 20 pages. First he posits his so-called 'Rotten Kid Theorem' (there is no 'theorem' that any mathematician would recognize, but let that pass): 'Each beneficiary, no matter how selfish, maximizes the family income of his benefactor and thereby internalizes all effects of his actions on other beneficiaries' (1981:183). What does this have to do with gift-giving? It takes a little economics training to see that this is the *inversion* of the impossibility of the gift: however selfish the individual member of the *oikos*, Becker says that the assembled kinship unit will end up where it would have done in any event, with the maximization of its household utility function. This is just a rehash of the conventional welfare theorem in neoclassicism that is supposed to reveal the superior efficacy of the market, with Becker's added insistence upon the intrusion of virtual markets into every nook and cranny of experience. But if the paterfamilias cannot taketh away, by symmetry, neither can he giveth; altruism is thus equally neutralized in this scheme of things. Becker, unfortunately, has some difficulty seeing through his own little model, since on pp. 194–5 he proceeds to argue that, 'altruism is less common in market transactions and more common in families because altruism is less "efficient" in the marketplace and more "efficient" in families' [NB – his own scare quotes]. Becker's subsequent forays into sociobiology in order to rationalize what he calls 'altruism' thus was born under a doubly bad sign: not only did he betray a tenuous grasp of the biology, but he was, in addition, attempting to explain something which he himself had shown not to exist.

This game of acknowledging the existence of something called 'altruism', only to then explain it away as simultaneously Natural and nonexistent, has become one of the major academic pastimes of our upbeat *fin-de-siècle* scene. Through the instrumentality of sociobiology, which is just neoclassical economics foisted upon some innocent unsuspecting animals and insects, it reveals its ambitions to become a Theory of Everything (Ridley, 1996). It is easy to learn as any proleptic two-step: posit an ontology of 'individuals' (selfish genes, isolated consciousnesses, strategic organisms, anomic atoms), and then run the numbers in a 'disguised self-interest' narrative. This game of 'gotcha' resonates nicely with a certain free-floating paranoia which itself thrives in the interstices of the Information Age.

Lest I be accused of picking upon economists of a certain political persuasion, let me choose for my third example Kenneth Arrow's response to Richard Titmuss's book *The Gift Relationship* (1971). Titmuss's book was an attack upon the then-contemporary American blood collection system, which was at that time roughly 25 per cent commercial. Titmuss argued that paying for blood led to problems of high rates of blood-borne illness (then hepatitis), but also that it degraded the population of donors in both psychological and structural ways. Arrow, who in the 1960s was concerned to foster the nascent field of 'health economics' as an offshoot of neo-Walrasian welfare theory, was uncharacteristically roused to ire by Titmuss's book. His retorts were a curious hodgepodge: for instance, he attacked the quality of Titmuss's empirical work in general terms, even resorting to the codewords 'precise and empirical language of empirical sociology,' though he himself had never done any comparable empirical work. He smugly pointed to the fact that 'only' 6 per cent of the eligible British population ever gave blood, as though that were prima facie proof of the aberrant nature of a voluntary provision system. He brought in that theorist's favorite bludgeon, conjectural history: 'It may be that the spread of commercial services in the United States was itself due to the failure of voluntary services to supply enough blood...it would not show that commercial bloodgiving was a cause rather than an effect' (1975: 19). He opined that the problem 'really' was one of uncertainty and asymmetric information between buyer and seller, which he would assert economists were learning to handle. He then tried to twin Titmuss with Friedrich von Hayek, which in the early 1970s (before the Nobel) was by no means a compliment (p.27). But the real objection behind all the persiflage surfaced in the exact center of the article: 'The aspect of Titmuss's work that will probably have the most striking effect both immediately and in the long run is his argument that a world of giving may actually increase efficiency in the operation of the economic system. This is on the face of it a direct challenge to the tenets of the mainstream of economic thought [s]ince the time of Adam Smith.' (1975: 20.)

Ignoring for the moment the attempt to saddle poor Adam with something he never intended, herein lies the heart of the matter. For Arrow, as for any other neoclassical in good standing, it is simply impossible that gift-giving, *if it exists*, could outperform the market in any way, shape or form. Could Arrow really just be Joel Waldfogel with a human face? In the Arrow shooting gallery it seems the ducks woodenly resist regimentation in a disciplined row: sometimes he accepts Titmuss's assertion that gifts do exist, but insists that his empirical data is wrong; sometimes he wants to deny the existence or at least the widespread prevalence of gift-giving; and sometimes he opts to treat the gift as epiphenomena of hidden market forces or as deceptively disguised individual optimization. The best he could manage is a separate-but-unequal brand of segregationist liberalism: 'I think it is best on the whole that the requirement of ethical behavior be confined to those circumstances where the price system breaks down as suggested above' (1975: 22).

While Arrow's fusillade contra Titmuss did subsequently provoke a small academic literature, mainly in philosophy, it did not have any effect on the health provider community. Instead, in response to Titmuss's book, the US Department of Health, Education and Welfare in 1973 announced a national blood collection policy discouraging the sale of blood, and the system moved decisively towards a donor provision basis (so much for Arrow's empirical instincts!), although the situation has since been complicated by the appearance of AIDS and the rise of a commercial plasma and blood products sector in more recent times (Piliavin and Callero, 1991). There was not much in the way of a field of health economics in the early 1970s, but as we perhaps have learned to our dismay from the national health care debate of 1994, neoclassical economists now have managed to gain much more of a purchase upon public policy towards the medical sector, and consequently the treatment of the 'gift' becomes more urgent.

The futility thesis on the impossibility of the gift is endemic in modern economics, even though Arrow and Becker seem only to have a semi-conscious appreciation of its force. Is this merely some sort of ideological bad faith, a crude apologetics for the status quo, or is something more complicated going on here? I shall adopt the latter position, for essentially three reasons: (1) There is nothing written in the smooth convex surfaces of the equations of neoclassicism which dictates that the gift must be treated in any specific manner. How it enters into the neoclassical equations is thoroughly underdetermined. (2) While neoclassicals seem to instinctively agree upon the impossibility of the gift, the exact way that this is realized in practice is not at all a subject of agreement. Indeed, as we have seen, one can get two or more different stories within the same article. (3) The futility thesis is not the sole province of neoclassical economists. Many diverse thinkers proposing their own rival theories of exchange also seem to run up against the thesis, though perhaps not with the verve and variety of the neoclassicals. It is their conundrum to which we now turn.

Who is the leader of the club that is made for you and me?

In economic anthropology, all roads to the gift lead back to Marcel Mauss. All the major anthropological theorists of exchange from Sahlins to Gregory, from to Douglas to Parry, from Strathern to Gudeman, feel impelled to make their peace with Mauss. More strikingly, many major protagonists of French structuralism and poststructuralism take their departure from Mauss: Levi-Strauss, Bataille, Baudrillard, Lyotard, and Derrida in his *Given Time*. The urge to shake this shaman's rattle, this 1925 essay, one more time before venturing forth to do battle with the spreading ectoplasm of bourgeois capitalism is a phenomenon which cannot be explained in any simple manner. The enduring legacy of Durkheimian sociological theory in the guise of the 'total social fact' certainly is a part of the story. The role of Mauss in providing a contemporary critique of Bolshevik socialism is another (Gane, 1992). Nevertheless, the primary attraction of *The Gift* is, self-reflexively, it's radical undecidability. People just don't know what they have hold of when they pick up *The Gift*. In the anthropological literature, one can encounter the most bizarre readings of the essay, such as the claim that Mauss demonstrated that 'there is no such thing as a free gift' (Parry, 1985: 455; Douglas, 1990: viii). If a postwar social theorist cannot tell the difference between Marcel Mauss and Gary Becker, then it really must be the end of history.

But of course, it is not. What is needed instead of eschatology is some real history, a narrative account of the sequence of anthropological texts on exchange, something I have tried to initiate in *Tit for Tat* (1994a). The story, all too briefly, goes like this: the question of the gift effectively begins in anthropology with Bronislaw Malinowski, in his classic *Argonauts of the Western Pacific* (1922). Therein Malinowski described the now-famous Kula ring in an attempt to make the case that Western approaches to economics were too limited to comprehend such apparently non-utilitarian practices. As a part of his project to propose an alternative analytical framework, he posited that the polar antithesis to market exchange was the 'gift.' Mauss's essay, not an ethnography but rather a historical survey of work on interpreting the gift, was critical of Malinowski's treatment; indeed, Malinowski's book clearly had elicited the essay. Uncharacteristically, Malinowski took Mauss's strictures to heart, and in his next work, *Crime and Custom in Savage Society* ([1926]1985: 40), he explicitly repudiated the theoretical importance of the gift. In many respects, it was Malinowski's abrupt summary of Mauss which was primarily responsible for the 'no free lunch' interpretation of Mauss's essay.

Mauss, however, had produced a much more complex set of propositions. The *Essai sur le don* was written roughly at the same time as a series of articles on Bolshevism in *Le Monde Slave* (see Gane, 1992: 165–211) and interventions in debates about socialism (see Mauss, 1969: 675). Furthermore, it bore more than a passing resemblance to texts in the German Historicist tradition, laced with a Durkheimian concern over the role of the sacred. Although there was no evidence that Mauss was intimately acquainted with neoclassical doctrines, he did regard himself as undermining

Malinowski's tendency to taxonomize exchanges by degrees of interest or disinterest. Mauss sought to explain the logic of obligation in such ethnographic oddities as the potlatch and Maori hau as a corollary of the principle that the things themselves have souls: 'Hence it follows that to make a gift of something to someone is to make a present of some part of oneself' (1990: 12). In other words, Malinowski stood accused of an insufficient appreciation that the distinction between things and persons was eminently a Western one. Having recourse to philology, the history of ancient law, and ethnographies, Mauss insisted that gifts were usually a species of aggression: 'through such gifts a hierarchy is established. To give is to show one's superiority, to be more, to be higher in rank, *magister*. To accept without giving in return, or without giving more back, is to become client and servant, to become small' (1990: 74). Hence, what enforces the reciprocation is not some utilitarian calculation, but rather the personality of the giver invested in the partible object; indeed it was the giver incarnate, hovering menacingly over the life of the receiver. The religious overtones were intended by Mauss, for they expressed the Durkheimian penchant for uncovering the religious origins of economic value (Parry,1985: 470).

One aspect of the radical undecidability in reading Mauss is that he attacks Malinowski by rendering the gift less of a polar opposite to commodity exchange than in *Argonauts*, but only subsequently to insist that there existed such a thing as a 'gift economy' which could be counterpoised to a modern exchange economy. An example of the former assimilative moment is his claim that the (then conventional) distinction in anthropology between barter and money economies was misleading, because the origins of credit could be found in gifts rather than in goldsmith's receipts (Gregory, 1982: 19). An example of the latter disjunctive moment would be his schema of the three stages of 'total prestation gift', and modern economies (p.20). This dual thesis – that the gift is not what it at first seems, obscuring the calculus of power and aggression which lay just beneath the surface; but, per contra, the gift is an earlier and kinder, gentler form of economic organization (Mauss,1990: 77–8) to be contrasted to the rapacity of developed market culture – this is what allows anyone to walk away from *The Gift* taking whatever they want from it. Nonetheless, in retrospect *The Gift* and the gift mirror and reinforce one another. For, as Mauss was one of the first to point out, the etymology of the English word gift is itself ambivalent. In Old High German, the word is derived from one meaning 'poison' – surely an antonym for the meaning conventionally assigned in modern dictionaries. Or is it? In the OED, the etymology is traced from an Old English word meaning 'payment for a wife'; and definition 3 reads: 'Something, the possession of which is transferred to another without the expectation or receipt of an equivalent' and definition 3c reads: 'a fee for services rendered.'

Well, what is it? Can we even begin to conceptualize 'something for nothing' without backsliding into 'trade of equivalents' or worse, 'self-interested manipulation'?

How the gift poisoned economic anthropology

Most people who went into anthropology in the postwar period did so partly out of a skepticism about the universality of their own culture's categories and preoccupations; and most shared a worry that the spread of the capitalist market would sooner or later wipe out the diversity of cultures which they cherished. The smaller tribe who decided to become directly engaged in the project of an 'economic anthropology' were therefore predisposed to regard the neoclassical orthodoxy as suspect, along with its third-world offshoot known as 'development economics' (Lodewijks, 1994). But where would an alternative framework for understanding such phenomena come from? By and large, that postwar generation saw its clan organization split between two opposed totems: Malinowski and Mauss. The former, as we have suggested, had essentially repudiated the gift as anthropological category; and this taboo in turn led to forays into Marxism and the structuralism of Levi-Strauss. (The fortunes of this clan, however fascinating, lie beyond our present purview.) The latter group, the Maussketeers, regarded the former as being insufficiently distanced from Western preoccupations, descrying a 'tendency to see exchanges as essentially dyadic transactions between self-interested individuals, as premised on some kind of balance, the tendency to play down supernatural sanctions, and the total contempt for questions of origin – all these constituted an important legacy of Malinowski's teachings' (Parry, 1985: 454). The rallying cry became therefore 'back to Mauss!' for many postwar economic anthropologists. However, the huzzah might as well have been 'quaff the hemlock!', since each and every aspiring theorist of the gift in economic anthropology ended up dispirited and dejected (and I do mean every Maussketeer from Malinowski to Sahlins; there are signs it is beginning with the feminists), essentially repudiating the possibility of a theory-driven economic anthropology. The detailed narrative of how this happened still awaits its historian, although I have made a first stab at exploring the terrain in (Mirowski, 1994a). Here we shall restrict ourselves to briefly indicating how this happened with two pre-eminent theorists, Marshall Sahlins and

Chris Gregory; a synoptic view would find the field crowded with notables such as Marilyn Strathern, Tim Ingold, Annette Weiner, Nicholas Thomas, Jonathan Parry, and yes, even Mary Douglas.

Marshall Sahlins' *Stone Age Economics* (1972) still stands as a landmark for postwar economic anthropologists, so it is all the more distressing to observe that Sahlins has in the interim apparently given up on the conceptual possibility of such an endeavor. His most recent pronouncements, such as (1992), have been reduced to generic mantras that cultural homogenization cannot triumph in the economic sphere. The earlier Sahlins was much more feisty:

> If the problem in the beginning was the 'naive anthropology' of Economics, today it is the naive economics of Anthropology...[I]t is a choice between the perspective of Business, for the formalist method must consider the primitive economies as underdeveloped versions of our own, and a culturalist study that as a matter of principle does honor to different societies for what they are...the attempt in the end is to bring the anthropological perspective to bear on the traditional work of microeconomics, the explanation of exchange value.
>
> (1972: xi, xii)

Sahlins proceeded to divide primitive exchange into centralized redistribution vs. reciprocity, à la Karl Polanyi, and insist for the latter category that, 'it is precisely through scrutiny of departures from balanced exchange that one glimpses the interplay between reciprocity, social relations and material circumstances' (p.190). His objective was to specify how a continuum from gift to balanced reciprocity to negative reciprocity would be conditional upon a set of inherently cultural factors, primarily kinship and clan/political distinctions. If successful, Sahlins could then have shown that exchange ratios could not be indicators of any single state of primal scarcity or disembodied forces of 'supply and demand'; indeed, the ratios themselves would need to be embedded within an expanded vector of considerations, losing their abstract calculative functions. Equivalence would be no longer dyadic, but rather systemic or multiply attainable. What moderns think of as allocation decisions would be replaced by local orderings inherent in cultural structures. The structure of the argument might be summarized in Figure 21.1.

Intrinsic to the argument is the existence of a benchmark of 'equivalence' in exchange and a polar extreme of 'gift' where calculations of equivalence have no place. The ability to array objects along this continuum (and beyond, to market-like exchange where a surplus is realized) is provided by a sort of proto-calculational device (a Turing machine?) inherent in the patterns of inclusion and exclusion to be found

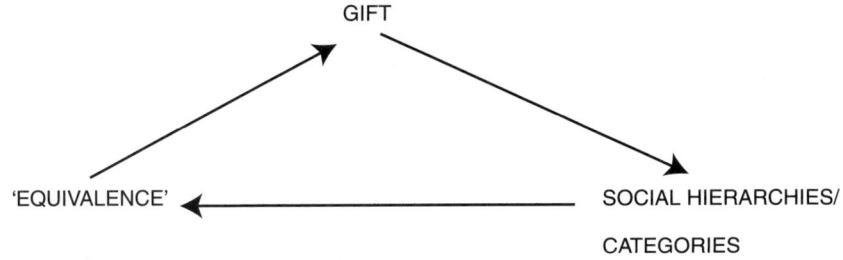

Figure 21.1 Sahlins causal structure
Source: Sahlins, 1972

in kinship ties, clan membership, etc. But the valiant attempt begins to deconstruct itself right at the end of Sahlins's text: 'Everything depends upon the meaning and practice of that capital principle, 'generosity.' But the meaning is ethnographically uncertain, and therein lies the weakness of our theory' (1972: 307). What is the nature of the weakness? To put it in slightly formal terms, the ability to posit an equivalence class somewhere in the system is heavily dependent upon the location of the invariant in the system. For Sahlins, initially this resides in kinship relations and the like. But then he proceeds to argue that in the event of a pronounced scarcity or other dislocation (shades of the economist's 'external shock'), 'a supply-demand imbalance is resolved by pressure on the trade partners rather than exchange rates' (p.311). And here is where the corrosive essence of the gift eats away at his system. The role of the gift is to *alter* many of the cultural equivalence classes, such as kinship, political affiliation and the like, and not simply to ratify prior relationships. Think of the 'gift' of women, or the 'gift' of territory. In these situations, the cultural patterns are *not invariant* with respect to the system of exchange, and therefore the presumption of an equivalence class is undermined. Value deliquesces at the initiative of the Other; or perhaps worse, it is dissolved in the downpour of external Noise. Nevertheless, from a Western perspective, there remains some notion of intentionality, and perhaps even self-interest, motivating gifts and exchanges; and the temptation is to lodge that intentionality and that calculative index somewhere deep in the human psyche. But, *mirabile dictu*, we are back at the neoclassical theory we tried to escape, or as Sahlins puts it, 'In many respects the opposite of market competition, the etiquette of primitive trade may conduct by a different route to a similar result'.

Sahlins prefaced his effort with the disclaimer, 'I do not attempt here a general theory of value' (1972: 277). Perhaps that was part of the reason for the collapse of his edifice. However, another more direct cause was his attempt to incorporate the gift into his anthropological economics. One detects a kind of rueful acknowledgment of this in his Radcliffe-Brown Lecture: 'And why the necessity for the reconciliation that Mauss discovered in *The Gift*? A pervasive sense of underlying chaos, a kind of Radcliffe-Brownian movement of self-interested atoms, weights like a nightmare on the brains of the living' (1988: 26). Or at least upon one of the living.

The case of Chris Gregory is equally instructive, because he was coached by his mentors at Cambridge (UK) in Sraffian economic theory as a rival tradition to neoclassicism, and subsequently sought to forge an alliance between neo-Ricardianism and Marcel Mauss to produce a theoretically informed economic anthropology. Gregory's *Gifts and Commodities* (1982) returns once more to Melanesia (the primal stomping grounds for economic anthropology ever since Malinowski) in order to analyze the difference between a 'gift economy' and an 'exchange economy'. He begins by insisting that, 'The concepts 'gift' and 'commodity' have no meaning within the [neoclassical] approach' (p.9), an assertion which some earlier sections of this paper suggest is perhaps a bit too draconian. Then, getting down to business, we are told, 'commodity exchange establishes objective quantitative relationships between the objects transacted, while gift exchange establishes personal qualitative relationships between the subjects transacting' (p.41). Here one detects the influence of Piero Sraffa, although some familiarity with the literature might raise doubts about the hard and fast nature of the dichotomy. The project of the neo-Ricardians to ground prices in the 'external' or 'physical' world of technological production specifications was always rather ambivalent as to the historical/institutional referent to which it applied; in their quest for an 'objective' economics it is not so clear how much they differed in this regard from the neoclassicals whom they otherwise so despised.

Nevertheless, for Gregory the Sraffian theory served as a polar opposition to a specification of the gift economy. In the central section of his text he proceeded to list a number of criteria for the gift economy, as a prerequisite for an anthropological theory of exchange. These benchmarks were:

1   People in a gift economy exist in a state of reciprocal dependence, in contrast to the relative independence of market participants (p.42).
2   'Commodities are *alienable* objects transacted by aliens; gifts are *inalienable* objects transacted by non-aliens' (p.43).
3   'Things are anthropomorphized in a gift economy' (p.45).
4   'Gift exchange is the exchange of like-for-like…commodity exchange is different because it involves the exchange of unlike-for-unlike' (pp.46–7).

5   Gift exchange is intrinsically extended through time, unlike commodity exchange (p.47).

The culmination of these considerations is two somewhat variant statements of the 'economic' difference between gift and exchange economies, although both appear on the same page (p.47):

> Simple commodity exchange establishes a relation of equality between heterogeneous things at a given point in time while gift exchange establishes a relation of equality between homogeneous things at different points in time...Commodity exchange – the exchange of unlike-for-unlike – establishes relations of equality between the objects exchanged...Gift exchange – the exchange of like-for-like – establishes an unequal relationship of domination between the transactors.

We are very close to the work of Sahlins here, a proximity which Gregory acknowledges. It is indeed possible to argue that the resemblance extends much further, in that, within the confines of the single text, the project to theoretically specify the gift economy deconstructs itself in roughly the same manner. Like Sahlins, Gregory admits that the five dichotomies above are better thought of as continua: for instance market transactors are not always alien uncorrelated atoms, alienability may be restricted by convention in a market economy, the exchange of commodities extends across time, and so on. Some of the dichotomies are even a little tendentious: Marx argued that anthropomorphism was rife even under the capitalist mode. But the crucial issue in detecting the parallel is that Gregory is striving to establish equivalence classes much in the style of Sahlins, as can be observed from the above quote. What purportedly demarcates like from unlike, equivalent from nonequivalent, are prior cultural structures: relations of reciprocal dependence, alienability classes, local specifications of identity of objects, agreement on time orderings. However, just as with Sahlins, it is precisely at this point that the corrosive character of the gift seeps into the structure, dissolving difference.

Recall Gregory's final claim that the exchange of like-for-like in the guise of gifts allows the assertion of dominance between transactors. This, of course, is intended to capture Mauss's notion of gift as aggression. As for any good Sraffian, the objective equivalence of things will then serve to underwrite some less specific equivalence class between persons. But is there not here lurking a suspicious circularity, the cultural equivalents determining the equivalence classes of objects underwriting the destabilization of cultural equivalents? The following passage suggests Gregory caught a whiff of the deliquescence of his system: 'So who is superior to whom? This is the problem of rank and the answer depends, in the first instance, on the rank of the objects, ie., their exchange order. Objects as gifts have this exchange order rather than exchange-value, because the relation between them is ordinal rather than cardinal' (p.48). This ploy of summoning the dreaded cardinal/ordinal distinction to conjure away the thorny problems of value theory is really unavailing, if not also excruciatingly embarrassing for Gregory, since it is precisely the same move made by the neoclassicals. Combined with the clear possibility that the gift can alter its own equivalence class, Gregory's theory foray tumbles into unceremonious rout:

> Thus the principle of like-for-like must be interpreted as rank-for-rank...This adds a further complication because it means that some gift exchanges appear as commodity exchanges...The redefinition of like-for-like as rank-for-rank also calls for a redefinition of inalienability. While it is conventional to interpret this in a literal sense at the level of pure theory, in practice this must be modified and interpreted in more of a metaphorical sense...Strictly speaking, like-for-like exchanges are impossible.
> (p. 50)

Once the gift is given its due, everything that distinguishes it from the commodity melts into air.

How did Gregory go on to write another 150 pages after this Brest-Litovsk? Careful examination of his subsequent work on the 'velocity theory of gifts', the trade of women, and so forth reveals that he falls back upon a rather inflexible Sraffian theory of value, in effect treating all value as an embodied 'standard commodity'. The spectacle of such a timeless physicalist theory supposedly underwriting a culturally sensitive and diverse economic anthropology is enough to make even an economist squirm. Skepticism about a natural invariant inscribed in the commodity (neoclassicals would rather locate it in the 'mind') is one of the primary reasons for the failure of neo-Ricardianism in economics.

Dissemination of the gift, or what Jacques saw

Jacques Derrida is justly renowned for his notion of the 'dissemination' of meaning. For us non-technocrit types, it is enough for this to be defined as a situation where supposedly opposing concepts merge to form a persistently undecidable exchange of attributes, often within the ambit of a single text. This concept was exemplified in his essay 'Plato's Pharmacy' (Derrida, 1991), where the ambivalence of the meanings of *Pharmakon* as both 'poison' and 'remedy' reverberated throughout Plato's dialogue 'Phaedrus.' Given the dual meanings of gift as 'beneficial donation' and 'poison', it is not surprising that the same sort of analysis might be deployed here, or indeed, given the numerous critical readings of Levi-Strauss, that Derrida himself would carry it out in his *Given Time*. But rather than quote Derrida, it would probably be more helpful for economists to rephrase his insights in more (deceptively?) prosaic terms. The task is to see how the endless displacement of the meaning of the gift obscures, frustrates, and baffles most of those seeking an alternative to neoclassical understandings of exchange.

What do people seem to think a gift is? Most commonly, the gift carries connotations of being the polar opposite of market exchange, that is, a species of non-exchange. Dig a bit deeper, and you will find that what qualifies it for the status of nonexchange is some value principle, because a gift is often defined as a transfer without reciprocal or commensurate value received in exchange. So this must be why the various theorists of the gift economy surveyed above find themselves impelled to discuss equivalence classes, rank orderings, continuua of reciprocities, and the like. However, the difficulties of rendering the value principle or principles explicit are not merely the result of some oversight, but rather inherent in the concept of the gift. Consciousness and intentionality are the source of the problem.

Suppose I drop a $20 bill on the sidewalk. (Derrida does an even more convoluted version of this with Baudelaire's tale of the donation of a counterfeit coin to a beggar.) Is that a gift? Certainly not if I am blissfully unaware that I dropped it – it would simply be a loss. Alternatively, there might be a baroque account where I knew what I was doing when the currency slipped from my grasp. In any event, the gift must have an intentional aspect to be a gift. But one dissemination leads to another with alarming alacrity in this instance. If we tend to conflate intentionality with calculation (and this is the very hallmark of Western thought), then this intentionality immediately undoes the gift and instead situates it squarely in the category of market exchange. The gift is poison if it is self-interested; but it is no gift at all if no attention is devoted to future consequences. As Douglas (1990) insists, to give with no discernable interest as to consequences is to deny the very existence of social ties.

Perhaps there is nonetheless some way to circumvent this paradox of intentionality with regard to the gift. Suppose a donor attempts to short-circuit the paradox with profuse expressions of disinterest and grand gestures devoid of self-seeking character (as is quite frequent in ethnographic accounts). In mild versions of this behavior, the contradiction remains quite clear, with the recipient thrust into the unhappy situation of realizing that protestations of disinterest are direct evidence of interest, or at least calculation. This is why the gift is frequently associated with aggression in anthropology and in art from Lascaux to *Lear*. (As a Midwesterner, I recommend Jane Smiley's *A Thousand Acres*.) The ludicrousness of the situation sometimes whips the donor into an even greater frenzy of self-abasement, whereupon one observes orgies of destruction like the potlatch, or complete and utter abnegation of the donor beyond all cultural parameters, like the hermits of Christian hagiography. But this frenzy of disinterest is all for naught, for it appears that the only successful way to transcend rational calculation is to exit from it, and that is why Western ethnographers often regard orgies of destruction and self-immolation as anti-economic or *irrational*, whereas true asceticism tends to be viewed as the lethargy, indolence and shiftlessness of traditional societies. We thus come full circle to Durkheim's religious basis of exchange: for Westerners the only true gift is the transcendental gift, the one which cannot be given by earthly mortals.

And now Jacques: 'If the gift is annulled in the economic odyssey of the circle as soon as it appears as gift or as soon as it signifies itself as gift, there is no longer any "logic of the gift"…One can go so far as to say a work as monumental as Marcel Mauss's *The Gift* speaks of everything but the gift' (1992: 24).

Is Jacques a stock character from Molière, speaking liturgical Latin unawares? Russell's set theoretic paradox has got nothing on this.

The holocaust of the vanities

The following is taken from Bresnick's *The Six Million Dollar Man*:

> *Schindler's List* uses the Holocaust as its setting, but its affective power may be understood to derive largely from what I take to be the core fantasy of philanthropy – the notion that a gift can be, in the words of Schindler's accountant Itzhak Stern, 'an absolute good'. The belief in a morally unambiguous philanthropy is writ large in the film's climactic moment…the film's apotheosis of Schindler depends on the notion of heroic philanthropy as the only visible way of solving society's ills, whether that society is

Nazi Germany or post-Cold War United States. The film is thus truly the product of its historical moment, for in the wake of the eradication of socialism as a viable political and economic counter-system, capitalism is the only game in town, and for those who enjoy the market's spoils, philanthropy is the most potent means of dispelling the moral disquiet occasioned by the enormous disparities of wealth that capitalism produces. Philanthropy, in this account, turns out to be the salve of liberalism's bad conscience, and it is no surprise that Spielberg, who made something on the order of $100 million in 1993, should have directed a film in which the philanthropist is the hero, regardless of the fact that the money that Schindler shells out to save his *Schindlerjuden* accrued to him by virtue of being a war profiteer.

(1997: 18)

Bresnick begins his article with the observation: 'At the deepest level of its fantasy, Hollywood would like to believe that it is essentially a philanthropy; that what it offers its mesmerized public is the gift of pleasure and, at certain exalted moments, the gift of consciousness itself.'

Donner un rien

A frequent complaint against postmodern writers is that they toy with politics, but that their postmodern play serves mainly to avoid political commitment or difficult social analysis. No Tinseltown enthusiasm for those practiced in the arts of reflexivity! While this may be the case, reasoned political action harbors its own paradoxes.

Derrida, more than other writers, is acutely aware of these paradoxes, for he revels in them. In *Given Time* he presents the paradox of intentionality and the resulting impossibility of the gift. He does this primarily through close reading of texts by Mauss and Baudelaire, giving a wide berth to the precincts of social theory in which this paradox becomes painfully apparent. In response, it might be then permitted to put this question to him: To whom does he bequeath his insight, and what is the intended content of his own 'gift'?

An obvious retort would be that he does not control the uses of his text, and that he has no idea of who might be on the receiving end of his missive, dissemination being endemic to the project. In other words, he might plead disinterest and ignorance of the consequences of his gift – but he is too smart for that. Tracing the boomerang of reflexivity, that option is closed to him, for it is

> precisely that reaction which he has relegated to the status of impossibility.
>
> Rather, and characteristically, Derrida chooses consistency in the face of dissemination. In *Given Time* and in much of his other work, he gestures towards the impossibility of the gift, he dances around it, he peers at it from many angles, takes relevant texts from others, appropriates ideas from across centuries as if they were all intended for his edification; but in the final accounting, he leaves us with nothing. Or, as he says, 'The general equivalent would be a transcendental signified or signifier' (1992: 52). Yes, we should all be wary of Pie in the Sky, but how about the Gift on the Ground?
>
> And fragging Fukayama after the colonial wars are over hardly constitutes an endorsement of any novel ambitions for social theory (Derrida, 1994).
>
> Could it be that Jacques Derrida is the Joel Waldfogel of philosophy?

The road to perdition

Contrary to Derrida, there is at least one immediate corollary of the impossibility of the gift, and it is a political one. It is that the supposed trade-off between equity and efficiency in economics is literally meaningless; and furthermore, the attempt to define liberal or left politics as creating a space within economics for ethics or communal goals or generosity or compassion is a tender trap. It is treacherous because it is premised upon the notion that the right is smugly selfish and coldly calculative, whereas the left alone is both capable of and predisposed towards giving a gift. This, of course, is just a replay of the paradox of intentionality, modulo the question of the ontological character of the fundamental actor. As soon as these ideas are mooted in the public arena, they are neutralized by the rhetoric and reality of political endeavor. For to 'give' communally one must 'give' reasons to get support, and then the protagonists become desperately embroiled in the calculations of cost and benefit, the apparent antithesis of the gift. This constitutes one of the great logical contradictions of democratic political life in the late twentieth century.

The prognosis that one might draw from the paradox of intentionality is that any combination of gift theory and neoclassical economics is not any sort of viable language for discussing politics. Arrow's attempts to reconcile his vestigial socialist instincts with his Walrasian general equilibrium theory are simply incoherent, and this has nothing to do with his own technical 'Impossibility Theorem'. The attempt of the 'liberal' George Akerlof to present a repackaged neoclassicism with a human face must likewise be judged a minor and insignificant diversion. Indeed, his use of Marcel Mauss to motivate the idea of 'labor contracts as partial gift exchange' (1984: 152) only goes to show that an interdisciplinary neoclassical is an oxymoron. The movement by the economics orthodoxy to 'take ethics seriously' (Hausman and McPherson, 1993) proposes the Sissyphyssian task of rolling the gift up onto the utility gradient. Finally, the whole massive literature which endlessly disputes the possibility and nature of altruism (Paul et al., 1993) in an economic or rational-choice framework are merely make-work projects designed to keep a few underemployed academics busy, and should be one of the first priorities in any impending budget cuts. These amendments to rational choice theory serve mainly to make the individual theorists pride themselves in their nobility and broad-mindedness; they make no substantial alteration to the 'two-step' explanations so prevalent in the culture. (The implications for applied policy areas like 'health economics' will be left to the imagination of the reader.)

But does this mean that the death of the gift is the triumph of the theorist of rational self-interest? Is it Joel Waldfogel or nothing? Not at all.

Gift theory and value theory

Derrida asserts that the existence of a general equivalent would be tantamount to the existence of a transcendental signifier. I think this is where he goes wrong, no matter whether one regards it as a rehash of Durkheim or else a translation of Saussure's appropriation of Walrasian general equilibrium. My excursions into economic anthropology, literary criticism and unorthodox economics were meant to suggest that: (a) their resort to gift theory in order to provide themselves with an alternative theory of exchange has left them hobbled and vulnerable to incursions by neoclassical economists; and (b), the crux of the problem, perhaps unrecognized by all these parties, resides in the specification of the quality and character of the *invariants* which are presumed to govern the actions and interpretations of the participants. To recap: the very definition of the gift is predicated upon some such invariant, but the gift corrodes and undermines all the posited invariants. Thus far I agree with Derrida. Where we part company is the implication, never fully explicit in Derrida, that the project of a value theory is futile.

The neoclassicals have a retort to this skepticism, which is why they generally do defeat their rivals. Value invariance, they insist, exists in the mental recesses of the individual; their orderings, while idiosyncratic and personal, are inviolate; thus self-interest is the only possible language suited to the discussion of exchange. The cogency of this response has been attacked and defended *ad nauseam* in the twentieth century; we shall simply pass it by here. Let's save it for another day, a day when the neoclassicals may have read a little bit more than the *AER*.

I should like to propose another possible response to this skepticism, one which resonates much more harmoniously with the prior theoretical inclinations of the anthropologists, critical theorists and feminists. It posits that value invariance is a socially constructed phenomenon, centered upon the institutions of monetary creation and control, one which is simultaneously acquiesced in and undermined by the self-seeking activities of transactors (Mirowski,1991; 1994b). It displays both elements of intentionality and unintended consequences; indeed, the tensions between the bottom-up and top-down forces are what allow it to be cast in the language of self-organized criticality. Value invariance is enforced from the top down by various monetary and accounting controls; it is homeostatically maintained from the bottom up by means of arbitrage operations. Value invariance is compromised from the top down by the expansion of debt and the need for macroeconomic expansion; it is challenged from the bottom up by all manner of devices aimed at circumventing budget constraints, from transactions innovations to theft. Putative psychological regularities of the transactors play no essential role in the structure. 'Value' here simply refers to the outcomes of a system of exchange organized in this manner.

While I have framed some formal aspects of a social theory of value elsewhere, here we will restrict ourselves to the consequences of this framework for the concept of the 'gift'. They fall under four categories: (1) Demonstration that the gift is yet one more instance of a bottom-up activity which impugns the strict integrity of the value invariant; (2) The relationship of the gift to monetary phenomena is central to its evolution and significance; (3) Gifts are an attempt to simultaneously operate outside the network of exchange and yet remain within it; and as such, stand as yet another class of pragmatic balancing acts which encompass the larger paradox of treating the value unit as invariant while all along acknowledging that it is not; and (4) Norms of beneficence and reciprocity are self-referential devices, such as those found in any recursive computational system. Thesis (1) will be sketchily described in this section, while theses (2–4) will be covered in the following 3 sections.

One can use some of the mathematics of networks of the social theory of value to demonstrate that a true gift, *should it exist*, would present obstacles to the numerical constitution of the value invariant. Briefly, imagine that the nodes of a directed graph are associated with commodities, while the arcs between them designate permitted exchanges. Attached to each arc is a rational number which represents the bilateral barter exchange ratio between the commodities. If the exchange were to be characterized as a gift, then that rational number would either be zero or infinity. While such attributions are technically permissible, they would effectively prevent any circuit of completed arbitrage in the section of the graph encompassing that commodity path. No completed arbitrage means no value invariant; therefore, gifts impugn the integrity of the value principle.

It is important to be clear about what this technical result does and does not mean. It is not a 'proof' that gifts don't exist in a capitalist exchange system. Rather, it highlights how gifts will necessarily appear as incompatible with a well-developed market value system. In a sense, it explains why the culture from time to time produces a Joel Waldfogel or Jacques Derrida: people clearly think about and act upon a category of gift activities, but simultaneously are forced to subsume them under the system of commodity exchanges when engaging in valuation. It is the *frisson* of paradox which accompanies this realization which can then be capitalized upon by the irony of a Derrida or a Waldfogel.

No gifts without payment systems

Another implication of the social theory of value is that the very category of 'gift' can only have meaning when contrasted to a prior payments system and an instituted value invariant. Thus the great error of anthropologists from Mauss to Gregory, or feminists from Cixous to Strathern, or sociologists of science like Hagstrom, is to posit the existence of a 'gift economy' which is somehow prior to and counterpoised against an exchange economy. Undoubtedly much of this tendency derives from a problem endemic to the definition of gifts, namely, should they be restricted to closed spheres of exchange which *exclude* money? The uneasy coexistence of gifts and monetization has been shown very nicely for the history of the USA by Viviana Zelizer (1994). Nevertheless, one should not confuse the synchronic quarantine of money from gifts with some diachronic precedence of gifts over money. Gifts are an attempt to transcend the system of value; but that system transcendence already presupposes some form of monetary structure. Without money (or some similar imposition of equivalence classes), there is no 'outside' to which to escape.

The major theoretical implication of the gift as a function of a money-based value schema is that the circularity of definition which bedevils other attempts at gift theory (Sahlins, Gregory) is neutralized. One of the signal characteristics of monetary exchange is that gifts do not alter the fundamental algebraic structures, as they often do with exchanges divided into equivalence classes along kinship, clan or other lines. While gift-giving is antithetical to the stability and integrity of the value invariant, that stability and integrity is maintained outside the sphere of the gift, in markets, banking institutions and accounting entities.

Unwrapping the gift

As Derrida reminds us, gifts are an attempt to be both intentional and disinterested, simultaneously a-rational and rational, friendly and hostile. Perhaps a better way to capture the paradox is that the category of gift transactions tries to use the system of social valuation to get outside the system of social valuation. At the most prosaic level, have you ever wondered why modern transactors wrap their gifts before presentation? From this vantage point, the explanation would involve stylized obfuscation. To put it differently, the market origins and the calculation of intentions cannot of course be effectively banished from the act of gift-giving in a market culture, but they can be disguised in such a way that the donor signals his willingness to suppress those phenomena. The wrapping of a gift pretends that it is temporarily extracted from the mundane level of commerce, and that its identity and its value (don't leave those price tags on!) are irrelevant to the occasion. The fact that the wrapping of gifts is a custom indicates that an interim solution to the paradox of intentionality, just as with the paradox of value invariance, must equally take place at the societal level. Giftwrap, like accounting, is elevated to the status of a transpersonal semiotic system. No individual protestations of disinterest, no rational argument however impassioned, can have any effective purchase on the paradox; but *institutions* can.

The importance of something for nothing

The final task of value theory is to explain why gifts exist at all if they are merely excrescences of a market-based value principle. Here we take a brief look at possible extensions into computational theory. The paradigm of the social theory of value is a vast transpersonal algebra, a kind of finite automata with the configuration of exchanges themselves as the analogue of the hardware, allowing the calculation of consequences of economic activities. Anyone familiar with this literature will realize that there is a whole range of results, from Gödel to Turing to algorithmic intractability to complexity theory, which suggest that some results capable of being stated within the system cannot be proven or even calculated within the system. This is especially true in the class of recursive functions, or statements made within the system about statements in the system. In other words, there are some truths which can be discerned from 'outside' the system which cannot be adequately encompassed from within its ambit.

I should like to suggest that the category 'gift' tends to occupy this relationship to the price system, and that the sociologist Alvin Gouldner essentially realized this in a brace of essays written in the 1960s on 'The Norm of Reciprocity' and 'The Importance of Something for Nothing'. In the first, he made the telling observation that functionalist social theory must presuppose a purely balanced reciprocity; and if the balance is in any way felt to be lacking, the analyst re-imposes it by inventing additional classes of calculative considerations. (This is the best summary of the structure of Gary Becker's style of sociology I have ever encountered, all the more impressive because it was proposed well before the fact.) The equivalent in Gödel's Theorem would be the *post hoc* inclusion of the undecidable statement into the previous structure as a new axiom of the revised system. Nevertheless, this is a mug's game, as Gouldner points out: it is an irreducibly arbitrary procedure, and creates a false sense of comprehensive explanation. Moreover, the achievement of pervasive balance in exchange is also a dead end, in the sense that it creates a rational impasse as to any further motivation to exchange (1973: 252). The vexing 'no-trade theorems' of rational expectations theory merely illustrate this point.

In his second essay, Gouldner suggests that the category of gift, or 'something for nothing', is the mechanism which breaks the deadlock. A system of pure value invariance, which implies pervasive equivalence in exchange, zero arbitrage, and complete balance, is a paradoxically unstable social system. (If this short circuits some neoclassical neurons, just think of the 'no-trade theorems' of Grandmont and Stokey in the rational expectations literature.) The condition which both initiates new exchange and keeps the system of exchange functioning is the possibility of something outside the value sphere, namely, the gift. It is the gift which injects the promise of irrationality, the mirage of transcendence, into the heart of Weberian *Zweckrationalität*. 'The self that wants something for nothing seeks an existence without alienation...it wants to be loved for itself' (1973: 271). It is the fabled return to childhood, or perhaps the nostalgia for the lost history of a barely imagined precapitalist era. It is the proposition which can be stated within the system (something for nothing needs a value invariant) but which cannot be computed within the system (the paradox of the gift).

But just as Gödelian paradoxes have led to further fruitful and interesting mathematics in the realm of recursive functions, the paradox of the gift leads to further social structures, perched atop the original institutions of value and exchange. 'The paradox of elites is this...they exploit and take something for nothing. But what transforms them from merely powerful strata into a legitimate elite, in short, what transforms their domination into hegemony, is that they can and sometimes do give something for nothing' (1973: 274).

No, No, Not Nietzsche!

He who...actually practices requital – is, that is to say, grateful and revengeful – is called good; he who is powerful and cannot requite is called bad. The good are a caste, the bad a mass like grains of sand. Good and bad is for a long time the same thing as noble and base, master and slave. On the other hand, one does not regard the enemy as evil: he can requite.

(Nietzsche, 1986: 37)

Acknowledgements

This paper was prepared for a conference on 'Postmodernism and Economics' at University of California-Riverside. The author has benefitted from comments of previous audiences at Duke University and COPEC XIII, Northeastern University. I would like to thank Esther-Mirjam Sent, James Drake, Ann Jennings, Arjo Klamer, Jack Amariglio and David Woodruff for comments, and Steve Gudeman for making it a conversation.

References

Akerlof, George (1984) *An Economic Theorist's Book of Tales*, New York: Cambridge University Press.
Anderson, Elizabeth (1993) *Value in Ethics and Economics*, Cambridge: Harvard University Press.
Andreoni, James (1990) 'Impure Altruism and Donations to Public Goods,' *Economic Journal*, 100: 464–77.
Arrow, Kenneth (1975) 'Gifts and Exchanges' in E. Phelps, (ed.) *Altruism, Morality and Economic Theory*, New York: Sage.
Bataille, Georges (1988) *The Accursed Share*, New York: Zone.

Becker, Gary (1981) *A Treatise on the Family*, Cambridge: Harvard University Press.
Booth, William (1993) *Households*, Ithaca: Cornell University Press.
Bresnick, Adam (1997) 'The Six Billion Dollar Man,' *Times Literary Supplement*, July 18: 18–19.
Caillé, Alain (1994) *Don, intérêt, et desinterressement*, Paris: Editions la decouverte.
Cixous, Helène (1976) 'The Laugh of the Medusa,' *Signs*, (1): 875–99.
—— (1991) *Coming to Writing, and Other Essays*, Cambridge: Harvard University Press.
Derrida, Jacques (1991) *A Derrida Reader: Between the Blinds*, (ed.) Peggy Kamuf, New York: Columbia University Press.
—— (1992) *Given Time I: Counterfeit Money*, Chicago: University of Chicago Press.
—— (1994) *Spectres of Marx*, New York: Routledge.
Douglas, Mary (1990) 'Foreword' to Maus, *The Gift*, New York: Norton. Miller.
Gane, Mike (ed.) (1992) *The Radical Sociology of Durkheim and Mauss*, London: Routledge.
Gouldner, Alvin (1973) *For Sociology*, New York: Basic.
Gregory, Chris (1982) *Gifts and Commodities*, New York: Academic.
—— (1994) 'Economic Anthropology' in Tim Ingold, (ed.) *Routledge Companion Encyclopedia of Anthropology*, London: Routledge.
Hagstrom, W.O. (1965) *The Scientific Community*, New York: Basic.
Hausman, Dan and McPherson, Michael (1993) 'Taking Ethics Seriously' *Journal of Economic Literature*, (21): 671–731.
Held, Virginia (1990) 'Mothering versus Contract' in Jane Mansbridge, (ed.) *Beyond Self-Interest*, Chicago: University of Chicago Press.
Herring, Hubert (1994) 'Dislike those Suspenders?' *New York Times* Sunday, Dec. 25.
Hyde, Lewis (1983) *The Gift*, New York: Vintage.
Kolm, Serge-Christophe (1984) *La bonne économie: La reciprocité generale*, Paris: Presses Universitaires de France.
Landa, Janet Tai (1994) *Trust, Ethnicity and Identity*, Ann Arbor: University of Michigan Press.
Lodewijks, John (1994) 'Anthropologists and Economists: Conflict or Cooperation?', *Journal of Economic Methodology*, (1): 81–104.
Malinowski, Bronislaw (1922) *Argonauts of the Western Pacific*, London: Routledge.
—— ([1925]1985) *Crime and Custom in Savage Society*, Totawa: Rowman and Allanheld.
Mauss, Marcel (1969) *Oeuvres*, vol. 3, Paris: Editions de Minuit.
—— (1990) *The Gift*, trans. W. Halls, New York: Norton.
Miller, Daniel (ed.) (1993) *Unwrapping Christmas*, Oxford: Clarendon Press.
Mirowski, Philip (1991) 'Postmodernism and the Social theory of Value', *Journal of Post Keynesian Economics*, (13): 565–82.
—— (1994a) 'Tit for Tat: Concepts of Exchange, Higgling, and Barter in Two Episodes in the History of Economic Anthropology' in Neil de Marchi and Mary Morgan, (eds) *Higgling. Supplement to History of Political Economy*, Durham: Duke University Press.

—— (1994b) 'Some Thoughts on Arbitrage, Symmetries and the Social Theory of Value,' in Amitava Dutt, (ed.) *New Directions in Analytical Political Economy*, Aldershot: Elgar.
Nietzsche, Friedrich (1967) *On the Genealogy of Morals*, trans. W. Kauffmann, New York: Vintage.
—— (1986) *Human, All too Human*, Cambridge: Cambridge University Press.
Parry, Jonathan (1985) 'The Gift, the Indian Gift and the "Indian Gift"', *Man*, (21): 453–73.
Paul, Ellen *et al.* (eds) (1993) *Altruism*, New York: Cambridge University Press.
Piliavin, Jane and Callero, Peter (1991) *Giving Blood*, Baltimore: Johns Hopkins University Press.
Posner, Richard (1980) 'A Theory of Primitive Society', *Journal of Law and Economics* (23): 1–53.
Ridley, Matt (1996) *The Origins of Virtue*, New York: Viking.
Sahlins, Marshall (1972) *Stone Age Economics*, Chicago: Aldine.
—— (1988) 'Cosmologies of Capitalism' *Proceedings of the British Academy*, (74): 1–51.
—— (1992) 'Economics of Develop-Man in the Pacific' *Anthropology and Aesthetics*, (22): 12–25.
Strathern, Marilyn (1988) *The Gender of the Gift*, Berkeley: University of California Press.
Sugden, Robert (1982) 'On the Economics of Philanthropy,' *Economic Journal*, (92): 341–50.
Titmuss, Richard (1971) *The Gift Relationship: From Human Blood to Social Policy*, New York: Vintage.
Waldfogel, Joel (1993) 'The Deadweight Loss of Christmas' *American Economic Review*, (83): 1328–37.
Zelizer, Viviana (1994) *The Social Meaning of Money*, New York: Basic.

22

POSTMODERN GIFTS

Stephen Gudeman

The Gift, by Marcel Mauss ([1925] 1990), is the 'master narrative' of economic anthropology, and anthropology's gift to neoclassical economics. Many in the field secretly believe that this present from the French master disrupts exchange theory in neoclassical economics. If only we could get economists to read it, they might carry out some fieldwork!

But the idea of a gift also represents economic anthropology's postmodern moment, for it seems to elude every fixed understanding we erect, as Mirowski makes clear in his contribution to this volume. We cannot seem to decide what a gift really is or what it implies for the idea of shared values or commensuration. Derrida (1992), by suggesting that the gift is a synthetic, local category, and not a universal one, heightens the discomfort, for he turns anthropology's critical stance back on itself. Is the claim that gifts exist an ideology that inverts the market experience of balanced exchange, and provides a false grounding for understanding nonmarket economies?

Mauss's small volume, elliptical and packed with learning, is admittedly difficult to read. It interweaves several themes. A gift, argues Mauss, always has an ambiguous status. If it is truly freely given, the gift has no social impact, because no social obligations are set in motion. The free gift conveys no history or social memory (which is one of Derrida's 1992 themes). But if the recipient of a gift is obligated to make a return (which is Mauss's argument), then we need to explain why this is so and to say something about the nature of the required return. The requital also may be delayed. For example, we may be invited to someone's house for dinner, which sets up the obligation to reciprocate. But when? And what constitutes a return? Surely there must be a shared standard by which to judge the exchange of dinners (which is the issue that troubles Mirowski). But if a standard of value exists, what makes a gift transaction different from a market exchange? And why do people such as the Trobriand Islanders (Malinowski [1922] 1961) carefully distinguish reciprocity in the kula from the regular trade of objects (*gimwali*)?

Let us begin with the terms, *gift* and *reciprocity*, because they are used differently by economists and anthropologists. For economists, reciprocity refers to two-directional exchanges; a market trade is reciprocal. Anthropologists use reciprocity for a more restricted set of practices. They reserve it for noncash, nonmarket exchanges and set it in opposition to the trade of commodities for cash. Often anthropologists equate reciprocity with the gift on the argument that a gift obligates the recipient to offer a return, setting in motion a temporal, lasting cycle of obligations, which is reciprocity. This sense of the term comes from Mauss who spoke of three linked obligations: to give, to receive and to return. Sometimes anthropologists avoid the term *gift*, however, because in a market economy gift has the connotation 'without obligation' which is not what Mauss intended. For this reason, there has been much discussion over the years about translating Mauss's (French) title, *Le Don*, as The Gift. For economists, there are no free lunches; for anthropologists there are no free gifts.

I use reciprocity for nonmarket, lasting, two-way exchanges, and gift for an initial present. An unrequited offering remains a gift. (Of course, uncertainty about whether the recompense will occur, not to mention delays in making it, blurs the line between reciprocity and the gift.) The examples of reciprocity are many: teenage friends in the USA share clothes; the Trobriand Islanders pass valuable necklaces and armbands along paths that link their kula communities; Tiv farmers of northern Nigeria send yams to kinsmen in times of lean (Bohannan and Bohannan 1968); some Latin American agriculturalists offer tithes to the church when the harvest has been bountiful. I think it is not accidental that we conceive of the 'real' unrequited gift – a gifted person, the gift of grace, the gift of fertility – as divinely inspired, for ultimately who can repay the gift of life?

The many cases of reciprocity recorded by anthropologists challenge the idea that material life must be completely organized by market practices. But into what theoretical framework should we fit reciprocity? Most of the theorizing on reciprocity was set in motion by Mauss, who is given a new reading by each generation of anthropologists. They usually argue that reciprocity is the pillar of social life. According to the accepted wisdom, reciprocity is the primary building block of community, because it makes and perpetuates dyadic relationships that lie at the core of society. Neoclassical theorists, developing a different view, visualize dyadic ties as evolving from individual motivations and interests that are infrasocial or prior to the development of social forms.

In contrast to these views, I shall argue that anthropologists are caught in a dialectic with neoclassical economists. Both offer essentialist or modernist perspectives: one is relational, the other atomistic. One side emphasizes altruism, the other self-interest. In opposition to both, I think offering gifts and enacting reciprocity are tactical acts that extend the shared values of a community. As tokens of apportionment and forays in expanding a community's borders, they are secondary processes. Not a rule but a process, reciprocity is one way of groping with uncertainty at the limits of a community: making a gift secures, probes, and expands the borders of a group. Thus, the gift is not opposed to the commodity nor would their opposition provide a typology of all economies, such as 'the gift economy' and 'the commodity economy' (Gregory 1982: 19). Economies are built on the interlocked regimes of communal and commercial value, not gift versus commodity. Communal allotment or distribution, which is not reducible to dyadic ties of reciprocity, signifies mutuality and shared identity before the act of giving extends them.

Genealogies

I want to set these themes into a broader conversation on exchange before developing my own argument in greater detail. Broadly, two discourses about reciprocal transactions have developed. The neoclassical one starts with Adam Smith, runs through Ricardo, and is still being embellished. For example, in the *Wealth of Nations* ([1776] 1976), Adam Smith offers three reasons why people exchange. In the first chapter, he sketches a model of the division of labor using the example of the pin factory to suggest that specialization by task leads to increased productive efficiency and wealth. The argument points to the development of interdependence, or exchange *within* a production unit. In the second chapter, Smith says that humans have a propensity 'to truck, barter, and exchange' (Smith [1776] 1976: 17). This rationale for exchange refers to transactions *between* market actors or units. Finally, Smith observes that we do not get our dinner from the benevolence of the baker or brewer. Their avarice impels market trade ([1776] 1976: 18); but from such self-interest, facilitated by the market, everyone benefits and the wealth of nations increases. This third rationale for exchange – involving notions of self-interest, profit-seeking, and maximizing one's gains – underpins much of neoclassical theory today.

Anthropological explanations of reciprocity developed in this century. There have been many contributions, especially in the last decade or so, but I shall attend to a principal strand that begins with Malinowski and Mauss, includes Lévi-Strauss, and counts as legatees Polanyi and Sahlins.[1] Many of the more recent contributions build on their voices. Like the discourse of the economists, the anthropologists' is essentialist but with a difference in the selected foundations.

In *The Gift* Mauss implicitly uses an evolutionary perspective. Drawing on the available ethnography, especially from the Trobriand Islands and the Northwest Coast, as well as classical texts, he often reads variation in space as a product or representation of temporal change: the cross-cultural comparison has a historical scent. As Parry has acutely pointed out, *The Gift* contains many speculations on evolution and betrays a deep interest in origins (Parry 1986: 457). In fact, Mauss's method was Aristotelian – according to which the genealogy of the observed pattern, made available by analysis of its components, points to the original or basic social form.

For Mauss, the initial exchange was that of total prestations in which individuals and entire groups, such as clans, 'exchange everything with one another', including food, goods, rituals, dances, women, and children (1990: 70). This 'ancient system', this 'elementary type', or 'base', *provides the morality for all instances of the gift*, but can hardly be found today (1990: 7, 70; see also 36, 42, 46).[2] Afterward, as society developed, the gift appeared. The gift is a transaction between individuals as representatives of groups. It does not involve whole groups – though it occurs between them – and is more limited than a total prestation: not everything comes and goes. The gift itself consists of objects, services, or performances. After the gift appeared, credit, barter, and then market exchange developed. Mauss hangs the argument on a logico-temporal ordering from total prestations to the gift, credit, barter, and market transactions. The gift makes and reinforces the mutuality that once was expressed by total prestations, whereas market exchange – being disconnected from all social ties – disrupts communality. Mauss's solution to what he perceived to be anomie in modern society partly caused by the predominance of market trade was to reinstate the morality inherent in gift exchange.

Mauss, like Aristotle, provides a genetic argument. Its correspondence with Aristotle's (1946) evolutionary 'history' that runs from families to villages to the polis to trade, from inside to outside, and from mutuality to alienation, is very close. Mauss does not claim that market trade is the teleological end of the gift, but he does link his synchronic and structural description, with its layers that vary from moral to self-interested exchange, to a diachronic account of the gift's appearance and evolution.

If we read Mauss's genetic scheme backwards, however, an absence becomes apparent. Turning the arrow in reverse from market exchange to gift to total prestations, we are led to ask: what preceded the stage of total prestations? This moment must constitute the big bang or original period of society. Mauss says little about this antecedent time, but he does offer a hint by referring, at the essay's close, to 'the basis of society...our common life, the conscious direction of which is the supreme art, *Politics*, in the Socratic sense of the word' ([1925] 1990: 83). Prior to the stage of total prestations between groups, communities themselves must be in place: clans, lineages, households, villages. The unvoiced component of *The Gift* is an intact community economy with its norms of distribution. The morality of reciprocity develops from this social form.

Mauss did not originate the idea of reciprocity. He used Malinowski's ([1922] 1961) Trobriand ethnography to develop his general argument, and Malinowski himself had pointed to the importance of reciprocity. In a central chapter of *Argonauts of the Western Pacific*, Malinowski observes that 'the whole of tribal life is permeated by a constant give and take' ([1922] 1961: 167) and proclaims:

> The view that the native can live in a state of individual search for food, or catering for his own household only, in isolation from an interchange of goods, implies a calculating, cold egotism...[Such views] ignore the fundamental human impulse to display, to share, to bestow. They ignore the deep tendency to create social ties through the exchange of gifts. Apart from any consideration as to whether the gifts are necessary or even useful, giving for the sake of giving is one of the most important features of Trobriand sociology, and, from its very general and fundamental nature, I submit that it is a universal feature of all primitive societies.
>
> ([1922] 1961: 175)

The difference with Mauss is slight but important. Mauss argues that reciprocity occurs within all social formations; Malinowski sees it as a characteristic of one class of societies that he labels 'primitive'. This equation of the primitive with reciprocity, and of the modern with the market, still finds its way into discussion.

Lévi-Strauss, in *The Elementary Structures of Kinship*, develops the reciprocity argument of Mauss but in a Cartesian direction. For Lévi-Strauss, reciprocity reflects basic forms of the human mind ([1949] 1969: 75) which are three: first, the necessity of the rule, then

> the notion of reciprocity regarded as the most immediate form of integrating the opposition between the self and others; and finally the synthetic nature of the gift...[which makes] individuals into partners.
>
> ([1949] 1969: 84)

For Lévi-Strauss, reciprocity is the kernel of the social contract: no reciprocity, no society. It is the foundation of all human institutions, which imperfectly express it ([1949] 1969: 76). By this argument, which asserts the universality of reciprocity across all societies, Lévi-Strauss not only expanded the Malinowski view but rid himself of Mauss's concern with origins. He also decisively raised the stakes in the battle between anthropologists and economists over the origins of economic forms: after Lévi-Strauss the choice was set between two essentialisms – irreducible dyadic bonds (for the anthropologists) and atomic individuals (for the economists).

Karl Polanyi has to be added to this story, because he has been so influential in anthropology and because we cannot fully understand Sahlins's later argument without grasping Polanyi's contribution on which it is based. Perhaps Polanyi did not write with the erudition of Mauss, the grace of Malinowski, or the force of Lévi-Strauss, but he is persuasive for his ideas if not his data. Here is my summary.

First, Polanyi is an empiricist. He surveyed the literature on 'ancient' and 'primitive' economies to extract underlying features in the data and construct typologies (1944, 1968). Polanyi offers a tripartite typology of all economic forms with an ill-fitting appendix. The divisions are these. First, there is reciprocity, which is built on the principle of symmetry and found in societies where kinship is dominant. These are 'primitive' societies. Second, there is redistribution. Built on the principle of centricity (or inward and outward movements), redistribution is encountered in systems where political or religious institutions are dominant, such as 'ancient' societies. Finally, market exchange, built on haggling, is characteristic of modern market society. Polanyi admits that the three patterns may be found together, but one is always dominant and colors the others. He does not develop a theory of their co-presence, however, and implies that they are connected by historical development. The first two forms – reciprocity in the context of kinship systems and redistribution in the context of politico-religious systems – are instances of the 'embedded' economy: material functions are carried out through kinship, religious, or political relationships. Only the market, in contemporary society, constitutes a 'disembedded' economy.

Hidden in Polanyi's comparative typology is a historical and evolutionary perspective that starts with reciprocity in primitive societies, moves to redistribution in archaic ones, and finishes with market exchange in modern economies. This scheme of development (from the embedded to the disembedded economy) fits the general anthropological argument that reciprocity lies underneath and before the market and redistribution.

An especially problematic feature of Polanyi's theory, however, was the economic form that could not be placed in any of his categories. A careful reader of Aristotle and of ethnographic texts, Polanyi knew that some economic units were inspired by the model of autarky. He called it 'householding', although the principle of achieving self-sufficiency can be applied at any level. Where can this economic form be fitted? Because Polanyi's typology is formed around modes of exchange, the self-sufficient economy has no place in it, as Polanyi uncomfortably recognized. Community economy was relegated to a position off the typological map.

Finally, there is the contribution of Marshall Sahlins (1972). In many respects, his argument is Polanyi's but stripped of time and laid out in space. Sahlins presents a scale that would correlate reciprocity and trade with close and distant social relations. At one end, there is generalized reciprocity, which refers to 'putatively altruistic' transactions such as the maternal suckling of children (1972: 193–4). Kinship obligations fall into this class as well. (This equation of female + sharing + community = non economy reproduces the standard view that economy is the realm of males.) Moving away from such closeness, there is balanced reciprocity – the give and take of the gift – which is less personal and 'more economic' (1972: 195). At the greatest social distance lies negative reciprocity, the attempt to get something for nothing, as expressed in barter and theft.

For Sahlins, reciprocity is the explanatory force behind the entire scheme, as demonstrated by his stretching of the verbal category to encompass all transactions from altruism at mutuality's core to stealing at its periphery. Thus Sahlins takes Polanyi one step further, by deriving communal sharing, allotment, and redistribution from reciprocity. For Polanyi, reciprocity in kinship is historically and logically prior to redistribution within a polity, and both come before competitive exchange in the market. Sahlins, in his reformulation of Polanyi's argument, locates communal allotment as a secondary phenomenon or example of generalized reciprocity: the domestic sharing of foods, household pooling, and maternal care are all forms of reciprocity. Chiefly dues and tribute are instances of reciprocity as well, because when power relations come to dominate material processes, prior bonds of reciprocity are brought together by a central authority and transformed to a scheme of redistribution which is only

> *an organization of reciprocities, a system of reciprocities* – a fact of central bearing upon the genesis of large-scale redistribution under chiefly aegis. But this most general understanding merely suggests concentration in the first place on reciprocity.
> (1972: 188)

Reciprocity for Sahlins is the building block of exchange, economy, and society.

The Argument

In different ways Polanyi, Sahlins, and Mauss hint that reciprocity may not constitute the foundation of economy and society, leaving an opening in the anthropological discourse. I suggest that economic institutions and acts have no single foundation – as modern models suggest – but that there are two ways of organizing material processes which are found separately, in shifting combinations, and in tension. For one part, production and distribution processes are carried out by individuals or units that engage in anonymous transactions or trade. In elaborated form these transactions are money-mediated and take place in complex and large markets. A variety of different economic theories have been developed to describe how such markets operate. But processes of production and distribution also may be socially mediated or take place through established institutions, such as families, household groups, great estates, lineages, villages, or nation states. In practice, most economic processes draw on the two in a variety of combinations. I call the two realms market economy and community economy. Market theorists tend to focus on one form; economic anthropologists look at the other, and at their dialectics.

The community form of economy has several important features. It offers, first, a degree of self-sufficiency. The production, distribution and consumption of a crop, such as rice, yams or potatoes may be kept within the unit. Traded occasionally, if at all, the crop may be viewed as a necessary and fundamental food plus mark of identity. A community also has a base or commons that it shares. Such a base might be water rights and canals, or land; it can be a flock, stock of foods, or other resource. The base more broadly consists of the legacy or patrimony of a people – their accumulated knowledge and skills – and in this sense the people themselves. A base is made up of humans and things together, and is not divided between subjects and objects, or culture and nature. Breaking what a people share or their commons fractures their community as quickly as breaking their social relationships.

In addition to maintaining a degree of self-sufficiency and a base, a central act in community economy consists of allotting or distributing parts of the base for use or consumption. This division may consist of portioning rights to use water or land, or it may mean dividing up a flow of goods, such as a harvest or game animal. The rights may be parcelled by different rules from gender to age to kinship to civil status to authority. Sometimes there is an emphasis on equity or necessity, and sometimes relative portions are determined by the exercise of power. Such distribution of resources and product is very different from market allocation that works through individual and separate offers and bids, and leads to systemic efficiency (in neoclassical theory).

By theorists of both the market and of community, however, reciprocity is usually construed as the basis of economy. In the market case, reciprocity refers to an exchange of equivalents, or balanced commodity exchange. In the community case, reciprocity refers to delayed transactions that may or may not reach a balance over time (though the concept of imbalance implies that a common standard of value exists).

I would displace reciprocity from a central position in the realm of community economy. Certainly, it is opposed to market trade as an act of community, but it resembles trade as a practice that reaches outside a unit. Reciprocity is an expression of community, and a way of expanding it, but community itself – contingent and vulnerable – and the base it holds – material or immaterial, spiritual or natural – together with the allotment rules it maintains – negotiated and contested – are the materials on which it operates. Distribution or apportionment of the commons is an act of making and maintaining community, and without it there can be no reciprocity. Communal allotment – contra the anthropological theorists – does not come 'after' reciprocity; rather, moments of reciprocity or the gift are tokens of existent community.

Reciprocity (or more exactly, an initial gift) distributes the base and projects it to others. The gift extends the commons to someone outside community, offering temporary participation or even permanent inclusion. Reciprocity is never contained within a community. The gift and reciprocity are used to probe across its borders, for a variety of motives, such as establishing mutuality and peace, expressing dominance, manipulating to advantage, displaying power or wealth, and bringing in new members. The gift is always an experiment and a secondary transaction in making community. It suggests the possibility of changing a community's boundaries by including new people within the allotment or by creating a larger and new association. The gift is a probe into uncertainty that can make community or evolve into trade. Always disruptive of the accepted, it has no single meaning but shifts with its use. To this extent, I agree with Mirowski that the gift disrupts a value sphere, but my placement of reciprocity at the margins of community is different.

Consider again the dinner party. We invite a circle of friends to dinner, and later they invite us back. This round of invitations surely exemplifies reciprocity – or does it? A dinner offered is commensality, because it represents the sharing of foodstuffs that sustain a household. Raised to a higher standard of cuisine than a normal supper and often the product of hand labor, the convivial dinner distributes a household's base and puts it on display. 'Eat what you want and still there will be leftovers', states the household. This is apportionment or distribution of the base outside the group's borders.

But a dinner party usually incurs an obligation which raises the question: what should be returned, and when? In some circles, guests bring their host a bottle of wine; usually it remains unopened through the evening. The wine is like an intermediary gift that signals acceptance of the dinner and promises further reciprocation, but it is not the full return itself. So we have two cycles; distinct parts of the base – wine and food –

are circulated against one another; one is consumed, the other is held. Indeed, I harbor images of a few unopened bottles of wine endlessly circulating among households. As for the food, sometimes a dinner is not reciprocated, and the wine alone must constitute the reciprocation: embarrassment lingers while status is gained and lost by the different parties. Sometimes the relative status of host and guest determine whether meals are even reciprocated. Usually, the dinner is returned (along with a countervailing bottle of wine carefully selected to be different from the one received); because the return dinner cannot be measured exactly against the original, however, the double cycle is perpetuated in this play of gaining status and making community with others. (A dinner, of course, may also represent an attempt to form community for business purposes.)

Gifts, thus, extend community to others, including them as users of the base, which is another way of expressing what Mauss meant by 'the spirit' of the gift. To worry about Mauss's use of the word *spirit* for the Maori term *hau*, and whether his interpretation, translation, and generalization of a local word is valid, misses the significance of the argument (Sahlins, 1972). The spirit of the gift is the offering of community by sharing its base or its most sacred holdings. In this respect, Mauss was perceptive to commingle objects and people as things to be exchanged, because together they make community ([1925] 1990: 14); they are base.

My argument partly overlaps that of Annette Weiner (1992), who offered an important contribution to the reciprocity debate.[3] She distinguishes two kinds of goods: alienable and inalienable possessions. The latter constitute sacra of the community or the core of the commons. For Weiner, to part with these goods is to lose something of one's identity, and she emphasizes that inalienable possessions are 'for keeping'.

On turning to reciprocity, Weiner thus speaks of keeping while giving, identifying this dynamic as the 'universal paradox' in exchange (1992: 5). She argues that things given away often are only loans because the objects are inalienable. As a real loss of inalienable possessions would diminish the self, one must keep as one gives and give only to attract more back. In the case of the Trobriand Islands, where Weiner has undertaken extensive fieldwork, land and decorations may be given away, but they are loans to others – being closely tied to the identity of matrilineages whose possessions they are – and must be returned.

But Weiner adds, though she does not fully develop, that such loans of inalienable possessions are ways of 'making kin of non-kin' (1992: 26) – and surely this is a central point. Goods kept do not necessarily give power or identity to the self or community; their possession must be recognized by others, and by the self knowing that others recognize them. In this negotiation, the power of community is expanded by including others in it or by compelling them to recognize its place. This strategic act is forceful because the gift is a token of the base and community.

One can never know if an offered gift will be accepted and returned. If the gift is reciprocated, the return says much the same as the offering, and more. The return accepts the commensality, yet signals difference and independence. The result, or reciprocity, is two overlapping bases. For this reason, in many situations reciprocity is an exchange of inequivalents; because each gift is a token of a base that belongs to a distinct community and the two bases are incommensurate, the exchange is made up of unmatched things.

But this reciprocal extension of communality suggests the possibility of forming a larger, encompassing community. Each fragment of a base offered is both a part of a whole (the existent community) – for gifts kept in circulation are a distributed base – and a part within a possible whole (the imagined community). The wine, unopened and continuously circulated, comes to stand for the hospitality of all dinner parties in a potential community. Similarly, when high school and college students borrow one another's clothes, and use and keep them for long intervals, in complicated exchanges, they are distributing their bases and making a new community in the doing – all from the bits and pieces of their domestic ones. The pragmatic act of reciprocity incorporates this tension between separation and unity, self-sufficiency and interdependence. There is always a delicate balance between distance and closeness, detachment and warm sentiments in the double act.

The unhingeing of this tension converts reciprocity to separate communities, to commercial trade, or to war. For example, Harrison (1992), describing group rituals or ceremonies as a kind of communal property, notes that victors in war often seize the tutelary gods or ceremonial privileges of the vanquished, such as names, dances, masks, and designs, that have been used in reciprocal exchanges. In this seizure, the core of the opponent's commons is destroyed, and so is community and the possibility of extending it to others.

On the other hand, to sell communal valuables that are used in reciprocal exchanges converts the realm of social value and wellbeing to that of commercial value and just living. Thus at a dinner party, the price tag on the gift of wine must be rubbed off, and the prices of the food, linen, glassware, and silver at the dinner table cannot be revealed, except at the cost of disgrace. Contemporary stories and films that feature the selling of the nonsaleable sacra – the upright public servant who allows himself to be bribed for a just cause, the spouse who sells her sexual access to save her impecunious husband – shock the viewer not for the high price that some services command but for the commensuration that is established between different spheres of value. These are morality tales, and they cut several ways, for it is equally shocking when wealthy people convert public sacra to domestic goods by shooting rare animals to secure household trophies, by purchasing a famous painting for private viewing, by taking an archaeological stela from Guatemala, or by buying the rights to log rare trees. In reverse, to hold and revere an old car model converts ordinary market goods to sacra – a contemporary process recognized by Warhol in his satiric painting of a soup can.

An initial gift, then, is a trial-and-error practice, because the giver operates in the realm of uncertainty about its acceptability and appropriateness, and whether it will be returned. Gifts are converted to reciprocity for different reasons. Reciprocity can cement a relationship and establish community. The gift may express affection and mutuality but also a power difference, for the giver is able to cede part of her base without requiring a requital. The dinner party establishes commensality, and it may be a token in the struggle for status where the giver's ability to gather resources, from money to cultural skills, are put on display. Accepting such hospitality without reciprocation signals acceptance of inferiority (see also Herzfeld 1987). So, for tactical reasons such as gaining power, keeping mutuality, and maintaining independence, reciprocity occurs. Similarly, refusal to reciprocate can indicate lack of desire to create mutuality, or it may signal inability to do so. Not a rule or norm of social life, not a feature of mind, a function of self-interest, or an essential foundation of society, reciprocity is part of a system of practices in which participants express, conserve, lose, and gain position in the sphere of social value.[4]

Sister-exchange

An ethnographic example showing how reciprocity functions in relation to communal apportionment has recently been provided by the late Alfred Gell. Having produced a fine study of the Umeda of New Guinea some years ago (1975), Gell (1992) reformulated his understanding of their marriage practices in a way that comes close to my thesis.

The Umeda live in West Sepik Province of Papua New Guinea. In pre-contact times, the Umeda were self-sufficient. Dependent on hunting and gathering, they made stone tools and sago-pounders, and produced salt, paint, and lime as needed. Umeda worked in family groups, and within each family, items were 'shared'. For example, a hunter could not eat any part of game he killed; the meat was divided among his matrikin and his wife's kin. Gell calls this social form an Indigenous Service Economy; quite simply, it was a community economy, within which there were asymmetrical relationships between husband and wife, and parents and children.

Pre-contact Melanesia also was criss-crossed by trade routes. Trade took place between groups, especially ones that did not intermarry; and goods moved, via trade partnerships, up to 50 miles. In highland areas, most goods traded were not subsistence articles: trade was not impelled by the need to overcome ecological deficiencies, and groups did not depend on it for their persistence. External trade was a source of excitement, exotic imports were esteemed, and exchange relationships themselves were valued (Gell 1992: 149, 148). In many cases, local specialization in the production of goods did not precede trade but was fostered, encouraged, and elaborated in response to the possibility of expanding impersonal exchange, much as neoclassical theorists might surmise.

The Umeda also practiced bride-service. Each new son-in-law had to live with and work for his wife's family for an extended period, hunting and pounding sago for them; and he was sustained by them. A son-in-law was incorporated, for a time, within the communal economy of his wife's family. Even after, when an independent and mature hunter sent portions of meat to his wife's parents, these were not considered to be gifts from an outsider but 'shares' to which they had rights (Gell 1992: 155).

The Umeda practiced sister-exchange as well, and a relatively high proportion of marriages were arranged between sets of siblings. When a man was able to effect a sister-exchange, he owed no bride-service to his wife's parents.

The existence of these two marriage transactions raises the question: was sister-exchange 'primordial' and an example of the reciprocal exchange that lies at the base of society, or did it develop after the institution of bride-service? Reciprocity theory in anthropology, from Lévi-Strauss onward, suggests that sister-exchange constitutes the weld of Umeda society; the reciprocal exchange of women (regarded as the supreme gift) was the original or foundational transaction between separate families. For the Umeda, therefore, bride-service is only a substitute payment for the central gift, a woman. In his reconsideration of the ethnography, however, Gell points out that sister-exchange was never an ideal or rule among the Umeda; it may even have begun very recently. Sister-exchange developed as a substitute for serving a woman's family – because men deem the latter to be onerous, even oppressive. Being compelled to live with and serve one's in-laws is shaming (in fact, the word for brother-in-law is 'shame' [Gell 1992: 154]). For a young man, having to work for his bride's father's group conflicts with his own desire to become an independent hunter and family head. Exchanging sisters, thus, is a way of escaping the obligation to work for another community, a strategy for establishing one's own, and a method for moderating, if not eliminating, the loss of social esteem.

Let me fit the ethnography more closely to my argument. The 'original' exchanges in Umeda were redistribution within household families and trade between them – or community and market transactions. A marriage transgresses a community's borders, and among Umeda the receipt of a spouse obligates males to participate in and become subservient to another household by contributing labor to its commons while subsisting from its flows. For young men, the simultaneous exchange of sisters was a way of solving the contradiction between the subservience they experienced when owing labor to another community and the esteem they sought as heads of their own. Exchanging sisters was a way of more quickly building a base.

The Umeda ethnography fits my argument that the gift and reciprocity are strategic moves across the borders of community. The gift of a woman, by obligating the groom to return labor, benefited the bride's community at the expense of the groom's. Returning a sister was a way of avoiding loss of prestige while quitting the obligation and helping to establish the groom's community more expeditiously. Gell himself argues that sister-exchange was modeled after the impersonal, external commodity exchanges that Umeda had long undertaken. He sensed correctly, I think, that community and trade interact, and that by exchanging sisters young men could liberate themselves from long-term obligations. But reciprocity and the gift are not pale reflections of commercial trade; they arise from the strategic negotiations that a community makes when using its base.

The badge of society

In an effort to counter the culturally compelling arguments of economists, anthropologists after Mauss have seized perhaps too eagerly on the concept of reciprocity. They might have looked more profitably to the precedent notion of community, for the gift is a foray across group boundaries. It connects incommensurate social worlds or islets of incommensurability within a plural universe.

There is no single way to calculate the return to be made at holiday time when our neighbors bring their personally canned jam for our enjoyment. What did it 'cost' them to make it? How much pleasure does it give us? Do we want to offer a return and continue the relationship? The contingencies in a gift are many, the uncertainties for both parties cannot be calculated and reduced to numerical risk. But the gift is filled with information, and what we do know is that with a gift of jam neighbors are saying something about connections between their household and ours; they are expanding their commons to include us. They are distributing their base outside its normal circle so that the bringing itself is unexpected – why else do we wrap presents except to say that the present, the prestation, is a surprise? Of course, reciprocity can also be an ideology that masks material imbalances in an exchange (George

1996: 78). And there are Trojan Horse gifts and poisoned gifts (Parry 1989; Raheja 1988). But why not, for to invoke Schumpeter ([1950] 1975), giving gifts is a mode of 'creative destruction'.

The gift, through the mutuality it extends or the antagonism it engenders, expresses one or another aspect of community. Prestations, done by touch and feel, are trials of extending community and its commons. I think this way of viewing the gift actually brings us closer to Mauss's view, in which the notion of community and the commons plays a central if silent part. Nothing mystical, no sacred force in the gift causes it to be given, received, and returned; the gift is a gesture of commensality, yet filled at times with countervailing impulses of competition. Strictly a secondary and composite phenomenon, reciprocity is not the core of society but its expression. Anthropological theories have it backwards: reciprocity is neither a primitive isolate nor the atom of society but its badge. If the gift is an unstable or uncertain category that is only because it is 'about' uncertainty itself – which makes it a preeminent category of any postmodern economics.

Notes

1 For some of the more recent discussions, see Gregory (1982), Parry (1986, 1989), and Strathern (1988).
2 'The system that we propose to call the system of "total services"…constitutes the most ancient system of economy and law that we can find…. It forms the base from which the morality of the exchange-through-gift has flowed' (Mauss [1925] 1990: 70).
3 For a discussion of Weiner, see Godelier (1995a, 1995b).
4 From a different perspective and in a different way, Bourdieu (1977) has well argued exactly this point.

References

Aristotle (1946) *The Politics of Aristotle*, trans. Ernest Barker, London: Oxford University Press.
Bohannan, Paul and Bohannan, Laura (1968) *Tiv Economy*, London: Longmans.
Bourdieu, Pierre (1977) *Outline of a Theory of Practice*, trans. Richard Nice, Cambridge: Cambridge University Press.
Derrida, Jacques (1992) *Given Time*, trans. Peggy Kamuf, Chicago: University of Chicago Press.
Gell, Alfred (1975) *Metamorphosis of the Cassowaries*, London: Athlone Press.
—— (1992) *Inter-tribal Commodity Barter and Reproductive Gift-Exchange in Old Melanesia*, in Caroline Humphrey and Stephen Hugh-Jones (eds), *Barter Exchange and Value*, Cambridge: Cambridge University Press, 142–68.
George, Kenneth M. (1996) *Showing Signs of Violence: The Cultural Politics of a Twentieth-Century Headhunting Ritual*, Berkeley: University of California Press.
Godelier, Maurice (1995a) 'L'énigme du don, I. Le legs de Mauss', *Social Anthropology* 3:15–47.

—— (1995b) 'L'énigme du don, II. De L'existence d'Objets Substituts des Hommes et des Dieux', *Social Anthropology* 3: 95–114.

Gregory, C.A. (1982) *Gifts and Commodities*, London: Academic Press

Harrison, Simon (1992) 'Ritual as Intellectual Property', *Man* (N.S.) 27: 225–44.

Herzfeld, Michael (1987) *Anthropology Through the Looking Glass*, Cambridge: Cambridge University Press.

Lévi-Strauss, Claude ([1949]1969) *The Elementary Structures of Kinship*, London: Eyre and Spottiswoode.

Malinowski, Bronislaw ([1922]1961) *Argonauts of the Western Pacific*, New York: Dutton.

Mauss, Marcel ([1925]1990) *The Gift*, trans. W. D. Halls, London: Routledge.

Parry, Jonathan (1986) 'The Gift, the Indian Gift and the "Indian Gift"', *Man* (N.S.) 21: 453–73.

—— (1989) 'On the Moral Perils of Exchange', in J. Parry and M. Bloch (eds) *Money and the Morality of Exchange*, Cambridge: Cambridge University Press, 64–93.

Polanyi, Karl (1944) *The Great Transformation*, New York: Rinehart.

—— (1968) *Primitive, Archaic, and Modern Economies*, (ed.) George Dalton, Garden City: Anchor Books.

Raheja, Gloria (1988) *The Poison in the Gift*, Chicago: University of Chicago Press.

Sahlins, Marshall (1972) *Stone Age Economics*, Chicago: Aldine.

Schumpeter, Joseph A. ([1950]1975) *Capitalism, Socialism and Democracy*, New York: Harper and Row.

Smith, Adam ([1776]1976) *The Wealth of Nations*, (ed.) Edward Cannan, Chicago: University of Chicago Press.

Strathern, Marilyn (1988) *The Gender of the Gift*, Berkeley: University of California Press.

Weiner, Annette (1992) *Inalienable Possessions*, Berkeley: University of California Press.

23

GIFTS AND TRADE
Mirowskian, Gudemanian, and Milbergian themes

John Davis

> The grand narrative has lost its credibility, regardless of what mode of unification it uses, regardless of whether it is a speculative narrative or a narrative of emancipation.
> (Lyotard, 1984: 37)

Saying that there is no master discourse allows us to see the space of discourse as constituted out of competing discourses, each of which may itself claim to be a master discourse. A postmodern interrogation of rivalrous discourses may proceed by granting each a temporary, relative integrity, so as to represent the whole space they occupy as an interaction between claimant master discourses, the interaction between them tending to reinforce or erode the identity of each. The relative integrity of each individual discourse may then be investigated in terms of its current conceptual structure, a network of compulsory meanings and allowable inferences between meanings. Discourses' identities are transient, because these structures do not endure. Their reconstruction or collapse is driven by their interaction with rival discourses and by internally discovered structural incoherences, either of which may undermine stability of meaning, cause its dissemination, and necessitate the rebuilding of new meaning structures, shifting or creating discourses' identities.

Philip Mirowski tracks the rise and fall of the postwar economic anthropological discourse on the gift that treated the meaning of giving the gift as polar alternative to the meaning of reciprocal exchange. For Marshall Sahlins and Chris Gregory, the meanings of both gift and exchange are embedded in a social-cultural concept nest: [kinship ties/clan distinctions/social political hierarchies], which determines allowable inferences regarding where material transfers fall on a single continuum from gift to balanced reciprocity to even negative reciprocity (or agression). In effect, the discourse's structure makes the social-cultural concept nest arbitrate inferences regarding how we classify material transfers. The inferential vehicle by which this arbitration occurs is the discourse's premising inclusion-exclusion membership patterns in social-cultural groups as the central invariant in the system. Gifts are then classified as what is transferred between or within 'like' social groups. Where 'like' social groups do not come into play, material transfer operates according to principles of reciprocal exchange, that is, according to the abstract logic of pure value equivalence.

For Sahlins and Gregory, however, this alternative principle of invariance must be thought subordinate to the social likeness group principle of invariance. When we make social group likeness our focus, abstract value equivalence appears as a socially disembedded form of material transfer. Thus the social-cultural concept nest arbitrates inferences regarding how we interpret gifts and exchanges, and in particular defines reciprocal exchange as 'non-gift' transfer.

Yet Mirowski argues, on closer scrutiny the discourse's proposed social group likeness principle of invariance lacks stable meaning. Sahlins and Gregory's texts are unable to develop and sustain the concept of inclusion–exclusion membership in a social group, and even add to its conceptual instability by retreating to market concepts of scarcity and exchange to 'help' explain what increasingly becomes the 'gift economy.' Even worse, they allow that gifts alter social-cultural groupings, thereby undermining the very idea of social group likeness as a distinct principle of system invariance.

Left standing, the victor by default, is abstract value equivalence as the system's only principle of invariance explaining material transfers. The gift in its original sense as non-reciprocated transfer is now simply the 'other', the non-commodity. But emptied of independent content it cannot be understood but as part of 'gift exchange' (except perhaps as briefly disguised by giftwrap – price tags discreetly removed of course).

The implication of Mirowski's argument is that postwar economic anthropological discourse on the gift was corrupt from the outset. But this is not a Derridean corruption, an irresistable displacement of meaning that frustrates any settled interpretation of the meaning of the gift whatsoever. Rather the source of the corruption lies in the discourse's determination to set the meaning of the gift as 'non-exchange material transfer alternative to reciprocal exchange', a conceptual apparatus rather at the heart of market economy discourse.

Having begun in this way, economic anthropological discourse found itself saddled with an alien conceptual structure. In particular, 'material transfers' presupposed 'principles of invariance', which would then need to be drawn from the social-cultural concept nest that constituted the pre-existing conceptual apparatus of economic anthropological discourse. But this concept nest (it should perhaps have been recognized) does not readily accomodate invariance principles. Inevitably then, it must also fail as an arbiter of material transfer classifications, thereby ultimately causing collapse of the discourse's conceptual structure.

It was consequently the interaction of the two discourses that undermined the temporary relative integrity of economic anthropology, poisoning/disseminating its concept of the gift, and eroding its transient identity as a discourse distinct from market economy discourse. But how on this view of relatively distinct discourses in competition does Mirowski understand neoclassical economic theory?

Following Alvin Gouldner, he argues that a system of pure value equivalence, with pervasive balance in exchange, zero arbitrage, and 'no trade' theorems everywhere, is an unstable conceptual system because it provides no reason for trade – its own paradox of intentionality. The 'no free lunch' crowd accordingly cannot resist the concept of the gift without return, because it is precisely the concept of gain from trade needed in but absent from the bloodless conceptual apparatus of exchange of equivalent for equivalent. We might, then, imagine that contact with anthropological discourse has contaminated neoclassical discourse in a manner not dissimilar to the manner in which neoclassicism has corrupted economic anthropology.

But this does not seem to be Mirowski's argument. Rather his Goedelian argument, in two steps, is that (a) any formally definite system must contain results stateable but not provable within the system, and (b) post hoc, sleight-of-hand inclusions of undecidable statements into formal systems is a mug's game, an irreducibly arbitrary procedure that creates a false sense of comprehensive explanation. Thus it is neoclassicism's conceptual pretension to structural completeness, an internal incoherence, that ultimately betrays it, not the vitality of an alternative discourse. Indeed, neoclassicism's appropriation of anthropology's gift concept of unrequited gain is opportunistic and gratuitous, since the discourse's structural strategy of closure by addition of undecidable statement creates an open field of concepts from which to select, a point made especially evident by the jack-of-all trades development of game theory.

Pol. [Behind] What, ho! help, help, help!
Ham. [Drawing] How now! a rat? Dead, for a ducat, dead!
[Makes a pass through the arras.]
Pol. [Behind] O, I am slain!
[Falls and dies.]

Modernism rests securely upon a paradox. (1) It (modernism) begins by supposing that reality anchors language, and gives language its intelligibility. Truth is ordinarily and widely thought of as a correspondence between statements, propositions, or sentences and states of affairs in the world. Individual terms and expressions are typically thought to acquire their meanings according to what they stand for, refer to, or pick out from the world. Thus reality both lies behind language and regulates language. (2) Yet because reality can only be described in language, we are never able to consult reality apart from language to determine whether language does indeed describe reality. We attempt to turn from language to the real, but only discover language once again. Thus it seems that language cannot be about reality. (3) But what is language about if it is not about reality? To say language is about language seems to say little, if anything at all. (4) [Return to (1)].

Gudeman sees economic anthropologists and neoclassical economists as both offering essentialist and modernist approaches to understanding gifts and reciprocity, the former basing their analysis on altruism, and the latter basing theirs on self-interest. The generation of anthropologists since Marcel Mauss has regarded reciprocity as a pillar of social life, because they believe reciprocity accurately reflects the character of dyadic relationships between individuals that anthropologists believe to be at the core of society. Neoclassical economists also regard reciprocity as a pillar of social life, but alternatively believe reciprocity reflects the play of individual motivation in dyadic relationships that neoclassical economists regard as being at the core of society. Both then, believe their respective discourses rest on real economic and social foundations. These foundations regulate what they may each say about reciprocity, exchange, and gifts by determining the truth of the statements they make and the meanings of their individual terms and expressions. These real world foundations also validate their respective characterizations of reciprocity, exchange, and gifts, since each view is judged, preferred to the other in virtue of its more accurately capturing underlying real world foundations. Of course it makes little sense to suppose that two discourses that contradict one another are both correct and accurate reflections of one and the same real world. Yet neither anthropologists nor economists can consult the world apart from the discourse in which they operate to compare language and reality, and then demonstrate their view to be correct and their opponent's mistaken. Both of course claim to get at the essentials of reciprocity, but neither is acquainted with anything more than a concept of the essential.

Indeed since every attempt to acquire access to the real world must produce but another concept of the real world, for essentialists the real must always appear in endless retreat from possible capture in language. But let us bring this tedious story to a close. Since any attempt to penetrate the veil of language and grasp the real world must destroy the object sought, we should abandon the notion that discourses rest on real world foundations, and ask how else we might understand gifts and reciprocity.

Gudeman's view is that economic processes may be seen to be organized in two distinct ways that appear separately, in shifting combinations, and in tension with one another. There are production and distribution processes that economists study as the market economy, but these processes are also socially mediated through families, household groups, villages, nations, etc. that anthropologists study as the community form of the economy. Reciprocity consequently needs to be understood differently according to the operant perspective. But it is a mistake to think that this means reciprocity simply corresponds to different things for economists and anthropologists.

For Gudeman reciprocity does not correspond to any set of institutions or processes in the community form of the economy, but is rather a way of making community. First, the gift extends the commons to someone outside a community. The gift transforms social relationships. Second, if the gift is reciprocated, the return both accepts commensality, yet also signals difference and independence. The reciprocal exchange of gifts consequently creates a larger, encompassing community in which there always remains a fragile balance between distance and closeness, detachment and warmth. Thus, if the gift in anthropological discourse is 'about' anything, it is about the uncertainty of community. But then we should not attempt to understand the language of gifts and reciprocity as a reflection of something behind discourse. Reciprocity is not at the core of society. Reciprocity is an expression of social economic processes – a secondary phenomenon, a badge worn, if briefly, upon the giving of the gift.

> Link to Local Home Page
> This goes on every page. Given the nature of the Web, you can't assume that everyone is beginning at the same starting point and following the links down. The user could be bailing in from some other link to somewhere deep in the dusty corners of the sprawl. The user may be completely lost, or may assume that your page is part of the company he or she just branched from. This can also happen with users using bookmarks to specific pages. Always show them a way home.
> (Cearley, 1998: 187)

Modernist metanarratives require centers of gravitation. They anchor a conceptual apparatus by identifying points of entry that channel passage to other conceptual sites. Those latter sites thus come with genealogies. A concept-site first gains meaning in terms of its association with the concept-sites previously visited; it gains additional meaning in terms of associations with concepts-sites subsequently visited. The entire narrative is understood in terms of its point of entry. At the same time, concepts-sites that cannot be accessed from a network of conceptual sites are impaired in their meaning from the perspective of the network. They either fall entirely outside the network, or should they be accessible, they inherit the genealogy of the network with its original center of gravitation. That is...unless the network's travellers pass far enough out upon the network's periphery that the gravitational pull of its center ceases to operate. Then one might even pass to another network whose links are designed to direct the traveler to this new network's center of gravity. Preventing escape from a conceptual network, casual or intentional, thus requires that it be centripetally constructed. 'Always show them a way home.'

William Milberg knows the way home in 'neoclassical international economics'. At the top of the neoclassical home page it reads, 'the economy as market'. From there one goes to 'competition' where one learns about 'equilibrium'. Having visited these sites one is then sufficiently prepared to click on 'general equilibrium competitive analysis', from which one can finally access 'the theory of international trade', including such otherwise accessible sites as 'Heckscher-Ohlin', 'Stolper-Samuelson', and 'Rybczinski' (all accompanied by easy links to the necessary bio sites). A convenient feature of the network as a whole is that it is designed to return the visitor from any particular concept-site to other concept-sites of importance. Or, one always has the option of simply returning to 'home', and then passing down through any of the pathways in the network one chooses. An egalitarian feature of the network is that accidental visitors to any of the network's concept-sites are treated no differently than regular visitors. The highly developed character of the network is reflected in the fact that these accidental visitors are encouraged at every possible point to go to 'home' so as to be able to learn the network from its point of entry.

Of course discourses are always under (re)construction. Their producers are ever in search of ways to better organize their concept-sites, and this process continually reveals new implications and connections not previously imagined that then require integration into the overall network. However there are risks involved. Because reconstruction is initially focused on a particular concept-site in the network, the consequences of its reconstruction are often not immediately apparent.

Milberg asks us to consider the case of site foreman, Paul Krugman, founder of the 'new international economics'. For a long time the 'theory of international trade' site was closely connected to the 'competition' site. Krugman wondered whether it might not be possible to link the former site to an infrequently visited one, 'imperfect competition'. From there he imagined further connections to 'game-playing man' (replacing visits to 'rational economic man') and 'trade-oriented industrial/commercial policies' (replacing visits to *laissez faire*/free trade'). Krugman's argument for re-connecting the 'theory of international trade' in these ways was based on the importance of intra-industry trade and the apparent success of trade-orientated policies in Japan and South Korea.

Yet as Milberg explains, Krugman soon found that these strategies for developing the 'neoclassical international economics' site met with considerable disfavor from others involved in the maintenance and reconstruction of both this site and the 'economy as market' site in which it is embedded. The issue was later cast as a technical problem involved in re-building the 'theory of international trade' site: 'the models were too sensitive to particular assumptions, and they encouraged unrealistic attempts to fine tune the activities of the state'. But Milberg identifies a more serious problem with Krugman's strategies. His proposed connections seemed to involve stronger links to other home pages than to the 'economy as market' home page. Indeed, upon arriving at the 'imperfect competition' site one does find connections to 'transnational corporations' and 'the state', which in turn have close links to the 'political economy' home page.

Krugman, it seems, originally failed to appreciate how far out on the periphery of the 'economy as market' network the 'transnational corporations' and 'the state' sites lay. But to his credit he soon recognized that visiting those sites was incompatible with the centripetal nature of the 'economy as market' network. At least in the short run, then, until a fuller structure of links through the 'optimization' site could be created for 'transnational corporations' and 'the state', he agreed that work would have to be discontinued in this area.

But lest the implications of all this be misunderstood, note that Milberg does not recommend a politics of constructing a rival 'political economy' home page with peripheral links designed to invade the 'economy as market' home page and lure its visitors away. In fact, he tells us that a postmodern theory of international trade must lack a central metaphor and cannot be rendered into a single metanarrative.

There seems to be both positive and normative reasons for thinking this. From a positive point of view, it is naive to suppose that the center can hold in any discourse for any extended period of time. Discourse is always decentering itself, because the opportunity to explore in ways that may take one outwards from any given site will always constitute an attraction. From a normative point of view, on the other hand, it seems we ought also resist the modernist impulse to compel conceptual traffic to follow rigidly predetermined pathways. Indeed, we ought to encourage travellers to visit the 'free trade in ideas' site (one, it turns out, without links to the neoclassical 'economy as market' site). They should travel prepared, however. The 'free trade in ideas' site is always under construction.

References

Cearley, Kent (1998) *HTML 4 INTERACTIVE COURSE*, Corte Madera, CA: Waite Group Press.

Lyotard, Jean-Francois (1984) *The Postmodern Condition: A Report on Knowledge*, Mineapolis: University of Minnesota Press.

NAME INDEX

Abel, N. 222
Abu-Lughod, L. 209, 217n
Adelstein, Richard P. 119
Adorno, Theodor 6
Aeschylus 124
Agarwal, Bina 256, 313
Akerlof, George 450–1
Allais, M. 180, 181
Allen, R.G.D. 144
Althusser, Louis 31, 32, 33, 148, 149, 160, 307
Altieri, Charles 106, 107, 112, 122
Amariglio, Jack 29, 62, 65, 66, 69, 70, 73, 83, 84, 105, 110–1, 112, 135, 149, 180, 182, 183, 187, 192, 222, 290
Anleu, S.R. 235, 236
Apfel-Marglin, Frederique 210
Appiah, Kwame Anthony 47n
Aquinas, Thomas 108
Aristotle 95–6, 122–3, 462, 464
Armstrong, N. 250
Arrow, K.J. 73, 87, 109, 130, 150, 153, 156, 158, 182, 183, 188, 191, 342, 436–7, 450
Ashmore, William 78
Auerbach, Paul 412
Austin, J.L. 433

Backhouse, Roger 46n
Bacon, Francis 105, 108, 111, 112, 113
Bakker, Isabella 297
Balibar, Etienne 32, 148, 150
Balzac, Honoré de 174, 175
Barber, Bernard 411
Barnes, Barry 28
Barthes, Roland 338, 345, 347, 348
Bataille, Georges 159, 438
Baudelaire, Charles 185, 447, 449
Baudrillard, Jean 121, 122, 159, 351n, 355, 438
Becker, Gary 7, 31, 252–3, 266, 305, 435–6, 439, 455
Beckson, Karl 187
Beerbohm, Max 185
Bell, Clive 114
Belsey, Catherine 411–12
Beneria, Lourdes 216n
Beniger, James 42n
Bennett, Arnold 114
Bentham, Jeremy 111, 117
Bergmann, Barbara R. 222, 286, 298, 327
Berkeley, George 72, 177
Berlin, Isaiah 116, 351n
Berman, Marshall 131, 354, 402
Bern, Sandra L. 291
Beuys, Joseph 86
Biewener, Carole 327
Binmore, K. 393, 394
Black, Max 123
Blank, Rebecca 305
Blaug, Mark 37, 45n, 66, 67, 338, 347, 348, 349
Blinder, Alan 298
Bloch, Marc 171
Bohannan, Laura 460

Bohannan, Paul 460
Bohr, Niels 39n
Boland, L.A. 67
Booth, Wayne C. 102, 103, 105, 120
Bordo, Susan 111, 227, 228, 234, 236, 263, 287, 288, 301, 329
Breo, D.L. 228
Bresnick, Adam 448, 449
Brolin, Brent C. 103, 107
Brown, Ronald 422
Brown, Stephen 20, 40n
Burczak, Ted 111
Burke, Kenneth 118
Busch, Johann Georg 191
Butler, Judith 33, 327
Butler, Samuel 33

Caldwell, Bruce 47n
Callero, Peter 438
Carey, John 113–14
Carlyle, Thomas 188
Carroll, Lewis 286
Cartland, Barbara 108
Castells, Manuel 40n
Cearley, Kent 479
Chandler, Alfred 425
Charusheela, S. 246–56
Chia, Sandro 86
Chick, V. 69, 71
Chomsky, Noam 307
Chydenius, J. 174
Cilliers, Paul 41n
Cixous, Helène 453
Clark, J.B. 339
Clower, Robert 39n
Coase, Ronald 111
Coddington, A. 74
Cohen, Avi 337
Cohen, M. 222
Cohen, Ruth 341
Comte, Auguste 108, 111, 116, 118
Condorcet, Marquess of 108
Cooper, Brian 42n, 251
Cornell, D. 221
Cosgel, Metin 109
Crawford, V. 389
Cucchi, Enzo 86
Cullenberg, Stephen 44n, 180, 216n, 400–1, 402, 403, 404
Culler, J. 222

Dallery, A.B. 223
Darwin, Charles 277
Dasgupta, Indraneel 400–1, 402, 403, 404
Davidson, Donald 399
de Man, Paul 307
de Marchi, N. 66
Deardoff, Alan 413
Debreu, Gérard 87, 150, 153, 155, 157, 158, 182, 183, 188, 191, 342
Degler, Carl 280
Deleuze, Gilles 159
Derrida, Jacques 16–17, 32, 87, 106, 118, 178, 180–1, 230, 262, 263, 307, 329, 375, 395, 400, 433, 434, 438, 446, 449, 450, 451, 453, 454, 459

NAME INDEX

Descartes, René 111, 138, 173, 316
Dewey, John 269
Diprose, R. 224, 228, 230, 231, 235, 240
Dobb, Maurice 159
Dodds, S. 228, 230
Douglas, G. 238
Douglas, Mary 364, 438, 439, 442, 447
Dow, Sheila 35, 62, 63, 67, 71, 73, 129, 130–132, 133, 135, 136, 139, 300, 337
Drakopoulos, S. 72
Drucker, P. 166
Dubois, D. 71
Durkheim, Emile 448, 451

Easterlin, Richard 46n, 49n
Eco, Umberto 105, 108
Edgeworth, Maria 250
Edgeworth, Richard Lovell 250
Einstein, Albert 104
Eisenstein, Z.R. 230
Eliot, T.S. 107, 113
Elster, Jon 157
Ely, Richard 268–9
England, P. 223, 314, 315–16
Erasmus 79
Escobar, A. 211
Esteva, Gustavo 41n

Faigley, Lester 43n
Farrell, J. 387, 389, 390, 391
Feiner, S.F. 238
Ferber, Marianne 328
Ferguson, Adam 3
Feyerabend, Paul 28, 29, 106
Feynman, Richard 39n
Fischl, Eric 86
Fish, Stanley 123, 308, 309, 329
Flax, Jane 33, 328
Fogel, Robert 104, 105, 109
Folbre, N. 222, 312, 313, 314, 315, 316
Foucault, Michel 15, 27–8, 32, 33, 138, 148, 149, 150, 182, 233, 262, 263, 271, 278, 331, 355, 362, 375, 378, 399
Franklin, S. 226, 227, 228, 230
Friedman, Jeffrey 122, 123–4
Friedman, Milton 26, 83, 90, 111, 118

Gablik, Suzi 85
Gane, Mike 439
Garegnani, P. 343, 350, 401
Garnett, Robert F., Jr. 48n
Gatens, M. 230, 232, 235, 238
Gell, Alfred 470–2
George, Kenneth M. 472–3
Gergen, Kenneth 11–12
Gibbons, R. 389
Gibson-Graham, J.K. 40n
Giddens, Anthony 44n
Gilman, Charlotte Perkins 36, 261–80, 331–2
Goebbels, Joseph 117
Goethe, Johann Wolfgang von 188
Gouldner, A. 455, 477
Goux, J.-J. 178, 180, 191, 192
Gramsci, Antonio 83
Grand, Sarah 186

Grandmont, J. M. 455
Grapard, Ulla 328, 331–2
Gray, Richard T. 190, 191
Grayson, D.R. 248, 249
Greenberg, Clement 85
Gregory, Chris 438, 440, 442, 444, 445–446, 453, 454, 461, 475, 476
Grewal, I. 255
Grosz, Elizabeth A. 33, 223
Guattari, Felix 159
Gudeman, Stephen 438, 478, 479
Güth, W. 391, 392
Guthrie, W.K.C. 117

Habermas, Jürgen 107, 235
Hacking, I. 64, 249
Hagstrom, W.O. 453
Hahn, F.H. 73, 91, 150, 156
Halberstam, Judith 183
Hall, Stuart 338, 344–5, 349
Haraway, Donna 183
Harcourt, G.C. 343, 344, 350, 401
Harding, Sandra 28, 288, 294, 316, 329, 330
Hargreaves Heap, Shaun 37, 363, 369, 401–2, 403, 404
Harrison, Simon 469
Harsanyi, John 48n
Hartmann, H. 312, 313, 314, 315, 316
Hartsock, Nancy 263, 312
Hartung, William 422
Harvey, David 399
Hassan, Ihab 86
Hausman, Dan 451
Hayek, Friedrich von 83, 111, 124, 138, 437
Hegel, Georg 130, 375
Heidegger, Martin 378
Held, Virginia 241
Hemingway, Ernest 104
Henderson, Willie 20
Herbert, C. 254
Herring, Hubert 433
Herzfeld, Michael 470
Hesse, Mary 123
Hewitson, Gillian 33, 222, 223, 224, 238, 246–256
Hicks, Sir John 86, 87, 144
Hilferding, Rudolf 178
Hill, Mary A. 269
Hirschman, A. 363, 412
Hirshliefer, Jack 48n
Hobbes, Thomas 111, 314, 316
Hollinger, David 47n
Horkheimer, Max 6
Hugo, Victor 175
Hume, David 72, 73, 363
Hunt, M. 254, 255
Hutchison, T.W. 4

Ingold, Gim 442
Ingrao, Bruna 46n
Irigaray, Luce 121, 223

Jaeger, Werner 117
James, Henry 106
Jameson, Fredric 6, 7, 12, 106, 122, 407
Jencks, Charles 69, 85, 86, 103

NAME INDEX

Jennings, A. 313
Jevons, W. Stanley 145, 146, 155–6, 177, 178
John of Salisbury 122
Johnson, Anna 237
Johnson, Mark 290, 291
Johnson, Samuel 108
Jones, K. 228, 230
Jones, Ronald 413
Joyce, James 103
Judd, Donald 86

Kahneman, D. 392
Kalai, E. 369, 401–2
Kant, Immanuel 123, 184, 363, 367–8
Karpin, I. 227
Katz, Elizabeth 313
Katzner, Donald 43–4n
Kayatekin, Serap 40n
Keane, N. 228
Keller, Catherine 293
Keller, Evelyn Fox 288, 294, 329
Kerferd, G.B. 117, 118
Keynes, John Maynard 3, 42n, 62, 69, 72, 73–74, 83, 84, 87, 114, 145, 161, 306
Kilbourne, 314, 315–16
Klamer, Arjo 20, 68, 70, 73, 81, 82, 95, 103, 105, 109, 129, 130–131, 132, 134, 135, 136, 137, 139–40, 184, 376, 412
Klein, Daniel 47n
Klein, Lawrence 109
Knetsch, J. 392
Knight, Frank H. 83, 84, 117–18
Kolb, David 103
Koopmans, Tjalling 39n, 43n
Koritz, Amy 41n
Koritz, Douglas 41n
Kreps, David 46n, 364
Krugman, Paul 415, 480
Kuhn, Thomas 28, 110, 265, 316
Kuiper, Edith 297
Kurtzman, J. 166

Lacan, Jacques 121, 169, 364, 403–4
Laffer, Arthur 118
Lakatos, Imre 265
Lake, M. 235, 238
Lakoff, George 290, 291
Lane, Ann 279
Lanham, Richard 118, 120–1
Laqueur, T.W. 233
Larkin, Philip 112–13
Larousse, Pierre 167
Lasch, Christopher 81
Laslett, Barbara 104
Latour, Bruno 28
Lavoie, Don 20, 109, 111
Lawrence, D.H. 114
Lawson, Tony 46n
Le Corbusier (Charles Jeanneret) 103
Leamer, Edward 109
Ledger, Sally 186
Lévi-Strauss, Claude 307, 438, 441, 447, 461, 463, 464, 471
Livingston, Ira 183
Lloyd, G. 235

Locke, John 72, 185, 224, 314, 316
Lodewijks, John 441
Lodge, David 103
Longino, Helen 294
Lucas, Robert 87, 88, 92, 103, 111
Lukács, Georg 6
Lukes, S. 362
Lupton, Ellen 106
Lyotard, Jean-François 8, 10, 12, 15, 32, 85, 91, 94, 121, 263, 356, 357, 368, 379, 399, 403, 409, 424, 438, 475

McCloskey, D. 20, 35, 36, 65, 66, 67, 69, 70, 71, 73, 80, 83–11, 108, 111, 121, 129, 130, 131–132, 133, 134, 135, 136–7, 138, 139–40, 298, 306, 308, 318, 329, 337–8, 400, 412, 413
MacIntyre, Alisdair 80, 96
McKeon, Richard 121
McPherson, Michael 451
Madison, Gary 124
Malinowski, Bronislaw 439–5, 441, 459, 461, 463–4
Malthus, Thomas 158, 246, 249, 250, 254, 435
Mandel, Ernest 6
Marcuse, Herbert 6
Marglin, Stephen 210
Marshall, Alfred 412
Martineau, Harriet 250, 254
Marx, Karl 130, 138, 148, 149, 159, 160, 166, 167, 169, 177, 185, 188–5, 192, 268, 270, 277, 339, 445
Matthau, Walter 115
Mauss, Marcel 433, 438, 439, 440, 441, 444, 448, 449, 451, 453, 459, 461–7, 463, 465, 468, 472, 473, 478
Mead, George Herbert 120
Mehta, Judith 17–18, 37, 356, 370, 377, 402–4
Menger, Carl 145, 306
Merleau-Ponty, Maurice 93
Milberg, William 70–8, 480–1
Mill, James 250
Mill, John Stuart 143, 145, 267, 269, 270
Mirowski, Philip 64, 93, 146, 302, 306, 441, 452, 459, 467, 475, 476, 477
Mises, Richard von 111
Mitchell, Wesley Clair 119
Mohanty, C. 211
Mohanty, S.P. 209, 216n
Molière 448
Mondrian, Piet 90, 93, 103
Montaigne, Michel de 83, 130–1
Moore, George 114, 186
Morgan, D. 238
Mulkay, Michael 124
Muller, Adam 190, 191, 192
Murphy, Margeuritte 42n
Musil, Robert 93
Mykitiuk, R. 226, 228, 229, 238

Nash, J. 376–377, 402
Nelson, Julie A. 223, 289, 292, 317, 328, 329–30, 331, 332, 412
Neurath, Otto 105, 108, 109
Newman, Charles 114–15
Nietzsche, Friedrich 33, 180, 431, 432, 456
Nixon, Richard 177
Norton, Bruce 40n

NAME INDEX

Novalis (Friedrich von Hardenberg) 191, 192
Nussbaum, Martha 96, 210

Oakeshott, Michael 107
Olmsted, J.C. 218n
O'Neill, O. 367, 368
Oppenheimer, Robert 104, 107
Osteen, M. 20

Pareto, Vilfredo 186
Parker, Charlie 'Bird' 112–13
Parry, Jonathan 438, 439, 440, 441, 442, 462, 473
Parsons, Talcott 307
Pateman, C. 222, 224, 225, 228, 230, 232, 235, 236
Paul, Ellen 451
Pearson, Karl 108, 114
Petchesky, R.P. 226, 227
Phelps, E.S. 73
Picasso, Pablo 103, 106, 112
Pickering, Andrew 45n
Pietrykowski, Bruce 40n
Piliavin, Jane 438
Planck, Max 3
Plato 108, 115–18, 123, 138, 235, 431, 433
Polanyi, Michael 179, 409, 442, 461, 464–5
Pollock, Jackson 104
Poovey, Mary 227, 228, 230–1, 235, 290
Posner, Richard 31, 111, 118, 222, 224, 225, 236–7, 238
Pound, Ezra 104, 112
Prade, H. 71
Prakash, Madhu Suri 41n
Pratt, M.L. 255
Prigogine, I. 71
Pujol, M.A. 222

Quetelet, Adolphe 257n

Raby, P. 254
Rachline, F. 180
Raheja, Gloria 473
Rawls, J. 366
Resnick, Stephen 31, 36, 133, 134, 180
Ricardo, David 73, 145, 148, 339, 413, 461
Richardson, Angelique 186
Ridley, Matt 436
Robinson, Joan 340–1, 342, 345–6, 350, 401
Roof, J. 238
Rorty, Richard 106, 111, 263, 308, 318, 356–7
Rosen, Stanley 110
Ross, Edward 268
Rossetti, Jane 40n, 62, 119, 289, 328, 329, 330, 332
Roth, A. 377
Rousseau, Théodore 108
Rubinstein, Ariel 376, 377, 391, 392
Ruccio, David F. 20, 29, 40n, 69, 73, 83, 135, 149, 180, 182, 183, 187, 192, 222, 290, 302
Ruskin, John 108–9, 110, 185, 186
Russell, Bertrand 73, 103, 108, 111, 448

Sahlins, Marshall 438, 441–5, 454, 461, 465, 468, 475, 476
Salanti, A. 61, 352n
Salle, David 86
Samuels, Warren 18–19, 20

Samuelson, Paul 3, 4, 5, 36, 37, 82, 86, 87, 90, 102, 103, 108, 109, 112, 130, 144, 145, 151–2, 153, 158, 306, 338, 340, 343, 344, 347, 348, 349, 409
Sand, George 185
Sandler, Irving 41n
Sap, Jolande 297
Sass, Louis 42n
Saussure, Ferdinand de 89–90, 178–9, 262, 338, 410
Schelling, T. 385, 391
Schmittberger, R. 391
Schreiner, Olive 186
Schultz, Theodore 109
Schumacher, E.F. 94
Schumpeter, Joseph A. 83, 473
Schwarze, B. 391
Scott, Joan 208, 263, 264, 270, 271, 278
Screpanti, E. 61
Secomb, L. 225, 226, 230, 235, 238
Seiz, J.A. 312, 314–5, 317, 318, 319
Selden, Raman 119
Sen, Amartya 41n, 43n, 45n, 152, 212n
Shackle, G.L.S. 161
Shaked, A. 393, 394
Shakespeare, William 188–9
Shanley, M.L. 225, 235
Shannon, Claude E. 99
Shaw, George Bernard 114
Shiller, Robert 109
Simon, Herbert 39n 42n
Singer, L. 237
Smiley, Jane 448
Smith, Adam 3, 36, 62, 69, 72, 73, 96–7, 143, 145, 148, 149, 158, 183, 184, 185, 188, 191, 192, 253–254, 314, 339, 409, 410, 437, 461
Smorodinsky, M. 369, 401–2
Sobel, J. 389
Sokal, Alan 400
Solomon, King 234
Solow, Robert M. 20, 45n, 67, 130, 338, 342, 343–344, 347, 348, 349
Sorkow, Judge (US) 236
Spencer, Herbert 269, 279
Spielberg, Steven 449
Spinoza, Benedict de 111
Spivak, Gayatri Chakravorty 47n, 121, 204–5
Sraffa, Piero 341, 342, 348, 444
Stengers, I. 71
Stern, Itzhak 448
Stern, Mrs 237
Steuart, Sir James 177
Stevens, Wallace 107
Stigler, George J. 111
Stiglitz, J.E. 338, 343, 344, 347, 348, 349
Stocking, G.W., Jr. 254
Stokey, 455
Strathern, Marilyn 438, 442, 453
Stravinsky, Igor 103
Strawson, P.F. 183
Sugden, Robert 435
Summers, Larry 298
Sutton, J. 393, 394
Symons, Arthur 187
Tapper, M. 232
Taylor, Michael 117
Thaler, R. 392

486

Thomas, Nicholas 442
Thünen, J.H. von 83
Tintner, Gerhard 109–10
Titmuss, Richard 436–8
Toulmin, Stephen 83
Tribe, Keith 35
Turgot, A.R.J. 45*n*

Valenze, D. 250
Valery, Paul 175
Van der Rohe, Mies 80, 85
Van Gogh, Vincent 106
Varoufakis, Yanis 37
Veblen, Thorstein 149
Vilar, Pierre 169, 170, 174, 176

Waldfogel, Joel 432, 433, 437, 450, 451, 453
Waller, W. 313
Walras, M.E.L. 83, 145, 146, 177, 178, 180
Ward, Lester 268, 269
Warhol, Andy 7, 84–5, 108, 470
Waring, M. 222, 305
Weedon, Chris 47*n*
Weiner, Annette 442, 468–9
Weiner, Myron 256
Weintraub, E. Roy 19, 39*n*, 46*n*, 66
Wells, H.G. 113–14
Wendt, Paul 66, 110, 112
Wheale, Nigel 20
White, M.V. 145
Whitehead, Mary Beth 238
Wildavsky, Adam 47*n*
Wilde, Oscar 185–6
Williams, R.M. 311, 314, 318, 319
Winch, D. 73
Wise, M. Norton 41*n*
Wittgenstein, Ludwig 92, 364
Wolff, Richard 31, 36, 133, 134, 180
Wollstonecraft, Mary 213*n*
Wood, Cynthia 313, 314, 318, 319
Woodmansee, Martha 20, 108
Woolf, Virginia 102, 103, 114
Wright, Frank Lloyd 80
Wriston, W. 180

Yeats, W.B. 107
Young, A. 228, 233
Young, I.M. 226

Zein-Elabdin, E. 218*n*
Zelizer, Viviana 453
Žižek, Slavoj 400
Zola, Emile 174, 175

SUBJECT INDEX

Note: italicised page numbers indicate tables and figures

Aaron's Rod (Lawrence) 114
abortion debate (US) 227, 228, 230, 235
abstraction: and economics 93, 147, 160; and representation 90, 176; and token-money 176
account money 168–9, 170, 171
action (human): in economic thinking 94–7; and morality 95–7, 99
actions: and cross-cultural judgments 206; instrumental model 362, 364, 365; and preferences 364–5
activity analysis 154, 200–1, 201
Adam Smith's Discourse (Brown) 20
After Virtue (MacIntyre) 80
agents/agency: and Aristotelean values 210; and the body 247–8; and choice 197, 200, 251, 252; choice-theoretic framework of actions 201; contracting 223, 239; female 202–4, 211, 263, 266; in feminist poststructuralism 246; neoclassical 229; and non-Western women 207–8, 251, 252–3; and the 'other' 221, 240; and personhood 248; and political economists 254; postmodern 402; pregnant woman as 223
aggregate outcomes 198
agricultural products: US export of 421–2
agriculturalists 254
altruism 7; as a feminine trait 288; and gift-giving 436, 460–1, 465, 478; and self-interest 302, 460–1
American Economic Review (AER) 432
American Economics Association (AEA) 432
analysis: activity 154, 200–1, 201; economic 143, 152, 210–11, 222, 229, 240, 255, 266, 305, 317–18, 393, 414; of the family 408; Malthussian 250; market 410–12; time-series 91
ancient Egypt: and evaluation of goods 167, 169–5, 171, 172, 176
ancient Greece: and status of money 170
androcentrism 315, 316, 318, 322, 330
anthropology: economic 438, 441–8, 451, 475–82; and gift-giving 439, 459, 460, 461, 463, 468; humanist 160; models/theories 184, 473; and reciprocity 461, 470–3
antimodernism and postmodernism 21–4
archetype-money 167–8, 169, 171; and symbolism 176
architecture: influence on economics 103; and modernism 103, 107; and postmodernism 69, 85
Argonauts of the Western Pacific (Malinowski) 439, 463
Arrow-Debreu model 151, 154
art: and consumption models 187; feminine associations of 104; neo-expressionist and neo-traditionalist 85–6; and postmodernism 84–5

SUBJECT INDEX

arts: and optical realism 171; problem of reference 175–6; and sciences (modernist) 82, 83
Austrian economists 149, 154
authoritarianism 138
authority: rejection of 72
autonomy: cultural 206–7; and women 198, 251

Baby Johnson surrogacy case (US) 237–8, 249–50
Baby M surrogacy case 236–8, 249–50
bank-money 179
banknotes: as political system 179
banks: power of 180
barbarism/destruction: contribution of science and technology 10–11
bargaining: behaviour 376–9, 381–95; and fairness 377–8, 379, 392, 393; games 377, 379–95, 383; theory 358–9; and universability 369
barter: and gift-giving 440, 453, 461
behaviour: bargaining 376–9, 381–95; ethical 254; laws of 306; rational 375; and social change 270
behaviourism: and positivism 187
beliefs 308–9
Beyond Economic Man (Ferber and Nelson) 328
binary oppositions 300, 301, 347, 408, 409
blood donor system (US) 436–8
body (human): and corporate bodies 183; in neoclassical economics 145; pregnant: as two persons 226–31, 239–40; sexed 221–41, 246, 247–8, 249, *see also* individualism
body/mind: in economic behaviour 152; problem 182–3
Bolshevism 439
brain: left/right thought processes 72

Caesarean section 228, 233
Cambridge capital controversy 337–50, 400–1; analysis 343–4; major issues 339–43; metaphors/myths distinction 338, 344–6; rhetorical structures 346–50, 400
'Can the Subaltern Speak?' (Spivak) 204–5
capital: and distribution theory 340, 341; theories of 339, 340, 341; womb-as 221
capital-output ratio 341
capital-reversal: and reswitching 341, 342, 400
capitalism 254; and Cambridge capital controversy 340; global 6, 138, 160; late 6, 8–9; postmodern 6–8, 139, 166–81
case law: Baby M/Baby Johnson surrogacy cases (US) 236–8, 249–50; and bodily integrity 234; *Roe v. Wade* abortion case (US) 230
categories/categorization: and dualities 309; and economic analysis 4–5, 315–17, 320; of gift/gift-giving 455, 459; and postmodernism 4–5; of women 263–4, 300, 314, 329–30
Centre Pompidou: Paris 85
characterization: in economics 78–80
'Chartism' (Carlyle) 188
chemistry: and open systems 71
Chicago Tribune 432–3
choice 200, 205, 252, 374; and agents/agency 197, 200, 201, 251, 252; and constraints and desires 199–200, 202–4; consumer 151–2, 157; and enthnocentrism/relativism 197–218; expressive 200, 202–4; and gender issues 315;

neoclassical conception of 197, 199–202; theories of 152, 246, 252, 374, 376, 377, 384–95, 402–3; utility-maximising 224–5; and women 197–218
cigarettes: as perfect commodity 185–6
clothing: and agent action 251–2; gender markers in 202–4, 209–10
Coase theorem 435
Cobb-Douglas production function 341–2
codes: and Cambridge capital controversy 344–6, 349–50; consumer 157; and decoding 204, 403; and language 399; oppositional 400; in production theories 155; in symbolic figuration 174; technological 157
coercion: and persuasion 117; in rhetoric 117, 139
cognition 295, 300
coins: as monetary tokens 170, 178
collaboration: interfirm 419–21
colonialism: and cultural autonomy 206–7; and subjectivity 208–9, 255
commercial images: and cultural artifacts 7
commercial surrogacy 221–41
commodities 6–8; demand for 157; exchange-value of 159, 445; and monetary distinction 173; people as 190; and reciprocity 460, 466–7; value of 167
commodity-money 171, 176, 177
commonality of human nature theory 73
communication 26, 169
communism: and postmodernism 139
community economy: and reciprocity 465–73, 479
comparative advantage: law of 413
Complete Works (Beerhohm) 185
Complexity and the Postmodern (Cilliers) 41*n*
computer language: and economic analysis 98
computer technology 8
Condition of Postmodernity, The (Harvey) 40*n*
conflicts: and language 376; narrative 354–6, 357–9; postmodern 357–9, 371, 401–2; of preference 360–6; Utilitarian/Rawlsian 360–1, 361, 369
consciousness: and dualisms 83; social 267, 274, 276
Consequences of Economic Rhetoric, The (Klamer et al.) 20
Consequences of Pragmatism, The (Rorty) 318
constraints: on choice 199–200, 202–4; and desires 251; gender-based 202–4, 209–10, 251
constructivism: social 36
consumers: choice 151–2, 157; codes 157; role of 153, 154
consumption 150, 155–6, 306; as decadence 186; and time 156
contracts: and motherhood 231–9; social 232; surrogacy 236–41, 248
Control Revolution, The (Beniger) 42*n*
convergent thinking 94
Conversations with Economists (Klamer) 20
conviction: and persuasion 112
Crime and Custom in Savage Society (Malinowski) 439
Critical Inquiry 122
Critical Legal Studies 123
critics/criticism: literary 118, 122, 338
Critique of Judgment (Kant) 184

488

SUBJECT INDEX

cultural autonomy: and self-determination 206–7
cultural diversity: and knowledge 13–14
cultural history: and the individual 183–4; and production/consumption models 187
culture(s): and gender dualisms 292; and marketing of commercial images 7; and modernism/postmodernism 23, 138, 409; phallocentric 238; and political economists 254–5
currencies: coins 170, 178; paper 179, 191
cyberfinance 180

'Deadweight Loss of Christmas, The' (Waldfogel) 432
decentering 17; of discourse 481; of poststructural thought 309; of self 12–13
deconstruction 17, 89, 92, 118, 399; and dualisms 289–90, 294–5, 309–10; and economics 92, 180–1, 290, 378; and feminist economics 287, 306–11, 321–3; and language/linguistics 307, 328; and late modernism 88; and literary/writing styles 16–17, 21, 118–19; and postmodernism 15–21, 118–20; and poststructuralism 307, 399, 400–1
demand: law of 413
desire: and choice 199–200, 202–4; in economic theory 146–7; and need 186; and resources 251
determinism 24, 30–2, 63
development: and transcendence 131
dialectics 68–74, 129–30, 135; Hegelian 130, 133
difference: and feminist poststructuralism 246
'différend, the' 356, 368, 401
Différend, The (Lyotard) 356
diffusion: of the individual 158
discipline 123, 125, 139
Discipline and Punish (Foucault) 182
discourses 475, 481; economic 29, 140–63, 144, 148; economic anthropological 475–82; exclusion in 375; feminist 305–6; and gender issues 262, 265–7; macroeconomic 86; and metadiscourse 29
discrimination: theories of 256
distribution 150
dollar 191; inconvertibility of 177–8
dualisms 61, 62, 288–302; altruism/self-interest 302; categorization/opposites 309; and cognition 300; and consciousness 83; and feminist economics 311–12; gender/value compass 292, 293–302; hierarchical 291, 311; man/nature 296; masculine virtues/feminine vices 296; mind/body 302; modernist 81, 289; modernist/postmodernist debate 69–70, 131–2, 293–4, 300, 300; and multiplicity of dimensions 293–5; objectivity/subjectivity 288, 294; separation/connection 294; a third way 129–40; unity/multiplicity 301–2, 301

econometrics: feminist input 297
economic anthropology 438, 441–3, 451, 475–82
economic man 222–3, 224, 228, 247–8, 250, 253, 300, 481; and motherhood 231–4; and 'others' 255, 256
Economic and Philosophic Manuscripts (Marx) 190
economic processes: and Marxians 64; and neo-Austrians 64
economic transactions: dehumanization of 192

economics 5, 65, 67, 72, 109, 246; and abstraction 93, 192; 'alternative' 332; analysis 143, 152, 210–11, 222, 229, 240, 255, 266, 305, 317–8, 393, 414; androcentric 315, 316, 318, 322, 330, 332; and the arts 88, 103, 107; and characterization 78–80; and deconstruction 92, 180–1, 290, 378; definitions of 289, 295–6; discourses 29, 144, 148, 162; and education 247, 250–1; and feminism 162, 210–1, 286–302; gay 321; history of 147, 148, 246–56, 263, 339; humanism in 149, 159, 160; and the individual 143–63; language of 89, 403; and late modernism 84–7; masculine bias of 295, 327–8; Max U character 93–4, 99, 135; models 87, 90, 181, 221, 224–31, 239, 256, 323; modernist 24, 67, 78–99, 83, 136, 147; political 62, 246–7, 249, 250, 254, 411, 481; postmodernist 20, 34–8, 78–99, 121–2, 163, 261–5, 354–71; Samuelsonian 84, 90, 103, 135, 136, 152; schools of thought 65, 129–40, 159; as a science 91–2, 111, 144, 146, 408, 411; and social change 295–9; theories 29–30, 91, 145, 147, 150, 151, 154, 162, 163, 253, 319–20, 466; use of mathematical models/terms 296, 298, 376, *see also* feminist economics; international economics; neoclassical economics
Economics as Discourse (Samuels) 20
Economics and Hermeneutics (Lavoie) 20
Economics and Language (Henderson et al.) 20
'Economics as a Postmodern Discourse' (Amariglio) 84
economies: community 465–70, 479; global 8; virtual/real 166–81, 178–9
Edinburgh school of sociology of knowledge 78
education: of children 256; and economics 247, 250–1; and socialization 200; of Victorian women 276, 279
Elementary Structures of Kinship, The (Lévi-Strauss) 463
elitism: and anti-elitism of postmodernists 114–15; of modernism 112–15
empiricism 27
Enlightenment: French 73, 110, 138; Scottish 61–2
Enlightenment, the 9, 14, 147; and choice theory 252; concept of humanity 197, 200–1, 251, 254; and feminism 197–8, 328–9; and modernism 124; and narrative conflicts 354–5; and postmodernism 355; and self-conception 204, 206; and subjectivity 252
epistemes (Foucault) 32, 262
epistemology 20, 62, 63–4, 132, 261; feminist 330–1
equal relative concession principle 369, 370
equality: and feminism 205; and feminist poststructuralism 246; gender 264, 269, 271–2, 277, 331; and James Mill 250
equilibrium 340, 387, 388, 389, 390, 391, 480; general equilibrium concept 151, 153–4, 407, 409, 413, 480; international 422–3, 423; and market economy metaphor 407–8, *see also* Nash equilibrium
essentialism 24–6, 29, 35–6, 464
ethnocentrism: and choice 252; and relativism 204–6, 246, 251
evaluation modes 173
evolution: importance of females 273–4
evolutionary theories 264; and Charlotte Perkins Gilman 269, 271–2

489

exchange 172, 442; and gift-giving 433–4, 438–40, 444–5, 451–2, 461, 466–73; and money 168, 191; and own-body ownership 224–5; of services 225; of sexed body property 235, 239; surrogate motherhood 221–41, 247–51; theories of 246, 444, 459, *see also* reciprocity
existentialism 5, 32
experiment: bargaining game 379–95, 383
Export-Import Bank (US) 421
exports: US agricultural/military equipment shipments 421–2

factor services 156, 157
family: analysis of 408; boundary definitions 250; and conception 247–51; economic theories of 246, 251, 265, 266; in feminist economics 312–3; in industrial activity 277; models of 256; nuclear 233; and reproductive technologies 249; and status of women 275
Faust (Goethe) 188, 190
feminism 24, 33–4, 118, 149, 158–62; and autonomy 204–5; and economic anthropology 441; and ethnocentrism/relativism binarism 197–218; and evolutionary theories 269, 271; French 264; gender issues 222, 311–18; liberal 327; non-Western Third World 206; poststructuralist 222–3, 229, 240, 246, 247; and production 186
Feminist Economics 48n, 297, 328
feminist economics 286–95, 311–21; and market forces 412; modernism to deconstruction 306–11; and postmodernism 305–11, 321–3, 327–32
'fetology' 226
fetus: as individual agent 226–31; personhood of 236; rights 227, 228, 230–1, 233; viability of 228, 233
fiduciary money 169
Finance Capital (Hilferding) 178
firms: in international transations 416–22
First World War period 62, 72, 102; and gold-standard system 176–7
flexible specialization 8
Fordism 40n
formalism 24, 26; as criterion of modernism 83; and Ricardo 73
Foucaultian ideas/theories 262, 331, 362, 378, 399
foundationalism 24, 27
fragmentation: of reality 68; of self/individual 13, 37, 63, 158, 161, 187, 240, 300; of social life 11, 12
Frankfurt School of sociocultural analysis 6
free market/trade concept 407, 409, 413, 425–6; and neoclassical economics 149; and rhetoric 138–9
freedom: positive and negative 117–18
French Enlightenment 73, 110, 138
From a Broken Web: Separation, Sexism, and Self (Keller) 293
fundamentalism 81
'futility thesis' 435–41

game theory/theorists 17–18, 84, 90, 144, 256, 364, 376, 384, 386, 477
game-theoretic prediction 391

games: bargaining 377, 379–95, 383; one-shot 394; strategies 386, 391
gay economics 321
gender: and cultural constraints 202–4, 209–10, 251; dualisms 287–302; and feminism 222, 311–18; identity 33, 202–3, 232, 263, 264, 321, 331; and individualism 312; inequality 264, 269, 271–2, 277, 331; roles 201–2, 267; and science 288
gender/value compass 292, 293–302
General Competitive Analysis (Hahn) 150
general equilibrium analysis 151, 153–4, 480; and international economics 407, 409, 413
Giffen goods 348, 352n
Gift Relationship, The (Titmuss) 436
Gift, The (*Essai sur le don*: Mauss) 439, 440, 444, 448, 459, 461, 462–3
Gifts and Commodities (Gregory) 444
gifts/gift-giving 431–56, 459–73; concept/theory of 8, 433–4, 447, 450, 451–3, 454, 472; dual meaning of 440–8, 477; and economic anthropology 439, 459, 460, 461, 463, 468; economy 440, 444, 453, 476; and exchange 433–4, 438; and futility thesis 435–41; impossibility of 449–51; and intentionality 447–8, 449, 452, 454; and native cultures 439–40, 459–63, 468; and neoclassical economics 432; Sahlins' causal structure 443, 465; and self-interest 443, 447, 451–2; spirit of 468; and trade 475–82, *see also* reciprocity
Given Time (Derrida) 449, 450
Given Time I: Counterfeit Money (Derrida) 434, 438
global economy 8
globalization: and postmodernity 6, 14; and symbolic economy 178
Gödel's theorem 98, 455
gold: as a measure of value 167; as treasure-money 168
gold-money 174, 176
gold-standard system 176–7, 178, 190, 191
good: social 184
goods: evaluation of 167–8, 170, 185; and services 166
Gorgias (Plato) 115–16
Grammar of Science, The (Pearson) 114
growth theories 253, 256, 340

health economics (US) 437, 438, 451
Hegelian dialectics 130, 133
Heisenberg's uncertainty principle 21
high modernism 7, 144
historicism 118
history: cultural 183–4, 187; economic 147, 148, 246–56, 263, 339; political 263; postmodernism 5
History of Sexuality (Foucault) 182
homo economicus 32, 34, 408
How to Observe: Morals and Manners (Martineau) 254
human action: in economic thinking 94–7; and morality 95–7, 99
human agency conception 197
Human Fertilisation and Embryology Authority (UK) 249

SUBJECT INDEX

humanism: in economics 149, 159, 160, 192; theoretical 24, 32–4, 161; and value 153
humanities: and feminist theory 262; mysticism connotation of 104, 105
humans: and evolutionary forces 274–5; female dependency in 272–3
hypercredit 191
hypermarkets 191

IBM: and interfirm collaboration 419–20
ideality: in postmodern capitalism 166–81
identity: fractured 183; and gender issues 33, 202–3, 232, 263, 264, 321, 331; individual 235, 408; and knowledge 13–14; national 255
ideology 169
immanence thesis 112
'Importance of Something for Nothing, The' (Gouldner) 455
impossibility theorem 450–1
income and wealth distribution 159
individuals/individualism: disembodied/fragmented 13, 37, 63, 158, 161, 187, 240, 300; fetal 226–31; and gender issues 312; humanistic 183; and identity 235, 255; liberal 229–30, 232; methodological 157; and modern economic discourse 143–63; and normality 150, 159, 182; patriarchal 228; and the pregnant body 226–31; and sexed bodies 249; and states/society 143, 182; universal 12–13, 221, 226, 232, 238
Industrial Revolution 72
industries: multifirm 414
inequality: gender 264, 269, 271–2, 277, 331
information systems: and postmodernism 188
Institute for Advanced Study: Princeton 104, 115
institutionalism 24, 34, 149
instrumental model of action 362, 364, 365
intentionality: and gifts/gift-giving 447–8, 449, 452, 454
interest: conflict over resource 359; and narratives 359–60
interfirm collaboration 419–21; airline computer reservations systems 421, 422
International Association for Feminist Economics 297
international economics 407–26, 480–1; with decentered markets 424–6; and free markets 407; and general equilibrium analysis 407
international economy: and markets/market system 412–15
international trade 416–22, 481; US government intervention 421–2
intra-firm integration of production 420
intra-firm trade 414, 416–19, 418, 424
intra-industry trade 415
investment: bankers 192; foreign 414; theory 145

Japan: transnational corporations 418
Journal of Political Economy 432
justice: theory of 366–7

Kalai-Smorodinsky principle 369, 401–2
Keynesian economics 84, 88, 136, 161; and public welfare 98
knowledge 133; and cultural diversity 13–14, 202; foundations for 26–8; identity-based 13–14; Kantian views of 367–8; Keynes' views of 73; and knowledge makers 264–5; and language 65, 400; and neoclassical theory 247; objective/subjective 310–11; phallocentric 231; problem of 20; and science 64–5; and sexual inequality 269; as a social force 9–10; systems of 188; theory of 63, 64–5, 73, *see also* methodology
Knowledge and Persuasion in Economics (McCloskey) 20
kula communities: and gift-giving 439, 459, 460

labour: distribution of 159; international division of 414, 426; and Marxism 159–60; services 156; sexual division of 252, 267, 268, 272; as a source of value 145; theory of value 184–5
Lacanian triplicate of imaginary: symbolic and real 168
language/linguistics 307–8, 374–5, 399, 402; and binary dualisms 289–302; and Cambridge capital controversy 344–6, 400; as code 399; computer 98; and conflict resolution 376; creation of 292–3; and deconstruction 307, 328; of economics 89, 403; figural 410; international stick-figure 105–6; and knowledge 65, 400; and methodology 66; and modernism 81; and reality 477–8, 479; and representation 25, 26, 173, 175; and semiology 344–6, 364; as a system 89–90, 179; theory of 117, 172; and thought 307–8; and truth 25, 374–5, 477–8
late capitalism 6, 8–9
late modernism 84–7, 135
Law and Literature: A Misunderstood Relation (Posner) 118
laws/legislation: of behaviour 306; and bodily integrity 234; of comparative advantage 413; of demand 413; and reproduction technologies 248–9; *Roe v. Wade* abortion case (US) 230; and surrogacy 236–8, 248–9
leisure 156
liberalism 9; feminist 197–8, 327; postmodern 118; and postmodern economics 121–2; and rhetoric 122
Libidinal Economy (Lyotard) 42n
literary critics/criticism 118, 122, 338
literary modernism 103, 107
literary styles: and deconstruction 16–17, 21, 118–19
literature: and modernist elitism 112–14; postmodern 69; problem of reference 175–6
London: A Book of Aspects (Symons) 187
'Look at Me Look at You' (Mehta) 17
Lord of the Flies, The (Golding) 123

macroeconomics: and deconstruction 92; discourse 86; and feminist input 297; founders of 87; growth theory 256; and masculine bias 298; methodology 298–9; rationalism 295; and trade balance 413
man/nature dualism 296
'manthropomorphizing' 226
marginal productivity theory 339–40, 343–4
marginalist revolution 153
marginalist school 178

SUBJECT INDEX

market economy metaphor 407–8, 410, 412, 416, 424–5
markets/market system 407–26; analysis of 410–12; decentering of 423, 424–6; and equilibrium 411–12; and international economy 412–15; and postmodernism 408–12; as a social construct 410; and states 415
Marxian economics 64, 68, 149, 151, 158–62, 159–60, 312–13, 327, 328
Marxism 9, 24, 34, 122, 133, 138; and economic anthropology 441; productionist bias 159
mathematics: and communication of truths 26; and economics 89, 146, 181; models 296, 298, 376; and open systems 71–2
Max U character 93–4, 99, 135
medieval economy: and exchange of goods 171, 172, 173, 176
men: development of social consciousness 267, 274, 276
metadiscourse: and discourse 29
metanarratives 409; and international economics 426; modernist 85, 91–2, 480; and postmodernism 355; and social progress 9, 11, 12
metaphors: and Cambridge capital controversy 338, 344–6; economic 409–10; market economy 407–8, 410, 412, 416, 424–5; and money 189–90; and truth 122–3; womb-as-capital 221, 224–31, 247–8
methodology 62, 63, 65–8, 330; detachment and engagement 298; in macroeconomics 298–9; in modernist economics 67–8; pluralist 65–6, 133; synthetic approach 64, 66–7, 68, 71, 132
Methodology of Mathematical Economics and Econometrics (Tintner) 110
microeconomics 92, 442
Middle Ages *see* medieval economy
Mike Fletcher (Moore) 186
military equipment: US export of 421–2
mind games 119
mind/body dualism 182–3, 302
models: anthropology 184, 473; Arrow-Debreu 151; consumption 187; econometric 91; economic 29–30, 87, 90, 181, 221, 224–5, 239, 256, 323; family 256; Keynesian 90; mathematical 296, 298, 376; one-sex 221, 224–31, 239; preference-satisfying 362–3; Samuelson's multiplier-accelerator 90
Models and Analogies in Science (Hesse) 123
Modern Language Association 106
modernism 7, 24–34, 144, 477–8; 1910 modernism 102–6, 115; aesthetic 179; architectural 103, 107; and arts and sciences 82, 105; characteristics of 81–2; and characterization 78–83; and dualisms 81, 105, 299–300; early forms of 108–15; and economics 5, 24, 67, 77–99, 136; elitism of 112–15; and Enlightenment 115; literary 103, 107; and metanarratives 85, 91–2; methodology 67–5; and monism 61, 64, 71; and Plato 115–18; and postmodernism 22, 102–25, 133, 138, 355; two kinds (literary/architectural) 103–6
Modigliani-Miller theorem 435
Mon Coeur Mis à Nu (*My Heart Laid Bare*: Baudelaire) 185

Monde Slave, Le (Mauss) 439
monetary systems: and gold-standard 177; Greco-Roman 170, 171, 174; in medieval Europe 170, 171
money/monetary systems 166–92; as an evil 190; and exchange 168, 191; inconvertibility of 177–8; and metaphor 189–90; theory of 191; triadic 166–81
monism 61, 64, 71, 132
morality: and human action 95–7, 99
mother/fetus as two persons 226
motherhood 279; and contracts 231–9; real/self-interested 232–5, 240; status of 238; surrogate 221–41, 247–51; and theories of exchange 247–51
'Mothering versus Contract' (Held) 241
multiculturalism 301–2
multifirm industries 414
myths: and Cambridge capital controversy 338, 344–6; semiology of 345

name-money 169
narratives: conflict over a resource 359; and postmodernism 354–6, 357–9; rational choice theory 384–95
Nash equilibria 377, 386, 390–1, 394, 402, 433
National Bioethics Advisory Commission (US) 248
National Bioethics Consultative Committee 236
need: and desire 186
neo-Austrians 64, 68
neo-traditionalism 80–1, 99, 135
neoclassical economics 143–63, 339, 401–2, 480; and androcentric categorization 315–16; and deconstruction 290; discourses on women/motherhood 235–9, 265–7; equilibrium approach 340; and feminists/feminism 246, 247, 328; and gifts/gift exchange 432–56, 459, 478; instrumental model of action 362, 364, 365; and international trade 412–13; masculinity of 222–3, 239–41; and monism 71; and one-sex model 221, 224–31, 239; phallocentric nature of 223, 239; reconstruction of 415; and sexed body 221–41; tensions and contradictions of 77, 86–7; theories 160–1, 414, 477; and transactions-cost approach 424
'netput' vector conception 154, 157
New Economic Criticism, The (Woodmansee and Osteen) 20
'New Home Economics, The' (Becker) 266
New York Times 106, 118, 122, 433
Newtonian era 72
Nichomachean Ethics (Aristotle) 96
no-trade theorems 455
nominal money 169, 172
non-modernism: and postmodernism 22–3
'Norm of Reciprocity, The' (Gouldner) 455
nuclear family 233
'numéraire' theory 177

object-commodity-money 169
objectivity 287–8, 315, 329; and subjectivity 409
obligations: and gift-giving 459, 460, 467–8; logic of 440
Old Chicago school 80, 83–4

492

SUBJECT INDEX

one-sex model: in neoclassical economics 221, 224–31, 239; and womb-as-capital metaphor 224–31
Only Paradoxes to Offer (Scott) 264
ontology 62, 63–4, 133
open systems in chemistry and mathematics 71–2
ophelimities 186
oppression of women 197, 199–200, 210, 269
optical realism: and the arts 171
order/chaos duality 71
Organization for Economic Cooperation and Development (OECD) 423
other/Other 314; and economic man 255, 256; and gift-giving 476; and women 221, 240, 262, 314
'Our Better Halves' (Ward) 268
Out of the Margin (Kuiper and Sap) 297
overdeterminism 31

Pareto optimality 377, 409
people as commodities 190
personhood: legal 230–1; of mother and fetus 226–31; of sexed body 248
persuasion 113, 116; in ancient Greece 117; and conviction 112; theory of 117
Phaedrus (Plato) 116
phallocentrism 33, 223, 230, 231, 232, 239
phenomena: characterization of 78–9
philosophy: and deconstruction 17; and French Enlightenment 73; and Scottish Enlightenment 72; similarities with new classical economics 92; Western 228–9
Picture of Dorian Gray, The (Wilde) 185–6
'Plato's Pharmacy' (Derrida) 446–7
pluralism 61, 62–8; in economics 63; in postmodernism 70–1, 132–3, 134, 356–7, 366–71
Pluralism in Economics (Salanti and Screpanti) 44n
policies: industrial 415
political economy 62, 246–7, 249, 254, 481; nineteenth-century 250, 254
political history 263
Politics (Aristotle) 96
Polyani's typology of economic forms 464–5
poor relief 435
pop-art 89
positivism 27, 187
post-Keynesianism 48n, 133, 149, 158–62, 161; and Cambridge capital controversy 337
postcolonial theory 47n, 246
Postmodern Condition: A Report on Knowledge, The (Lyotard) 9, 409
postmodernism 4–38, 106–8, 399–404, 475; and 1910 modernism 102–6; anti-elitism 114–15; and antimodernism 21–4, 61; and arts 84–5; and capitalism 6–8; categorization of 4–5; as a condition 8–15; definition of 102, 108; and dualism 69–70; and economics 34–8, 121–2, 163, 354–71; and feminism 261–5, 299–302; and feminist economics 305–11, 321–3, 327–32; genealogy of 102–25; and markets 408–12; and modernism 61, 131–2, 133, 138, 355; narrative conflicts 354–6, 357–9; new theories 74; and pluralism 70–1, 132–3, 134, 356–7, 366–71; refutation of 122–5; styles 15–21; toggling ideas 120–1, 134

poststructuralism 16, 307, 400; and deconstruction 399; feminist 222–3, 229, 240, 246, 247, 262
potlatch 440, 448
pound (*livre*): as a standard pricing unit 170–1
power: concept of 362–3
Praise of Folly (Erasmus) 79
precious metal: economic functions 166–7
prediction 110–11
preference-satisfying models 362–3
preferences 408; and action 364–5; conflicts of 360–6; and consumers 153, 157; and individual interests 363–4; model 362–3; revealed 144–5, 152
pregnancy issues: mother/fetus dichotomy 238–9; surrogacy contracts 235–41
producers: role of 153–5
production: activities 156; creative 186; economic/non-economic 319; and feminism 186; functions 340–3, 345; gender issues of 311–14, 315; inputs/outputs 155–6, 413; intra-firm integration 420, 425; models 183, 187; organization/reorganization of 424; and profit 341; and technology 155, 157; theories 150, 155
Production of Commodities by Means of Commodities (Sraffa) 341
'Production Function and the Theory of Capital, The' (Robinson) 340
profit-maximising conditions 156, 157
Prometheus Bound (Aeschylus) 124
property: evolution of 253; sexed body as 235
psychosocial unity and fragmentation 11, 12, 13
public welfare and Keynesian economics 98

quality: and quantity 349

Rand Corporation 104
rational behaviour 375
rational choice theory 374, 376, 377, 395, 402–3; narrative 384–95
rational economic man *see* economic man
rational-agent optimization 415
rationalism 27, 111, 323; and irrationalism 124; in Newtonian era 72
Real, the 403–4
reality: as a characteristic of modernism 81; fragmentation of 68; and gold-money 176; and language 477–8, 479; non-metaphorical 122–3; in postmodern capitalism 166–81; and virtual/symbolic economies 168–9, 178–9, 180; vision of 62–4, 71
reason: and choice 205
reciprocity: and community economy 465–70, 479; genealogy of 461–5; and gift-giving 459–61, 475; and sister-exchange 470–2
reductionism as criterion of modernism 83
reflexivity 89–91, 449–50
regulatory capture theorem 435
relativism 191, and choice 252; and deconstruction 118; and ethnocentrism 204–8, 246, 251; and feminism 204, 329; and rhetoric 80
Renaissance economies 171, 176
representation 24–6, 376–9; and behaviour 378; and language 173, 375; and modernism 81, 82
reproduction: gender roles 272–3; technology 248–9

SUBJECT INDEX

Republic (Plato) 116
resources: conflict 359; and desires 251
reswitching and capital-reversal 341, 342, 348, 400
revealed preference 144–5; theory 152
rhetoric: and coercion 139; as a discipline 123; and free market exchange 138–9; importance of 73; and liberalism 122; and modernism 110–11, 137; and relativism 80; and sophistry 115; as a third way 138
Rhetoric (Aristotle) 122
Rhetoric of Economics, The (McCloskey) 20, 298, 318
Ricardian equivalence 435
rights: fetal 233, 249
Robinson Crusoe: as universal individual 226, 257*n*
Roe v. Wade abortion case (US) 230
Romanticism 107, 190

Sacre du Printemps 103
Samuelsonian economics 84, 103, 135, 136, 152
Santa Monica: USA 104
Saussure's linguistics 89–90
Schindler's List 448–9
schools of thought 65, 129–40, 159
Science 116
science: definition of 288; and destruction 10–11; economic 13, 122; and knowledge 64–5; and literature 122; masculine bias of 288, 291; and the postmodern condition 9–11; and scientism 28–30
scientism 24, 28–30
Scottish Enlightenment 61–2, 72, 97
self: fragmentation of 13, 37, 63, 158, 161, 300; gendered 262–3, 293; relational 300; unified and decentered 12–14
self-conception: and decentering 206; and the Enlightenment 204, 206; of women 318
self-consciousness 306, 403; and deconstruction 89; of postmodernism 19–20
self-determination: and cultural autonomy 206
self-interest 288, 302, 314; and gifts/gift-giving 443, 451–2, 460–1; motivation of academics 297; and social good 184–5
self-organising systems theory 71
self-referential systems 90
self-reflexivity: and non-Western women 209; and postmodernism 15–21; and writing styles 21
semiotics 191, 344–6
sexed body exchanges 239–41
sexual differences: phallocentric construction of 230, 232, 239
Siemens: and interfirm collaboration 419–21
sign-money 169
Silent Scream (film) 227
sister-exchange 470–2
'situated subjects' 208–10; in feminist economics 210–11
Six Million Dollar Man, The (Bresnick) 448–9
social change/evolution 9, 11, 269–70, 278–9, 295–9
social constructivism 36
Social Darwinism 269, 279
social engineering 137
social good: and self-interest 184–5

social life: fragmentation of 12; and reciprocity 460, 475–6
social relations 187–8; and money 190
social sciences 306; and concept of power 362; and feminist theory 262
social theory of value 452–6
socialization: and educational levels 200; of gender roles 201–2
society: decentering of 13–14; and division of labor 158; and the individual 143; progress of 276–7
sociobiology 436
sophists/sophistry 115, 116–17, 118, 120
speculation: and stock market 180
standards 123–4, 125, 169–70, 317–19; fixed 167–8; gold 176–7, 178, 190, 191
states: and individualism 182; and international trade 416–22; and issue of banknotes 179; and markets 415; roles in international trade 421–2, 481
stock market: and speculation 180
Stoic theory of the sign 174
Stone Age Economics (Sahlins) 442
Stones of Venice (Ruskin) 185
Strategic Silence, The (Bakker) 297
structuralism 34, 307, 441
Structure of Scientific Revolutions, The (Kuhn) 110, 316
'Subjection of Women' (Mill) 269
subjectivity 315, 375; conception of 208–10; and Enlightenment 252; as a feminine trait 234–5, 288; and feminist poststructuralism 246; neoclassical 255; and objectivity 409; and political economists 254; postcolonial 255
surrogacy: commercial 221–41; contracts 235–9, 248
Sweden: transnational corporations 418
symbolism: and monetary systems 166–92
synthetic approach: and dualism 64, 66–7, 68, 71, 132

technology 8, 10–11; interfirm collaboration in 419–21; of production 155, 157; of reproduction 248–9
theories 96, 143, 144, 145, 149; and action 136; capital and distribution 339, 340; of choice and exchange 152, 246, 252; of commonality of human nature 73; of discrimination 256; economic 29–30, 91, 145, 147, 150, 162, 163, 253, 319–20, 477; evolutionary biology 264, 269, 271–2, 331; of exchange 247–51; of the family 246, 251, 265, 266; feminist 327, 329–32; game 17–18, 84, 90, 144, 256, 364, 376, 384, 386, 477; general equilibrium 151, 153–4; growth theories 253, 256, 340; investment 145; of justice 366–7; of knowledge 63, 64–5, 73; of language 117, 172; marginal productivity 339–40, 343–4; of modernist economics 82–3, 109, 137; of money 191; neoclassical 150, 151, 154, 160; numéraire 177; of persuasion 117; postcolonial 246; production 150, 155; rational choice 374; of revealed preference 152; of self-organising systems 71; value 144, 146, 150
Theory of Moral Sentiments, The (Smith) 96, 143, 144, 149

SUBJECT INDEX

Theory of Political Economy (Jevons) 145
Theory of Value (Debreu) 150
Third World: and female agency 207–8; and feminism 206; and women's choices 199–202
thought: dualistic/non-dualistic modes 72; and language 307–8; postmodern 310–11; poststructural 309
Thousand Acres, A (Smiley) 448
time: and consumption 156; and space compression 11–12
time-series analysis 91
Timon of Athens (Shakespeare) 188–9
Tit for Tat (Mirowski) 439, 441
token-money 168, 169, 173, 176
Toshiba: and interfirm collaboration 419–21
trade: and gifts/gift-giving 475–82; international 416–22; intra-firm 414, 416–19, 418; intra-industry 415
trade balance: cumulative 423, 423; and macroeconomics 413
trade theories 414
tradition: and modernism 81
transcendence 125, 131, 137, 139–40; and traditional dialectics 132, 135
transnational corporations (TNCs) 416–19, 417, 424, 481
travel: and concept of culture 254–5
treasure-money 168, 169
Treatise on the Circulation of Money (Muller) 191
Treatise of the Family (Becker) 435
Trobiand Islanders: and gift-giving 459, 460, 461, 463, 468
Truth/truths 107, 116, 117, 122, 123; communication of 25, 26; and language 25, 374–5, 477–8; and metaphor 122–3; and postmodernism 306–7, 354; pursuit of 118, 131
Turing machine 442, 455

Umeda of New Guinea 470–2
uncertainty 110–11; Keynes discussion of 73, 161
understanding 375, 376, 378–9
unified self 12–13
United Nations 418, 421, 422
United Nations Centre for Transnational Corporations 418
United States: blood donor system 436–8; Department of Health, Education and Welfare 438; government intervention in international trade 421–2; health economics 437, 438; transnational corporations 418

universability principle 369–70, 401–2
universal individual 12–13, 221, 226, 232, 238
University of Chicago Press 109–10
uterus *see* womb
utilitarianism 32, 111
utility: and choice 200; and disutility 145; functions 157; of futility 435–41; and labour theory of value 184–5; principles of 158; womb as 224
utility-maximisation 224–5, 374

Value of Culture, The (Klamer) 184
value(s): aesthetic 184; of commodities 167; and humanism 153; measures/standards of 172, 176; theory 144, 146, 159, 184, 443–4, 451–3; variance 452
veiling practices and gender-based constraints 202–4, 209–10, 251
virtual economy and real economy 178–9, 180
vision of reality 62–4, 71, 132, 134

Wall Street Journal 106
Waste Land, The (Eliot) 103, 113
Wealth of Nations, The (Smith) 96–7, 108, 253–4, 461
What is Post-Modernism (Jencks) 85
Woman Question, The (Schreiner) 186
womb as rentable space 225, 236, 238
womb-as-capital metaphor 221, 224–31, 247–8
women: as agents 202–4, 207–8, 211, 223, 251, 252–3, 263, 266; autonomy of 198, 251; categorization of 263–4, 300, 314, 329–30; choices and enthnocentrism/relativism 197–218; dependency on men 272–6; in economic analyses 267–9, 311–12; and 'economic man' 248, 250; emancipation of 270–1, 278; and feminism/postmodernism 261–5; and gender inequality 264, 269, 271–2, 277, 331; and motherhood 221–41, 234–5, 238, 247–51, 279; non-Western Third World 207–8, 314; and one-sex body 221, 224–31, 239–41; oppression of 197, 199–200, 210, 269; as the 'other' 221, 240, 262, 314; self-understanding of 318; and sexed-body exchange 239–41; stereotyped roles 293; subjectivity 234–5; subordination of 268, 272, 273–4, 276, 278, 279; Victorian 270–1
Women and Economics (Gilman) 261, 264, 269–78, 331
writing styles: postmodern 16–17, 18, 21, 106–8

495